The Oxford Handbook of
Evidence-Based Management

OXFORD LIBRARY OF PSYCHOLOGY

OXFORD LIBRARY OF PSYCHOLOGY

Editor-in-Chief PETER E. NATHAN
Editor, Organizational Psychology STEVE W. J. KOZLOWSKI

The Oxford Handbook of Evidence-Based Management

Edited by

Denise M. Rousseau

OXFORD
UNIVERSITY PRESS

Oxford University Press is a department of the University of Oxford.
It furthers the University's objective of excellence in research, scholarship,
and education by publishing worldwide.

Oxford   New York
Auckland   Cape Town   Dar es Salaam   Hong Kong   Karachi
Kuala Lumpur   Madrid   Melbourne   Mexico City   Nairobi
New Delhi   Shanghai   Taipei   Toronto

With offices in
Argentina   Austria   Brazil   Chile   Czech Republic   France   Greece
Guatemala   Hungary   Italy   Japan   Poland   Portugal   Singapore
South Korea   Switzerland   Thailand   Turkey   Ukraine   Vietnam

Published in the United States of America by
Oxford University Press
198 Madison Avenue, New York, NY 10016

Library of Congress Cataloging-in-Publication Data
The Oxford handbook of evidence-based management / edited by Denise M. Rousseau.
p. cm. — (Oxford library of psychology)
ISBN 978-0-19-976398-6 (hardcover); 978-0-19-936626-2 (paperback)
1. Decision making.   2. Business intelligence.   3. Management.
I. Rousseau, Denise M.
HD30.23.O955 2012
658.4'03—dc23
2011036150

SHORT CONTENTS

FOREWORD

We have a very long way to go to make management practice evidence-based. A few years ago, while serving on the compensation committee for a publicly traded NASDAQ company, we were considering what to do about the CEOs' stock options and our stock-option program in general. Just that day, articles appeared in the mainstream business press on Donald Hambrick's research showing that stock options led to risky behavior (Sanders & Hambrick, 2007). That research added to the growing body of evidence demonstrating that many executive pay practices not only did not enhance company performance (Dalton, Certo, & Roengpitya, 2003), but led instead to misreporting of financial results (Burns & Kedia, 2006). The finding that options led to riskier actions is logical. Once an option is out of the money, there is no further economic downside for executives. Therefore, there is every incentive for managers to take big risks in the hope that the stock price will go up, thereby giving those once previously worthless options economic value.

At the meeting, a vice president from Aon Consulting who was advising the compensation committee replied, "No," without any hesitation or embarrassment when I asked him, first, if he knew about this research, and, second, if he was interested in my sending him the original articles or other information about the extensive research on stock options and their effects. What is particularly telling is that many people from other compensation consulting firms to whom I have related this story said it could have been their firm, too—that the perspective reflected is typical. Meanwhile, my colleagues on the compensation committee seemed to believe that the fact that our professional advisor was both unknowledgeable about and, even worse, uninterested in sound empirical research that might inform our compensation policy decisions should not in any way affect our continued reliance on his "advice." This consulting example is all too typical of the perspective of numerous, particularly U.S., executives, many of whom value their "experience" over data, even though much research suggests that learning from experience is quite difficult and much of such presumed learning is just wrong (e.g., Denrell, 2003; Mark & Mellor, 1991; Schkade & Kilbourne, 2004).

Yes, it is true that there is much recent interest in investing in "big data" start-ups and technology and in building software to comb through large data sets for analytical insights, such as how to improve margins through pricing optimization. However, as Jim Goodnight, the CEO of SAS Institute, a business analytics and business intelligence software company, recently told me, that analytic work is mostly done by professionals fairly far down in the company hierarchy who sometimes have trouble getting the CEO interested in implementing their results. Few companies or their leaders seem to see that information and data-driven business insight can be a competitive advantage. Although it may seem ironic that companies invest in analytical capabilities and software that they don't fully use, such a circumstance is far from unusual. David Larcker, a well-known cost-accounting professor, has said that few companies turn all the data they have collected in their enterprise resource-planning systems into business intelligence but instead use most of that information simply for purposes of control. And purveyors of marketing research also tell a similar tale: companies purchase their services but then don't act on the results when the recommendations conflict with the preexisting views of senior management.

The problems confronting building evidence-based practice in management are scarcely unique to this domain. It has taken more than 200 years for evidence-based medicine to become a normative standard for professional practice. The objections to applying standards of practice—protocols—in medicine are eerily similar to those encountered in advocating evidence-based management: that each situation is different; that practitioners' wisdom, experience, and insight is more valuable than aggregated data-based information; and that statistical evidence pertains to what happens "on average," but that the particular individual speaking is, of course, much above average and not, therefore, bound by the results of aggregate information—a phenomenon reliably observed in psychology and called the above-average effect (e.g., Williams & Gilovich, 2008). Although there are evidence-based movements in various policy domains ranging from criminology to education, resistance to implementing science, particularly when that science conflicts with belief and ideology, looms large.

Failure to adhere to clinical guidelines in medicine, unfortunately still quite common, costs lives and money (e.g., Berry, Murdoch, & McMurray, 2001). Pressures for cost containment and the documented instances of literally hundreds of thousands of lives lost from preventable medical errors have seemingly turned the tide so that evidence-based medical practice now seems to be inevitable. However, the absence of similar pressures in management means that the quest to bring evidence-based practice into organizations still faces a long and tortuous journey. In the meantime, damage occurs to both people and companies. According to Conference Board surveys, job satisfaction is at an all-time low; most studies of employee engagement and distrust of management portray a dismal picture of the typical workplace; and the failure to heed the evidence about the physiological effects of workplace stress, economic insecurity, and long working hours contributes to employee mortality and morbidity (Pfeffer, 2010). Companies suffer from having disengaged workforces with excessive turnover even as they neglect the science and information that could improve their operations and profitability (e.g., Burchell & Robin, 2011).

Simply put, there is a profound "doing-knowing" problem in management practice: many managers make decisions and take actions with little or no consideration of the knowledge base that might inform those decisions. *The Oxford Handbook of Evidence-Based Management* intends to change this situation. It contains more than just a review of the literature on evidence-based management (EBMgt). The *Handbook* recognizes the need to provide information on how to teach EBMgt in classes and executive programs and also the requirement to provide role models—illustrations of practitioners who have embraced an evidence-based approach—so that practicing leaders can see how evidence-based principles might be applied in real organizations. Because EBMgt is relevant in both the for-profit and nonprofit worlds, the handbook has examples from both. With its focus on changing the practice of management, this work examines the important topic of how to get research findings implemented in practice and the barriers to connecting science with practice. *The Oxford Handbook of Evidence-Based Management* provides a comprehensive overview of the information required to understand what EBMgt is, how to teach it, how to apply it, and how to understand and overcome the barriers that stand in the way of basing management practice on the best relevant research. It represents an important step on the road to building an EBMgt movement.

It is scarcely news that management is not a profession, even though it might and should be. There are two elements that define a profession, one of which is the development and adherence to specialized bodies of knowledge. Sometimes specialized knowledge is reflected in licensing examinations. However, licensing is not the only path to ensuring that people know and implement knowledge and standards of professional practice. What may be even more important are social norms and public expectations and the sanctions for violating those expectations. As the opening example—and hundreds of others—make clear, there is, at the moment, neither the expectation that professionally educated practitioners will know relevant management research nor any sanctions that punish their ignorance. Consequently, management, and indeed, much of the popular management literature, is beset with myths, dangerous half-truths (Pfeffer & Sutton, 2006), and rules of thumb often based on little more than publicity, repetition, and belief. Organizations and their leaders do a profound disservice to society and even to themselves by not being more committed—not just in rhetoric but in their behavior—to implementing management science.

In this project of professionalization, the role of educational institutions looms large, which means that it is important that the handbook includes so much material on teaching EBMgt and on linking science with practice. At the moment, however, there is little to suggest that even in business-school classrooms, much attention is paid to EBMgt. Business schools are increasingly staffed by part-time and adjunct faculty who have no requirement to know, let alone contribute, to the science of management. Courses often use case examples as a primary pedagogic focus, and relatively few business schools impart the critical thinking and evaluation of ideas and the skills necessary to separate good management science from quackery. A recent review of more than 800 syllabi of required courses from some 333 programs found that only about one-quarter utilized scientific evidence in any form (Charlier, Brown, & Rynes, 2011). The fact that even business school instructors often inhabit the world of folk wisdom rather than the domain of science has sparked notice and commentary (e.g., Pearce, 2004).

If EBMgt is to become a reality in professional practice, business schools at both the undergraduate and MBA levels will need to play an important role. That's because it is in school where students not only begin to learn about the relevant research and theory but also come to understand standards of science and what constitutes evidence and the sound basis for making decisions. It is interesting that business schools are currently evaluated in many ways—the extent to which they raise their graduates' salaries, how "satisfied" they make their students and the companies that recruit them, their adherence to guidelines that specify what they must teach and the proportion of their faculty with terminal degrees, their reputations as perceived by their peers, and various other criteria. What is not measured is the extent to which they impart the science of management and critical-thinking skills to their graduates, or the extent to which the graduates actually practice EBMgt. If we are serious about implementing a science of management, we need to measure and evaluate both schools and their graduates, at least to some degree, using these metrics.

We live in an organizational world. Decisions made in and by organizations profoundly affect the working lives and economic well-being of people all over the globe. As the financial crisis of 2007–2008 well illustrates, many of those decisions are all too frequently characterized not just by venality but also by profound incompetence (Lewis, 2010). As scholars and as practitioners whose work affects so many lives in so many ways, we have a sacred obligation and responsibility to develop and use the best knowledge possible to make the world a better place. It is only through embarking on the goal of building an evidence-based body of knowledge linked to professional practice that this obligation can be fulfilled. In that regard, *The Oxford Handbook of Evidence-Based Management* makes both a profoundly important contribution and lays out a statement of intent to make EBMgt a reality.

—Jeffrey Pfeffer

References

Berry, C., Murdoch, D. R., & McMurray, J. J. V. (2001). Economics of chronic heart failure, *European Journal of Heart Failure, 3,* 283–291.

Burchell, M., & Robin, J. (2011). *The great workplace: How to build it, how to keep it, and why it matters.* San Francisco, CA: Jossey-Bass.

Burns, N., & Kedia, S. (2006). The impact of performance-based compensation on misreporting, *Journal of Financial Economics, 79,* 35–67.

Charlier, S. D., Brown, K. G., & Rynes, S. L. (2011). Teaching evidence-based management in MBA programs: What evidence is there? *Academy of Management Learning and Education, 10,* 222–236.

Dalton, D. R., Certo, S. T., & Roengpitya, R. (2003). Meta-analyses of financial performance: Fusion or confusion? *Academy of Management Journal, 46,* 13–28.

Denrell, J. (2003). Vicarious learning, undersampling of failure, and the myths of management, *Organization Science, 14,* 227–243.

Lewis, M. (2010). *The Big Short: Inside the Doomsday Machine,* New York: W. W. Norton.

Mark, M. M., & Mellor, S. (1991). Effect of self-relevance on hindsight bias: The foreseeability of a layoff, *Journal of Applied Psychology, 76,* 569–577.

Pearce, J. (2004). What do we know and how do we really know it? *Academy of Management Review, 29,* 175–179.

Pfeffer, J. (2010). Building sustainable organizations: The human factor, *Academy of Management Perspectives, 24,* 34–45.

Pfeffer, J., & Sutton, R. I. (2006). *Hard facts, dangerous half-truths, and total nonsense: profiting from evidence-based management.* Boston: Harvard Business School Press, 2006.

Sanders, W. M., & Hambrick, D. C. (2007). Swinging for the fences: The effects of CEO stock options on company risk-taking and performance, *Academy of Management Journal, 50,* 1055–1078.

Schkade, D. A., & Kilbourne, L. M. (2004). Expectation-outcome consistency and hindsight bias, *Organizational Behavior and Human Decision Processes, 49,* 105–123.

Williams, E. F., & Gilovich, T. (2008). Do people really believe they are above average? *Journal of Experimental Social Psychology, 44,* 1121–1128.

OXFORD LIBRARY OF PSYCHOLOGY

The *Oxford Library of Psychology*, a landmark series of handbooks, is published by Oxford University Press, one of the world's oldest and most highly respected publishers, with a tradition of publishing significant books in psychology. The ambitious goal of the *Oxford Library of Psychology* is nothing less than to span a vibrant, wide-ranging field and, in so doing, to fill a clear market need.

Encompassing a comprehensive set of handbooks, organized hierarchically, the *Library* incorporates volumes at different levels, each designed to meet a distinct need. At one level are a set of handbooks designed broadly to survey the major subfields of psychology; at another are numerous handbooks that cover important current focal research and scholarly areas of psychology in depth and detail. Planned as a reflection of the dynamism of psychology, the *Library* will grow and expand as psychology itself develops, thereby highlighting significant new research that will impact on the field. Adding to its accessibility and ease of use, the *Library* will be published in print and, later on, electronically.

The *Library* surveys psychology's principal subfields with a set of handbooks that capture the current status and future prospects of those major subdisciplines. This initial set includes handbooks of social and personality psychology, clinical psychology, counseling psychology, school psychology, educational psychology, industrial and organizational psychology, cognitive psychology, cognitive neuroscience, methods and measurements, history, neuropsychology, personality assessment, developmental psychology, and more. Each handbook undertakes to review one of psychology's major subdisciplines with breadth, comprehensiveness, and exemplary scholarship. In addition to these broadly conceived volumes, the *Library* also includes a large number of handbooks designed to explore in depth more specialized areas of scholarship and research, such as stress, health and coping, anxiety and related disorders, cognitive development, or child and adolescent assessment. In contrast to the broad coverage of the subfield handbooks, each of these latter volumes focuses on an especially productive, more highly focused line of scholarship and research. Whether at the broadest or most specific level, however, all of the *Library* handbooks offer synthetic coverage that reviews and evaluates the relevant past and present research and anticipates research in the future. Each handbook in the *Library* includes introductory and concluding chapters written by its editor to provide a roadmap to the handbook's table of contents and to offer informed anticipations of significant future developments in that field.

An undertaking of this scope calls for handbook editors and chapter authors who are established scholars in the areas about which they write. Many of the nation's and world's most productive and best-respected psychologists have agreed to edit *Library* handbooks or write authoritative chapters in their areas of expertise.

For whom has the *Oxford Library of Psychology* been written? Because of its breadth, depth, and accessibility, the *Library* serves a diverse audience, including graduate students in psychology and their faculty mentors, scholars, researchers, and practitioners in psychology and related fields. Each will find in the *Library* the information they seek on the subfield or focal area of psychology in which they work or are interested.

Befitting its commitment to accessibility, each handbook includes a comprehensive index, as well as extensive references to help guide research. Because the *Library* was designed from its inception as an online as well as a print resource, its structure and contents will be readily and rationally searchable online. Further, once the *Library* is released online, the handbooks will be regularly and thoroughly updated.

In summary, the *Oxford Library of Psychology* will grow organically to provide a thoroughly informed perspective on the field of psychology, one that reflects both psychology's dynamism and its increasing interdisciplinarity. Once published electronically, the *Library* is also destined to become a uniquely valuable interactive tool, with extended search and browsing capabilities. As you begin to consult this handbook, we sincerely hope you will share our enthusiasm for the more than 500-year tradition of Oxford University Press for excellence, innovation, and quality, as exemplified by the *Oxford Library of Psychology*.

Peter E. Nathan
Editor-in-Chief
Oxford Library of Psychology

ABOUT THE EDITOR

Denise M. Rousseau is the H. J. Heinz II University Professor of Organizational Behavior at Carnegie Mellon University. Recognized for developing psychological contract theory, she has twice won the Terry Award for best management book and is a founder of the Evidence-Based Management Collaborative.

Dedicated to the Visionaries Who First Recognized
the Possibility of Evidence-Based Management:

Mary Parker Follett
Herbert A. Simon
Peter Drucker

Maturity means doing something even
our elders think is a good idea.

ACKNOWLEDGMENTS

This handbook grew out of the deliberations of the Evidence-Based Management Collaborative, a community of innovators inaugurated in 2008. Many of its participants have written handbook chapters. All contributed to the ideas herein. We are especially grateful to Mark Wessel and Ken Dunn who, as deans at Carnegie Mellon's Heinz College and the Tepper School of Business, provided support at a critical time in the Collaborative's formation. Paul Goodman provided incisive comments on many chapters and brought greater clarity to our thinking. Cathy Senderling did her usual excellent work editing several chapters. Mary Ann O'Brien did a wonderful job of producing a finished manuscript. We thank Abby Gross, our Oxford editor, for her faith and patience.

CONTRIBUTORS

Richard Adams
Cranfield School of Management
Cranfield University
Bedfordshire, UK

Eric Barends
University of Amsterdam
Amsterdam, the Netherlands

Jean M. Bartunek
Carroll School of Management
Boston College
Boston, MA

Andreas Bausch
Department of Economics
University of Giessen
Gießen, Germany

John Boudreau
Center for Effective Organizations
University of Southern California
Los Angeles, CA

Rob B. Briner
School of Management
University of Bath
London, UK

Wendy R. Carroll
School of Business
University of Prince Edward Island
Charlottetown, Prince Edward Island, Canada

David Denyer
Cranfield School of Management
Cranfield University
Bedfordshire, UK

Lex Donaldson
School of Business
University of New South Wales
Sydney, Australia

Michael Frese
Department of Management and
    Organisation
National University of Singapore
Sinapore

Tamara L. Giluk
Williams College of Business
Xavier University
Xavier, OH

Jodi S. Goodman
College of Business and Economics
West Virginia University
Morgantown, WV

Lee A. Green
Department of Family Medicine
The University of Michigan
Ann Arbor, MI

Gerard P. Hodgkinson
Warwick Business School,
    University of Warwick, UK

Severin Hornung
Department of Management and
    Marketing
The Hong Kong Polytechnic University
Hong Kong

Frank Huisman
University of Amsterdam
Amsterdam, the Netherlands

R. Blake Jelley
School of Business
University of Prince Edward
    Island
Charlottetown, Prince Edward
    Island, Canada

Rüdiger Kabst
Department of Economics
University of Paderborn
Paderborn, Germany

Anthony R. Kovner
Robert F. Wagner Graduate School of
    Public Service
New York University
New York, NY

Opal Leung
Department of Management
Bentley University
Waltham, MA

Ravi Madhavan
Joseph M. Katz Graduate School of
Business
University of Pittsburgh
Pittsburgh, PA

Joseph T. Mahoney
College of Business
University of Illinois at
Urbana-Champaign
Urbana, IL

James O'Brien
Aubrey Dan Program in Management and
Organizational Studies
The University of Western Ontario
London, Ontario, Canada

Jone L. Pearce
Paul Merage School of Business
University of California, Irvine
Irvine, CA

Georges A. Potworowski
Department of Family Medicine
University of Michigan
Ann Arbor, MI

Andreas Rauch
Department of Psychology
University of Giessen
Gießen, Germany

A. Georges L. Romme
Department of Industrial
Engineering & Innovation Sciences
Eindhoven University of Technololgy
Eindhoven, the Netherlands

Denise M. Rousseau
Heinz College and Tepper School of
Business
Carnegie Mellon University
Pittsburgh, PA

Sara L. Rynes-Weller
Tippie College of Business
University of Iowa
Iowa City, IA

Paul Salipante
Mandel Center for Nonprofit
Organizations
Case Western Reserve University
Cleveland, OH

Peter Schmidt
Institute for Political Science
University of Giessen
Gießen, Germany

Ann Kowal Smith
Weatherhead School of Management
Case Western Reserve University
Cleveland, OH

Jayne Speicher-Bocija
Pradco, Inc.
Columbus, OH

Steven ten Have
University of Amsterdam
Amsterdam, the Netherlands

Joan Ernst van Aken
Department of Industrial
Engineering & Innovation Sciences
Eindhoven University of
Technology
Eindhoven, the Netherlands

Roye Werner
Hunt Library
Carnegie Mellon University
Pittsburgh, PA

J. Frank Yates
Department of Psychology
University of Michigan
Ann Arbor, MI

John Zanardelli
President & CEO
Asbury Heights
Mount Lebanon, PA

CONTENTS

PREFACE

What field is this?
- "There is a large research-user gap."
- "Many practices are doing more harm than good."
- "Practitioners do not read academic journals."
- "Academics not practitioners are driving the research agenda."
- "Practice is being driven more by fads and fashions than research."

The fact is, these quotes all come from the early days of evidence-based medicine (Sackett et al., 2000). More recently the same comments have been about the (lack of) use of scientific evidence in management practice; no wonder, because management practice today is as poorly aligned with organization and management research as medicine and science were then. Scientific knowledge identifies what we know and what we don't know about the natural and human-made world. It is the bedrock of all evidence-based approaches to practice. From medicine to education, each area of evidence-based practice has needed to confront these criticisms and work to make such comments descriptions of things past.

Evidence-based management (EBMgt) is the science-informed practice of management. It's about using scientific knowledge to inform the judgment of managers and the nature, content, and processes of decision making in organizations. Its practice reduces the costs of unaided judgment and limited and biased human information processes. EBMgt allows managers, consultants, and other practitioners to overcome these impediments through use of decision aids, practices, and frameworks to support better quality decisions.

The notion of evidence-based practice is relatively new, but the vision of management informed by science is not. Mary Parker Follett a renowned management consultant in the early twentieth century was perhaps the first to recognize the power of social science to inform management. Much of her influence today has been channeled through the writings of Peter Drucker, her self-proclaimed disciple, who advised practitioners to pay attention to scientific research and to pursue feedback on the outcomes of their decisions more deliberately in order to learn and perform better. Herbert Simon, the quintessential scientist and founder of such fields as computer science, artificial intelligence, and robotics, identified the limits of unaided human decision making as well as the potential for science and practice to partner in designing preferred conditions for our human-made world.

As we shall explore in this handbook, EBMgt is an adaptive evidence-informed family of practices relevant to anyone seeking to improve how people and organizations are managed. This handbook is intended to promote EBMgt's broad use in for-profit businesses, nonprofit organizations, and government. Management means getting people together to accomplish some objective. This handbook is intended for anyone in an organization who steps up to make things happen by organizing people, tasks, and processes. That includes executives, officers, and department heads as well as by proactive workers and volunteers.

Throughout history, management has reflected fundamental beliefs about what people can and should control in organizations. Manufacturing firms had no designated workplace safety function in the first 100 years after the industrial revolution began. Accidents were viewed as an act of God and, hence, could not be reduced or managed. Periodically, through scientific and practice innovations, such beliefs have changed. In its day, the notion of a planful enterprise manager was a Utopian view, scarcely evident in the loosely tied small job shops that comprised pre-industrial age shipbuilding or textile manufacturing. Practices promoting efficiencies in organizations became management's job over subsequent centuries, and by the twentieth century its functions included innovation and marketing (Drucker, 2003). Through all these developments, the habits of mind and knowledge used in the practice of management also changed.

The emergence of EBMgt in the twenty-first century parallels in some ways the systematization of finance and accounting in the last century. Management concepts have evolved over time and with them the mental models of managers and other practitioners. Nineteenth-century organizations for the most part lacked fundamental concepts like the time-value of money. In the early twentieth century, the concept of return on equity was developed and its components explicated in order to better assess and analyze company performance. Finance and accounting today have well-specified logics that lead to wider consistency in their practice and shared understandings of their meaning. In contrast, the logics that executives, managers, human-resource staff, and others use in managing people, structuring organizations, and making strategic decisions are far more inconsistent and ad hoc (Boudreau, 2010). EBMgt offers evidence-informed logics for effective management practice that complement other business disciplines.

Why Now? Drivers of Evidence-Based Management

We can never understand the total situation without taking into account the evolving situation. And when a situation changes we have not a new variation under the old fact, but a new fact.

—*Mary Parker Follett*

The time is ripe for the emergence of EBMgt. A confluence of factors (in italics in the following sentence and the following paragraphs) provides unparalleled opportunity to reconsider the fundamentals of managing organizations. Since World War II, *a large body of social science and management research has investigated the individual, social, and organizational factors that impact managerial performance and organizational effectiveness.* It has produced hundreds of well-supported evidence-based principles relevant to organizational decisions and practices. Awareness of the large volumes of research relevant to real-world decisions is a major factor in the current zeitgeist of evidence-based practice across innumerable professions (e.g., Armstrong, 2010; Locke, 2009).

The Internet offers broad access to scientific knowledge. From electronic libraries to listservs, the Internet offers findings from organizational and management science and opportunities to participate in communities interested in applying them. Medicine and nursing, among other fields, have undergone their own Internet-based transformations toward evidence-based practice. Using online sources, physicians and nurses regularly find information about problems and decisions they face. The result has been science-informed patient-care protocols, guidelines, and procedures, turning clinical research into better patient outcomes. In our field, management research is becoming widely accessible through Google.scholar and other web-based resources. Broadly available management research and summaries provide the basis for more effective mental models, processes, and practices. These make it easier for managers to apply the products of scientific knowledge daily in organizations.

Increasing awareness of the consequences from managerial decisions prompts widespread concern with improving its quality. Advancements in human knowledge give people new resources for tackling what once appeared to be intractable problems. Schools and criminal-justice institutions have been early adopters of evidence-based practice, perhaps no surprise given that their reliance on public dollars can require greater accountability (Orszag, 2010). Similarly, health-care managers are being challenged to use the same evidential approach that their clinical practitioners are using for patient care (Walshe & Randall, 2001). The movement toward accountability is likely to grow, fueled by widely available information regarding consequential decisions made with increasing global interdependence.

An evidence-based practice zeitgeist results from these forces across fields as diverse as medicine, education, criminal justice, and public policy. Each of these evidence initiatives reflects a recognition that the well-being of people, organizations, and society in an increasingly vulnerable and interdependent world may depend on how effectively we act on evidence. In the context of management, the potential benefits from evidence use are no less.

This Handbook's Organization
This handbook is designed with three goals in mind. First, it provides an overview of key EBMgt concepts and puts them in context of broader efforts promoting evidence-based practice and the closing of research-practice gaps. Second, it addresses the roles, contributions, and concerns of EBMgt's three core constituents: practitioners, educators, and scholars, providing perspectives and resources for each. Third, it incorporates critical perspectives to raise awareness of alternative views and possible unintended consequences and to stimulate future EBMgt innovations. EBMgt's development, adoption, and future progress depend on the related efforts of managers, consultants, and other practitioners who perform EBMgt; the educators who help develop the professional skills on which EBMgt rests; and the scholars who provide the basic research, summaries, and partnerships with practitioners that make EBMgt possible.

From health care to education, the many fields that now base core practices on research findings all began with the early adoption of evidence-informed practices by a small percentage of professionals (Rogers, 1995; Proctor, 2004). For this reason, this handbook targets the early adopters in all three groups, that is, those self-improving practitioners, educators, and scholars interested in learning and innovating. The handbook is intended to inform all three communities, offering perspective, food for thought, and guides to action.

The Introductory section provides an overview of EBMgt and its facets and puts these in context. I first present its central elements and functions in my chapter on envisioning EBMgt. Then, because evidence-based practice began in the field of medicine, Barends, ten Have, and Huisman compare and contrast EBMgt and its medical counterpart, addressing the commonalities as well as false beliefs and misapprehensions regarding their association. The introductory section concludes with van Aken and Romme's chapter on design science, a broadly applicable process originally developed by Herbert Simon (1997) that enables the use of scientific knowledge to solve practical problems through the collaborations between practitioners and scientists.

The Research section provides both resources and tools relevant to the role of scholars and academic research in promoting EBMgt. Its first set of chapters present core domains of management and organizational research, addressing what we know now and what we can do in future to advance each domain's uptake and use in EBMgt. "Micro" organizational behavior (OB), which I describe, is perhaps the most mature research field with a 100+ year history and considerable body of cumulative research. OB has yielded a host of evidence-based principles to guide practice. "Macro" organizational theory and strategy, as Madhavan and Mahoney detail, is a more recent field of study characterized by disciplinary disputes regarding the value of novelty versus cumulative research. They call for attention by macroscholars to moving this field toward greater integration and synthesis. Lastly, Frese, Bausch, Schmidt, Rauch, and Kabst describe the field of entrepreneurship, which has fostered cumulative research on critical issues related to creating and managing start-ups and developing entrepreneurial capabilities.

Other Research chapters describe techniques and approaches to help make research more accessible and useful to practice. A core aspect of all evidence-based practice is systematic reviews (SRs). These are summaries of a comprehensive body of research undertaken to address a specific managerial (and sometimes, too, scholarly) question. Briner and Denyer describe how SRs are conducted and their role in making useful knowledge more readily available. The next two chapters provide insights into how researchers can make their work more informative and useful to practice. Giluk and Rynes present lessons learned from evidence-based medicine to help us appreciate why practitioners might not believe, accept, or act on the best available evidence, and how to overcome these barriers. Leung and Bartunek address how scholarly research can be more effectively presented so that practitioners find it more memorable and easy to use.

The Practice section targets the realities of everyday management practice and the role EBMgt can play in improving decision making and well-being of employees and organizations. Practicing EBMgt involves overcoming a variety of hurdles. A first set of Practice chapters provides resources for understanding practice issues.

This section begins with the first-hand experiences of two practitioners. Long-standing EBMgt advocate Kovner discusses the resistance and opportunities he witnessed in EBMgt's infancy. An evidence-based manager with two decades of experience leading an evidence-based organization, Zanardelli recounts how he and his organization have used scientific evidence and logic models in his everyday management practice, and he describes the developmental activities undertaken to help his staff use evidence. Insofar as contemporary firms offer up both obstacles and facilitators to evidence-based practice, the next two chapters address how organizational dynamics affect EBMgt's adoption and use. Potwoworski and Green provide insight into the role that organizational culture plays in influencing the meaning, function, and use of evidence. Speicher-Bocija and Adams take the vantage points of managers at various levels, describing how evidence can have different meanings and value to chief executives, middle managers, and first-line supervisors.

Other Practice chapters offer tools practitioners can use. Roye Werner, Carnegie Mellon's business librarian, describes how practitioners can access the best available scientific evidence, especially in the form of online information. Yates and Potwoworski delineate an evidence-based framework for making quality decisions and walk the reader through ways to apply it. Important to making decisions based on meaningful facts, Donaldson details how the reliability and validity of business data can be improved by applying basic principles of statistics and data analysis. Boudreau demonstrates how the use of logic models, including frameworks derived from finance and related fields, can help managers make better use of evidence.

The Education section targets educators in their roles as instructors, curriculum designers, and textbook writers. Education is a central concern in EBMgt given the importance of creating an inaugural generation of evidence-based management practitioners. First, educators themselves need to be evidence-based practitioners and, thus, Goodman and O'Brien present evidence-based principles regarding teaching and learning. Jelley, Carroll, and Rousseau build on these principles to detail their methods and lessons learned in teaching EBMgt as an integrated part of the curriculum and as a stand-alone course. Salipante and Smith then discuss the education of EBMgt practitioners in the context of an executive doctoral program. Lastly, Pearce's chapter addresses how textbooks and textbook writing are impacted by the movement toward evidence-based management practice and provides a first-hand report of her experiences in writing the inaugural management textbook based wholly on scientific evidence.

The final Critique section recognizes that virtually no problem's solution fails to generate other problems. Being only in its 1.0 phase, EBMgt will undoubtedly undergo testing, development, and refinement over time. Presenting critical views at this early stage serves to remind us that potential unintended consequences must be addressed before EBMgt can fully realize its full promise. First, motivated by the concern that EBMgt focuses too much on managers and not enough on employees and the public, Hornung calls for balance in the interests that research on management and organizational practices serves. Second, Hodgkinson explores the politics of evidence and ways to reconcile threats that use of evidence might pose to the interests of various constituencies. Both critiques suggest constructive ways of balancing and expanding the influence of constituents so that EBMgt's benefits are broadly shared.

Our hope is that this handbook motivates readers to contribute to EBMgt's use, advancement, quality, and scope. Thank you for considering what we have to say.

Denise M. Rousseau
Sitka, Alaska
June 2011

References

Armstrong, J. S. (2010). *Persuasive advertising: Evidence-based principles*. New York: PalmgraveMacmillan.

Boudreau, J. W. (2010). *Retooling HR*. Cambridge, MA: Harvard Business Publishing.

Drucker, P.F. (2003). *On the profession of management*. Boston, MA: Harvard Business Review Books.

Follett, M. P. (1918). *The new state—Group organization, the solution for popular government*. New York: Longmans, Green.

Locke, E. A. (2009). *Handbook of principles of organizational behavior: Indispensable knowledge for evidence-based management*. New York: Wiley.

Orszag, P. (2010). Malpractice methodology. *New York Times, October 20*, p. A39.

Proctor, E. K. (2004). Leverage points for the implementation of evidence-based practice. *Brief Treatment and Crisis Intervention, 4*, 227–242.

Rogers, E. M. (1995). *Diffusion of innovation*. New York: Simon and Schuster.

Sackett, D. L., Straus, S. E., Richardson, W. S., Rosenberg, W., & Haynes, R. B. (2000). *Evidence-based medicine: How to practice and teach EBM*. New York: Churchill Livingstone.

Simon, H. A. (1996). *Science of the artificial* (3rd ed.). Cambridge, MA: MIT Press.

Walshe, K., & Rundall, T. G. (2001). Evidence-based management: From theory to practice in healthcare. *The Milbank Quarterly, 79*, 429–457.

PART 1

Introduction

Envisioning Evidence-Based Management

Denise M. Rousseau

Abstract

Evidence-based management (EBMgt) is an evolution in the practice of management. It is a knowledge-intensive, capacity-building way to think, act, organize, and lead. Its practice incorporates (1) use of scientific principles in decisions and management processes, (2) systematic attention to organizational facts, (3) advancements in practitioner judgment through critical thinking and decision aids that reduce bias and enable fuller use of information, and (4) ethical considerations including effects on stakeholders. It is a no-fad, no-fluff approach to developing better managers and leading effective and adaptive organizations. EBMgt is a product of the distinct yet interdependent activities of practitioners, educators, and scholars. This chapter discusses how each contribute to the advancement and use of EBMgt.

Key Words: Scientific evidence, organizational facts as evidence, systematic decision making, ethics, critical thinking, decision aids, cognitive repair, logic models, cognitive bias, bounded rationality, practice-oriented research

"Management" means, in the last analysis, the substitution of thought for brawn and muscle, of knowledge for folklore and superstition, and of cooperation for force...
—*Peter Drucker*

In science you need to understand the world; in business you need others to misunderstand it.
—*Nassim Nicholas Taleb*

The world is complex and experience meager.
—*James G. March*

Evidence-based management (EBMgt) is the systematic, evidence-informed practice of management, incorporating scientific knowledge in the content and process of making decisions. Part of a broad movement to make better use of scientific knowledge in everyday life, EBMgt is an evolution in management practice and the way professional

managers are educated. It deploys well-established scientific findings regarding critical thinking, human judgment, and decision making to aid managers in obtaining quality information and putting it to use. The set of practices that make up EBMgt achieve better-quality results in organizations by improving the practitioner's knowledge, judgment, and competencies. EBMgt offers no one-size-fits-all solutions. It does not oversimplify problems and their solutions in the way that management fads tend to do (Huczynski, 2006). Instead, it supports practitioners in making fuller use of their human, social, and technological capabilities. EBMgt is developed and mastered over a career, not a course.

This chapter first introduces the basic facets of EBMgt and how they can be practiced. It then describes how evidence-based approaches can be adapted to the broad array of situations managers face. It concludes by describing the roles of EBMgt's three critical constituencies: (1) the managers, consultants, and others who practice EBMgt and the (2) educators and (3) scholars who provide it critical support. But first, to help the reader envision what EBMgt practitioners actually do, let's meet two of them: Frances Tan, an executive in a global corporation, and Normand Mathieu, a middle manager in a regional bank. What practices are they using that seem "evidence-based" to you?

Frances Tan is the marketing vice president of an international container and packaging firm. She is on the lookout for ways to improve how her division organizes work and makes decisions. Frances champions her staff's development and their efforts to make better decisions. She and her direct reports collaborated with a consulting psychologist to turn a set of principles from decision-making research into practical guidelines for improving their decisions. These covered advance preparation, processes for making an actual decision, and managing its aftermath. At meetings and when she teaches in the company's in-house leadership program, Frances reinforces these principles. At the end of meetings where decisions are made, her staff now takes a few minutes to talk about how they applied the principles and what they learned. These discussions have helped adapt and expand the use of evidence-based decision principles to the division's array of decisions. The results so far include (1) more consistent decision follow-through and (2) fewer unexpected customer or employee problems as a consequence of decisions.

Normand Mathieu is the institutional research director for a large bank. As part of his role, Normand regularly analyzes bank data to help address critical questions the bank's top management team has raised. Searching for ways to improve his

management practice, he uses the bank's electronic library to follow research in relevant areas. Recently he looked into the research on demographic diversity. These studies led Normand to examine the results of a naturally occurring experiment inside the bank: comparing units that had included diversity in their performance goals to those that hadn't. Findings from this analysis demonstrated that certain practices led to better retention and advancement of women and minorities at the bank. They also highlighted ways to reduce backlash from white men to the bank's diversity efforts. As a result, Normand changed certain practices in his own group and provided senior management with information on diversity-promoting practices that work at the bank.

Appendix 1 lists evidence-based practices used by these two practitioners. As we go through the chapter, I will provide more details about how they practice EBMgt. The practices Frances and Normand use reflect EBMgt's four facets.

The Four Facets of EBMgt

Think for yourself upon rational lines, hypothesize, test against the evidence, never accept that a question has been answered as well as it ever will be.
Billy Beane

EBMgt combines four fundamental activities in the everyday exercise of management judgment and decision-making (Figure 1.1):

1. Use of the best available scientific findings.
2. Gathering and attending to organizational facts, indicators and metrics in a systematic fashion to increase their reliability and usefulness.

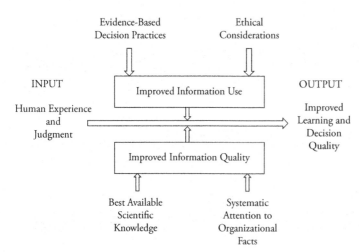

Fig. 1.1 EBMgt Facets and Functions.

3. On-going use of critical, reflective judgment and decision aids in order to reduce bias and improve decision quality.

4. Consideration of ethical issues including the short- and long-term impact of decisions on stakeholders.

These facets are implemented in ways that surmount the limitations and constraints that operate on unaided human judgment (Simon, 1997). EBMgt's features are intended to improve information quality while providing cognitive aids and decision tools to repair and develop practitioner judgment and decision making (cf. Heath, Larrick, & Klayman, 1998).

Use of Best Available Scientific Findings

Research is to see what everybody else has seen, and to think what nobody else has thought.
—*Albert Szent-Györgi*

It's not that I'm so smart, it's just that I stay with problems longer.
—*Albert Einstein*

Scientific knowledge is the bedrock of all evidence-based approaches to practice, from medicine (Sackett, Straus, Richardson, Rosenberg, & Haynes, 2000) to criminology (Sherman, 2002) to education (Ambrose, Bridges, DiPietro, Lovett, & Norman, 2010; Thomas & Pring, 2004). EBMgt is built on the scientific premise that there is an underlying degree of order in which a common set of basic physical, biological, social and psychological processes occur. The distinctive value of scientific evidence is the explicit knowledge it provides regarding how the world operates. This includes the natural world and the human-made sphere of organizations (Simon, 1996).

Scientific knowledge is distinct from other forms of knowledge. It is based on controlled observations, large samples sizes (N), validated measures, statistical controls, and systematically tested and accumulated understandings of how the world works (i.e., theory). Scientists are human and are generally subject to the same biases and value judgments of other people. The important difference is that the scientific method and related processes I describe in this chapter provide checks and balances to reduce these biases, enabling a fuller understanding of the world.

Problems to Overcome

The information that managers use is limited by human biases in interpreting the world and our experiences of it. To take the best advantage of scientific knowledge, it is necessary to overcome these limitations.

Individuals are prone to see patterns even in random events, from the clouds in the sky to the leaves at the bottom of a teacup (Nickerson, 2002). The patterns that individuals see often reflect systematic misinterpretations that, over time, may come to be accepted as fact. One kind of misinterpretation, for example, is the "attribution bias," that is, the tendency to adopt self-enhancing views of failure and success (Zuckerman, 1979). If a slew of customer complaints come in after hiring a new customer-service agent, her boss may well blame the new hire, even if complaints have come in bunches before. On the other hand, if sales went up that month, the boss might see that good news as a sign that his commitment to hiring and training great agents has paid off. In either case, there is a real possibility that the observed changes are merely random fluctuations. The fact is that randomness exists everywhere. Our minds, on the other hand, seek certainty and look for patterns and explanations that create more of it. An EBMgt practitioner confronted with the forementioned complaint and sales data is conscious of the possibility of random fluctuation—and less likely to draw an unsubstantiated conclusion.

Two very different kinds of uncertainty exist: irreducible and reducible. Randomness creates irreducible uncertainty; it is intrinsic to the phenomenon and cannot be eliminated. *Reducible* uncertainty is that which can be diminished through learning (Montague, 2007). Customer complaints and sales data involve both.

Scientific evidence based on large numbers of observations identifies both random (irreducible) and systematic (predictable and reducible) variation. Knowing how to obtain and use scientific evidence and reliable business knowledge helps practitioners respond effectively to the uncertainty they face everyday in organizations. Customer complaints may be related to staff turnover (the people the new agent might have replaced), which can erode service quality. The EBMgt practitioner who is aware of the effects of turnover on service quality (e.g., Schneider & Bowen, 1985) is less likely to rush to blame the service agent inappropriately and better able to appreciate sources of fluctuation in business outcomes. The same goes for the EBMgt practitioner who has gathered data on historical drivers of company sales, making that person better able to judge whether the sales increase is meaningful or explained by outside forces (e.g., the weather or the economy). These practitioners use evidence to make informed judgments. On the other hand, the non-evidence-based practitioner who unjustly blames the new agent for complaints or takes credit for apparent successes is likely to repeat the same mistaken judgments time and again.

Despite the fact of randomness, greater predictive power and more reliable knowledge are possible. Aggregated events often can be predicted when individual events cannot. Scientific evidence capitalizes on the predictability of averaged data by gathering many observations in a single study. Science's reliance on multiple studies is even more powerful in finding the best explanation that accounts for known facts. Scientific research and careful attention to aggregated information can uncover patterns our unaided minds miss. Nonetheless, there is no such thing as a "scientifically proven" phenomenon (Rovelli, 2011):

> The very foundation of science is to keep the door open to doubt…a good scientist is never "certain"…Knowledge itself is probabilistic in nature….Better understanding of the meaning of probability, and especially realizing that we never have, nor need, "scientifically proven" facts, but only a sufficiently high degree of probability, in order to take decisions and act, would improve everybody's conceptual toolkit.

It has long been understood that the assumptions managers make can be stumbling blocks on the road to organizational effectiveness. William Redfield, the first Secretary of Commerce in the United States, long ago pointed out:

> EFFICIENCY means keen self-criticism. It means to go out into the shop and find nothing there that is sacred or fixed. It means that the shop six months ago shall be ancient history. It means the dropping of history, the forgetting of ghosts, the questioning of everything.
> (Redfield, 1912)

The human dilemma is that we actually see the world *through* our assumptions (Dawes, 2001). Chinese research subjects, born and raised in a highly collectivist society, were asked to look at pictures of fish and were found to commonly see a school of fish moving an individual fish along. American subjects, raised in a more individualistic society, tended to interpret the same picture as depicting a brave little fish leading the others (Morris & Peng, 1994). This is just one illustration of how virtually impossible it is for people to view events without making assumptions about them. Those assumptions reflect and reinforce preexisting beliefs—a

phenomenon referred to as confirmation bias. At the same time, one purpose of scientific research is to investigate the assumptions people make in interpreting the world to better understand how the world works and also how human tendencies affect it and its organizations. Becoming able to recognize and think critically about one's assumptions leads to better judgment.

Using the Best Available Scientific Knowledge

Scientific knowledge is potentially applicable to every aspect of management practice. An evidence-based practitioner is familiar with basic research in his or her area of practice. This familiarity is often based on training, self-guided reading, and contact with well-informed sources. A practitioner seeking to make more evidence-based decisions is in the habit of obtaining the best available scientific evidence on issues that matter (Zanardelli, chapter 11 of this volume). Research in the organization and management fields affirms some personal judgments (like the "commonsense" notion that employees derive job satisfaction from the rewards they receive, Porter & Lawler, 1968) and challenges others (pay for performance can actually reduce performance, Ariely, Gneezy, Loewenstein, & Mazar, 2009). As described earlier, science is less biased than unaided human judgment and thus provides, in general, more valid knowledge.

Frances Tan, the marketing vice president at the packaging corporation, is good at getting the assumptions behind business proposals and practices out in the open. Reacting to the investor press's recent questioning of the firm's growth potential, the CEO of Frances's firm had brought up the need to dominate the competition by getting their market share up. Frances took her boss aside and asked him, "Is market share the kind of growth we need?" Questioning assumptions is fundamental to good evidence-based practice. The craft of it is how to raise the issue especially when it's the boss making assumptions. Frances raised this question at a break in a meeting. She went on to explain that a lot of conventional thinking about market share is wrong (she actually said "not supported by the evidence"). In fact, the market share of firms whose stated objectives focus on beating out their competition is negatively related to their financial returns. Frances's basic point was informed by studies on the costs and benefits of market share. Firms pursuing profitability garner greater returns than those focused on gaining market share (Armstrong & Collopy, 1996; Armstrong & Green, 2007). This isn't to say market share never matters. It's just not a simple linear X→Y connection (i.e., firms perform better when they pursue market share if they are niched businesses or have lower expansion costs).

The advantage science has over individual experience is that scientific research is essentially a project involving many thousands of people using systematic methods to understand the world. Personal experience is plagued by the problem of small numbers: it reflects an individual's interpretation of events in his or her life. With its scale and scope, science can counter the human tendency to overinterpret small bits of information and underestimate randomness. Scientific research on management and organizations is conducted worldwide and is a project of many thousands of researchers. For instance, the Academy of Management, the most prominent research association of management scholars, educators, and practitioners, has, at this writing, more than 19,000 members from more than 60 countries. Such science-oriented organizations operate worldwide, made up of researchers studying organizations and the behavior of people associated with them.

Scientific knowledge relevant to management and organizations depends on two practices that give it different meaning and utility from other sorts of information, the peer-review process and the systematic review (SR).

Peer Review

The peer review process is a central means of establishing the credibility of scientific evidence (Werner, chapter 15 of this volume). Independent scientists anonymously review research to determine whether it merits publication in a scientific journal. A big part of this review is to establish the validity of findings by critically evaluating whether bias and alternative explanations can be ruled out. Peer review involves an authentication of research methods, findings, and conclusions prior to a scientific paper's acceptance and publication in a journal. (N.B.: certain scholarly books may also undergo critique similar to peer review as in the case of this handbook, published by a university press). It's good practice to first look to peer-reviewed sources when seeking out what is known about an issue or problem.

The advice to rely upon peer-reviewed sources also applies to popular management books available from a bookstore or online retailer. Go to the bookstore and pull a few books off the shelf that look like they might be useful to a manager. Flip to their reference sections and check out the extent to which the sources authors have used would pass our basic

(peer review) quality test. My own students, who do this as a class exercise, find that the majority of business books make limited use of research evidence. Most fail to use peer-reviewed journals as sources. A few writers like Malcolm Gladwell (2005) measure up quite nicely, offering reader-friendly translations of scientific findings previously published in peer-reviewed journals. The fact remains, however, that most management books rely on popular articles or the opinions of famous people, while ignoring scientific evidence. Peer-reviewed findings merit a degree of confidence, whereas non-peer-reviewed work and its derivatives must be treated with greater skepticism.

Systematic Reviews

SRs also play an important role in providing evidence for practice (Briner & Denyer, chapter 7 of this volume). An SR analyzes all studies relevant to a particular question in an explicit, transparent fashion in order to provide the best available answer. An SR avoids the (often subconscious) cherry picking of individual studies chosen for their support of the reviewer's preferred position. Because any single study has limitations, the best evidence comes from multiple studies with different kinds of designs and conducted by different scientists, thus providing independent corroboration that a finding is real. Research summaries based on a body of evidence, thus, are more valuable, because multiple studies can cancel out the limits of any one. As one example, a recent SR on employee involvement revealed its positive effects on employees, work groups, companies, and countries (e.g., outcomes included greater individual satisfaction, group and firm performance, and societal participation in democratic processes) and the importance of training and development to making employee involvement effective (Wegge et al., 2010).

SRs need to possess certain features if they are to be informative and useful (Briner & Denyer, chapter 7 of this volume). These include careful formulation of the managerial question and a willingness to adapt that question as the review process sheds light on the underlying issues. SRs also pay attention to data quality, to assess whether the body of studies has successfully ruled out possible bias. Under time pressure, a modified SR in the form of a rapid review can be conducted to identify the gist of what the evidence says.

Implications

By using peer review to critique single studies and SRs to answer important questions, we can identify the best available reliable knowledge. Knowledge vetted in this way is explicit and easily communicated. The specific products such knowledge yields include general principles (e.g., specific goals tend to lead to higher performance than do general goals; Latham & Locke, 2002) as well as action guides—such as the specific steps to follow in making a quality decision (Yates & Potwoworski, chapter 12 of this volume). Such knowledge products to support EBMgt are increasingly available. For example, Armstrong's (2010) *Persuasive Advertising: Evidence-Based Principles* contains 194 principles marketers and advertisers can use to formulate effective advertising. Locke's (2009) *Handbook of Principles of Organizational Behavior: Indispensible Knowledge for Evidence-based Management* contains more than 100 principles managers and human-resource (HR) professionals can use in developing effective practices for managing employees and organizing work. The scientific knowledge explosion is likely to increase the number and scope of these compendia in future. (Note: EBMgt is not about putting a hundred principles in play at one time! It is about learning the principles useful to your practice and looking into additional ones when new situations arise. See Rousseau and Barends, 2011.)

Systematic Use of Organizational Facts

A man should look for what is, and not for what he thinks should be.
—*Albert Einstein*

Facts are stubborn things.
—*Ronald Reagan*

Organizations and their decisions are as much structured by the information they pay attention to as by formal roles and reporting relationships. Identifying organizational facts that are critical to making important decisions requires systematic practices to overcome both the decision maker's cognitive limits and the unreliability of information.

Organizational facts describe the organization, its outcomes, and its environment. They come in many forms. These include basic metrics for assessing the health of an organization (cash flow and liquidity) or monitoring its business outcomes (e.g., EBITA, ROI) and customer/client impacts (e.g., for hospitals, the infection rate per patient days or severity adjusted mortality). Other facts pertain to the many factors contributing to performance, such as market- or customer-related competencies, employee and customer satisfaction (Drucker, 2003), and

organizational processes related to coordination and problem solving (Goodman, 2001). Additional information related to decisions includes the expected returns from allocating people or money to projects and environmental information relevant to strategy. A major value of all this information is that it can help to surface questions about assumptions and expectations (Drucker, 2003, pp. 95–98). This information, then, serves as a guide to more reflective managerial decisions and actions.

Problems to Overcome

Making fact-based decisions in organizations is not easy. The word *fact* connotes a verifiable truth; however, the basic metrics, outcomes, and indicators start out as raw data generated by the efforts of organization members or people outside the organization. Raw data can omit important information (e.g., counting the number of errors made in an air traffic facility doesn't tell whether the errors are consequential or insignificant or whether they were made by one person or many). Data are also contaminated in that information may be biased. For example, because business managers might be inclined to underestimate next year's revenues in order to avoid a shortfall, their forecasts may not be reliable.

A second challenge in using business facts is figuring out what they mean. Facts are subjectively interpreted. How they are understood can depend on the practitioner's job or functional background. In the early years of managerial decision research, Dearborn and Simon (1958) observed that the same business case tended to be seen as a personnel problem by HR people, a cash flow problem by finance people and an operations problem by production managers. Entrepreneurs may read opportunities into business situations in which bankers see only the risks (Sarasvathy, Simon, & Lave, 1998). Nonmanagerial employees make judgments about the trustworthiness of management based on the business information shared with them (Ferrante, 2006).

Facts are also political. The business information that managers rely on can be highly politicized. Reporting can be spun, framed, or downplayed, depending on the responses anticipated. From mundane concern for how a CEO will react to a performance problem to the catastrophe that followed Enron's "cooking the books" (McLean & Elkind, 2003), the channels through which facts about the organization's health and well-being must travel can resemble baffles rather than conduits of information. In the words of one administrator confronted with problems from a restructuring, "I don't want to know. If you give me data, I will have to act on it."

The facts managers use reveal what they pay attention to. The adage that "what gets measured gets managed" holds true (Cyert & March, 1992). Figuring out what facts to obtain and how to use them is a critical matter. Recalling the issue Frances Tan raised with her boss, the evidence suggests that market share growth is a less important objective than pursuing profitability. Armstrong (2007) says, "The objective should be profitability. In view of all the damage that occurs by focusing on market share, companies would be better off not measuring it." Still, it is no mean feat to collect useful and accurate information. Organizations are made up of different coalitions whose interests are often widely (even wildly) different (Hodgkinson, chapter 23 of this volume; Potwoworski & Green, chapter 16 of this volume). A responsible manager has a lot of ground to cover in figuring out what data might be useful and then to obtain them (Barnard, 1938). An evidence-based manager takes certain steps in analyzing organizational data in order to overcome their inherent limitations.

FACTS DIFFER IN THEIR RELIABILITY

Organizational facts may reflect measurement error and randomness. Donaldson (2010; chapter 14 of this volume) describes strategies for obtaining reliable organizational data. Small firms may need different strategies than large ones, but some general principles hold. The "small-numbers" problem means that data based on a single point in time are more likely to reflect random processes. A wise manager is skeptical of one-shot or single-time data. Instead, it may be better to collect data over time. It can also be important to interpret certain event data, such as accident or errors, in terms of ratios (e.g., errors divided by the number of transactions) rather than absolute counts. Base rates matter to the meaning of certain events. Sixty errors in a hospital that occur over the course of 15,000 patient days (a rate of 0.004 errors per patient day) may indicate safer health care than the 16 errors that occurred over just 1,000 patient days (an error rate of 0.016 errors per patient day—four times the rate of the other hospital).

CAUSAL AMBIGUITY

Causal ambiguity compounds the problems associated with organizational data in that identifying the key factors driving outcomes can be difficult. It can take considerable intelligence-gathering and analysis to figure out the real factors that account for fluctuating results, or the reasons why one department does something one way and gets a good result, while another tries it and doesn't. The higher up the manager is, the more likely that the data flowing in are aggregated. Though aggregated data can be useful, aggregation can disguise important variations. If revenues vary month to month, is this fluctuation across all parts of the organization, or is one area less stable than the rest? So too, fluctuations mean different things if results stem from independent actions by a firm's branch offices or the highly interdependent operations within an investment bank. In the past decade, we have seen very smart executives make big mistakes because they didn't understand the context in which they were operating (Goodman, 2001; McLean & Elkind, 2003).

All these characteristics of organizational data and their context need to be taken into account and managed in order to make informed decisions. Andrew J. Hoffman, a social scientist who has researched the cultural and social underpinnings of the backlash against climate change, has said, "(W)hen I hear scientists say, 'The data speak for themselves,' I cringe. Data never speak. And data generally and most often are politically and socially inflected" (Barringer, 2011).

Systematically Using Organizational Facts

Making decisions based on facts requires a set of supporting practices that increases the reliability and usefulness of available data. A useful first step involves a decision aid known as a logic model. A logic model spells out the process by which an organizational intervention, program, or strategy is expected to produce certain outcomes. In making expectations (its logic) explicit, a logic model helps identify the kinds of data needed to indicate if an intervention is working and whether actions are needed to revise or correct it. Such models may take the form of a framework describing resource flows (e.g., input→throughput→output) or any structured way of organizing and thinking about key factors in managerial decisions (e.g., Goodman, 2001; Zanardelli, chapter 11 of this volume).

One logic model used with success is the type illustrated in Figure 1.2a. This logic model, from the University of Wisconsin Extension Program Development (Taylor-Powell & Henert, 2008), can be used to lay out the process of implementing a strategy, a program, or a project. In the case of developing a new instructional program in a public outreach agency, practitioners can use a logic model to specify the program's important inputs (people, resources, knowledge) its outputs (activities and participants who engage in them), and desired outcomes (results measured in the short term, moderate, and long term; Figure 1.2b). Once specified, the concepts and ideas that populate a particular decision's logic model can be used to identify data that can be gathered to diagnose problems and inform the decision. For instance, short-term program outcomes include participant learning and motivation of the participants to use their learning. Medium-term outcomes include changes in their actual decisions and behavior. Longer-term outcomes are broader societal changes over time. A logic model helps identify the facts and metrics that provide important information to decision makers. At the same time, it calls attention to assumptions regarding the mechanisms whereby one stage affects the next. Since program activities and participants (as output) lead directly to the short-term outcomes of learning and motivation to use that learning, decision makers are alerted to the need to ensure that the participants are appropriately motivated. Since we cannot assume that learning and use are inevitable outcomes of participating in the program, the logic model calls attention to the need for interventions that promote both. Logic models make the assumptions and details of a decision more explicit. Models can be updated or revised based on what the decision maker learns in the course of their use.

With a logic model mapped out, the second step is an analytic plan that transforms data into reliable information (Donaldson, chapter 14 of this volume). As described earlier, data typically are raw observations, and are not necessarily reliable or informative in themselves. Such data may need to be aggregated and/or examined over time to determine their meaning.

The third step involves developing the ability to interpret information so that it can become actionable knowledge. To be actionable, knowledge must involve an understanding of the context of information. In the case of customer complaints, for example, an evidence-based manager can construct a model of the organization's approach to customer satisfaction, including its inputs, outputs, and outcomes, to diagnose what might be causing the complaints and take corrective action. The model

may specify that the organization's customer-service strategy is predicated on having a stable customer-service capability, as for the case in which employees know the customer and have latitude in how they provide service. When a personalized relationship is the basis of service, complaint trends might be examined in relation to changes in staffing or employee satisfaction, since turnover intentions and dissatisfaction among employees are known to reduce customer service (e.g., Schneider & Bowen, 1985). Assessing business facts in this case can call attention to staffing issues that must be addressed to ultimately resolve the problem.

As a technical manager in a regional bank, Normand Mathieu headed a department that was having trouble attracting and retaining women and minorities. He first looked for information within the bank, and he identified that units with diversity goals in their annual performance assessments were more successful in promoting women and minorities. Persuaded that greater diversity could be achieved in his department, too, Normand began working with his supervisory staff to develop and support diversity goals. Among other things, he sent several of his staff to interview managers in other units, in order to find out the sort of practices units emphasizing diversity had used to meet their goals. The supervisors reported on a variety of practices. Not being sure which of these worked best, given the small-numbers problem, Normand then searched in an online library database to find whether scientific evidence indicated that any of these practices worked to promote diversity. Research evidence indicated that two practices the successful departments employed were known to be effective in promoting diversity: clear performance expectations and staff development plans (Cox, 1994). Normand and his direct reports implemented them both. At the same time, Normand created a logic model to guide future diversity planning and assessment, based on the research he had read and what he had learned from investigating diversity activities within the bank (Figure 1.2c). The model helped Normand figure out what data to gather in order to monitor and improve diversity efforts in his unit and, subsequently, across the bank.

Implications

Reliance on organizational facts in EBMgt requires on-going effort to both identify relevant data and transform them into useful knowledge. Learning to resolve the qualities of data that

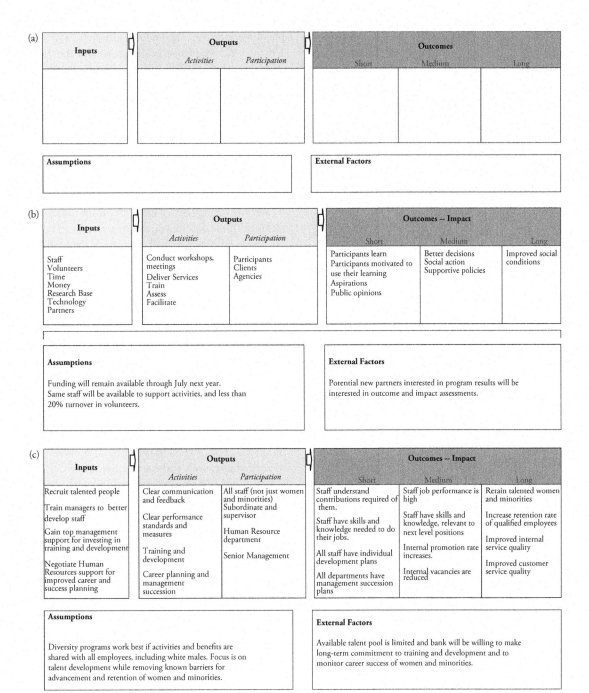

Fig. 1.2 a. Logic Model Template (University of Wisconson Extension, Taylor-Powell & Henert, 2008). b. Logic Model for Extension Program Strategy (adapted from University of Wisconson Extension, Taylor-Powell & Henert, 2008). c. Logic Model Applied to Diversity Issues.

introduce error and unreliability helps practitioners make better judgments regarding business indicators (Donaldson, 2010). Finally, gathering useful organizational data is aided by developing frameworks or logic models that help identify the information a decision requires (Zanardelli, chapter 11 of this volume).

Reflective and Thoughtful Judgment Processes

Compared with what we ought to be, we are only half awake...

We are making use of only a small part of our possible mental resources...which only

exceptional individuals push to their extremes of use.
—*William James*

(L)ack of certainty is perceived as a sign of weakness, instead of being what it is: the first source of our knowledge.
—*Carlos Rovelli*

The ways decisions are made in EBMgt practice reflects perhaps the most dramatic difference from business as usual today. Managers will always need to make decisions under conditions of incomplete information and unknowable futures—yet most decisions fail to take advantage of what is actually known or knowable about the content and process of good decision making. An EBMgt approach involves paying greater attention to the ways a decision might be made, the issues that frame it, and the facts that inform it. This approach seeks to overcome what Yates (2003) has termed "decision neglect," failure to use fully the resources at hand that could help make a good decision.

Advances in management science and research have not spread evenly over the varied domain of decision making (Simon, 1986). These advances have had their greatest impact on decisions that are well structured, deliberative, and quantitative; an example would be the case of financial decisions, though these are not without their own issues (Kaplan, 2011). Evidence-based and related practices have less impact when decisions are loosely structured, intuitive, and qualitative. EBMgt overcomes decision neglect in two ways: first by increasing the practitioner's capacity for decision awareness, and second by developing and using processes based on scientific research, which improve the quality of a manager's decisions and what he or she learns from experience.

Problems to Overcome

Science-based practices that drive quality decision making have been identified, but executives, midlevel managers, and supervisors are inconsistent in whether and how well they apply them (Yates, 2003). The practice of EBMgt makes use of a number of "repairs" to overcome cognitive limits and biases (Heath et al., 1998). In the context of decision making, three additional limitations are targeted for repair and development.

BOUNDED RATIONALITY

Unaided human judgment cannot fully use the array of information relevant to most decisions, a phenomenon known as bounded rationality (Simon, 1967). It manifests in sporadic use of available facts and considerations (e.g., options, impact on others, ease of implementation, risks) because people can only pay attention to and process a limited amount of information at any one time. It also means that people lack decision awareness and cannot make accurate reports on their decision processes (Nisbett & Ross, 1980).

OVERVALUING PRIOR EXPERIENCE

Relying on experience can suffer from the small-numbers problem, in which what occurs may be random or misunderstood, but we believe otherwise. Because we tend to give credence to what we have seen with our own eyes, we assume our own experiences are typical. Relying on prior experience in place of more systematic knowledge has a lousy track record (March, 2010). We give ourselves explanations for why one decision worked (our good judgment, careful planning, the right timing) and another didn't (bad luck, wrong partners). We veer toward accounts that confirm our beliefs and filter out explanations that challenge them. In talking with other people about our experiences, we gravitate toward like-minded others, from the people we talk with at work to preferred columnists and writers whose views endorse our own. Even drawing on the past is uncertain. People generally recall experiences incompletely, if not also inaccurately and in self-serving ways, making it difficult to truly "learn from experience" (March, 2010). Experience may lead at least as often to confirmation of existing beliefs as it does to valid learning. Science offers a good understanding of the world and can help people make better sense of their experiences.

Valid and reliable learning to make decisions can certainly come from experience. It is greatest in specialized domains (e.g., making decisions in driving or cooking, practicing accounting or law) where good performance is well understood and the learner repeatedly practices certain core processes. Experiential learning works well in domains in which complete and accurate knowledge of results is readily available and the learner is motivated and capable of interpreting feedback thoughtfully (Ericsson, Kramp, & Tesch-Römer, 1993; Ericsson & Lehmann, 1996). Unfortunately, management is widely practiced without any special training in making good decisions. Its decision consequences can take years to materialize and involve so many stakeholders that "complete and accurate knowledge of results" is a pipedream.

RELIANCE ON INTUITION WHILE IGNORING FACTS

Relying on intuition to make decisions in unstructured, diverse domains, such as general management, is associated with poorer outcomes when compared against the results of systematic decision making (Meehl, 1954; Highhouse, 2008). A classic example of a problematic reliance on intuition is the baseball scouts who travel the United States look for promising rookies among high-school and college ballplayers. Lewis's (2004) book *Moneyball* describes how Oakland A's manager Billy Beane built a successful team on a smaller budget than other teams by the careful analysis of individual performance data. He didn't have to worry that other teams would copy his strategy: Analyzing performance data to make managerial decisions was not a common practice in the sport. His statistician commented, "It's hard to tell what the scouts make of these numbers. Scouts from other teams would almost surely say: who gives a shit about the guy's numbers. . . . You need to *look* at the guy. *Imagine* what he might become." (p. 32). The Oakland A's performance far exceeded their resources because their manager relied on facts important to success in baseball, whereas other teams continued to relied on "feel." In doing so, Billy Beane was able to recruit players with critical capabilities that were not well understood by other teams.

Making Reflective, Thoughtful Judgments

An evidence-based approach involves developing one's judgment. No new approach can be effective unless it takes human imperfections into account. The repair for unaided human judgment entails checking the logic and the supporting facts related to a decision to be made or a problem to solve. Concern for facts and logic mean that EBMgt practice often takes the form of active questioning and skepticism, a habit of mind reflecting a critical, rigorous way of thinking that expands use of available information. This habit of mind is referred to as "mindfulness," that is, a heightened sense of situational awareness and a conscious control over one's thoughts and behavior relative to the situation (Langer, 1989).

CRITICAL THINKING

Critical thinking is at the core of evidence-based management. The word *critical* is a loaded word. This usage doesn't mean being negative or oppositional. It means to devote one's attention to thinking, including raising awareness of hidden values, beliefs, and assumptions—those of others and our own. Critical thinking involves questioning assumptions, evaluating evidence, and testing the logic of ideas, proposals, and courses of action. More than a cognitive skill, it involves the courage to pursue reason and logic to where they lead. Given the limitations to how people process information, critical thinking in EBMgt makes use of heuristics, thinking aids, and decision tools to more mindfully make judgments and decisions. These aids and tools constitute another form of cognitive repair that scientific evidence indicates improves judgment and decisions (Heath, Larrick, & Klayman, 1998; Larrick, 2009).

A useful heuristic includes questions probing the logic underlying assumptions and proposals. In their book on EBMgt, Pfeffer and Sutton (2006) raise powerful questions. A key one is why do management practitioners think that a past practice they intend to use again has been effective. Their point is that if you cannot specify the logic of why you believe a practice works, it is unlikely that you know whether it really does work. It is important to be thorough in any logical analysis of practical matters. The evidence-based decision maker pays attention to the kinds of information being used to formulate a policy or practice, and he or she actively scrutinizes assumptions to see if they are reasonable.

SYSTEMATIC DECISION-MAKING

EBMgt is predicated on paying explicit attention to actual decision processes (Yates, 2003; Yates & Potwoworski, chapter 12 of this volume). As the example of Frances Tan illustrates, the process by which evidence-based practitioners make decisions is itself guided by research. Of course, no process can ever guarantee a perfect outcome. Considerable research demonstrates that certain considerations in making decisions can improve their quality, leading, on average, to better outcomes. These include attention to alternatives, risks, and stakeholders, and advance specification of criteria for a successful decision (Yates & Potwoworski, chapter 12 of this volume). Decision quality can be improved by using evidence-informed action guides such as Yates and Potwoworski propose, and by feedback from decision tracking.

Decision tracking, obtaining feedback on the outcomes of decisions, is a way of getting accurate feedback on results in order to improve both learning and the decision process. Decision makers record a decision they have just made along with the outcomes they anticipate from it, and they later read that document to reflect on and learn from the decision's consequences. Repeating this practice over time helps develop better decision processes (Drucker, 2003; Evans & Wright, 2009). Divisions of Bosch, the automotive parts manufacturer, use tracking to improve both business and engineering decisions. Tracking supports another important aspect of decision management: monitoring the aftermath of a decision to see if its steps and timeframe are being followed (Yates, 2003). The feedback and reflection that decision tracking supports improves decisions by promoting critical thinking and awareness of decision processes.

Frances Tan provides an example of how these practices can be used. Frances and her staff, with the help of a consultant, built a decision framework or guide to help them touch all the important bases in making a good decision. She first familiarized her direct reports with the reasons that improved decision processes were important. They agreed to try using the framework, and after exploring what issue would be best to begin with, Frances and her staff elected to test out the framework by piloting it on a set of changes required by new governmental regulations. They gathered preliminary information regarding the new requirements and benchmarked what other facilities were doing. Ultimately, they chose to make one coherent set of changes to reduce disruptions over time. In the core decision process, they considered a set of alternatives and how employees, customers, and regulators would likely react to each approach. They developed a plan that assigned responsibilities and created milestones. Included was a series of follow-up meetings to monitor progress. At one meeting, several team members talked about what they were learning from the decision process and the adjustments they'd made in making their own decisions. These discussions led to use of an adapted version of the framework, suited to the division's particular decisions.

Evidence-based managers like those I describe in this chapter use scientific findings in two ways. First, they make decisions and develop practices informed by scientific evidence and reliable organizational facts. Second, they build standard procedures based on what the evidence and their data say works. The kinds of scientific knowledge that might be used in making an evidence-based decision cover the waterfront from research in marketing, operations, finance, and information systems to knowledge of human behavior in organizations.

Implications

The basic work of management is decision making. Refining one's judgment and using decision aids is essential to improving decision quality. Indeed, decision makers at the top of the pyramid are known to more commonly use decision techniques to improve quality (Pavic, 2008). Such techniques have value at all organizational levels.

Ethics and Stakeholder Considerations

There is surely nothing quite so useless as doing with great efficiency what should not be done at all.
—*Peter Drucker*

The hardest hit, as everywhere, are those who have no choice.
—*Theodor Adorno*

Ethics are standards of conduct that guide our actions as human beings and as professionals. Business schools have discussed ethics since there have been business schools (Khurana, 2007). Ethics is not science per se; they are moral standards that promote goodness, justice, and fairness. Evidence-based practitioners, by virtue of their awareness of how things work, have considerable power to impact the lives and well-being of many, and a professional obligation to make ethical decisions. Indeed, ethical considerations are part of the decision process that Yates details (Yates, 2003; Yates & Potwoworski, chapter 12 of this volume). Nonetheless, rather than treat ethics as part of systematic decision making, its importance warrants its own place in our discussion of EBMgt.

Problems to Overcome

Making ethical managerial decisions is subject to the array of human biases already described. Ethical decision making is effortful in the face of role demands, situational pressures, and conflicting interests, standard fare in modern organizations. As managers advance up the organizational hierarchy, changes in role and vantage point are known to shift their views regarding the stakeholders important to their decisions. Managers at lower levels are inclined to focus on their subordinates and supervisors (Hill, 2003), whereas those at higher levels tend to pay attention to issues important to the top management team (Sutcliffe & Huber, 1998). Given the salience of local concerns, ethical decision making requires both mental effort and information gathering in order to avoid one's limited vantage point creating a disservice to others. Research has identified one antidote: Seeking the opinions of "reasonable third parties." These are people without vested interests in the situation who can offer perspective on what may be fair, ethical, and appropriate conduct (Bok, 1978).

Practicing Ethical Decision Making

Stakeholder considerations are an inherent feature of systematic decision models (Yates, 2003). Attention to the often-diverse interests of stakeholders helps managers appreciate how their organization fits into its larger environment and how its standard operating procedures affect stakeholders, within the company (employees, managers, stockholders), immediately beyond (customers, suppliers, financiers), as well as the general public. Stakeholders can differ with respect to the immediacy with which organizational decisions impact them. Thus, it can be important to broaden the time frame considered in weighing the consequences of corporate decisions. In particular, broader time frames call attention to "externalities," outcomes borne by others not party to the decision. Some externalities are positive, such as the corporate development activities that bring jobs to an impoverished neighborhood. Negative externalities create costs or burdens for others, such as pollution or job loss.

Heuristics and frameworks, like the action guides for decisions already described, exist for making ethical decisions (e.g., Makkula Center, 2009). Such frameworks advise developing a trained sensitivity to ethical issues and a practiced method for exploring the ethical implications of a decision. As with decision making generally, it is easier to regularly attend to ethics in making decisions when a framework outlining decision steps or a heuristic specifying important questions is available.

Consider the tough call Admiral William J. Fallon, head of the American military in the Middle East, made in 2007. A stream of intelligence reports showed Al Qaeda and Taliban leaders would be meeting in the Tora Bora region of Afghanistan. *New York Times* reporters Eric Schmitt and Thom Thanker (May 5, 2011) wrote that there had been hints that Bin Laden might travel there to hatch suicide attacks against Europe and North America. The U.S. military planned a large strike with bombers, attack helicopters, and artillery targeting this mountain valley along the Afghanistan border with Pakistan. Six B-2 bombers had made it halfway to their target when they were ordered to return to base. The size of the mission, coupled with the ambiguity of the intelligence, alarmed some senior United States commanders, including Admiral Fallon. "Fallon's view was you're swatting a fly with a 16-pound hammer," said a senior American officer familiar with the commander's thinking. "This was carpet bombing, pure and simple," said another top military officer who had openly voiced disagreement with the operation. "It was not precision-targeted. There was no way to separate the Al Qaeda leadership that might be on hand, and the fighters, from the local population and the camp followers." In place of a huge air strike that might kill hundreds of civilians, a smaller attack was carried out, killing dozens of militants. Osama bin Laden was not there. These deliberations, made at a time of considerable pressure, when ethical decision making could have taken a back seat to the immediacy of the goal of taking out one of America's most-sought-after enemies, later informed the successful 2011 commando raid that culminated in the killing of Bin Laden in his urban hideout in Pakistan.

Implications

Ethical considerations in decision making primarily pertain to the impact of decisions and organizational actions on stakeholders, particularly with regard to how costs and burdens are allocated to various groups. In line with other aspects of EBMgt practice, critical thinking and regular use of evidence-based heuristics and frameworks can call attention to ethical issues in organizational decisions. Careful exploration of the problem, aided by the insights and perspectives of others, helps practitioners make ethical choices.

Adaptive Practices Within EBMgt

We aren't going to be more wrong than the way we did it before.
—*Billy Beane*

Science is organized knowledge. Wisdom is organized life.
—*Immanuel Kant*

EBMgt practice is not a cookbook or a formula. It is a variety of science-informed approaches that can be adapted to make better-quality decisions in the service of organizations, their members, stakeholders, and the public. Indeed, it may be that calling this array of practices "evidence-based" puts people off, making it sound like the evidence decides and managers just comply. Nothing is further from the truth. Evidence is not answers. It is input to the information and processes that help practitioners to make better judgments and decisions. It doesn't matter if a manager or consultant using these practices labels them differently. Feel free to call them "evidence-informed," "adaptive decision making," or whatever you like ("scientific management," of course, is taken). In real-world use, thoughtful practitioners will adapt EBMgt's four facets as needed. Here are some common circumstances in EBMgt's adaptive practice.

Situations Where Lots of Scientific Evidence Exists

Scientific findings provide considerable guidance for certain decisions. However, using science requires practitioners to interpret the evidence and turn it into useful practices. For example, a hospital's chief executive initiated an innovative labor-management arrangement in response to the increase in employees seeking early retirement. After considering various approaches, he learned from a consulting psychologist about findings from research that colleagues and I have done on flexible arrangements negotiated between workers and their employers (Hornung, Rousseau, & Glaser, 2008; Rousseau, Hornung, & Kim, 2009). To motivate his employees to stay rather than take early retirement, the CEO and his HR staff met with managers and employees to encourage them to negotiate development plans and flexible arrangements.

The process this CEO and his staff created adapted the general findings of research on negotiated flexibility to the hospital's circumstances (e.g., a fund was created for each individual employee that could be expended only via discussion with the immediate manager). The approaches used in the settings on which past research were based had focused more on informal negotiations between employee and supervisor. In the context of this hospital, located in the Netherlands, a more formal approach was considered culturally more acceptable. In keeping with the spirit of EBMgt, after an evaluation of this intervention, a more comprehensive program was developed to promote both greater development and flexibility via negotiation.

Critical thinking and use of evidence are not limited to executives. Subordinates can bring evidence and related issues to the attention of their bosses, the organization's board, or others in a position to make decisions. The CEO and top management team in one firm had long participated in in-house education on research evidence. Sometimes local university faculty gave workshops, and other times senior management led the sessions. When the company president indicated his intention to cut back on employee benefits, the president's executive assistant decided to contact two business-school faculty members who had led recent workshops. Her question to the faculty was what research suggested as the likely implications of such a cut. A conference call was then organized that included the CEO and two business-school professors. On that call, the executive assistant raised her concerns about how various stakeholders would be affected by the planned cut. She worried that employees would think the cuts were unfair and find the sudden change too drastic. With the CEO listening, the executive assistant probed the issues of fairness and justice (Tyler, 2006) and psychological contract violation (Rousseau, 1995), resulting in the president's decision to delay a change in benefits until staff were informed of the company's financial predicament and alternative ways of reducing costs were explored. The result was a less-radical health-insurance change (adding a modest employee co-pay) plus considerable savings achieved through employee efforts to reduce inefficiencies. A by-product was increased employee awareness of the organization's economic predicament. This awareness made subsequent changes more acceptable.

In both examples, it wasn't the evidence that solved the problem; rather, it was individual managers and employees who sought out evidence to answer a particular question and then presented it to others. Judgments still need to be made and the facts in the situation taken into account. In doing so, practitioners develop skills in applying evidence. These skills lead to practices that suit the situation while acting on the underlying principles the evidence supports (e.g., Parnas & Clements, 1986).

Using Evidence from Very Different Populations and Settings

Adapting evidence from one population to another requires thoughtful judgment. Veterinarians face this situation frequently. The shortage of clinical research on animals has led veterinarians to regularly use studies conducted on humans in caring for dogs and cats (and a host of other animals). As veterinarians come to use evidence much as physicians do (e.g., Olivery & Mueller, 2003), this adaptation leads to special care in its application, including attention to the animal's body size and metabolism.

Asking questions about how evidence from one domain might apply to another can lead to new angles of thinking and ways to solve problems. The U.S. Army implemented a program to train more than a million soldiers in emotional resiliency (Carey, 2009). Its basis is a program developed by Martin Seligman to reduce mental distress in children and teens. At this time, there is no evidence that mental toughness can be taught in a classroom; nonetheless, the experiences of veterans of the Iraq War and incidence of posttraumatic stress syndrome upon returning home have motivated the Army to make use of the "best available evidence" and careful monitoring of outcomes (Carey, 2009). Soldiers at all levels participate in this training (Lester, 2010), which emphasizes "the immutables" of positive psychology including focusing on one's strengths, knowing what is controllable and what's not, recognizing positive outcomes even in negative events, and building strong relationships. Evaluation of this training's effectiveness is ongoing, and tools have been developed to assess outcomes over time.

Lots of Organizational Data but Little Relevant Research

Practice decisions can involve circumstances for which little research exists. Benchmarking against other settings is sometimes used in these circumstances (Kovner, Fine, & D'Aquila, 2009). Practitioners should also step back and ask whether relevant facts are available in-house or easily obtainable to help understand the issue.

Consider the case of whether a hospital should continue its palliative care unit (White & Cassel, 2009). Consultants were brought in to help manage the unit's costs without compromising quality. Their initial analysis indicated that their hospital's cost per patient discharged from palliative care was considerably greater than the reimbursement they received from insurance agencies and other payers, and they recommended that the unit be closed. At the time, virtually no published literature existed on the financial contributions that palliative-care programs made to hospitals. Some articles offered the opinion that financial viability was unlikely unless the average daily occupancy was over 70 percent (this unit's utilization fluctuated between 55 percent and 77 percent). Careful re-analysis of hospital cost data indicated that the consultants had assigned all the costs of each patient's treatment to the palliative-care unit, including any inpatient days prior to admission to the unit. However, patients typically did not transfer into palliative care until after 10 days or more of hospitalization. Analyzing costs day by day following patient transfer to palliative care, the unit's management realized that its costs were considerably lower than those incurred from previous stays in other units, a savings of several hundred thousand dollars per patient. They then used a "what-if" analysis to explore the implications if more of the hospital's terminally ill patients were transferred to palliative care after spending two weeks or more in conventional treatment. Evidence suggested considerable additional savings. Based on this assessment, the program continued. Further, having become sophisticated in analyzing outcome data, the unit's managers were able to turn their attention to assessing and improving the quality of care. This case illustrates that, even with little scientific evidence on the decision itself, the process for making decisions can be informed by reliable local information, with attention to decision formulation, framing of alternatives, and stakeholder concerns.

Novel Decisions with neither Evidence nor Experience

The future is uncertain, and complex interactions can cause events never before seen, including technology-related disasters and economic catastrophes. Scientific study on unpredictable environments has identified several findings of use to managers in these circumstances.

Novel, unpredictable events may require us to adjust to them once they occur, rather than to try and anticipate them (Taleb, 2010). According to current evidence, such events are likely to be best addressed by high levels of situational awareness. Situational awareness involves scanning the situation in order to interpret its features in discriminating, observant ways (Weick & Sutcliffe, 2006). In this process, the decision maker generates a large number of distinctions that helps to refine his or her existing concepts or create new ones to better understand the uncertain situation. A danger in dealing with truly novel and potentially consequential events (e.g., a tsunami that generates a nuclear disaster) is that decision makers will focus on some aspect of the situation that seems familiar and generalize from it to things that remain unobserved. For example, treating a financial crisis today in the same way one responded the last time might ignore fundamental differences in their causes and consequences. A more informed approach is to keep an open mind and pursue multiple avenues for action, since any understanding can only be tentative (Weick & Sutcliffe, 2006).

Implications

Evidence-based approaches can apply whether a decision's circumstances are recurrent or novel, replete with prior research, or radically new. The preceding examples illustrate that the practice of EBMgt can differ depending on the decision and the relevance of existing knowledge and scientific evidence. New circumstances may have little research to illuminate them, yet practitioners can still take advantage of scientific findings on judgment and decision making. The practice of EBMgt depends on its practitioners' informed judgment in choosing those EBMgt approaches that best apply.

EBMgt's Three Communities

As the saying goes, "Vision without execution is hallucination." In offering our vision of evidence-based management, we recognize that execution is both important and difficult. Making EBMgt a reality requires contributions from practitioners, educators, and scholars and, in many ways, requires collaborations among all three of these groups. Evidence-based practice is what practitioners do. However, the infrastructure required to make EBMgt possible involves the combined efforts of practitioners, educators, and researchers.

The Most Diverse Category: Practitioners

Practitioners—including consultants, managers, and others working in organizations—are EBMgt's central actors. Ultimately, its success lies with them. Not only must practitioners embrace the concept to make it work, they will largely determine how it is practiced. From the present early stages of "EBMgt 1.0," like software and other knowledge products, EBMgt will undoubtedly evolve.

Practitioners are not monolithic. Insofar as practitioners are diverse in their roles, settings, and attributes, EBMgt will take an array of forms. Management is as much an activity as a role or group of people. People make decisions on their organization's behalf at all levels, from the ground floor to the executive suite. The organizations for which they make decisions include single-person businesses, mom-and-pop shops, midsize concerns, global corporations, and networked organizations existing in cyberspace. Across these organizations EBMgt will mix and match various processes and practices. Practitioners should feel free to adopt, adapt, and innovate (and evaluate the outcomes!).

Management is not a profession in the traditional sense. Unlike medicine or accounting, there are no required credentials, agreed-upon base of knowledge, or code of conduct. Like parenting, people can become managers without education or preparation. The results of management decisions echo those of parenting: they are consequential, sometimes beneficial to individuals and the broader society, and sometimes not. The movement promoting EBMgt aspires to promote better-quality decisions and organizational practices by developing our capacity to use what we can know more effectively. Management may not be a profession, but an individual manager can be a professional.

Managers committed to EBMgt must sometimes make their way in settings not particularly friendly to evidence (see Speicher & Adams, chapter 17 in this volume). In doing so, it might be best to focus first on improving one's individual decision-making skills and knowledge of evidence (Rousseau & Barends, 2011). This entails priming the pump by developing a more critical mindset. Learning how to access evidence is a next step (Werner, chapter 15 of this volume), keeping in mind that when confronted with a demanding situation, decision makers tend to go with the information in hand. It can help to identify in advance where evidence might be especially useful. Targeting reading and seeking out evidence-informed consultants and scholars as contacts can enable rapid reviews on important practice issues. Such activities help the individual practitioner deepen his or her expertise as an evidence-based professional.

Building a more evidence-supportive organization starts with awareness about the existence and utility of scientific research for organizational decisions (see Rousseau & Barends, 2011 for more details). Getting the word out can involve discussing new findings in conversations and meetings, citations used in memos to present evidence-based ideas, and a host of other small but cumulative acts.

Basing one's professional practice on evidence often involves managing up as well as down. It is less about becoming an evidence fundamentalist and more a process of influencing by education, persuasion, and example. Two practices apply in managing up as well as down. The first is asking the important questions, "Why do you think that? Do we have the best evidence?" The second is commissioning and/or conducting SRs of evidence on important practice questions. The latter gets people involved in the search for and synthesis of evidence and builds their capacity for critical thinking. Similarly, certain routines such as feedback gathering and systematic decision making can improve a manager's practice while helping him or her learn better from experience. Consultants who ground their practice in science, such as those at Ten Have Change Management in Europe and Valtera in North America, can provide organizational leaders with the procedures and tools that translate evidence into solutions.

Educators

The obituary of long-time dean of the Harvard Medical School, Daniel Tosteson, quotes him as saying, "Knowing people would have long careers and that so much will be proven wrong, we cannot have a curriculum based only on facts, but on making learning and expanding knowledge a part of the process" (Weber, 2009, A25). Tosteson was renowned for shifting the teaching of medicine away from "ingestion and regurgitation of vast amounts of information, and more on patient care and problem solving" (p. A25). Combining scientific knowledge with solving problems and updating repertoires as new knowledge emerges are as challenging for self-improving managers as for physicians. The professional schools that educate them face the same difficulties.

A big gap exists between what management educators teach and what the research says. The founding of the first business school, Wharton, preceded the first management research by several decades. What existed then were how-to manuals and industry examples, including the structures of railroads and retail stores. Insofar as management education emphasized practices used in existing firms, management was taught as a craft. The emergence of management research (Frese et al., chapter 6 of this volume; Madhavan & Mahoney, chapter 5 of this volume; Rousseau, chapter 4 of this volume) brought scientific knowledge into the business-school curriculum. Yet business schools typically have difficulty balancing practice and research (Simon, 1967). The evidence-teaching gap in business schools remains especially problematic in courses in strategy, organizational behavior, and HR (Charlier, Brown, & Rynes, 2011).

Contemporary practitioners, even those with MBAs, tend to lack fundamental management knowledge. Not being a formal profession, management has not been subject to the forces in place in other fields to promote use of evidence. No licenses or credentials exist to guarantee that managers have certain requisite professional knowledge. Credentialing bodies such as the Association to Advance Collegiate Schools of Business focus more on faculty education and research productivity than on the quality of knowledge taught. Reasons for educators failing to teach evidence include the fact that many management educators don't know the evidence themselves. They also fail to help students learn how to access and make use of research to be produced after they graduate.

Teaching Evidence, Search and Use

Management education needs to help students think critically and pursue learning goals aligned with the features of EBMgt (Jelley, Carroll, & Rousseau, chapter 19 of this volume). This includes teaching evidence-based principles and decision processes as well as how to obtain reliable and useful business information. Fortunately, there is a new effort to develop evidence-based textbooks and teaching materials (Pearce, chapter 21 of this volume), which will ease the process.

A major challenge for educators is preparing managers to update their knowledge as the evidence base expands. A key task that educators face is preparing practitioners to learn how to obtain important scientific knowledge in a timely way when decisions are at hand. EBMgt requires the capacity and willingness to search for and evaluate evidence. Much has been made of speed as a business resource, but using research can take time. It is important that professionally educated managers acquire a sound knowledge base about human behavior, decision making, and organizational design during their formal education. At the same time, we need to prepare them to access information while on the job, too. A good deal of information on how to obtain relevant scientific evidence is provided in this handbook (Barends et al., chapter 2 of this volume; Briner & Denyer, chapter 7 of this volume; Werner, chapter 15 of this volume) and elsewhere (Rousseau & Barends, 2011). Such preparation is nontrivial, as practitioners often need to learn how to state their question at a level of abstraction suitable for searching in research databases.

Teaching in an Evidence-Informed Fashion

Teaching evidence well coincides with teaching well, period. By this I mean teaching in an evidence-informed fashion, incorporating effective teaching principles into the design of courses and learning experiences (Goodman & O'Brien, chapter 18 of this volume). An educator goes into a certain field because he or she is good at the kind of thinking it requires and his or her expertise in that area has deepened over time. However, being deeply expert at something can at times interfere with one' ability to recognize that barriers exist for new learners. Middendorf and Pace (2004) point out that having faculty from other disciplines sit in on one's classes can make it easier to identify key concepts, termed "threshold concepts," that the experts have mastered but many learners never grasp. For a molecular biology professor, the recognition may be to teach students to visualize complex molecular structures. In the case of learning how to diagnose an employee performance problem, learners may need to develop a mental representation of the individual, group, and organizational factors that affect employee behavior.

Evidence is easy to ignore or misunderstand when poorly taught. Useful findings can be at odds with users' values or mindsets. Effective teaching may require the use of motivating stories and attention to the applications of evidence. Learners need to practice turning using evidence into appropriate problem solutions.

Researchers

Scholars have four important roles to play in EBMgt. The first is to conduct research that explicates the actual content and processes of decisions made in organizations. Field research on the way actual decisions are made is especially needed. Closing the gap between research and practice in this and other areas requires greater researcher contact with the problems and decisions practitioners face.

The second is to support evidence use in the ways scholars approach peer review. This peer-review process should include attention to the implications a particular study has for practice. Scholars have begun advocating for more explicit prescriptions in management research publications (Bazerman, 2005). I concur, while recognizing that there are difficulties with this idea. The education level required to read the "Implications for Practice" sections in management journals increased by nearly a full grade (from 16.6 to 17.5 years) between 1992–1993 and 2003–2007 (Bartunek & Rynes, 2010). Most of the advice offered says "be aware of *x* or *y*"—that is, what *not* to do—rather than explaining what to do, when, and how. Scholars are trained to be critical and are often reluctant to claim benefits from acting upon evidence. Such caution is justified by an important factor: A single finding in itself may be neither reliable nor generalizable. In this regard, practice implications in research articles should reflect the balance of evidence, a matter that

scholars supporting EBMgt may be in a position to assess and provide useful comment. More balance in the review process may be achieved by including reviewers who are knowledgeable practitioners (e.g., consultants and experienced managers with a PhD or executive doctorate)—something that practice-oriented research publications (e.g., *Academy of Management Perspectives* and *Human Resource Management*) already do.

Third, researchers can support and participate in SRs, including meta-analyses, to identify conclusions the evidence supports. In my teaching, I am repeatedly struck by the usefulness of meta-analyses and SRs for giving nonscholars more ready understanding (and confidence) regarding research findings. At the same time, many subfields of management research, including organizational theory and strategy, place less emphasis on the accumulation of findings (Madhavan & Mahoney, chapter 5 of this volume). This is a source of repeated frustration for practitioners seeking research-based facts on strategy, organizational design, and organizational-environment relationships. Scholars can advance both practice and their own fields by doing more to build cumulative bodies of research and evaluate what we can know from them.

Research in organizations has always been motivated by practical problems (Rousseau, 1997; Rousseau, chapter 4 of this volume). In the nineteenth century, it identified causes and remedies for telegrapher's cramp, an occupational injury comparable to carpal tunnel syndrome today (Telegrapher's Cramp, 1875). Now after decades of management and organizational research, bodies of evidence exist relevant to a host of practical matters, from incentive pay to organizing, and from mergers to downsizing. Innovative techniques for answering practical questions fuel the growth of meta-analyses and SRs to overcome the academics' reluctance to draw practical conclusions (Rousseau, Manning, & Denyer, 2008). This zeitgeist is aided by the fact that more practitioners, particularly executives and consultants, are raising questions for research reviews to answer. Executive programs for practicing managers, such as Cranfield in the United Kingdom and Case Western Reserve University in the United States (Salipante & Smith, chapter 20 of this volume), increasingly have participants conduct SRs as part of their education.

The last important scholarly contribution to EBMgt is the weakest link: practice-oriented research deliberately undertaken to provide scientific knowledge that informs practice. Practice-oriented research examines how practitioners currently practice. In its various forms, practice-oriented research provides information about conditions and support practices that make scientific knowledge more useful. Its purposes are twofold: (1) to find solutions to practical problems, and (2) to ease their adoption by identifying required supports while reducing factors that work against their adoption or effective implementation. In medicine, this kind of research has been termed "translation science." At one time, progress in medicine was almost exclusively from basic research on the biology of disease. Turning these advances into clinical practice was slow and sporadic. Progress has only recently been made in the rate of improvement in evidence-based clinical practice (Ebell, Barry, Slawson, & Shaughnessy, 1999). Translation science, that is, practice-oriented research targeting the needs of clinicians, has increased the quality of clinical practice by making evidence-based medicine easier to practice. In management, too, most advances have been from general scientific knowledge, and these are slow in reaching both management education and practice. Practice-oriented research exists but it is limited. The management equivalent of translation science begs for further development.

Design science is a form of practice-oriented research that has made inroads in organizational and management scholarship (van Aken & Romme, chapter 3 of this volume). It is a collaborative approach involving managers, engineers, scholars, and others to develop practical knowledge out of scientific research. It field tests research-based principles and develops its own "grounded technological rules" to be used in designing, configuring, and implementing solutions to specific problems. Design science and practice-oriented research generally are essential to better inform evidence-based management as well as to alert scholars to significant research questions that can only be identified in practice.

Practitioners, Educators, and Researchers Working Together

Whether research findings are used depends a lot on the quality of the relationships between researchers and users, the timeliness of the research's availability to nonresearchers, and whether users believe they have control over the factors research identifies as important (Beyer & Trice, 1982). In working to make research findings easier to access and use, organizational scholars may need to develop even deeper understandings of the phenomena they study. This understanding can be fostered by organizations as they encourage greater collaboration with researchers (Cyert & Goodman, 1997; Mohrman, Gibson, & Mohrman, 2001). Educators who provide practitioners with basic scientific knowledge and coach them in applying it contribute to the practitioners' lifelong learning in evidence-based practice. Those consultants grounded in science have a special role to play as knowledge brokers, by helping organizations apply evidence effectively. By making evidence-based decisions and practices possible, scholars, educators, and consultants all have a key contribution to make in building the essential supports for the practice of EBMgt. At the same time, it is in managerial work and everyday organizational practice where EBMgt is performed.

The absence of a critical mass of evidence-based managers today translates into pressures to conform to more ad hoc and experience-based approaches. Physicians historically practiced in much the same fashion of those who trained them, with little updating except occasional new ideas picked up from other doctors. The same is true of managers. The fact is that most new ideas gain momentum by contagion and ease of uptake—somebody tells another about an idea that is easy to try. Otherwise, changes come about via generational shifts supported by education, media, and other institutions. (The television show *House* portrays an evidence-based physician who ultimately holds all the answers. No word yet on the managerial equivalent, but the show *Office* is not it.) Mainstreaming new professional practices takes time. An entire generation of managers educated to use and access evidence may be needed before organizations make wide use of behavioral science. Until that time, networks among evidence-based practitioners can help individual practitioners develop their knowledge and skills. Partnerships with researchers and educators also provide on-going access to the latest research while helping practitioners learn how to turn evidence into action (see Zanardelli, chapter 11 of this volume).

Conclusion

As we round out this discussion of EBMgt, some concluding remarks are in order. EBMgt is a very different thought world from that of conventional managers (the same can be said for conventional management researchers and educators, too). There is an historical, cultural perspective that management is self-taught and learned from hands-on experience. Business history and lore are filled with companies built by college dropouts (Bill Gates,

Steve Jobs, and Charles Schwab to name a few). The idea that academic research can inform business decisions simply doesn't fit this image. EBMgt introduces new dimensions to what it means to be a manager.

Would-be EBMgt practitioners must confront some psychic costs. Making one's management practice more evidence-based can be emotionally threatening. The systematic processes advocated by EBMgt can feel like they take control away from practitioners (e.g., Dipboye, 1992). They can threaten a manager's self-image as a person of good judgment (Highhouse, 2008). When first starting to practice EBMgt, it can seem like another layer of evaluation and pressure in a busy manager's life (e.g. Dipboye, 1992). EBMgt requires engaging in a learning process that may ultimately move through the stages of novice, intermediate, and expert. It takes time, effort, and good support to become an evidence-based professional manager.

Not everyone is motivated to use evidence. Some people fail to learn new things because they don't want to make the effort. Non-evidence-based practices tend to be the norm for decisions regarding managing people, structuring work, and developing business strategy—and people tend to be comfortable with the status quo (Kahneman & Tversky, 1979). People who are confident about the quality of their own expertise and performance tend to see no need to change. Ironically, it is poor performers who are most likely to overestimate their expertise. Their lack of ability makes recognizing their personal deficits difficult (Ehrlinger, Johnson, Banner, Dunning, & Kruger, 2008). EBMgt is not for everybody.

EBMgt is for practitioners at the opposite end of the spectrum: those willing to invest time and effort to expand their knowledge, expertise, and personal depth. Practitioners attracted to EBMgt are its innovators and early adopters, drawn to it because of the benefits it offers and less threatened (or perhaps more intrigued) by the personal changes it involves. Interpreting and acting on evidence requires active thinking and reflection, a certain curiosity or hunger for understanding (cf. McAuliff & Kovera, 2008). EBMgt equips those prepared to work at it with an exciting and productive professional career over the course of ever-deeper experience and substantive learning.

EBMgt is a family of adaptive practices, inspired by the improved decision outcomes that using research evidence makes possible. EBMgt focuses educators on helping practitioners become critical thinkers, acquire relevant scientific knowledge, and apply evidence-informed methods to make better decisions. It calls for scholars to pay more attention to the cumulative nature of research and to make their findings more accessible and easier for practitioners to use. It engages managers in a deliberative, life-long effort to develop their professional knowledge, judgment, and impact. Turning EBMgt into a mainstream practice ultimately changes what managers, educators, and scholars do—for the greater advancement of all.

Author's Note

Eric Barends, John Boudreau, Paul Goodman, James O'Brien, and Susanne Schrader provided comments that developed this chapter. Cathy Senderling did her usual superb job of editing.

References

Ambrose, S.A, Bridges, M.W., DiPietro, M., Lovett, M.C., & Norman, M.K. (2010). *How learning works: Seven research-based principles for smart teaching.* San Francisco: Jossey-Bass.

Ariely, D., Gneezy, U., Loewenstein, G., & Mazar, N. (2009). Large stakes, big mistakes. *Review of Economic Studies, 76,* 451–469.

Armstrong, J. S. (2007) quoted in Knowledge @ Wharton. The 'Myth of Market Share';: Can Focusing Too Much on the Competition Harm Profitability? http://knowledge.wharton.upenn.edu/article.cfm?articleid=1645 (accessed October 25, 2011).

Armstrong, J. S. (2010). *Persuasive advertising: Evidence-based principles.* New York: Palgrave Macmillan.

Armstrong, J. S., & Collopy, F. (1996). Competitor orientation: Effects of objectives and information on managerial decisions and profitability. *Journal of Marketing Research, 32,* 188–199.

Armstrong, J. S., & Green, K. S. (2007). Competitor-oriented objectives: The myth of market share. *International Journal of Business, 12,* 117–136.

Barnard, C. I. (1938). *Functions of the executive.* Cambridge, MA: Harvard University Press.

Barringer, F. (2011) Q. and A. Taking on climate skepticism as a field of study. https//greenblogs.nytimes.com (Accessed April 9.)

Bartunek, J. M., & Rynes, S. L. (2010). The construction and contributions of I-implications for practice: What's in them and what might they offer? *Academy of Management Learning and Education, 9,* 100–117.

Bazerman, M. H. (2005). Conducting influential research: The need for prescriptive implications. *Academy of Management Journal, 30,* 25–31.

Beyer, J. M., & Trice, H. (1982). The utilization process: A conceptual framework and synthesis of empirical findings. *Administrative Science Quarterly, 27,* 591–622.

Bok, S. (1978). *Lying: Moral choice in public and private life.* New York: Random House.

Carey, B. (2009). Mental Stress Training Is Planned for U.S. Soldiers. *New York Times,* August 17.

Charlier, S. D., Brown, K. G., & Rynes, S. L. (2011) Teaching evidence-based management in MBA programs: What evidence is there? *Academy of Management Learning and Education, 10,* 222–236.

Cox, T. (1994). *Cultural diversity in organizations: Theory, research and practice.* San Francisco: Berrett Koehler.

Cyert, R., & March, J. G. (1992). *A behavioral theory of the firm,* 2nd ed. Oxford: Blackwell.

Cyert, R.M. & Goodman, P.S. (1997). Creating effective university-industry alliances: An organizational learning perspective. *Organizational Dynamics, 25 (4),* 45–57.

Dawes, R. M. (2001). *Everyday irrationality: How pseudo-scientists, lunatics and the rest of us systematically fail to think rationally.* Boulder, CO: Westview.

Dearborn, D. C. & Simon, H. A. (1958). Selective perception: A note on the departmental identifications of executives. *Sociometry, 21,* 140–144

Dipboye, R. (1992). *Selection interviews: Process perspectives.* Cincinnati, OH: South-Western.

Donaldson, L. (2010). *The meta-analytic organization: Introducing statistico-organizational theory.* Armonk, NY: M.E. Sharpe, Inc.

Drucker, P. F. (2003). *On the profession of management.* Boston: Harvard Business Review Books.

Ebell, M. H, Barry, H. C., Slawson, D. C., & Shaughnessy, A. F. (1999). Finding POEMs in the medical literature—Patient-oriented evidence that matters, *Journal of Family Practice,* May, *48,* 350–355.

Ehrlinger, J., Johnson, K., Banner, M., Dunning, D., & Kruger, J. (2008). Why the unskilled are unaware: Further explorations of (absent) self-insight among the incompetent. *Organizational Behavior and Human Decision Processes, 105,* 98–121.

Ericsson, K. A., Krampe, R. T., & Tesch-Römer, C. (1993). The role of deliberate practice in the acquisition of expert performance. *Psychological Review, 100,* 363–406.

Ericsson, K. A., & A. C. Lehmann, A. C. (1996). Expert and exceptional performance: Evidence on maximal adaptations on task constraints. *Annual Review of Psychology, 47,* 273–305.

Evans, C., & Wright, W. (2009). How to make effective decisions. *The British Journal of Administrative Management,* Autumn, 32–33.

Ferrante, C. J. (2006). Innovative sharing: Shared accounting information as a facilitator of trust and performance. *Journal of Engineering and Technology Management, 23,* 54–63.

Gladwell, M. (2005). *Blink: The power of thinking without thinking.* New York: Little, Brown.

Goodman, P. S. (2001). *Missing organizational linkages.* Thousand Oaks, CA: Sage.

Heath, C., Larrick, R. P., & Klayman, J. (1998). Cognitive repairs: How organizational practices can compensate for individual shortcomings. *Review of Organizational Behavior, 20,* 1–38.

Highhouse, S. (2008). Stubborn reliance on intuition and subjectivity in employee selection. *Industrial and Organizational Psychology: Perspectives on Science and Practice, 1,* 333–342.

Hill, L. A. (2003). *Becoming a manager: How new managers master the challenges of leadership.* Boston: Harvard Business School Press.

Hornung, S, Rousseau, D. M., & Glaser, J. (2008). Creating flexibility through idiosyncratic deals. *Journal of Applied Psychology, 93,* 655–664.

Huczynski, A. (2006). *Management gurus.* Rev. ed. London: Routledge.

Kahneman, D., & Tversky, A. (1979). Prospect Theory: An analysis of decision under risk. *Econometrica, 47,* 263–292.

Kaplan, R. S. (2011). The hollow science. *Harvard Business Review,* May, 15–16, 18.

Khurana, R. (2007). *From higher aims to hired hands: The social transformation of American business schools and the unfulfilled promise of management as a profession.* Princeton, N.J.: Princeton University Press.

Kovner, A. R. Fine, D. J., & D'Aquila, R. (2009). *Evidence-based management in healthcare.* Chicago: Healthcare Administration Press.

Langer, E. J. (1989). *Mindfulness.* Reading MA: Addison-Wesley.

Larrick, R. K. (2009). Broaden the decision frame to make effective decisions. In E.A. Locke (Ed.), *Handbook of principles of organizational behavior: Indispensable knowledge for evidence-based management.* Chichester, UK: Wiley, pp. 461–515.

Latham, G., & Locke, E.A. (2002). Building a practically useful theory of goal setting and task motivation. *The American Psychologist, 57,* 705–717.

Lester, P. A. (2010). Resilience training in the U.S. Army. Harvard Business Review Spotlight: Examining leadership lessons from the military. http://blogs.hbr.org/frontline-leadership/2010/10/resilience-training-writ-large.html (accessed October 25, 2011).

Lewis, M. E. (2004). *Moneyball: The art of winning an unfair game.* New York: Norton.

Makkula Center (2009). *A framework for ethical decision making.* http://www.scu.edu/ethics/practicing/decision/framework.html (accessed October 25, 2011).

March, J. G. (2010). *The ambiguities of experience.* Ithaca, NY: Cornell University Press.

McAuliff, B.D., & Kovera, M.B. **(2008).** Juror need for cognition and sensitivity to methodological flaws in expert evidence. *Journal of Applied Social Psychology, 38,* 385–408.

McLean, B., & Elkind, P. (2003). *The smartest guys in the room: The amazing rise and scandalous fall of Enron.* New York: Penguin.

Meehl, P. (1954). *Clinical versus statistical prediction: A theoretical analysis and a review of the evidence.* Minneapolis: University of Minnesota Press.

Middendorf, J., & Pace, D. (2004). Decoding the disciplines: A model for helping students learn disciplinary ways of thinking. *New Directions for Teaching and Learning, 98,* 1–12.

Mohrman, S. A., Gibson, C. B., & Mohrman, A. M. (2001). Doing research that is useful to practice: A model and empirical exploration. *Academy of Management Journal, 44,* 357–375.

Montague, R. (2007). *Your brain is (almost) perfect: How we make decisions.* New York: Plume.

Morris, M. W., & Peng, K. (1994). Culture and cause: American and Chinese attributions for social and physical events. *Journal of Personality and Social Psychology, 67,* 949–971.

Nickerson, R. S. (2002). The production and perception of randomness. *Psychological Review, 109,* 330–357.

Nisbett, R. E., & Ross, L. (1980). *Human inference: Strategies and shortcomings of social judgment.* Englewood Cliffs, NJ: Prentice-Hall.

Olivery T. & Mueller, R. S. (2003). Evidence-based veterinary dermatology: A systematic review of the pharmacotherapy of canine atopic dermatitis. *Veterinary Dermatology, 14,* 121–146.

Parnas, D. L., & Clements, P. C. (1986). A rational design processes: How and why to fake it. *IEEE Transactions on Software Engineering, SE12,* 251–256.

Pavic, I. (2008). Business Review, Cambridge, *10,* 199–206.

Pfeffer, J., & Sutton, R. I. (2006). *Hard facts, dangerous half-truths, and total nonsense*. Boston: Harvard Business School Press.

Porter, L. W., & Lawler, E. E. (1968). *Managerial attitudes and performance*. Homewood, IL: Dorsey Press.

Redfield, W. (1912). http://www.careers-in-business.com/consulting/hist1800.htm

Rousseau, D. M. (1995). *Psychological contract in organizations: Understanding written and unwritten agreements*. Newbury Park, CA: Sage.

Rousseau, D. M. (1997). Organizational behavior in the new organizational era. *Annual Review of Psychology, 48*, 515–546.

Rousseau, D. M., & Barends, E. (2011). Becoming an evidence-based manager. *Human Resource Management Journal, 21*, 221–235.

Rousseau, D. M., Hornung, S., & Kim, T.G. (2009). Testing idiosyncratic deal propositions: Timing, content, and the employment relationship. *Journal of Vocational Behavior, 74*, 338–348.

Rousseau, D.M., Manning, J. & Denyer, D. (2008). Evidence in Management and Organizational Science: Assembling the field's full weight of scientific knowledge through reflective reviews. *Annals of the Academy of Management, 2*, 475–515.

Rovelli, C. (2011) The Uselessness of Certainty http://toolsforthinking.blogspot.com/2011/03/uselessness-of-certainty.html (Accessed April 1, 2011).

Sackett, D. L., Straus, S. E., Richardson, W. S., Rosenberg, W., & Haynes, R. B. (2000). *Evidence-based medicine: How to practice and teach EBM*. New York: Churchill Livingstone.

Sarasvathy, S., Simon, H. A., & Lave, L. (1998). Perceiving and managing business risks: Differences between entrepreneurs and bankers. *Journal of Economic Behavior and Organizations, 33(2)*, 207–225.

Schneider, B., & Bowen, D. E. (1985). Employee and customer perceptions of service in banks: Replication and extension. *Journal of Applied Psychology, 70*, 423–433.

Sherman, L. W. (2002). Evidence-based policing: Social organization of information for social control. In E. Waring and D. Weisburd (Eds.), *Crime and social organization*. New Brunswick, NJ: Transaction Publishers, pp. 217–248.

Simon, H. A. (1967). The business school: A problem of organizational design. *Journal of Management Studies, 4*, 1–16.

Simon, H. A. (1986). Behaving like a manager. All Academy Address, Academy of Management meetings, August. Chicago.

Simon, H. A. (1996). *The sciences of the artificial* (3rd ed.). Cambridge, MA: MIT Press.

Simon, H. A. (1997). *Administrative behavior: A study of decision-making processes in administrative organization* (4th ed.). New York: The Free Press.

Sutcliffe, K. M., & Huber, G. P. (1998). Firm and industry as determinants of executive perceptions of the environment. *Strategic Management Journal, 19*, 793–807.

Taleb, N. N. (2010). *The black swan: The impact of the highly improbable*. New York: Random House.

Taylor-Powell, E., & Henert, E. (2008). Logic model template. Madison, WI: University of Wisconsin.

Telegrapher's Cramp (1875). *Chicago Journal of Nervous & Mental Disease: 2 (3)*, 455. http://journals.lww.com/jonmd/Citation/1… (Accessed June 7, 2011).

Thomas, G., & Pring, R. (2004) *Evidence-based practice in Education*. Maidenhead, UK: Open University Press.

Tyler, T. (2006). *Why people obey the law*. Princeton, NJ: Princeton University Press.

Wegge, J., Jeppesen, H. J., Weber, W.G., Pearce, C.L., Silva, S. A., Pundt, A., et al. (2010). Promoting work motivation in organizations: Should employee involvement in organizational leadership become a new tool in the organizational psychologist's kit? *Journal of Personnel Psychology, 9(4)*, 154–171.

Weber, B. (2009). Daniel C. Tosteson, Longtime dean who reshaped Harvard Medical School, Dies at 84. *New York Times*, p. A25, June 3.

Weick, K. E., & Sutcliffe, K. M. (2006). Mindfulness and the quality of organizational attention. *Organization Science, 17*, 514–525.

White, J. R., & Cassell, J. B. (2009). The business case for a hospital palliative care unit: Justifying its continued existence. In A.R. Kovner, D. Fine and R D'Aquila, *Evidence-based management in healthcare*. Chicago: Health Administration Press, pp. 171–189.

Yates, J. F. (2003). *Decision management*. San Francisco: Jossey-Bass.

Zuckerman, M. (1979). Attribution of success and failure revisited: Or the motivational bias is alive and well in attribution theory. *Journal of Personality, 47*, 245–287.

Learning from Other Evidence-Based Practices: The Case of Medicine

Eric Barends, Steven ten Have *and* Frank Huisman

Abstract

Evidence-based practice is all around us. Not only has medicine embraced its principles, but so have education, social welfare, criminal justice and, last but not least, management. With only slight exaggeration, Evidence-based practice can be said to be emblematic of the modern professional. This chapter addresses the implications of this trend toward evidence-based practice, by taking a close look at its first introduction, in medicine. Given evidence-based medicine's almost paradigmatic status, we then will cover the similarities and the differences between the two professional fields. In doing so, we will show that the hindrances that block the further development of evidence-based management today are the same hindrances that blocked the development of evidence-based medicine two decades ago.

Key Words: evidence-based medicine, differences from evidence-based medicine, hierarchy of evidence, evidence-based practice, clinical judgment, systematic review, best available evidence, randomization, causality, PICO, trust in professionals, Cochrane Collaboration

The Rise of Evidence-Based Medicine

As a concept, "evidence-based medicine" was coined in the 1990s. It was defined as "the conscientious, explicit and judicious use of current best evidence in making decisions about the care of individual patients" (Sackett, Rosenberg, Gray, Haynes, & Richardson, 1996). This definition is striking, because it implies that the practice of medicine was not always "conscientious, explicit, and judicious." In the 1960s and 1970s, people like Alvan Feinstein, Archie Cochrane, and Henrik Wulff—generally considered as the pioneers of the evidence-based medicine movement—were struck by the fact that clinical practice was characterized by much diversity. In clinical decision making, experience, intuition, and the wisdom of former teachers seemed to be more important than scientific first principles. Feinstein, Cochrane, and Wulff found this intellectually disturbing, and tried to remedy

this situation by writing books that became classics to the movement: *Clinical Judgment* by Feinstein (Feinstein, 1967), *Effectiveness and Efficiency* by Cochrane (Cochrane, 1972) and *Rational Diagnosis and Treatment* by Wulff (Wulff, 1976). Parallel to this self-reflection by physicians, there was growing criticism on medicine and physicians from outside medicine. Physicians were accused of being inconsistent in diagnosis and treatment, causing iatrogenic damage, and for being responsible for a cost explosion in health care. This situation was especially disturbing because the average life expectancy at birth had remained much the same during the second half of the twentieth century.

An evaluation of the effectiveness and efficiency of health care was called for, and this is exactly what happened. A new discipline was created: clinical epidemiology. Epidemiology, a branch of medical science dealing with factors affecting the health and illness of large populations, had existed for many years, but it was associated with public health. Because of its political implications, public health was viewed with suspicion by both biomedical researchers and clinicians. Therefore, something new had to be created, to appeal to both groups and provide a viable solution to the problems of intraphysician variability in behavior and decisions and the cost explosion in health care at the same time. This is what clinical epidemiology set out to do: although the research questions of the new discipline were supplied by the clinic, its methods were solid enough to appeal to basic researchers and applicable to medically defined clinical populations. In the process, it moved from the periphery to the center of the medical enterprise. Epidemiology—once considered to be a rather irrelevant discipline by clinicians—had become *clinical* epidemiology.

The new discipline was developed at McMaster's University in Canada, by a team of clinicians, biostatisticians, engineers, and health economists headed by David Sackett. Greatly inspired by the work of Feinstein, Sackett successfully launched a program in which

problem-based medical research was translated into a problem-based medical curriculum. The practical questions of medical students were taken as a starting point. The new approach was embraced and funded by the Rockefeller Foundation, and successfully exported to other western countries. It didn't take too long before clinical epidemiology was institutionalized in a handbook, a journal, and a network. In 1985, David Sackett, Brian Haynes, Gordon Guyatt and Peter Tugwell published *Clinical Epidemiology: A Basic Science for Clinical Medicine* (Sacket, Haynes, Guyatt, & Tugwell, 1991). Two years later, the *Journal of Chronic Diseases* was rechristened the *Journal of Clinical Epidemiology*, and finally, an INternational CLinical Epidemiology Network (INCLEN) was established to support clinical epidemiology worldwide.

Things were taken even a step further by Gordon Guyatt, an early graduate of the Department of Clinical Epidemiology and Biostatistics at McMaster University. In an article published in the *Journal of the American Medical Association* in 1992, he inaugurated the concept of "evidence-based medicine." The article was subtitled "A new approach to teaching the practice of medicine." It sprang from his need to justify the training program in the McMaster's medical school (Evidence-Based Medicine Working Group, 1992). Physicians of the future needed to be educated differently. Instead of

being knowledge and teacher based, their education needed to be problem and patient based. To do so, physicians should be able to judge the value and the applicability of published research. On top of that, they needed to be able to identify the relevant articles from a plethora of literature. In this respect, Guyatt claimed that evidence-based medicine represented a paradigm shift for medical practice. Whereas the old paradigm had valued pathophysiologic first principles, teacher authority, experience, and unsystematic clinical observation, the new paradigm stressed their fallibility. Clinicians should henceforth rely on evidence, and they should be able to decide what constitutes reliable evidence and what does not. To do so, they should be able to search, evaluate, and apply original medical literature. The underlying belief was that physicians could gain the skill to make *independent* assessments of evidence—that is: without the guidance of external authorities (e.g., their teachers) or the weight of tradition.

A few years after Guyatt's article, his mentor Sackett published *Evidence-Based Medicine: How to Practice and Teach EBM* (Sackett, Richardson, Rosenberg, and Haynes, 1997), a book he again co-authored with Brian Haynes. In 1995, the bimonthly journal *Evidence-Based Medicine* was founded, published by the American College of Physicians. Today, this journal scans over 100 journals and around 50,000 articles a year so that it can identify the most important and valid 120 research articles. Practicing clinicians assess the clinical relevance of the best studies. Key details of these studies are included in a succinct, informative expert commentary on their clinical application. In other words, the journal summarizes published findings from other journals to promote access to research that is relevant to patient treatment. This outlet allowed proponents of evidence-based medicine to develop and apply criteria of critical appraisal, in order to reduce the mass of published material and boil it down to the two percent of articles that are both valid and of immediate clinical use.

The Domain of Management

The modern era of medicine began at the end of the eighteenth century. Organizational science as a discipline emerged more than 150 years later, during the first half of the twentieth century. This period saw the introduction of mass production, which was popularized in the 1910s and 1920s by Henry Ford's Ford Motor Company. Managers began to ask questions surrounding the production of large amounts of standardized products on assembly lines and operational process efficiency. These questions were answered by organization experts of the time, who include Frederick Taylor and Henri Fayol. Seen from a management perspective, classic organizational science developed over the course of the twentieth century with the help of such concepts as systems and contingency thinking. During that time, the field was joined by the social sciences—sociology, organization sociology, psychology, and social and organization psychology in particular. The contributions from these disciplines often resulted from the questions or problems organizations faced in their internal and external environments. Whereas at the turn of the twentieth century Taylorism was the answer to the day's predominant production issue, psychological insights offered help when problems surrounding employee motivation and profiles demanded attention in the management of organizations. When seen in terms of such disciplines as general and organization sociology, the management world, by the 1980s, had considerable high-quality evidence at its disposal. The associated knowledge and insights were developed through the codification of experience *and* high-quality empirical research conducted in the previous decades. It was chiefly toward the end of the 1960s and the start of the 1970s that evidence in the organization sociology field saw accelerated advancement. Nevertheless, the professional field we call management still appears to be in its infancy, as far as empirical foundations are concerned. Why is this, and is it really true? There are three possible explanations for this appearance of "infancy."

First, universal recipes for success drove out attention for contingencies. During the 1980s, popular, universalistic recipes for success increasingly replaced the previously carefully cultivated and nuanced contingency thinking of the 1960s and 1970s (Burns & Stalker, 1961; Lawrence & Lorsch, 1967; Woodward, 1958). This line of thought, into which notions of "the excellent organization" (Peters & Waterman, 1982) fit, flourished through the 1990s and the start of this century. During this period we encounter popular concepts such as "visionary companies" (Colins & Porras, 1995), "good to great organizations" (Collins, 2001) and "high- performance organizations" (Holbeche, 2005). The fact that people speak of "the holy grail of management" in relation to these concepts, thus invoking the suggestion that there is a universal recipe for success, illustrates this development nicely. Comparable suggestions are made with respect to leadership and strategy, for example. In all cases, these

were studies that had the necessary impact in terms of publicity, and among managers they were then subject to serious criticism. This criticism varied from comments on the tenability of the conclusions, as in the case of the excellent organizations (*Business Week,* 1984), to fundamental criticism on the methodological quality of the research by Collins and Porras (Rosenzweig, 2007) and the concept of high-performance organizations (ten Have, 2007). Moreover, the one-size-fits-all character of these concepts does not do justice to the context, history, and characteristics of individual organizations. In contrast, an evidence-based practice approach treats the question, "What works?" as less relevant than "What works, for whom, with which problem, in which context?"

Second, management is a synthetic field constituting an array of disciplines; as such, in itself, it is neither very cumulative nor integrated. In addition to the search for universal solutions at the expense of attention to context, the nature of the management field itself provides an explanation for its image of infancy. Management, in its connection to business administration, is a field that, like communication and change management, is an integration sciences: a science or professional field composed of, supplied by, or dependent on other sciences or professional fields. In the case of business administration, this usually concerns such fields as economics, psychology, organizational science, sociology, and strategy. With regard to psychology, it has been noted earlier that this is a field with a strong empirical basis. Thus, the field of social psychology is characterized by scientific research with a high "level of evidence." The question is, however, how to assess the business administration field and its associated management discipline using these "strong" suppliers of evidence. Is it a matter of tallying up the supplier's collective track records and research contributions? Or should management be chiefly assessed as a separate domain based upon its own reliance on empirical evidence? Various authors point to limited progress, which some attribute to a form of "balkanization" within the professional field. James March describes this phenomenon as follows:

> … Energized subfields have tended to seal themselves off, each seemingly eager to close further minds of the already converted, without opening the minds of others
> (March, 1996).

Other authors express themselves in similar terms and summarize this development under the term "compartmentalization" (Goia and Pitre, 1990).

March looks back to around 30 years after the conclusions he drew halfway though the 1960s and notes that, since that time, very little in the professional field has changed: "Plus ca change, plus c'est la meme chose." Management's image of stagnation and absence of empirical foundation can be partially attributed to the fragmentary approach to research within the professional field itself.

A third possible explanation for this appearance of infancy is the strong normative view of what organizations are, of what they can do, and the associated resistance against concepts such as "systematic and methodical" and "evidence-based." In this view, much emphasis is placed on the human factor and the limits of (or limits to) the rational perspective and its associated concepts such as "planning," "design" and "steering." Then again, concepts such as "learning" and "development" are prized very highly by the followers of this approach. This contrast still appears to be current and touches on the possibilities and limits that the role that "design" and its associated concepts, such as "systematic and methodical" and "evidence based," have in relation to the field's professionalization (chapter 3 of this volume).

Peter Drucker views the professionalization of management as the most important technological development of the twentieth century. He links the enormous economic growth that took place in the nineteenth century to the development of "the management profession." His position is that, without professionalization of the field, economic growth would have been significantly lower and organizations would have not been able to make the contribution that is so common in our societies:

> But surely if management had not emerged as a systematic discipline, we could not have organized what is now a social reality in every developed country: the society of organizations and the "employee society". (Drucker, 1985).

Drucker stresses that organizations are systems in which a whole range of activities are consciously and purposefully coordinated. Moreover, an organization's right to exist is determined by its capacity to coordinate economic activities more efficiently than the market can. Joseph Bower notes this in connection to the assignment that managers have in relation to this right to exist and the action and operational orientation that is needed for that purpose:

> It is one thing to recognize that a corporation is a complex non-linear system interacting with a very rich and changing environment. It is another

to provide a map of that system that permits managers to act in an intentionally rational fashion (Bower, 2000).

We know, of course, that intention rationality means trying to engage in systematic thoughtful decision making, despite human limits and, in particular, bounded rationality. Intentional rationality is the same as rationality per se. Drucker argues for a kind of management practice in which people work "systematically and methodically," and he makes mention of the "management profession." However, Drucker's attribution of professionalization to management raises a critical question: if despite human limitations, attempts to be intentionally rational aided management and organizations in the twentieth century, how do we continue to develop management as a profession in the twenty-first? One answer is the more systematic use of evidence in management and organizational decisions, in particular, scientific evidence.

Comparing Medicine and Management: Implications for Evidence-Based Management
Levels of Professionalism: A Naïve Image of the Discipline of Medicine

One side of this issue is the common view that management is not really a profession, unlike medicine, which is a discipline that is regarded by many as the archetypal profession (Barker, 2010; Khurana, Nohria, & Penrice, 2005; Sutton, 2007; Walshe & Rundall, 2001). Walshe and Rundall, for example, argue that medicine, in contrast with management, has a formal body of knowledge which is shared by all members in the professional group and which acts as a common frame of reference during discussions and debates within the discipline. Moreover, access to the discipline is restricted in the case of medicine: only those who have studied medicine at a recognized university are qualified to be a physician. Even then they may not be allowed to perform certain medical procedures until they have had further training, during which the physician acquires greater knowledge and skills in a specific area of his discipline. To guarantee the quality of specialized training courses, training is periodically assessed by fellow specialists in a system of peer review and visits. A training course or institute can lose its accreditation unless it meets the specialty's quality criteria. Many countries subject practicing physicians to an ongoing system of evaluation. For a physician to be allowed to continue practicing medicine, he or she must demonstrate each year that he/she has had further training and met the formal minimum standard with respect to certain medical procedures.

It is often suggested that the situation in the field of management is quite different. Walshe and Rundall point out there are no formal or legal rules that set conditions for using the title of manager, so anyone can call him/herself a manager. Managers are, therefore, a diverse group, and they come from various disciplines, often with a widely varying training and education background. Thus, according to Walshe and Rundall, an employee who after some years of experience (without any formal training) rises to management belongs to the same professional group as the CEO who received an MBA degree at a renowned business school and then gained experience in various sectors for years. Because of this difference in training, education, and experience, managers do not have a common language, and there are huge differences in their familiarity with the body of knowledge. Concomitantly, it is suggested that there is little consensus about which management techniques would be the best to apply, in which way, and in which situations. As a result, management practice varies considerably, not only between countries or organizations, but even within divisions or departments, and personal experience and self-generated knowledge play an important part in that. Finally, it is often pointed out that, by and large, the training of managers takes place within the confines of the training institute and that students, upon graduating, can take up a management position immediately, without any related work experience. This is, according to the authors, in sharp contrast to medicine, in which graduates, after their formal training at a university, first have to hone their skills under the supervision of a senior colleague before they are allowed to practice independently. On these grounds, it is implied that management is not a profession and, in consequence, the application of the principles of evidence-based medicine in management practice is barely possible.

The portrait just presented reflects a naïve image of the discipline of medicine, one which some writers espouse. In fact, medical practice is far from uniform. Clinical decisions and results of medical interventions can vary enormously from one physician to the next, in spite of shared educations and knowledge (O'Connor et al., 1999). These differences cannot be explained by the seriousness of the illness or the patient's preference and must, therefore, be the result of the physician's personal style,

behavior, and experience. And although it is true that within each medical specialism clinical practice guidelines exist that physicians are required to follow, research demonstrates that sometimes reality is a far cry from this lofty ideal. For example, asthma is a disorder for which there is an official guideline in the United States, but a study among physicians responsible for emergency aid in hospitals revealed that four years after publication of the guideline, only 45 percent of the physicians had heard about it and a mere 24 percent had actually read it (Crain, Weiss, & Fagan, 1995). A study among American pediatricians even showed that although 88 percent stated they were aware of the guideline, only 35 percent actually followed it (Flores, Bauchner, & Kastner, 2000). Similar percentages crop up in studies with respect to other guidelines, leading to articles with titles such as "Why don't Physicians follow Clinical Practice Guidelines?" (Cabana et al., 1999). Also, the statement that anyone without a formal education or formal training can become a manager proves to be somewhat at odds with reality. Although never formally investigated, it is not likely that there are many top managers in big corporations without formal management training. Even managers of smaller companies and nonprofit organizations, such as hospitals, tend to be well educated. The majority has completed advanced studies. Because there is a great demand for well-trained managers, a self-regulating system has developed in most Western countries, emphasizing education credentials. As such, people without any formal management training face difficulties qualifying for a manager's job. This is partly why management courses and training have sky-rocketed over the past few decades and various large international organizations now warrant the quality of MBA and other management courses through accreditation.

Unfortunately, this increasing professionalization doesn't say much about the levels of expertise of managers. Several authors are right in pointing out that, in general, management training leaves future managers ill-prepared, at least with the current form in which the training is given (Mintzberg, 2005; Rousseau & McCarthy, 2007). The content of management training seems to be heavily influenced by fads, fashionable topics, and theories based on poor evidence presented by management gurus. Ghoshal rebuked such renowned business schools as Harvard and Stanford for teaching pseudo-scientific management models (Ghoshal, 2005). This criticism is comparable to David Sackett's observation in the 1990s with respect to the medical training:

> A group of us came together in the late sixties, rebels with a cause. We said, "We know a lot of stuff about medical education, we think it's crap and we ain't going to do any of that." So we set up our own Medical School. We attracted a lot of brilliant young minds because what we were doing was so iconoclastic: it allowed them a way of questioning the pervasive authority of leading clinical teachers...Attitudes to medical authority changed as students started asking their teachers, respectfully, "Why are you doing this with this patient? What is the evidence you have for this?"
> (Daly, 2005).

The (correct) observation that in the present management training little attention is paid to scientific research and promoting systematic procedures in management practice also is a parallel to medicine. However, this situation is comparable to the situation in medicine only two decades ago. Witness a comment made by Gordon Guyatt in 1990:

> The problem isn't clinical experience: the problem is that we (physicians) are so unsystematic, intuitive, and with no notion of scientific principles in our accumulation of clinical experience.
> (Daly, 2005)

The current situation with training managers bears a great resemblance to the medical training situation in the 1990s, which could constitute an argument in favor of educating management students in the principles of evidence-based practice. In that sense, Drucker's 1985 plea for a systematic and methodical approach can be regarded as prophetic (Drucker, 1985). However, there remains one important obstacle to this, an obstacle that impedes the field's development of evidence-based management.

Sociology has developed various criteria that characterize a profession. A number of these criteria have already been highlighted earlier, such as formal training, certification, and quality control. An important criterion not yet mentioned here is the existence of a common body of knowledge. A profession needs to be based on a clearly defined domain of well-organized and systematized knowledge, a domain that forms the basis for the training and development of professionals (Khurana et al., 2005). Admittedly, this body of knowledge is amply available in the field of management (Pfeffer and Sutton [2006] have even argued that there is too much evidence), but it is still insufficiently systematized and also insufficiently

accessible. As such, the body of relevant management knowledge does not yet act as a common frame of reference for managers. The lack of this common frame of reference also impedes the development of peer pressure supporting managerial use of this body of knowledge. To develop into a genuine profession, management needs better integration and accessibility of this body of knowledge into its practitioners' training. The assumptions developed by Sackett and Guyatt regarding evidence-based medicine are an important starting point: educating managers and students based on self-learning and problem-based instruction in small groups that provide intensive, hands-on instruction on how to find the best available evidence, how to critically appraise the evidence, and how to integrate the evidence in (management) practice.

Misconceptions about the Researchability of Management Practice

The Western world recognizes various sciences. A distinction is made between fundamental and applied sciences, and sciences are also divided into humanities, the natural sciences, and social sciences. The humanities, also called the liberal arts, include disciplines such as philosophy, history, anthropology, and literary theory. The humanities occupy a special place in the spectrum, as these are less suited to experimental research and, therefore, use techniques from logic to construct internally consistent theories. Natural sciences, also called exact sciences, are different from other sciences in that they are based on the laws of nature and theories that are more suited to be tested in experimental research. Examples are physics, chemistry, and biology. The social sciences are a halfway house so to speak. These disciplines, also known as social studies, include sciences that are focused on man and his environment, e.g., sociology, pedagogic or educational theory, psychology, economics, business administration, and law. From this perspective, management is squarely in the social sciences camp. In the natural sciences, experiments are conducted that allow the researcher to control all the conditions and factors that may influence the result. This often takes place in a controlled environment such as a laboratory. This is why the term *cause*, as used in the natural sciences, has the same meaning in common parlance. In the social sciences, the results of studies are often influenced by multiple variables that affect each other as well and causality is not often demonstrable. For this reason, terms such as *cause* and *effect* are avoided by social scientists, who prefer to use terms such as *correlated* or *related with* (Hunt, 1997). Because of the multirelational nature of the social sciences, it is possible to demonstrate that certain variables under certain conditions bear on a certain result, but often it is not possible to show that that relationship exists in all or even most cases.

The practical value of management research's results is limited because of this tangle of multirelational connections whose potential cause-effect connections are not teased apart. As a counterexample, medicine is often used, where strongly focused research questions are allegedly used that can be answered unequivocally in double-blind randomized studies and where strong, monocausal links exist. That is why medicine is often considered to be the more scientific discipline, as well as why it is concluded that the practices of evidence-based medicine do not apply to management. However, there are three comments to be made here.

RANDOMIZED RESEARCH IS WIDELY USED IN MEDICINE, BUT LESS THAN WE THINK

As early as 1926, Ronald Fisher, the founding father of modern statistics, described the use of randomization in agricultural experiments (Fisher, 1926). The first medical randomized controlled trial (RCT) was not conducted until the end of the 1940s (Medical Research Council Streptomycin in Tuberculosis Trials Committee, 1948); however, RCTs are now applied worldwide and regarded as the gold standard. All the same, most evidence in medicine is based on nonrandomized and observational research. One reason for this is that blinding is not always possible in medicine. With surgical procedures for example, it is blindingly obvious to the patient and the researcher that an operation has taken place. The same is true for pharmacological research in which the long-term side effects of the drug to be tested are such that blinding is pointless. Moreover, randomization is not always feasible in medicine. Sometimes randomization is not possible for practical reasons, but more frequently, objections of an ethical nature come into play, for example in research into the effects of smoking on the development of lung cancer. Additionally, quite often it is not possible to conduct experimental research in medicine. This is the case in research into disorders that afflict only a very small part of the population, research into the side effects of drugs, and research into the mortality rate of certain diseases or treatments. In fact, even in the natural sciences, experimental research is not always the most appropriate method for providing evidence, for instance, in the

field of astronomy or astrophysics. In all these cases, observational research is used, where the researcher merely observes but does not intervene, with the intention of finding correlations among the observed data. Such research too can lead to robust empirical foundations, particularly when repeated frequently and under varying conditions (Petticrew & Roberts, 2003). One form of observational research widely used in medicine is cohort research. In this type of research, large groups of people are followed over a long period to see (prospectively) whether differences occur among the groups. Another type of observational research that is frequently used is case-control research. In this type of research, one group of patients with a particular disorder is compared retrospectively with a group that does not have this disorder (Schulz & Grimes, 2002).

In management research too, randomization and experimental research is often hard to carry out for practical reasons. In spite of this, cohort research or case-control research is used relatively little. This is remarkable as case-control research could be applied in management relatively easily. These observations force the conclusion that the research practice of medicine shows extensive similarities with that of management, and that, yet, the extent and the methodological repertoire of management research is significantly smaller.

Causality is complicated in medicine, not just in management. A second comment must be made with respect to the assumption that there are strong, monocausal connections in medicine. For example, it is a well-known fact that a person's blood pressure is influenced by a dozen variables and that the effect of a treatment for high blood pressure is modified by a range of factors (Friedman et al., 2001). Even with an intervention that seems unequivocal at first sight, such as a hip replacement, its success is determined not only by variables such as the quality of the prosthesis or the surgeon's experience, but also by numerous less obvious variables, such as the patient's nutritional situation, living conditions, social support, state of mind, and the ability to cope with setbacks. In medicine, too, there is a tangle of multirelational links that are also difficult to measure or to control. Even natural sciences like physics are not as exact, objective, and free of experimenter bias as they are purported to be. Therefore, the most important difference between research practice in medicine and management is less the nature of that practice and more the degree of variation in shared meaning within each discipline. For researchers to be able to carry out a study in the discipline, they must attach t he same meaning to concepts and models and strive to eliminate ambiguity and achieve value freedom. Every physician knows what is meant by fever, and a standardized measurement tool has been developed even for a subjective concept such as pain, so that it can be used globally as a hard outcome measure for research. This is in contrast to the management practice, where much use is made of multi-interpretable abstractions such as "dynamic capabilities," "change capacity," "organizational learning," and "level-five leadership." Such abstractions are far from unambiguous and difficult to operationalize and thus hinder the development of a common frame of reference.

Evidence-based practice is about "best available" evidence. The third and most important comment involves the assumption that evidence-based practice is only possible if the discipline has a research practice with a high level of evidence. This is a common fallacy. With evidence-based practice, whether it involves medicine, education, justice, or management, it is all about the "best available evidence." If evidence is available on the basis of multiple systematic reviews of double-blind randomized studies, that is great, but often the results of observational research, surveys, or even case studies are the best available evidence. The level of evidence in itself does not say anything about the extent to which an evidence-based decision is possible, because a decision based on the opinion of experts can also be an evidence-based decision. In many cases, there is even insufficient evidence, so a professional has no option but to make a decision based on experience or intuition. Therefore, the scientific status or developmental phase of a field does not determine the applicability of the principles of evidence-based practice. If research is conducted within the field, and a decision is to be made, a professional can establish whether there is sufficient evidence to underpin this decision and in doing so apply the principles of evidence-based practice.

A Closer Look at the Practice—Knowledge Gap

The management field shows a broad consensus on the existence of a deep chasm between knowledge and practice. Journals frequently feature articles on the gap between practitioners and researchers and the authoritative *Academy of Management Journal* even dedicated special issues to this subject. Most publications point out that researchers and practitioners live in separate worlds and seldom communicate (Cohen, 2007; Rynes,

Bartunek, & Daft, 2001; Rynes, Giluk, & Brown, 2007; Shapiro, Kirkman, & Courtney, 2007). Consequently, results from scientific studies are hardly ever applied in practice. There is little consensus about the causes of this gap or about the best way to bridge it.

As for the cause, many authors look to medicine again, and they are right to observe that the culture among managers is very different from that of physicians (chapter 8 of this volume). Physicians regard medicine as a scientific domain, combining natural and social sciences. Consequently, much attention is given in their medical training, to research and methodology, and the scientific method is regarded as the basis for developing medical knowledge. In the hierarchy of the discipline, physicians who participate in research or who have done research for a doctorate have a higher status than physicians who only practice. Many medical consultants, therefore, have a career in both research and clinical practice, so the communities of researchers and practitioners in medicine overlap each other to a large degree. That is why physicians, unlike managers, recognize the importance of scientific research and appreciate the results of studies. This combination of scientific knowledge and practice-based experience enables physicians to assess the results of research critically and to translate these into their daily practice and into individual patient cases.

Managers on the other hand seldom see research results during their training, which is one reason for their minimal knowledge in this area. Only a small number of managers read academic journals; the majority gain their knowledge from colleagues, popular management books, authoritative consultants, or success stories about well-known CEOs (Cohen, 2007). Students also tend to have strong normative beliefs and ideas about what they need as future managers, and they are primarily interested in current company practices and experiences of corporate leaders (Rousseau & McCarthy, 2007). Or to put it differently, managers rate face validity and readability more highly than methodological validity and evidence based on scientific research. However, a closer look at the practice-knowledge gap reveals that this cultural difference does not just exist between managers and physicians but also between management researchers and their medical counterparts. In medicine, a researcher is typically a physician as well, which means that he or she has completed a medical training and has had years of experience working with real patients, so he or she knows what the daily practice of a physician is about.

Management researchers on the other hand tend to be people who have never worked in management themselves and who, therefore, have no experience of the issues a manager has to address in practice. Moreover, management researchers often cherish an Aristotelian perspective, that is, the importance of an internally consistent theory explaining the observed phenomena. Put differently, management researchers strive to explain how things work, whereas managers (like physicians) seek to know whether things work.

Of course, there is no evidence-based practice without theory about how things work. If we do not understand the world, we can neither anticipate it nor take purposive effective action. Even more, practitioners need some theoretical understanding of why something works to make evidence "stick" (Rousseau & Boudreau, 2010). However, the degree to which the question "Why?" is adequately answered appears to differ between managers and researchers. As parents of small children know, the question "Why?" can be asked ad infinitum. In general, managers seem to settle for answering the first "Why?" Researchers, on the other hand, will find this answer unsatisfactory and will repeat the question "Why?" a few more times in order to find out more about the underlying mechanisms. This also might be the reason that management researchers tend to publish hard-to-read articles in which a disproportionate number of pages are dedicated to theory and hypothesis formation, only a few pages to research results, and none to implications for practice (Kelemen & Bansal, 2002). Even more, in some management journals it is almost impossible to publish scientific research without an underlying theory, even if the study's outcome is relevant for practice.

The practice-knowledge gap has also existed in medicine and still exists today. Several studies reveal that, late into the 1990s, the publication of either relevant research results on the basis of RCTs or systematic reviews in a widely read journal was no guarantee for practical application. As a result it sometimes took many years before relevant research results were included in guidelines or were recommended by experts (Antman, Lau, Kupelnick, Mosteller, & Chalmers, 1992). This situation has significantly improved during the last two decades, particularly thanks to the influence of evidence-based medicine through which a more pragmatic attitude was adopted. As a result, research articles in medical journals are significantly shorter, written in easy-to-read English, and the theoretical underpinning of the research outcomes is of secondary importance to the practical relevance and applicability.

Foreground and Background Questions

The gap between practice and knowledge in medicine had its origin—to a considerable degree—in the very kind of research conducted. Until the late 1970s, the most important medical research consisted of biomedical laboratory research, the nub of which was the pathophysiology of diseases, but it had limited possibilities for application and limited relevance for clinical practice. Here too, researchers concentrated mostly on explaining how certain diseases and disorders are caused, whereas physicians mainly want to know which clinical interventions work. Also due to the influence of evidence-based medicine, this situation has changed slowly but steadily, and the focus in medical research has shifted to the most important task of physicians: treating patients. Evidence-based medicine has played an important part in that shift by emphasizing the difference between foreground and background questions (Sackett et al., 1997). Background questions are about general knowledge of the biomedical aspects of a disease or disorder. A typical background question would be, "How does congestive heart failure lead to swollen feet?" or "What causes migraines?" Background questions usually begin with an interrogative pronoun such as who, what, when, where, how, and why. Background questions are usually asked because of the need for basic information about a disease or disorder. It is not normally asked because of a need to make a clinical decision about a specific patient. The outcome of a background question is sometimes referred to as disease-oriented evidence (DOE) (Geyman, 1999). This kind of evidence is found in textbooks and handbooks or even medical information sites on the Internet.

Foreground questions on the other hand are about specific knowledge that can be used in a clinical decision about the treatment of a patient. A typical foreground question is "Would adding medication X to the standard therapy for adults with heart failure reduce morbidity from thromboembolism over three to five years?" A well-formulated foreground question consists of four elements: the patient's condition, the population or the actual problem (P), the intervention (I), the intervention with which the comparison is made (optional) (C), and the outcome one is interested in (O). These four letters form the acronym PICO, which is used the world over by medical researchers, physicians, and students as a mnemonic to describe the four elements

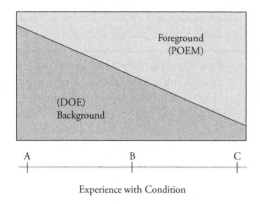

Fig. 2.1 Knowledge needs depend on experience with condition.

of a good clinical foreground question. The use of the PICO acronym has even become established in social sciences as well, usually with the addition of an additional letter C for context (PICOC). The acronym is also helpful for physicians to evaluate the relevance, usefulness, and meaningfulness of the research outcome to their patient. The outcome of a foreground question is sometimes referred to as patient-oriented evidence that matters (POEM). This kind of evidence is found within the information contained in published research studies, which are accessible through databases like MEDLINE. Foreground questions tend to be more difficult to answer than background questions because they require the synthesis of a wide range of knowledge.

The evidence-based medicine movement stresses that physicians need both background and foreground knowledge, and that the need for foreground knowledge grows with experience with respect to a certain disorder or disease (see Figure 2.1). A medical student who has just begun his/her studies (point A) will benefit mostly from knowledge about the genesis of diseases and the underlying pathophysiological processes, but an experienced medical consultant (point C) will need practical knowledge about the clinical treatment of his/her patients. Note that the position of the diagonal line implies that a practitioner is never too green to learn foreground knowledge, or too experienced to outlive the need for background knowledge (Straus, Richardson, Glasziou, & Haynes, 2005). Because medical researchers focused on background questions until the late 1970s, most medical research did not meet the physician's need for foreground knowledge, resulting in the gap between practice and knowledge. For that reason, evidence-based medicine is critical of the dominance of laboratory

research investigating biomedical processes and a plea for research on the effect of clinical interventions aimed at real patients. In other words: bring research back from the bench to the bedside.

The Accessibility of Evidence

To a large degree, evidence-based medicine is justified by the enormous explosion of research literature. As early as 1994, it was estimated that over 40,000 medical scientific journals were published each year, containing over one million research articles (Olkin, 1995). In the field of coronary heart disease alone, over 3,600 articles are published annually, and this means that a cardiologist would have to read more than 10 articles each day just to keep up with developments. For a general practitioner or family physician, this number is many times higher yet. The problem with evidence-based medicine is not so much a lack of evidence, but rather its surplus: for any individual physician, there is too much evidence to take into consideration in daily clinical practice. Pfeffer and Sutton (2006) were justified in pointing out that this is not different for the field of management. The number of research articles on management published annually will be significantly lower, but even then, too many research articles are published for a manager to keep abreast of the latest knowledge. As a consequence of this gigantic scientific output, it is not just the volume that increases but the diversity of the research results as well, so much so that it becomes impossible for researchers and practitioners to find their way in the mass of evidence. This results in a situation in which researchers no longer base their research on the cumulative knowledge in the discipline but on their subjective perception of only a fraction of this knowledge, and practitioners ignore (sometimes contradictory) research results and rely instead on their personal experience and intuition. This soon led to the realization within the evidence-based medicine movement that evidence-based practice is only feasible if two crucial preconditions are met.

First, access to evidence must be quick and easy, via online databases. The enormous development of the Internet has been an important driver in the development and spread of evidence-based practice within medicine. A great number of bibliographical databases are now available via the Internet and they often contain thousands of indexed journals and many millions of research articles. This enables physicians to search relevant research articles using Key Words, text words in the title or abstract, and using the embedded filter to limit the research results to research type or level of evidence. One of the most famous databases in medicine is MEDLINE, which allows the user to search publications from as far back as1966 in over 4,000 journals. Thanks to Internet access to these databases, every physician can go online to find the most up-to-date studies and every consultation room has an immense virtual library containing the latest studies (chapter 15 of this volume).

Second, aggregate evidence needs to be available in forms such as systematic reviews, synopses, summaries, and evidence-based guidelines. The intention behind a systematic review is to identify as fully as possible all the scientific studies of relevance to a particular subject and to assess the validity and authority of the evidence of each study separately. As the name indicates, a systematic review takes a systematic approach to identifying studies and has the methodological quality critically appraised by multiple researchers independently of each other. The use of statistical-analysis techniques in a systematic review to pool the results of the individual studies numerically in order to achieve a more accurate estimate of the effect is termed a "meta-analysis."

Systematic reviews are crucial for the development of a well-systematized and organized body of knowledge (Denyer & Tranfield, 2009). They efficiently summarize the available evidence on a certain subject (eliminating the need to read individual studies on this topic). They also call attention to gaps in our knowledge and the areas for which little or at best only weak evidence is available, and in turn, help shape the field's research agenda. The most important database for systematic reviews is that of the Cochrane Collaboration. Synopses are succinct descriptions of primary studies and systematic reviews and summaries are summaries of multiple systematic reviews on one medical topic. Summaries and synopses can be searched via special databases such as Trip, Sumsearch, DARE and Bandolier. Evidence-based guidelines are the highest form of aggregate evidence and they consist of systematically developed statements to assist practitioner and patient decisions about appropriate health care for specific clinical circumstances. Guidelines are not legally binding regulations, but insights and recommendations informed by as much evidence as possible regarding what physicians need to do to provide quality care. A well-known American database containing guidelines is the National Guideline Clearinghouse. Thanks to the availability of online databases with systematic reviews, synopses, summaries and guidelines, the massive amount of evidence in medicine is organized and well-indexed, so researchers, physicians and medical students can find the evidence they need with relative ease.

These two preconditions are not met yet in the field of management. Although research articles are quickly accessible via databases such as ABI/INFORM, Business Source Premier, Science Direct and PsycINFO, most managers cannot benefit from this wealth of information for the simple reason that the companies and organizations they work for do not have a license. On top of that, these databases are organized and indexed differently from the medical databases, which rules out filtering on research design or level of evidence, and a search often turns up mostly irrelevant articles. More importantly, though, is the fact that aggregate evidence is almost non-existent in management: the number of well-executed systematic reviews that can stand the methodological test of criticism is severely limited and synopses, summaries and evidence-based guidelines do not yet exist. The absence of aggregate evidence can be attributed to a large part to the diverging character of management research: contrary to medicine, where research is repeated as often as possible and under different conditions, so as to obtain the highest possible level of evidence, research in management is often isolated and unrelated and does not build enough on previous studies, so aggregation of research results through systematic reviews is difficult (Denyer & Tranfield, 2009). This makes for a heavily fragmented body of knowledge with a low level of evidence. This divergent character is partly caused by the fact that research in management is strongly driven by academic interests and there is insufficient consensus on the most important questions in the field that need answering. This situation could be resolved if researchers began to focus more on the foreground questions of managers rather than the background questions of academics, and, also, if management research developed into a discipline driven by problems and questions that relate to the daily practice of managers.

Side Effects of Evidence-Based Practice
Evidence as a Higher Form of Truth

In *Evidence-Based Medicine and the Search for a Science of Clinical Care* by Jeanne Daly (2005), a famous anecdote is told about how David Sackett used evidence to settle a professional dispute:

> It concerns a consensus conference where it was difficult to reach agreement because authoritative clinical experts saw their own clinical view as definitive.

Unable to persuade them otherwise, the McMaster people at the conference sent for Sackett. He proposed that experts be encouraged to make any recommendations they chose, but that they also rate on a scale the quality of evidence to back the recommendation. If a recommendation was based on evidence from randomized clinical trials with sufficient power, it would head the list. If the evidence was a case report, the recommendation would still be accepted, but it would be rated as a lower grade of evidence. Thus was born the hierarchy of evidence.

(p. 77)

In evidence-based medicine, the term *evidence* is used deliberately instead of *proof*. This emphasizes that evidence is not the same as proof, that evidence can be so weak that it is hardly convincing at all or so strong that no one doubts its correctness. It is, therefore, important to be able to determine which evidence is the most authoritative. So-called levels of evidence are used for this purpose and specify a hierarchical order for various research designs based on their internal validity (Phillips, 2001). The internal validity indicates to what extent the results of the research may be biased and is, thus, a comment on the degree to which alternative explanations for the outcome found are possible. The pure experiment in the form of a randomized controlled trial is regarded as the "gold standard," followed by non-randomized controlled trials (quasi-experiment) and observational studies such as cohort and case-control studies. Surveys and case studies are regarded as research designs with the greatest chance of bias in their outcome and, therefore, come low down in the hierarchy. Right at the bottom are claims based solely on experts' personal opinions. Experiments in the form of RCTs are only suitable for assessing the effectiveness of interventions. To evaluate serious side effects and the long-term effects of an intervention, one needs longitudinal and observational research and for the assessment of the effect on the quality of life for example, qualitative research is sometimes more suitable.

However, as RCTs are at the top of the hierarchy of evidence, medical research largely has focused on topics that could best be researched using experimental research designs, and, until recently, only evidence based on RCTs was treated as real evidence. This restrictive view of evidence led to medical research dominated by experimentation and aimed at hard, quantifiable outcome measures. It meant that research with a lower level of evidence, often aimed at side effects, the long-term effect, or

social-psychological success factors—such as the patient's coping skills, the level of support from his environment, and the perceived quality of life—were largely left out of the equation. Another problem that resulted from this one-sided focus on experimental research was limited generalizability. In research designs with a high level of evidence such as RCTs, there are often strict inclusion criteria that exclude patients with co-morbidities (for example, overweight or excessive alcohol consumption) or certain demographical properties (e.g., age), so that the research outcome only applies to a specific patient population, which limits the generalizability. Observational studies and noncomparative research, on the other hand, have lower internal validity, but are sometimes more generalizable. One drawback of the levels of evidence is that they do not say anything about the research result's external validity (generalizability), and they take insufficient account of the methodological suitability of the particular research design to the research question at hand. Alvan Feinstein and Henrik Wulff accused the people at the McMaster University openly of being obsessed with RCTs and reproached them for promoting RCT as a higher form of truth when, in fact, it is only a means to determine the effectiveness of an intervention. In management, too, the negative effects of the levels of evidence and the dominance of RCTs are frequently pointed out. For example, in his article "*Evidence-Based Management: A Backlash Against Pluralism in Organizational Studies*," Mark Learmonth expresses concern that the popularity of evidence-based management can lead to a one-sided view of evidence at the expense of funding observational and qualitative research (Learmonth, 2008).

In 1996, David Sackett and his colleagues responded to mounting criticism with an editorial in the *British Medical Journal*, called "Evidence-Based Medicine: What It Is and What It Isn't" (Sackett et al., 1996). In this article they argue that

Evidence-Based Medicine is not restricted to randomised trials and meta-analyses. It involves tracking down the best external evidence with which to answer our clinical questions. Without clinical expertise, practice risks becoming tyrannised by evidence, for even excellent external evidence may be inapplicable to or inappropriate for an individual patient.

In our field Briner, Denyer and Rousseau pointed out that the same counts for evidence-based management (Briner, Denyer, & Rousseau, 2009).

In the past few decades, the focus on RCTs in evidence-based medicine has waned slowly but steadily and by now it is generally acknowledged that a clinical decision should not only be based on scientific evidence with respect to the effect of the treatment, but also on evidence regarding the long-term effect, the chance of harmful side effects, the way patients experience their illness, the quality of life, and other outcome measures relevant to patients. Partly because of this, the National Institute for Health and Clinical Excellence (NICE), the biggest source of evidence-based guidelines in the world, always involves two patients in the production of a guideline, which always includes a chapter on patient experience. The importance of the levels of evidence has also drastically decreased by now and they have been partly replaced by the GRADE approach (GRADE Working Group, 2008). In this approach, evidence is weighed not just on the basis of the internal validity of the research design, but also the size of the effect detected is taken into account, as well is the subjective interest that a patient assigns to the outcome and the possible side effects (Guyatt et al., 2008). This approach has led to a revaluation of research designs with a lower level of evidence such as observational and qualitative research and initiatives like the establishment of the Cochrane Qualitative Research Methods Group and the Joanna Briggs Institute.

Trust in Numbers

Trust is essential for any discipline; it can be said to be a precondition for the social mandate that facilitates professionals to do their job. But what is the source of this trust? What is it that separates common knowledge from professional expertise? Why would lay people be prepared to abstain from their own intuitions and rely on the expert judgment of a professional? How does professional authority reduce uncertainty about any problem and pacify social unrest? In his widely acclaimed book *Trust in Numbers. The Pursuit of Objectivity in Science and in Public Life*, Theodore Porter is addressing these intriguing questions (Porter, 1995). Wondering how social trust is organized, he discusses the appeal of quantification in the nineteenth and twentieth centuries. He argues that quantification is no inherent quality of science, but rather the result of compromise, that becomes necessary when a discipline is experiencing external social pressure and distrust. It is interesting to apply this line of reasoning to evidence-based practice. In his book, Porter introduces an analytical distinction between two sorts of objectivity. Whereas disciplinary objectivity relates to consensus among professional experts, mechanical objectivity is referring to formalized knowledge to satisfy the general public. This is not just an analytical distinction but a chronological one as well. Over time, personal trust in professionals in face-to-face communities faded, to be replaced by "trust in numbers" in democratic mass societies. This development was not only derived from the understanding that expert judgment of professionals tends to be imprecise and unreliable, but was also the result of public distrust. Professionals no longer made a difference; instead, standardized and transparent guidelines became the instruments in the hands of bureaucrats and managers. Quantification and calculation were a response to an emerging political and social culture marked by distrust of elites and experts:

> Quantification grows from attempts to develop a strategy of impersonality in response to pressures from outside.
> (Porter, 1995)

Applied to medicine, this means that evidence-based medicine did more than reduce clinical uncertainty. It also created or expanded public accountability. At the end of the twentieth century, physicians faced an exploding volume of literature, the rapid introduction of technologies, a deepening concern about burgeoning medical costs, and increasing attention to the quality and outcomes of medical care. There was an urgent need to address these challenges, but medicine could not do this by itself. Greg Stoddart and George Torrance, two members of the Department of Clinical Epidemiology and Biostatistics at McMaster's realized this, when in 1988, they founded the Centre for Health Economics and Policy Analysis. The aim of the new Center was to develop and apply methods for the economic evaluation of specific services and to design and evaluate systems of health-care delivery. The Center sought to study decision making in health care: not just by health providers, but by consumers and policy makers as well. In doing so, Stoddart and Torrance took decision making to a higher level of aggregation: from the clinic to society at large. The market—so they argued—should be organized on the basis of analyses of technical efficiency *and* cost-effectiveness (Drummond, Stoddart, & Torrance, 1987).

Over the course of the 1970s and 1980s, the protagonists moved from basic science to applied clinical epidemiology, and from there to health economics and health policy. Gradually, the implications of evidence-based medicine became clear: it was obvious that a tool now existed that facilitated intrusion by third parties, who generally were medical lay people like civil servants and health insurers. In a sense, clinical epidemiology, evidence-based medicine, and health economy have been instrumental in making medical practice transparent and open to public scrutiny. Evidence-based medicine introduced new notions regarding autonomy, objectivity, medical jurisdiction, and risk. By making medical decision more transparent, it changed the relationship between preventive and curative interventions, between rights and duties of citizens, and between physician and patient. The boundaries between science, politics, and society faded, and the stakeholders had to position themselves and articulate their goals continuously.

The creation of public accountability is a current issue in management, too. Managers have to endure a great deal of criticism from various directions. Misuse of the position of power to one's own benefit, and failure and mismanagement are the charges most commonly heard. In a number of Western countries such as the Netherlands, this criticism is not restricted to the manager involved but is extended to the profession as a whole:

> Staff in the private and public sectors are addressed on a daily basis in a language which does not express their own specific reality but the make-believe world of managers. This make-believe world is dominated by objectives couched and repeated in a theatrical rhetoric: top quality, excellence, and continuous innovation.
> (Pessers, 2005)

As a result of this increasing social pressure, there is an external drive for transparency which fosters an upheaval for "objective opinion" and even "objective evidence." It is, therefore, to be expected that the acceptance of evidence-based management will not only be promoted by the need to improve the quality and professional standing of the profession, but will also, in particular, be used to increase managers' public accountability.

Cost Control as a Driver

As we saw in the previous section, evidence-based medicine is not just about clinical decision making but also about cost containment, recourse allocation, and distributive justice. In health economy, it is imperative to stand back from specific medical interventions and consider their place in the bigger picture. At the end of the twentieth century, governments and insurance companies were facing soaring health-care costs. In many Western countries, these costs rose faster than the growth of the economy allowed, and the costs sometimes ran over 10 percent of the gross domestic product.

In addition, many diagnostic and clinical interventions were found wanting in their effectiveness and many medical treatments were considered superfluous. Against this background, governments and insurance companies felt the need to regulate medical care, and evidence-based medicine could cater to that need. Governments, therefore, hailed evidence-based medicine as an external evaluation tool for the professional activities of health- care professionals. Insurers now embraced evidence-based guidelines set up by the professional group itself as a criterion for compensation. Consequently, the freedom of action for physicians was drastically curtailed. In the United States, this development has given rise to a situation in which physicians first have to seek permission from insurers for many medical interventions. Applications are assessed by trained employees without medical background via simple protocols. As a result, physicians no longer run the show in clinical decisions in the United States, as they have had to relinquish some power to insurers and managers. As a consequence, the discussion on evidence-based medicine has not only been politicized but also strongly polarized. In this discussion, advocates of evidence-based medicine see it as the tool to save health care: use the best available evidence to determine the best treatment and eliminate all superfluous and unnecessarily expensive medical intervention. Opponents see evidence-based medicine as cookbook medicine, where the patient's need is no longer the main concern; rather the need of governments and insurers to keep costs down is the determinant. In their view, cost control instead of medical necessity has become the justification for the assignment and distribution of care. In his article "Evidence-Based Medicine: What It Is and What It Isn't" Sackett warns against this depiction of evidence-based medicine, which he feels is an oversimplification:

> Evidence-based medicine is not "cookbook" medicine. Because it requires a bottom up approach that integrates the best external evidence with individual clinical expertise and patients' choice, it cannot result in slavish, cookbook approaches to individual patient care. Some fear that Evidence-Based Medicine will be hijacked by purchasers and managers to cut the costs of healthcare. This would not only be a misuse of evidence based medicine but suggests a fundamental misunderstanding of its financial consequences. Physicians practising Evidence-Based Medicine will identify and apply the most efficacious interventions to maximize the quality and quantity of life for

individual patients; this may raise rather than lower the cost of their care (Sackett et al., 1996).

Implications for Further Development of Evidence-Based Management
Recapitulation

This chapter provided a short history of evidence-based medicine's development and that of the professional field of management. It has also extensively covered the similarities and the differences between the two professional fields and the hindrances that block evidence-based management's further development. It has also demostrated the untenability of the view that evidence-based practice in our professional field is not possible because management is not a profession. The most important argument to support this statement, namely the lack of a body of knowledge that functions as a common frame of reference, says more about the developmental phase than about the nature of the professional field: medicine's body of knowledge failed to provide a common frame of reference until the late 1980s; the introduction of evidence-based practice promises to be the ultimate gamechanger.

We demonstrated why evidence-based practice needs to become part of the management curriculum. The current supply-driven management educational system must make way for problem-based teaching and hands-on instruction for finding the best available evidence, critically appraising it, and then integrating it into management practice. The problems managers struggle with in practice must take center stage in educating and developing managers.

With regard to scientific research, we revealed that our professional field shows a striking amount of similarities with medical science. Research results in both professional fields are determined by several variables, and there are weak links and often a large number of factors that modify the effect. It is noted that the methodological repertoire of management research is significantly less broad than that of medical science. Evidence-based management should, therefore, imitate its medical colleague and promote the application of other research designs. Management researchers must stimulate the exploration of the possibility of comparative research and further randomization within the professional field. Because comparative research is only possible in homogenous categories, researchers, instructors, and managers will also need to put in the effort to push back the use of multi-interpretable abstractions within the professional field. Both aspects, a limited

methodological repertoire and a large meaning variance, are characteristic of our professional field's development phase, but they do not form a hindrance to applying the principles of evidence-based practice. As remarked earlier, within every professional field in which research is conducted, a professional can, when making a decision, establish whether there is evidence to underpin this decision and in doing so apply the principles of evidence-based practice.

The same is true for the gap between practice and science. The observation that researchers and practitioners live in separate worlds and that, because of this, the research results are not applied in practice, proves after further examination to be a better argument for evidence-based practice than against it. Just as it can in medical science, evidence-based practice can act as a catalyst in our professional field and make researchers concentrate more on managers' foreground questions instead of academics' background questions. This means management research can develop into a problem- and demand-driven discipline that aligns closely with daily practice. As we pointed out, one important precondition here is for practice-driven and repeated research in academic centers to be held in higher regard and for authoritative management journals, like medical journals, to focus more on its relevance to practice.

Further Development and Dissemination: Lessons to Learn from Medicine

It has been concluded in the paragraphs preceding that the present situation in management shows a striking number of similarities with the situation in medicine two decades ago. It is, thus, reasonable to expect that the initiatives that ensured the propagation of evidence-based practice in medicine will also make the difference in the management field. If we look at the historical development of evidence-based medicine, we see that the key drivers are:

• The development of courses on evidence-based practice and the integration of the five-step approach of evidence-based practice into the medical curriculum.
• The publication of a handbook on how to practice and teach evidence-based medicine.
• The introduction of the levels of evidence, which weigh evidence on the basis of the internal validity of the research design, and the GRADE approach, which weighs evidence on the basis of the subjective interest that a patient assigns to the outcome, and using them as a way to "flag" the vast array of available research.

- The introduction of the concept of foreground and background knowledge and disease-oriented evidence (DOE) and patient-oriented evidence that matters (POEM), as a way to promote more research on the effect of clinical interventions aimed at real patients.
- The foundation of the Center for Evidence-Based Medicine to promote evidence-based health care and to provide free support and resources to doctors, clinicians, teachers, and others.
- The creation of databases with aggregated evidence to improve the accessibility of evidence.

All these initiatives can be translated directly to the management field and are potentially, therefore, an important driver in the further development and propagation of evidence-based management. The first and last initiatives, in particular, are crucial in light of the contribution that these initiatives have made to the paradigm shift that has occurred within medicine in the past two decades. In view of the many initiatives that have already been implemented in this field, it is reasonable to suppose that it must be possible to set up courses on evidence-based practice and integrate the five-step approach of evidence-based practice into the curriculum of universities and business schools in the decade ahead. The creation of databases with aggregated evidence to improve the accessibility of evidence is expected to be very difficult to achieve.

The Main Challenge: Improving the Accessibility of Evidence

In the section "The Accessibility of Evidence" we considered the limited availability of online databases and the lack of aggregated evidence. Both preconditions form one absolute condition for the development and application of evidence-based practice in our professional field. In this respect, too, we can learn from evidence-based medicine. The journal *Evidence-Based Medicine* was mentioned earlier in this chapter. It publishes the 120 best and most relevant research articles every year. The journal's editors summarize these articles and provide them with commentary in which they give a great deal of thought to the implications for their use in practice. Such a journal does not exist in our professional field, but it could be a first step to bringing well-conducted and practical, relevant studies to managers' attention in an accessible way. In addition to this journal, the Cochrane Collaboration is the paragon of excellence in the promotion, production and dissemination of aggregated evidence. The Cochrane Collaboration has, in the meantime, been copied within the social sciences in the form of the Campbell Collaboration. The idea for the initiative was thought up in London in 1999 during a meeting of 80 scientists. A number of these scientists were linked to the Cochrane Collaboration, where the need had arisen for a sister organization "that would produce systematic reviews of research evidence on the effectiveness of social interventions" (The Campbell Collaboration, 2010). The ambition to establish a separate organization to this end was widely supported by a large number of social and behavioral scientists and led, in the year 2000, to the formal establishment of the Campbell Collaboration.

There is a pronounced need within the evidence-based-management movement for an organization such as the Cochrane or Campbell Collaboration. To give evidence-based practice a shot at success within management, management education needs to promote the availability and accessibility of aggregated evidence. According to Gordon Guyatt, who introduced the term "evidence-based medicine":

> When I started, I thought we were going to turn people into evidence-based practitioners, that they were really going to understand the methodology, that they were really going to critique the literature and apply the results to clinical practice. I no longer believe that. What I believe now is that there will be a minority of people who will be evidence-based practitioners, and that the other folk will be evidence users who will gain a respect for the evidence and where it comes from and a readiness to identify evidence-based sources that summarize the evidence for them.
> (Daly, 2005)

References

Antman, E. M., Lau, J., Kupelnick, B., Mosteller, F., & Chalmers, T. C. (1992). A comparison of results of meta-analyses of randomized control trials and recommendations of clinical experts: Treatments for myocardial infarction. *Journal of the American Medical Association, 268*, 240–248.

Barker, R. (2010). No, management is not a profession. *Harvard Business Review, July-August*, 52–60.

Bower, J. (2000). The purpose of change, a commentary on Jensen and Senge. In M. Beer, N. Nohria (Eds.), *Breaking the code of change*. Boston, MA: Harvard Business School Press, 83–95

Briner, R., Denyer, D., & Rousseau, D. M. (2009). Evidence-based management: Concept cleanup time? *Academy of Management Perspectives, 23*(4), 19–32.

Burns, T., & Stalker, G. M. (1961). *The management of innovation*. London: Travistock Publications.

Business Week (1984, November 5). Oops. Who's excellent now? pp. 76–88.

Cabana, M. D., Rand, C. S., Powe, N. R., Wu, A. W., Wilson, M. H., Abboud, P-A., & Rubin, H. R. (1999). Why don't physicians follow clinical practice guidelines? A framework for improvement. *Journal of the American Medical Association, 282*(15), 1458–1465.

The Campbell Collaboration. (2010). www.campbellcollaboration.org/background (Retrieved March 22, 2011).

Cochrane, A. L. (1972). *Effectiveness and efficiency: Random reflections on health services.* London: Nuffield Provincial Hospitals Trust.

Cohen, D. J. (2007). The very separate worlds of academic and practitioner periodicals in human resource management: Reasons for the divide and concrete solutions for bridging the gap. *Academy of Management Journal, 50*(5), 1013–1019.

Colins, J. C., & Porras, J. I. (1995). *Built to last: Succesful habits of visionary companies.* New York: Harper Business.

Collins, J. C. (2001). *Good to great: Why some companies make the leap and others don't.* London: Random House Books.

Crain, E. F., Weiss, K. B., & Fagan, M. J. (1995). Pediatric asthma care in U.S. emergency departments. *Archives of Pediatric and Adolescent Medicine, 149*(8), 893–901.

Daly, J. (2005). *Evidence-based medicine and the search for a science of clinical care.* Berkeley, CA: University of California Press.

Denyer, D., & Tranfield, D. (2009). Producing a systematic review. In D. A. Buchanan & A. Bryman (Eds.), *The SAGE handbook of organizational research methods* (pp. 671–689). London: SAGE Publications.

Drucker, P. (1985). *Innovation and entrepreneurship.* New York: Harper & Row.

Drummond, M. F., Stoddart, G. L., & Torrance, G. W. (1987). *Methods for the economic evaluation of healthcare programs.* Oxford, England: Oxford University Press.

Evidence-based medicine Working Group (1992). Evidence-based medicine: A new approach to teaching the practice of medicine. *Journal of the American Medical Association, 268*(17), 2420–2425.

Feinstein, A. R. (1967). *Clinical judgment.* Baltimore, MD: Williams & Wilkins.

Fisher, R. A. (1926). The arrangement of field experiments. *Journal of the Ministry of Agriculture, 33,* 503–513.

Flores, M., Bauchner, H., & Kastner, B. (2000). Pediatricians' attitudes, beliefs, and practices regarding clinical practice guideline: A national survey. *Pediatrics, 105(3).*

Friedman, R., Schwartz, J. E., Schnall, P. L., Pieper, C. F., Gerin, W., Landsbergis, P. A., & Pickering, T. G. (2001). Psychological variables in hypertension: Relationship to casual or ambulatory blood pressure in men. *Psychosomatic Medicine, 63,* 19–31.

Geyman, J. P. (1999). POEMs as a paradigm shift in teaching, learning, and clinical practice. Patient-oriented evidence that matters. *The Journal of Family Practice, 48*(5), 343–344.

Guyatt, G., Oxman, A. D., Kunz, R., Vist, G. E., Falck-Itter, Y., Schünemann, H. J., & Group, f. t. G. W. (2008). What is "quality of evidence" and why is it important to clinicians? *British Medical Journal, 336*(7651), 995–998.

Ghoshal, S. (2005). Bad management theories are destroying good management practices. *Academy of Management Learning and Education, 4*(1), 75–91.

Goia, D. A., & Pitre, E. (1990). Multiparadigm perspectives on theory building. *Academy of Management Review, 15*(4), 584–602.

GRADE Working Group (2008). GRADE: An emerging consensus on rating quality of evidence and strength of recommendations. *British Medical Journal, 336* (7650), 924–926.

Holbeche, L. (2005). *The high performance organization: Creating dynamic stability and sustainable success.* Oxford, England: Elsevier, Butterworth Heinemann.

Hunt, M. (1997). *How science takes stock: The story of meta-analysis.* New York: Russel Sage Foundation.

Kelemen, M., & Bansal, P. (2002). The conventions of management research and their relevance to management practice. *British Journal of Management, 13,* 97–108.

Khurana, R., Nohria, N., & Penrice, D. (2005). Management as a profession. Chap. 3 in J. W. Lorsch, L. Berlowitz, & A. Zelleke (Eds.), *Restoring trust in American business.* Cambridge, MA: MIT Press.

Lawrence, P., & Lorsch, J. (1967). *Organization and environment: Managing differentiation and integration.* Cambridge, MA: Harvard University Press.

Learmonth, M. (2008). Evidence-based management: A backlash against pluralism in organizational studies? *Organization, 15*(2), 283–291.

March, J. G. (1996). Continuity and change in theories of organizational action. *Administrative Science Quarterly, 41,* 278–287.

Medical Research Council Streptomycin in Tuberculosis Trials Committee. (1948). Streptomycin treatment for pulmonary tuberculosis. *British Medical Journal, 2,* 769–782.

Mintzberg, H. (2005). *Managers not MBAs: A hard look at the soft practice of managing and management development.* San Francisco, CA: Berrett-Koehler.

O'Connor, G. T., Quinton, H. B., Traven, N. D., Ramunno, L. D., Dodds, T. A., Marciniak, T. A., & Wennberg, J. A. (1999). Geographic variation in the treatment of acute myocardial infarction: The cooperative cardiovascular project. *Journal of American Medical Association, 281*(7), 627–633.

Olkin, I. (1995). Meta-analysis: Reconciling the results of independent studies. *Statistics in Medicine, 14,* 457–472.

Pessers, D. (2005). Managers undermine the professional pride of employees. *De Volkskrant,* June 26th.

Peters, T. J., & Waterman, R. H. (1982). *In search of excellence: Lessons from America's best-run companies.* New York: Harper & Row.

Petticrew, M., & Roberts, H. (2003). Evidence, hierarchies and typologies: Horses for courses. *Journal of Epidemiology and Community Health, 57,* 527–529.

Pfeffer, J., Sutton, R. (2006). Evidence-based management. *Harvard Business Review, 84*(1), 63–74.

Phillips, B., Ball C., Sackett D., Badenoch D., Straus S., Haynes B., Dawes M. (2001). *Levels of evidence.* Oxford, England: Oxford Centre for Evidence-Based Medicine.

Porter, T. M. (1995). *Trust in numbers: The pursuit of objectivity in science and public life.* Princeton, NJ: Princeton University Press.

Rosenzweig, P. (2007). *The halo effect and the eight other business delusions that deceive managers.* New York: Free Press.

Rousseau, D. M., & Boudreau, J. W. (2010). Sticky findings: Research evidence practitioners find useful. Chap. 14 in E. E. Lawler & S.A. Mohrman (Eds.), *Useful research 25 years later.* San Francisco, CA: Berret-Koehler.

Rousseau, D. M., & McCarthy, S. (2007). Educating managers from an evidence-based perspective. *Academy of Management Learning & Education, 6*(1), 84–101.

Rynes, S. L., Bartunek, J. M., & Daft, R. L. (2001). Across the great divide: Knowledge creation and transfer between academics and practitioners. *Academy of Management Journal, 44*, 340–355.

Rynes, S. L., Giluk, T. L., & Brown, K. G. (2007). The very separate worlds of academic and practitioner periodicals in human resource management: Implications for evidence-based management. *Academy of Management Journal, 50*, 987–1008.

Sacket, D. L., Haynes, R. B., Guyatt, G. H., & Tugwell, P. (1991). *Clinical epidemiology: A basic science for clinical medicine.* Boston, MA: Little, Brown.

Sackett, D. L., Richardson, S. E., Rosenberg, W. M., & Haynes, R. B. (1997). *Evidence-based medicine: How to practice and teach EBM.* New York: Churcill Livingstone.

Sackett, D. L., Rosenberg, W. M., Gray, J. A., Haynes, R. B., & Richardson, W. S. (1996). Evidence-based medicine: What it is and what it isn't. *British Medical Journal, 312*, 71–72.

Schulz, K. F., & Grimes, D. A. (2002). Case-control studies: Research in reverse. *Lancet, 359*(9304), 431–434.

Shapiro, D. L., Kirkman, B. L., & Courtney, H. G. (2007). Perceived causes and solutions of the translation problem in management research. *Academy of Management Journal, 49*, 249–266.

Straus, S. E., Richardson, S. E., Glasziou, P., & Haynes, R. B. (2005). *Evidence-based medicine: How to practice and to teach EBM.* Edinburgh, Scotland: Elsevier Churchill Livingstone.

Sutton, B. (2007, 2010). Why management is not a profession. http://bobsutton.typepad.com/my_weblog/2007/09/more-evidence-t.html. Accessed March 5, 2012.

ten Have, S. (2007). The essence of the high performance: Knowing the organization and context as a basis for good organization. *Management & Organization, 51*(7), 5–20.

Walshe, K., & Rundall, T. G. (2001). Evidence-based management: From theory to practice healthcare. *The Milbank Quarterly, 79*, 429–457.

Woodward, J. (1958). *Management and technology.* London: HM Printing Office.

Wulff, H. R. (1976). *Rational diagnosis and treatment.* Oxford, England: Blackwell Scientific Publications.

A Design Science Approach to Evidence-Based Management

Joan Ernst van Aken *and* A. Georges L. Romme

Abstract

In this chapter we adopt a design-science approach to demonstrate how evidence-based management can extend experience-based management by judiciously gathering, validating, selecting, and using knowledge. The creative processes in which valid knowledge is used in designing *and* creating preferred futures are discussed, as well as the nature of the design knowledge needed for this. This includes knowledge on possible interventions with expected outcomes and on the mechanisms producing these outcomes.

Key Words: design science, collaboration between scientists and practitioners, design propositions, spin-offs, preferred future, professional practice, technical rationality

Design is (…) the principal mark that distinguishes the professions from the sciences. Schools of engineering, as well as schools of architecture, business, education, law, and medicine, are all centrally concerned with the process of design.
—*Simon (1996, p. 111)*

This chapter builds on the idea proposed by Nobel laureate Herbert Simon that organization and management research is a science of design. In keeping with this idea, evidence-based management (EBMgt) is a design process that individuals and teams use to solve real-life organizational problems through the use of scientific evidence and validated local facts.

EBMgt itself is a family of approaches to the practice of management, all of which use relevant scientific evidence (Rousseau, 2006; Briner, Denyer, & Rousseau, 2009). In this chapter, EBMgt is positioned in the context of the design-science paradigm in management and organization science (e.g., Bate, 2007; Boland & Collopy, 2004a; Jelinek, Romme & Boland, 2008; Romme, 2003; Van Aken, 2004). As such, we argue that EBMgt

is much more than rational decision making; it is about changing the actual into the preferred, with research-informed designing as the core activity. This perspective draws on the conceptualization of EBMgt as research informed, organizational problem solving (Tranfield, Denyer, & Smart, 2003) and a design-science approach (Romme, 2003; van Aken, 2004).

A design-science approach to EBMgt has the following three key features:

• Design-science research produces a critical part of the evidence to be used in EBMgt.

• This evidence is not to be used as a set of instructions or fixed protocols, but as input to the creative and innovative process of designing structures, processes, or interventions.

• Research-informed designing is the core activity in a complex process of changing the actual into the preferred: EBMgt involves acting, rather than (only) decision making, on the basis of evidence.

By positioning EBMgt in the context of management as a design-oriented discipline, this chapter draws on two seminal books, namely Herbert Simon's (1969/1996) *The Sciences of the Artificial,* and Donald Schön's (1983) *The Reflective Practitioner,* both building on the work of James (1907), Dewey (1929), and Peirce (1955) on pragmatism. Schön analyzed the more science-based professions like medicine and engineering, as well as the (somewhat) less science-based professions like architecture, management, and psychotherapy. Following Schön, professional work in all these disciplines entails much more than the model of pure technical rationality implies. In the latter model, professional practice largely boils down to instrumental problem solving on the basis of explicit knowledge, made rigorous by applying scientific theory and technique. The classic example of pure technical rationality is the engineer who uses a formula to calculate the maximum load for a building's construction. By contrast, professionals use rich repertoires of explicit and tacit knowledge in a creative process of reflection in action. These repertoires contain tacit knowledge, developed through personal experiential learning, as well as explicit knowledge, derived from their academic discipline.

This chapter thus develops the following key ideas:

• The core process in EBMgt is research-informed designing of structures, processes, or interventions, which entails a creative process of developing situation-specific solutions to design issues, combined with a more analytic process of evaluating these solutions.
• This process of designing "on paper" is an essential part of the very complex and challenging process of changing the current (organizational) world into a preferred one.
• The design process draws on multiple forms of knowledge, including tacit as well as explicit knowledge, through a creative process of reflection in action.
• Design-science research produces a critical part of this explicit knowledge.
• Personal and interpersonal experiential learning are central to developing both tacit and explicit knowledge for use in designing.

We first describe the design science perspective and then discuss a key component in the design process: the role of reflection-in-action. The chapter then describes the general process of changing the actual into the preferred, and subsequently compares and contrasts designed-based changes in the material and social worlds. Then, we explore the

nature of generic evidence for design, and contrast it with the nature of evidence in the social world, setting the stage for a discussion of EBMgt from a design science perspective. The chapter subsequently illustrates the EBMgt approach to design in a study of creating university spinoffs. Finally, we give recommendations for both practitioners and organizational researchers in advancing EBMgt as a design process.

The Design-Science Perspective

Designing a future is fundamentally different from describing and explaining the present. Simon's (1969/1996) *The Sciences of the Artificial* has played an important role in recognizing the centrality of design in applied disciplines, by demonstrating the fundamental differences between describing and explaining "what is" and designing and evaluating "what can be." Scholars often emphasize "describing and explaining the present" as the core research mission of any academic discipline. By contrast, designing "what can be" is a core activity in architecture and the arts, and also in research-based engineering. Yet, an increasing number of disciplines now resonate with Simon's recognition that the human world is artificial and that design activity is essential in making this world.

The primary mission of academic disciplines like medicine and engineering is the creation of preferred futures—for example, restoring health in the case of pneumonia or creating a more fuel-efficient car. This mission is realized through knowledge produced by research as well as through the actions of the professionals trained in these disciplines. Because design plays a central role in the creation of preferred futures, one may call disciplines for which design is central design sciences, as opposed to explanatory sciences. The mission of an explanatory science, like physics and sociology, is to describe and explain the world as it is. Explanatory research is largely driven by a quest for knowledge as an end in itself. The iconic research product here is the causal model. A causal model is assessed in terms of descriptive validity, that is, how well it accounts for the observed world.

Mainstream research in a design science is driven by field or real-world problems. Field problems are situations in reality that, according to influential stakeholders, can or should be improved. Knowledge development here is instrumental in solving field problems; students are thus trained to become professionals, using the knowledge of their discipline to explore, design, and create preferred futures.

Whereas explanatory research typically uses an "independent observer" perspective, design-science research (DSR) draws on a participant-observer perspective that requires knowledge of intervention-outcome-context combinations to be able to make judgments on the (likely) outcomes of interventions in specific cases.

With disciplines like medicine and engineering as inspiration, one can define DSR as a family of approaches to research that are driven by field problems, use a participant-observer instead of the independent observer perspective, and pursue a solution orientation. This implies that design-science researchers are not satisfied with describing field problems and analyzing their causes, but also develop alternative general solution concepts for these field problems. In medicine and engineering the participant-observer perspective does not pose specific problems because most researchers in these disciplines are, or have been, practicing professionals. In management research, this is typically not the case. Therefore, DSR in this discipline often draws on research strategies like collaborative or interventionist research (e.g., Romme and Endenburg, 2006).

The iconic research product of DSR is a well-tested solution concept, that is, a generic intervention to solve a generic field problem, tested in the laboratory and in the field of its intended use. In medicine, for example, solution concepts for a certain dysfunction (the field problem) can include types of drugs or surgery. In engineering, solution concepts to design a particular electronic equipment can include types of electrical circuits or programmable logic for their operation. In management, for example, solution concepts for creating cooperative arrangements can include types of contracts and procedures for assessing the fit between the prospective parties. A solution concept is assessed in terms of its real-world practical use, that is, pragmatic validity (Worren, Moore, & Elliott, 2002). For example, solution concepts for organization design problems are: "hierarchy" as an unambiguous sequence of accountability levels and "circularity" for organizing the flow of power and information (Romme & Endenburg, 2006).

The logic of applying the solution concept is the design proposition (also called technological rule). The design proposition puts the solution concept into its application context. It runs like this: if you want to achieve a given outcome for this generic problem in context, then use this generic intervention. For example: "if you want to achieve

a successful entry in a rather inaccessible foreign market by way of a cooperative arrangement with a local company, then use this particular type of contract." The most powerful design proposition is the field-tested and grounded one: the intervention is tested in its intended field of application and is grounded in an understanding of the generic mechanisms—that is, the cause-effect relations—that produce the outcome (van Aken, 2004). Therefore, in the example of the proposition regarding the type of contract (given earlier), one would like to have it tested through actual applications and grounded in a theoretical explanation of why this type of contract is superior in this particular context. The logic of the field-tested and grounded solution concept is called the CIMO-logic (Denyer, Tranfield, & Van Aken, 2008), a combination of problem in context, intervention, generative mechanisms producing the outcome, and outcome.

A discipline is called a design science if DSR approaches are firmly positioned in its mainstream. This is the case in fields like medicine, architecture and engineering. However, the importance of design has also been acknowledged in other fields, for example, IT (March & Smith, 1995; Hevner, March, & Park, 2004), accounting (Kasanen, Lukka, & Siitonen, 1993; Labro & Tuomela, 2003) and education (Kelly, 2003; Collins, Joseph, & Bielaczyc, 2004). Moreover, there is a growing interest in developing knowledge for design among management researchers. For example, inspired by architect Frank Gehry's approach to design, Boland & Collopy (2004a) brought together a group of people from very different backgrounds to explore the potential of design for management studies. The design science perspective to organization and management studies was initially developed by, among others, Romme (2003) and Van Aken (2004), and later, also, in special issues of the *Journal of Applied Behaviorial Science* (Bate, 2007) and *Organization Studies* (Jelinek, Romme, & Boland, 2008).

Like EBMgt, DSR can, thus, be regarded as a family of approaches: driven by field problems, using a participant-observer perspective, and pursuing a solution orientation.

Research-Based Designing and Reflection in Action

The core activity of designing consists of synthesis-evaluation iterations. A possible solution to the design problem is created or synthesized, typically by contextualizing an appropriate solution concept. The designed solution is then evaluated "on paper" to determine how well it solves the problem. Evaluation is the basis for choosing among alternative solutions to a design issue; evaluation "on paper" means judging the extent to which a design meets its desired specifications, before that design is actually implemented. Evaluation may also take place by engaging in small experiments or pilot studies to try out one or more alternative designs. If the result is not satisfactory, the solution is redesigned and evaluated again, an iterative process that continues until a satisfactory design is obtained.

Engineers, psychotherapists, managers, and other design professionals draw on their creativity, skills, and repertoires of tacit and explicit knowledge. They engage with a specific situation and treat their case as a unique one. At the same time, in a creative process of reflection in action they draw on an extensive repertoire of, among others, examples, models, theories, and solution concepts in order to make sense of their case and to design alternative solutions (Schön, 1983). In this respect, the designer draws on a repertoire as a kind of "grab bag" of knowledge, sometimes consciously but more often largely unconsciously, to synthesize and evaluate alternative designs.

The repertoires of junior professionals are largely the result of their initial formal training. These initial repertoires consist of internalized formal theory and tacit "clinical experience," obtained through personal experiential learning. Subsequently, professionals continually enrich their repertoires with further personal experiential learning, usually combined with efforts to keep their formal disciplinary knowledge up to date.

The use of explicit disciplinary knowledge demands creativity and considerable expertise: general knowledge has to be translated toward the specific context in question. DSR is not really intended for use by the layperson but rather by experienced and well-educated professionals. That is, design-science results are best used by professionals, having mastered the body of knowledge of their discipline, having the ability to locate and obtain (new) knowledge that is relevant in their work setting, the ability to contextualize explicit knowledge, and the ability to develop intimate knowledge of the case under consideration and its context. For example, physicians adapt their use of patient care protocols to individual circumstances and needs, and professional experience and judgment are key elements in designing context-specific solutions.

The degree to which explicit knowledge can support the design and realization of preferred realities varies by profession. In engineering, this role is so inherent and self-evident that evidence-based engineering is a nonissue. Engineers do not want to reinvent the wheel. In medicine, the role of explicit knowledge is also important, but compared to engineering more professional judgment is needed to contextualize generic knowledge in designing and choosing interventions. In some cases, this need for contextualization is fairly low, allowing for a crisp definition of best practices. In other instances, this need is so high that it is impossible to define unambiguous best practices, and the role of the practitioner's judgment thus becomes more pervasive (Goodman, 2010). Both engineering and medicine (largely) operate in the material world, although laws in physics are more general and less contingent than those in biology (Mitchell, 2000). This allows engineering to evaluate designs more unambiguously than medicine (e.g., evaluating the maximum load of alternative constructions in designing a building versus evaluating alternative interventions in the case of a brain tumor).

Next to the generic knowledge of the professional repertoire, the core process of designing requires case-specific inputs: the formulation of the design problem, the specifications the design has to satisfy, (likely) root causes of the problem, and an analysis of the problem context. However, designs cannot be derived from these inputs in a number of logical steps. Designing typically entails a creative leap from inputs to design; this may be a small leap, but more often it is a large one (cf. logic of abduction; Peirce, 1955). For example, new product development teams draw extensively on past knowledge, but only as a jumping board for creating radically new products. Designing is, thus, creatively exploring possible futures. It deploys accumulated knowledge and experience, without becoming locked into the past.

Changing the Actual into the Preferred in the Material World

The core process of designing, as previously described, is a key part of the overall process of changing the actual into the desired. This section explores this process in the material world, using engineering design as an exemplar. As such, this serves to identify key elements of design and change processes, and this discussion will later be used to understand how design processes in the social world differ from those in the material world.

Prior to starting the core process of designing, designers engage with principals and users to formulate the design problem and its specifications. These specifications can change during the design process, as the understanding of the problem and its setting deepens; moreover, time and cost constraints may make it impossible to meet initial specifications (which may then be adjusted downward). Alternatively, developments in technology or competitive conditions may lead to specifications being adjusted upward. If the design problem and specifications can be well defined, the development of specifications can be readily separated from the core process of designing. If design problem and specifications cannot be defined unambiguously, because both problem formulation and design specification are strongly intertwined with designing; designing then involves exploring alternative futures in close collaboration with various stakeholders. For instance, many people find it rather difficult to unambiguously specify the home furnishing they want, so interior decorators have to design interiors in close interaction with their clients.

An intense dialogue may be needed with those that will produce and implement the design, to produce designs that are easy or inexpensive to realize. In a wide range of routine settings (e.g., designing and producing shoes), design for manufacturing can be readily accomplished using explicit knowledge about manufacturing requirements. Otherwise, a focused dialogue between designers and producers is necessary.

Changing the actual into the preferred involves creating an action net (Lindberg & Czarniawska, 2006), a network of actors—individuals, groups, organizations—working together to create something new. This action net can be emergent in nature, occurring in an ad hoc, as-needed fashion. However, if an action net does not emerge spontaneously, design professionals need to deliberately develop it.

A design can be defined as a model to be realized. In engineering design, evaluating alternative designs "on paper" is typically done with the help of mathematics (e.g., analytically or through simulation modeling). As discussed later, using mathematical models for evaluation purposes is enabled by the fact that key mechanisms in the material world can be described in terms of universal and invariant laws. However, even in the material world it is not always possible to develop models of future entities that can be analyzed mathematically. If the entity being designed is too complex to be adequately modeled in mathematical terms, case-based reasoning is useful (e.g., Leake, 1996; Watson, 1997). In case-based

reasoning, the design is evaluated by comparing it with similar, previously realized designs—just as lawyers assess their cases on the basis of case law. If the entity involves such a high level of complexity that even case-based reasoning cannot be applied, small-scale pilot experiments with the alternative designs might be used to test and evaluate them.

Evidence for Design in the Social World

A design-science approach is a pragmatic one. It is not about developing "true" propositions about reality. Rather, it develops propositions that inform people about how to create preferred realities. This does not imply that design-science approaches merely aim at "instrumentalistic" propositions (Archer, 1995: 153), informing agents about interventions producing preferred realities without informing them about why these interventions would work. On the contrary, the answer to the why question is essential for effective and thoughtful usage of a design proposition. As discussed, in the implementation stage, a design proposition always has to be adapted to the specific context of application; in designing the adapted version, one has to know why the intervention works in order not to lose its power in the adaptation process. Nevertheless, the pragmatism of design science deeply influences the kind of evidence used for designing in the social world: evidence is needed on how, when, and why the particular intervention works.

Design-science research produces knowledge of solution concepts for solving field problems. The key scientific claim with respect to a design proposition is that it predicts the outcomes of the use of the solution concept in question (in the given context). In applied research in the material world, this prediction is enabled by universal and invariant mechanisms governing the behavior of matter—even if these are contingent on this world (Mitchell, 2000). An electron does not have the freedom today to behave differently from yesterday, nor can it act differently in Amsterdam than in New York. A machine tested in Barcelona will perform similarly in Buenos Aires—assuming that the human operator cannot significantly influence the machine's performance. Because of these universal and invariant mechanisms, responses identified in past/current tests can reliably be used to predict responses in the future.

Human agency creates the social world and is subject to interactions with the behavior of others. People do have the freedom to act on the basis of anticipated effects of their actions. Thus, no universal and invariant mechanisms exist in the social world. However, human behavior has patterns and regularities as a result of human nature and nurture. These patterns and regularities can be uncovered and then used in predicting—within certain ranges—the outcomes of interventions in the social world. In fact, predicting human behavior is an almost universal human competence (almost universal: autistic people lack this competence, showing how important and rather generic it is). Starting from the day we are born, we learn over the years what we can do to get what we want from others—that is, experiential learning (see Kolb, 1984).

The repertoires of professionals (both in the material and in the social world) contain the explicit knowledge of their discipline and the results of their personal experiential learning in real-world settings. We argue that for applied disciplines in the social world, given the absence of universal and invariant laws, knowledge production should be largely based on the strategy of experiential learning (see also van Aken, 2010). However, knowledge production in this case should result from objectified experiential learning, based on, among other things, controlled observations (following protocols and using methods like triangulation), comparative case analyses, and validation of designed interventions by alpha- and beta-testing (van Aken, 2004) in the intended field of application. Objectified experiential learning in academic research can, for instance, be done through the comparative case study, resulting in a rich understanding of context, intervention, and outcome. However, other approaches to objectified experiential learning can also be of value.

According to Bhaskar (1998) it is the nature of the object that determines the form of its possible science. In engineering design, the available science is such that one often can evaluate alternative designs by means of calculations of their expected performance. However, in social-system design, the nature of the designed system implies that the evaluation of alternative designs proceeds through experience-based judgment of expected performance. To support this judgment, objectified experiential learning is a powerful knowledge-production strategy.

Problems arising in organizations are not limited to purely social dimensions. They can also refer to socio-technical systems, as in operations management. The smaller the social component in such a system, the stronger are the universal and invariant mechanisms governing system behavior, and, thus, the stronger the potential for adequate mathematical modeling of the system (of an existing as well as a newly designed one). Designing socio-technical systems with a small social component is more similar to engineering design than to social system design, making math-based evaluation tools more useful. For instance, the design and evaluation of a scheduling or inventory control system can be largely based on mathematical modeling and analysis if the human operator can be expected to quite closely follow the instructions from the information system. However, if the operator must make frequent, significant adaptations to the schedules calculated by the system (e.g., because the dynamic complexity of the context leads the operator to make frequent exceptions to the built-in rules), any evaluation effort has to draw on experiential learning as well as mathematical modeling. Thus, if the social component of the system is large, one has to largely rely on experience-based prediction of the performance of the designed system; if the social component is small, one may fairly predict this performance on the basis of calculations.

EBMgt in Action: Operating in the Swamp of Practice

Schön (1983) argued there is the high ground of theory and there is the lowly swamp of practice. The ambition of EBMgt is to provide some firm ground in the swamp through the use of valid evidence. This will not drain the swamp: The use of this evidence still needs a substantial level of competence, experience and creativity.

In the following section we discuss EBMgt in the swamp of organizational change, particularly in design-based organizational change. This discussion will highlight several important aspects of EBMgt that draws on a design-science perspective.

EBMgt: Dealing with Major Managerial Challenges

Managers deal with most problems "on the fly." However, in this chapter we discuss ways of dealing with major managerial challenges in a more or less organized way, allowing for the deliberate use of EBMgt. An "organized way" implies giving sufficient attention to following various process steps, to relevant stakeholders, as well as to the information needed and its quality. This can result in a formally organized project with a principal, a project team, a project leader, a project assignment and a project plan. Major challenges can also be engaged within the framework of a series of regular management meetings in which the incumbent issue is part of the normal agenda—possibly supplemented by assignments on aspects of these issues completed between meetings or by "break-out sessions" for more focused discussions.

In the following we give a generic process model of formal or informal solution design projects (for more details: Van Aken, Van der Bij, & Berends, 2007). These projects deal with a significant issue, like a revision of strategy, a merger, a reorganization, or starting a large, high-risk product-development project. Typically, the project is preceded by a fuzzy front end, in which some stakeholders start to recognize the issue and try to obtain support for addressing it. Weick (2004) characterizes the experience of entering and engaging a new project as "being thrown" into a continuously evolving and ambiguous context. This fuzzy stage may result in an explicit acknowledgement of the issue by major stakeholders and the decision to start a major effort to deal with it. If one decides to adopt an organized process, then a project definition step is initiated. The products of this step should include:

- The problem definition.
- The project assignment, giving, among other things, the specifications for the intended outcomes of the project.
- The project plan that outlines the approach to analysis, design, and realization, and provides a time line for these activities.
- The project team, project leader, and reporting structure.

If a less organized approach is chosen, a sound problem definition is critical and its importance cannot be overstated. The rest of the project brief may be less detailed and formalized, but agreement is still needed on what will be done, by whom, and when. If using EBMgt, an essential part of these agreements refers to the efforts to be spent on collecting validated local knowledge as well as explicit scientific knowledge on the issue in question through systematic review and research synthesis.

Another key issue is the intended realization. If it is a significant issue, already at the project-definition step, one needs to develop a rough idea of who the possible change recipients are as well as their involvement in the design and realization processes. The entire process should lead to the development of a strong action net (Lindberg & Czarniawska, 2006), as previously discussed, to realize the designed solution.

The process steps following project definition, generally, are:

- Problem analysis (elaborating the initial problem analysis, made at the problem-definition step), which involves a process of naming and framing (Schön, 1983). This naming and framing will give pointers to relevant scientific literatures, and the analysis will include a diagnosis of the causes of the problem and the background of the issue.
- Context analysis, involving both the internal and external organizational context.
- The core process of designing the solution and the change plan.
- Realization, that is, the actual changes in roles, role structures, and activities.
- Learning for performance by the change recipients.
- Interpretation of and reflection on the results, design process, and change process —with the intent to capture the main lessons learned, to be used next time.

Typically, the project will not follow such an undisturbed process, because of delays or accelerations in the process, resulting from the interactions with the daily operations in the organization. Other urgent issues may demand attention or the issue itself suddenly may increase in urgency.

The Core Process: Designing

The basic process steps for solution design and change planning are:

- Sketching, by informally and creatively exploring possible solutions.
- Actually designing alternative solutions through a process of synthesis-evaluation iterations, resulting in the outline design and in a change plan to realize it.
- Detailing the outline design and change plan.

Usually the actual design process is not a linear one. Rather, the design process will use iterations and explorations. In an iteration, one may return to a previous step, because new insight reveals that more information is needed. There may even be a need to change the project objectives at such an iteration. In an exploration, one jumps to a step further in the process, for example, to understand what information is needed to design and evaluate alternative solutions.

In organizational-solution design, many people may be involved. There may be a lead designer or main sponsor (e.g., the CEO or his/her delegate), but, in all cases, a group of people will work together on the issue. The composition of this group may change over time. In the remainder of this section, we will call this group of tightly or loosely coupled people the design group.

For major issues, this design group generally should be multidisciplinary. The quality of the designed solutions depends on the extent to which this group uses its members' expertise effectively and efficiently. The quality of the designed solution strongly depends on the performance of the Transactive Memory System (TMS) of this group (Wegner, 1986; Peltokorpi, 2008). That is, in terms of Schön's repertoire notion, the quality of the design depends to a large extent on the quality of the design group's shared repertoire.

With respect to the actual designing (i.e., the synthesis-evaluation iterations), we distinguish between a decision mode and a design mode (cf. Boland & Collopy, 2004b). In the more-common decision mode, the emphasis is on the evaluation part of the iterations, and it is fairly tangible, allowing the use of familiar analytic scientific methods. In the design mode, on the other hand, the creative but much less tangible synthesis part is emphasized.

Boland and Collopy give an interesting illustration of the working-in-design mode (Boland & Collopy, 2004b). This illustration concerns the design of the Lewis building for the Weatherhead Business School, by the architectural firm of Frank Gehry. Toward the end of the design process, the floor space had to be reduced by 4,500 square feet, a really major change. At that point, the project architect Matt Fineout took two days to discuss this design problem with a representative of the client, going into many details and into many alternative detail solutions, making a lot of drawings. But to the complete astonishment of the client, at the end of the second day, as the client thought the problem had largely been solved, the architect tore these drawings up and threw them in the trashcan. The client had expected that the design would emerge through a process of successive detailing, each intermediate design coming closer to the eventual design. But the architect's behavior in this case demonstrated two key principles of designing:

• Designing is playing with alternatives (don't marry the first design idea).
• Assign the main effort to the outline design (start the time- and resource-consuming detailing only after the key design dilemmas are solved).

The architect needed discussions with the client to become familiar with the design dilemmas he faced, but he was not yet ready to resolve these dilemmas in an outline design, being still in the phase of creatively synthesizing alternative solutions. In organizational problem solving in the design mode, participants, therefore, need to take time to play with alternatives and put a lot of effort into making a sound outline design. In managerial settings, too, often the design group becomes entrapped in the first feasible solution found, and then shifts all its effort in detailing it.

As said previously, one cannot deduce the design from the inputs; there always is a creative leap from input to design. However, the inputs to the design process are of critical importance to the design's quality. The explicit inputs include:

• The problem analysis and diagnosis.
• The context analysis.
• Solution concepts and ways to evaluate them.

In the synthesis steps, the design group merges these explicit inputs with their tacit and explicit knowledge to subsequently synthesize alternative solutions to design issues in a process of reflection in action. In the same way, tacit and explicit knowledge is used to evaluate the alternative designs against the specifications, the most important being that the solution should solve the problem. As in very complex situations in engineering design that are rather difficult to model, case-based reasoning is an important alternative approach to evaluate organizational designs "on paper."

Design-Based Change in the Social World

The overall process of changing the actual into the preferred in organizations has similarities to engineering design. Much of the process is comparable: problem analysis, development of specifications, interactions with the various stakeholders, the building of an action net to realize the solution. Fundamental differences also exist.

Foremost among the differences is the need to contextualize generic knowledge. How teams, meetings, or policies are thought of and operate in one firm differs from those in another. Thick, rich, and detailed descriptions are, therefore, needed for the various solution concepts, the contexts in which these concepts have been tested, and the nature of the (intended and unintended) outcomes. Furthermore, the evaluation of alternative designs is done differently. Many engineering designs can be adequately modeled, so engineers can use their impressive array of engineering mathematics to evaluate their designs on paper. This typically is not the case in the social world. An experiential learning approach, like case-based reasoning, therefore, has to be used to evaluate designs. For instance, to evaluate the design for an account-management system in a sales department, the design group can draw on data on the performance of implemented account-management systems in other sales departments (within or outside the same company).

Finally, a fundamental difference exists in realizing the design. In engineering, the design determines the realized entity and, thus, also its behavior. In management and organizational settings, realizing any design always involves the ultimate redesign and adaptation of the initial design by the change recipients; their behavior depends on how they interpret the design. Their collective interpretation can produce social realities at odds with the design group's intentions, and thus different outcomes. A nursing group implementing a new self-managing team approach, developed at the level of the hospital at large, may distrust the given protocol and still appoint a group leader. In engineering design, this dilemma is solved in the design-for-manufacturing approach. In management and organization, however, the design group needs to facilitate the interpretation and enactment of their design by frequently interacting with change recipients during the design process as well as by staying involved in the entire subsequent process of change and learning for performance.

In this process of participation by the change recipients, EBMgt can make another contribution by informing the design group as well as the broader stakeholder audience of the design and change—thereby supporting interpretation, enhancing credibility, and generating confidence in the endeavor's future outcomes.

Other Contexts of EBMgt

Earlier, we discussed EBMgt in design-based organizational change. EBMgt can also be of great value in issues not necessarily involving major organizational change, as in decision-making on large investments or technology-driven innovations. Moreover, in organizational change there are important alternatives to design-based change. In some situations, one cannot design a preferred end state, because, for instance, the available knowledge is insufficient or because organizational politics make it ill-advised to do so. In such cases, one may prefer to adopt a step-by-step approach, each step based

on the results of the previous one. In other cases, change objectives are difficult to realize by designing preferred end states (e.g., in cultural change). In each of these alternative settings, however, there still is a lot of design to do—for example, defining the objectives and set-up of the next step of the change process or the type of intervention to be used.

The Contribution of EBMgt

EBMgt intends to extend and build on intuitive, experience-based managerial problem solving. It does so by:

- Giving attention to the informational inputs to the problem-solving process.
- Enhancing the shared repertoire (or Transactive Memory System) of the design group.
- Providing significant content to the design process.

In the course of problem and context analysis, the design group gathers a lot of case-specific information, with respect to both the organization and its environment. EBMgt promotes a rigorous approach to collecting information, calling attention to scientific evidence as well as local facts and experiences, and adopting a critical attitude toward the information collected. EBMgt thus enhances the quality of the inputs to the process of designing solutions to organizational problems.

An EBMgt approach emphasizes not just the solution to a single problem, but also enhances the organization's readiness to address issues in future. Thus, it also aims to make full use of the explicit knowledge of the members of the design group and to make their tacit knowledge as explicit as possible (e.g., see the case in the next section), thus creating a shared repertoire for the design group. This is an important issue, especially because design groups for significant organizational issues often represent many different disciplines. Making knowledge explicit and critically assessing its quality can significantly enhance the design group's performance by promoting knowledge sharing and deeper understanding.

The primary contribution of EBMgt, however, is to produce valid generic knowledge on a particular issue, based on rigorous scientific research, including the outcomes of DSR. This explicit knowledge can support problem analysis and diagnosis, context analysis, and, especially, design, both for synthesis and for evaluation. Naming and framing at the problem-definition step gives pointers to the literatures to be searched. The synthesis step of the design process proper can be supported by identifying a range of generic solution concepts along with their indications and contra-indications. Evidence from the literature arising from testing the solution concepts in various settings can support the subsequent evaluation step. As in engineering design, the evaluation and justification of designs in management and organization may draw on case-based reasoning.

The process of producing this valid generic knowledge is systematic research synthesis (Denyer & Tranfield, 2006; Denyer et al., 2008; Briner & Denyer, chapter 7 of this volume). Quantitative meta-analysis may be a powerful way to synthesize quantitative research outcomes in the material world. In the social world, however, a highly effective knowledge-production strategy is to synthesize research outcomes on the basis of an objectified experiential learning approach. At each step of the literature review, the basic question is this: What have we learned until now to understand our problem and to synthesize alternative solutions, and what evidence have we generated to enable us to judge what the outcomes of these solutions would be in our specific context?

As discussed in the section on evidence for design in the social world, if the system to be designed has a significant material component, designing is more like engineering design. In that case, the knowledge-production strategy can make more use of quantitative approaches to research synthesis.

The results of the systematic-research synthesis are shared within the design group, thus further adding to the group's shared repertoire. These results can also be shared with the prospective change recipients. This serves to create an even broader shared repertoire, which can be of great value in realizing the design—as will be discussed in the next section.

EBMgt in Developing University Spin-offs

To illustrate evidence-based solution design in the context of organization and management, we draw on a study of a university spin-off creation by Van Burg, Romme, Gilsing & Reymen (2008). This study provides an example of designing and developing policies, informed by codifying and synthesizing practitioners' experiences and the academic body of knowledge inferred from an extensive literature review.

The problem was how to create university spin-offs, that is, business start-ups that commercialize technologies developed at the incumbent university.

Its particular context is the common case where the focal university resists any deviation from its core teaching and research processes. The assignment to develop evidence-based guidelines for spin-off creation was given to a research team by a Dutch university—Eindhoven University of Technology (TU/e). The spin-off creation project was already underway when this assignment was given. Three years earlier, TU/e had started the development of a new venturing incubation unit. In a quest to realize some early results, this was done without giving much attention to the literature on the subject. After some time the University board and the incubator director became interested in how their incubator system compared to those at other (leading) universities and in what the scientific literature had to say about it. In other words, the incubator was set-up without using EBMgt, but after some time the key players became interested in it. This way of starting EBMgt meant that the research team (in which one of the authors of this chapter participated) could benefit from the initial practitioners' learning outcomes and experiences (i.e., reflection in action). On the other hand, arriving in the middle of the project meant that the design group—the group actually involved in designing—consisted, not only of the research team, but also included the university staff members already engaged in developing university spin-offs. Thus, the research team faced the challenge of transforming an ongoing, largely emergent design process into a more deliberate one. A further challenge was, as always in evidence-based solution design, the need to contextualize any generic findings of a systematic literature review to take into account the features specific to TU/e.

In view of these challenges, a design-science-driven EBMgt approach was adopted in which two key notions connected professional practices and research findings (cf. Romme & Endenburg, 2006): design propositions and solution concepts (as discussed in the section The Design-Science Perspective). Design propositions can be based on research, but can also be derived from successful professional practice. The research-based propositions serve as tangible artifacts that allow different groups of people to focus on and create shared understandings (Romme & Endenburg, 2006). That is, these explicit propositions allowed participants from diverse backgrounds to focus on a common set of issues in the design process (cf. boundary objects).

The research team developed design propositions for the university spin-off creation by separately developing propositions based on practice (practice-based propositions) and propositions based on scholarly knowledge (research-based propositions). The synthesis of these propositions subsequently resulted in design propositions, which thus provides a body of knowledge that is grounded in research as well as tested in practice (cf. Van Aken, 2004). Thus, the key steps in developing design propositions were as follows (Van Burg et al., 2008):

1. So-called practice-based propositions were developed by converting the largely tacit knowledge of key actors in the university spin-off creation into explicit propositions.

2. Propositions were derived from a review of the literature; these research-based propositions then served to help understand (and possibly improve) practices and solutions already in place as well as to create entirely new solutions.

3. Finally, the research team synthesized the practice-based and research-based propositions in a set of design propositions – defined as propositions that are tested in practice as well as grounded in the existing body of research.

The practice-based propositions were derived from the data by means of a careful coding and reduction process (Strauss & Corbin, 1990). First, the research team coded all different practices and experiences reported by initial design-team members and support advisors as well as described in key documents. Next, the coded practices were clustered and reduced to a small number of categories. For each category, crucial elements of the solutions and any common denominators were identified. Finally, for each practice-based proposition the different experiences of support staff and entrepreneurs were listed. For example, some of the practice-based propositions identified by Van Burg et al. (2008: 122) were as follows:

> Create arrangements for starters to use university labs and other resources; (…) enable starters to use the academic network of the university; establish a network around the support organization of investors, industry contacts and financers.

The research team derived research-based propositions by means of a systematic literature review using a qualitative metasynthesis approach (Denyer & Tranfield, 2006). The domain of this review was defined in terms of all research in the area of university spin-offs. The purpose of the review was to derive normative (generic) propositions rather than to provide a comprehensive overview.

The findings from the review were synthesized in a number of key concepts and a preliminary set of propositions. Subsequently, this set of research-based propositions was linked to general theories, to explain the key mechanisms addressed by these propositions (according to the CIMO logic, advocated by Denyer, Tranfield, & Van Aken, 2008, as outlined earlier in this chapter).

Finally, Van Burg et al. (2008) developed a set of design propositions by confronting and comparing the list of practice-based propositions with the list of research-based propositions. This resulted in the following set of design propositions for building and increasing capacity for creating spin-offs; in this respect, a (European) university should design and implement practices that:

1. Create university-wide awareness of entrepreneurship opportunities, stimulate the development of entrepreneurial ideas, and subsequently screen entrepreneurs and ideas by programs targeted at students and academic staff.

2. Support start-up teams in composing and learning the right mix of venturing skills and knowledge by providing access to advice, coaching and training.

3. Help starters in obtaining access to resources and developing their social capital by creating a collaborative network organization of investors, managers, and advisors.

4. Set clear and supportive rules and procedures that regulate the university spin-off process, enhance fair treatment of the parties involved, and separate spin-off processes from academic research and teaching.

5. Shape a university culture that reinforces academic entrepreneurship by creating norms and exemplars that motivate entrepreneurial behavior (Van Burg et al., 2008: 123).

This set of emerging design propositions was shared with the design group as a whole. They were discussed repeatedly with startup advisors, the incubation unit manager, entrepreneurship professors, and other TU/e stakeholders. This ongoing dialogue also served to reposition and fine tune two specific TU/e incubation practices. The first involved a program in which Master of Science students worked in teams to develop value propositions and business models for a particular university-developed technology. The second practice was a regional incubator network in which investors, banks, incubators of local companies (including Philips Electronics), applied research institutes, and regional developments agencies collaborate with the start-up advisors of the TU/e to provide access to resources, network contacts, and other facilities to entrepreneurs engaging in spin-off projects. The design propositions developed by Van Burg et al. (2008) served to create awareness and understanding of each of the elements of the TU/e approach to spin-off creation, by placing these in a broader framework.

The set of design propositions exposed blind spots and major opportunities for improvement and development. Moreover, they helped to create a shared repertoire of knowledge on university spin-offs for the various parties concerned. Thus, the EBMgt project by Van Burg and co-authors served to define the lack of an entrepreneurial university culture (cf. design proposition 5) at the TU/e as the main weakness of its spin-off creation capability. Throughout the university, the awareness of this deficiency grew, and several new initiatives and projects were used to expose the TU/e community to role models (e.g., successful entrepreneurs among the TU/e alumni) and to motivate entrepreneurial behavior (e.g., by creating attractive financial benefits for scholars whose patented technologies are used in successful spin-offs). The university's senior management and other key stakeholders were well aware of the long-term effort required here, because universities tend to be rather conservative in view of their long-standing commitment to academic research and education.

This evidence-based project on spin-off creation, set up in 2005, is still going on at this writing. The preliminary results of the project are as follows. First, the TU/e increased its spin-off rate from zero in the late 1990s and about 5 per year around 2005, to the current rate (in 2010–2011) of about 15 new firms exploiting Intellectual Property (IP) of the university per year. The design framework developed by Van Burg et al. (2008), in combination with this boost in the spin-off rate, motivated the university's top management to increase its ambitions—to double the spin-off rate in the next 5 years. Of course, it is not possible to determine precisely to what extent the EBMgt project of Van Burg et al. (2008) contributed to the increase in the spin-off rate at the TU/e. It is not unlikely that without this EBMgt project the TU/e would also have increased its performance in creating spin-offs. Moreover, any EBMgt project is embedded in a continuously evolving and ambiguous socioeconomic system. The spin-off creation project at the TU/e, however, does illustrate that EBMgt serves to

build a systematic, theory-driven understanding of a rather complex managerial issue, which previously was dealt with on the basis of common wisdom and personal experiences.

Another, more academic, upshot of this project is that the design propositions developed by Van Burg et al. (2008) served to reflect on the comprehensiveness of (previous) research and theory development. In this respect, Van Burg et al. (2008) observed that some of their design propositions are not yet (firmly) incorporated in the university spin-off literature. For example, the proposition referring to clear and supportive rules and procedures was not previously identified, and as such not grounded in any theoretical frameworks. In turn, this finding motivated a new study exploring the role of transparency and fairness in university spin-off formation. Moreover, other research teams have adopted and replicated the design framework developed by Van Burg et al. (2008), for example Barr, Baker, Markham and Kingon (2009) in the context of several U.S.-based universities.

Discussion

The term evidence-based management (EBMgt) may evoke a picture of rational decision making (like *The Rational Manager* of Keppner & Tregoe, 1965), with academic research findings as its main input, replacing intuitive, experience-based management. Instead, this chapter demonstrates and illustrates a design-science approach in which EBMgt involves extending intuitive, experience-based management. This extension draws on scientific evidence as a source of design propositions and for creating a design process that effectively makes use of a broad array of knowledge and perspectives. EBMgt itself involves identifying and using those business practices that work, according to the best available evidence.

EBMgt demands a significant effort in gathering valid information for designing solutions for management and organization problems. As yet, research-based information on many managerial and organizational issues is not readily accessible; our academic community thus needs to engage in a systematic literature review and synthesis on each significant managerial challenge that practitioners are facing. In medicine, the Cochrane database (www.Cochrane.org) provides professionals with the evidence to design and optimize their interventions for a broad range of disorders. As long as there is no such equivalent in the field of management and organization, EBMgt in this field needs to focus on major issues and challenges for which it is feasible to invest in an extensive systematic-research synthesis.

Even so, practitioners need persuasion and incentives to engage in EBMgt, since its added value appears less obvious than in some other disciplines. We already observed that the value of valid, explicit knowledge is self-evident in engineering. Interestingly, in the social world we have a similar example: law practice. Evidence-based law practice simply is a nonissue; lawyers and judges have to extensively use the law, case-law, and all available evidence to get their job done. On the other hand, experienced medical doctors sometimes need to be seduced to acquire and use state-of-the-art explicit knowledge. They may feel that their initial training in the medical discipline, complemented with their rich tacit knowledge gained through experiential learning, is quite sufficient to operate as a medical practitioner. The challenge here is to demonstrate the added value of recently developed evidence to medical professionals.

A similar problem occurs for experienced managers and management consultants: the added value of research-based knowledge is not always self-evident to them (and experienced managers may also have different views on what counts as evidence; see Potwoworski & Green, chapter 16 of this volume). The community of management and organization researchers and educators must take charge of this challenge, by building a strong case for EBMgt, by creating attractive conditions for practitioners to join collaborative EBMgt projects, and especially by giving much attention to EBMgt in management training.

The term *evidence* suggests a decision mode; that is, the idea that the main challenge is to choose between known alternatives. This implies that the main contribution of evidence-based practice is to produce the evidence for making a rational choice between these alternatives. As previously argued, EBMgt will typically address major managerial issues. For such issues, we advocate a design mode that puts substantial effort in the design of alternative solutions or arrangements of solutions, thus crafting a high-quality outline design before going into details. Academic research can provide significant support for this type of design effort by providing a range of well-tested solution concepts.

A final comment relates to the roots of the evidence-based practice movement in medicine: it is both an asset and a liability. As an asset, it provides a link with a well-respected design science. It is also a liability that evokes criticism by those perceiving EBMgt as a solely technical-rational approach to managerial issues (e.g., Denzin, 2009). Or the criticisms leveled by Morrell (2008) of, among other things, having a commitment to positivism (which is not the case), having simplistic ideas on the nature of evidence and on accumulation and progress in social science knowledge, and of being troubled by "physician envy" (as opposed to the "physics envy" in some other social-science arenas). This chapter serves to argue that this is not necessarily the case. In this respect, a design science approach suggests that effective EBMgt is complementary to experience-based management, by giving research evidence a productive role in management as a complex professional process.

One of the characteristics of a design-science approach to EBMgt is that a significant part of the general evidence to be used is produced by DSR, an approach to research that has three defining characteristics: it is driven by field problems, it uses a participant-observer perspective, and it adopts a solution orientation. As such, DSR differs from the (in the social sciences) far more common explanatory research. But DSR is not foreign to management research: both observe reality, both analyze observations, and both draw grounded conclusions. Explanatory research studies the world as it is, DSR is interested in what the world can be. But it does so by developing knowledge from experimenting with these future states and observing and learning from these experiments. In its methods, DSR is therefore not fundamentally different from explanatory research. Furthermore, almost every actual DSR project starts with an explanatory part, describing and analyzing the type of field problem at hand, and only then does it start to develop alternative solutions. If there is a substantial body of knowledge about the field problem in question, the DSR part can be large; if little is known, the explanatory part needs to be larger, leaving much work for DSR in follow-up projects. Finally, DSR is not discipline specific. In disciplines like medicine and engineering it is an important part of mainstream research, but in other disciplines one can do DSR equally well.

Implications for Practice and Research

As Bismarck once said, "fools learn from their experience, I prefer to learn from the experience of others." EBMgt does not replace intuitive, experience-based management; EBMgt extends it by judiciously gathering, validating, selecting, and using knowledge of the incumbent organization, its environment, and the types of issues at stake. In a design-science approach to EBMgt, a critical part of the general evidence to be used is produced by DSR. Moreover, one deals with these significant issues in a design rather than in a decision mode: the emphasis is on designing and creating a preferred future, rather than on using evidence to choose from existing alternatives. EBMgt is not about finding exact interventions in the literature but about interrogating scientific evidence to obtain valid input for the design of managerial initiatives, interventions, and systems.

Next to practitioners, educators and researchers also have an important role in advancing and applying EBMgt. MBA as well as DBA programs should include rigorous training in EBMgt, including systematic review and research synthesis, preferably, also, in real-life settings. Researchers can support EBMgt by including design science in their repertoire of research strategies, in order to develop field-tested solution concepts for significant managerial issues. In the medical discipline, the Cochrane database does not only give practitioners diagnoses of dysfunctions; it also gives field-tested alternative treatments. Likewise, EBMgt should (ideally) be able to draw on a body of valid knowledge on alternative solutions to types of field problems.

EBMgt can and should become part of mainstream managerial thinking, just as Total Quality Management became part of this mainstream after the hype surrounding it had abated. For this to become reality, a strong partnership between interested practitioners, educators, and researchers is needed.

References

Archer, M. S. (1995). *Realist social theory: The morphogenetic approach*. Cambridge, England: Cambridge University Press.

Barr, S. H., Baker, T., Markham, S. K., & Kingon, A. I. (2009). Bridging the valley of death: Lessons learned from 14 years of commercialization of technology education. *Academy of Management Learning and Education, 8*, 370–388.

Bate, P. (2007). Editorial to the special issue "Bringing the design sciences to organization development and change management". *Journal of Applied Behavioral Science, 43*, 8–11.

Bhaskar, R. (1998). *The possibility of naturalism: A philosophical critique of the contemporary human sciences* (3rd ed.). New York: Routledge.

Boland, R., & Collopy, F. (2004a) (Eds.). *Managing as designing*. Stanford, CA: Stanford University Press.

Boland, R., & Collopy, F. (2004b). Design matters for management. In R. Boland & F. Collopy (Eds.), *Managing as designing* (pp. 3–18). Stanford, CA: Stanford University Press.

Briner, R. B., Denyer, D., & Rousseau, D. M. (2009). Evidence-based management: Concept cleanup time? *Academy of Management Perspectives, 23*, 19–32.

Collins, A., Joseph, D., & Bielaczyc, K. (2004). Design research: Theoretical and methodological Issues. *Journal of the Learning Sciences, 13*, 15–42.

Denyer, D., & Tranfield, D. (2006). Using qualitative research synthesis to build an actionable knowledge base. *Management Decision, 42*, 213–227.

Denyer, D., Tranfield, D., & Van Aken, J. E. (2008). Developing design propositions through research synthesis. *Organization Studies, 29*, 249–269.

Denzin, N. K. (2009). The elephant in the living room; or extending the conversation about the politics of evidence. *Qualitative Research, 9*, 139–160.

Dewey, J. (1929). *The quest for certainty: A study of the relation of knowledge and action*. New York: Minton, Balch.

Goodman, J. (2010). Healthcare: Who knows best? *The New York Times Review of Books, 57*(2).

Hevner, A. R., March, S. T., & Park, J. (2004). Design science in information system research. *MIS Quarterly, 28*, 75–105.

James, W. (1907). *Pragmatism, a new name for some old ways of thinking*. New York: Longmans, Green.

Jelinek, M., Romme, A. G. L., & Boland, R. J. (2008). Introduction to the special issue "Organization Studies as a Science for Design:" Creating collaborative artifacts and research. *Organization Studies, 29*, 317–329.

Kasanen, E., Lukka, K., & Siitonen, A. (1993). The constructive approach in management accounting research. *Journal of Management Accounting Research, 5*, 243–263.

Kelly, A. E. (2003). Research as design. *Educational Researcher, 32*, 3–4.

Keppner, C. H., & Tregoe, B. J. (1965). *The rational manager*. New York: McGraw Hill.

Kolb, D. A. (1984) *Experiential learning: Experience as the source of learning and development*. Englewood Cliffs, NJ: Prentice-Hall.

Labro, E., & Tuomela, T-S. (2003). On bringing more action into management accounting research. *European Accounting Review, 12*, 409–442.

Leake, D. B. (1966). *Case-based reasoning: Experiences, lessons and future directions*. Menlo Park, CA: American Association for Artificial Intelligence.

Lindberg, K., & Czarniawska, B. (2006). Knotting the action net, or organizing between organizations. *Scandinavian Journal of Management, 22*, 292–306.

March, F. T., & Smith, G. F. (1995). Design and natural science research on information technology. *Decision Support Systems, 15*, 251–266.

Mitchell, S. D. (2000). Dimensions of scientific law. *Philosophy of Science, 67*, 242–265.

Morrell, K. (2008). The narrative of "evidence based" management: A polemic. *Journal of Management Studies, 45*, 613–635.

Peirce, C. S. (1955). *Philosophical writings of Peirce*. Selected and edited by J. Buchler. New York: Dover.

Peltokorpi, V. (2008). Transactive memory systems. *Review of general Psychology, 12*, 378–394.

Romme, A. G. L. (2003). Making a difference: Organization as design. *Organization Science, 14*, 558–573.

Romme, A. G. L., & Endenburg, G. (2006). Construction principles and design rules in the case of circular design. *Organization Science, 17*, 287–297.

Rousseau, D. M. (2006). Is there such a thing as evidence-based management? *Academy of Management Learning and Education, 31*, 256–269.

Schön, D. A. (1983). *The reflective practitioner.* London, England: Temple Smith.

Simon, H. A. (1996/1969). *The sciences of the artificial* (3rd ed.). Cambridge, MA: MIT Press.

Strauss, A. & Corbin, J. (1990). *Basics of qualitative research: Grounded theory procedures and techniques.* Newbury Park, CA: Sage.

Tranfield, D., Denyer, D., & Smart, P. (2003). Towards a methodology for developing evidence-informed management knowledge by means of systematic review. *British Journal of Management, 14*, 207–222.

Van Aken, J. E. (2004). Management research based on the paradigm of the design sciences: The quest for field-tested and grounded technological rules. *Journal of Management Studies, 41*, 219–246.

Van Aken, J. E. (2010). Donald Schön's legacy to address the great divide between theory and practice. *Planning Theory and Practice, 11*, 609–613.

Van Aken, J. E., Van der Bij, H., & Berends, H. (2012). *Problem solving in organizations: A methodological handbook for business and management students.* Cambridge, England: Cambridge University Press.

Van Burg, E., Romme, A. G. L., Gilsing, V. A., & Reymen, I. M. M. J. (2008) (2nd ed). Creating university spin-offs: A science-based design perspective. *Journal of Product Innovation Management, 25*, 114–128.

Watson, I. (1997). *Applying case-based reasoning: Techniques for enterprise systems.* San Francisco, CA: Morgan Kaufman Publishers.

Wegner, D. M. (1986). Transactive memory: A contemporary analysis of the group mind. In B. Mullen & G. R. Goethals (Eds.), *Theories of group behavior* (pp. 185–208). New York: Springer Verlag.

Weick, K. E. (2004). Designing for thrownness. In R. Boland & F. Collopy (Eds.), *Managing as designing* (pp. 74–78). Stanford, CA: Stanford University Press.

Worren, N., Moore, K., & Elliott, R. (2002). When theories become tools: Toward a framework for pragmatic validity. *Human Relations, 55*, 1227–1250.

PART 2

Research

Organizational Behavior's Contributions to Evidence-Based Management

Denise M. Rousseau

Abstract

Organizational Behavior (OB) is a social science that has discovered general principles regarding the organization and management of work. One of management research's more mature fields, OB's contribution to evidence-based Management (EBMgt) stems from its large body of programmatic, cumulative research. This chapter provides an overview of OB research, including its history, standards for evidence, and domains of study. It distinguishes between science- and practice-oriented OB research and their respective evidence criteria to better show different ways OB research can inform EBMgt. OB research has identified several hundred evidence-based principles to inform practice, and this chapter provides examples. The chapter concludes by discussing how OB scholars, educators, and practitioners can further EBMgt practice.

Key Words: organizational behavior, principles, science-oriented evidence criteria, practice-oriented evidence criteria, hiring talent, goal setting, making decisions, motivating people

Organizational Behavior's Contribution to Evidence-Based Management

This chapter provides an overview of the background and focus of the OB field and its findings. It uses examples of well-established findings to demonstrate the sort of actionable principles OB contributes to guide evidence-informed practice. It then assesses the state of OB practice and education. The chapter concludes with implications for how practitioners, educators, and researchers can further the development and use of OB knowledge in evidence-based management (EBMgt).

Organizational behavior has been a mainstay in professional management education for decades. The field's goals are to understand human behavior in organizations and provide knowledge useful to practitioners. These two goals often coincide. Here's an example from one manager's experience: Jim Fuchs, a midlevel manager in an American firm, came up to me after a session on change

management in my business school's executive program. "Let me show you what I do when I see a need to convince the supervisors reporting to me that we need to change something about how we manage our people," he said, going over to one of the classroom's flip charts. "I learned Porter and Lawler's model of motivation back while I was an undergraduate [business major]," he said, as he sketched out a diagram (Figure 4.1). "First, to get people to put out effort in new ways, they have to see that a certain kind of new behavior is more likely to bring them rewards [effort-reward probability] they care about [value of reward]. Then, they need to put out the right kind of effort to produce the performance we need [effort→performance accomplishment], which means they need to know what new thing they're supposed to be doing [role perceptions] and have the ability to do it [abilities and traits]. If you put the right rewards, skills, and expectations in place, you get the right results and your employees

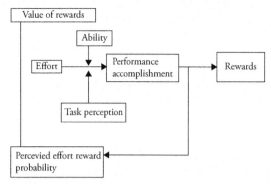

Fig. 4.1 Jim Fuch's diagram for discussing design and change adapted from Porter and Lawler.

At this writing, OB is arguably one of the more developed bodies of scientific knowledge relevant to management practice. Like the broader field of managerial and organizational research of which it is a part, OB is a social science. MBA and undergraduate business programs incorporate a good deal of the field's evidence into courses on decision making, leadership, and teams (Chartiers, Brown & Rynes, 2011). Along with other research-oriented fields such as marketing and advertising (Armstrong, 2011), OB offers a substantial research base to inform management education and practice. Some OB findings are already distilled into useable form (e.g., Locke, 2009) for management education, professional and personal development, and problem solving. At the same time, making it easier for practitioners to know about and use the OB evidence base continues to be a work in progress.

stay motivated." I commented that this might be one of the best examples of how an undergraduate OB course can be useful. Jim laughed and said, "At this point, my supervisors know this model by heart."

This classic evidence-based motivation model, as Lyman Porter and Edward Lawler (1968) formally presented it, is a bit more detailed (Figure 4.2) than Jim's diagram—consistent with the large and diverse body of evidence on which it is based. Yet Jim's adaptation of it has the essentials. Importantly, Jim drew upon this scientifically developed framework in his day-to-day management practice, applying it wherever he judged it to be useful. By using this model regularly, his staff learned how to think more systematically about why employees do what they do on the job and how to motivate them to do more and do better. Jim Fuchs's approach fulfills an important objective of science: to think clearly about the social and physical world and make informed interventions in it. It also exemplifies a simple but adaptable way in which OB research (and well-supported theory) can contribute to EBMgt.

A Century of Research

Research on fundamental processes in organizing and managing work began with the activities of OB's parent disciplines, industrial-organizational psychology (known as work and organization psychology in Europe; Munsterberg, 1913), industrial sociology (Miller & Form, 1951), public administration (Follett, 1918; Gulick, & Urwick, 1937; Simon, 1997) and general management (Drucker, 1974; McGregor, 1960). Early empirical work focused on employee selection, testing, vocational choice, and performance (Munsterberg, 1913); group dynamics, supervisory relations and incentives (e.g., Hawthorne studies, Roethlisberger & Dickson, 1939); worker attitudes (Likert, 1932; Kornhauser, 1922); and leadership, authority, and control (Selznick, 1945; Braverman, 1974).

The formal label "organizational behavior" emerged in the 1960s and 1970s, as business schools

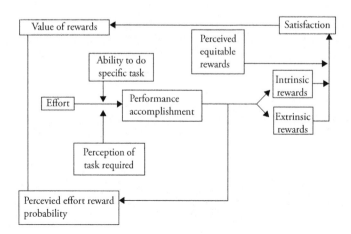

Fig. 4.2 Porter and Lawler's motivational model.

responded to criticism that what they were teaching was more opinion and armchair theorizing than validated knowledge (Gordon & Howell, 1959). Schools began hiring social scientists to promote the use of research to understand and solve organizational problems and provide more science-based business education (Porter & McKibbin, 1988). OB departments sprang up where once stood more eclectic "management" or "personnel" units.

Today's OB researchers come from many fields. Some identify OB as their home discipline, typically completing doctorates in business schools. Others originate in and often continue to identify with psychology, sociology, human development, or economics. All these researchers share an interest in how humans behave in organizations. As just one example of the cross-pollination between behavioral science and business disciplines prevalent in OB, the author of this chapter is an OB professor with a doctorate in industrial-organizational (I-O) psychology who has taught in both psychology departments and schools of business and public-sector management.

Today, OB research is prevalent worldwide, with thousands of researchers currently at work expanding the OB knowledge base. The largest professional association focused management research is the Academy of Management. In 2011, the Academy had over 19,000 members. Its OB division had nearly 4,000 active academic members and more than 400 executive/practitioner members, and the human-resources division, whose research (and some of its members) overlap OB, had almost 2,500 academic members and 300 executive/practitioner members. Other professional associations outside the United States also have members who are actively adding to the OB knowledge base.

Forces at multiple levels drive how humans behave in organizations. OB research investigates individual and group behavior along with formal and informal organization-wide dynamics. The types of phenomena that intersect the OB field range from the oil-rig worker trying to decide whether to report hazardous job conditions to the conflict-ridden top- management team whose infighting undermines how the company's frontline managers perform. As a multi-level field, OB scholarship rides the organizational elevator from individual personality, beliefs, and behavior to group dynamics to organizational- and industry-level practices that affect how people act and respond in organizations.

The largest body of OB research addresses individual and group behaviors and their ultimate causal connections with organizational performance and member well-being. This wide array of studies on individuals and groups is the reason academics sometimes refer to OB scholars and their research as "micro" (as opposed to more "macro" areas of organizational theory or strategic management, see Madhavan & Mahoney, chapter 5 of this volume), as in "she's a micro person." However, the term *micro* is not a particularly accurate description for the OB field (Rousseau, 2011). A good deal of OB research examines such organization-level phenomena as culture or change implementation (e.g., Schein, 2010), but the micro/macro distinction remains common in academic OB-speak.

OB Research Philosophy and Objectives

The research philosophy underlying OB is largely in-line with evidence-based management (Briner, Denyer & Rousseau, 2009; Rousseau, chapter 1 of this volume), with its aspiration to improve organization-based decision making and to tackle applied problems in ways that balance economic interests with the well-being of workers (Argyris, 1960; Katz & Kahn, 1966; Munsterberg, 1913; Viteles, 1932).

Historically, OB research has been responsive to business trends and practice concerns. Over time, its emphasis has shifted—from productivity to global competitiveness and quality; from employee security to employability (see Rousseau, 1997, for an assessment of trends from 1970s to 1990s). Indeed, critics inside and outside the field have long argued that it tends to emphasize managerial and performance-related concerns over the concerns of workers and other stakeholders (Baratz, 1965; Ghoshal, 2005)—an appraisal echoed by Hornung (chapter 22 of this volume) and other critical theorists.

On the other hand, OB research addressed the worker experience on the job even prior to the famous Hawthorne studies at Western Electric (Roethlisberger & Dickson, 1939) or the popularity of work-satisfaction questionnaires (originally developed for Kimberly Clark by Kornhauser and Sharp (1932; Zickar, 2003). Since then, a good deal of research concentrates on the effects of work and organizations on the well-being of workers, families, clients, and the general public (e.g., Gardell, 1977; Karasek, 2004, Kossek & Lambert, 2005). More recently, the "Positive Organizational Behavior" movement has expanded both the goals of organizational research and the outcomes it studies to include how workers can thrive in organizational settings (Dutton & Ragins, 2006). The large and growing body of OB research is wide-ranging in its economic and social implications.

Focus on Cumulative Findings

My sense is that supporting EBMgt comes relatively naturally to many OB scholars and educators. As Chartier and colleagues (2011) report, OB educators typically rely on evidence more than do faculty in the fields they surveyed, such as international business or strategy. Part of this reliance is attributable to the cumulative findings in certain core OB research areas. The field's history and tendency toward sustained interest in particular topics makes possible the cumulative research that is generally valued in the evidence-based practice movement (Barends, ten Have, & Huisman, chapter 2 of this volume). OB's accumulated findings contrast with newer management-research fields, such as strategy and organizational theory (Madhavan & Mahoney, chapter 5 of this volume) where less attention has yet been paid to creating integrative knowledge (cf. Whitley, 1984; 2000). As such, OB scholars have, over time, pulled together and built on the available evidence on an array of management issues. The result provides evidence-informed practitioners and educators with numerous well-supported principles of human behavior, organizing, and managing, with considerable practical value (e.g., Locke, 2009). I present examples of these principles later, after discussing a key reason that cumulative findings in OB research can produce these principles, that is, the largely agreed-on norms for what constitutes evidence in the OB field.

Criteria for Evidence

Generally speaking, the OB field has certain widely held norms about what constitutes sufficient evidence to make claims regarding the truth of a research finding. Norms are particularly well articulated for what I refer to here as OB's "science-oriented evidence." These norms, exemplified by the seminal work of Cook and Campbell (1979), emphasize the value of (1) controlled observations to rule out bias and (2) consistency with the real world to promote the generalizability of findings. Classic academic or scholarly research is motivated to understand the world (i.e., to develop and test theory). Less widely discussed or, perhaps, agreed upon, are the norms or standards for OB's "practice-oriented evidence." Practice-oriented research investigates what practitioners actually do in organizations. In particular, a practice orientation demonstrates what happens when scientific evidence is acted upon in real-world settings. The goals of science- and practice-oriented research differ. Thus, each necessarily emphasizes somewhat different indicators of evidence quality.

Note that the same study can have both science and practice goals. For example, employee participation systems have been investigated to test scientific theories of voice and motivation as well as such systems' practical impacts on productivity and their sustainability over time (e.g., the Rushton project, Goodman, 1979). Equitable pay practices have been examined to evaluate equity and justice theories and impact on employee theft (Greenberg, 1990). Job enrichment interventions have tested both theory regarding optimal levels of job autonomy and impact on the quality of wastewater treatment (Cordery, Morrison, Wright, & Wall, 2010). Such studies are proof that science and practice goals can go hand-in-hand.

Criteria for Science-Oriented OB Evidence

The general goal of science-oriented research is to interpret and understand. OB research pursues this goal by relying largely on a *body of studies*, rather than on the results of any single study, in evaluating a particular finding's validity. Because all studies are limited in some fashion, no single study is sufficient to establish a scientific fact. Good evidence constitutes a "study of studies," where individual or primary studies are considered together in order to allow the credibility of their overall findings to be assessed (Briner & Denyer, chapter 7 of this volume; Rousseau, Manning, & Denyer, 2008. Systematically interpreting all relevant studies is the general standard for determining the merit of any claims regarding evidence (Hunter & Schmidt, 1990). (N.B.: Practitioners are more likely to use rapid reviews, that is, quick searches through a few studies to see if agreed-upon findings exist, and other expedient assessments of published evidence when no systematic review is available.) The most common form of systematic review in OB is the *meta-analysis*, a quantitative analysis of multiple studies to determine the overall strength or consistency of an observed effect (e.g., job satisfaction's effect on performance). It is not unusual for OB meta-analyses to review hundreds of studies, combining results for 30,000+ individuals—as in the case of the impact of general mental ability on occupational attainment and job performance (Schmidt & Hunter, 2004). OB's roots in psychology have shaped its research methods and aligned its culture of evidence largely with that of psychology, where use of meta-analysis is common. Say, for example, that 90 studies exist on the relationship of flexible work hours with staff retention and performance. Meta-analysis standards typically mandate examination of all 90 studies—whether published or not—to see what findings, if any, the studies together support and to examine the nature of any inconsistencies across the studies.

There is a world of difference between a systematic review of a body of studies (e.g., a meta-analysis) and a more casual or "unsystematic" literature review. A systematic review has a methods section that details how the review was conducted and what specific technical requirements were used (Briner & Denyer, chapter 7 of this volume). In contrast, conventional literature reviews are highly vulnerable to the biases authors display in their choice of studies to include. Studies included in conventional literature reviews reflect the author's priorities and focus and, thus, may not represent the body of research. In conducting a systematic review of science-oriented studies, the following indicators of evidence quality are evaluated.

1. *Construct validity: Is the purported phenomenon real?* A basic requirement of evidence is construct validity, which asks whether the underlying notion or concept jibes with the observed facts. In the case of flexible hours, is there a set of common practices companies pursuing flexible hours actually use? Or do many different kinds of practices go by the label "flexible hours"? Do we have reason to treat the "flexible hours" of a 4/40 workweek as the same as the flexibility workers exercise over their own daily stop-and-start times? If research findings reveal that the 4/40 work week and personal control over work hours differ in their consequences for workers and employers, we are likely to conclude that "flexibility" in reality takes several distinct forms. As in the case of flexibility's potential effects on worker motivation or company performance, any test of cause-effect relationship needs to first establish a clear meaning and construct validity for the concept of interest. In the case of flexibility, concepts of flexibility with clearer construct validity are "reduced hours"—where the hours worked are fewer than the normal work week—and "working-time control"—where workers exercise personal control over when they work (not how many hours *per se*).

As illustrated, the term "flexible hours" can have so many different meanings that it is not a single coherent construct. Similar issues exist for popular notions like "morale" or "emotional intelligence," phrases used colloquially to refer to a variety of things. Morale can mean group *esprit de corps* or

individual satisfaction, each driven by very different forces in organizations. Similarly, emotional intelligence (EI) is used to refer to an emotional competency (Goleman, 1995) or a form of intelligence in social relations distinct from general intelligence (Mayer, Salovey & Caruso, 2000). Further, some object to equating emotion and reason, arguing that EI cannot be a form of intelligence (Locke, 2005). As with the preceding flexibility example, the key is to develop a clear definition of the construct being studied, so that the study's findings can best be interpreted and used by others.

Because scholars tend to be concerned with construct clarity (terminology, definition, and distinctions), practitioners looking into the OB literature to answer a practice question usually need to try a variety of key words or seek out an academic for guidance, in order to identify the proper scientific terms (which may include some jargon specific to the field) that the relevant research uses (Werner, chapter 15 of this volume).

2. *Internal validity: Do the observed effects or relationships indicate causality?* Internal validity is the degree to which a study's results are free of bias (Cook & Campbell, 1979). If bias cannot be ruled out, then any relationship we observe, such as a correlation between rewards and performance, may be due to measurement error, methodological problems, or some uncontrolled third variable like the state of the economy. It's unlikely any single study will be bias-free. In contrast, several studies with different settings, methods, and so forth can cancel out potential biases. Internal validity is established when a body of studies show comparable findings across different research designs, such as experiments and longitudinal studies. As we are able to use these comparable findings to rule out the potential effects from measurement error, methodological problems, and other alternative explanations, it is more likely that the observed effect is real and caused by the particular factor(s) investigated.

3. *External validity: How widespread is the effect? Why does it hold sometimes and not others?* External validity (sometimes called generalizability) refers to the extent to which a result holds across populations, settings, procedures, and time periods (Cook & Campbell, 1979). A study might provide information about the conditions under which a phenomenon is likely to be observed or repeated elsewhere. Attention to the circumstances surrounding the finding helps us understand its generalizability and provides information regarding *why* a finding

might apply in some circumstances and not others. Relevant details can tell us if there are conditions, not part of the phenomenon itself, which influence its occurrence or consequences. Such is the case where the effects of rewards on performance depend on the way rewards are distributed (to all employees vs. only high performers vs. various employees, but unsystematically, Lawler, 1971; 1990) or the extent to which the effects of high-involvement work systems depend on appropriate workforce training and rewards (cf. MacDuffie, 1995). Another way context impacts generalizability is by changing the meanings people give to the event, behavior, practice, or phenomenon studied. Prior events or historical factors, such as a previously failed change, can lead an otherwise promising practice to fail because people view the new practice through the lens of that previous failure. Or, society itself can give the phenomenon a distinct meaning: how people experience "close supervision" in the relatively authoritarian culture of Turkey is likely to differ from egalitarian Norway (House, Hanges, Javidan, Dorfman, & Gupta, 2004). The same set of directive behaviors from a boss might appropriately coordinate work in one culture but be viewed as controlling micromanagement in the other.

Criteria for Practice-Oriented OB Evidence

The goals of practice-oriented research are to identify what works (or doesn't) in real-life settings and to learn which circumstances affect how those practices work. Both scholars and practitioners conduct practice-oriented research. Scholars seek to obtain information on how practitioners approach the decisions they make and the actions they take. Practitioners conduct their own research, often in the form of pilot tests or evaluation studies, to gauge the impact of a company policy or program. Practice-oriented research is directed toward particular problems and settings that practitioners care about. Design science's collaborations among academics, end users, and an organization's technical experts are a form of practice-oriented research (Van Aken & Romme, chapter 3 of this volume). Key criteria for practice-oriented evidence are discussed next.

1. *Detailed description: What are the conditions of practice?* Practice-oriented evidence is useful in part because it describes what practitioners actually do and the conditions under which they do it. Data can be gathered in many ways: via interviews, observations, and surveys, in forms both qualitative and quantitative. Perlow's (1997) study of how

a company implemented its flexibility policy used interviews and observations. This study uncovered how employees received mixed signals about the acceptability of flexibility and the role that position and status in the company played in determining whose requests for flexibility were granted.

Another example of practice-oriented research is investigations of how practitioners actually use an evidence-based process. Pritchard, Harrell, DiazGranados & Guzman (2008) investigated why differences existed in the results of an organizational analysis and assessment system known as PROMES. Their investigation revealed the kinds of implementation behaviors that affected PROMES's outcomes. The extent to which PROMES implementers adhered to the system's specified procedures affected their overall productivity gains, as did the quality of the information they provided the organization.

Given the widespread variation in how organizations implement routines (e.g., performance appraisals) or interventions (e.g., quality programs) there is a lot of value in practitioner-oriented studies that examine how sensitive the expected outcomes are to whether practitioners adhere to specified procedures. In medical research, for example, practice-oriented research indicates that diabetics who adjust or fine-tune their regimen for self-testing and administering insulin enjoy better health outcomes than those strictly following their clinicians' orders (e.g., Campbell et al., 2003). Despite this example, noncompliance with standard procedures can be associated with poorer outcomes as in the case of PROMES just mentioned. Practice-oriented research provides crucial information about the sensitivity of interventions and practices to variability in compliance.

The variability in adherence to prescribed processes and procedures is referred to as *implementation compliance*. Implementation compliance is a major issue in implementing evidence-based practices. In the case of PROMES, consultants and managers who implemented the technique but did not fully follow its standard instructions oversaw programs with fewer performance gains than did those who adhered more closely to the specified PROMES procedures. Companies that follow fads have been known to "implement the label" but not the actual practices on which the evidence is based. So-called engagement or talent management programs, for example, might really be the same old training and development activities the company has always followed, with a catchy new name. Attention to the actual activities implemented is critical to understanding what works, what doesn't, and why.

2. Real-world applicability: Are the outcome variables relevant to practice? Practice-oriented research focuses on end points that are important to managers, customers, employees, and their organizations. In recent years, research/practice gaps in health care have been reduced by more patient-oriented research, tapping the patient outcomes that clinicians and their patients care about, such as morbidity, mortality, symptom reduction, and quality of life. This focus on practice-oriented outcomes in medicine contrasts with the theory-centric outcomes of science- (or disease-) oriented medical research. In the latter, outcomes typically take the form of specific physiological indicators (e.g., left ventricular end-diastolic volume or the percentage of coronary artery stenosis [Ebell, Barry, Slawson, & Shaughnessy, 1999]). Similarly, practice-oriented OB evidence includes outcomes of practical significance, such as the level of savings or improved employee retention, data often available from an organization's own records. In contrast, theory-centric outcomes in OB research might include interpersonal organizational citizenship behavior or employee role-based self-efficacy, typically using indicators that academics have developed.

As part of his executive master's thesis, banker Tom Weber took up the challenge of testing whether a leadership training program for the bank's managers would actually change their behavior and the bank's performance. In contrast to the typical large sample sizes of academic research, this study relied on numbers more typical of the bank's actual training programs. Using a sample of 20 managers, 9 were randomly assigned to the training group, and the remainder to the control group, which received no training. To provide the kind of support training often required in a busy work setting, leadership development ("the treatment") consisted of a one-day group session followed by four individual monthly booster sessions. Results demonstrated that subordinates of the trained managers reported increases in their managers' charisma, intellectual stimulation, and consideration than did subordinates of control-group managers. Using archival data from his bank's branches, Weber found that the training led to increased personal loan and credit card sales in the branches supervised by the trained managers. These outcomes were selected for their real-world relevance, rather than theoretical interest (cf. Verschuren, 2009). This study, undertaken because a practicing manager questioned the practical value of transformational leadership training, ultimately was published in a major research journal (Barling, Weber, & Kelloway, 1996).

3. Effect size: How strong is the effect or relationship? The effect size is a measure of the strength of the relationship observed between two variables (Hedges & Okin, 1985). It is a statistical criterion useful to practitioners and academics. Academic researchers rely on effect sizes to interpret experimental results. For example, where two or more treatment conditions are manipulated, effect sizes can tell which treatment is more powerful. Effect sizes are also central to meta-analyses and allow comparison of the relative effects of several factors (e.g., whether personality or intelligence is more important to worker performance).

From a practice perspective, a large effect size for the relationship between mental ability and job performance means that increasing the general intelligence of the workforce can have substantial impact on worker contributions to the firm. Small effect sizes can mean that practitioners looking for an intervention that improves outcomes ought to look elsewhere. Such is the case in a study of software engineering, where a collection of technologies used in actual projects had only a 30 percent impact on reliability and no effect on productivity (Card, McGarry, & Page, 1987). Instead, human and organizational factors appear to have stronger effects on software productivity than tools and methods (Curtis, Crasner, & Iscoe, 1988).

In the context of practice, effect sizes are often most useful when judged in relation to costs. Even a small effect can be important in practice. If it can be gained at minimal cost, it may be worth the slight effort required. For example, it is relatively easy to create a general sense of group identity (where co-workers in a department view themselves as an in-group, distinct from others). Group identity is positively related to willingness to help peers (and negatively related to helping outsiders.). Its benefits (and costs) are relatively easy to induce, one reason why logos and group nicknames are so popular (Gaertner & Dovidio, 2000). Systematic research reviews can be very useful to practice when they provide both effect sizes and cost/benefit information. Now we turn to the kinds of well-established findings OB research produces.

Some Well-Established OB Findings

The primary knowledge products of OB research are *principles*, that is, general truths about the way the world works. Massive amounts of data have been accumulated and integrated to develop these principles, each of which sums up a regularity manifest in organizations and their members. For purposes of this chapter, a few well-established OB principles are summarized to illustrate OB's relevance to the practice of EBMgt. (Additional evidence-based OB principles are summarized in Cialdini, 2009; Latham, 2009; and Locke, 2009).

Readers will note that these principles take one of two forms. The majority are forms of declarative knowledge ("what is")—facts or truth claims of a general nature, such as the goal-setting principle, "Specific goals tend to be associated with higher performance than general goals" (Latham, 2009). Less often, these principles represent procedural knowledge ("how to"); these are task behaviors or applications found to be effective in acting on the general principle or fact. As an example, take the finding, "The goal and the measure of performance effectiveness used should be aligned," as is the case when a goal of 15 percent increase in logger productivity is measured as the number of trees cut down divided by the hours it takes to cut down those trees (Latham, 2009, p.162). By its very nature, declarative knowledge tends to be general and applicable to lots of different circumstances. Specific goals can take many forms across countless work settings. In contrast, procedural knowledge is more situation-specific and may need to be adapted as circumstances change (Anderson, 2010). In some situations, no single goal may be adequate to reflect productivity, and thus more than one measure of performance effectiveness may need to be used.

Making Decisions

Decision making is a fundamental process in organizations. Making decisions is the core activity managers perform. A prominent principle in management education is bounded rationality: *Human decision makers are limited in the amount of information they can pay attention to at one time and in their capacity to think about and process information fully* (Simon, 1997). Indeed, such are the limits of individual decision-making capabilities that *having too much choice tends to keep people from making any decision at all* (Schwartz, 2004, pp. 19–20). Schwartz's research demonstrated that giving shoppers at an upscale grocery only six choices (in this case, of jam) increased the likelihood that they would choose to buy some, in contrast to giving them 24 choices. In the case of Schwartz's study of customer choices, these findings also have practical utility in terms of both boosting sales and making the best use of shelf space.

The pervasive effects of bounded rationality make it necessary for EBMgt practices to be structured in a fashion that is compatible with our cognitive limits as human beings. To aid more systematic and informed decisions, another evidence-based principle of a procedural nature applies, that is, *develop and use a few standard but adaptable procedures or tools to improve the success of organizational decisions* (Larrick, 2009). Decision supports are pragmatic tools that can be designed to aid practitioners in making evidence-informed decisions. A checklist, for example, might use Yates's 10 Cardinal Rules (Yates, 2003; Yates & Potwoworski, chapter 12 of this volume) as steps to follow in making a good decision. Evidence-informed decision-making procedures need to be simple to use, because complexity or perceived difficulty can keep people from using them. Contemporary medical practice has numerous decision supports (Gawande, 2009) such as patient care protocols, handbooks on drug interactions, online decision trees, and specific tests indicating whether a course of treatment applies. In contrast, business practices in OB's domain appear to make limited use of decision supports (e.g., hiring, giving feedback, running meetings, dealing with performance problems, etc.).

Hiring Talent

In the long history of selection research (e.g., Munsterberg, 1913), perhaps the most prominent principle is that *unstructured interviews are poor predictors of job performance.* Interviewers using their own idiosyncratic questions have low inter-interviewer agreement on applicants and virtually no reliable capacity to identify the candidate who is best able to do a job. Recruiters, personnel interviewers, and the people who manage them are known to be quite limited in the information they gather (Highhouse, 2008). In addition, because they typically lack quality feedback on their success rates in identifying good employees, interviewers are unaware of their own poor performance in hiring talent. On the other hand, *structured interviews using well-designed job-related questions can be good predictors of job performance* (Stevens, 2009). This second principle in evidence-based selection provides a basis for improving the way personnel decisions are made, by developing specific interview questions directly tied to job content and success on the job.

Other evidence-based principles for hiring talent reflect the kind of individual qualities known to widely predict future job success. A third principle is that *general mental ability is the single best predictor of individual productivity* and other job performance indicators. It is thus the case that for skilled jobs, top workers can produce 15 times as much as the poorest performers (Schmidt, 2009). A fourth principle is that *hiring people who are conscientious and emotionally stable is typically a better decision than hiring agreeable people who try to get along with others* (Barrick & Mount, 2009). Employers spend a lot of time screening potential recruits for interpersonal fit, yet the fact is that getting along with others tends to be far less valuable for performance than having sufficient self-discipline to work in a thoughtful manner (conscientiousness) and being free of anxiety and neuroticism (emotional stability).

Motivating People

Motivating employees is a critical managerial concern. A central factor in individual and group performance is the existence and acceptance of challenging performance goals (Locke & Latham, 1984). The likelihood that *setting specific, challenging goals improves performance* is as high as 0.90 (Latham, 2009). Moreover, *accurate feedback generally increases both performance and learning.* Feedback effects are nuanced (Kluger & DeNisi, 1996): Performance is increased when the feedback focuses on providing task-related information rather than self-referencing information. Thus, the subordinate receiving feedback that highlights the goals she attained and those on which she fell short tends to demonstrate performance improvement whereas another subordinate who is told that her personality is great with customers but annoys her colleagues probably will not. Similarly, *performance feedback aids learning when given intermittently rather than constantly,* to allow learners to reflect on their learning (see Goodman & O'Brien, chapter 18 of this volume).

Another body of research indicates that *money does motivate people under certain conditions*; in particular, pay for performance can increase the particular type of performance targeted if money is important to the performer (Rynes, Gerhart & Parks, 2005). However, the effects of individual-level pay for performance are limited. *Incentive pay increases*

individual performance in tasks that are not cognitively challenging (Ariely, Gneezy, Loewenstein, & Mazar, 2009) Similarly, *pay for individual performance doesn't work very well when employees have a lot to learn before performing at a desired level* (Durham & Bartol, 2009) *or when employees are highly interdependent* (Shaw, Gupta, & Delery, 2002).

There are other motivation outcomes, such as commitment and job satisfaction. *Offering rewards that create a compelling future, such as development opportunities, engender greater commitment to the organization than short-term rewards* (Hornung, Rousseau, & Glaser, 2009; Rousseau, Hornung, & Kim, 2009). *Job satisfaction is an important predictor of life satisfaction in general—and mental challenge is a key cause of job satisfaction* (Judge & Klinger, 2009). The optimal level of challenge to promote job satisfaction depends on the individual's mental ability and skills (what's known as an inverted-U-shaped distribution).

How managers behave affects their capacity to direct the attention and behavior of others. One well-established principle is that *managers need to cultivate power or influence beyond the authority that comes with their position* (Yukl, 2009). Gaining the respect of subordinates, co-workers, and superiors gives managers an important source of influence. *Top managers who set a vision for their organization typically outperform executives who don't* (Kirkpatrick, 2009). Such managers develop and reinforce values and norms that affect how employees behave.

Additional Research Findings

These well-established findings from a small set of OB's many research areas have broad practical use. Additional findings are found in Locke's (2009) compendium detailing 33 sets of practitioner-oriented findings, *Handbook of Principles of Organizational Behavior: Indispensable Knowledge for Evidence-Based Management* and Latham's (2009) guide to *Becoming the Evidence-Based Manager: Making the Science of Management Work for You.* Pearce's textbook (2009) *Organizational Behavior: Real Evidence for Real Managers* provides other generalizable OB principles (see Pearce, chapter 21 of this volume, for a discussion of the role of textbooks in EBMgt).

Current Use of OB Findings in Practice

Given the facts that OB research offers about decision making, hiring talent, and motivating people, is there any evidence that practitioners actually use this knowledge? No definitive indicators exist to assess the extent to which educated managers use OB's knowledge base. Without actual data on evidence use, I looked for other practice-related indicators likely to occur with use of OB evidence. First, I surmise that OB evidence use is more likely when practitioners hold beliefs consistent with the OB findings regarding management practices. Second, I surmise that practitioners who conduct OB-related research themselves are more likely to apply such evidence in their own professional decisions. Thus, this chapter presents two kinds of information to assess the likelihood that practitioners make use of OB research: whether practitioners are aware of relevant OB findings and whether they undertake or participate in practice-oriented OB research themselves.

Practitioner Awareness of OB Findings

Of all the conditions needed to motivate practitioners to use evidence-based practices, perhaps the most basic is awareness of research findings (see Speicher-Bocija & Adams, chapter 17 of this volume, for other conditions). To examine the extent of practitioner knowledge of OB findings, Rynes, Colbert, and Brown (2002) developed a quiz regarding 35 well-established findings in OB related to the effectiveness of various company practices. (These findings were selected because management professors think them to be important.) Nearly 960 midlevel managers and senior executives who were members of the Society for Human Resource Management (SHRM) took the quiz. They averaged 13 years of experience in management or HR.

Results revealed wide gaps between replicated OB research findings and practitioner beliefs. The greatest gaps involved research findings about hiring talent. For example, the item, "Companies that screen job applicants for values have higher performance than those that screen for intelligence," is false. Only 16 percent of practitioner respondents got it right. In emphasizing values over ability, respondents may actually be reflecting the preference for informal methods to size up job applicants and make personnel decisions (Highhouse, 2008), which, as we now know, is less effective than using structured interviews. People in general (not just HR folks), are known to be reluctant to substitute scores and formulas for their own intuitions, despite consistent evidence that intuition is a poor substitute for evidence-based indicators. The preference to rely on personal judgment instead of systematic criteria has a long history (Grove & Lloyd, 2006; Highhouse, 2008; Meehl, 1954). Interestingly,

criminal profilers who attempt to identify serial killers from the details of crime scenes turn out to be only slightly more accurate at the task than lay people (Snook, Eastwood, Gendreau, Goggin, & Cullen, 2007).

On other topics, SHRM members gave more research-consistent answers. A full 96 percent accurately rated as false the item, "Leadership training is ineffective because good leaders are born, not made." A total of 88 percent of SHRM respondents accurately answered as true, "Teams with members from different functional backgrounds are likely to reach better solutions to complex problems than teams from a single area;" as did a total of 81 percent who correctly answered true to, "Most employees prefer to be paid on the basis of individual performance rather than on a group or organizational performance." Similarly, 62 percent correctly answered true on two items related to specific management practices and performance: "There is a positive relationship between the proportion of managers receiving organizationally based pay incentives and company profitability," and, "Companies with vision statements perform better than those without them."

The average SHRM sample score on this quiz was 57 (based on the percentage of items answered correctly). Still, there was a lot of variation. Beliefs consistent with the research findings were greatest for practitioners in higher organizational positions, for those with advanced certification in HR, or for those who read the academic literature. For example, practitioners who indicated that they usually read HR journals averaged 3 points (i.e., 11%) higher. Notably, more than 75 percent of those surveyed indicated they had never read any of the top three OB journals.

Sanders, van Riemsdijk, and Groen (2008) replicated the SHRM study in a survey of 646 Dutch HR managers. Their results are similar to SHRM's American sample. Again, the greatest differences between beliefs and evidence were for items related to employee selection and recruiting. Dutch HR managers scored higher when they were more highly educated or read journals, as did the SHRM members. In addition, Dutch respondents scored more highly when they held positive attitudes toward research and evidence use.

Additional studies tested the generalizability of these findings to other populations. Pepitone (2009) assessed the knowledge of 336 mid- to high-level U.S. organization managers using the same quiz Rynes and her colleagues developed.

His findings reveal virtually identical knowledge levels, with the same average of 57 percent correct. Timmerman (2010) found a similar knowledge level among undergraduate college students (58% average), although MBAs scored slightly but significantly higher (62%). Undergraduates and MBAs consistently missed the same seven items, which overlapped six of the most commonly missed items by HR managers. Across all four groups, the pattern of right answers (from highest percentage correct to lowest) was similar.

These results, if representative of the larger populations from which participants are drawn, suggest that none of these groups is particularly aware of OB findings. Note that the test items focus on common organizational practices, not arcane or rarely needed information. The items are in no way esoteric. It is also the case that MBA education may modestly increase knowledge levels, a finding that provides educators a ray of hope.

These results beg the question, Why do educated managers believe what they do? Results from the quiz may be due to lack of knowledge. Or, it may be that practitioner misperceptions and false beliefs develop prior to their becoming managers, consultants, or HR professionals—and unless education focuses considerable attention on evidence, what "they know that ain't so" remains unchallenged. How we can effectively address this "awareness problem" depends on its underlying cause. If the pattern of results stems from fundamental contradictions between evidence-based principles and deeply held beliefs, merely providing more information may be insufficient to change minds (Highhouse, 2008).

Practitioner Involvement in Research

Part of the professional activities of practitioners in evidence-informed fields is participation in research. In medicine and nursing, practicing physicians and nurses frequently are involved in carrying out both basic research and clinical studies. In much the same way, organizational practitioners have the potential to conduct and/or participate in research. Indeed, historically practitioners have been quite active in OB research. As reported by Anderson, Herriot, and Hodgkinson (2001), between 1949 and 1965 practitioners authored 36 percent of the articles in one of the field's most prestigious journals, *Journal of Applied Psychology* (JAP), including 31 percent of articles written by practitioners alone. Tom Weber's study evaluating leadership training, described earlier, is one such study. More recently, from 1990 to 2000 (the terminal year of

the Anderson et al. survey), practitioners authored only 4 percent of JAP articles (1% by practitioners alone). Other similar journals manifest a comparable decline in practitioner-authored research. Where in-house researchers and external consultants once actively contributed to OB research, academics now dominate.

Why have practitioners gone missing from OB research? This shift toward academic production of OB research has several reasons. First, the decline in practitioner research coincided with the rise in global competition and a short-term business focus during the last quarter of the twentieth century. I suspect that one reason for the decline in practitioner-oriented research in our journals is the reduced support for in-house research on management and organizational practices. Historically, industry sponsorship has been a major source of support, funding, and expertise for OB research. From ATT to Sears, to the military in the United States, to Cadbury in the United Kingdom, to myriad consulting firms in North America and Europe, practitioners both sponsored and produced organizational research. I suspect that cutbacks in practitioner-conducted research ceded journal pages to academics. Over time, academics exerted stronger control over the publication criteria for journals by virtue of the predominance of their work within those journals, making it more difficult to publish practitioner-conducted research. Interestingly, practitioner-oriented journals (e.g., *Harvard Business Review*, *California Management Review*) are major consumers of academic research, especially from the applied psychology area that overlaps OB (McWilliams, Lockett, Katz, & Van Fleet, 2009).

Despite the aspiration for OB research to be useful to practice, lack of practitioner involvement in research is a big problem. Without practitioners helping to focus research on the actual conditions and challenges they face, we know less than is optimal to make findings actionable. Science-oriented OB research tends to tell us about a single effect in isolation. Thus, we may know that A tends to increase B, yet a real situation can also involve C, D, and Z (perhaps adding the layers of a challenging job, limited information, and several people with a say in the situation). A decision maker trying to take all these matters into account doesn't have a straight path to an answer—a problem that confronts evidence use in other fields, too. DeAngelis (2008) notes that practicing clinical psychologists face such problems in treating their patients. Mental-health service providers can confront patients who are not only depressed but interpersonally challenged and substance-abusing, too. Little basic research can prepare mental-health professionals to treat this combination of patient conditions. Practice conditions aren't as neat and tidy as the effects that targeted, science-oriented studies identify. Without practitioner participation in the research process, we are less likely to know the kinds of actual everyday decisions they face for which evidence is needed. Thus, lack of practitioner involvement in research is a double whammy for EBMgt. Their low participation levels suggest that practitioners typically don't see organizational research as useful or relevant. Further, their nonparticipation exacerbates the research-practice gap by limiting the kind of research that gets done. The result is research even less widely known, used, or useful in the eyes of practitioners.

Implications

Evidence suggests that OB research is not widely used. This research-practice gap has motivated many calls for EBMgt (e.g., Latham, 2007; Rousseau, 2006; Rynes, Giluk, & Brown, 2007). The gap has multiple explanations, including the lack of knowledge on the part of many practitioners about what might be called basic "OB 101." At the same time, awareness and knowledge aren't quite the same. Practitioners can be familiar with what the science says but not *believe* it. Taken-for-granted beliefs that are at odds with scientific evidence are at the core of Pfeffer and Sutton's (2006) well-stated notion that EBMgt's challenge isn't just what practitioners don't know but "what they know that isn't so."

Practitioner involvement in research, endemic in other evidence-based professions, is nearly absent in management. Limited practitioner involvement in research limits real-world managers' exposure to research ideas. It also affects the very nature of the research available to help tackle managerial and o problems. Thus, we are likely to have both a communication and a knowledge-production problem. At the same time, evidence exists that companies whose HR managers read the academic literature perform better than companies where they don't (Terpstra & Rozell, 1997). We next consider what we can do to turn the evidence-informed practice of a few savvy managers into a way of life for more practitioners in contemporary organizations.

So What Next?

The central mission of EBMgt is not new to OB: to conduct research that both advances scientific inquiry and enlightens practice. So how might we best proceed to realize this heretofore "elusive ideal" (Van de Ven, 2007)? I suspect the necessary steps involve things we already do, as well as some new activities. Because EBMgt is something that practitioners do with the support of researchers and educators, let's explore the contributions each might make to closing OB's research-practice gap.

Practitioners

Regardless of the management field involved, the need to close the research-practice gap has many of the same implications for practitioners. Recommendations of a more general nature are presented in Rousseau (chapter 1 of this volume) and Speicher-Bocija and Adams (chapter 17 of this volume). Here, I offer two recommendations that capitalize on the reasonably advanced state of OB's knowledge base.

The first is learning fundamental evidence-based OB principles. Formal training, directed reading, and developing a network of evidence-savvy contacts are some ways evidence-based managers acquire this knowledge (see Zanardelli, chapter 11 of this volume). In a similar fashion, Locke's *Handbook of Principles of Organizational Behavior* (2009) offers and gives guidance for how to use its practitioner-friendly research summaries. Such reading can help develop a more sophisticated understanding of why certain practices work and others don't. Practitioners—managers in particular—often need to act quickly. Thus, evidence use comes more readily to the practitioner, like Jim Fuchs in our opening discussion, who acquired the knowledge before it was needed. User-friendly models and other heuristics that help busy practitioners recall and use evidence-based findings can support both learning and use (Larrick, 2009; Rousseau, chapter 1 of this volume).

Second, practitioners can become involved in research themselves. This involvement can take many forms. Pilot studies can be used to test interventions suggested by scientific evidence for use in a particular work setting. For example, to see how best to implement flexible hours, a group of supervisors might be trained in ways to promote flexible schedules. Then, the resulting outcomes (new scheduling arrangements, employee satisfaction, attendance, etc.) can be contrasted with the outcomes of a comparable group of supervisors not yet trained. Or, managers can collaborate with local academics to obtain evidence via systematic review or new research on a practice question. No matter the approach taken, direct experience with research problem formulation, design/measurement, testing, and interpretation is a powerful tool for enhancing critical thinking and knowledge of what works and how. Providing a site for research in collaboration with academic researchers can be a way to ease into this mode of professional practice (Zanardelli, chapter 11 of this volume). Many OB-related practice questions are particularly well suited to a single firm or work setting as Barling, Weber, and Kelloway (1996) demonstrate.

Educators

Educators are inadvertently contributing to the research-practice gap by not teaching the evidence or teaching it in a fashion that is not readily applied (Rousseau & McCarthy, 2007). Primary reading materials in many management programs include popular writings by armchair theorists and nonscientific opinion pieces by consultants and executives. In an evidence-based curriculum, students would learn both the principal research findings relevant to a practice area as well as how to apply them (Rousseau & McCarthy, 2007). Educator neglect of OB's well-established evidence base undermines the professional development of organizational practitioners. It fosters reliance on gut and intuition over facts and systematic knowledge. In contrast, teaching with an emphasis on evidence-based practice helps students identify and pursue the goal of greater cumulated knowledge and expertise over the course of their careers.

OB courses need to be taught by faculty familiar with relevant research. In their study of the evidence base of MBA teaching, Chartier et al., (2011) found that faculty lacking PhDs did not base their courses on evidence. Adjuncts often taught these non-evidence-based courses and based their teaching upon their own experiences. There were no effects on the teaching of OB evidence from the nature of the business school itself, its rankings, or whether it had a doctoral program or research-active faculty. These findings suggest that our central concern should be that the faculty teaching in OB courses are knowledgeable about OB research and know how to teach that evidence. Evidence-based textbooks (Pearce, chapter 21 of this volume) and research syntheses (Briner & Denyer, chapter 7 of this volume) are useful in helping faculty to update their teaching with relevant research. Otherwise popular textbooks, reputed to present up-to-date research findings, often fail to meet to mark (Rynes & Trank, 1999; Trank & Rynes, 2003).

Specific teaching practices in OB can reinforce the relevance of evidence to the well-informed practitioner. In-class demonstrations of research findings play to the tendency to value what we experience ourselves. A good illustration of this tendency is demonstrating the effects of positive illusions, where people tend to harbor overly positive beliefs about themselves on attributes for which they receive little feedback (Taylor & Brown, 1988). Ask students to write down the percentile at which they stand individually compared to people in general on driving skills, looks, and intelligence. (The average answer is almost never less than 70–80 percent! On driving skills, no less!) Class participation in research also drives home core behavioral principles and stimulates the critical questioning that deepens understanding. Consider Latham's (2007, p. 1029) approach of involving managers in executive programs and MBA students in his research:

> I present a question to them in the classroom (e.g., Do you think bias can be minimized, if not eliminated, in a performance appraisal?). I encourage strong debate among them regarding the questions I pose. Then I immediately involve them in an experiment to obtain the answer... [they] love the suspense as much as I do in seeking the answers. Anecdotal evidence suggests that the research results are subsequently applied by the managers in their respective work settings. Of further benefit is the participants' newfound appreciation of how the answers were obtained—through systematic empirical research.

Transferring this knowledge from the classroom to real-world practice needs to be woven into the fabric of our courses. Concepts and principles should be presented in ways consistent with how they will be used in practice (Ambrose, Bridges, DiPietro, Lovett, & Norman, 2010; Goodman & O'Brien, chapter 18 of this volume). Articulating a vision is a case in point. As noted earlier, successful managers commonly convey a vision for the future to their organization's members. However, accompanying support practices, such as goal setting and rewards aligned with the vision, are probably used a lot less frequently and possibly not very effectively. Teaching concepts in modules that demonstrate how they can be used together can increase their effective use. For example, concepts such as vision, reward contingencies, and goal setting combine to form a bundle of mutually supportive practices in shaping behavior. Such factors can, for example, be presented as facets of change implementation (Goodman & Rousseau, 2004) or part of the infrastructure for high-performance teams (MacDuffie, 1995). Helping practitioners think through the connections among sets of concepts or practices can make it easier to apply them successfully.

Lastly, educators need to more actively investigate the conditions that promote or interfere with student acquisition of knowledge and skills in our educational settings. Identifying how lay beliefs influence reactions to research may prove key to improving our ability to help students acquire and apply OB-related knowledge. Given the social and interpersonal nature of OB research, practitioners are particularly likely to have developed their own beliefs about OB phenomena—beliefs that fall into Pfeffer and Sutton's category of what we know that isn't so. Thus, OB education has to recognize and work to overcome false beliefs learners hold and then to more effectively educate them in threshold concepts, insights that, if not acquired, keep students from fully understanding certain basic OB principles. Consider why intuition, though a poor prognosticator, remains so seductive. It turns out that most people reason backward ("the person I hired was successful, so I made the right decision"). People tend to forget that in the real world, decisions are made looking forward, without the results in hand. We typically have no information about what might have been if we had hired the people we chose not to at the time. Management educators need to identify and overcome such likely impediments to learning We then need to develop activities that lead to insight and mastery of threshold concepts (e.g., forward focus). Both may be critical in order for learners to understand, accept, and be willing to use evidence (cf. Ambrose et al., 2010).

Researchers

I have three recommendations specific to OB researchers. First, let's capitalize on the field's strengths—namely, its accumulation of programmatic research—and more systematically review and evaluate the conclusions that can be drawn from its bodies of evidence. OB's cumulative advantage contrasts with other management fields that are less concerned with replication and cumulative findings (Mone & McKinley, 1993). Replication and cumulative findings in OB have not always been viewed positively. Critics have raised concern that the field lacks openness to innovative topics (cf. O'Reilly, 1991). I don't believe that is a valid criticism (Rousseau, 1997) and see OB's focus on the accumulation of knowledge as a sign of the field's maturity and scientific values (Whitley, 2000). Along these lines, OB's body of work is methodologically diverse, with many of its principles derived from findings that hold across experiments, cross-sectional and longitudinal studies, and in-depth qualitative work. As such, research demonstrating convergent findings across multiple methodologies characterizes the more advanced sciences (Whitley, 1984, 2000). At this juncture, contributing to EBMgt offers OB opportunities to expand its activities to include greater research synthesis and greater involvement in and support for practice-based evidence.

A huge volume of potentially relevant OB research findings awaits synthesis to figure out what we know, what we don't know, and the concomitant implications for practice (Barends, ten Haven & Huisman, chapter 2 of this volume; Briner & Denyer, chapter 7 of this volume). Ensuring practitioners have access to summaries of OB evidence is a major stumbling block to the field's EBMgt contribution. Journals can be expensive. It also is difficult to draw conclusions from the single studies they tend to publish. Systematic reviews about important practice questions are in short supply, despite the available research base. When they are undertaken, these summaries and syntheses need to go beyond quantitative meta-analyses. In many cases, practice questions necessitate syntheses of qualitative information (Denzin, 1978; Van de Ven, 2007). Research synthesis takes many forms (Rousseau, Manning, & Denyer, 2008). All are valid components in the EBMgt repertoire and in advancing our science. Researchers, beginning with their doctoral training, can contribute to our knowledge accumulation and capacity to ask new and important questions by more adequately synthesizing existing research to figure out what we already know now. We may know more than we think we do. (N.B. Orlitzky, Schmidt, and Rynes (2003) do a nice job of demonstrating this point in their meta-analysis of the link between corporate social responsibility and firms' financial outcomes.)

The practical goals of OB are more readily accomplished with better understanding of the conditions of practice and practitioner needs. EBMgt implementation, as in the case of EBMgt teaching discussed earlier, would benefit from greater insight into practitioner intuitions and beliefs. Such research can help identify the conditions and perceptions that interfere with or aid the uptake of evidence-based practices. Practice-oriented research lends itself to collaboration. It can bring practitioners and academics together to make sense of and solve real-life problems. Practitioner participation is key to insights into organizations, real-world practices, and conditions of use (Vermeulen, 2005, 2007). Practice-oriented research also allows the testing of practitioner "(lay)" theory, since false knowledge is a barrier to effective practice (Pfeffer & Sutton, 2006). Persistent faith in the accuracy of intuition is perhaps the most significant (and most often incorrect) lay belief (Highhouse, 2008). Research is needed to investigate both the conditions that sustain ineffective practice and those that facilitate effective practice. Significant opportunities for knowledge generation and application lie in the intersection of research/education, education/practice, and research/practice.

A final research implication is the need to begin developing knowledge products particularly focused on the end user: action guides and implementation manuals based on evidence. Action guides provide procedural knowledge about ways to act upon evidence-based facts (the declarative or what-is knowledge described earlier). These guides help make effective practice easier by taking organizational facilitators and barriers into account. Frese and his colleagues (chapter 6 of this volume) describe a series of studies evaluating implementation manuals developed to support evidence-based practice among African entrepreneurs (Koop, De Reu, & Frese, 2000; Krauss, Frese, Friedrich, & Unger, 2005). These action guides detail steps in proactive business planning, relevant metrics for success, and ways to correct or adapt plans that failed or were difficult to implement. Their development benefits from researcher-practitioner collaboration.

Picking up our example of the impact of flexible scheduling on workers and firms, recall Perlow's (1997) study of the kinds of problems flexible schedules create. An action guide might be developed based on such research to address how to carry out flexibility effectively. A guide of this nature might describe the kinds of adjustments flexible schedules need if their initial implementation creates problems. The guide's use can then be evaluated and redesigned for impact on effective practice, according to the approach taken by Frese and his colleagues (Koop et al., 2000; Krauss et al., 2005). With its focus on the actual practices managers and organizations use, OB's practice-oriented evidence can aid training and development to support implementation and provide insights into the facilitators, barriers, and adjustments that affect it.

Conclusion

Hundreds of evidence-based principles from OB contribute to the scientific basis of EBMgt, a foundation that continues to expand and deepen. OB's scientific research can be relevant to practice, just as its practice research can produce valid knowledge in the scientific sense. Recognizing the value of both types of research promotes new forms of knowledge. Such knowledge makes it easier to create and inform evidence-based decision making and practices. Furthering OB's contribution to EBMgt requires certain activities on the part of practitioners, educators, and researchers: greater involvement by practitioners in research creation, interpretation/translation, and use; greater effort by OB educators in helping practitioners learn to use evidence; and the union of their forces with researchers to better evaluate, synthesize, and make available OB research to practitioners. Making the use of OB evidence a reality requires the complementary and joint efforts of practitioners, educators, and researchers.

References

Ambrose, S. A., Bridges, M. W., DiPietro, M., Lovett, M. C., & Norman, M. K. (2010). *How learning works: Seven Research-based principles for smart teaching*. San Francisco, CA: Jossey-Bass.

Anderson, J. R. (2010). *Cognitive psychology and its implications* (7th ed.). New York: Worth.

Anderson, N., Herriot, P., & Hodgkinson, G. P. (2001). The practitioner–researcher divide in Industrial, Work and Organizational (IWO) psychology: Where are we now, and where do we go from here? *Journal of Organizational and Occupational Psychology, 74*, 391–411.

Argyris, C. (1960). *Understanding organizational behavior*. Homewood, IL: Dorsey.

Ariely, D., Gneezy, U., Loewenstein, G., & Mazar, N. (2009). Large stakes, big mistakes. *Review of Economic Studies, 76*, 451–469.

Armstrong, J. S. (2010) *Persuasive advertising: Evidence-based principles*. New York: Palgrave Macmillan.

Baratz, L. (1965). *Servants of power*. New York: Wiley.

Barling, J., Weber, T., & Kelloway, K. (1996). Effects of transformational leadership training on attitudinal and financial outcomes: A field experiment. *Journal of Applied Psychology, 81*, 827–832.

Barrick, M. R. & Mount, M. K. (2009). Select on conscientiousness and emotional stability. In E.A. Locke (Ed.), *Handbook of principles of organizational behavior* (2nd ed., pp. 19–39). Malden, MA: Blackwell.

Braverman, H. (1974). *Labor and monopoly capital: The degradation of work in the 20th century*. Danvers, MA: Monthly Review Press.

Briner, R. B., Denyer, D., & Rousseau, D. M. (2009). Evidence-based management: Concept cleanup time? *Academy of Management Perspectives, 23*(4), 19–32.

Campbell, R., Pound, P., Pope, C., Britten, N., Pill, R., Morgan, M., et al. (2003). Evaluating meta-ethnography: A synthesis of qualitative research on lay experiences on diabetes and diabetes care. *Social Science and Medicine, 56,* 671–684.

Card, D. N., McGarry, F. E., & Page, G. T. (1987). Evaluating software engineering technologies. *IEEE Transaction Software Engineering, 13,* 845–851.

Chartier, S. D., Brown, K. G., & Rynes, S. L. (2011). Teaching evidence-based management in MBA programs: What evidence is there? *Academy of Management Learning and Education, 10,* 222–236.

Cialdini, R. B. (2009). *Influence science and practice.* Boston: Pearson.

Cook, T. D., & Campbell, D. T. (1979). *Quasi-experimentation: Design and analysis for field settings.* Chicago, IL: Rand McNally.

Cordery, J. L., Morrison, D., Wright, B. M., & Wall, T. D. (2010). The impact of autonomy and task uncertainty on team performance: A longitudinal field study. *Journal of Organizational Behavior, 31,* 240–258.

Curtis, B., Krasner, H., & Iscoe, N. (1988). A field study of the software design process for large systems. *Communications of the ACM, 31,* 1268–1287.

DeAngelis, T. (2008). When do meds make the difference? *Monitor on Psychology, 39,* 48.

Denzin, N. K. (1978). *The research act: A theoretical introduction to sociological methods.* New York: McGraw-Hill.

Drucker, P. F. (1974). *Management: Tasks, responsibilities and practices.* New York: Harper.

Durham, C. C. & Bartol, K. M. (2009). Pay for performance. In E. A. Locke (Ed.), *Handbook of principles of organizational behavior* (2nd ed., pp. 217–238). Malden, MA: Blackwell.

Dutton, J. E., & Ragins, B. (2006). *Exploring positive relations at work: Building a theoretical and research foundation.* Mahwah, NJ: Lawrence Erlbaum.

Ebell, M. H., Barry, H. C., Slawson, D. C., & Shaughnessy, S. F. (1999). Finding POEMs in the medical literature—Patient-oriented evidence that matters. *Journal of Family Practice, 48*(5), 350–355.

Follett, M. P. (1918). *The new state: Group organization the solution of popular government.* New York: Longmans, Green and Co.

Gaertner, S. L., & Dovidio, J. F. (2000). *Reducing intergroup bias: The common in-group identity mode.* London: Psychology Press.

Gardell, B. (1977). Autonomy and participation at work. *Human Relations, 30,* 515–533.

Gawande, A. (2009). *The checklist manifesto: How to get things right.* New York: Metropolitan Books.

Ghoshal, S. (2005). Bad management theories are driving out good management practices. *Academy of Management Learning and Executive, 4,* 75–91.

Goleman, D. (1995). *Emotional intelligence: Why it can matter more than IQ.* New York: Bantam.

Goodman, P. S. (1979). *Assessing organizational change: The Rushton quality of work experiment.* New York: Wiley.

Goodman, P. S., & Rousseau, D. M. (2004). Organizational change that produces results: The linkage approach. *Academy of Management Executive, 4*(18), 7–21.

Gordon, R. A., & Howell, J. E. (1959). *Higher education for business.* New York: Columbia University Press.

Greenberg, J. (1990). Employee theft as a reaction to underpayment inequity: The hidden cost of pay cuts. *Journal of Applied Psychology, 75,* 561–568.

Grove, W. M., & Lloyd, M. (2006). Meehl's contribution to clinical versus statistical prediction. *Journal of Abnormal Psychology, 115,* 192–194.

Gulick, L. J., & Urwick, L. (1937). *Papers on the science of administration.* New York: Institute of Public Administration.

Hedges, L. V. & Olkin, I. (1985). *Statistical methods for meta-analysis.* San Diego: Academic Press.

Highhouse, S. (2008). Stubborn reliance on intuition and subjectivity in employee selection. *Industrial and Organizational Psychology, 1,* 333–342.

Hornung, S., Rousseau, D. M., & Glaser, J. (2009). Creating flexibility through idiosyncratic deals. *Journal of Applied Psychology, 93,* 655–664.

House, R. J., Hanges, P., Javidan, M., Dorfman, P. W., & Gupta, V. (2004). *Culture, leadership, and organizations: The GLOBE study of 62 societies.* Thousand Oaks, CA: Sage.

Hunter, J. E., & Schmidt, F. L. (1990). *Methods of meta-analysis: Correcting error and bias in research findings.* Thousand Oaks, CA: Sage Publications.

Judge, T. A. & Klinger, R. (2009). Promote job satisfaction through mental challenge. In E.A. Locke (Ed.), *Handbook of principles of organizational behavior* (2nd ed., pp. 107–121). Malden, MA: Blackwell.

Karasek, R. (2004). Job socialization: The carry-over effects of work on political and leisure activities. *Bulletin of Science, Technology & Society, 24,* 284–304.

Katz, D. & Kahn, R. (1966). *Social psychology of organizations.* New York: Wiley.

Kirkpatrick, S. A. (2009). Lead through vision and values. In E.A. Locke (Ed.), *Handbook of principles of organizational behavior* (2nd ed,, pp. 367–387). Malden, MA: Blackwell.

Kluger, A. N., & DeNisi, A. (1996). The effects of feedback interventions on performance: Historical review, meta-analysis and preliminary feedback intervention theory. *Psychological Bulletin, 119,* 254–284.

Koop, S., De Reu, T., & Frese, M. (2000). Sociodemographic factors, entrepreneurial orientation, personal initiative, and environmental problems in Uganda. In M. Frese (Ed.), *Success and failure of microbusiness owners in Africa: A psychological approach,* pp. 55–76. Westport, CT: Quorum.

Kornhauser, A. W. (1922). The psychology of vocational selection. *Psychological Bulletin, 19,* 192–229.

Kornhauser, A. W., & Sharp, A. (1932). Employee attitudes: Suggestions from a study in a factory. *Personnel Journal, 10,* 393–401.

Kossek, E. E., & Lambert, S. (2005). *Work and life integration: Organizational, cultural and psychological perspectives.* Mahwah, NJ: Lawrence Erlbaum.

Krauss, S. I., Frese, M., Friedrich, C., & Unger, J. (2005). Entrepreneurial orientation and success: A psychological model of success in Southern African small scale business owners. *European Journal of Work and Organizational Psychology, 14,* 315–344.

Larrick, R. P. (2009). Broaden the decision frame to make effective decisions. In E.A. Locke (Ed.), *Handbook of principles of organizational behavior* (2nd ed., pp. 461–480), Malden, MA: Blackwell.

Latham, G. (2007). A speculative perspective on the transfer of behavioral science findings to the workplace: "The times they are a changin." *Academy of Management Journal, 50*(5), 1027–1032.

Latham, G. (2009). *Becoming the evidence-based manager: Making the science of management work for you.* Boston, MA: Davies-Black.

Lawler, E. E. (1971). *Pay and organizational effectiveness: A psychological view.* New York: McGraw- Hill.

Lawler, E. E. (1990*). Strategic pay: Aligning organizational strategies and pay systems*. San Francisco, CA: Jossey-Bass.

Likert, R. (1932). A technique for the measurement of attitudes. *Archives of Psychology, 22* (140), 1–55.

Locke, E. A. (2005). Why emotional intelligence is an invalid concept. *Journal of Organizational Behavior, 26*, 425–431.

Locke, E. A. (2009). *Handbook of principles of organizational behavior: Indispensible knowledge for evidence-based management*. New York: Wiley.

Locke, E. A. & Latham, G. P. (1984). *Goal setting: A motivational technique that works*. Englewood Cliffs, NJ: Prentice-Hall.

MacDuffie, J. P. (1995). Human resource bundles and manufacturing performance: Organizational logic and flexible production systems in the world automobile industry. *Industrial and Labor Relations Review, 48*, 197–221.

Mayer, J. D., Salovey, P., & Caruso, D. R. (2000). Emotional intelligence as zeitgeist, as personality and as mental ability. In R. Bar-On & J. D. A. Parker (Eds.), *Handbook of emotional intelligence* (pp. 92–117). San Francisco, CA: Jossey-Bass.

McGregor, D. (1960). *The human side of enterprise*. New York: McGraw-Hill.

McWilliams, A., Lockett, A., Katz, J., & Van Fleet, D. D. (2009). Who is talking to whom? The network of intellectual influence in academic research. *Journal of Applied Management and Entrepreneurship, 14* (2), 61–81.

Meehl, P. E. (1954). *Clinical versus statistical prediction: A theoretical analysis and a review of the evidence*. Minneapolos, MN: University of Minnesota Press.

Miller, D. C., & Form, W. H. (1951). *Industrial sociology: An introduction to the sociology of work relations*. New York: Harper & Row.

Munsterberg, H. (1913). *Psychology and industrial efficiency*. Boston: Houghton Mifflin.

Mone, M. A., & McKinley, W. (1993). The uniqueness value and its consequences for organizational studies. *Journal of Management Inquiry, 2*, 284–296.

O'Reilly, C. A. (1991). Organizational behavior: Where we've been, where we're going. *Annual Review of Psychology, 42*, 427–458.

Orlitzky, M., Schmidt, F. L., & Rynes, S. L. (2003). Corporate social and financial performance: A meta-analysis. *Organization Studies, 24*, 403–441.

Pearce, J. L. (2009). *Organizational behavior: Real research for real managers*. (2nd ed.). Irvine, CA: Melvin & Leigh.

Pepitone, J. S. (2009). Survey of organization managers' knowledge supporting evidence-based human resource management. *Dissertation Abstracts International Section A: Humanities and Social Sciences, 70*(6-A), 2138.

Perlow, L. (1997). *Finding time: How corporations, individuals and families can benefit from new work practices*. Ithaca, NY: Cornell.

Pfeffer, J., & Sutton, R. I. (2006). *Hard facts: Dangerous half-truths & total nonsense*. Boston, MA: Harvard Business School Press.

Porter, L. W. & Lawler, E. E. (1968). *Managerial attitudes and performance*. Homewood, IL: Irwin.

Porter, L. W. & McKibbin, L. E. (1988). *Management education and development: Drift or thrust into the 21st century*. New York: McGraw-Hill Book Company.

Pritchard, R. D., Harrell, M. M., DiazGranados, D., & Guzman, M. J. (2008). The productivity measurement and enhancement system: A meta-analysis. *Journal of Applied Psychology, 93*, 540–567.

Roethlisberger, F., & Dickson, W. J. (1939). *Management and the worker*. Cambridge, MA: Harvard University Press.

Rousseau, D. M. (1997). Organizational behavior in the new organizational era. *Annual Review of Psychology, 48*, 515–546.

Rousseau, D. M. (2006). Is there such a thing as "evidence-based management"? *Academy of Management Review, 31*(2), 256–269.

Rousseau, D. M. (2011). Reinforcing the micro/macro bridge: Organizational thinking and pluralistic vehicles. *Journal of Management, 37*, 429–442.

Rousseau, D. M., Hornung, S., & Kim, T.G. (2009). Testing idiosyncratic deal propositions: Timing, content, and the employment relationship. *Journal of Vocational Behavior, 74*, 338–348.

Rousseau, D. M., Manning, J., & Denyer, D. (2008). Evidence in management and organizational science: Assembling the field's full weight of scientific knowledge through syntheses. *The Academy of Management Annals, 2*, 475–515.

Rousseau, D. M., & McCarthy, S. (2007). Educating managers from an evidence-based perspective. *Academy of Management Learning and Education, 6*(1), 84–101.

Rynes, S. L., Colbert, A. E., & Brown, K. G. (2002). HR professionals' beliefs about effective human resource practices: Correspondence between research and practice. *Human Resource Management, 41*(2), 149–174.

Rynes, S. L., Gerhart, B., & Parks, L. (2005). Personnel psychology: Performance evaluation and pay for performance. *Annual Review of Psychology, 56*, 571–600.

Rynes, S. L., Giluk, T. L., & Brown, K. G. (2007). The very separate worlds of academic and practitioner periodicals in human resource management: Implications for evidence-based management. *Academy of Management Journal, 50*(5), 987–1008.

Rynes, S. L., & Trank. C. Q. (1999). Behavioral science in the business school curriculum: Teaching in a changing institutional environment. *The Academy of Management Review, 24*, 808–824.

Sanders, K., van Riemsdijk, M., & Groen, B. (2008). The gap between research and practice: A replication study on the HR professionals' beliefs about effective human resource practices. *International Journal of Human Resource Management, 19*(10), 1976–1988.

Schein, E. (2010). *Organizational culture and leadership*. New York: Wiley.

Schmidt, F. L. (2009). Select on intelligence. In E. A. Locke (Ed.), *Handbook of principles of organizational behavior* (2nd ed., pp. 3–17). Malden, MA: Blackwell.

Schmidt, F. L., & Hunter, J. (2004). General mental ability in the world of work: Occupational attainment and job performance. *Journal of Applied Psychology, 86*, 162–173.

Schwartz, B. (2004). *The paradox of choice: Why more is less*. New York: ECCO.

Shaw, J. D., Gupta, N., & Delery, J. E. (2002). Pay dispersion and workforce performance: Moderating effects of incentives and interdependence. *Strategic Management Journal, 23*, 491–512.

Simon, H. A. (1997). *Administrative behavior* (4th ed.). New York: The Free Press.

Snook, B., Eastwood, J., Gendreau, P., Goggin, C., & Cullen, R. M. (2007). Taking stock of criminal profiling: A narrative review and meta-analysis. *Criminal Justice and Behavior, 34*, 437–453.

Stevens, C. K. (2009). Structure interviews to recruit and hire the best people. In E.A. Locke (Ed.), *Handbook of principles of organizational behavior* (2nd ed., pp. 41–56), Malden, MA: Blackwell.

Selznick, P. (1957). *Leadership in administration: A sociological interpretation.* New York: Harper Row.

Taylor, S. E., & Brown, J. (1988). Illusion and well-being: A social psychological perspective on mental health. *Psychological Bulletin, 103,* 193–210.

Terpstra, D. E. & Rozell, E. J. (1997). Sources of human resource information and the link to organizational profitability. *The Journal of Applied Behavioral Science, 33*(1), 66–83.

Timmerman, T. A. (2010). Misconceptions about HRM start early. *Journal of Human Resources Education, 4,* 31–40.

Trank, C. Q., & Rynes, S. L. (2003). Who moved our cheese? Reclaiming professionalism in business education. *Academy of Management Learning & Education, 2,* 189–205.

Van de Ven, A. (2007). *Engaged scholarship: A guide for organizational and social research.* New York: Oxford University Press.

Vermeulen, F. (2005). On rigor and relevance: Fostering dialectical progress in management research. *Academy of Management Journal, 48,* 978–982.

Vermeulen, F. (2007). "I shall not remain insignificant:" Adding a second loop to matter more. *Academy of Management Journal, 50*(4), 754–761.

Verschuren, P. J. M. (2009). *Why methodology for practice-oriented research is a necessary heresy.* Nijmegen, Netherlands: Radboud University.

Viteles, M. S. (1932). *Industrial psychology.* New York: Norton.

Whitley, R. (1984). The scientific status of management research as a practically-oriented social science. *Journal of Management Studies, 21*(4), 369–390.

Whitley, R. (2000). *The intellectual and social organization of the sciences* (2nd ed.). Oxford, England: Oxford University Press.

Yates, J. F. (2003). *Decision management.* San Francisco: Jossey-Bass.

Yukl, G. (2009). Use power effectively to influence people. In E. A. Locke (ed.), *Handbook of principles of organizational behavior* (2nd ed., pp. 349–365). Malden, MA: Blackwell.

Zickar. M. J. (2003). Remembering Arthur Kornhauser: Industrial psychology's advocate for worker well-being. *Journal of Applied Psychology, 88*(2), 363–369.

CHAPTER 5

Evidence-Based Management in "Macro" Areas: The Case of Strategic Management

Ravi Madhavan *and* Joseph T. Mahoney

Abstract

Despite its intuitive appeal, evidence-based management (EBMgt) faces unique challenges in "macro" areas such as organization theory and strategic management, which emphasize actions by organizations and business and corporate leaders. The inherent focus on complex, multilevel and unique problems presents serious challenges that EBMgt scholars must address. EBMgt will nurture the establishment of a new model of research that is not only cumulative in its knowledge building but also promotes engaged scholarship. Further, the uncertainty and conflict that characterize "macro" decision contexts heighten the need for EBMgt. We put forward four recommendations to advance EBMgt: (1) using more sophisticated meta-analyses, (2) providing syntheses that go beyond quantitative summaries, (3) engaging in a disciplined conversation about our implicit "levels of evidence" frameworks, and (4) developing decision supports.

Key Words: strategic management, organizational theory, systematic review, collaborative research, decision supports, engaged scholarship

Evidence-based management (EBMgt) involves a community of practice whose members learn by respectfully collaborating among practitioners, educators, and researchers (Rousseau, 2007). Over time, EBMgt will be iterative, transforming research findings into shared understandings, structures, and best practices (Aram & Salipante, 2003; Carlile, 2004). Evidence suggests constructs and if-then relationships possessing both internal and external validity, which informs the decision process. Evidence is enhanced by an accumulated body of learning and by triangulation across methods and types of studies (Jick, 1979; Mahoney, 1993; Van de Ven, 2007). EBMgt not only emphasizes the use of evidence but also focuses on making organizational decisions that take into account practitioner experiences. Although all meaningful research is eventually aimed at influencing practice, the EBMgt movement has the potential to significantly change how we do research in the "macro" subfields of (business and corporate) strategy and (organizational design in) organization theory (OT), since the macro side of the aisle—more so than in micro fields such as organizational behavior and human-resource management—is characterized by multi-level phenomena and divergent approaches. EBMgt can help to bring some harmony and discipline to this research.

Since first articulated by Rousseau (2006), EBMgt has evolved through successive conceptualizations. Starting with the definition "translating principles based on best evidence into organizational practices" (Rousseau, 2006, p. 256), the initial characterization of EBMgt highlights learning about cause-effect connections, isolating variation that affects outcomes, building an evidence-respecting culture and community, developing decision supports that incorporate evidence, and focusing on the practice of management as informed by the best evidence. Subsequently, Rousseau, Manning, and Denyer (2008) consider the role of the scholarly community in developing the ingredients of EBMgt. Systematic reviews are identified as the preferred mode of evidence synthesis, with elaboration of four forms of synthesis— aggregative, integrative, interpretive, and explanatory. Tranfield, Denyer, and Smart note that: "Systematic reviews differ from traditional narrative reviews by adopting a replicable, scientific and transparent process…that aims to minimize bias through exhaustive literature searches of published and unpublished studies…(2003, p. 209).

More recently, conceptualizing EBMgt as a family of approaches that support decision making, Briner, Denyer, and Rousseau (2009) assert that it is something that is done by practitioners, not scholars, whose role is to provide the infrastructure. In this chapter, we differ somewhat from Briner, Denyer, and Rousseau's (2009) position that the relevance of EBMgt to scholars is largely from the standpoint of providing infrastructure. For example, the EBMgt movement can substantially change how we do research in strategic management.

To explore this theme, the paper proceeds as follows. The next section considers the challenges of EBMgt in strategic management and why EBMgt is needed. The subsequent section provides implications for EBMgt in strategic management. The final section provides discussion and conclusions.

Challenges of EBMgt in Strategic Management

Although well established in several disciplines, EBMgt runs into some unique challenges in more "macro" areas, and especially in the field of strategic management. We classify these special challenges into three categories: philosophical, methodological, and institutional.

At the philosophical level, EBMgt connects to a central feature of strategic management, which is its emphasis on the integrative view, the general management perspective, and on large, unique, history-dependent problems (Eisenhardt, 1989; Mahoney & McGahan, 2007). Some implications of such emphasis include the continuing dominance of case studies in research as well as teaching, multilevel narratives that meld together individual leaders with firm-level factors set in historical contexts, and the integration of economic and behavioral perspectives (Gimeno, Folta, Cooper, & Woo, 1997; Mahoney, 2005).

To illustrate the emphasis on unique events,—such as lessons learned from the Columbia Shuttle disaster or by examining first-mover advantages achieved by Coca-Cola internationally during WWII—a key paper about the challenges of learning in a "macro" context was titled, "Learning from Samples of One or Fewer" (March, Sproull & Tamuz, 1991). This issue goes beyond the bias to novelty remarked on by Rousseau, Manning, & Denyer identifying, as a key driver of our failure to use evidence well, the habit of "overvaluing novelty to the detriment of accumulating convergent findings" (2008, p. 476) in management and organization science. The emphasis on unique problems, settings, and historical pathways is endemic to the strategic management field. A recent example of this orientation is the problem-finding/problem-solving perspective (Heiman, Nickerson, & Zenger, 2008; Nickerson & Zenger, 2004), which departs from the conventional framing of strategy as the search for competitive advantage to one of how leaders find new problem-solution pairings that have the potential to yield substantial and continuing value streams. The co-existence of, on the one hand, research examining unique events, and, on the other hand, an emphasis on reductionist research that can push for overly simplified theory that fails to capture complex contextual interactions of importance, contributes to the "split personality" of the field. In a nutshell, the "macro" nature of the field exacerbates the problem of dueling models determining what is knowable from rich contextual research and from reductionist methodologies that can run roughshod over institutional and contextual factors.

At the methodological level, a fundamental question is raised by the fact that "macro" fields are characterized by the near-total absence of experimental studies, because it is difficult to set up experiments in which complex organizations are randomly assigned to different conditions and their outcomes are compared. Thus, whether qualitative (case studies) or quantitative (large-sample) studies, most empirical evidence in strategy stems from observational studies. In contrast, the "micro" disciplines are rich in experimental studies. This contrast raises an interesting question: How might doing meta-analysis—a key tool for synthesizing findings in the EBMgt toolkit—on nonexperimental data be different from doing meta-analysis on experimental data? Some controversy exists in evidence-based medicine about the relative status of meta-analysis of experimental data and meta-analysis of observational data. The main issue, then, is whether meta-analyses of micro studies based on randomized trials will be inherently superior to meta-analyses of macro studies based on observation data. Concerning this issue, Egger, Schneider, & Smith (1998, p. 141) make the following argument:

> Meta-analysis of randomized trials is based on the assumption that each trial provides an unbiased estimate of the effect of an experimental treatment, with the variability of the results between the studies being attributed to random variation. The overall effect calculated from a group of sensibly combined and representative randomized trials will provide an essentially unbiased estimate of the treatment effect, with an increase in the precision of this estimate. A fundamentally different situation arises in the case of observational studies. Such studies yield estimates of association which may deviate from true underlying relationships beyond the play of chance. This may be due to the effects of confounding factors, the influence of biases, or both.

Although the position espoused by Egger, Schneider, & Smith (1998) is by no means the final word on the topic,—especially as methodologies utilizing observational data continue to advance—it does offer food for thought from the standpoint of EBMgt in the "macro" subfields of management. In observational studies that are the norm in strategy and OT, confounding factors may distort results. Further, recall that even when the original research studies may have controlled for a variety of factors, the meta-analysis does not take such controls into effect, because the primary input for the meta-analyst is the effect strength—most often, the raw correlation between X and Y.

At the institutional level, a significant "re-education" campaign may be necessary to disseminate the true role of systematic reviews and meta-analyses. Those of us who have tried to publish meta-analyses in the management field have found, to various degrees, pressure from reviewers and editors to use meta-analyses as yet another tool for theory building, not for genuine evidence accumulation.

Why Bother With EBMgt Then?

Why should "macro" scholars and practitioners adopt an EBMgt orientation despite these challenges? We provide two reasons in favor of such adoption. First, EBMgt will allow for the emergence of an engaged scholarship model that balances rigor and relevance to flourish in the strategic management field. Achievement of this goal is important in order for research to emerge in the "Pasteur's quadrant" (Stokes, 1997), in which improved fundamental understandings and applications of findings are achieved (Tushman & O'Reilly, 2007). Second, EBMgt will mitigate barriers to learning that exist in complex organizations, which often pose significant problems in the form of cognitive biases in strategy. EBMgt can help practitioners to evaluate research results better. Practitioners may also better appreciate the research process, including the identification of research problems and the relevance of research findings to practice.

Van de Ven's (2007) book, *Engaged Scholarship*—in which research scholars are the focal audience—provides a compelling model for thinking about impactful research in a way that emphasizes the interaction between scientists and practitioners. Scholars are not the only group to whom scholarship matters; practitioners, as sources of problems and data, as well as users of solutions devised by scholars, are important stakeholders in scholarship (Lawrence, 1992). Thus, Van de Ven calls for "Engaged scholarship [, which] is a participative form of research for obtaining the advice and perspectives of key stakeholders (researchers, users, clients, sponsors, and practitioners) to understand a complex social problem" (2007, p. ix). Van de Ven (2007) suggests that engaged scholarship produces more penetrating and insightful knowledge than would emerge if scholars and practitioners work in isolation. This view is consistent with the aspiration of EBMgt to close the "great divide" (Rynes, Bartunek, & Daft, 2001; Rynes, Giluk, & Brown, 2007) between research and practice. The diamond model (see Figure 5.1) proposes a process of (1) *problem formulation* (Delbecq & Van de Ven, 1971; Volkema, 1983), (2) *theory building* (Bacharach, 1989; Whetten, 1989), (3) *research design* (Denzin, 1978; Kaplan, 1964), and (4) *problem solving* (Ackoff, 1978; Polya, 1957). Such an approach is a participative form of research for obtaining the counsel and perspectives of key stakeholders (e.g., educators, researchers, and practitioners) for improved understandings of problems that are often of high complexity (Hodgkinson & Rousseau, 2009).

Van de Ven's (2007) diamond model of engaged scholarship emphasizes an iterating cycle comprising four steps that show how theories, models, and research designs combine to produce solutions to problems that emerge from reality: (1) problem formulation, (2) theory building, (3) research design, and (4) problem solving. In the problem formulation

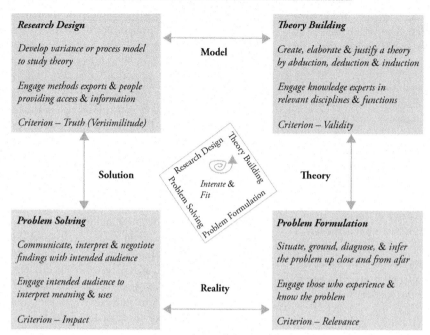

Study Context: Research problem, purpose, perspective

Research Design

Develop variance or process model to study theory

Engage methods exports & people providing access & information

Criterion – Truth (Verisimilitude)

Model

Theory Building

Create, elaborate & justify a theory by abduction, deduction & induction

Engage knowledge experts in relevant disciplines & functions

Criterion – Validity

Solution

Research Design Theory Building

Problem Solving Problem Formulation

Interate & Fit

Theory

Problem Solving

Communicate, interpret & negotiote findings with intended audience

Engage intended audience to interpret meaning & uses

Criterion – Impact

Reality

Problem Formulation

Situate, ground, diagnose, & infer the problem up close and from afar

Engage those who experience & know the problem

Criterion – Relevance

Fig. 5.1 The engaged scholarship model. Adapted from Van de Ven (2007).

phase, the goal is to identify and understand a real-life problem worth solving through engagement with those who experience and know the problem first hand; relevance is the key criterion. Relevance is found in generating insights that practitioners find useful for understanding their own organizations and situations better than before (Vermeulen, 2005, 2007). In the theory-building phase, the goal is to construct and justify a theory that fits the identified problem, through engagement with knowledge experts in the disciplines relevant to the theory; validity is the key criterion. In the research-design phase, the goal is to develop a variance or process model to test the theory, through engagement with methods experts as well as those others who provide data access; verisimilitude is the key criterion. Finally, in the problem-solving phase, the goal is to share and shape the findings with the intended audience; impact is the key criterion here. By linking the worlds of science and practice in this instructive iterative model, Van de Ven (2007) cuts the Gordian knot posed by the rigor versus relevance paradox that has plagued the macro field for so long.

In many ways, we can conceive of EBMgt as an approach that will advance the agenda of engaged scholarship, and help anchor strategy scholarship in the concerns of our stakeholders and, ultimately,

in reality. The central mission of the enterprise of EBMgt and engaged scholar-ship is to conduct research that both advances scientific inquiry and enlightens practice (Simon, 1976). Van de Ven (2007) notes, however, that this mission is an elusive ideal. Indeed, studies show that practitioners often fail to adopt the findings of management research (Rynes, Bartunek, & Daft (2001); Tranfield, Denyer, & Smart, 2003). Criticisms for this great divide between theory and practice have flowed in both directions (Argyris & Schön, 1978; Hodgkinson, 2001; Van de Ven & Johnson, 2006). Management educators and researchers, for example, are criticized for not adequately considering how to put their abstract knowledge into practice (Bartunek, 2003; Beyer, 1997; Beyer & Trice, 1982). Practicing managers, as well, are criticized for not being aware of relevant research and not appreciating enough the "know-why" of practice (Latham, 2007; Van de Ven, 2002; Weick, 2001). Part of the reason here may be that educators typically do not educate managers to know or use scientific evidence (Rousseau, 2006: 262).

Often the gap between theory and practice is characterized as a knowledge transfer problem in which we simply need to translate and diffuse knowledge into practice (Cascio, 2007; Hambrick, 1994; Kelemen & Bansal, 2002). A deeper understanding of the challenges, however, is required (Kieser & Leiner, 2009; Schön, 1983; Simon, 1996). For example, Polanyi (1962) and Nonaka (1994) make important distinctions between explicit scientific knowledge and more tacit practical knowledge. The knowledge of science and practice are typically *complementary.* Rather than regarding tacit practical knowledge as a derivative of scientific knowledge, practical knowledge is regarded as a distinct mode of knowing in its own right (Pearce, 2004; Van de Ven & Johnson, 2006). Indeed, Van de Ven maintains that:

> Exhortations for academics to put their theories into practice theories into practice and for managers to put their practice into theory may be misdirected because they assume that the relationship between knowledge of theory and knowledge of practice entails a literal transfer or translation of one into the other. Instead, I suggest taking a pluralistic view of science and practice as representing distinct kinds of know-ledge that can provide complementary insights for understanding reality. (2007, p. 4)

Motivating practitioners to give attention to scholarly evidence will be impossible unless our research is seeded by a real-life problem that is worth solving. The validity of theories will be difficult to justify in the theory-building phase unless we have knowledge of the cumulative empirical support that theories enjoy. The research design phase, as well as its key criterion, verisimilitude, is difficult to address in the absence of clear links to extant evidence. Finally, sharing the results of the research with practitioner stakeholders in ways that take note of their interpretations as well as motivate them to deploy the solution found is also a critical set of steps that are integral to EBMgt.

Going further still, the gap between theory and practice may be a knowledge-production problem (Huff, 2000; Huff, Tranfield, & Van Aken, 2006). There is not only a knowledge- transfer problem, in which relevant management research does not reach practitioners (the "lost-in-translation problem") but also a knowledge-production problem in which managerial relevant knowledge is not even created (the "lost-*before*-translation problem") (Markides, 2007; Shapiro, Kirkman & Courtney, 2007). To aid in mitigating the knowledge-production problem, various forms of engaged scholarship are required and can range from attached insiders to detached outsiders (Bartunek, 2007; Evered & Louis, 1981; Lewin, 1951) to help connect the process and product of research (Kor & Mahoney, 2000; Mahoney

& Sanchez, 2004; Simon, 1978). Three types of engaged scholarship suggested by Van De Ven (2007) are considered here: (1) informed basic research; (2) collaborative research; and (3) design/ evaluation research.

Informed Basic Research. Informed basic research resembles a traditional form of social science where the academic researcher adopts a detached outsider perspective of the social system being examined, but solicits advice and feedback from key stakeholders and informants (Gulati, 2007). Ouchi's (2003) research on making schools work better, and Van de Ven's (2007) engaged-scholarship model are exemplars of this research approach.

Collaborative Research. Collaborative research entails the genuine sharing of power among researchers and stakeholders (Amabile, Patterson, Mueller, Wojcik, Odomirok, et al. 2001). Collaborative research teams are typically composed of insiders and outsiders who jointly share in activities in order to co-produce basic knowledge that describes or explains a complex problem (Bartunek & Louis, 1996; Louis & Bartunek, 1992; Mohrman, Gibson & Mohrman, 2001).

Design/ Policy Evaluation Research. A third form of engaged scholarship is the focus of the current chapter, in which research is undertaken to examine questions dealing with the design and evaluation of policies for solving practical problems (Denyer, Tranfield, & Van Aken, 2008 Simon, 1996), such as designing a better business school. This design/ policy-evaluation research goes beyond describing or explaining a social problem and seeks to obtain evidence-based knowledge of the efficacy or relative success of alternative solutions to applied problems (Romme, 2003; Romme & Endenburg, 2006; Van Aken, 2004, 2005). A pragmatic emphasis is placed on systems thinking and actionable knowledge (Morrell, 2008; Tranfield & Starkey, 1998; Whitley, 1984). Design/policy-evaluation research differs from the informed-basic and collaboration research because it not only evaluates what has been done in the past, but it also is forward thinking, using principles to imagine next steps for an improved design for solving problems, such as designing a better bridge.

The engaged scholarship model (Van de Ven, 2007) also resonates with Boyer's (1990) powerful articulation of four forms of scholarship: discovery, integration, application/practice, and teaching/ dissemination. In Boyer's (1990) terms, the scholarship of discovery is the traditional research model, in which knowledge is sought for its own sake or for practical purposes through systematic modes of inquiry. The scholarship of integration is designed to synthesize extant research, bringing meaning to isolated findings, and developing new perspectives or connections across disciplines. The scholarship of application/practice is represented in the performance of service-related activities requiring specialized knowledge from one's discipline of expertise. The scholarship of teaching/disseminating comprises those creative activities that stimulate active learning and encourage students to be critical, creative thinkers. Thus, in Boyer's (1990) conception, scholarship comprises the distinct, yet overlapping functions of discovery, integration, application, and teaching. Much as EBMgt can play the role of connective tissue between the four stages of Van de Ven's (2007) model, it can also play a critical role in linking Boyer' (1990) four types of scholarship. The evidence that emerges from the scholarship of discovery activities today often languishes without explicit linkage to the other types of scholarship (Abbott, 2004; Ladd, 1987). When attempts are made to integrate such evidence, those attempts are often poorly structured, subjective, and unreliable. Systematic reviews, including meta-analyses, a central element of EBMgt (Rousseau, Manning, & Denyer, 2008), provide a much more compelling way to approach the scholarship of integration. A relentless focus on the implications of research for specific management problems is critical (Bartunek & Rynes, 2010; McGahan, 2007). EBMgt also provides the glue for connecting the scholarship of discovery with the scholarship of application—in the form of the decision aids that constitute another important element of EBMgt. Finally, directly leveraging empirical research findings into the MBA classroom provide one route to linking discovery with dissemination.

Our second argument is that the practice and culture of EBMgt will help mitigate barriers to learning and adaptive capacity, which hamper success in many complex organizations. Strategic decision making is rife with cognitive and organizational imperfections, such as groupthink (Janis, 1972) and organizational politics (Allison, 1971). Although all human behavior is subject to biases of various kinds, the phenomena studied in the "macro" fields are especially prone.

March's (1999) characterization of three "elementary problems" that plague organizations in their pursuit of success is illustrative. The first problem is that of ignorance. Not only is the future uncertain, but peoples' anticipations of the future are also divergent. The past is also uncertain, because it is dimly, inaccurately, or differently recalled. Ignorance about the causal structure of the world expresses itself in *post hoc* socially constructed explanations that shift often. The second problem is that of conflict. Multiple, nested actors interact over multiple, nested time periods on the basis of very different—often discordant—preferences that may themselves change over time. The third problem is that of ambiguity. The preferences of the actors may be ambiguous and only crudely measurable. In combination, uncertainty, conflict, and ambiguity serve to throw up extraordinary challenges in how organizations process "macro" issues, such as strategic choices, resource allocation, and external dependence. Therefore, the pathologies associated with the bounded rationality (Simon, 1976) and human biases (Kahneman, Slovic, & Tversky, 1982) endemic to all of management are likely to be exacerbated in the "macro" fields.

Given this, we propose that the need for EBMgt is also greater in strategic management. At a practical level, among the solutions offered by consulting organizations, such as McKinsey, to the problem of ambiguous strategic choices is "fact-based" decision making, with the implicit promise that expensive consultants will provide objective, fact-based decision guidelines that will lead to better strategic decisions. The consultants may very well be on to something here: evidence may be just the antidote. Indeed, that is just the argument that Pfeffer & Sutton (2006) make in their pioneering book on EBMgt. A commitment to fact-based decision making is at the core of their conception of EBMgt, and EBMgt is essentially a set of practices, systems, and cultural norms that make it possible to base decisions on sound facts rather than on casual benchmarking, superstitious learning, or untested ideologies. In this sense, the need for EBMgt is all the more pressing in the "macro" fields because of what is at stake. Such a practitioner-based approach to EBMgt is complementary to a more science-based approach to EBMgt of informed, collaborative, and evaluative research designs, just discussed.

Before the strategy field can provide supportive EBMgt infrastructure for strategists, however, scholars may need to rethink how we do our research. We turn to this topic next.

Implications for EBMgt In Strategic Management

Building on the preceding observations, we make four specific recommendations:

1. Devote research resources to understanding both the limitations of meta-analysis in our context and how to adapt it to the type of problems and research designs we work with.

2. Learn more about (and/or develop) synthesis approaches other than meta-analyses—for example, systematic ways to synthesize case studies and qualitative data.

3. Engage in a clarifying conversation about levels of evidence in our field.

4. Devote research resources to developing and testing decision supports (e.g., checklists) for strategy problems.

Toward a More Sophisticated Understanding of Meta-Analysis

Perhaps the most immediate implication has to do with improving the use of meta-analysis given the preponderance of observational data that is characteristic of our field. While working on this chapter, we conducted a quick assessment of the influence of the meta-analytic approach in strategic management by searching for extant meta-analyses in the leading journals relevant to the field (see Table 5.1). Although by no means an exhaustive list of all published meta-analyses in strategic management, the results are instructive.

Overall, meta-analysis appears to be well represented in the field's top journals. Over the 21-year period between 1989 and 2010, at least 17 studies appeared in the top journals, covering core topics such as first-mover advantage, generic competitive strategy, diversification, mergers and acquisitions, and corporate governance. By comparison, Geyskens, Krishnan, Steenkamp, & Cunha (2009) identified 69 meta-analyses published in a broader set of 14 management journals over the 1984–2007 period. Further, meta-analytic studies appear to be well cited by scholars in strategic management, with citations for key studies being in the mid to high hundreds. In certain core areas, such as the planning-performance relationship and mergers and acquisitions, multiple meta-analyses have been published in the top journals. Yet, given the inherent complexity of strategic management phenomena and the relative youth of the field, it is not surprising that few meta-analyses appear to provide a final, comprehensive answer to key questions (Dalton & Dalton, 2005). Rather, in many of the studies, the attempt is less to provide the last word in terms of quantitative effect-size summaries and

more to stimulate further theoretical development by identifying new moderators and directions for further inquiry. Paradoxically, this use of meta-analysis implies that it is difficult to list many well-established strategy findings as emerging from meta-analytic studies.

We conclude that the meta-analytic approach (Geyskens, Steenkamp & Kumar, 2006; Hunter & Schmidt, 1990) is well on its way to becoming an established element in the strategic management toolkit, but that significant roadblocks remain. As familiarity with the approach diffuses through the field, efforts are under way to improve meta-analytic practices, as in, for example, Geyskens et al.'s (2009) review and evaluation, which identifies a set of eight sequential decisions involved in meta-analysis (from choosing the effect-size metric to dealing with publication bias) and proposes a set of best practices.

The criticism of meta-analyses of observational data cited earlier (Egger, Schneider, & Smith 1998) suggests a whole set of productive questions that "macro" scholars should ask. Are there indeed critical differences in the statistical properties of meta-analyses as applied to controlled trials as against to observational studies? Are there ways to account for possible selection bias and endogeneity effects when conducting meta-analyses of observational studies? Our point here is not that meta-analyses are inappropriate but that we need to approach them with greater sophistication. The following comments from Egger, Schneider, & Smith (1998: 142. 143) are instructive:

Some observers suggest that meta-analysis of observational studies should be abandoned altogether. We disagree, but we think that the statistical combination of studies should not generally be a prominent component of reviews of observational studies. The thorough consideration of possible sources of heterogeneity between observational study results will provide more insights than the mechanistic calculation of an overall measure of effect, which will often be biased. The suggestion that formal meta-analysis of observational studies can be misleading and that insufficient attention is often given to heterogeneity does not mean that researchers should return to writing highly subjective narrative reviews. Many of the principles of systematic reviews remain: a study protocol should be written in advance, complete literature searches carried out, and studies selected and data extracted in a reproducible and objective fashion. This allows both differences and similarities of

Table 5.1. Illustrative List of Meta-Analytic Studies in Strategic Management

No.	Year	Author(s)	Journal	Topic	Citations[1]
1	1989	Datta & Narayanan	*J. of Management*	Concentration-performance relationship	14
2	1990	Capon, Farley, & Hoenig	*Management Science*	Determinants of financial performance	535
3	1991	Miller, Glick, Wang, & Huber	*Academy of Management J.*	Technology-structure relationships	73
4	1991	Damanpour	*Academy of Management J.*	Organizational innovation	2280
5	1991	Boyd	*J. of Management Studies*	Planning-performance relationship	198
6	1992	Datta, Pinches, & Narayanan	*Strategic Management J.*	Wealth creation from M&A	226
7	1994	Miller & Cardinal	*Academy of Management J.*	Planning-performance relationship	328
8	1997	VanderWerf & Mahon	*Management Science*	First-mover advantage	148
9	1999	Dalton, Daily, Johnson, & Ellstrand	*Academy of Management J.*	Number of directors and firm performance	725
10	2000	Palich, Cardinal, & Miller	*Strategic Management J.*	Diversification-performance relationship	342
11	2000	Campbell-Hunt	*Strategic Management J.*	Generic competitive strategy	176
12	2003	Dalton, Daily, Certo, & Roengpitya	*Academy of Management J.*	Financial performance and equity	215
13	2003	Combs & Ketchen	*J. of Management*	Franchising as entrepreneurial strategy	103
14	2004	King, Dalton, Daily, & Covin	*Strategic Management J.*	Postacquisition performance	243
15	2005	Rhoades, Rechner, & Sundaramurthy	*J. of Managerial Issues*	Effects of executive and institutional ownership on performance	21
16	2008	Crook, Ketchen, Combs, & Todd	*Strategic Management J.*	Strategic resources and performance	55
17	2010	Lee & Madhavan	*J. of Management*	Divestiture and firm performance	4

[1]As of March 2011, per *Google Scholar*.

the results found in different settings to be inspected, hypotheses to be formulated, and the need for future studies, including randomized controlled trials, to be defined.

Thus, it may be wise to use caution in generating combined estimates of effect strength, taking due care to evaluate the appropriateness of doing so in light of possible sources of heterogeneity. In a broader sense, "macro" scholars intrigued by EBMgt should not only stay away from potentially misleading combined estimates in meta-analyses and give more attention to the unique features of the input studies in their fields. One response to this imperative may be to develop ways to do syntheses that go beyond mechanistic meta-analyses.

Syntheses of Case Studies and Qualitative Data

Given that the unique features of "macro" data include not only observational data but also case studies and qualitative narratives, it may be appropriate for "macro" scholars to evaluate methods to synthesize such data. In nursing research, for example, there is a significant tradition of qualitative research, and Patterson, Thorne, Canam, and Jillings (2001) have proposed an approach to integrating such data, labeled "metastudy." At its core, metastudy is an attempt to develop an analog to meta-analysis for the synthesis of qualitative data. Primary qualitative research is the beginning, and then there are three pathways that converge on metasynthesis. Path 1 is the metadata analysis of research findings. Metadata analysis is processing the processed data (Zhao, 1991), and is not merely aggregative, but also interpretive (Noblit & Hare, 1988). Path 2 is metamethod for research methods. Metamethod focuses on the rigor and epistemological soundness of the research methods used in the underpinning studies. Path 3 is metatheory for theoretical and analytical frameworks. Metatheory is the analysis of the underpinning structures on which the source research is grounded: philosophical, cognitive, theoretical perspectives and assumptions.

Similarly, in public administration, Jensen and Rodgers (2001) proposed a meta-analytic approach to the integration of case study data, which identifies two types of prior integrative effort based on case studies: patchwork case studies and comparative studies of cases. Patchwork studies integrate several prior case studies that have examined a given entity at various points in time into a composite summary (e.g., Roethlisberger & Dickson's (1939) summary of the Hawthorne studies). In contrast, a comparative study of cases typically seeks to integrate examinations of different entities in order to identify underpinning commonalities (e.g., Allison 1971). Central to Jensen and Rodger's (2001) meta-analysis model for case studies is the insight that structured reporting of case-study particulars facilitates the accumulation of case-study evidence, leading to their recommendation that universal standards be adopted for the reporting of case studies—quantitative and qualitative.

Closely related to the task of synthesis approaches for case study and qualitative data is the challenge of learning how to perform integrative, interpretive, and explanatory research syntheses (Rousseau, Manning, & Denyer, 2008). Aggregative syntheses of quantitative studies (i.e., meta-analyses) are not the only legitimate synthesis even in the current EBMgt toolkit. The goal of integration in research synthesis refers to the attempt to answer specific questions by combining across different methods. Triangulation across multiple studies and methods, relying on reviewer judgment, is central (Denzin, 1978; Van de Ven, 2007). The goal of interpretation in research synthesis refers to the attempt to build higher-order theoretical constructs by combining and interpreting extant research. The data are primarily descriptive, and they seek to incorporate the interpretations of the primary researchers. The goal of explanation in research synthesis refers to the attempt to generate new theory by creating explanations and discerning patterns behind extant claims of explanation. Rousseau, Manning, and Denyer's (2008) discussion makes it clear that these approaches to research synthesis are valid members of the EBMgt team, although aggregative statistical meta-analysis may be the best known.

Engaging in a Conversation about Levels of Evidence in Strategy

Fields, such as medicine, in which evidence-based approaches have gained traction, appear to have achieved some measure of consensus about the relative value accorded to different types of evidence. For example, the center for evidence-based medicine at Oxford University provides five different levels of evidence, with systematic reviews of randomized controlled trials at the highest level (i.e., the best evidence) and expert opinions along with reasoning based on first principles at the lowest level. Although there will no doubt be some differences of opinion among medical scientists and practitioners about the nuances of such a hierarchy of evidence, its broad features provide some commonality to the field. We propose that the "macro" fields should engage in an explicit conversation about what a corresponding evidence hierarchy would be for our field. Such a conversation should cover the following questions, among others:

• What types of evidence do we give attention to? Case studies, process descriptions, large-sample quantitative analyses based predominantly on archival data, practitioner war stories, and so on, would surely surface.

• If these types of evidence were to conflict with each other in addressing a particular evidence, under what conditions would we believe one type versus the other?

- Which of those types are most EBMgt-friendly? It would appear to be quantitative analyses although with the aforementioned limitations of observational data.
- What should we do with the evidence-types that are not EBMgt-friendly, such as unique events and evidence that relies exclusively on nonexperimental data? Perhaps we would figure out other ways to discipline our conversations about them.

Developing and Testing Decision Supports for Strategists

One of the central features of evidence-based approaches identified by Rousseau and McCarthy (2007) is the availability (or not) of decision supports. Decision supports are pragmatic tools designed to serve as scaffolding for practitioners to make decisions that are informed by current best evidence (e.g., checklists). Medicine is characterized as having "numerous" decision supports (Rousseau & McCarthy, 2007), such as patient care protocols, handbooks of drug interactions, online decision trees, and so forth. In contrast, business disciplines have few decision supports available to students and practitioners. Where concrete decision supports exist, they are not in the public domain—for example, companies may capture their internal learning in decision-support tools, but those are treated as intellectual property and guarded zealously. One way in which "macro" scholars can begin to incorporate EBMgt thinking is to develop decision supports that are based on research findings. Such decision supports may be as simple as checklists (Gawande, 2009) that encapsulate the steps to follow in making a decision, or the criteria to be employed in evaluating an outcome. Such checklists may, in turn, give rise to further research opportunities, such as empirically evaluating whether their use helps to improve performance.

Conclusion

In brief, we have proposed that EBMgt faces some unique challenges on the "macro" side of the aisle. An inherent bent toward complex, multi-level and unique problems presents a philosophical challenge and the preponderance of observational studies presents a methodological challenge. Yet, there are compelling reasons that "macro" scholars need to take EBMgt seriously. On the one hand, EBMgt will nurture the establishment of a new model of research that is not only cumulative in its knowledge-building but also promotes engaged scholarship that reduces the unfortunate opposition between rigor and relevance. On the other hand, the uncertainty, conflict and ambiguity that characterize "macro" decision contexts also exacerbate the organizational pathologies that are present across the subfields of management and heighten the need for EBMgt as a countermeasure. Based on the this reasoning, we have put forward a set of recommendations to help scholars advance the EBMgt agenda in strategy and organizational theory.

References

Abbott, A. (2004). *Methods of discovery: Heuristics for the social sciences.* New York: W.W. Norton.

Ackoff, R. L. (1978). *The art of problem solving.* New York: Wiley.

Allison, G. T. (1971). *Essence of decision: Explaining the Cuban missile crisis.* Boston, MA: Little, Brown.

Amabile, T., Patterson, C., Mueller, J., Wojcik, T., Odomirok, P., Marsh, M., et al. (2001). Academic-practitioner collaboration in management research: A case of cross-profession collaboration. *Academy of Management Journal, 44*(2), 418–435.

Aram, J. D., & Salipante, P. F. (2003). Bridging scholarship in management: Epistemological reflections. *British Journal of Management, 14*(3), 189–205.

Argyris, C., & Schön, D. (1978). *Organizational learning: A theory of action perspective.* New York: McGraw-Hill.

Bacharach, S. B. (1989). Organizational theories: Some criteria for evaluation. *Academy of Management Review, 14*(4), 496–515.

Bartunek, J. (2003). A dream for the Academy. *Academy of Management Review, 28*(2), 198–203.

Bartunek, J. M. (2007). Academic-practitioner collaboration need not require joint or relevant research: Towards a relational scholarship of integration. *Academy of Management Journal, 50*(6), 1323–1333.

Bartunek, J. M., & Louis, M. R. (1996). *Insider/outsider team research.* Thousand Oaks, CA: Sage Publications.

Bartunek, J. M., & Rynes, S. L. (2010). The construction and contribution of implications for practice: What's in them and what might they offer? *Academy of Management Learning and Education, 9*(1), 100–117.

Beyer, J. M. (1997). Research utilization: Bridging a cultural gap between communities. *Journal of Management Inquiry, 6*(1), 17–22.

Beyer, J. M., & Trice, H. M. (1982). The utilization process: A conceptual framework and synthesis of empirical findings. *Administrative Science Quarterly, 27*(4), 591–622.

Boyd, B. (1991). Strategic planning and financial performance: A meta-analytic review. *Journal of Management Studies, 28*(4), 353–374.

Boyer, E. L. (1990). *Scholarship reconsidered: Priorities of the professoriate.* San Francisco, CA: Jossey-Bass.

Briner, R. B., Denyer, D., & Rousseau, D. M. (2009). Evidence-based management: Concept cleanup time? *Academy of Management Perspectives, 23*(4), 19–32.

Campbell-Hunt, C. (2000). What have we learned about generic competitive strategy? A meta-analysis. *Strategic Management Journal, 21*(2), 127–154.

Capon, N., Farley, J., & Hoenig, S. (1990). Determinants of financial performance: A meta-analysis. *Management Science, 36*(10), 1143–1159.

Carlile, P. R. (2004). Transferring, translating, and transforming: An integrative framework for managing knowledge across boundaries. *Organization Science, 15*(5), 555–568.

Cascio, W. F. (2007). Evidence-based management and the marketplace for ideas. *Academy of Management Journal, 50*(5), 1009–1012.

Combs, J. G., & Ketchen, D. J. (2003). Why do firms use franchising as an entrepreneurial strategy? A meta-analysis. *Journal of Management, 29*(3), 443–465.

Crook, T. R., Ketchen, D. J., Combs, J. G., & Todd, S. Y. (2008). Strategic resources and performance: A meta-analysis. *Strategic Management Journal, 29*(11), 1141–1154.

Dalton, D. R., Daily, C. M., Certo, S. T., & Roengpitya, R. (2003). Meta-analyses of financial performance and equity: Fusion or confusion? *Academy of Management Journal, 46*(1), 13–26.

Dalton, D. R., Daily, C. M., Johnson, J. L., & Ellstrand, A. E. (1999). Number of directors and financial performance: A meta-analysis. *Academy of Management Journal, 42*(6), 674–686.

Dalton, D. R., & Dalton, C. M. (2005). Strategic management studies are a special case for meta-analysis. *Research Methodology in Strategy and Management, 2*, 31–63.

Damanpour, F. (1991). Organizational innovation: A meta-analysis of effects of determinants and moderators. *Academy of Management Journal, 34*(3), 555–590.

Datta, D. K., & Narayanan, V. (1989). A meta-analytic review of the concentration-performance relationship: Aggregate findings in strategic management. *Journal of Management, 15*(3), 469–483.

Datta, D. K., Pinches, G. E., & Narayanan, V. K. (1992). Factors influencing wealth creation from mergers and acquisitions: A meta-analysis. *Strategic Management Journal, 13*(1), 67–84.

Delbecq, A. L., & Van de Ven, A. H. (1971). A group process model for problem identification and program planning. *Journal of Applied Behavioral Science, 7*(4), 466–492.

Denyer, D., Tranfield, D., & Van Aken, J. E. (2008). Developing design propositions through research synthesis. *Organization Studies, 29*(3), 393–413.

Denzin, N. K. (1978). *The research act: A theoretical introduction to sociological methods.* New York: McGraw-Hill.

Egger. M., Schneider, M., & Smith, G. D. (1998). Spurious precision? Meta-analysis of observational studies. *British Medicine Journal, 316*, 140–144.

Eisenhardt, K. (1989). Building theories from case study research. *Academy of Management Review, 14*(4), 532–550.

Evered, R., & Louis, M. R. (1981). Alternative perspectives in the organizational sciences: Inquiry from the inside and Inquiry from the outside. *Academy of Management Review, 6*(3), 385–395.

Gawande, A. (2009). *The checklist manifesto: How to get things right.* New York: Metropolitan Books.

Geyskens, I., Krishnan, R., Steenkamp, J-B. E. M., & Cunha, P. V. (2009). A review and evaluation of meta-analysis practices in management research. *Journal of Management, 35*(2), 393–419.

Geyskens, I., Steenkamp, J-B. E. M., & Kumar, N. (2006). Make, buy, or ally: A transaction cost theory meta-analysis. *Academy of Management Journal, 49*(3), 519–543.

Gimeno, J., Folta, T. B., Cooper, A. C., & Woo, C. Y. (1997). Survival of the fittest? Entrepreneurial human capital and the persistence of underperforming firms. *Administrative Science Quarterly, 42*(4), 750–783.

Gulati, R. (2007). Tent poles, tribalism, and boundary spanning: The rigor-relevance debate in management research. *Academy of Management Journal, 50*(4), 775–782.

Hambrick, D. C. (1994). What if the Academy really mattered? *Academy of Management Review, 19*(1), 11–16.

Heiman, B., Nickerson, J. A., & Zenger, T. (2008). Governing knowledge creation: A problem finding and problem solving perspective. In N. J. Foss & S. Michailova (Eds.), *Knowledge governance: Processes and perspectives* (pp. 25–47). Oxford, England: Oxford University Press.

Hodgkinson, G. P. (Ed.) (2001). Facing the future: The nature and purpose of management research reassessed. *British Journal of Management, 12,* S1-S80.

Hodgkinson, G. P., & Rousseau, D. M. (2009). Bridging the rigour-relevance gap in management research: It's already happening! *Journal of Management Studies, 46*(3), 534–546.

Huff, A. S. (2000). Changes in organizational knowledge production. *Academy of Management Review, 25*(2), 288–293.

Huff, A., Tranfield, D., & Van Aken, J. E. (2006). Management as a design science mindful of art and surprise. *Journal of Management Inquiry, 15*(4), 413–424.

Hunter, J. E., & Schmidt, F. L. (1990). *Methods of meta-analysis: Correcting error and bias in research findings.* Thousand Oaks, CA: Sage Publications.

Janis, I. L. (1972). *Victims of groupthink: Psychological studies of policy decisions and fiascoes.* New York: Houghton Mifflin.

Jensen, J. L., & Rodgers, R. (2001). Cumulating the intellectual gold of case study research. *Public Administration Review, 61*(2), 235–246.

Jick, T. M. (1979). Mixing qualitative and quantitative methods: Triangulation in action. *Administrative Science Quarterly, 24*(4), 602–611.

Kahnemann, D., Slovic, P., & Tversky, A. (1982). *Judgment under uncertainty: Heuristics and biases.* Cambridge, England: Cambridge University Press.

Kaplan, A. (1964). *The conduct of inquiry: Methodology for the behavioral sciences.* New York: Chandler Publishing.

Kelemen, M., & Bansal, P. (2002). The conventions of management research and their relevance to management practice. *British Journal of Management, 13*(2), 97–108.

Kieser, A., & Leiner, L. (2009). Why the rigour-relevance gap in management research is unbridgeable. *Journal of Management Studies, 46*(3), 516–533.

King, D. R., Dalton, D. R., Daily, C. M., & Covin, J. G. (2004). Meta-analysis of post-acquisition performance: Indicators of unidentified moderators. *Strategic Management Journal, 25*(2), 187–200.

Kor, Y. Y., & Mahoney, J. T. (2000). Penrose's resource-based approach: The process and product of research creativity. *Journal of Management Studies, 37*(1), 109–139.

Ladd, G. W. (1987). *Imagination in research.* Ames, IA: Iowa State University Press.

Latham, G. (2007). A speculative perspective on the transfer of behavioral science findings to the workplace: The times they are a changin. *Academy of Management Journal, 50*(5), 1027–1032.

Lawrence, P. R. (1992). The challenge of problem-oriented research. *Journal of Management Inquiry, 1*(2), 139–142.

Lee, D., & Madhavan, R. (2010). Divestiture and firm performance: A meta-analysis. *Journal of Management, 36*(6), 1345–1371.

Lewin, K. (1951). *Field theory in social science.* Oxford, England: Harpers.

Louis, M. R., & Bartunek, J. M. (1992). Insider/outsider research teams: Collaboration across diverse perspectives. *Journal of Management Inquiry, 1*(2), 101–110.

Mahoney, J. T. (1993). Strategic management and determinism: Sustaining the conversation. *Journal of Management Studies, 30*(1), 173–191.

Mahoney, J. T. (2005). *Economic foundations of strategy.* Thousand Oaks, CA: Sage Publications.

Mahoney, J. T., & McGahan, A. M. (2007). The field of strategic management within the evolving science of strategic organization. *Strategic Organization, 5*(1), 79–99.

Mahoney, J. T., & Sanchez, R. (2004). Building management theory by integrating processes and products of thought. *Journal of Management Inquiry, 13*(1), 34–47.

March, J. G. (1999). *The pursuit of organizational intelligence.* Malden, MA: Basil Blackwell.

March, J. G., Sproull, S., & Tamuz, M. (1991). Learning from samples of one or fewer. *Organization Science, 2*(1), 1–13.

Markides, C. (2007). In search of ambidextrous professors. *Academy of Management Journal, 50*(4), 762–768.

McGahan, A. M. (2007). Academic research that matters to managers: On zebras, dogs, lemmings, hammers and turnips. *Academy of Management Journal, 44*(2), 357–375.

Miller, C. C., & Cardinal, L. (1994). Strategic planning and firm performance: A synthesis of more than two decades of research. *Academy of Management Journal, 37*(6), 1649–1666.

Miller, C. C., Glick, W. H., Wang, Y.-D., & Huber, G. P. (1991). Understanding technology-structure relationships: Theory development and meta-analytic theory testing. *Academy of Management Journal, 34*(2), 436–448.

Mohrman, S., Gibson, C., & Mohrman, A. (2001). Doing research that is useful to practice: A model and empirical exploration. *Academy of Management Journal, 44*(2), 357–375.

Morrell, K. (2008). The narrative of evidence-based management: A polemic. *Journal of Management Studies, 45*(3), 613–635.

Nickerson, J. A., & Zenger, T. R. (2004). A knowledge-based theory of the firm—The problem-solving perspective. *Organization Science, 15*(6), 617–632.

Noblit, G. W., & Hare, R. D. (1988). *Meta-ethnography: Synthesizing qualitative studies.* Thousand Oaks, CA: Sage Publications.

Nonaka, I. (1994). A dynamic theory of organizational knowledge creation. *Organization Science, 5*(1), 14–37.

Ouchi, W. (2003). *Making schools work: A revolutionary plan to get your children the education they need.* New York: Simon Schuster.

Palich, L. E., Cardinal, L. B., & Miller, C. C. (2000). Curvilinearity in the diversification-performance linkage: An examination of over three decades of research. *Strategic Management Journal, 21*(2), 155–174.

Patterson, B. L., Thorne, S. E., Canam, C., & Jillings, C. (2001). *Meta-study of qualitative health research: A practical guide to meta-analysis and meta-synthesis.* Thousand Oaks, CA: Sage Publications.

Pearce, J. L. (2004). What do we know and how do we know it? *Academy of Management Review, 29*(2), 175–179.

Pfeffer, J., & Sutton, R. I. (2006). *Hard facts: Dangerous half-truths & total nonsense.* Boston, MA: Harvard Business School Press.

Polanyi, M. (1962). *Personal knowledge.* Chicago, IL: University of Chicago Press.

Polya, G. (1957). *How to solve it: A new aspect of mathematical method.* Garden City, NY: Doubleday.

Rhoades, D. L., Rechner, P. L., & Sundaramurthy, C. (2000). Board composition and financial performance: A meta-analysis of the influence of outside directors. *Journal of Managerial Issues, 12*(1), 76–92.

Roethlisberger, F., & Dickson, W. J. (1939) *Management and the worker.* Cambridge, MA.: Harvard University Press.

Romme, A. G. L. (2003). Making a difference: Organization as design. *Organization Science, 14*(5), 558–573.

Romme, A. G. L., & Endenburg, E. (2006). Construction principles and design rules in the case of circular design. *Organization Science, 17*(1), 287–297.

Rousseau, D. M. (2006). Is there such a thing as evidence-based management? *Academy of Management Review, 31*(2), 256–269.

Rousseau, D. M. (2007). A sticky, leveraging, and scalable strategy for high-quality connections between organizational practice and science. *Academy of Management Journal, 50*(5), 1037–1042.

Rousseau, D. M., Manning, J., & Denyer, D. (2008). Evidence in management and organizational science: Assembling the field's full weight of scientific knowledge through syntheses. *The Academy of Management Annals, 2*, 475–515.

Rousseau, D. M., & McCarthy, S. (2007). Educating managers from an evidence-based perspective. *Academy of Management Learning and Education, 6*(1), 84–101.

Rynes, S. L., Bartunek, J., & Daft, R. L. (2001). Across the great divide: Knowledge creation and transfer between practitioners and academics. *Academy of Management Journal, 44*(2), 340–356.

Rynes, S. L., Giluk, T. L., & Brown, K. G. (2007). The very separate worlds of academic and practitioner periodicals in human resource management: Implications for evidence-based management. *Academy of Management Journal, 50*(5), 987–1008.

Schön, D. A. (1983). *The reflective practitioner.* New York: Basic Books.

Shapiro, D. L., Kirkman, B. L., & Courtney, H. G. (2007). Perceived causes and solutions of the translation problem in management research. *Academy of Management Journal, 50*(2), 249–266.

Simon, H. A. (1976). *Administrative behavior: A study of decision-making processes in administrative organization* (pp. 335–356). New York: Free Press.

Simon, H. A. (1978). Rationality as process and as product of thought. *American Economic Review, 68*, 1–16.

Simon, H. A. (1996). *The sciences of the artificial* (3rd ed.). Cambridge, MA: MIT Press.

Stokes, D. E. (1997). *Pasteur's quadrant: Basic science and technological innovation.* Washington, DC: Brookings Institution Press.

Tranfield, D., Denyer, D., & Smart, P. (2003). Toward a methodology for developing evidence-informed management knowledge by means of systematic review. *British Journal of Management, 14*(3), 207–222.

Tranfield, D., & Starkey, K. (1998). The nature, social organization and promotion of management research: Towards policy. *British Journal of Management, 9*(4), 341–353.

Tushman, M., & O'Reilly, C. (2007). Research and relevance: Implications of Pasteur's quadrant for doctoral programs and faculty development. *Academy of Management Journal, 50*(4), 769–774.

Van Aken, J. E. (2004). Management research based on the paradigm of the design sciences: The quest for field-tested and grounded technological rules. *Journal of Management Studies, 41*(2), 219–246.

Van Aken, J. E. (2005). Management research as a design science: Articulating the research products of mode 2 knowledge production in management. *British Journal of Management, 16*(1), 19–36.

Van de Ven, A. (2002). Strategic directions for the Academy of Management: This Academy is for you! *Academy of Management, 27*(2), 171–184.

Van de Ven, A. (2007). *Engaged scholarship: A guide for organizational and social research.* New York: Oxford University Press.

Van de Ven, A., & Johnson, P. (2006). Knowledge for science and practice. *Academy of Management Review, 31*(4), 802–821.

Van der Werf, P. A., & Mahon, J. F. (1997). Meta-analysis of the impact of research methods on findings of first-mover advantage. *Management Science, 43*(11), 1510–1519.

Vermeulen, F. (2005). On rigor and relevance: Fostering dialectical progress in management research. *Academy of Management Journal, 48*, 978–982.

Vermeulen, F. (2007). I shall not remain insignificant: Adding a second loop to matter more. *Academy of Management Journal, 50*(4), 754–761.

Volkema, R. J. (1983). Problem formulation in planning and design. *Management Science, 29*(6), 639–652.

Weick, K. E. (2001). Gapping the relevance bridge: Fashions meet fundamentals in management research. *British Journal of Management, 12(Special issue)*, S71-S75.

Whetten, D. (1989). What constitutes a theoretical contribution? *Academy of Management Review, 14*(4), 490–495.

Whitley, R. (1984). The scientific status of management research as a practically-oriented social science. *Journal of Management Studies, 21*(4), 369–390.

Zhao, S. (1991). Meta-theory, meta-method, meta-data analysis. What, why, and how? *Sociological Perspectives, 34*(3), 377–390.

Evidence-Based Entrepreneurship (EBE): A Systematic Approach to Cumulative Science

Michael Frese, Andreas Bausch, Peter Schmidt, Andreas Rauch *and* Rüdiger Kabst

Abstract

The concept and aim of an evidence-based entrepreneurship (EBE) is discussed as a strategy to overcome the divide between knowledge developed in the field of entrepreneurship and its use in practice. Evidence constitutes the best summary of knowledge based on several sources of information (several studies, several different research groups, several different methodological approaches, among them the best methods available), all of which go beyond individual experience and isolated studies. We argue that meta-analyses can and should be used in entrepreneurship research (and that it should also be used for qualitative work). Meta-analyses establish certain relationships; these should then be summarized in well-founded models and theories that can be translated into action principles. These action principles can then be used by EBE's constituents. These include scientists, professionals who regularly deal with entrepreneurs (bankers, consultants, venture capital providers), policy makers (e.g., government), students of entrepreneurship, and, last but not least, the entrepreneurs themselves. Once, a set of action principles have been developed from science, the application of them can be tested with the help of further evidence on the efficacy of interventions (including meta-analyses on the interventions). Evidence-based entrepreneurship (EBE) has the potential to change research, teaching, and practice.

Key Words: evidence-based entrepreneurship, entrepreneurs, systematic review, meta-analysis, action plans, training

The ideas of economists and political philosophers, both when they are right and when they are wrong are more powerful than is commonly understood... Indeed the world is run by little else. Practical men, who believe themselves to be quite exempt from any intellectual influences are usually the slaves of some defunct economist....
It is ideas, not vested interests, which are dangerous for good or evil.
—*(Keynes, 1953), p. 306)*

As Keynes acknowledged, we assume that scientific knowledge often gets translated into practice

This article is a shortened version of an article by the same authors (2012). Evidence-based Entrepreneurship (EBE): Cumulative science, action principles, and bridging the gap between science and practice. *Foundations and Trends in Entrepreneurship, 8,* 1–62. By permission of *Foundations and Trends in Entrepreneurship*

without the practitioners even noticing their dependency on those ideas. The tasks of science are to generate new knowledge, to answer essential questions, and to develop a good knowledge base that can make practice more effective and efficient and that protects practice from making wrong decisions. To accomplish these tasks, science typically produces scientific models and theories to integrate knowledge, conducts empirical studies, and reports incremental new knowledge. To help these tasks, science provides literature reviews on the current state of scientific knowledge and on the scientific knowledge of the efficacy of interventions. In short, the function of science is to produce evidence for propositions and to integrate this evidence into some kind of systematic theory or model. An important function of science is to support practice in becoming more effective and efficient. To do this, it needs to develop good methods of summarizing the current knowledge and to let develop from this knowledge prototypical interventions; these interventions should be derived from the most current scientific knowledge and should be more effective than traditional interventions. Practically useful knowledge needs to be accessible and must be based on the best summary of available knowledge in the field.

In this article, we would like to introduce the concept of EBE, discuss the implications of EBE, and sketch out the opportunities and limitations connected to EBE. Who should be users of EBE? At the least, these are users of EBE: the scientists themselves, professionals who deal with entrepreneur, policy makers, students of entrepreneurship, and, last but not least, the entrepreneurs themselves.

If the development of evidence is the function of science, why should we talk about EBE? As a first definition, evidence is the best summary of knowledge based on several sources of information (several studies, several different research groups, several different methodological approaches, among them the best methods available), which clearly goes beyond individual experience and a few isolated studies. What is the difference between what entrepreneurship science has been doing all along and what constitutes EBE? We argue that evidence-based science and evidence-informed practice is the next logical step of developing science and is, indeed, appreciably different from what science and practice has been doing up to this point. The field of entrepreneurship can be advanced if it uses examples from evidence-based approaches found in the fields of medicine and work and organizational psychology. We are optimistic that it is possible to achieve the ideal of science-informed practice and a scientific approach that provides the best evidence for practitioners and policy makers. Thus, we want to argue that scientific suggestions for practice should be evidence-informed. To do this, the field of EBE needs to be developed. This evidence can then be used to inform practice. Practice can never be fully based on evidence; therefore, we talk about evidence-*informed* practice and evidence-*based* research suggestions. We think that EBE provides a great opportunity that is both relevant for practice and policy while strengthening the empirical and theoretical bases of entrepreneurship research (Rauch & Frese, 2006).

Scientists can use EBE by targeting new research in a much more precise way. A good summary of the literature in the sense of a meta-analysis, provides clear knowledge on what is known, but also what is not known. One frequent result of meta-analyses is, for example, that the results are heterogeneous and that it is, therefore, useful to search for moderators. Also, it can be established from meta-analyses that a relationship is strong, but often the mediation processes are still unknown. Moreover, there are often gaps in the literature that are shown as a result of meta-analyses. Finally, meta-analyses may show that some relationships are more important than others—this may imply that theories have to cope with this information and incorporate the size of relationship into their theories. All this information is useful for scientists to develop new studies and theories. Moreover, science will profit from EBE by encouraging scientists to do more theory-based interventions and to evaluate them in a meaningful way.

By developing EBE, we also heed recent calls in general management to advance evidence-based management (Pfeffer & Sutton, 2006; Rousseau, 2006; Rynes, Giluk, & Brown, 2007; Tranfield, Denyer, & Smart, 2003) and we think of EBE as one part of this emergent development. Both management and entrepreneurship show a gap between knowledge and practice—the knowledge-doing gap (Pfeffer & Sutton, 2000). Managers as well as entrepreneurs or professionals who deal with entrepreneurs (such as bank employees, business angels, analysts, policy makers, etc.) do not routinely take note of scientific evidence when making decisions and acting on them. Empirical research has shown that managers often take actions that are uninformed and sometimes even diametrically opposed to empirical evidence (Rynes et al., 2007). In the area of entrepreneurship, one can often hear open disdain for scholarly work because professors have not yet "made their first million"—the foremost argument seems to be that only experience counts. We suggest that professionals who deal with entrepreneurs can profit from evidence-informed practice. Venture capitalists who often work with models developed from their individual and idiosyncratic experiences as a base for their funding decisions; meta-analyses show that the efficacy of selection of good entrepreneurs of venture capital providers is often negligible outside the knowledge on general industry effects (Rosenbusch, Brinckmann, & Mueller, 2012 in press). This knowledge may encourage venture capital firms to develop new procedures and experiment with them (and evaluate their own experiments).

Institutions that are supposed to support entrepreneurship often develop policies that have not been adequately empirically tested. For example, the German government spent millions of euros in East Germany to develop networks for small businesses. This was done as a result of a few studies showing a relationship between social network size and entrepreneurial success. However, the studies did not examine whether networks were useful for only those businesses that had actively developed their own networks themselves. In these cases, an active approach with high initiative was the variable that causes network size and success (Frese, 2009; Zhao, Frese, & Giardini, 2010). These studies also did not examine the reverse causality hypothesis: maybe business social networks are not the cause of business success but, instead, they are the results of business success (successful businesses rise in attractiveness and are, therefore, in more networks or more central in networks). Moreover, the intervention itself was not rigorously evaluated. This is not an isolated example. Many countries invest many millions of dollars into programs for their small business owners. Most of them do not develop evidence on whether these programs (or part of them) are successful.

Similarly, textbooks do not teach EBE. For example, a cursory look at popular textbooks of entrepreneurship (of the years 2007–2011) shows that none of the ones we examined even mentioned meta-analyses in their index. This is not surprising because there are very few meta-analyses, despite calls for these analyses in the area (Rauch & Frese, 2006) (a simple search for entrepreneurship and meta-analysis in *Business Source Premier* produced a number of published or in-press meta-analyses, cf. Table 6.1; more on this later). Often meta-analyses have direct effects on how students are educated. For example, there has been a debate about whether business plans really are useful. Meta-analyses have settled this matter—the evidence is clear that business plans can be useful (Brinckmann, Grichnik, & Kapsa, 2010; Schwenk & Shrader, 1993). However, the relationship between doing formal business plans and success is highly variable. Thus, there are clearly moderators in this relationship. Thus, students (and educators) should be encouraged to experiment with how to teach business plans and how to do business plans, and they should evaluate these experiments. Moreover, there may be some plans that have negative consequences. Again, students need to know that and be allowed to experiment on these but with the general knowledge that, by and large, it is more successful to have a business plan available when starting a business.

Entrepreneurs are the prime targets of EBE: They should know what works and what does not on average. For example, they should know that innovativeness does carry positive results and that these results are larger for new firms and not so important for older firms (Rosenbusch, Brinckmann, & Bausch, 2011). However, they should also know that there are many exceptions to this rule (in other words, these correlations are heterogeneous) and that innovativeness is not the most important predictor of growth and income—for example, the overall stance of entrepreneurial orientation (which includes the attempt to be innovative) may be more important (particularly for young and small enterprises) (Rauch, Wiklund, Lumpkin, & Frese, 2009).

It is surprising how often recommendations, suggestions, curricula, and policies are developed without recourse to rigorous objective studies and meta-analyses. Most of the recommendations in entrepreneurship are either based on individual studies (often completed by the person recommending the policy) or they are based on so-called narrative reviews—reviews that present the considered opinion of somebody who has studied the literature. The narrative reviews often draw conflicting conclusions about the evidence, making it difficult for practitioners to rely on scientific evidence.

Providing Sufficient Scientific Evidence for Practice

We shall first discuss the usefulness of meta-analyses, then the development of interventions and the rigorous testing of them. We shall also acknowledge the constraints of evidence-informed practice. Recently, the first author of this chapter went to a physician for a painful knee condition. The physician prescribed some medicine that, he said, according to his experience had helped well; when the first author looked up the medicine in the abstracts of the Cochrane Foundation, he found that this drug had been shown not to be efficacious and he threw it away (by the way the drug was also shown not to have any negative side effects—thus, the physician may have been right in giving it to patients as a placebo—but more likely than not, the physician did not know that it worked only as well as a placebo). This incident provides a good example of how customers of professionals can use information that is accessible and that constitutes the best summary of current knowledge in a field. The publicly accessible abstracts of quantitative reviews on the Cochrane web site provide the best available evidence at any

Table 6.1. Meta-Analyses in Entrepreneurship Research

References	Meta-Analysis or Systematic Review	Content
Mwasalwiba, E. S. (2010). Entrepreneurship education: A review of its objectives, teaching methods, and impact indicators. *Education & Training, 52,* 20–47.	Systematic review, vote counting	$K = 108$, semi-systematic literature review. The study addresses educational objectives, target audience, teaching methods, and impact indicators.
Henrekson, M., & Johansson, D. (2010). Gazelles as job creators: a survey and interpretation of the evidence. *Small Business Economics, 35*(2), 227–244.	Systematic review, vote counting	$K = 20$, semi-systematic literature review; although different definitions of gazelles exist, segments of all industries have fast growing firms that are usually young.
Westlund, H., & Adam, F. (2010). Social capital and economic performance: A meta-analysis of 65 studies. *European Planning Studies, 18*(6), 893–919.	Systematic review, vote counting	$K = 65$; study investigates relationship between social capital and economic performance for different levels; on firm level (including households) strong evidence for positive relationship, contradictory results of studies on national and regional levels; results based on narrative review and vote counting only.
Rauch, A., Wiklund, J., Lumpkin, G. T., & Frese, M. (2009). Entrepreneurial Orientation and Business Performance: An Assessment of Past Research and Suggestions for the Future. *Entrepreneurship: Theory & Practice, 33*(3), 761–787.	Meta-analysis	$K = 53$ samples, overall relationship between entrepreneurial orientation and performance $r_c = 242$. Effect sizes are highest for micro businesses and for high tech businesses. Additional moderators are suggested.
Stewart, W. H., & Roth, P. L. (2001). Risk propensity differences between entrepreneurs and managers: A meta-analytic review. *Journal of Applied Psychology, 86,* 145–153.	Meta-analysis	$K = 14$ samples, the difference between managers and entrepreneurs is $d_c = .36$. Moderators identified include type of entrepreneur and type of risk assessment.
Miner, J. B., & Raju, N. S. (2004). Risk Propensity Differences Between Managers and Entrepreneurs and Between Low- and High-Growth Entrepreneurs: A Reply in a More Conservative Vein. *Journal of Applied Psychology, 89*(1), 3–13.	Meta-analysis	$K = 28$ studies, $d = .12$, ns. This article opened a meta-analytical dispute with Stewart & Roth (2001/2004) about the risk propensity differences between entrepreneurs and managers.
Stewart, W. H., & Roth, P. L. (2004). Data quality affects meta-analytic conclusions: A response to Miner and Raju (2004) concerning entrepreneurial risk propensity. *Journal of Applied Psychology, 89,* 14–21.	Meta-analysis	This study is a response to Miner & Raju (2004). The combined results of $K = 18$ samples revealed an effect size of $d_c = 0.23$. Notably, projective measures of risk-taking produced negative effects, while objective instruments produced positive effects.
Collins, C. J., Hanges, P. J., & Locke, E. A. (2004). The relationship of achievement motivation to entrepreneurial behavior: A meta-analysis. *Human Performance, 17*(1), 95–117.	Meta-Analysis	$K = 41$, need for achievement correlated with career choice $r = 21$ and performance $r = 0.31$.

(Continued)

Table 6.1. Continued

References	Meta-Analysis or Systematic Review	Content
Stewart, W. H., & Roth, P. L. (2007). A meta-analysis of achievement motivation differences between entrepreneurs and managers. *Journal of Small Business Management, 45*(4), 401–421.	Meta-Analysis	$K = 17$, analysis indicates that entrepreneurs are higher in achievement motivation than are managers; differences are influenced by the entrepreneur's venture goals, by the use of U.S. or foreign samples, and, to a less clear extent, by projective or objective instrumentation; when analysis is restricted to venture founders, difference between entrepreneurs and managers on achievement motivation is substantially larger.
Zhao, H., & Seibert, S. E. (2006). The Big Five Personality Dimensions and Entrepreneurial Status: A Meta-Analytical Review. *Journal of Applied Psychology, 91*(2), 259–271.	Meta-analysis	$K = 23$, classified studies along the Big Five Personality traits. Effect sizes ranged from $d_c = 45$ (conscientiousness) to $d_c = -.37$ (neuroticism). Some facets of the Big Five Traits produced higher effect sizes (achievement).
Rauch, A., & Frese, M. (2007). Let's put the person back into entrepreneurship research: A meta-analysis on the relationship between business owners' personality traits, business creation, and success. *European Journal of Work & Organizational Psychology, 16*(4), 353–385.	Meta-analysis	$K = 62$ for business creation and $K = 54$ for business success. Effect sizes were stronger for traits matched to the tasks of entrepreneurs (e.g., $r_c = .238$ for matched traits and business success and $r_c = .027$ for nonmatched traits). The traits matched to entrepreneurship correlated well with entrepreneurial behavior (business creation, business success), such as need for achievement, generalized self-efficacy, innovativeness, stress tolerance, need for autonomy, and proactive personality.
Zhao, H., Seibert, S. E., & Lumpkin, G. T. (2010). The Relationship of Personality to Entrepreneurial Intentions and Performance: A Meta-Analytic Review. *Journal of Management, 36*(2), 381–404.	Meta-analysis	$K = 66$; discusses intention to entrepreneurship and performance of entrepreneurial unit; some overlap with Rauch & Frese, 2007; however, constructs are coded as to where they would fall to the Big Five Factors.
Schwenk, C. B., & Shrader, C. B. (1993). Effects of Formal Strategic Planning on Financial Performance in Small Firms: A Meta-Analysis. *Entrepreneurship: Theory & Practice, 17*(3), 53–64.	Meta-analysis	$K = 14$, strategic planning correlates positively with growth and return, $d = .20$. Further, the results indicate the presence of moderators. However, the authors did not attempt to identify such moderator variables.
Combs, J. G., & Ketchen Jr., D. J. (2003). Why do firms use franchising as an entrepreneurial strategy?: A meta-analysis. *Journal of Management, 29*(3), 443–465.	Meta-analysis unclear how large SMEs or entrepreneurial companies	$K = 44$, 10 hypotheses, general support for agency theory; no relationship between franchising and growth; no relationship between resource scarcity and franchising.

Reference	Method	Results
Song, M., Podoynitsyna, K., van der Bij, H., & Halman, J. I. M. (2008). Success factors in new ventures: A meta-analysis. *Journal of Product Innovation Management, 25*(1), 7–27.	Meta-analysis New technology ventures	$K = 31$, 4 years survival rate: 36%; frequently factor meta-analyses are based on very few studies and therefore, confidence interval includes 0; clearest positive results for market scope, financial resources, firm age, patent protection, size of founding team, supply chain partnering ($k<5$ results not listed here).
Crook, T. R., Ketchen, D. J., Combs, J. G., & Todd, P. M. (2008). Strategic resources and performance: A meta-analysis. *Strategic Management Journal, 29*, 1141–1154.	Meta-analysis unclear how large SMEs or entrepreneurial companies	$K = 125$, Overall for resources with firm performance $r_c = 0.22$; human resources rc = 0.30, tangible resources rc = 0.08, and intangible resources $r_c = 0.24$.
Rosenbusch, N., Brinckmann, J., & Mueller, V. (2010). *Does Acquiring Venture Capital Pay Off for the Funded Firms? A Meta-Analysis on the Relationship between Venture Capital Investment and Funded Firm Financial Performance.* Paper presented at the Babson, Lauzanne.	Meta-analysis	$K = 65$, overall a very low but significant correlation of $r_c = 0.075$ of VC money in the firm vs. not and returns for these companies; when industry is controlled, this correlation becomes 0 which means that VC firms are not able to predict returns for the firms but are able to predict industry returns
Rosenbusch, N., Brinckmann, J., & Bausch, A. (2011). Is innovation always beneficial? A meta-analysis of the relationship between innovation and performance in SMEs. *Journal of Business Venturing.*	Meta-analysis	$K = 42$, innovation has a positive effect on the performance of SMEs ($r = 0.13$); innovation-performance relationship positively influenced for new ventures (compared to mature firms) and cultures with low/medium individualism; for both moderators credibility interval does not include zero. Further moderators are related to type and measurement of innovation: internal/external, innovation process input/innovation process output.
Unger, J. M., Rauch, A., Frese, M., & Rosenbusch, N. (2011). Human capital and entrepreneurial success: A meta-analytic review. *Journal of Business Venturing.*	Meta-analysis	$K = 70$, overall relationship between human capital and success $r_c = 0.098$. Effect sizes were higher for human capital outcomes, for task related human capital, for young businesses.
van der Sluis, J., van Praag, M., & Vijverberg, W. (2005). Entrepreneurship Selection and Performance: A Meta-Analysis of the Impact of Education in Developing Economies. *World Bank Economic Review, 19*(2), 225–261.	Meta-analysis Unusual methods used, combining vote counting with regression-analysis	$K = 203$; results cannot be compared to the usually used corrected correlations. One year additional education in developing countries increases enterprise income by 5.5%.

(Continued)

Table 6.1. Continued

References	Meta-Analysis or Systematic Review	Content
Read, S., Song, M., & Smit, W. (2009). A meta-analytic review of effectuation and venture performance. *Journal of Business Venturing, 24*(6), 573–587.	Meta-analysis, search restricted to *JBV* 1985–2007	Tests four predictions of effectuation. Means based, better resources lead to better outcomes (tested in what I know, who I am, whom I know) with effect sizes of $r_c = .11$ ($k = 24$) to 0.23 ($k = 10$); partnership: $r_c = 0.17$ ($k = 14$); affordable loss: nonsignificant; leverage contingency $r_c = 0.07$ ($k = 5$).
Boyd, B. K. (1991). Strategic planning and financial performance: A meta-analytic review. *Journal of Management Studies, 28*(4), 353–374.	Meta-analysis	$K = 29$; moderate correlations between planning and nine performance measures; the overall effect of planning on performance is $r = 0.151$; largest effect sizes are produced for earnings per share growth ($r = 0.282$) and sales growth ($r = 0.246$); smaller effect sizes are found for return on investment ($r = 0.105$) and return on equity ($r = 0.081$); growth measures revealed very wide ranges of estimates across studies, profitability measures generally yielded smaller, but more consistent effect size measures.
Miller, C. C., & Cardinal, L. B. (1994). Strategic planning and firm performance: A synthesis of more than two decades of research. *Academy of Management Journal, 37*(6), 1649–1665.	Meta-analysis	$K = 26$; planning positively related to growth ($r = 0.17$) and profitability ($r = 0.12$); results suggest that methods factors are primarily responsible for the inconsistent planning-performance findings reported in the literature.
Brinckmann, J., Grichnik, D., & Kapsa, D. (2010). Should entrepreneurs plan or just storm the castle? A meta-analysis on contextual factors impacting the business planning–performance relationship in small firms. *Journal of Business Venturing, 25*, 24–40.	Meta-analysis	$K = 51$. Average $d_c = 0.20$ between business planning and firm performance; moderator analyses show that established firms have higher effect sizes $d_c = 0.24$ ($k = 36$) than new firms $d_c = 0.13$ ($k = 15$); there is no difference in effect sizes between business planning outcome (having a business plan) and business planning process (doing planning along the way).
Daily, C. M., Certo, S. T., Dalton, D. R., & Roengpitya, R. (2003). IPO underpricing: A meta-analysis and research synthesis. *Entrepreneurship: Theory & Practice, 27*(3), 271–295.	Meta-analysis; however, strategy of selecting articles not described and unclear whether and how independence of samples was assured	$K = 241$. Average $r_c = 0.022$ with a high variance; this means that direct relationships of various predictors of underpricing of IPOs are zero. (e.g., risk factors and underpricing or prestige of underwriter and underpricing).

point in time. The Cochrane web site displays several thousand systematic reviews (most of them meta-analyses) in medicine. In addition, there are several thousand more meta-analyses in other medical literature. Furthermore, there is also a social science web site that is similar to the Cochrane Collaboration, but the Campbell Collaboration web site is unfortunately not as prolific as the Cochrane Collaboration's.

Evidence-based medicine—defined as "the process of systematically finding, appraising, and using contemporaneous research findings as the basis for clinical decisions" (Rosenberg & Donald, 1995, p. 1122)—has quickly developed into an accepted approach to practice in medicine. Similarly, clinical psychology, criminology, nursing, education, and work and organizational psychology have started to use meta-analyses to answer important questions of theory and practice.

The Usefulness of Meta-Analyses and Systematic Reviews

Meta-analyses (which are quantitative systematic reviews) can be compared to the other major approaches for accumulating knowledge—the narrative review. The scientific field of entrepreneurship tends to produce many narrative reviews with its accompanying problems: The psychology of decision making has shown conclusively that non-quantitative judgment (also often called clinical judgment) is inferior to statistical decision making (regression analysis based decision making) (Grove & Meehl, 1996). This is also the case when we summarize the literature. Narrative literature reviews put together the literature in an unsystematic and often biased way (e.g., emphasizing certain journals or even restricting the search to only some journals and not starting out the literature search in a systematic fashion without a handbook of which search terms to use). After the articles are assembled for the review, the summarizing of the literature may also be influenced by stereotypes and biases because of our cognitive and emotional constraints (Hunter & Schmidt, 2004). Memory load is very high when summarizing a voluminous literature. We need strategies to reduce memory load. Scholars tend to evaluate some studies as better than others and this influences their thinking about the whole body of the literature. Also, reviewers of the literature have theoretical preferences for certain studies, study designs, choice of operationalization, and so forth (often colored by their own studies, their own experiences, and their professional background).

This leads to highly conflicting conclusions of the literature, making it difficult for practitioners to rely on scientific evidence. (Note that meta-analyses can also come to different conclusions; however, because every step of the meta-analysis can be reproduced, these differences can often be resolved (examples include: Judge, Thoresen, Bono, & Patton, 2001; Stewart & Roth, 2004).

The defense of narrative reviews often centers on the importance of one or a few particularly good studies—after all, should we not be influenced by just the very best studies and leave others aside? However, any one study invariably has limitations. There is simply no perfect study (Hunter & Schmidt, 2004, p.17), because every study has its own sampling error (random deviations from the true value of the population); error of measurement (both objective and subjective measures include errors); and deviation from high validity, internal validity problems, or range restriction, and issues of generalization (Scherpenzeel & Saris, 1997). All these factors make it unlikely that any one study can overcome all the potential problems. Thus, researchers need to include all studies into a meaningful summary of the literature, and they should correct for systematic problems inherent in the studies. Thus, good evidence implies that we need to look at the convergence of knowledge from several studies (and preferably from *all* studies done). The overall set of studies tends to cancel out the weaknesses of each individual study. In other words, the whole set of empirical findings has a higher likelihood to identify the true effect than any single study. Any given set of studies will show an approximation to a normal curve around a mean of correlations.

As an alternative form to the narrative reviews, reviewers developed systematic reviews without a meta-analysis in which the number of significant results was counted (so-called vote counting). These are clearly useful because they are careful to base conclusions on several studies, and they also approach the selection of the reviewed studies systematically without leaving out studies that need to be included; inclusion criteria on eligibility and relevance of articles are developed before the start of the literature search. Unfortunately vote counting often leads to the conclusion that many studies did not show significant effects. Most researchers are constrained by lack of time and resources and, therefore, have to rely on small samples. Of course, the significance test is influenced by statistical power, which depends on sample size. Therefore, a high number of nonsignificant findings may be an artifact of the low sample size of these studies. Power is usually not configured into the mental formula that narrative reviews use. We suggest, with others (Combs, Ketchen, Crook, & Roth, 2011; Rynes et al., 2007), that these problems should be dealt with by using meta-analyses (which should always include a systematic search for articles). Meta-analyses provide a good summary of several studies because they reduce these biases (Hunter & Schmidt, 2004; Rauch & Frese, 2006).

An Example: Meta-Analyses and Narrative Reviews in the Area of Personality and Entrepreneurship

In the area of personality and entrepreneurship, narrative reviews have concluded from the literature that personality effects are unimportant for starting a firm and for the success of entrepreneurs (Aldrich & Widenmayer, 1993). Gartner (1989, p. 48) concluded from such a narrative review: "I believe that a focus on the traits and personality characteristics of entrepreneurs will never lead us to a definition of the entrepreneur nor help us to understand the phenomenon of entrepreneurship." Gartner's hypothesis can be examined by meta-analysis. First, the meta-analysis would have to establish if there is correlation between personality and entrepreneurship at all; entrepreneurship would be defined by whether people start a company (e.g., comparing managers with owners of start-up firms) and whether personality is related to entrepreneurial success. Most likely, the overall correlation between personality and entrepreneurship is small because some personality traits are related to entrepreneurship and some others not. Moreover, different studies probably produce different results; thus, heterogeneity of the correlations is high (and, therefore, moderators should be examined). Meta-analysis has indeed, shown that there are some sizeable correlations but that other correlations with personality are low (Rauch & Frese, 2007; Zhao & Seibert, 2006). This seems to corroborate the conclusion that it does not pay off to search for personality factors. However, once one examines potential moderators, the results turn out to be very different. One obvious moderator from personality theory (Tett & Guterman, 2000) is whether a personality factor matches the tasks of the entrepreneur. Once this differentiation is made, the results are eye-opening: we asked experts in the field of entrepreneurship which personality factors are matched to the tasks of entrepreneurs and which ones are not. For example, traits like generalized self-efficacy, need for achievement,

and proactive personality are matched to the tasks of entrepreneurs, whereas traits such as dogmatism, shyness, and rigidity were not matched with entrepreneurship. When matching to entrepreneurial tasks is used as a moderator in the meta-analysis, the results become quite clear: those traits not matched show a low correlation to business creation and business success, whereas personality factors that are matched to entrepreneurship produce a sizeable correlation with business creation and business success (Rauch & Frese, 2007). If we look at the most clearly matched traits—need for achievement, proactive personality, and generalized self-efficacy, the correlations are much higher and reach correlations of 0.23 (need for achievement and business success) and even 0.34 (generalized self-efficacy and business creation) (Rauch & Frese, 2007). When need of achievement is further differentiated into cultures with high-performance orientation and those with low-performance orientation, there is a high correlation of need for achievement with starting a company (Zhao & Seibert, 2006).

Thus, entrepreneurs are higher in need for achievement, innovativeness, and internal locus of control compared to other populations (Collins et al., 2004; Rauch & Frese, 2007). These personality traits are additionally related to business success. Thus, the empirical evidence reviewed in this chapter leads to the conclusion that all those who have called for the end of doing research on personality traits because of lack of important relationships with entrepreneurship were clearly wrong. Why have narrative reviews been so wrong? The answer is that there simply is a lot of distracting "noise" in the data: Some relationships are, indeed, very small—for example, the relationship of risk taking with both business creation and success or the relationship between business creation and broad personality measures. More importantly, whenever scientists throw all sorts of personality variables and all sorts of dependent variables into a correlation matrix, the correlations appear to be quite small. Moreover, there are large variations in the size of the reported relationships and many studies are based on small samples. All this made it difficult to detect the true relationships. It should be added that comparing the results of the meta-analysis on personality and entrepreneurship with, for example, medical meta-analyses shows personality to have comparably high predictive validity. The correlations between need for achievement or generalized self-efficacy and business success is similar to the relationship of taking sleeping pills and temporary relief of insomnia or of the effectiveness of Viagra for the sexual functioning of men (Meyer et al., 2001); these medications tend to be on the high side of medical interventions.

Drawing wrong conclusions from narrative reviews clearly had negative effects on research and practice. Because researchers and practitioners were so convinced that personality plays little role in entrepreneurship (Aldrich & Martinez, 2001), governments invested (like the German government) in developing networks for entrepreneurs without testing the hypothesis that the effects of networks were dependent on the entrepreneurs' personality (Klein, Lim, Saltz, & Mayer, 2004); obviously, if network effects are a spurious effect of personality, government help for networks would not increase entrepreneurial success. Moreover, selection of entrepreneurs (e.g., for sparse starting capital by banks) was not done with personality tests but, instead, rough indicators of human capital were preferred that clearly demonstrate much smaller correlations with success (Unger, Rauch, Frese, & Rosenbusch, 2011) than personality.

Conducting Meta-Analyses in the Field of Entrepreneurship

The function of science is to produce evidence without biases; science has forever driven the process to reduce biases. The meta-analytic approach is just one way to help with this endeavor when reviewing the literature. The starting point of any meta-analysis is to ask a relevant research and practice question. At this stage, it is often useful to consult with colleagues on whether there is a certain degree of homogeneity of measures of the concepts in question and whether there is a large enough body of empirical articles to warrant a meta-analysis. It may also help to ask practicing entrepreneurs' consultants which question can have potential implications for them. Once the research question has been determined, a systematic search for articles to be included follows (every meta-analysis implies that there is a systematic search for articles). First, one needs to develop a codebook with all the terms used in scientific article that are related to the current research question. Also, it is not necessary to do a wide and systematic approach to finding both published and unpublished articles (unpublished articles need to be included to be sure that a potential publication bias does not lead to skewed results). If at all possible, foreign language publications should be included as far as possible. Moreover, both methodologically weak as well as strong articles should be included (however, methodological weakness should

be coded)—thus, it is counterproductive to search for articles from only prestigious journals or articles utilizing only the most sophisticated methods, and so forth. Once the full number of articles has been assembled, it is necessary to decide which of these articles need to be excluded. Articles that may use the same terminology but are really based on a different conceptual or operational approach to the research question, articles that do not report effect sizes or equivalent empirical indicators, articles that use the same sample as another article on the same subject can all be excluded. All criteria that lead to inclusion or exclusion of articles have to be systematically developed and clearly described. In case of doubt, it makes sense to be as inclusive as possible, because one can test whether different methodology, different operationalizations of the dependent and independent variables, and different conceptualizations of key concepts lead to different results (moderator analysis in the meta-analysis).

In entrepreneurship research, a large body of knowledge is based on qualitative studies. This has led some scholars to argue against meta-analyses because they are solely based on quantitative studies. Fortunately, the instrument of meta-analysis is so versatile that qualitative studies (e.g., case studies) can be coded so that they can also be meta-analyzed (Bullock & Tubbs, 1990; Larsson, 1993). We believe that the instrument of meta-analysis may be even more important for qualitative studies in entrepreneurship than for quantitative ones, so that researchers can move from a knowledge detecting mode (e.g., in the sense of grounded theory) to examining the evidence for a specific hypothesis and its theory based on qualitative material.

Theoretically and empirically, an important question is whether meta-analytic results are homogenous or not. Most frequently, the relationships uncovered by meta-analyses in entrepreneurship are heterogeneous. As a matter of fact, we have never seen nonheterogeneous meta-analytic results in entrepreneurship research. There are various empirical indicators of the homogeneity of the effect sizes used by meta-analyses (Q-statistics, credibility interval, 75 percent rule). Heterogeneity of results suggests that it makes sense to search for moderators. This can be done in the meta-analysis but it is also required in future original research. For practitioners it means that they can and should experiment with the conditions that have an effect on their best results. For example, there is a large credibility interval for new firms for the positive effect of innovation (Rosenbusch et al., 2011); although the effect size itself shows that something important is going on indicating that, on average, it pays for new firms to be innovative, the heterogeneity of the effect sizes implies that some innovation practices do not really work out well, whereas others do. So, the entrepreneur could take the advice that innovativeness is useful, but the entrepreneur would know that it pays to experiment to receive even larger returns. A conversion from the $r = 0.206$, which was used in this meta-analysis (Rosenbusch et al., 2011), to Cohen's d provides us with an estimate of $d = 0.42$. Thus, the entrepreneur knows that the average innovation should produce about 42 percent of a standard deviation better profit rate than a noninnovative procedure.

Moderators are of importance in entrepreneurship because the context often decides whether a certain idea will work or not. For example, human capital is more important for success in developing countries than in the developed world (Unger et al., 2011). Therefore, the role of moderators is essential in entrepreneurship research.

Additionally, because entrepreneurship research is much less cohesive and there are more debates on the right methodological approach than in medicine, the issue of methodological sophistication needs to be addressed explicitly in entrepreneurship research. Whereas medicine often selects only those articles that meet the gold standards of randomized controlled experiments, work and organizational psychology and the field of entrepreneurship are better off rating the quality of each article and using this quality rating as a moderator, testing whether a relationship is more frequently found in "good" articles or in articles of a lower quality. Thus, the issue of what constitutes a methodologically and otherwise good study has to be empirically proven by the authors of meta-analyses (and methodological sophistication of the study is treated as a moderator).

A typical problem for meta-analyses in fields such as entrepreneurship is that different definitions and operationalizations of key variables are employed (this is also true of work and organizational psychology). This implies that meta-analyses should test explicitly whether differences in theoretical terms and operationalization produce differences in the results (again this is a methodological moderator) (Stewart & Roth, 2004; Zhao & Seibert, 2006). Moreover, it is sometimes fruitful to code the theoretical orientation of the authors and examine whether the theoretical orientation has an influence on the results. For example different theoretical orientations have led to very different

inclusion criteria in meta-analyses on risk and entrepreneurship (Miner & Raju, 2004; Stewart & Roth, 2001; Stewart & Roth, 2004).

There are different approaches to testing moderators (Hunter & Schmidt, 2004; (Geyskens, Krishnan, Steenkamp, & Cunha, 2009). Both the subgrouping approach and the regression approach should be used concurrently, because they answer different questions. The subgroup approach (Hunter & Schmidt, 2004) relates to the size of the correlations for different values of the moderator; the regression approach answers the question how important each moderator is among the set of moderators that were examined in this study (of course, the regression approach is strongly affected by which moderators can and have been included in this meta-analysis, and the relative strength of the moderator effect will strongly depend on which moderators are included).

Meta-analyses help to improve the degree of scientific professionalism in a field and to develop higher standards in an area of science. Because meta-analyses often show quantitatively different effect sizes for well-designed versus not-so-well-designed studies (Carlson & Schmidt, 1999), there is pressure on researchers to utilize better designs. Moreover, the use of meta-analyses leads entrepreneurship journals to provide all relevant statistical data (particularly, mean, standard deviation, intercorrelations of variables) that can be used as raw material for additional analyses. Last but not least, meta-analyses reveal when authors use the same samples and variables more than once (because they can only be entered once in a meta-analysis).

Finally, interventions may be suggested on the basis of meta-analyses. However, EBE should not be restricted to meta-analyses.

What Is Evidence in Entrepreneurship?

"Evidence in the broadest sense, refers to anything that is used to determine or demonstrate the truth of an assertion."(Wikepedia on evidence, http://en.wikipedia.org/wiki/Evidence). Thus, an assertion has to be tested so that there is evidence in the sense of objective and unbiased knowledge. We have already established that good evidence should be based on several studies and several observations rather than only on one observation or on one study. Because every study has its own problems, good evidence needs to be based on a summary of several studies.

Compared with other areas of research, such as medicine, criminology, education, work, and organizational psychology, the area of entrepreneurship has produced comparatively few meta-analyses and those that exist have not yet been as influential as they should. This is all the more problematic because entrepreneurship research is often utilized in the support of policy decisions, for example, tax decisions, government decisions.

Apparently, it was easier to introduce evidence-based approaches in medicine. One of the most important events was the article by Antman et al. (Antman, Lau, Kupelnick, Mosteller, & Chalmers, 1992), which pointed out how many lives could have been saved had medicine used cumulative meta-analysis to test certain drugs, thus allowing an earlier onset of the use of these drugs.

Calls for evidence-based management and entrepreneurship argue that it would help economic development if entrepreneurs, companies, and policy makers would take an evidence-informed approach in their day-to-day management (Pfeffer & Sutton, 2006). However, entrepreneurship research seems to be so different from medicine. Tranfield, Denyer, and Smart (2003) have discussed the differences between medicine and management, which also apply to entrepreneurship research. Medicine is not only more cohesive in its epistemological approac but it is also more formalized. In approach, entrepreneurship research is much less cohesive in its approach. There are lively debates on the best empirical approach in entrepreneurship. Entrepreneurship research emphasizes the influence of the specific context on whether entrepreneurial decisions are effective. The most important difference is certainly that medicine examines interventions with the help of randomized controlled experiments. As a matter of fact, many protocols used in the most famous site for systematic reviews and meta-analyses—the Cochrane Collaboration—eliminate those studies that are not based on controlled randomized experiments from their database that they utilize for their meta-analyses. In contrast, most research in entrepreneurship is based on field studies that need to control for alternative explanations; even longitudinal studies are rare in entrepreneurship research. Moreover, large-scale data sources are often "milked" by several research groups, leading to a high alpha error in their research (assuming that something is true although it may not be so); there is often less emphasis on developing new databases than on developing new theoretical approaches to analyze the same data set again.

When it comes to interventions, there are practically no controlled randomized experiments that have been done in entrepreneurship research. We agree with recent calls for more of such experiments in management and entrepreneurship (Reay, Berta, & Kohn, 2009). However, meta-analyses need to utilize the article present; and in entrepreneurship research the typical research is based on correlations and only infrequently on interventions. All of this speaks against using the medical analogy in entrepreneurship research. EBE may be better off following the example of other disciplines on how to do meta-analyses. The better model for entrepreneurship research may not be the medical field but work and organizational psychology (Anderson, Herriot, & Hodgkinson, 2001; Hodgkinson, Herriot, & Anderson, 2001). Work and organizational psychology often systematically compares different theoretical approaches and different methods. Work and organizational psychology is, also, often based on nonexperimental field studies or on quasi-experiments. In field studies, the question is often asked whether a new construct will add explained variance in a dependent variable of importance (e.g., in the field of entrepreneurship this may be starting a company or entrepreneurial success). It makes sense to ask the question whether an additional predictor (derived from theory or from empirical evidence) explains additional variance in comparison to known predictors in the area of entrepreneurship research (a good example of work and organizational psychology is presented by Schmidt & Hunter, 1998).

Theory testing on full models with the inclusion of mediators can also be done on the basis of meta-analyses. In order to test whole theories, researchers may choose to not just present correlational results of two variables but to base meta-analytic regression analyses on meta-analytically derived correlation matrixes that can then support meta-analytic path analyses to test theoretical models. Such meta-analyses are particularly useful to examine mediation effects (Colquitt, Scott, & LePine, 2007; Shadish, 1996; Viswesvaran & Ones, 1995) and to test full theories (Cheung, 2008).

EBE is not restricted to doing meta-analysis; EBE involves tracking good empirical evidence for practical and theoretical questions. But what constitutes good empirical evidence? Most evidence-based approaches posit some kind of hierarchy of evidence—often ranging from anecdotal evidence experienced by experts via consensus by experts up to meta-analysis. We liked the ideas developed in clinical psychology (based on Chambless & Hollon, 1998):

- The important relationship has to be shown to exist in at least three studies from at least two different research groups.
- Causal analysis has to be done on the basis of longitudinal studies that exclude plausible alternative hypotheses or by developing evidence on the basis of randomized experiments.
- Outcome measures have to come from different sources than the independent variables, and all measures need to be reliable and valid.
- A clear definition of samples have to be given.
- If there is conflicting evidence, then meta-analytic evidence, which possibly explains with the help of moderators why there is conflicting evidence, should be provided.
- In addition to quantitative research, there should be qualitative case material that describes the configurational and contextual situations under which a certain intervention may work.

Clearly, we need to be skeptical toward "naïve" forms of evidence. "We've…suggested no less than six substitutes that managers…often use for the best evidence—obsolete knowledge (based on college education obtained many years ago, added by the authors of this article), personal experience, specialist skills, hype, dogma, and mindless mimicry of top performers …" (such as benchmarking) (Pfeffer & Sutton, 2007), p. 16). Probably we should also add that experience per se has been shown to be limited in its usefulness. As long as the experiences are relatively uniform, the learning curve levels off after a few months or years. Research comparing top performers with average performers has shown that experience is only valuable if it is highly varied (Sonnentag, 1998) or if it is based on so-called deliberate practice—a form of learning strongly oriented toward practicing those parts of the skills that are underdeveloped (Ericsson, Krampe, & Tesch-Römer, 1993; Sonnentag & Kleine, 2000; Unger, Keith, Frese, Hilling, & Gielnik, 2008). Thus, it is highly questionable to use one's "simple" experience as evidence. We are also worried when consensus of experts is used as evidence; a few years ago a certain consensus was reached among entrepreneurship researchers that personality cannot be conceptualized to be a factor for success for entrepreneurs (prior to meta-analyses showing this consensus to be false).

Examples of the Use of Meta-Analysis in EBE

Table 6.1 describes a number of meta-analyses that were developed in the area of entrepreneurship.

This is not an exhaustive table. It is also not meant to provide all the information. However, the table shows that there are already some meta-analyses in entrepreneurship and that this number is growing rapidly.

One area that has stimulated a high degree of controversy in entrepreneurship is the role of a business plan. This is also an interesting issue because, here, meta-analysis is used to evaluate how well a potential intervention works: getting people to develop a business plan, as is routinely done in business schools. In practice, there are numerous business-plan competitions that attract potential entrepreneurs and the media. A popular example is the "meet the dragon's project," which allows potential entrepreneurs globally to pitch their business plan to investors. So the big question is this: Is the business plan worth its hype? Some academic scholars argue that fully developed business plans are not functional to success (Honig & Karlsson, 2004; Sarasvathy, 2001) and that entrepreneurs should better proactively and quickly exploit their business idea. As Table 6.1 shows, there are two meta-analyses on the effectiveness of business plans (Schwenk & Shrader, 1993; Brinkmann, Grichnik, & Kapsa, 2010). These meta-analyses show that the effect size is sizeable enough to make a difference ($d = .20$) and that effect sizes vary considerably. Moderator analyses showed that effect sizes are larger for established enterprises as compared to young enterprises.

Can this evidence be used in practice? The answer is yes. The meta-analysis shows that it makes sense for entrepreneurs to produce business plans and to plan in the process of managing a firm—there are only very few cases in which business planning has negative effects (although they do exist). The moderator analysis shows, in addition, that having a business plan available is as effective as it is to do planning during the management of the firm.

However, some reservations need to be described, as well: First, the evidence shows having a business plan and managing with clear plans is better for established firms than for new ones. This may be a time effect—it pays off long term; therefore, only established firms profit more highly from having a business plan. There may be a second reason: communication in the firm is easier when one has clear plans available—and that may be more important in the established firms than in the new firms. These are questions of mediation: Which factors are responsible for producing the positive effects of business planning? Third, one has to acknowledge that there are very few controlled randomized experiments that test whether business planning has a positive effect on success (most studies are not based on randomized experiments in this area). Thus, the present evidence has not yet established the causal structure. Fortunately, a longitudinal study has shown that planning leads to success and success leads to more planning (Van Gelderen, Frese, & Thurik, 2000); thus, both causal effects may be operative to produce long-term effects of the kind shown in the meta-analysis. However, this is only one longitudinal study—more of them need to be done. Moreover, in the last analysis, experiments could be done and could produce better data on the effectiveness of an intervention, such as teaching business planning. However, the overall practice implication is clear from this meta-analysis: teach business plans (and for entrepreneurs, learn how to do business planning and use this skill).

Unfortunately, not every meta-analysis has clear-cut implications for practice. For example it is much more difficult to determine what an entrepreneur can learn from the evidence on personality discussed earlier? Unfortunately, it is highly unlikely that one can change one's personality traits; it is not impossible but an extremely hard undertaking, partly because they are genetically determined (Judge, Higgins, Thoresen, & Barrick, 1999) and partly because personality effects are stable across time (Costa & McCrae, 1997; Roberts, Walton, & Viechtbauer, 2006). However, it may be possible to *manage* one's personality. One of the best ways is to manage one's personality by integrating others into the firm and getting people who can compensate for one's own weakness. Indeed, having partners is useful for success, as shown by a meta-analysis (Read, Song, & Smit, 2009). It is also possible to change more specific behavioral examples of traits. For example, the meta-analysis by Rauch and Frese (2007) has shown that generalized self-efficacy and achievement motivation is important to predict performance. Task-specific self-efficacy can be changed by training entrepreneurs' self-efficacy, for example, on how to attract customers (Eden & Aviram, 1993). Similarly, achievement motivation can be increased by training (Miron & McClelland, 1979). Moreover, bankers, professionals who work with entrepreneurs, will profit from knowledge about personality effects.

Thus, some research questions can be translated into practice more easily than others. It pays to develop theories that are explicit on the mediating mechanisms that lead to positive effects. One of the best-known theories in this regard is the theory of goal setting, which suggests that high and specific goals lead to higher performance and is explicit about the mediation and moderator processes and has been summarized in a meta-analysis (Latham, 2004; Wood, Mento, & Locke, 1987).

Bridging the Knowledge-Doing Gap: How to Make Knowledge Doable

All forms of evidence including meta-analyses provide the basis for the development of effective interventions. Once there is evidence for a relationship, interventions that change the target variable should be attempted (e.g., teaching personality management or selecting people to receive support for their entrepreneurial unit based on their personality). Of course, each new intervention needs to be empirically evaluated as part of EBE. The best instrument to examine such interventions is the randomized controlled experiment (Reay et al., 2009). This means that an intervention is given to one group; a second group of participants—the control group—does not get the intervention, but provides data on their development. The two groups have to be randomly divided. Often, the control group gets the same intervention at an appropriate time (e.g., after a year). Once a number of interventions studies have been done, they can also be meta-analyzed. Meta-analyses can, for example, examine how far courses of personality management are positively related to success and whether they generalize across situations, across people, and across methods of teaching. Often, new research needs appear as a result of such meta-analyses of interventions (e.g., Is it possible to improve methods of teaching personality management?).

A similar approach can be used in policy making. Recommendations to policy makers should be based on meta-analyses. Policy makers are also often interested in knowing which factors are the most influential. This can only be accrued across studies, because no individual study can investigate all relevant variables. When there is good meta-analytic evidence for a specific variable to have a high influence, then it is useful to develop an intervention through policy changes (Campbell, 1969).

Unfortunately, it sounds much easier than it is to decipher from meta-analytic results clear policy implications or other interventions. There is always a hiatus between knowledge and action. A meta-analysis may answer which variable needs to be changed; however, it does not necessarily answer how this can be done. Even if there is meta-analytic evidence of how something needs to be changed, action is, by necessity, situationally embedded; the meta-analytic evidence is often highly abstracted from the situational conditions. For this reason, we suggest to develop implementation manuals as explicit manuals of how knowledge can be translated into practice.

Action Principles and the use of Implementation Manuals

Good evidence should lead to good practice. We suggest that good practice and good intervention research can be supported by implementation handbooks (similar to treatment handbooks in clinical psychology; Luborsky & DeRubeis, 1984). These implementation handbooks are based on good empirical evidence, including meta-analysis, and they describe how implementation can be accomplished in entrepreneurial firms. Implementation manuals should describe the evidence and the theoretical foundation. It is also helpful if they include qualitative cases of successful implementation of a policy. These cases should comprise potential pitfalls and difficulties when implementing evidence-informed ideas and policies. Thus, the manual needs to describe the contexts in which changes take place and how such changes can be supported.

One of the main concepts that help to put theory into practice is the concept of action principle (Frese, Beimel, & Schoenborn, 2003) (a good example of a book that develops action principles from theory has been edited by Locke; Locke, 2004). Examples for action principles are provided by goal-setting theory, which argues that goals need to be high and specific. These are clearly action-guiding ideas and are both theoretical as well as practical (Latham, 2009). Thus, the manuals should be based on principles of action that have been shown to be important for successful implementation of evidence. Importantly, the manuals should explain how the success and failure of the procedures can be measured; business owners should attempt to get this feedback so that they can recognize whether they are on the "right track." Such manuals may be accompanied by interviews with business owners who have successfully implemented a certain idea or policy and who describe the problems that needed to be solved on the way toward the goal. We foresee that there will be a big market for such implementation manuals in the future.

Implementation manuals are not trivial results of known empirical relationships. Rather, additional evidence and theoretical concepts have to be considered, most often in the form of action principles that explain how to translate a theory into effective

action. These action principles can then be translated into action hypotheses—hypotheses about which actions produce which effects—and then entrepreneurs or policy makers can make choices about which conditions they need to change to affect changes (Bamberg & Schmidt, 2001).

Such implementation manuals can be tested with a true experimental or quasi-experimental design. Companies that participate in the study can be matched to other companies that function as control group. Additional process measures examine how much companies conform to or deviate from the implementation manuals; crucial changes in the companies' behaviors and cognitions can be described (DeRubeis, Tang, & Gelfand, 2000). If the implementation manual is useful, a higher degree of conforming to the implementation manual should lead to better results and the experimental group should show better results in important theoretical variables (e.g., profitability) than a control group. Similar approaches have been used in clinical psychology. Research has shown that cognitive behavioral interventions for depression started to work when patients developed certain cognitions and when the therapists conformed to implementation manuals (Hollon, DeRubeis, & Evans, 1987; Tang, DeRubeis, & Beberman, 2005). Potential positive effects of deviation from the implementation manuals can lead to additional research on which aspects of the implementation manuals are not successful, and this may lead to changes in theory and calls for new meta-analyses.

We have tried in one series of publications to walk through the full process from developing evidence, via developing a meta-analysis, to developing an implementation manual, to testing such a manual with the help of a randomized experiment. We developed the concept of owners' proactive approach (and personal initiative), and we showed that it was related to success of the owners' firms (Koop, De Reu, & Frese, 2000; Krauss, Frese, Friedrich, & Unger, 2005). In a second step, we developed a theory of proactive behavior of entrepreneurs (Frese, 2009). In a further step we developed a training procedure. This included two aspects. First, it included a procedure of action training based on the development of action principles from theory and using them to directly influence individual behavior (Frese et al., 2003). This action training was then used to develop an intervention for entrepreneurs evaluated with a randomized controlled experiment (Glaub, Fischer, Klemm, & Frese, 2011). The experiment proved that the intervention was successful; over time the experimental group increased its success and the waiting control group reduced its success. The most important test of the theory was to examine whether those who actually learned most in the intervention were also the ones who had the highest success. A mediation model was shown to be correct: enhancing owners' proactive behavior by the intervention fully mediated the relationship between the intervention and the increase of business success. Similarly, meta-analyses on internationalization (Bausch & Krist, 2007; Schwens & Kabst, 2009a, 2009b) can be used to develop an implementation manual on how to internationalize a firm.

Translating Knowledge into Practice: Using Evidence as an Entrepreneur

Recent publications have pointed to the gap between scientific knowledge and how little it is translated into practice (Pfeffer & Sutton, 2000; Pfeffer & Sutton, 2006; Rousseau & McCarthy, 2007; Rynes et al., 2007). "Many companies and leaders show little interest in subjecting their business practices and decisions to the same scientific rigor they would use for technical or medical issues" (Pfeffer & Sutton, 2006, p. 12). Pfeffer and Sutton (2006) give example after example in the area of management to illustrate the desirability and even the necessity for managers to utilize evidence-based approaches. Rynes et al. (2007) show how often practitioners of management do not have the right knowledge—actually putting the right policies into place may be even less frequent.

Owners can use information from EBE in three ways: First, they can get inspiration and knowledge directly from empirical evidence, from multiple studies, systematic reviews, and meta-analyses. Most commentators on evidence-informed management have shown that it is unlikely that many business owners will have the time and expertise to read the scientific literature. It is somewhat more likely that owners might take a theoretical statement and use it to inspire organizational practices from such a theory. Sources of such models and theories may be journals that translate scientific findings or courses in business schools or science informed consultants. The second approach is to use implementation manuals. We urge entrepreneurship researchers to produce such implementation manuals as a way of making evidence practical. Third, business owners can collect evidence themselves. Pfeffer and Sutton (2006) provide a number of examples of how industry uses quantifiable evidence that exist in most firms. Examples include evidence on the

efficacy of advertisements, of different presentations of a homepage, or of HR strategies of hiring and retaining the best employees. Google proves that true experiments can be done, for example, around issues of presentation of computerized material for customers.

Limitations of the EBE Approach

These are the potential limitations of an EBE approach:

• Garbage-in/garbage-out: If badly designed studies define an area, the resulting meta-analysis will also lead to incorrect results. Cochrane meta-analyses often use inclusion criteria such that "good" studies are included into their meta-analyses—true experiments with random control and experimental groups and double-blind conditions. Their reviews are, therefore, often based on only a few studies. Hunter and Schmidt (2004) warn of this procedure because invariably biases may creep into the decision about which articles to delete. This is particularly so in entrepreneurship. We, therefore, suggest a different procedure for entrepreneurship—the following safeguards should be used: First, meta-analyses should differentiate between methodologically "sound" and not-so-good studies and test empirically whether the results are the same for the "good" and "bad" studies. Second, they can test whether more recent studies (possibly based on better methodology) have similar results to older ones. Third, meta-analyses should correct for certain problems in the literature, for example, unreliability of measures. Fourth, a meta-analysis can examine whether good (reliable, valid) measures show similar effects to not-so-good measures. Thus, meta-analyses should include a number of methodological moderators to examine such issues.

• Nonsignificant results are often not published and this may lead to biases in meta-analyses. Two countermeasures are used. First, reviewers attempt to find as many unpublished studies as possible (often doctoral studies) and compare their results to the published ones. Second, a so-called fail-safe index calculates how many unpublished null-effect studies would be needed to reduce the current results to nonsignificance (Rosenthal, 1979).

• One-size-fits-all. Meta-analyses often aggregate across various industries, measures, contexts. In contrast, entrepreneurship research often emphasizes the contextual dependency of entrepreneurship concepts. There are so many differences in owners, industries, consumer tastes, and so on. Often the same strategies in different contexts may lead to the different effects. In principle, these differences can be examined with meta-analyses as well (and often meta-analyses will actually find such effects) or at least point out the need for future moderator studies. However, the danger of a one-size-fits-all approach exists. Therefore, we suggest that implementation manuals should be combined with case studies and careful consideration of context variables. Moreover, we suggest developing theories of configurations and examining them empirically. Moreover, meta-analyses can be combined with qualitative reviews of contextual issues in the literature.

• Entrepreneurship often implies that an owner does something different from others. Particularly, small fledging entrepreneurial units use a niche approach that may be directly opposed to the typical approach of doing things. We agree with this statement. Fortunately, meta-analyses often examine processes and not the content of decisions. Success may come from being different in content but not necessarily different in processes from others. Obviously, this hypothesis needs to be tested both empirically and meta-analytically.

Implications for Entrepreneurship Research and Practice

EBE is full of new opportunities. Relevant consumers of EBE are scientists, consulting firms, CEOs, boards of directors, banks, institutions for developing nations (e.g., the World Bank), governments, and, last but not least, individual entrepreneurs. EBE does not mean that professional knowledge is invalidated (APA-Presidential-Task-Force-on-Evidence-Based-Practice, 2006); EBE is a necessary add-on for consultants, banks, entrepreneurs, and so forth—all of whom should consider the knowledge reported within EBE and then make their own autonomous and considered decisions.

EBE is not the same as empirical entrepreneurship research. Evidence implies that there is more than one source for an empirical relationship. We have emphasized meta-analyses because they can be used in those areas of entrepreneurship in which several studies are available (a rule of thumb may be that more than 10 empirical studies should be available as a literature base for a meta-analysis). We do not want to equate EBE with only meta-analyses because some areas of entrepreneurship are not mature enough to produce enough empirical articles. Therefore, we think that any type of triangulation should be used to derive evidence from empirical studies. Several studies (preferably with different methodology and from different authors and from different industry and cultural contexts) should be taken to derive evidence. The same also applies for qualitative studies. Rating procedures can be used in a similar way as meta-analyses to test whether evidence across different case studies can be accrued. Moreover, a set of studies that leads to similar findings can be taken as evidence in entrepreneurship research.

An evidence-based approach will change research and teaching in entrepreneurship (for teaching, please consult Rousseau and McCarthy, 2007). There are easy connections between evidence-based management and EBE. However, specific approaches that are more akin to entrepreneurship may complement the approach of evidence-based management. For example, bets may be placed on certain approaches, much like business angels place bets on certain entrepreneurial ideas. For example, an approach based on an implementation manual for an initial public offering may lead to better share prices than an approach that is not evidence based (Daily, Certo, Dalton, & Roengpitya, 2003). Investors may place bets on certain approaches by investing in approaches that are evidence based. One step beyond this idea, investing itself may be conceptualized to be evidence of an investor's belief that a certain idea may be viable in the future, much like the share price is a bet on future viability of a firm (Sarasvathy, 2001). Future research could establish the relationship of such bets and whether the behavior of the firms conforms to scientifically derived evidence and how deviations might be explained.

References

Aldrich, H. E., & Martinez, M. A. (2001). Many are called, but few are chosen: An evoluationary perspective for the study of entrepreneurship. *Entrepreneurship: Theory & Practice, 25*(4), 41–56.

Aldrich, H. E., & Widenmayer, G. (1993). From traits to rates: An ecological perspective on organizational foundings. In J. A. Katz & R. H. Brockhaus (Eds.), *Advances in entrepreneurship, firm emergence, and growth* (Vol. 1, pp. 145–195). Greenwich, CT: JAI Press.

Anderson, N., Herriot, P., & Hodgkinson, G. P. (2001). The practitioner-researcher divide in industrial,work and organizational (IWO) psychology: Where are we now, and where do we go from here? *Journal of Occupational and Organizational Psychology, 74*, 391–411.

Antman, E. M., Lau, J., Kupelnick, B., Mosteller, F., & Chalmers, T. C. (1992). A comparison of results of meta-analyses of randomized control trials and recommendations of clinical experts. *Journal of the American Medical Association, 268,* 240–248.

APA-Presidential Task Force on Evidence Based Practice. (2006). Evidence-based practice in psychology. *American Psychologist, 61,* 271–285.

Bamberg, S., & Schmidt, P. (2001). Theory driven subgroup-specific evaluation of an intervention to reduce private car use. *Journal of Applied Social Psychology, 31,* 1300–1329.

Bausch, A., & Krist, M. (2007). The effect of context related moderators on the internationalization-performance relationship: Evidence from meta-analysis. *Management International Review, 47,* 319–347.

Boyd, B. K. (1991). Strategic planning and financial performance: A meta-analytic review. *Journal of Management Studies, 28*(4), 353–374.

Brinckmann, J., Grichnik, D., & Kapsa, D. (2010). Should entrepreneurs plan or just storm the castle? A meta-analysis on contextual factors impacting the business planning–performance relationship in small firms. *Journal of Business Venturing, 25,* 24–40.

Bullock, R. J, & Tubbs, M. E. (1990). A case meta-analysis of gainsharing plans as organization development interventions. *Journal of Applied Behavioral Science, 26,* 383–404.

Campbell collaboration web site (http://www.campbellcollaboration.org/)

Campbell, D. T. (1969). Reforms as experiments. *American Psychologist, 24,* 409–429.

Carlson, K. D., & Schmidt, F. L. (1999). Impact of experimental design on effect size: Findings from the research literature on training. *Journal of Applied Psychology, 84,* 851–862.

Chambless, D. L., & Hollon, S. D. (1998). Defining empirically supported therapies. *Journal of Consulting and Clinical Psychology, 66,* 7–18.

Cheung, M. W.-L. (2008). A model for integrating fixed-, random-, and mixed-effects meta-analyses into structural equation modeling. *Psychological Methods, 13,* 182–202.

Cochrane foundation web site (http://www.cochrane.org/reviews/en/topics/index.html)

Collins, C. J., Hanges, P. J., & Locke, E. A. (2004). The relationship of achievement motivation to entrepreneurial behavior: A meta-analysis. *Human Performance, 17*(1), 95–117.

Colquitt, J. A., Scott, B. A., & LePine, J. A. (2007). Trust, trustworthiness, and trust propensity: A meta-analytic test of their unique relationships with risk taking and job performance. *Journal of Applied Psychology, 92,* 909–927.

Combs, J. G., Ketchen, D. J., Crook, T. R., & Roth, P. L. (2011). Assessing cumulative evidence within 'Macro' research: Why meta-analysis should be preferred over vote counting. *Journal of Management Studies, 48,* 178–197.

Combs, J. G., & Ketchen Jr., D. J. (2003). Why do firms use franchising as an entrepreneurial strategy?: A meta-analysis. *Journal of Management, 29*(3), 443–465.

Costa, P. T., & McCrae, R. R. (1997). Longitudinal stability of adult personality. In R. Hogan, J. Johnson, & S. Briggs (Eds.), *Handbook of personality psychology* (pp. 269–292). San Diego, CA: Academic Press.

Crook, T. R., Ketchen, D. J., Combs, J. G., & Todd, P. M. (2008). Strategic resources and performance: A meta-analysis. *Strategic Management Journal, 29,* 1141–1154.

Daily, C. M., Certo, S. T., Dalton, D. R., & Roengpitya, R. (2003). IPO underpricing: A meta-analysis and research synthesis. *Entrepreneurship: Theory & Practice, 27*(3), 271–295.

DeRubeis, R. J., Tang, T. Z., & Gelfand, L. A. (2000). Recent findings concerning the processes and outcomes of cognitive therapy for depression. In S. L. Johnson, A. M. Hayes, T. M. Field, N. Schneiderman, & P. M. McCabe (Eds.), *Stress, coping, and depression* (pp. 223–240). Mahwah, NJ: Lawrence Erlbaum .

Eden, D., & Aviram, A. (1993). Self-sefficacy training to speed reemployment: Helping people to help themselves. *Journal of Applied Psychology, 78,* 352–360.

Ericsson, K. A., Krampe, R. T., & Tesch-Römer, C. (1993). The role of deliberate practice in the acquisition of expert performance. *Psychological Review, 100,* 363–406.

Frese, M. (2009). Toward a psychology of entrepreneurship: An action theory perspective. *Foundations and Trends in Entrepreneurship, 5,* 435–494.

Frese, M., Beimel, S., & Schoenborn, S. (2003). Action training for charismatic leadership: Two evaluation studies of a commercial training module on inspirational communication of a vision. *Personnel Psychology, 56,* 671–697.

Gartner, W. B. (1989). "Who is an entrepreneur?" is the wrong question. *Entrepreneurship Theory and Practice, 1*(4), 47–68.

Geyskens, I., Krishnan, R., Steenkamp, J.-B. E. M., & Cunha, P. V. (2009). A review and evaluation of meta-analysis practices in management research. *Journal of Management, 35,* 393–419.

Glaub, M., Fischer, S., Klemm, M., & Frese, M. (2011). A theory based controlled randomized field intervention to enhance personal initiative in African small business owners – a contribution to evidence based management. *Manuscript submitted for publication.*

Grove, W. M., & Meehl, P. E. (1996). Comparative efficiency of informal (subjective, impressionistic) and formal (mechanical, algorithmic) prediction procedures: The clinical–statistical controversy. *Psychology, Public Policy, and Law, 2,* 293–323.

Henrekson, M., & Johansson, D. (2010). Gazelles as job creators: a survey and interpretation of the evidence. *Small Business Economics, 35*(2), 227–244.

Hodgkinson, G. P., Herriot, P., & Anderson, N. (2001). Re-aligning the stakeholders in management research: Lessons from industrial, work and organizational psychology. *British Journal of Management-Special Issue, 12,* S41–S48.

Hollon, S. D., DeRubeis, R. J., & Evans, M. D. (1987). Causal mediation of change in treatment for depression: Discriminating between nonspecificity and noncausality. *Psychological Bulletin, 102,* 139–149.

Honig, B., & Karlsson, T. (2004). Institutional forces and the written business plan. *Journal of Management, 30,* 29-48.

Hunter, J. A., & Schmidt, F. L. (2004). *Methods of meta-analysis: Correcting error and bias in research findings* (2nd ed.). Thousand Oaks, CA: Sage.

Judge, T. A., Higgins, C. A., Thoresen, C. J., & Barrick, M. R. (1999). The big five personality traits, general mental ability, and career success across the life span. *Personnel Psychology, 52*(3), 621–652.

Judge, T. A., Thoresen, C. J., Bono, J. E., & Patton, G. K. (2001). The job satisfaction-performance relationship: A qualitative and quantitative review. *Psychological Bulletin, 127,* 376–407.

Keynes, J. M. (1953). *The general theory of employment, interest, and money.* New York: Harcourt Jovanovich.

Klein, K. J., Lim, B.-C., Saltz, J. L., & Mayer, D. M. (2004). How do they get there? An examination of the antecedents of centrality in team networks. *Academy of Management Journal, 47,* 952–963.

Koop, S., De Reu, T., & Frese, M. (2000). Sociodemographic factors, entrepreneurial orientation, personal initiative, and environmental problems in Uganda. In M. Frese (Ed.), *Success and failure of microbusiness owners in Africa: A psychological approach* (pp. 55–76). Westport, CT: Quorum.

Krauss, S. I., Frese, M., Friedrich, C., & Unger, J. (2005). Entrepreneurial orientation and success: A psychological model of success in Southern African small scale business owners. *European Journal of Work and Organizational Psychology, 14,* 315–344.

Larsson, R. (1993). Case survey methodology: Quantitative analysis of patterns across case studies. *Academy of Management Journal, 36,* 1515–1546.

Latham, G. P. (2004). Motivate employee performance through goal-setting. In E. A. Locke (Ed.), *Handbook of principles of organizational behavior* (pp. 107–119). Oxford, England: Blackwell.

Latham, G. P. (2009). *Becoming the evidence-based manager.* Boston, MA: Davies-Black.

Locke, E. A. (Ed.). (2004). *Handbook of principles of organizational behavior.* Oxford, England: Blackwell.

Luborsky, L., & DeRubeis, R. J. (1984). The use of psychotherapy treatment manuals: A small revolution in psychotherapy research style. *Clinical Psychology Review, 4,* 5–14.

Meyer, G. J., Finn, S. E., Eyde, L. D., Kay, G. G., Moreland, K. L., Dies, R. R., et al. (2001). Psychological testing and psychological assessment: A review of evidence and issues. *American Psychologist, 56,* 128–165.

Miller, C. C., & Cardinal, L. B. (1994). Strategic planning and firm performance: A synthesis of more than two decades of research. *Academy of Management Journal, 37*(6), 1649–1665.

Miner, J. B., & Raju, N. S. (2004). Risk propensity differences between managers and entrepreneurs and between low- and high-growth entrepreneurs: A reply in a more conservative vein. *Journal of Applied Psychology, 89*(1), 3–13.

Miron, D., & McClelland, D. C. (1979). The impact of achievement motivation training on small business performance. *California Management Review, 21*(4), 13–28.

Mwasalwiba, E. S. (2010). Entrepreneurship education: A review of its objectives, teaching methods, and impact indicators. *Education & Training, 52,* 20–47.

Pfeffer, J., & Sutton, R. I. (2000). *The knowing-doing gap.* Boston, MA: Harvard Business School Press.

Pfeffer, J., & Sutton, R. I. (2006). *Hard facts, dangerous half-truths, and total nonsense.* Boston, MA: Harvard Business School.

Pfeffer, J., & Sutton, R. I. (2007). Evidence based management. *Public Management, 89,* 14–25.

Rauch, A., & Frese, M. (2006). Meta-analyses as a tool for developing entrepreneurship research and theory. *Advances in Entrepreneurship, Innovation, and Economic Growth, 9,* 29–51.

Rauch, A., & Frese, M. (2007). Let's put the person back into entrepreneurship research: A meta-analysis on the relationship between business owners' personality traits, business creation and success. *European Journal of Work and Organizational Psychology, 16,* 353–385.

Rauch, A., Wiklund, J., Lumpkin, G. T., & Frese, M. (2009). Entrepreneurial orientation and business performance: An assessment of past research and suggestions for the future. *Entrepreneurship: Theory & Practice, 33*(3), 761–787.

Read, S., Song, M., & Smit, W. (2009). A meta-analytic review of effectuation and venture performance. *Journal of Business Venturing, 24,* 573–587.

Reay, T., Berta, W., & Kohn, M. K. (2009). What's the evidence on evidence-based management? *Academy of Management Perspectives, 23,* 5–18.

Roberts, B. W., Walton, K. E., & Viechtbauer, W. (2006). Patterns of mean-level change in personality traits across the life course: A meta-analysis of longitudinal studies. *Psychological Bulletin, 132,* 1–25.

Rosenberg, W., & Donald, A. (1995). Evidence based medicine, an approach to clinical problem solving. *British Medical Journal, 310,* 1122–1126.

Rosenbusch, N., Brinckmann, J., & Bausch, A. (2011). Is innovation always beneficial? A meta-analysis of the relationship between innovation and performance in SMEs. *Journal of Business Venturing 26,* 441–457.

Rosenbusch, N., Brinckmann, J., & Mueller, V. (2010). *Does acquiring venture capital pay off for the funded firms? A meta-analysis on the relationship between venture capital investment and funded firm financial performance.* Paper presented at the Babson, Lausanne.

Rosenbusch, N., Brinckmann, J., & Mueller, V. (2012). Does Acquiring Venture Capital Pay Off for the Funded Firms? A Meta-Analysis on the Relationship between Venture Capital Investment and Funded Firm Financial Performance. *Journal of Business Venturing,* conditionally accepted.

Rosenthal, R. (1979). The "file drawer problem" and tolerance for null results. *Psychological Bulletin, 86,* 638–641.

Rousseau, D. M. (2006). Presidential address: Is there such a thing as "evidence-based management"? *Academy of Management Review, 31,* 256–269.

Rousseau, D. M., & McCarthy, S. (2007). Educating managers from an evidence-based perspective. *Academy of Management Learning and Education, 6,* 84–101.

Rynes, S. L., Giluk, T. L., & Brown, K. G. (2007). The very separate worlds of academic and practitioner periodicals in human resource management: Implications for evidence/based management. *Academy of Management Journal, 50,* 987–1008.

Sarasvathy, S. D. (2001). Causation and effectuation: Toward a theoretical shift from economic inevitability to entrepreneurial contingency. *Academy of Management Review, 26,* 243–263.

Scherpenzeel, A., & Saris, W. E. (1997). The validity and reliability of survey items. *Sociological methods and Research, 25,* 341–383.

Schmidt, F. L., & Hunter, J. E. (1998). The validity and utility of selection methods in personnel psychology: Practical and theoretical implications of 85 years of research findings. *Psychological Bulletin, 124,* 262-274.

Schwenk, C. R., & Shrader, C. B. (1993). Effects of formal strategic planning on financial performance in small firms: A meta-analysis. *Entrepreneurship: Theory and Practice* (Spring), 53–64.

Schwens, C., & Kabst, R. (2009a). Determinanten früher Internationalisierung: Eine Meta-Analyse ("determinants of early internationalization: A meta-analysis"). *Zeitschrift für Betriebswirtschaft, 19,* 1–26.

Schwens, C., & Kabst, R. (2009b). How early opposed to late internationalizers learn: Experience of others and paradigms of interpretation. *International Business Review, 18,* 509–522.

Shadish, W. R. (1996). Meta-analysis and the exploration of causal mediating processes: A primer of examples, methods and issues. *Psychological Methods, 1,* 47–65.

Song, M., Podoynitsyna, K., van der Bij, H., & Halman, J. I. M. (2008). Success factors in new ventures: A meta-analysis. *Journal of Product Innovation Management, 25*(1), 7–27.

Sonnentag, S. (1998). Expertise in professional software design: A process study. *Journal of Applied Psychology, 83,* 703–715.

Sonnentag, S., & Kleine, B. M. (2000). Deliberate practice at work: A study with insurance agents. *Journal of Occupational and Organizational Psychology, 73,* 87–102.

Stewart, W. H., & Roth, P. L. (2001). Risk propensity differences between entrepreneurs and managers: A meta-analytic review. *Journal of Applied Psychology, 86,* 145–153.

Stewart, W. H., & Roth, P. L. (2004). Data quality affects meta-analytic conclusions: A response to Miner and Raju (2004) concerning entrepreneurial risk propensity. *Journal of Applied Psychology, 89,* 14–21.

Stewart, W. H., & Roth, P. L. (2007). A meta-analysis of achievement motivation differences between entrepreneurs and managers. *Journal of Small Business Management, 45*(4), 401–421.

Tang, T. Z., DeRubeis, R. J., & Beberman, R. (2005). Cognitive changes, critical sessions, and sudden gains in cognitive-behavioral therapy for depression. *Journal of Consulting and Clinical Psychology, 73,* 168–172.

Tett, R. P., & Guterman, H. A. (2000). Situation trait relevance, trait expression, and cross-situational consistency: Testing a principle of trait activation. *Journal of Research in Personality, 34,* 397– 423.

Tranfield, D., Denyer, D., & Smart, P. (2003). Toward a methodology of developing evidence-informed management knowledge by means of systematic review. *British Journal of Management, 14,* 207–222.

Unger, J. M., Keith, N., Frese, M., Hilling, C., & Gielnik, M. (2008). *Deliberate practice in entrepreneurship: Relationships with education, cognitive ability, knowledge, and success.* Giessen: Manuscript submitted for publication.

Unger, J. M., Rauch, A., Frese, M., & Rosenbusch, N. (2011). Human capital and entrepreneurial success: A meta-analytic review. *Journal of Business Venturing, 26,* 341–358.

van der Sluis, J., van Praag, M., & Vijverberg, W. (2005). Entrepreneurship selection and performance: A meta-analysis of the impact of education in developing economies. *World Bank Economic Review, 19*(2), 225–261.

Van Gelderen, M., Frese, M., & Thurik, R. (2000). Strategies, uncertainty and performance of small business startups. *Small Business Economics, 15,* 165–181.

Viswesvaran, C., & Ones, D. S. (1995). Theory testing: Combining psychometric meta-analysis and structural equations modeling. *Personnel Psychology, 48*(4), 865–885.

Westlund, H., & Adam, F. (2010). Social capital and economic performance: A meta-analysis of 65 studies. *European Planning Studies, 18*(6), 893–919.

Wood, R. E., Mento, A. J., & Locke, E. A. (1987). Task complexity as a moderator of goal effects: A meta-analysis. *Journal of Applied Psychology, 72,* 416–425.

Zhao, H., & Seibert, S. E. (2006). The big five personality dimensions and entrepreneurial status: A meta-analytical review. *Journal of Applied Psychology, 91,* 259–271.

Zhao, H., Seibert, S. E., & Lumpkin, G. T. (2010). The relationship of personality to entrepreneurial intentions and performance: A meta-analytic review. *Journal of Management, 36*(2), 381–404.

Zhao, X.-Y., Frese, M., & Giardini, A. (2010). Business owners' network size and business growth in China: The role of comprehensive social competency. *Entrepreneurship & Regional Development, 22,* 675–705.

Systematic Review and Evidence Synthesis as a Practice and Scholarship Tool

Rob B. Briner *and* David Denyer

Abstract

Reviews of existing research evidence have the potential to inform both practice and scholarship. This opportunity is currently not being fully realized in management and organization studies due to the limitations of traditional methods of review, which fail to identify clearly what is known and not known about a given topic. For practitioners, systematic review can help address managerial problems by producing a reliable knowledge base through accumulating findings from a range of studies. For scholars, systematic review can enhance methodological rigor as well as highlight opportunities for further research. Systematic reviews are guided by a set of principles rather than a specific, inflexible, and restricted protocol. By revealing these principles, outlining a systematic review methodology, and offering examples, we hope that this chapter helps both practitioners and scholars to use systematic review to inform their practice.

Key Words: systematic review, systematic-review methodology, critical appraisal, Question formulation traditional, narrative literature review

How do experts know what they know and what they don't know? Academics and practitioners claim to possess expertise, which informs the opinions they offer and the decisions they make. But what is the basis for this expertise? One of the cornerstones and a prerequisite of evidence-based management (EBMgt) is that it draws on systematic reviews of existing knowledge and evidence to inform decisions about research or practice. A systematic review addresses a specific question, utilizes explicit and transparent methods to perform a thorough literature search and critical appraisal of individual studies, and draws conclusions about what we currently know and do not know about a given question or topic. *Systematic* simply means that reviewers follow an appropriate (but not standardized or rigid) design and that they communicate what they have done. In essence, conducting systematic reviews means applying the same level of rigor to the process of reviewing literature that we would apply to any well-conducted and clearly-reported primary research.

This apparently simple, straightforward, and even "commonsense" approach is widely used in many fields such as medicine, health care, social policy, and education, but it is rarely used in management and organization studies. Without conducting a systematic review, how do you know that the evidence that you are using to inform your research or practice is reasonable? What degree of certainty can you claim about your contribution, intervention, or decision? Could other evidence exist that refutes your current thinking or offers an entirely new insight or perspective?

In this chapter, we explain how systematic review can be used as a key tool for advancing scholarship in management and organization studies and improving the practice of management. In what follows, we explain how poor-quality reviews and syntheses can hinder scholarship and practice. We then consider current approaches to literature review in management. We next define and describe systematic reviews and their uses. We provide an overview and introduction to the processes involved in conducting a systematic review and research synthesis. We conclude by discussing how the findings of systematic reviews can be used to inform practice and scholarship and identify the prospects for systematic reviews in management. At the end of the chapter, we provide details about available resources and information useful for conducting systematic reviews.

Why Academics and Practitioners Need Systematic Reviews and Evidence Syntheses

The overall intent of management and organization studies is simultaneously to advance knowledge and to give insights into the practice of management. Currently both of these aims are being hindered by the inability of the field to effectively accumulate evidence across a body of previous research. The idea that research is formed on the basis of and by extending existing knowledge is well-expressed in Isaac Newton's statement—"If I have seen a little further it is by standing on the shoulders of giants"—even though the Giant metaphor overpersonifies knowledge. Given the importance placed on building on prior research by developing a deep understanding of the existing state of knowledge, it is somewhat surprising that management academics seem much more preoccupied with identifying new research questions than consolidating knowledge around a defined and agreed agenda. The emphasis on empirical contributions rather than reviews and syntheses has resulted in a voluminous, fragmented, and contested field.

Research-methods courses and textbooks focus almost exclusively on techniques for conducting primary research (collecting and analyzing new data) rather than secondary research (researching existing research). Few management researchers are trained in how to review literature. The result is primary research that is often informed by partial, haphazard, and opinion-driven syntheses of previous research findings.

Within business schools, the rigorous research that academics publish in high-quality journals is seldom used in management education. Programs such as the MBA, rarely train students in how to scrutinize literature around practice questions or

how to keep abreast of emerging research once out of school. This is in sharp contrast to other domains, such as medicine, law, and engineering, in which developing such skills forms the basis for exercising and sustaining professional judgment and expertise. In business and management, practitioners rarely access and use academic research. Instead, they are more likely informed by the "lessons learned," "best practices," "cutting-edge practices," and "world-class techniques" gleaned from single case studies frequently offered by consultancies, popular journals, and management books of apparently successful organizations. However, implementation of these recipes often produces outcomes that are unanticipated and potentially suboptimal.

As a consequence of these shortcomings, many academics and practitioners have a relatively patchy understanding of the current state of the body of knowledge relating to any given topic. Despite this, academics and practitioners often make quite broad and confident statements, such as "previous research has shown that team building improves performance" or "it has been demonstrated that management development is effective." Similarly, the existence of a relationship between two phenomena, such as "networking leads to increased innovation," is often stated as fact and then simply followed by a bracketed list of half a dozen or so citations to earlier studies or reference to admired and thriving organizations. For scholars and practitioners, statements like these should raise important and challenging questions such as: Did *all* previous research show this? What proportion of previous research? How many studies? How strongly or clearly or consistently was this shown? Were the study designs such that the conclusions reached could be justified? What did the authors do to avoid the biases of preexisting beliefs? We do not believe that the current approaches to reviewing literature in management and organization studies effectively address such questions.

Current Approaches to Reviewing Management Knowledge

Literature reviews are found mainly in five main contexts: (1) introductions to papers reporting empirical studies; (2) papers, chapters, or books whose principal aim is to review literature; (3) meta-analyses; (4) textbooks for students; and (5) trade and management practice books for practitioners. The literature review practices in each of these contexts will be considered in turn.

Literature Reviews Motivating Empirical Studies

Most literature reviews are short summaries at the beginning of empirical journal articles. Their main purpose is to build a case to explain why the research reported in the article is interesting, important, and fills gaps in knowledge. Because the aim of these reviews is to build an argument, they involve some cherry picking: published research that supports the rationale for the study is included but research that does not is omitted. Given space limitations in journal articles, these reviews rarely provide an in-depth, comprehensive, balanced, or detailed account of previous research. They rarely tell the reader how the review was conducted or how the authors arrived at their conclusions. Although the peer-review process is intended to screen out erroneous conclusions, the wide acceptability of unsystematic reviews suggests that management researchers take a fairly relaxed or ad hoc approach to building on previous research.

Formal Full-Length Literature Reviews by Academics

The purpose of full-length reviews is to provide an analysis and summary of existing literature on a particular topic. These are published in a range of outlets including specialist review journals (e.g., *International Journal of Management Reviews*, *Psychological Bulletin*) or regular review issues of journals (e.g., *Journal of Management*), annual series (e.g., *International Review of Industrial and Organizational Psychology*, *Annual Review of Psychology*) and book chapters. These often take the form of either an argument/thematic review or an expert review (Gough, 2007). Argument/thematic reviews explore and usually support a particular argument or theme and rarely claim to use explicit rigorous methods. An expert review is informed by the skill and experience of the reviewer in that particular field, but it has no clear method so open to hidden bias. Most reviews in management are of the argument/thematic or expert type. For example, in the majority of *Academy of Management Annals* articles, the methods of review are rarely discussed or considered. Some literature reviews in management and organization studies claim to be systematic but do not follow any particular methods, whereas others may use rigorous methods but these are not stated or explicitly discussed (see Gough, 2007 for a discussion of different review types).

Meta Analyses

Meta-analysis is a technique used to quantitatively combine the data from comparable individual studies that address the same topic in order to reach some general conclusions. In a meta-analysis research, studies are collected and data from each individual study is coded and interpreted using statistical methods similar to those used in primary data analysis. Meta-analyses can demonstrate that effects occur even if the individual studies that were included in the review lacked the power to show such effects (Ohlsson, 1994). The aim is to produce results that are generalizable and can be used to make reasonable predictions of future events. Although meta-analysis can be considered to be a form of systematic review, it is not being discussed in detail in this chapter mainly because it is a specific technique and considerable guidance is available elsewhere (e.g., Hunter & Schmidt, 2004; Geyskens, Krishnan, Steenkamp & Cunha, 2009).

Reviews in Current Textbooks

A fourth category of publications that reviews literature and previous research is textbooks aimed at the mass-education market. Given the purposes of textbooks, their audience, and the very limited space available to discuss a large number of topics, it is inevitable that they tend to choose pieces of research that the author believes best exemplify an area of research. There are no criteria for textbook quality or adequacy. In some fields, certification bodies authorize books. However, in the management field, literature cited in texts can be from newspapers and magazines or from scholarly works combined with business articles. In general, instructors choose which text to adopt perhaps more on the basis of whether they will appeal to students than the quality of referencing.

Research findings are inevitably presented in an over-simplified way in order to present a clear and coherent narrative about how research has developed and what has been found emphasizing the linear development and progress of knowledge and the importance of a few key individuals in the style of the "Great Man" theory of history.

Reviews in Popular Management Books

Popular management-practice books vary considerably, but most aim to provide practical advice or insights to managers and other practitioners. Although reviews of literature or the exploration of previous research findings are not usually central aspects of such books, they do, nonetheless, draw on published research or unpublished research from case studies or testimonials that support the use of the particular ideas or approaches that the book promotes. These and similar popular books rarely claim to offer a comprehensive or balanced review of the literature. Again, extensive cherry picking of research is the norm in order to support the books' claims. Unlike academic papers, there is no peer-review process to help identify any misrepresentation or inaccurate conclusions.

Popular management books advise practitioners to take up new, "leading-edge" or "cutting-edge" management techniques. However, by definition, these techniques are not well established enough to have been well researched. For example, in 1982, Tom Peters and Robert Waterman published *In Search of Excellence* claiming that there were eight keys to excellence that were shared by the 43 firms in their study. The book quickly became one of the most quoted management books and seemed to provide a blueprint for effective performance in a competitive market. However, critics have questioned the way Peters and Waterman conducted their research and the validity of their findings. For example, Hitt and Ireland (1987) re-examined the performance of Peters and Waterman's excellent firms by comparing them with a general sample of Fortune 1,000 firms. They discovered that only three of these excellent firms performed better than the average Fortune 1,000 firms, and several excellent firms did not exhibit the keys to excellence to a greater extent than other firms in the Fortune 1,000 sample. Without systematic reviews of research evidence, there is a danger that managers searching for "quick fixes" to complex problems may turn to popular books that seldom provide a comprehensive and critical understanding of what works, in which circumstances, for whom, and why.

What Are Systematic Reviews and Research Syntheses?

Systematic reviews have become an essential tool of evidence-based practice. They

> … differ from traditional narrative reviews by adopting a replicable, scientific and transparent process, in other words a detailed technology, that aims to minimize bias through exhaustive literature searches of published and unpublished studies and by providing an audit trail of the reviewers' decisions, procedures and conclusions.
> (Tranfield, Denyer, & Smart, 2003, p. 209)

The benefits of this approach to reviewing are that it is "systematic and replicable, giving confidence to the users it informs regarding the status of present knowledge on a given question" (Rousseau, Manning, & Denyer, 2008, p. 500). However, it is important to note that

systematic reviews never provide "answers". What they do is report as accurately as possible what is known and not known about the questions addressed in the review
(Briner, Denyer, & Rousseau, 2009, p. 27).

Systematic review involves five key steps: (1) planning the review, (2) locating studies, (3) appraising contributions, (4) analyzing and synthesizing information, and (5) reporting "best evidence." They also adhere to a set of core principles:

• Systematic/organized: Systematic reviews are conducted according to a system or method that is designed in relation to and specifically to address the question the review is setting out to answer.
• Transparent/explicit: The method used in the review is explicitly stated.
• Replicable/updatable: As with many forms of primary research, the method and the way it is reported should be sufficiently detailed and clear such that other researchers can repeat the review, repeat it with modifications, or update it.
• Synthesize/summarize: Systematic reviews pull together in a structured and organized way the results of the review in order to summarize the evidence relating to the review question.

It is important to note that systematic reviews are, therefore, different from the vast majority of literature reviews that currently exist and are undertaken in management research.

What do Systematic Reviews do?

Systematic reviews allow us to draw conclusions, though, of course, with varying levels of certainty, consistency, and confidence about what is known and not known about the answer to the review question. One important difference between systematic and the traditional forms of literature review described earlier is that such limitations are acknowledged and, as the review method is made explicit it can be seen and critically evaluated. "Being specific about what we know and how we know it requires us to become clearer about the nature of the evaluative judgments we are making about the questions that we are asking, the evidence we select, and the manner in which we appraise and use it" (Gough, 2007, p. 214).

Although the conclusions of systematic reviews do vary, it is not uncommon for reviews to find that there actually is far less evidence on a given topic than assumed, and that it is, in turn, more inconsistent and less robust than widely believed. People, including researchers, tend to form strong beliefs, even though information may be ambiguous and limited. One good example is a meta-analysis (De Dreu & Weingart, 2003) that showed that the relationship between task conflict, team performance, and team satisfaction was largely negative, even though both academic papers and textbooks regularly report that task conflict has a generally positive effect.

For a range of reasons, both individual researchers and research communities tend to emphasize their knowledge rather than their ignorance, their certainty rather than their doubt, and their ability to find something rather than find nothing. However, finding an absence of evidence (what we do not yet know) is equally important as finding "evidence" (what we currently know), though social science, in particular, does not usually recognize this (Collins, 2003). This leads to the cherry-picking approach found in some traditional literature reviews discussed earlier, which produces distorted and overconfident views about the state of knowledge, which then becomes widely accepted and the "taken as givens" of a particular field. Another consequence is publication bias whereby journals tend only to publish studies that show positive findings relevant to a given question. This, in turn, leads to the "file-drawer problem" in which researchers feel they cannot publish or use null or negative results from well-conducted studies, so they abandon such findings to their file-drawer (see Rosenthal, 1979; Geyskens et al., 2009).

In systematic reviews, researchers make extensive efforts to locate all studies, including those that show negative or contradictory findings. This is achieved by comprehensively searching the grey literature (working documents, conference papers, preprints, statistical documents, and other difficult-to-access materials that are not controlled by commercial publishers). When synthesized and taken together with these partial and positive findings, systematic reviews can produce a more mixed and less clear answer to the question than had been previously assumed. It is, therefore, not surprising that the conclusions from systematic reviews are sometimes received with something less than enthusiasm, because they often challenge established views and positions.

In spite of not providing *the* answer, particularly if one is looking for those that are clear, unambiguous, and definitive, systematic reviews are very useful and potentially very important for both research and practice in a number of ways, which will be discussed toward the end of the chapter.

The Use of Systematic Reviews in Other Areas

Management is a relatively late adopter of systematic review methods, with the first paper published discussing the use of systematic reviews in management by Tranfield et al. (2003) though their use in health-care management (Axelsson, 1998), organizational psychology (Briner, 1998), and human resource management (Briner, 2000) was advocated a little earlier. Some of the earliest formal attempts to conduct reviews in a systematic way and synthesize evidence, though small in number, can be found in psychology and psychotherapy research (Petticrew & Roberts, 2006). More recently, in the early 1990s, the Cochrane Collaboration was formed to produce systematic reviews to support the growing interest in evidence-based medicine. A social-policy equivalent, the Campbell Collaboration, was founded in 1999. Since this time, systematic reviews have been produced and discussed in a number of disciplines such as social- work research (e.g., Littell, Corcoran, & Pillai, 2008), education research (e.g., Davies, 2004), and criminology (e.g., Bennett, Holloway, & Farrington, 2006). A more complete list of other fields in which evidence-based approaches and the role of systematic reviews have been discussed can be found on Pfeffer and Sutton's Evidence-Based Management (2010) web site (http://www.evidence-basedmanagement.com/).

Because one of the main purposes of systematic reviews is to help practitioners access research, systematic reviews are often made available in on-line databases. For example, the Cochrane Collaboration focuses on health-care decision making, and publishes the Cochrane Database of Systematic Reviews (2010). In 1995 the database contained 36 reviews, 1,000 reviews by 2001, and by early 2010 over 4,000 reviews had been published. In 2008 its impact factor placed it fourteenth of 100 international journals in medicine (internal and general category). Other online databases include:

• The Campbell Collaboration (2010) whose current mission is to help people "…make well-informed decisions by preparing, maintaining and disseminating systematic reviews in education, crime and justice, and social welfare." Examples of topics covered by reviews include the impact of after-school programs on student outcomes, effects of closed circuit television surveillance on crime, and the effects of correctional boot camps on offending.

• The EPPI-Centre (2010) (Evidence for Policy and Practice Information and Co-ordinating Centre) conducts and publishes systemic reviews in a range of areas, such as education, health promotion, employment, social care, and crime and justice. Examples of review topics include children's views about obesity and body shape, effectiveness of interventions to reduce gang-related crime, and the impact of head teachers on student outcomes. The EPPI-Centre also develops tools and methods around systematic reviews and provides systematic-review training.

Examples of Systematic Reviews in Management

Given the growth of evidence-based medicine, it is not surprising that researchers in health-care management were among the first to apply the idea of evidence-based management (e.g., Kovner, Fine, & D'Aquila, 2009) and to consider how systematic reviews might be made more useful to health-care managers (Lavis et al., 2005).

In relation to management research more generally, Briner et al. (2009) provided some examples of management-relevant systematic reviews (some published and unpublished) funded by a range of organizations and government agencies. Table 7.1 provides further examples of systematic reviews published in management journals.

Although published and unpublished systematic reviews exist in management, they are few in number compared to medicine and policy-oriented areas of social science.

Conducting a Systematic Review

Although a fair amount has been written on how to conduct systematic reviews and research syntheses in medicine (e.g., Glasziou, Irwig, Bain, & Colditz, 2001; Khan, Kunz, Kleijnen, & Antes, 2003; Higgins & Green, 2008) and social science and social policy (e.g., Gough, Oliver, & Thomas, in press; Pawson, 2006; Petticrew & Roberts, 2006) there is relatively little writing on this topic in the area of management (with the exceptions being Denyer & Tranfield, 2009; Rousseau et al., 2008; Tranfield et al., 2003). There are fundamental differences between medicine and management and, as we have noted elsewhere (Briner et al., 2009), systematic-review techniques cannot and should not be simply transferred directly from medical research to management research. Review methods need to be adapted to fit the question the review is setting out to address and the underlying assumptions of the research being reviewed. Having said that, there is, however, broad consensus across all these areas about the stages or steps involved in systematic review (see Table 7.2). In practice these stages are often not as linear as implied and, given that so much depends on the review question, the process may vary quite a lot across reviews. Some stages may, for example, be particularly difficult, prolonged, or significant. Also, some stages may, in practice, actually involve a series of smaller and more detailed steps.

In addition to reading the guidance provided here and elsewhere about conducting systematic reviews, there are two other, perhaps more direct, ways of understanding how such reviews can be conducted. The first is to become familiar with a few systematic reviews (see earlier for examples) and the second is to plan or actually do one. Designing a review and thinking through in principle what would need to be done can give insight into the underlying principles and logic. Some of the key aspects of conducting a systematic review are described briefly in the following sections.

Identify the Review Question

As with any research, developing a precise, answerable, and meaningful question is both difficult and crucial: Difficult because questions that can initially seem clear and sensible often turn out to be not clear enough and not really the right question; crucial because a badly formulated or otherwise inappropriate question will produce a weak review. "A good systematic review is based on a well-formulated, answerable question. The question guides the review by defining which studies will be included, what the search strategy to identify the relevant primary studies should be, and which data need to be extracted from each study. Ask a poor question and you will get a poor review." (Counsell, 1997, p. 381).

So how can a good review question be developed and identified? Several techniques have been suggested. The first involves using an advisory group of experts and users to help shape and formulate the review question. Through discussing the purposes of the review with subject-area experts and potential users the review questions formulated will be both more answerable and relevant to the field and/or to practice. Using advisory groups is considered to be standard practice in contexts in which systematic reviews are more common, and they will be discussed in more detail later.

Table 7.1: Examples of Published Systematic Reviews Relevant to Management Research and Practice

Author	Title	Place of publication	Main findings
Hogh and Viitasara (2005)	A systematic review of longitudinal studies of nonfatal workplace violence	*European Journal of Work and Organizational Psychology*	16 longitudinal studies found. Different risk factors and outcomes assessed across studies. 5 studies showed exposure to violence has acute and long-term consequences. 2 found symptoms of posttraumatic stress disorder.
Adams, Bessant and Phelps (2006)	Innovation management measurement: A review	*International Journal of Management Reviews*	Large number of measures of innovation management measures found. Most lacked (predictive) validity. Many aspects of innovation management assumed to be important not assessed by any measures.
Egan et al. (2007)	The psychosocial and health effects of workplace reorganisation. 1. A systematic review of organisational-level interventions that aim to increase employee control	*Journal of Epidemiology and Community Health*	12 controlled prospective studies that met inclusion criteria found, plus 3 uncontrolled prospective and 3 retrospective. No negative effects of interventions. 8 of 12 controlled studies found evidence of health improvements. Most health measures self-reported and control of confounding variables limited.
Pittaway and Cope (2007)	Entrepreneurship education: A systematic review of the evidence	*International Small Business Journal*	Entrepreneurship education has had impact on student propensity and intentionality but not clear if it has had impact on number or effectiveness of graduate entrepreneurs.
Keupp and Gassmann (2009)	The past and the future of international entrepreneurship: A review and suggestions for developing the field	*Journal of Management*	179 relevant articles identified (representing 4.6% of all published entrepreneurship articles). Most focused on antecedents of international entrepreneurship and most in small and young firms. Half did not have clearly specified theoretical framework.
Walker (2010)	A systematic review of the corporate reputation literature: Definition, measurement, and theory	*Corporate Reputation Review*	54 articles and 1 book identified Fewer than half studies defined corporate reputation and a lack of consensus over definition Gaps between theoretical assumptions and measurement of corporate reputation
Joyce, Pabayo, Critchley and Bambara (2010)	Flexible working conditions and their effects on employee health and wellbeing	*Cochrane Database of Systematic Reviews*	10 longitudinal studies that met inclusion criteria were found. Studies included 6 different types of interventions including flexitime and self-scheduling of shiftwork. Three interventions types had no effect on well-being. Tentative conclusion that interventions that increase work control may be beneficial.

Table 7.2 Typical Systematic Review Stages

1. Identify and clearly define the question the review will address.
2. Consider forming an advisory or steering group.
3. Determine the types of studies and data that will answer the question.
4. Search the literature to locate relevant studies.
5. Sift through all the retrieved studies in order to identify those that meet the inclusion criteria (and need to be examined further) and those that do not and should be excluded.
6. Extract the relevant data or information from the studies.
7. Critically appraise the studies by assessing the study quality determined in relation to the review question.
8. Synthesize the findings from the studies.
9. Consider potential effects of publications or other biases.
10. Write up report.
11. Disseminate the review findings.

Adapted from Petticrew and Roberts (2006).

A second way of developing the review question, which may involve members of the advisory group or members of the review team itself, is to test the question logically. By this we mean examining whether, in principle, the question makes sense, is specific enough, and will facilitate the development of the review method by, for example, allowing reasonably clear judgments about what sorts of data from what types of sources might answer the question.

Table 7.3 illustrates some of the broad initial questions that a systematic review team might start with which then will be made more specific so they can be addressed in a systematic review.

Taking the last question—Does team-building work?—as an example, a range of other questions need to be asked first in order to narrow it down sufficiently to address it in a systematic review. Further questions such as:

• What is meant by "team," and what is not included as a "team?"
• What kind of teams?
• In which particular contexts or settings?
• What is "team building" and what is not "team building"?
• What does *work* mean?
• Why "work" compared to any other outcome?
• How does team building compare to any other intervention or taking no action at all?
• What outcomes are relevant?
• What are the mechanisms, processes, and theories that might account for possible effects of team building on outcomes?
• What time periods are relevant for observing any possible effects?
• What about possible negative effects or harm?

• What types of data from what sorts of designs would, in principle, provide good quality, medium quality, and poor-quality evidence?

The answers to these questions will help refine the review question, make it more specific and answerable, and, also, possibly break down the question into a number of review questions. It is not uncommon to find that what initially seems to be a single review question is actually several interlinked questions.

A third and similar means of making the review question more specific is to use a framework that helps focus the question. One used in systematic reviews in medicine (with the acronym PICO) where the review question is concerned with the effectiveness of an intervention asks the reviewer to consider: (1) The patient (P) group(s) with the condition or problem; (2) the intervention (I), action, or activity under consideration; (3) the comparison (C) or alternative to the intervention; and, (4) the possible outcomes (O) or effects of the intervention or activity (e.g., Higgins and Green, 2008). An example of such a PICO question might be: For children with earache, does taking antibiotics compared to not taking antibiotics reduce levels of reported pain?

A version of this framework adapted for social science is called SPICE (Booth, 2004) and considers setting (or context); perspective (of the stakeholder asking the question); and the intervention or phenomenon of interest, comparison, and evaluation (the way in which success is evaluated). Another social science version of this framework is that of Denyer and Tranfield (2009), drawing on Pawson's (2006) work on evidence-based practice from a realist perspective. Their CIMO framework

Table 7.3. Examples of Intitial Review Questions that Require much Greater Specificity

- What's the best way to designs jobs in call centers?
- Is introducing team-based working in a sales force a good idea?
- Does management development do anything?
- Are organizations that use management by objectives more effective?
- Why are there relatively few ethnic-minority employees at the top of organizations?
- Does having a strategy make organizations more successful?
- What causes resistance to organizational change?
- How different are leaders and does it matter?
- What are the most effective absence management techniques?
- Do higher-performing companies pay better salaries?
- How is trust between organizations broken and repaired?
- What are organizations' motives for introducing green policies?
- Is it worth trying to develop the emotional intelligence of our managers?
- Is EBMgt effective?
- How do managers use management information systems?
- What kinds of organizational communication fail?
- Does team-building work?

similarly includes context (C), interventions (I), and outcomes (O), but one crucial difference is the inclusion of a consideration of the mechanisms (M) through which the intervention may affect outcomes.

Last, review questions can be made more specific and revised by actually testing them through attempting to locate and select relevant studies. If no relevant studies are found, this does not mean the question needs to be changed because, if the question is reasonable, the absence of relevant data or evidence is, in itself, a potentially very important review finding. Rather, what may happen through the process of trying to use the question is that, for example, it becomes apparent that the intervention has been defined too narrowly or perhaps incorrectly, or that additional outcomes need to be considered, which hadn't initially been considered.

Locate and Select Relevant Studies

Before conducting the review and starting to search for relevant studies, a protocol based on and incorporating the review questions should be developed. A protocol is a project plan for the review. It is the equivalent of the method and design used in primary research and "includes a description of and rationale for the review question, and the proposed methods, and includes details of how different types of study will be located, appraised, and synthesized" (Petticrew & Roberts, 2006, p. 44). A protocol ensures that the review is systematic, transparent, and replicable—the key features of a systematic review. Having a protocol also means the review

method can be challenged, criticized, and revised or improved in future reviews.

When the review questions and objectives become reasonably clear, so, too, should be the types of studies that will be relevant, the criteria for including and excluding studies, and where such studies are more likely to be found. When relevant databases and search terms have been identified, a scoping study can help ensure that the search strategies are effective. Such a scoping study may show, for example, that the search strategy is picking up too many irrelevant studies, missing highly relevant ones, or may not have identified all the relevant search terms.

One important question that will strongly shape the search strategy is whether to include unpublished data and the grey literature. As systematic reviews should ideally include *all* studies and data relevant to the review question that meets the inclusion criteria, they should, therefore, ideally seek out as much unpublished data and grey literature as possible. Publication bias and the file-drawer problem are already well known in relation to quantitative data (e.g., Geyskens et al., 2009), and the same problem will also apply to qualitative research. Data that unequivocally support a particular theory or approach are more likely to get published than data that show mixed or no support for the theory, or even show the opposite of what was expected.

Searching electronic databases is unlikely on its own to be sufficient. Other techniques for identifying more studies include looking through the reference lists of published reviews; citation searches;

Table 7.4. Example Structure of a Systematic Review Protocol

Background to review
- Problem statement and problem importance/relevance
- Rationale for the review
- Previous review findings (if any exist)
- How will this review be different?

Objectives
- Precise statement of the review's primary objective
- Statement of main review questions and subquestions

Criteria for considering studies for this review (CIMO)
- Types of contexts
- Types of interventions
- Types of mechanisms
- Types of outcomes
- Types of studies – qualitative, quantitative, both
- Types of designs

Search strategy for identification of studies
- What databases and sources will be searched?
- What the time period?
- What search terms and key words?
- Will there be language restrictions?
- Will unpublished data be sought?

Eligibility
- What are inclusion/exclusion criteria for studies?
- How many reviewers will screen the articles for inclusion/exclusion?
- How will reviewer disagreements be resolved?
- Will articles be reviewed in a blinded manner?

Data collection
- How many reviewers will extract data?
- Exactly what data will be extracted?
- How will the reviewers resolve disagreements?
- What other study data will be collected?

Assessment of methodological quality
- What instrument or scale or criteria will be used to assess quality?
- How many reviewers will assess study quality?
- How will the reviewers resolve disagreements?
- How will the quality data be used?

Synthesis
- What sort of synthesis (e.g., aggregation, integration, interpretation, or explanation) will be used and why?
- How will quality of data be incorporated?
- How can data most clearly be represented to address review questions?

Adapted from Higgins and Green (2008).

and contacting researchers, research groups, and institutions known for conducting research relevant to the review question for unpublished or in-press studies.

Next, the inclusion and exclusion criteria need to be applied to each paper and study found to determine whether the paper is relevant to the review. This is usually done by at least two reviewers. Mechanisms also need to be in place to help resolve disagreements among reviewers. Typically, resolution is achieved through a process of discussion between the reviewers, but if this is unsuccessful, other reviewers can also become involved. Too many disagreements suggest that the reviewers need further training or that the inclusion and exclusion criteria are insufficiently clear.

Sometimes, enough information is provided in the abstract to know whether the study meets the inclusion criteria and does not meet any of the exclusion criteria. In other cases, full copies of the paper have to be obtained so that details such as the method, can be checked.

At the end of this stage, all those studies deemed to be relevant to the review question will have been selected. The next stage is to examine each of these in order to reach some conclusions about the quality of each study included in the review.

Critically Appraise the Studies

A key part of systematic review is that each study is critically appraised in relation to the quality criteria devised as part of the systematic review protocol. This allows review findings to state clearly the quality levels of the studies included in the review. So, for example, a systematic review might report that, of the 28 relevant studies found, four were appraised as meeting the highest-quality standards, eight were found to be of moderate to good quality, and the remainder were of relatively poor quality. This means the review can be quite specific in identifying what, if any, differences might be occurring across studies that are appraised as having different quality levels. It also provides a good overall sense of what the quality of evidence is in relation to the review question and the weight or confidence that can and should be placed on the review's findings.

When judging the quality of a study in more traditional forms of review, many of us are sometimes swayed by the "brand" of the journal in which the study is published, thus conflating journal properties that are believed to signal quality—such as impact factor (a rating based on the average number of times articles published in that journal are cited), rejection rate (the percentage of articles submitted to the journal which are not accepted for publication), and whether the journal is recognized in some way by highly ranked business schools—with the quality of an individual study that happens to be published in that journal. We may equally be swayed by the "brand" of the individual researcher. By applying quality criteria that have been designed in advance and in relation to the review question we can avoid such potential biases.

One contentious and potentially misleading idea is that the "hierarchy of evidence" used specifically in medicine to critically evaluate studies of the efficacy of interventions can also be readily applied in other areas and to studies that are not evaluating interventions. This hierarchy privileges randomized controlled trials (RCTs) and suggests that all other research methods are less valuable. However, even in medicine, there is growing recognition that RCTs may not be the best form of evidence for research questions that are not

about the effectiveness of interventions. The field of management and organization studies is notoriously methodologically eclectic, and so systematic reviews cannot be restricted to certain research designs but involve tracking down the best external evidence from a variety of sources with which to address the review questions. Because the issues confronted by managers are varied and multifaceted, which evidence is "best" depends on its pertinence to the question being asked (Boaz & Ashby, 2003). Some questions are addressed best via quantitative evidence, some qualitative evidence, some theory or a combination of all of these sources as noted elsewhere:

> ... it is unfeasible and undesirable for management research to simply adopt the benchmark of the Cochrane model or any other field's approach toward the review process or the hierarchy of evidence. All academic fields are different. Which evidence is "best" depends entirely on its appropriateness to the question being asked....
> (Briner et al., 2009, p. 26)

In other words, decisions about the design of the quality criteria and the critical appraisal process, as with every other design decision, are taken to ensure that the review is fit for purpose: to answer the review question.

Many checklists and tools have been devised to help with critical appraisal of many different study types (see Petticrew & Roberts, 2006) including qualitative studies of various kinds, observational studies, interrupted time series studies, and questionnaire surveys. The power of these qualitative contributions is their ability to help develop an understanding of participant experience and give insights into the nature of competing values issues. For qualitative research, quality checklists might include (depending on the orientation of the researchers in relation to ideas about the nature of knowledge) questions covering issues such as (Cohen & Crabtree, 2008):

- Research ethics.
- The theoretical and practical importance of the research.
- The clarity and coherence of the study report.
- The extent to which methods were appropriate and rigorous.
- The role of reflexivity or attending to researcher bias.
- Consideration given to establishing validity or credibility.
- Consideration of verification or reliability.

For a questionnaire survey, a quality or critical appraisal checklist would include questions covering areas such as:

- Clarity and basis of research question or hypotheses.
- Appropriateness of sample selection.
- Known reliability and validity of measures used and reliability and validity of measures as used in current study.
- Appropriateness of design to research question.
- Appropriateness of data analysis and inferences made.

For each study, one or more reviewers would answer each of the specific questions contained in the checklist, thus producing an overall quality score or rating or category.

As with each aspect of the systematic review process, the method used for critically appraising the studies needs to be explained in sufficient detail such that someone from outside the review team could replicate the method. Similarly, the rationale for the choice of quality criteria needs to be clearly described so that the reader can understand why some study designs and attributes are judged to reflect higher study quality. For example, if the review question is one about understanding *causes* or *processes* in relation to some phenomenon, then it would be reasonable to expect that study designs that allow for some inference of causality or process (e.g., longitudinal) would be appraised as having higher quality in relation to the review question than studies designs that do not allow for inference of causality (e.g., cross-sectional). In this particular example, studies with cross-sectional designs may have already been excluded from the review at the previous stage as not generating findings relevant to the review question.

Analyze and Synthesize the Findings from the Studies

Once all the studies relating to the review question have been collated and appraises, the next stage of the systematic review is analysis and synthesis. The aim of the analysis is to examine and dissect individual studies and explore how the components relate to one another. In contrast, synthesis is a process of putting the findings from individual studies together "into a new or different arrangement and developing knowledge that is not apparent from reading the individual studies in isolation" (Denyer & Tranfield, 2009, p. 685). The process usually

begins with the extraction of data from individual studies using data extraction forms, which are tailored to the specific requirements of each review. Examples of such forms can be found at the web sites, which produce systematic reviews such as Cochrane, Campbell, and EPPI. The data extraction forms allow the reviewer to explain in descriptive terms the nature of the field of study. For example, "who are the key authors, how many of the core contributions are from the USA, how many are European? What is the age profile of the articles? Can the fields be divided into epochs in terms of volume of orientation of study? Do simple categories divide up the field? For example, can the field be divided sectorally? By gender?" (Tranfield et al., 2003, p. 218). This information, when cross-tabulated and presented in the appendices of a systematic review, provides the reader with an extremely useful summary of the field.

The aim of synthesis is to bring together the "the findings on a chosen theme, the results of which should be to achieve a greater level of understanding and attain a level of conceptual or theoretical development beyond that achieved in any individual empirical study" (Campbell et al., 2003, p. 672).

There are numerous established methods of research synthesis. Dixon-Woods, Agarwall, Young, Jones, and Sutton (2004) identified almost 20 approaches to research synthesis. Rousseau et al. (2008) group the multitude of syntheses into four categories: aggregative, integrative, interpretation, and explanation. Each of these approaches adopts different principles and methods. Aggregative methods, such as meta-analysis, quantitatively combine the findings from multiple homogeneous single studies using statistical techniques. Meta-analysis, "allows for an increase in power and thus based on a summary estimate of the effect size and its confidence interval, a certain intervention may be proved to be effective even if the individual studies lacked the power to show effectiveness" (Ohlsson, 1994, p. 27).

Integrative approaches often incorporate qualitative and quantitative studies. For example, in many systematic reviews the findings of qualitative studies are summarized and compared with the findings of the quantitative studies. Bayesian meta-analysis goes further by combining the two data sets (Roberts, Dixon-Woods, Fitzpatrick, Abrams, & Jones, 2002). Interpretative synthesis involves translating and comparing the data across the studies to develop categories and higher-level themes (Noblitt & Hare, 1988). The explanatory approach to synthesis attempts to ascertain causal mechanisms in the data and explain how they function. The aim is to produce a transferable theory in the form of "what works for whom in what circumstances" (Pawson, 2006).

Although there are multiple novel and powerful approaches to synthesis, examples of their use in the management field are limited. As such, narrative synthesis remains the most common approach. Narrative synthesis attempts to take a collection of studies that address different aspects of the same phenomenon and build them into a bigger picture, map, or mosaic (Hammersley, 2001) or to "tell the story" of studies included in the review (Popay et al., 2006, p. 5) by, for example, describing how they fit within a theoretical framework and the size or direction of any effects found. Narrative synthesis is a flexible method that allows the reviewer to be reflexive and critical (Hart, 1998) through their choice of organizing narrative. However, it is often criticized because authors can privilege certain findings or studies over others, and it is feasible that two reviewers who synthesize the same set of studies using this method of synthesis could reach different conclusions (Rumrill & Fitzgerald, 2001).

So which approach should be adopted? As with other aspects of the systematic review process, the approach should be fit-for-purpose, taking into account the review question and the nature of the available evidence. Whatever the chosen method, the approach should be made explicit and a justification given for all decisions.

Disseminate the Review Findings

As one of the main purposes of systematic reviews is to make findings from research more accessible to practitioners, the dissemination of review findings is fundamental to the purpose of conducting a systematic review—whether those practitioners are other management researchers (in the case of a more research-focused review), managers and organizational decision makers, or both.

In medicine and other fields of practice where systematic reviews are common, there are relatively well-developed systems for getting the results of systematic reviews to practitioners (e.g., web sites, journals, summaries, secondary journals, continuing professional development, and professional bodies) and in forms that allow the results to be fairly directly applied to practice (e.g., guidelines, checklists, protocols).

For example, The UK's National Institute of Health Research Centre for Research and Dissemination (2010), in addition to producing systematic reviews, providing training, and developing systematic review methodology, also produces regularly updated databases of abstracts of systematic reviews published around the world. Its own guidance on undertaking systematic reviews (Centre for Reviews and Dissemination, 2009, p. 85) defines dissemination as "... a planned and active process that seeks to ensure that those who need to know about a piece of research get to know about it and can make sense of the findings" and recommends that a dissemination strategy be built into the review protocol.

The dissemination of systematic reviews in health care is far from simple or straightforward and, even where systematic reviews produce relatively unequivocal findings these are not, for a range of reasons, necessarily reflected in the practice of health-care professionals. The dissemination of systematic review findings in management presents even greater challenges. First, management research is very broad with limited consensus in some domains about what counts as evidence (Rousseau et al., 2008) or indeed the purposes of management research or the activity of managing. Second, the sorts of decisions managers make are not usually "life or death," as they may be for health-care practitioners, and thus the benefits of using research evidence and the costs of not using it are less salient. Third, as mentioned earlier, it appears that many areas of management practice are about adopting new or "cutting-edge" practices, which, by their nature, have not been researched or evaluated. Indeed, it may be the case that practices sufficiently researched to enable a systematic review are also those very practices that are perceived by organizations as old-fashioned and unappealing, even where review findings suggest they are effective. Fourth, in contrast to health care and other areas of practice, managers are not usually required to belong to regulated professional bodies that often prescribe the content of initial training, continuing professional development, and promote evidence-based practice among their members. One way to enhance the uptake and use of the findings of systematic reviews in management would be to teach evidence-based approaches in MBA programs, in order to help develop the critical appraisal skills that might help managers find systematic-review findings attractive and usable.

A final challenge for disseminating the findings of systematic reviews is that, at the present time, management researchers and management practitioners have almost no exposure to such reviews, and initial exposure to systematic reviews may not be a wholly positive experience. Compared to the sometimes overconfident and air-brushed presentation of research findings in more traditional reviews, systematic-review findings are more nuanced, qualified, and presented in a "warts-and-all" fashion, making them more difficult to swallow. However, this particular challenge should be overcome as more systematic reviews become available and are used in teaching, in training, and to help inform managerial decision making.

Using the Resources Available for Conducting Systematic Reviews

Some examples of guidance and help have been briefly described earlier, and at the end of the chapter are more details of how to access specific sources of support. Here, we consider some of the ways in which these resources can be used during the process of planning, conducting, and reporting the results of a systematic review.

As mentioned earlier, it is considered fairly standard practice in some fields to draw together a review advisory group. It consists of users or potential users of the review findings and might include, for example, users of services or those whom the intervention affects (e.g., employees and employee representatives), practitioners, and organizational policy makers (e.g., managers and directors), and other researchers. The Campbell Collaboration in social science suggests that the tasks of the group might include:

- Refining the review question.
- Identifying interventions and populations to be included.
- Setting priorities for outcomes to be assessed.
- Helping to interpret the findings of the review.
- Commenting on the review protocol and draft report.
- Advising on the dissemination plan and helping to disseminate findings.

The review team is the group of researchers who actually conduct the review and often consists of a mix of more senior researchers, research assistants, and/or PhD students. The team is vital, not only because it gets the work done, but, as discussed earlier, conducting a systematic review can be quite an iterative process and one that also requires judgments from several people about each paper and study identified. Understanding and articulating the bases of agreements and disagreements is an essential part of the process because these help refine and develop the design of the review. The quality of the final review depends a lot on how well the review team functions and develops a critical, challenging, though collaborative approach to their task.

Previous reviews of both the systematic and traditional types can be a useful resource in at least a couple of ways. First, simply studying how previous systematic reviews have been designed and conducted can help provide guidance about what to do—and, in some cases, what not to do. A review that addresses a similar sort of question found in other review protocols can be a useful template. Second, more traditional reviews often make claims about where gaps in knowledge are or where findings are relatively consistent. Such claims are a useful starting point for identifying systematic review questions where the aim is, in part, to test or challenge conventional wisdom. For example, if there appears to be general consensus in previous reviews that a particular theory has been well-supported by empirical evidence, a systematic review enables a more specific examination of how much and what sort of research exists, its quality, and what the findings of each study suggest individually and collectively.

Another important resource is information scientists and librarians (see Werner, chapter 15 of this volume). As noted earlier, management scholars are not usually trained in how to perform literature reviews and, therefore, have little technical knowledge about how to search the literature and find relevant publications. Information scientists, on the other hand, study the efficacy of different literature-search techniques. These can be more complicated in social science and management than medicine, not least because of the number of different terms used by social-science researchers for the same or very similar phenomenon. Most university librarians are trained in information science, and, in our experience, can provide very valuable information and guidance.

Strengths and Weaknesses of Systematic Reviews

The major strength of systematic reviews is that they attempt to establish in an explicit and methodical way what is known and not known in relation to a given question. Clearly, this knowledge has limits, but as the process of reaching conclusions is made clear, such limits should also be obvious.

Though systematic reviews do have weaknesses, we believe that many but certainly not all of the

Table 7.5. – A Critical Appraisal Checklist for Assessing the Quality of Systematic Reviews

- Was a rationale and need for the review stated in relation to previous research and reviews?
- Was the review question clearly defined in terms of population, interventions,
- Comparators, outcomes, and study designs (PICOS) or other relevant framework?
- Was the search strategy adequate and appropriate to the review question? Were there restrictions on language, publication status, or publication date?
- Were steps taken to minimize bias and errors in the study selection process?
- Were criteria appropriate to the review question used to assess the quality of the primary studies, and were steps taken to minimize bias and errors in the quality assessment?
- Were preventative steps taken to minimize bias and errors in the data extraction process?
- Were sufficient details presented for each of the primary studies?
- Were appropriate methods used for data synthesis? Were differences between studies assessed? Were the studies pooled, and if so was it appropriate and meaningful to do so?
- Do the authors' conclusions accurately reflect the evidence that was reviewed?

Adapted from the *Systematic reviews: CRD's guidance for undertaking reviews in health care* (2009) published by the Centre for Reviews and Dissemination.

perceived weaknesses (e.g., Learmonth & Harding, 2006; Morrell, 2008) are a result of some of the more popular myths that have developed around the purposes of systematic reviews, what they can and cannot achieve, and their status relative to other forms of review and primary research. Examples of these myths are discussed later.

Perhaps more relevant in the context of this book and this chapter is to consider how we can judge the quality of systematic reviews. As with any type of research, it may be done well or badly. So how can systematic review quality be judged?

One means of doing this is by using some sort of critical appraisal checklist such as the one in Table 7.5.

From some perspectives, systematic reviews are seen as intrinsically or fundamentally weak *in principle* and question the legitimacy and usefulness of this approach to reviewing literature. If, on the other hand, the idea of attempting to identify and critically appraise existing knowledge in relation to a specific question is seen as potentially useful then techniques such as the checklist in Table 7.5 can help ensure the systematic review is of reasonable quality and minimize weaknesses.

Using the Findings of Systematic Review

As discussed, the findings of systematic reviews set out what is known and not known about the review question. They are also explicit about what that knowledge is and the bases on which it is claimed to shed light (or otherwise) on the question. Systematic reviews usually start with a question from practice rather than a question from research. However, the findings from any sort of systematic

review have the potential to inform both practice and research.

Systematic reviews help identify the best available research evidence. However, it must be remembered that practitioner expertise and judgment, evidence from the local context, and the perspectives and views of those people who might be affected by the decision also play a critical role in management decisions (Briner, et al., 2009). As noted by the *Cochrane Handbook* (Higgins & Green, 2008, p. 167):

> the primary purpose of the review should be to present information, rather than offer advice. The discussion and conclusions should be to help people to understand the implications of the evidence in relationship to practical decisions.

Simply reporting the best available evidence is rarely enough to alter practice. Research in health care has shown that user involvement in systematic reviews greatly enhances the uptake and use of research evidence (Oliver et al., 2004). Our own work has shown that collaboration between the various stakeholders who use and create research evidence is at the heart of fostering effective EBMgt. Through this socialization, the best available research evidence can support, challenge, and combine with practitioner experience, tacit knowledge, and judgment.

In terms of research, systematic reviews can provide researchers with a solid understanding of the current state of knowledge in their field. A well-conducted systematic review can produce multiple outputs. For example, a systematic review on the relationship between networking and innovation

Table 7.6. Common Myths And Misconceptions About Systematic Review

- *Systematic reviews are exactly the same as ordinary reviews only bigger:* They share some features with the standard type of literature review found in management, but their use of an explicit method and the focus on a specific review question make them rather different. The complete version of a systematic review is often larger than a traditional review but they are also simultaneously published in other more-condensed formats.
- *Systematic reviews include only randomized control trials and quantitative data from quasi-experimental studies:* What is included or excluded in a systematic review depends on the review question and what the types of studies considered relevant. Given the nature of the questions asked in management and the design of most management research, it is unlikely that any systematic reviews in management would or even could include only randomized control trials or quasi-experimental studies.
- *Systematic reviews require the adoption of a positivistic scientific approach:* Systematic reviews can be conducted from many different science approaches depending, again, on the review question and the assumptions underlying it.
- *Systematic reviews necessarily involve statistical synthesis:* Statistical synthesis is only one way of synthesizing (quantitative) data. Systematic reviews can include qualitative data, quantitative data, or both.
- *Systematic reviews can easily be done without experienced information/library support:* Although they probably can be done without such support, doing so can make the process more difficult. Information scientists and librarians are trained in how to do systematic searches across multiple databases.
- *Systematic reviews provide definite answers to the review question:* Definite answers are rare. The answers produced by systematic reviews are more complete, more explicitly qualified, and, therefore, often less definite than the conclusions of traditional reviews.
- *Systematic reviews can only be done by subject matter and methodological experts:* Although subject matter and methodological experts are essential as members of the advisory group, they certainly do not need to be part of the review team. In fact, it can be argued that systematic reviews conducted by researchers who are not subject matter or methodological experts are more free from bias.
- *Systematic reviews are the best way to do literature reviews:* As emphasized in many places in this chapter, systematic reviews are just one method for conducting literature reviews. However, from an EBMgt perspective, it is likely that systematic reviews will be more useful than other forms of review.
- *Systematic reviews are a more important than doing good quality individual studies:* Neither is more important than the other, and both have central roles to play in developing understanding and insight.

Adapted from Petticrew and Roberts (2006).

(Pittaway, Robertson, Munir, Denyer, & Neely, 2004) was published as a working paper by the Advanced Institute of Management Research (AIM) together with a short "executive briefing" for managers. The review was then rewritten for publication in the *International Journal of Management Reviews* and has become one of the most cited papers in that journal. Subsequently, the systematic review was used by several of the authors to support their own empirical research.

Conclusion

In this chapter we have argued that many management scholars and practitioners claim to base their decisions at least in part on research evidence, yet the training of scholars and managers and the very limited availability of rigorous, relevant, and digestible summaries of research findings mean that they can only do so to a very limited extent. We have argued that systematic reviews are an efficient and effective method of developing an understanding of what we know and what we do not know about a given topic.

Systematic review methods are now well established in many other fields, and we believe that they are potentially of great value to both management researchers and management practitioners. However, the adoption and use of systematic reviews is constrained by objections based largely on myths and misconceptions (Briner et al., 2009). Tackling and discussing some of these, as described in Table 7.6, should encourage more management scholars to look more closely at the possible benefits of systematic review methods.

We have argued that systematic reviews are driven by a set of principles or a guiding logic rather than a single rigid and narrow protocol. By revealing these principles and outlining a systematic review methodology, we hope that this chapter helps reviewers to create a fit for a purpose-systematic-review approach that meets the specific requirements of their project. We believe that systematic reviews and syntheses of research evidence have the potential to inform both research and inform management practice by making known the best available academic evidence so that it can be integrated with judgment and experience of scholars and practitioners to help them make better decisions.

References

Adams, R., Bessant, J., & Phelps, R. (2006). Innovation management measurement: A review. *International Journal of Management Reviews, 8,* 21–47.

Axelsson, R. (1998). Toward an evidence-based healthcare management, *International Journal of Health Planning and Management, 13,* 307–317.

Bennett, T., Holloway, K., & Farrington, D. P. (2006). Does neighborhood watch reduce crime? A systematic review and meta-analysis. *Journal of Experimental Criminology, 2,* 437–458.

Boaz, A., & Ashby, D. (2003). *Fit for purpose? Assessing research quality for evidence based policy and practice.* London: ESRC UK Centre for Evidence Based Policy and Practice.

Booth, A. (2004). Formulating answerable questions. In A. Booth & A. Brice (Eds.), *Evidence-based practice: An information professional's handbook* (pp. 61–70). London: Facet.

Briner, R. B. (1998). What is an evidence-based approach to practice and why do we need one in occupational psychology? Proceedings of the 1998 British Psychological Society Occupational Psychology Conference, 39–44.

Briner, R. B. (2000). Evidence-based human resource management. In L. Trinder & S. Reynolds (Eds.), *Evidence-based practice: A critical appraisal.* London: Blackwell Science.

Briner, R. B., Denyer, D., & Rousseau, D. M. (2009). Evidence-based management: Construct clean-up time? *Academy of Management Perspectives, 23*(4), 19–32.

Campbell Collaboration (2010). Retrieved April 29, 2010, from http://www.campbellcollaboration.org/.

Campbell, R., Pound, P., Pope, C., Britten, N., Pill, R., Morgan, M., et al. (2003). Evaluating meta-ethnography: A synthesis of qualitative research on lay experiences of diabetes and diabetes care. *Social Science and Medicine, 56,* 671–684.

Centre for Reviews and Dissemination. (2009). Systematic reviews: CRD's guidance for undertaking reviews in healthcare [Internet]. York: University of York. Retrieved April 29, 2010, from http://www.york.ac.uk/inst/crd/systematic_reviews_book.htm.

Cochrane Database of Systematic Reviews. (2010). Retrieved April 29, 2010, from http://www2.cochrane.org/reviews/.

Cohen, D., & Crabtree, B. F. (2008). Evaluative criteria for qualitative research in healthcare: Controversies and recommendations. *Annals of Family Medicine, 6,* 331–339.

Collins, H. M. (2003). Lead into gold: The science of finding nothing. *Studies in History and Philosophy of Science, 34,* 661–691.

Counsell, C. (1997). Formulating questions and locating primary studies for inclusion in systematic reviews. *Annals of Internal Medicine, 127,* 380–387.

Davies, P. (2004). Systematic reviews and the Campbell Collaboration. In G. Thomas & R. Pring (Eds.), *Evidence-based practice in education* (pp. 21–33). Maidenhead, England: Open University Press.

De Dreu, C. K. W., & Weingart, L. R. (2003). Task and relationship conflict, team performance, and team member satisfaction: A meta analysis. *Journal of Applied Psychology, 88,* 741–749.

Denyer, D., & Tranfield, D. (2009). Producing a systematic review. In D. A. Buchanan & A. Bryman (Eds.), *The SAGE handbook of organizational research methods* (pp. 671–689). London: Sage Publications Ltd.

Dixon-Woods, M., Agarwall, S., Young, B., Jones, D., & Sutton, A. (2004). *Integrative approaches to qualitative and quantitative evidence.* Department of Health Sciences, University of Leicester. Department of Psychology, University of Hull. www.hda.nhs.uk

Egan, M., Bambra, C., Thomas, S., Petticrew, M., Whitehead, M., & Thomson, H. (2007). The psychosocial and health effects of workplace reorganisation 1: A systematic review of organisational-level interventions that aim to increase employee control. *Journal of Epidemiology and Community Health, 61,* 945–954.

EPPI-Centre. (2010). Retrieved April 29, 2010, from http://eppi.ioe.ac.uk/cms/

Evidence-Based Management. (2010). Retrieved April 29, 2010, from http://www.evidence-basedmanagement.com/

Geyskens, I., Krishnan, R., Steenkamp, J.-B. E.M., & Cunha, P. (2009). A review and evaluation of meta-analysis practices in management research. *Journal of Management, 35,* 393–419.

Glasziou, P., Irwig, L., Bain, C., & Colditz, G. (2001). *Systematic reviews in healthcare: A practical guide.* Cambridge, England: Cambridge University Press.

Gough, D. (2007). Weight of evidence: A framework for the appraisal of the quality and relevance of evidence. *Research Papers in Education, 22,* 213–228.

Gough, D., Oliver, S., & Thomas, J. (in press). *An introduction to systematic reviews.* London: Sage.

Hammersley, M. (2001). On "systematic" reviews of research literatures: A "narrative"response to Evans and Benefield. *British Educational Research Journal, 27,* 543–554.

Hart, C. (1998). *Doing a literature review: Releasing the social science research imagination.* London: Sage Publications.

Higgins, J. P. T., & Green, S. (2008) (Eds). *Cochrane handbook for systematic reviews of interventions* [updated September2009].RetrievedApril29,2010,fromwww.cochrane-handbook.org.

Hitt, M. A., & Ireland, R. D. (1987). Peters and Waterman revisited: The unended quest for excellence. *Academy of Management Executive, 1,* 91–98.

Hogh, A., & Viitasara, E. (2005). A systematic review of longitudinal studies of nonfatal workplace violence. *European Journal of Work and Organizational Psychology, 14,* 291–313.

Hunter, J. E., & Schmidt, F. L. (2004). *Methods of meta-analysis. Correcting error and bias in research findings (2nd Ed.).* Thousand Oaks, CA: Sage.

Joyce, K., Pabayo. R., Critchley, J. A., & Bambra, C. (2010). Flexible working conditions and their effects on employee health and wellbeing. *Cochrane Database of Systematic Reviews 2010, 2.* Art. No.: CD008009. DOI: 10.1002/14651858. CD008009.pub2.

Keupp, M. M., & Gassmann, O. (2009). The past and the future of international entrepreneurship: A review and suggestions for developing the field. *Journal of Management, 35,* 600–633.

Khan, K. S., Kunz, R., Kleijnen, J., & Antes, G. (2003). *Systematic reviews to support evidence-based medicine: How to review and apply findings of healthcare research.* London: Royal Society of Medicine.

Kovner, A. R., Fine, D. R., & D'Aquila, R. (2009). *Evidence-based management in healthcare.* Chicago, IL: Health Administration Press.

Lavis J. N., Davies, H. T. O., Oxman, A. D., Denis, J.-L., Golden-Biddle, K., & Ferlie, E. (2005). Toward systematic reviews that inform healthcare management and policy-making. *Journal of Health Services Research and Policy, 10* (1), 35–48.

Learmonth, M., & Harding, N. (2006). Evidence-based management: The very idea. *Public Administration, 84,* 245–266.

Littell, J. H., Corcoran J., & Pillai, V. (2008). *Systematic reviews and meta-analysis.* New York: Oxford University Press.

Morrell, K. (2008). The narrative of "evidence based" management: A polemic. *Journal of Management Studies, 45,* 613–635.

National Institute of Health Research Centre for Research and Dissemination. (2010). Retrieved April 29, 2010, from http://www.york.ac.uk/inst/crd/.

Noblit, G. W., & Hare, R. D. (1988). *Meta-ethnography: Synthesizing qualitative studies.* London: Sage Publications.

Ohlsson, A. (1994). Systematic reviews—theory and practice. *Scandinavian Journal of Clinical and Laboratory Investigation, 54,* 25–32.

Oliver, S., Clarke-Jones, L., Rees, R., Milne, R., Buchanan, P., Gabbay, J., et al. (2004). Involving consumers in research and development agenda setting for the NHS: Developing an evidence-based approach. *Health Technology Assessment, 8,* 1–148.

Pawson, R. (2006). *Evidence-based policy: A realist perspective.* London: Sage.

Petticrew, M., & Roberts, H. (2006). *Systematic reviews in the social sciences: A practical guide.* Oxford, England: Blackwell Publishing.

Pittaway, L., & Cope, J. (2007). Entrepreneurship education: A systematic review of the evidence. *International Small Business Journal, 25,* 479–510.

Pittaway, L., Robertson, M., Munir, K., Denyer, D. & Neely, A. (2004). Networking and innovation: A systematic review of the evidence. *International Journal of Management Reviews, 5/6,* 137–168.

Popay, J., Roberts, H., Sowden, |A., Petticrew, M., Arai, L., Rodgers, M., et al. (2006). *Guidance on the conduct of narrative synthesis in systematic review. A product from the ESRC Methods Programme.* Retrieved from http://www.conted.ox.ac.uk/cpd/healthsciences/courses/short_courses/qsr/NSguidanceV1-JNoyes.pdf

Roberts, K. A., Dixon-Woods, M., Fitzpatrick, R., Abrams, K. R., & Jones D. R. (2002). Factors affecting uptake of childhood immunisation: A Bayesian synthesis of qualitative and quantitative evidence. *Lancet, 360,* 1596–1599.

Rosenthal, R. (1979). The "file drawer problem" and tolerance for null results. *Psychological Bulletin, 86,* 638–641.

Rousseau, D. M., Manning, J., & Denyer, D. (2008). Evidence in management and organizational science: Assembling the field's full weight of scientific knowledge through syntheses. *Annals of the Academy of Management, 2,* 475–515.

Rumrill, P. D., & Fitzgerald, S. M. (2001). Speaking of research: Using narrative literature reviews to build a scientific knowledge base. *Work, 16,* 165–170.

Tranfield, D., Denyer, D., & Smart, P. (2003). Toward a methodology for developing evidence-informed management knowledge by means of systematic review. *British Journal of Management, 14,* 207–222.

Walker, K. (2010). A systematic review of the corporate reputation literature: definition, measurement, and theory. *Corporate Reputation Review, 12,* 357–387.

Systematic Review Resources
Websites

http://www.cochrane.org/ – The Cochrane Collaboration - database of systematic reviews relevant to healthcare and resources for conducting systematic reviews

http://www.campbellcollaboration.org/ – The Campbell Collaboration – library of systematic reviews related to education, crime and justice, and social welfare plus some guidance for conducting reviews

http://eppi.ioe.ac.uk/cms/ – Evidence for Policy and Practice Information and Co-ordinating Centre part of the Social Science Research Unit at the Institute of Education, University of London – a library of systematic reviews relevant to education and social policy. Also has guidance about conducting reviews and systematic review software.

Books

Glasziou, P., Irwig, L., Bain, C., and Colditz, G. (2001). *Systematic reviews in healthcare: A practical guide.* Cambridge, England: Cambridge University Press.

Gough, D., Oliver, S., and Thomas, J. (2012). *An introduction to systematic reviews.* London: Sage.

Higgins, J.P.T. and Green, S. (2008) (Eds). *Cochrane handbook for systematic reviews of interventions* [updated September 2009]. Retrieved April 29, 2010, from www.cochrane-handbook.org.

Littell, J.H., Corcoran J., and Pillai, V. (2008). *Systematic reviews and meta-analysis.* New York: Oxford University Press.

Petticrew, M. and Roberts, H. (2006). *Systematic reviews in the social sciences: A practical guide.* Oxford: Blackwell Publishing.

Research Findings Practitioners Resist: Lessons for Management Academics from Evidence-Based Medicine

Tamara L. Giluk *and* Sara L. Rynes-Weller

Abstract

We explore why practitioners resist scientific evidence and what academics—as researchers and educators—can do to promote its use. Evidence shows that practitioners often disbelieve, dismiss, or simply ignore findings from scientific studies. Drawing parallels between the fields of medicine and management, we discuss seven sources of resistance to research findings. Then, based on the relatively longer history of evidence-based medicine, we make recommendations for management academics wishing to more effectively advance evidence-based management.

Key Words: persuasion, practitioner resistance, practitioner distrust of academics, practitioner anxiety, inertia

Evidence-based medicine is flying with knowledge, instead of flying blind. Donald Berwick, M.D., Administrator, Medicare & Medicaid Services; former President and CEO, Institute for Healthcare Improvement
(PBS Newshour, November 2009*)*

The time is ripe for the "evidence-based" mantra to be silenced....if EBM (evidence-based medicine) does not fall spontaneously, it may need to be pushed. Bruce Charlton, MD
(Charlton & Miles, 1998, p. 373*)*

The movement toward evidence-based management (EBMgt) is gaining momentum. EBMgt is about making decisions that integrate the best available research evidence with practitioner expertise and judgment, evidence from the local context, and the perspectives of those who might be affected by the decision (Briner, Denyer, & Rousseau, 2009). However, history tells us that this movement is bound to encounter some resistance along the way (e.g., Johns, 1993; Rogers, 2003).

The parallel movement of evidence-based medicine (EBMed) has preceded that of management, with the term EBMed having been introduced in the early 1990s and the practice of EBMed growing phenomenally since then. The proportion of medical practice that is evidence-based, estimated to be about 10 percent in the late 1950s, is growing; more recent estimates range from 65 percent to 82 percent (Earle & Weeks, 1999). The *British Medical Journal* has called EBMed "one of our most important medical milestones" (Dickersin, Straus, & Bero, 2007, p. s10), on par with anesthesia, antibiotics, and the discovery of DNA structure. Clearly EBMed has "made it." Or has it? This chapter's opening quotes, both from physicians, illustrate the radically differing receptions that EBMed has received from various parties. For Berwick, EBMed provides information and clarity, whereas for Charlton, it serves as a call to arms.

What is at the root of such divergent views? In particular, what can explain such zealous reactions against evidence-based practice? A variety of criticisms have been leveled at EBMed over the years.

Some clinicians cite a lack of time and resources to practice EBMed (Straus & McAlister, 2000). Others claim a lack of evidence that EBMed actually "works," in other words, that the practice of EBMed actually improves patient outcomes (Norman, 1999; Straus & McAlister, 2000). From a more philosophical perspective, Kerridge (2010) has questioned whether EBMed seeks to perpetuate the dual authority of traditional medicine over complementary and alternative medicine and physicians over other health professions. Still other criticisms result from misperceptions regarding EBMed, for example, believing that it ignores patients' values and preferences, that it is a cost-cutting tool in disguise, or that it promotes a "cookbook" approach to medicine (Straus & McAlister, 2000). And some critics just do not like the "proselytizing zeal of EBMed proponents" (Charlton & Miles, 1998, p. 373) or their presumption that the practice of medicine "was previously based on a direct communication with God or by tossing a coin" (Fowler, 1997, p. 240).

Even more recently, Charlton (2009) characterized EBMed as "not driven by the scientific search for truth" (p. 930) but rather as a movement driven by the financial and personal interests of politicians, government officials, and managers who benefit from it. Charlton (2009) cites Goodman's (1998, p. 357) earlier assertion that "there is no evidence (and unlikely ever to be) that evidence-based medicine provides *better medical care in total* (emphasis in original) than whatever we like to call whatever went before" (p. 932).

Such criticism of EBMed gives us some idea of what to expect in reaction to EBMgt as it attempts to become common practice. In fact, similar criticisms have already been directed toward EBMgt. Critics have questioned the push for EBMgt before evidence exists to show that the practice of EBMgt would improve organizational performance (Reay, Berta, & Kohn, 2009). Others have expressed concern about the nature of the "the best scientific evidence" (e.g., the best evidence according to whom?; Learmonth, 2009), suspecting that the EBMgt movement might privilege certain types of research over others, both substantively (e.g., favoring research that endorses managerialist beliefs and reinforces managerial power) as well as methodologically (e.g., positioning meta-analysis as superior to qualitative research; Learmonth, 2006; Learmonth & Harding, 2006).

We would argue that one critical cause of resistance to evidence-based practice is resistance to the evidence itself. Consider the following example from medical research. *Effective Care in Pregnancy and Childbirth* (Chalmers, Enkin, & Kierse, 1991) is an extensive collection of meta-analyses—extensive being a two-volume, 1,516-page tome that reviews more than 3,000 randomized controlled clinical trials—that "has shaken obstetrics worldwide" (Naylor, 1995, p. 841). Mann (1990) describes some of the work's conclusions as well as its reception at the time. The research contained in the volumes clearly rejected such common practices as routine episiotomy (cutting the tissue between the vagina and anus to facilitate delivery) and repeating Cesarean sections routinely after a woman has had one (to avoid a rare risk of a C-section scar coming open during delivery and harming mother and baby). In contrast, it directly endorsed less common practices such as vacuum extraction (rather than forceps; used to facilitate delivery when the baby is "stuck"), the use of corticosteroids for women who are delivering prematurely (to prevent harm to the baby), and external turning for breech births (when the baby is coming out butt or feet first rather than the normal head first).

As with the opening quotes to the chapter, reactions to the book varied greatly. As cited in Mann (1990, p. 476), one medical journal called it "arguably the most important publication in obstetrics since William Smellie wrote *A Treatise on the Theory and Practice of Midwifery* in 1752." An editor of another medical journal wrote that "the price of £225 ($400) should protect aspiring registrars (medical residents) from acquiring too many confused ideas from its pages." A physician pronounced its authors "an obstetrical Baader-Meinhof gang," referring to one of post-World War II Germany's most violent left-wing organizations. The latter two comments indicate a disbelief or lack of acceptance of the research findings ("confused ideas"), with the visceral likening of the authors to a militant group in the vein of Charlton's earlier call to arms. The authors of the collection were not surprised at their critics, saying: "we have very strong evidence that obstetricians should do some things they are not doing, and we call into question the relevance of some of the things they are doing." Although this statement was made regarding obstetricians, we imagine that we could make similar statements about managers (see, for example, Rynes, Colbert, & Brown, 2002).

In this chapter, we explore why practitioners (of various fields) resist scientific evidence and what academics—researchers and educators—can do to promote EBMgt more effectively, given predictable resistance. What does it mean to "resist" evidence? Oxford English Dictionary (www.oxforddictionaries.com, 2010) defines *resist* as "withstand the action or effect of; try to prevent by action or argument; succeed in ignoring the attraction of (something wrong or unwise)." The various definitions indicate that resistance can take active (e.g., "try to prevent") or more passive (e.g., "succeed in ignoring") forms. In our chapter, we use the term generally, as resistance to evidence may take any of these forms.

During a planning conference for this *Handbook*, several chapter authors expressed concern about using the term *resist* or its derivatives in our chapters. The concerns seemed to center around the negative connotation of the term and, thus, the resulting admonishment of practitioners. We want to emphasize that our intent is not to target practitioners as the primary cause of the gap between practice and scientific evidence; academics must also accept responsibility. Thus, the potential solutions we discuss center on academics' roles and what they can do to facilitate the uptake of scientific evidence and thereby lessen the gap. Indeed, recent theoretical work (Ford, Ford, & D'Amelio, 2008; Piderit, 2000) challenges the negative connotation of the term *resistance*, arguing that positive intentions often motivate resistance and that resistance can make a positive contribution to a change effort. We generally agree, while noting that a discussion of this with respect to EBMgt is outside the scope of our chapter. In addition, Ford et al. (2008) note that change agents—those who identify the need for change and then create and drive the vision—contribute toward resistance to change through their own actions and inactions. In our chapter, we briefly note where academics contribute to resistance and discuss, in depth, their role in addressing resistance, no matter the source.

Our discussion must necessarily assume practitioners' awareness of research findings. Certainly this is often not the case, and we have discussed elsewhere the issue of practitioner lack of awareness of findings, its contribution to the academic-practice gap, and strategies to increase practitioner knowledge (e.g., Rynes, in press; Rynes et al., 2002; Rynes, Giluk, & Brown, 2007). However, after being exposed to relevant research, practicing managers may disbelieve, dismiss, or simply ignore the findings. What are the underlying sources of such behavior?

Rynes (in press) has previously considered this question in the context of industrial/organizational psychology after reviewing related research in the areas of utility analysis, selection procedures, and jury reactions to expert testimony. In this chapter, however, we will examine this question through the lens of evidence-based medicine and medical research. Because the field of medicine is further ahead than management on the path of evidence-based practice, we believe it can provide rich insights into resistance to research evidence. Our approach will also illustrate that resistance to research findings is not limited to the discipline of management, and occurs for reasons that are widely applicable across disciplines. Once we have explored the types of research findings practitioners find difficult to believe or accept, we turn to implications. In other words, given predictable resistance to evidence, what might academics do to promote EBMgt more effectively?

Sources of Practitioner Resistance to Research Findings
Distrust of Scientists, Statistics, and Special Interests

We start with perhaps the broadest source of resistance: distrust of academics or scientists, the statistics and scientific methods they use, and the role of sponsorship or special interests in the creation or presentation of research. This resistance strikes, not directly at the substantive content of the research findings, but rather at the creators of the research, their methods, and potential conflicts of interest. Because this source of resistance can color perceptions of all research findings, it is an important place to start. Although these three areas of distrust are related to some degree, they are also distinct, so we discuss them in turn.

Distrust of Academics/Scientists
Previous writings on the relationship between academics and practitioners have visualized the two groups as functioning in "separate worlds" (Rynes et al., 2007) or across a "great divide" (Rynes, Bartunek, & Daft, 2001). Indeed, academics and practitioners do exist in very different cultures. Murphy and Sideman (2006) argue that *practice-driven culture* emphasizes real-world problem solving. Practitioners are encouraged to take action ("get it moving"), even in the face of considerable uncertainty, drawing from any source necessary to devise a solution. The buy-in of end users and other stakeholders is crucial, so an important component of practice is an ability to persuade others of the value of one's proposed solution. The action orientation

ensures that the problem-solving process happens quickly.

Science-driven culture, on the other hand, emphasizes empirical confirmation and scientific caution ("get it right"). Theoretical support and linkages to prior research are critical, particularly when the only necessary buy-in is that of one's scientific peers. This emphasis on precision and method means that new academic findings develop and disseminate slowly. Practitioners and scientists do seem to live in separate worlds, and "understanding 'the other'... rarely happens without resistance" (Fisher, 2004/2005, p. 1).

The conception of academics as "other" not only creates a considerable credibility gap with practitioners, but also sets up a demonizing process, resulting in an "us-against-them" dynamic. Social-psychology research helps us to understand why this occurs. People view themselves as individuals, but they also have social identities, "their definitions of themselves in terms of their group memberships" (in this case, as practitioners or academics; Turner & Haslam, 2001, p. 25). Individuals categorize others with whom they share a group membership as part of their "in-group" and those who do not as part of an "out-group." In doing so, individuals tend to maximize similarities within and differences between the in-group and out-group (Gaertner et al., 2000). This social categorization of others—the mere acknowledgement that individuals belong to one group rather than another—can result in attitudes and behavior that favor the in-group and discriminate against the out-group (Tajfel, Flament, Billig, & Bundy, 1971). Such bias is more likely when the social identity is salient as well as when a group perceives its status to be under threat from another group (Turner & Haslam, 2001). Right now, EBMgt is a movement that is largely *driven* by academics and scientists, yet it is largely intended to *affect* managers or practitioners. In this context, EBMgt is likely a factor that not only makes salient the managers/practitioners' group identity, but it may also be perceived as a threat to their status or autonomy, suggesting that the "us-against-them" mentality may become particularly severe.

For a real-world illustration, consider a relatively recent controversy in the field of mental and behavioral health. In a review of the practice of clinical psychology, Timothy Baker and his colleagues (Baker, McFall, & Shoham, 2008) were highly critical of the impact of clinical psychologists on clinical and public health, citing their tendency to value personal experience over research evidence, to use

assessment practices with little to no psychometric support, and their failure to use interventions with strong evidence of efficacy. This prompted one popular science writer (Begley, 2009) to ask with respect to Baker et al.'s research, "Why do psychologists reject science?" Examination of almost 75 online reader comments (posted on *Newsweek.com,* 2009) about Begley's article proved rather illuminating. One of the first readers commented, "Amusingly, only 1 out of 3 authors of the paper has an actual license to practice Psychology in the state of their university." Implicit in this reader's statement is the notion that, because the authors are academics rather than licensed, practicing psychologists, they do not have the standing to critique practice. Another reader, noting a lack of research on the long-term effectiveness of "so-called evidence-based treatments," questioned the motives of academic researchers: "Most researchers are just looking to prove something quickly and have publications so they can obtain tenure at some university." Finally, another reader summed up his or her views by saying "If science had all the answers, I think we would see quite different conditions in all aspects of life and in our society." This virtual dismissal of science as a whole surely must also reflect this reader's view of those who create it.

Thus, practitioners' distrust of academics and scientists appears to reflect social categorization in action. However, recent theoretical and empirical work offers another explanation for such distrust and skepticism toward academics and scientists—a phenomenon that Kahan and colleagues (Kahan, 2010; Kahan, Jenkins-Smith, & Braman, 2010) call "the cultural cognition of expert consensus." Cultural cognition refers to the influence of group values—such as equality and authority, individualism and community—on risk perceptions and related beliefs. As Kahan (2010) notes, most people are not in a position to evaluate technical or scientific data on their own. As such, they tend to follow the lead of experts that they regard as credible. And who is considered credible?

Kahan and colleagues have found that the people whom laypersons see as credible are those whom they perceive to share their own values. To illustrate, in one study, Kahan, Braman, Cohen, Slovic, and Gastil (2010) investigated attitudes toward the human-papillomavirus (HPV) vaccine for girls. HPV is a sexually transmitted virus and the leading cause of cervical cancer. The Centers for Disease Control and Prevention (CDC) recommended in 2006 that all girls ages 11 and 12 (who presumably are not yet sexually active) receive the vaccine. Critics worry not only about harmful side effects of the vaccine, but also that it will encourage unsafe sexual activity. The CDC (2009) reports that only about a quarter of teenage girls received the vaccine in 2007 and that this proportion increased only slightly in 2008.

To study the possible reasons for the slow uptake of HPV research, Kahan and his colleagues (2010) created arguments for and against mandatory HPV vaccination. Arguments were then matched with fictional experts whose appearance and publication record were designed to be consistent with distinct cultural perspectives (e.g., hierarchical and individualistic versus egalitarian and communitarian). Their findings show that participants in the experiment aligned their views with the expert whom they perceived to share their values. Another experiment (Kahan et al., 2011) yielded similar results. Participants were asked to evaluate whether an individual of elite academic credentials (e.g., PhD from Harvard, professor at Stanford, member of the National Academy of Sciences) was a "knowledgeable and trustworthy expert." Again, participants' responses depended on the fit between their values and those of the expert. If the expert endorsed a position (on climate change, nuclear waste disposal, or handgun regulation) that was consistent with the position associated with participants' values, then he or she was more readily viewed as knowledgeable and trustworthy. In addition, participants also tended to overestimate the proportion of experts who held views consistent with their own views and values (a specific case of the egocentric bias; Turk & Salovey, 1985).

Although Kahan's work has examined only the cultural values just described, the broader implications for evidence-based practice are profound. Whether or not academics and scientists are viewed as credible and trustworthy is dependent on whether practitioners perceive them as sharing their values. As we saw from the contrast of practice-driven and science-driven cultures (Murphy & Sideman, 2006), academics and practitioners have quite different values, performance criteria, and audiences.

Of course, because of these cultural and value differences, one might think that academics and scientists would do everything they can to bridge the "great divide" (Rynes et al., 2001). Indeed, many do advocate or engage in such efforts (e.g., Van de Ven & Johnson's [2006] and Van de Ven's [2007] engaged scholarship, Bartunek's [2007] relational scholarship of integration). However, the efforts of academics to engage with laypersons often fail. As Begley (2010) notes in her *Newsweek* article, "Their Own Worst Enemies: Why scientists are losing the PR wars," scientists have "abysmal communication skills," at times exhibiting a "smarter-than-thou condescension" (p. 20). Latham (2007) agrees that most academics do not yet possess the skills to communicate with practitioners. He suggests that academics essentially need to "become bilingual" (p. 1029), mastering not only scientific language but also the translation of that language for practitioners. He gives examples of how he adjusts his language when communicating with practitioners (e.g., "hypotheses" become "ideas," results of F-tests and structural equation modeling become graphs that show "what happened where we did, versus where we did not, implement our ideas," p. 1029). Olson (2009) argues that communication is often more about telling a good story and engaging the audience's hearts (a skill at which scientists generally do not excel) than solely rational explanation of the data (see also Heath & Heath, 2008 on making ideas "stick").

As for academics' condescension toward nonscientists to which Begley (2010) refers, it is sometimes observed, even within our own field of management. For example, in response to the recommendation that the management field start doing and rewarding research that can be read and applied by business people, McKelvey (2006) asks, "Should management research be held hostage to people who seem mentally challenged when reading the *Harvard Business Review*?" (p. 823). Such queries are not likely to win any practitioners' hearts. Thus, in some respects, academics and scientists are their own worst enemies in building trust and credibility with practitioners.

One obstacle likely to be encountered in attempting to change this state of affairs is scientists themselves, who do not necessarily see the need for change. As one scientist reader commented on Begley's (2010) article: "I admit that I honestly didn't know it was supposed to be about winning or losing the PR wars as this article suggests. Spending most of my life in various scientific fields, I always thought science was about gaining knowledge. What an odd view by the author" (*Newsweek.com*, 2010).

Thus, the credibility and trustworthiness of academics is in question in part simply by virtue of who they are: a socially identified "other" with respect to practitioners, belonging to a culture emphasizing different values and performance criteria than that of practitioners, and communicating in a language and manner that practitioners do not always understand. Although the issue of communication is one that seems quite actionable, the others are not so easily remedied. Consequently, one important source of resistance to research evidence is practitioners' distrust of the creators of the research—that is, the academics or scientists themselves.

Distrust of Statistics and the Scientific Method

Practitioners are also generally skeptical of statistics and the scientific method—the foundation of research. This skepticism is nicely summed up in the phrase popularized by Mark Twain: "There are three kinds of lies: lies, damned lies, and statistics." According to Wikipedia, the phrase is used mostly by people who wish to disparage statistics that do not support their positions, or else to denounce the use of numbers in order to bolster weak arguments. Such distrust is a challenge for evidence-based practice, particularly given the evidence that having a positive attitude toward research is a strong predictor of using research findings in practice (e.g., Champion & Leach, 1989; Kenny, 2005; Lacey, 1994).

There are several reasons for this skepticism. First, individuals have a strong preference for intuitive or clinical decision making, despite the fact that statistical or actuarial methods outperform clinical judgments in a wide variety of circumstances (Ayres, 2008; Grove & Meehl, 1996; Grove, Zald, Lebow, Snitz, & Nelson, 2000). This preference may partially stem from the fact that the vast majority of people are fairly naïve about statistics (Best, 2001). Rynes (in press) discusses the preference for clinical judgment in the context of utility analysis, employee selection, and jury decisions. However, this preference is certainly evident in health-care-related areas as well—for example, clinical psychology.

Vrieze and Grove (2009) surveyed close to 200 clinical psychologists about the way in which they integrated patient assessment results to make decisions regarding diagnosis, treatment, or prognosis—using mechanical (formal, statistical) or clinical (informal, judgmental) methods. Ninety-eight percent of the clinical psychologists integrated assessment results using clinical methods, whereas only 31 percent used mechanical methods. (Percents are greater than 100 because respondents were given nine different options to describe how they normally combine data. Although mechanical and clinical prediction techniques are theoretically mutually

exclusive, the researchers wanted to allow for the fact that many respondents do not share this point of view). Respondents gave a variety of reasons that mechanical prediction methods were not used. The most common reason was simply that they did not believe they worked; mechanical methods could not possibly account for all of the factors that influence a prediction, substitute for a clinician's intuition, or be as accurate as other methods. (Such reasoning is consistent with Highhouse's (2008) argument for why managers prefer unstructured interviews to structured selection methods.) Others admitted that they were not familiar enough with mechanical methods to be comfortable using them or thought that they were simply too difficult to apply.

Second, skepticism also results from a perceived lack of generalizability of the findings. Practitioners find it difficult to reconcile the aggregate results provided in research to a specific case or situation. Charlton (1997), the critic of EBMed whose quote kicked off the chapter, believes that epidemiological data do not provide the information necessary to treat an individual patient. As he characterizes it, this is the intractable error of EBMed, and "no amount of statistical jiggery-pokery with huge data sets can make any difference" (p. 170). There is a flawed, unstated assumption in this assertion, however. Individuals criticize research as irrelevant because statistics can only give average probabilities (i.e., cannot make an exact prediction about a unique individual or circumstance). In doing so, they seem to imply that they, as clinicians, *can* make an exact prediction (Grove & Meehl, 1996). Of course, we know that this is very rarely the case.

Grove and Meehl (1996) respond to this assertion of average probabilities as irrelevant with a hypothetical example. They ask us to imagine that our physician has advised us to undergo surgery for some serious health condition. We ask whether the surgery will solve our health problem and how risky it is (i.e., Does it work? Will we die in surgery?). Most of us would look for an answer referencing statistical probability (e.g., it works 50 percent or 90 percent of the time; one in 1,000 patients or five in 100 will die during surgery). They ask, "How would you react if your physician replied, 'Why are you asking me about statistics? We are talking about *you*—an individual patient. You are unique. Nobody is exactly like you. Do you want to be a mere statistic? What differences do those percentages make, anyway?'" (p. 305). Clearly, none of us would be satisfied with such an answer, but those who claim that averages are irrelevant to a unique person or situation are essentially similar to a physician answering just that. As Rousseau (2006) points out, this belief that a patient or an organization and its problems are special and unique—termed the *uniqueness paradox* (Martin, Feldman, Hatch, & Sitkin, 1983)—is common. Unfortunately, it is a belief that works against the movement toward evidence-based practice.

Lastly, another reason that practitioners may distrust statistics and the scientific method is that the resulting evidence keeps changing. Shojania and colleagues (Shojania, Sampson, Ansari, Doucette, & Moher, 2007) examined 100 systematic reviews of medical research; systematic reviews are a highly recommended source of evidence to guide clinical decisions. They found that changes in evidence relevant to clinical decision making—changes often as drastic as a complete reversal of recommendation—occur in a relatively short time period. Within one year, 15 percent of reviews must be updated; within two years, 23 percent, and at five-and-a-half years, 50 percent of reviews are no longer correct.

Certainly, knowledge evolves in the management field as well. For example, research regarding teams and conflict at one time reflected the idea that relationship conflict (e.g., conflict about values or interpersonal style) was harmful to both team performance and satisfaction, whereas task conflict (e.g., conflict regarding procedures or resource distribution) could be beneficial (e.g., Amason, 1996, Jehn, 1995). In the introduction to a meta-analytic study of the issue, DeDreu and Weingart (2003) summarized this view before presenting their "new" results showing *both* task and relationship conflict to be equally disruptive. In all likelihood, of course, findings will continue to evolve as researchers attempt to develop an even more nuanced understanding of when, and under what circumstances, conflict is harmful or beneficial (though certainly much has already been done in this area, which we will not review here).

Those of us who do research understand that this changing landscape reflects the nature of research and the incremental process by which knowledge develops. As physicist Richard Feynman famously stated, "If you thought science was certain, well, that was just an error on your part." It does beg the question, however, of how often systematic reviews and guidelines to managers will have to be updated. Although knowledge has always changed and progressed, this may be particularly frustrating for managers, given that staying up to date on research is only one item in an extraordinarily long list of responsibilities (if it is on their list at all). Worse still, the progression of research knowledge often seems cyclical or back and forth, rather than linear, as illustrated by changes in results over time concerning, say, the relationship between hormone replacement therapy and women's cardiac health or the success of low-fat diets in treating obesity.

Distrust of Sponsorship and Special Interests

Our discussion of individuals' distrust of scientists and scientific research in general would be incomplete without understanding the role of sponsorship and special interests in adding to such distrust. First, research sponsorship (e.g., by an industry trade group) or related financial conflicts of interest (e.g., researchers having financial ties to an industry) cause people to have doubts about research findings; moreover, evidence tells us that this suspicion is warranted. Bekelman and colleagues (Bekelman, Li, & Gross, 2003) completed a systematic review of financial conflicts in biomedical research. They reviewed research from 1980 onward; 1980 was the year in which the Bayh-Dole Act passed, which encouraged academic institutions and researchers to partner with industry. Their findings reveal the prevalence of financial relationships among industry, scientists, and academic institutions: approximately 25 percent of researchers were affiliated with industry (e.g., received research funding from industry) over that period, and approximately 66 percent of academic institutions held equity in "start-ups" that sponsor research performed by their own faculty. Analysis of 1,140 studies examining industry sponsorship and research conclusions exposed a more worrisome, but perhaps not surprising, result: industry-sponsored research tended to draw pro-industry conclusions. Some specific examples will better illustrate their results.

Barnes and Bero (1998) investigated 106 reviews on the health effects of passive smoking (i.e., secondhand smoke). Of the 106 reviews, 37 percent concluded that secondhand smoke was not harmful to one's health; 74 percent were written by authors tied to the tobacco industry (defined as having received funding from the tobacco industry, submitted a statement to the government on behalf of the tobacco industry, or participated in multiple tobacco industry-sponsored symposia). The authors controlled for other potential explanatory factors, including article quality, peer-review status, article topic (e.g., specific type of health effect), and year of publication—tobacco industry affiliation was the only factor associated with concluding that second-hand smoke was not harmful to one's health.

Stelfox and colleagues (Stelfox, Chua, O'Rourke, & Detsky, 1998) came to similar conclusions regarding a different substantive area and industry. They examined research on the safety of calcium-channel antagonists (a class of drugs used to treat high blood pressure or angina/heart pain) and researchers' financial relationships with the pharmaceutical industry. They categorized each article as supportive, neutral, or critical of the use of calcium-channel antagonists. Results indicated that authors supportive of the drug class were significantly more likely than neutral or critical authors to have financial relationships with manufacturers of calcium-channel antagonists (96 percent versus 60 percent of neutral authors and 37 percent of critical authors) as well as with pharmaceutical companies in general (100 percent versus 67 percent of neutral authors and 43 percent of critical authors), regardless of which products they manufactured. Such relationships with pharmaceutical companies may also influence EBMed through creation of the clinical practice guidelines themselves. An initial study of this issue (Choudhry, Stelfox, & Detsky, 2002) found that the majority of authors had some form of interaction with the pharmaceutical industry—58 percent had received financial support to perform research, 38 percent had served as employees of or consultants to the pharmaceutical industry, and 59 percent had relationships with the companies whose drugs were considered in the guidelines they authored.

Authors of the reviews discussed (Barnes & Bero, 1998; Bekelman et al., 2003; Choudhry et al., 2002; Stelfox et al., 1998) advocate for clear disclosure of these conflicts of interest. Although one cannot automatically conclude that all conclusions of scientists with industry affiliations are biased or incorrect, readers must be able to take such relationships into account when evaluating an article's conclusions. Review authors also recommend further study to better understand the influence of industry affiliations and an effective policy approach to minimize research bias.

In addition to sponsorship and financial conflicts of interest, we must examine special interest groups (e.g., trade associations, professional associations, groups sharing views on a social/political issue such as the environment, gun control, etc.). Such groups generally have a vested political or financial interest in research conclusions as they relate to the group's position. Thus, they may choose to selectively promote research that supports their position, to actively spread "misinformation" to advance their position, or to deliberately interfere with the dissemination of research that counters their position.

Mooney (2005) relates an illustrative example of the industry groups representing sugar and high-fructose corn syrup. In 2002, the World Health Organization (WHO) convened an expert panel to review evidence relating diet and physical activity to health conditions such as obesity and Type 2 diabetes; in early 2003 the panel issued a report regarding its conclusions and recommendations (WHO, 2003). The recommendations emphasized increasing physical activity, eating more fruits and vegetables, and reducing intake of fat and sugars. With respect to sugar, the panel recommended limiting free sugars (those added to food as opposed to occurring naturally) to 10 percent of daily calories; it characterized the evidence linking sugar (particularly from sugar-sweetened beverages) to obesity as fairly consistent.

The U.S. Sugar Association (among other food industry groups) took action. It informed WHO that it would "exercise every avenue available" to challenge what it characterized as a "misguided, non-science-based report" (U.S. Sugar Association, 2003, p. 1). Indeed, the Association threatened to lobby congressional allies to withdraw all funding from the WHO. These same allies contacted the Health and Human Services Secretary to demand that WHO cease all promotion of the report. The Association also worked to discredit a particular scientist, Shiriki Kumanyika, who was a member of the expert panel that produced the report. She was also a member of the Food and Nutrition Board at the Institute of Medicine (IOM). This organization had produced a report on a similar topic, noting in its report that no more than 25 percent sugars should be consumed to prevent nutrient loss. The U.S. Sugar Association promoted this as a contradiction and Kumanyika as "speaking out of both sides of her mouth" (Mooney, 2005, p. 122); the IOM clarified that the 25 percent figure was not a dietary recommendation (i.e., it was not endorsing 25 percent sugar intake) but rather a maximum intake level to prevent nutrient loss, and, therefore, its conclusion did not contradict the WHO report. Mooney (2005) describes the data relating sugar, particularly sugar-sweetened beverages, to obesity as "especially troubling" and painting a "consistent picture" that our eating and drinking habits are making us obese (pp. 125–126). The U.S. Sugar Association states that, with respect to obesity, "there has to be a scapegoat…sugar is not part of the problem" (Pastor, 2010, p. 3, 4).

Current evidence suggests the debate could continue. Various meta-analyses exist summarizing the research on sugar-sweetened beverages and obesity. Some conclude there is a positive relationship and sufficient evidence to support public-health recommendations to reduce consumption (Malik, Schulze, & Hu, 2006; Vartanian, Schwartz, & Brownell, 2007); others conclude there is no relationship or that the science does not yet support such a dietary recommendation (Forshee, Anderson, & Storey, 2008; Gibson, 2008). Complicating the picture and consistent with our previous discussion is the finding that studies that are not funded by the food industry tend to find significantly larger effects than those that are funded by the food industry (Vartanian et al., 2007); at least one of the meta-analyses finding no relationship was sponsored by the American Beverage Association (Forshee et al., 2008).

One can see how sponsorship, conflicts of interest, and deliberate actions by special interest groups to obfuscate research findings can cloud the truth of what research actually says and create distrust of scientists and research in general. As Mooney (2005) observes, "If Americans come to believe you can find a scientist willing to say anything, they will grow increasingly disillusioned with science itself" (p. 11). Indeed, MacCoun (1998) notes that "the latter half of this century has seen an erosion in the perceived legitimacy of science as an impartial means of finding truth" (p. 259). Increasing disillusionment will only intensify a distrust of scientists and science that is already greater in the United States than in most of the rest of the world (Begley, 2010; Hofstadter, 1964). In sum, distrust of academics/scientists, the statistics, and scientific methods that they use, and the role of sponsorship and special interests in the creation and presentation of research serve as the foundation of resistance. This base of resistance is in place before practitioners even process the research itself—to think about the substantive content of the research findings and what the research might mean for themselves and their organizations.

Threatening or Anxiety-Provoking Findings

Moving to research findings *per se,* it appears that many types of findings provoke anxiety or are perceived as threats by practitioners or laypeople. For example, in the management field, threat is often illustrated with individuals' reactions to research regarding genetically heritable traits such as intelligence (e.g., Pinker, 2002). Rynes and colleagues (Caprar, Rynes, & Bartunek, 2010; Rynes, in press)

and Pinker (2002) argue that the idea that intelligence has a major role in vocational and financial success is a threat to individuals' self-image and deeply held personal beliefs. Indeed, research has the potential to threaten practitioners in a variety of ways, including self-image, role, status, or financial standing.

How do individuals tend to react to threat? When faced with an event that might have negative or harmful consequences, people experience increased stress, anxiety, and arousal; in response, they tend to become more rigid. The threat-rigidity thesis (Staw, Sandelands, & Dutton, 1981) suggests that this rigidity is exhibited in two ways. First, information processing is restricted; people narrow their attention and focus on what they currently know and believe. As a result, individuals become less open to new ideas or perspectives. Second, constrictions in control occur; in other words, people tend to behave in habitual ways or rely on dominant responses. In essence, individuals rely on both familiar knowledge and familiar behavior when under threat. Similar responses occur at the group and organizational levels, though they may manifest differently (D'Aunno & Sutton, 1992; Griffin, Tesluk, & Jacobs, 1995). Although this "bear down and stay the course" approach may be appropriate in stable and predictable environments, it is generally maladaptive in the dynamic and complex environments in which most individuals currently operate. It would seem to work heavily against thoughtful processing of new and evolving research evidence and integration of that evidence into practice, particularly if that integration requires changes in behavior or processes.

In one infamous case of medical research (Brownlee, 2007; Groopman, 2002), the threatened group fought back with a vengeance. The evidence concerned the treatment of low back pain. This would seem to be a crucial area of medicine in which to consider research evidence, as the condition affects many people: approximately two-thirds of adults will suffer from low back pain at some point in their lives, although many instances of back pain will simply go away on their own. When this does not occur, however, individuals turn to medical intervention.

The two most common surgical treatments are discectomy (in which a central portion of the disc is removed) and spinal fusion (which involves removing discs and mechanically bracing the vertebrae). In 1993, the federal Agency for Healthcare Policy and Research (AHCPR) convened a panel of 23 experts to evaluate the scientific evidence regarding treatment of low back pain and to formulate clinical guidelines for physicians. The panel did not explicitly consider spinal fusion, because its mission was focused only on treatment options for patients within the first three months of back pain. However, a member of the panel, Dr. Richard Deyo, had recently published a meta-analysis (Turner, Herron, & Deyo, 1993) of the results of spinal fusion, as well as a review of the treatment of low back pain (Deyo, Cherkin, Conrad, & Volinn, 1991). The meta-analysis concluded that spinal fusion lacked scientific rationale and required more and higher quality research, including comparison to nonsurgical and other surgical methods. In the review, the authors concur with the Institute of Medicine's (the health arm of the National Academy of Science) conclusion that "surgery for chronic back pain is overused and often misused" as an approach to the treatment of back pain (Deyo et al., 1991, p. 50). It is generally no more effective than nonsurgical treatment and often less effective; for patients undergoing repeated back surgeries, there are often severe adverse effects. In addition, spinal fusion is sometimes performed when the simpler discectomy would be sufficient (Deyo, Nachemson, & Mirza, 2004).

In the end, the panel concluded that nonsurgical interventions should be tried first, as there was little evidence to support surgery as first-line treatment. Spine surgeons rallied. Many sent letters to Congress contending that the agency's panel was biased. Dr. Neil Kahanovitz, a board member of the North American Spine Society, led a group of spine surgeons that lobbied Congress to cut off the agency's funding. Sofamor Danek, a manufacturer of screws sometimes used during spinal fusion, sought a court injunction to prevent publication of the guidelines. The agency survived the onslaught, but its budget was drastically cut. In an effort to protect the agency, its director worked to soften its mission to that of a "clearinghouse" for data, meaning it could no longer offer explicit guidance to Medicare as it determined coverage of treatments. The word "policy" was removed from the agency's name, which became the Agency for Healthcare Research and Quality (AHRQ). As Groopman (2002) notes, "the guidelines that were eventually published were medically conservative, but the furor surrounding the panel tainted its credibility, and its recommendations have had little impact on surgical practice" (p. 72). Indeed, Brownlee (2007) notes that between 1997 (three years after the guidelines were published) and 2006, "the number of spinal fusions went up 127 percent, from a little more than 100,000 a year to 303,000 annually" (p. 32).

What accounts for the quick mobilization and fairly drastic response of the spine surgeons to this panel, whose purpose was simply to critically examine the evidence and recommend supported treatment approaches? The panel's conclusions likely threatened the surgeons on multiple fronts. First, a research-based conclusion questioning or recommending against surgery would "hit them in the pocketbook." One physician puts it bluntly: "In medicine, if you are able to stick a needle into a person, you are reimbursed at a much better rate by the insurance company. So there is a tremendous drive to perform invasive procedures" (Groopman, 2002, p. 69). And even among surgeries, there is a financial hierarchy. In one physician's practice area, the surgeon's fee for a discectomy is between $5,000 and $7,000, but $20,000–$30,000 for a spinal fusion (Groopman, 2002, p. 70). The potential for financial damage should surgery fall out of favor as the preferred treatment option was clearly a tangible threat to the physicians.

A second threat, less tangible but perhaps even more severe, would target physicians' very identity. March's (1994) research in decision making suggests that individuals use two basic models to make decisions. In the *consequences* model, an individual weighs the costs and benefits of the alternatives and chooses the alternative providing the most benefit with the least cost. This reflects a rational approach to decision making, yet we know that individuals are not as rational as they are often painted (Ariely, 2009). In the *identity* model, individuals ask themselves three questions: Who am I? What kind of situation is this? What would someone like me do in this situation?

Think about this latter model in terms of how a spine surgeon might apply it to decisions regarding patient diagnosis and treatment recommendation. What would his or her answers to the three questions likely be? "I am an expert in surgery of the spine. This is a situation of a patient with low back pain. Someone like me performs spine surgery to treat low back pain." Aside from the lucrative nature of the profession, many spine surgeons likely take pride in their work and their ability to relieve patients' pain through surgery. But with respect to March's third question, what does "someone like a spine surgeon" do to treat patient low back pain, if not perform spine surgery? A panel recommending against such a decision threatens the surgeon's very identity.

The greatest perceived threat of any research finding, however, may be to practitioners' judgment and autonomy. As discussed previously, practitioners (including doctors) have a strong preference for intuitive or clinical decision making, despite its inferiority to statistical or actuarial methods (Ayres, 2008; Grove & Meehl, 1996; Grove et al., 2000). The superiority of actuarial methods is likely a threat to their self-image as individuals of sound judgment and intuition (Ayres, 2008). In addition, actuarial methods may also threaten doctors' power and control. Dopson and colleagues (Dopson, Locock, Gabbay, Ferlie, & Fitzgerald, 2003) observe that doctors may selectively resist evidence-based clinical guidelines depending on "whether doctors see them as authoritative, credible, professional documents that help them improve their practice, or as a form of management imposition and control" (p. 323). In illuminating the power struggles within the EBMed movement, Pope (2003) turns back to our own management literature to compare the resistance to EBMed by physicians to the efforts of other occupational groups to resist rationalization and the formal specification of work practices, such as the cooks described in Fine (1996), the technicians studied by Barley (1996), or the managers and professionals studied by Leicht & Fennell (2001). Harkening back to our earlier discussion on academic/scientist credibility, Dopson et al. (2003) suggest that doctors' view of guidelines as helpful or controlling often depends on the origin of the guidelines—that is, their perception of the credibility and motivation of the experts who created them.

We also previously discussed that some practitioners believe that aggregated research results are irrelevant to any particular unique set of circumstances. Another form of belief related to the generalizability of research evidence, however, seems to assert, not that research results are irrelevant, but that they can be relevant only when used in conjunction with expert clinical judgment. Miles (2009) wonders of EBMed advocates, "Do they not appreciate that navigating the huge inferential gap between the *general* and the *singular* has always been part of the exercise of judgment in medicine, which judgment necessarily appeals to sources of knowledge other than the results of empirical clinical research?" (p. 928). As we stated in the introduction, both EBMed and EBMgt aim for physicians/practitioners to integrate best available research evidence with clinical expertise and judgment; neither "cookbook medicine" nor "cookbook management" is being prescribed. Of course, some would question whether this "should"

be the case, as evidence suggests that the addition of clinical judgment generally deteriorates the quality of decision making (e.g., Highhouse, 2008). As Briner and colleagues (Briner et al., 2009) point out, judgment is an essential management skill. Critical appraisal of research—Is it valid and reliable? Is it relevant to this issue and this context?—is required for effective evidence-based practice.

To give just one example, there are myriad empirically supported strategies to enhance transfer of training, that is, the degree to which trainees apply the knowledge, skills, and attitudes they learn in training to the job (Burke & Hutchins, 2007). However, practitioner judgment will be necessary to determine, of the empirically supported strategies, which an organization can support from a resource perspective, which are most likely to be accepted by managers and employees, which align best with the organizational culture, and so on. The misperception that evidence-based practice is calling for a suspension of expert judgment in research persists, and as long as practitioners believe this, they will interpret research evidence as a threat to their judgment and autonomy.

Findings Contradictory to Personal Experience

Personal experience can serve as another source of resistance to research evidence. Individuals draw conclusions from their personal experience; management, in particular, is often learned primarily through experience (see Leung & Bartunek, chapter 9 of this volume). Consider the research on the link between sugar and obesity previously discussed in the U.S. Sugar Association example. As you read WHO's dietary recommendation to limit sugar intake to 10 percent of your calories based on this research, you may have nodded your head, "Yes, I have experienced this. When I have limited high-sugar food and beverages in my diet, I've lost a few pounds." In that case, your personal experience validated the research, and it was probably easy to "buy into" the research conclusion and dietary recommendation because it simply confirmed what you already believed to be true. However, what if your personal experience contradicted the research? As we discuss later, you may be much less likely to be persuaded. Individuals' personal experience is akin to their personal collection of anecdotes. Not only do individuals have a strong preference for anecdotal evidence (i.e., stories), but they probably also have a particularly strong need to believe in their own stories.

Stephen Gould has called humans "the primates who tell stories" (Dawes, 1999, p. 29). Indeed, narrative plays a central role in the human experience (Landau, 1984) and is a "primary and irreducible form of human comprehension" (Mink, 1978, p. 132). In other words, narratives (such as stories and anecdotes) are how we make sense of the world. We would argue that personal experience is the ultimate narrative, one's own individual story. And when it comes to stories versus statistics, people generally prefer the stories (Kida, 2006). Consistent with this preference, if individuals are presented with statistical evidence but are then confronted with a counterexample (i.e., an example contrary to the statistical evidence), they display a bias *against* the statistical information and *in favor of* the example (i.e., the base-rate fallacy; Allen, Preiss, & Gayle, 2006). In essence, individuals are influenced by salient, individual cases more so than generalized, abstract probabilities (e.g., Kahneman & Tversky, 1973). This is true regardless of whether the individual case is counter to research (as in the base-rate fallacy) or consistent with research.

For example, consistent with the base-rate fallacy, research on jury decision making shows that juries are more persuaded by expert testimony that focuses on individuating information (e.g., a concrete example that illustrates research) than on abstract summaries of research (e.g., Gabora, Spanos, & Joab, 1993; Kovera, Levy, Borgida, & Penrod, 1994; Schuller, 1992). In addition, Bornstein (2004) has found that experts who present anecdotal evidence are perceived as more credible than those who present nonanecdotal evidence, even after controlling for the expert's credentials. Concrete examples and anecdotes are useful for juries, particularly given the way they make decisions. Specifically, Pennington and Hastie (1988) found that juries tend to use a "story-based" model of decision making. In evaluating evidence, jurors essentially "construct a story structure summary of the evidence" (p. 527), creating a causal model that explains the facts they are given. Thus, anecdotes and stories have a sense-making purpose. Any subsequent decision is then based on this causal explanation (i.e., story) that the jurors have imposed on the evidence.

This preference for narrative is also seen in the area of health communications, a field in which researchers study how to persuade people to adopt health-related behavioral changes (e.g., quit smoking, use condoms). For example, De Wit and colleagues (De Wit, Das, & Vet, 2008) compared the effects of narrative and statistical evidence in persuading men who engaged in high-risk sex to obtain the hepatitis B vaccine. They found that men's perception of personal risk and intention to get vaccinated were highest in response to the narrative evidence, and posit that narrative evidence may be less subject to defensive responding.

Narrative may be particularly powerful when research contradicts one's beliefs. Slater and Rouner (1996) investigated the effectiveness of alcohol education messages (e.g., health risks, drunk driving) with college students. Statistical evidence was rated as more persuasive and believable by students whose beliefs and values about alcohol were consistent with the messages. However, students for whom the messages were inconsistent with existing beliefs and values were more persuaded by anecdotal evidence. In a review of narrative communication as a tool for health behavior change, Hinyard and Kreuter (2007) suggest that narrative communication not only is viewed as more personal, realistic, believable, and memorable (versus non-narrative forms such as statistics), but also appears to be processed differently. They argue that audience members become immersed in a narrative and connect to the characters within it, and thus are less likely to counter argue the key messages and more likely to allow the characters to influence their attitudes and beliefs.

Thus, research evidence supports that narrative—particularly vivid and concrete stories—has the power to trump statistical evidence. Heath and Heath (2008) make a persuasive case for "concreteness" and "stories" as two key qualities to make ideas "stick." We would propose that personal experience—in essence, one's own narrative—is likely one of the most powerful stories of all in terms of its ability to produce resistance to contradictory research evidence. First, it is well-documented that individuals have a need to view themselves positively (e.g., Allport, 1955; Epstein, 1973; Steele, 1988) and will both think and act in ways that maintain or enhance this self-image (e.g., Blaine & Crocker, 1993; Greenberg & Pyszczynski, 1985; Greenwald, 1980; Steele, 1988). Thus, in terms of practice—whether medical or management—individuals want to think of themselves as knowledgeable and good at what they do. Research evidence that suggests to people that what they know is wrong or what they do is ineffective puts their positive self-view into question. Second, individuals use their own behavior as a source of evidence for their beliefs and attitudes (Bem, 1972), and they also prefer consistency between their attitudes and behavior. When attitudes and behaviors conflict, individuals experience cognitive dissonance, or tension; they then adjust their attitudes or behavior to return to a state of consistency (Festinger, 1957). Thus, believing in one's practice, regardless of the evidentiary support for the practice, is not only a way of maintaining a positive self-image but also a way of reducing the dissonance that would be created by doing something in which one did not believe.

Two practitioners illustrate how belief forms with respect to what they do. London physician Richard Asher (Asher, 1972) described the following paradox in medicine, now known as Asher's paradox: "If you can believe fervently in your treatment, even though controlled tests show that it is quite useless, then your results are much better, your patients are much better, and your income is much better too. I believe this accounts for some of the remarkable success of some of the less gifted, but more credulous members of our profession, and also for the violent dislike of statistics and controlled tests which fashionable and successful doctors are accustomed to display" (p. 48). He suggests that most physicians mentally compromise; they believe enough in their practice to be able to maintain a positive view of themselves and keep their patients happy, while knowing, if they are completely honest, that their practice may be inadequate. Freidson (1970) suggests that such belief is necessary in order to practice, that the practitioner must believe "that what he does makes the difference between success and failure rather than no difference at all" (p. 168).

Coincidentally, this idea of needing to believe in what one is doing, regardless of the evidence, surfaced 40 years later in the management field. Richard Hanson, a former senior vice president of human resources for New York Life Insurance, provided commentary to the Rynes, Brown, and Colbert (2002) article that presented evidence of various discrepancies between research findings and practitioner beliefs in HR. His view illustrates the potential dominance of personal experience—of belief in one's stories—in the face of evidence. He states: "I think that, for most HR officers, *belief follows practice*. We tend to believe in those things we do and are able to implement…unfortunately, I don't think that greater exposure to the literature will have much impact on us" (p. 103; emphasis added). Interestingly enough, Hansen made this statement not only as a practitioner, but also as a former academic with a PhD. Clearly, what one does shapes one's beliefs, and believing in what one is doing both enhances self-image and maintains consistency between belief and behavior.

The primacy of personal experience—individuals developing their own narratives—creates a formidable challenge for evidence-based practice. In a recent book on clinical trials in psychiatry, Everitt and Wessely (2008) describe the slow movement in that field from reliance on expert opinion to clinical trials. In arguing for clinical trials as essential to evidence-based medicine, they note that "past experience can be misleading, and the plural of anecdote is not evidence" (p. 33). However, people like and believe in anecdotes, especially their own. Consequently, contradictory evidence will create resistance.

Findings that Require Change

It is well-known that individuals do not generally embrace change; inertia is a powerful force. People have a strong affinity for the status quo (Samuelson & Zeckhauser, 1988), and unless the incentive to change is compelling—although "compelling" is in the eyes of the beholder—they will tend to stick with what they are currently doing. In fact, they will often exert a great deal of effort to stay as they are, a tendency that Schön (1971) labeled *dynamic conservatism*.

In addition to reasons already discussed (e.g., loss of status, perception of threat), there are still other reasons why individuals resist change. For example, resistance to change has a dispositional component (Judge, Thoresen, Pucik, & Welbourne, 1999; Oreg, 2003; Wanberg & Banas, 2000): individuals who are risk averse or have a low tolerance for ambiguity tend to dislike change (Judge et al., 1999; Oreg, 2003), whereas those who are optimistic or have a strong sense of self-efficacy are more likely to accept it (Judge et al., 1999; Wanberg & Banas, 2000). However, although personality may be a factor in resistance to change, it is seldom the only important factor. Individuals selectively process information, taking in and interpreting information in ways that reinforce their existing knowledge, beliefs, and attitudes (Fiske & Taylor, 1984; Greenwald, 1980). Consequently, they may fail to perceive information supporting the need for change or may interpret information in such a way that the costs associated with change seem to outweigh its benefits. Lastly, individuals are reluctant to change simply because of habit. Habits are intrinsic to human nature (Dewey, 1922). The automaticity inherent in habits minimizes cognitive effort in information processing (Shiffrin & Schneider, 1977), and thus offers a way of coping with life's complexities. In addition, habits provide a sense of comfort and security in a turbulent environment (Dewey, 1922). In spite of a compelling incentive to change, then, the status quo often prevails.

Ayres (2008) tells the tragic story of Austrian physician Ignaz Semmelweis. In the 1840s, Semmelweis completed observations in a maternity ward. He noticed that deaths from childbirth (puerperal) fever were greater among women treated by doctors and medical students than those treated by midwives. In the mid-nineteenth century it was common for a doctor to move from one patient to the next, or from an autopsy to a patient, without washing his hands. Semmelweiss reasoned that doctors and students must be transferring some type of "particle" that was causing the deaths. He noticed that mortality rates dropped markedly if doctors washed their hands in chlorinated lime before treating each patient and, thus, ordered doctors to wash their hands prior to each examination.

The physicians were extraordinarily resistant. Hand washing would be a waste of their valuable time. In addition, because Semmelweis could not offer an explanation for why unwashed hands would cause death, physicians discredited his observations. Semmelweis endured much ridicule and was eventually fired. He ultimately suffered a nervous breakdown and was admitted to a mental hospital until his death in 1865. Ayres (2008) remarks on the resistance: "No one likes to change the basic way that they have been operating. Ignaz Semmelweis found that out a long time ago when he had the gall to suggest that doctors should wash their hands repeatedly throughout the day" (p. 111).

However, perhaps it was the lack of theory, the fact that Semmelweis could not explain *why* hand-washing worked, that drove their resistance? Alas, even today, when we clearly *do* know why hand washing works to prevent infection, doctors still do not wash their hands enough. Studies generally report that less than 50 percent of health-care workers wash or sanitize their hands as instructed, with physicians having lower compliance rates than nurses or other health-care workers (e.g., Lankford et al., 2003; Pittet, 2001; Pittet, Mourouga, & Perneger, 1999; Saba et al., 2005); a systematic review of 96 studies found an overall adherence rate of 40 percent (Erasmus et al., 2010). Interestingly enough, however, one barrier to hand hygiene compliance (as reported by health-care workers) is their perceived lack of scientific evidence showing that improved hand hygiene will lower hospital infection rates (Pittet, 2001). In other words, even today, Semmelweis might still have a fight on his hands.

In a nod to the power of personal experience, health-care providers who were asked to identify important obstacles to improving their compliance with hand-hygiene guidelines noted that they had rarely seen complications due to lack of hand washing (Grol, 1997). *Status quo* prevails, indeed.

Thus, the power of inertia and individuals' preference for the status quo (Samuelson & Zeckhauser, 1988) can work against evidence-based practice, particularly given our previous discussion on the changing nature of knowledge and evidence (e.g., DeDreu & Weingart, 2003; Shojania et al., 2007). Heath and Heath (2010) caution, however, that "what looks like a people problem is often a situation problem" (p. 3). We will discuss the latter idea (environment) in the next section and both of these ideas (people plus environment) in more detail in the implications section of the chapter.

Findings Unsupported by Context

Finally, research findings that are unsupported by local context—whether peers, management, or the structure of the environment—may provoke resistance. An individual practitioner does not make decisions to embrace or resist various research findings in a vacuum; rather the people, processes, structure, and culture that exist within or characterize their environments influence these decisions. Researchers have noted the importance of contextualization in conducting, interpreting, and reporting research (e.g., Bamberger, 2008; Johns, 2001, 2006; Rousseau & Fried, 2001). Thus, it will also be critical to consider context in individuals' reactions to research findings. As Johns (2001) notes, context can "provide constraints on or opportunities for behavior and attitudes in organizational settings" (p. 32). Relevant contextual factors (Rousseau & Fried, 2001) may include those at the individual (e.g., performance and reward criteria for role) and organizational (e.g., structure, culture) levels, within the external environment (e.g., legal/institutional impact, national culture), and related to time (e.g., contemporary events). In short, "context counts" (Bamberger, 2008, p. 839). Although a complete discussion of all relevant contextual factors is beyond the scope of this chapter, we discuss two exemplar contextual features relevant to individuals' reaction to research findings: others' acceptance and implementation of research findings and the structure of the broader environment.

Research in the areas of social identity (Turner & Haslam, 2001), social influence (Cialdini & Trost, 1998), and cognitive development (Luria, 1976;

Vygotsky, 1978) provide evidence that cognition and behavior are partially a function of social context. Cialdini (2009) asserts that a key way in which we become persuaded is "the principle of social proof," that is, we determine what is correct by finding out what others think is correct—and this principle is most powerful when the "others" from whom we take the lead are just like us. The idea of opinion leaders—individuals who influence others' attitudes and behaviors informally and with relative frequency (Rogers, 2003)—as important agents in change and the diffusion of innovations aligns with this principle. Opinion leaders' power comes, not through their formal position or status, but, rather, is earned by virtue of their competence, social accessibility, or other characteristics (Rogers, 2003). Within the EBMed movement, opinion leaders have been found to be effective promoters of evidence-based practice (Doumit, Gattellari, Grimshaw, & O'Brien, 2009).

The success of EBMed has been attributed in part to the fact that it was professionally led early on: driven from the bottom up by physicians and other health-care professionals rather than managers or policy administrators (Dopson et al., 2003). This fact helped limit resistance to adhering to research-based guidelines. For example, Locock and colleagues (Locock, Chambers, Surender, Dopson, & Gabbay, 1999, as cited in Dopson et al., 2003) interviewed health-care professionals in evaluating a national clinical effectiveness initiative to improve application of evidence. Their research validated the power of peer influence. One medical director noted: "What makes me change—it's not scientific, but when I know what my peers are doing. We meet, we talk, we look at publications" (p. 322). A general practitioner observed: "If the information is easily available, some people will change. When sufficient numbers of informed people make changes in their practice then peer pressure will make the rest change" (p. 322). Thus, the endorsement of peers and influential others can be an important factor in the uptake of research evidence.

However, opinion leaders can also contribute to resistance (Dopson, Fitzgerald, Ferlie, Gabbay, & Locock, 2002; Locock, Dopson, Chambers, & Gabbay, 2001). In Locock and colleagues' (Locock et al., 2001) evaluation of the national clinical effectiveness initiative just referenced, they found that the presence of opinion leaders who were ambivalent, resistant, or actively hostile tempered the level of positive influence that more enthusiastic opinion leaders could exert. Again, attesting to the powerful influence of others, one project manager noted of influential clinicians: "You don't have to be actively hostile to cause trouble—you can cause a lot of problems just by being neutral" (Locock et al., 2001, p. 754). It can be difficult to try to follow research evidence when others around you do not. To return to the spine-fusion controversy, Groopman (2002) tells of one physician who tried to be conservative, as the research suggested, and recommended against fusion surgery for back pain unless it was absolutely necessary. He eventually discovered that nearly all the patients he turned away went to other physicians who then agreed to do the surgery. In time, the physician just gave in—if the patients were going to get surgery anyway, he might as well be the one to do it.

However, even if there seems to be a consensus regarding some evidence-based practice among one professional group in a setting, lack of acceptance by other professional groups may slow the adoption of the practice. Ferlie, Fitzgerald, Wood, and Hawkins (2005) conducted two qualitative studies in the United Kingdom in which they traced the adoption of health-care practice innovations (e.g., use of heparin to prevent postsurgical blood clots after orthopedic surgery, and a new service delivery system for the care of women in childbirth). Their results showed that social and cognitive boundaries between different professions slowed the spread of the innovation. The authors argue that professional communities of practice develop *within* rather than *across* disciplines, with these communities "sealing themselves off" even from neighboring communities. For example, in the study of the use of heparin postsurgery, tension existed between the orthopedic and vascular surgeons' communities of practice (in spite of both sharing a broader identity as surgeons). Strong scientific evidence supported this practice, and vascular surgeons endorsed the practice as a safe way to prevent blood clots. Although orthopedic surgery did not have the same research base, it was resistant to using research knowledge acquired in the vascular and general surgery fields, viewing it as not directly applicable. The various professional groups also displayed different cultures, agendas, and concerns. In the study of the new service-delivery system for women in childbirth, the authors observed different definitions of risk and of what constituted both effective care and sufficient evidence among obstetricians, midwives, and social-advocacy groups. Thus, the level of support (or lack thereof) among *particular* others is one contextual feature that may play a significant role in practitioners' reactions to and implementation of research evidence.

At a higher level of analysis, another important contextual feature is the structure and systems of the surrounding environment in which one lives and works. Authors writing about successful change management invariably discuss the potential for one's environment to facilitate or inhibit change. For example, Kotter (1996) discusses barriers related to structure and systems (e.g., cultural norms, socialization processes, reward systems) as some of the biggest obstacles to successful change. As we mentioned previously, Heath and Heath (2010) note that what appears to be a people problem is sometimes a situation problem. We mistake the source of resistance because of our tendency to attribute individuals' behavior to internal rather than external causes (i.e., fundamental attribution error; Ross, 1977). However, individuals may resist research findings, not because they do not believe them, but because the environment does not facilitate successful uptake of the research findings.

An illustrative and inspiring example can be seen in the town of Albert Lea, Minnesota. Although we step away from our focus on practitioners for a moment in sharing this example, we would argue that the lesson is still applicable. Dan Buettner (2008) is founder of The Blue Zones Organization—an organization that creates lifestyle management tools to help people live longer, better lives—and author of *The Blue Zones: Lessons for Living Longer from the People Who've Lived the Longest*. Buettner—an author, explorer, and endurance bicyclist, among other things—collaborated with physicians and academics at the University of Minnesota's National Institute on Aging as well as other scientific experts to investigate four specific regions where populations were reaching age 100 at extraordinarily high rates. Their mission was to study the lifestyle behaviors that were contributing to these individuals' long lives. They identified common healthy behaviors related to diet (e.g., dine on plants; stop eating when 80 percent full), physical activity (e.g., find ways to move naturally), social networks (e.g., make family a high priority), and purpose (e.g., live your passion, participate in spiritual activities).

The Blue Zones organization and its team of scientists partnered with AARP and the United Health Foundation to effect a community transformation; Albert Lea, Minnesota served as the prototype community. The goal? "For the people of Albert Lea to adopt these healthy habits so naturally, so painlessly, they wouldn't even realize how radically they were changing their lives" (Blue Zones, 2010). Numerous structural and environmental changes were made. For example, the city laid new sidewalks connecting neighborhoods with schools and shopping centers; restaurants changed their menus to offer more healthy choices; schools stopped selling candy for fundraisers and sold wreaths instead; volunteers planted 70 community gardens; numerous workshops were offered on how to pursue talents and passions; the idea of "walking school buses" to escort kids to school on foot was introduced (Blue Zones, 2010; Willett & Underwood, 2010). Over 25 percent of the population participated.

The results speak to the power of a facilitative environment (and likely the positive influence of others, as we just discussed). Participants lost an average of 3 pounds and increased life expectancy by an average of 3.2 years; employers reported a 21 percent drop in absenteeism; city employees showed a 49 percent decrease in health-care costs (falling for the first time in a decade); kids walked the last mile to school every day with parents and volunteers using the "walking school bus" system (Blue Zones, 2010; Willett & Underwood, 2010).

Willett and Underwood (2010) note that "diet and exercise programs routinely fail, not for lack of willpower, but because the society in which we live favors unhealthy behaviors" (p. 42). The Blue Zones project in Albert Lea attempted to alter that society. Heath and Heath (2010) would describe the process in Albert Lea as "tweaking the environment"— essentially "making the right behaviors a little bit easier and the wrong behaviors a little bit harder" (p. 183). Thaler and Sunstein (2009) would call it a "nudge." The lessons from Albert Lea also apply to evidence-based practice. What looks like resistance to the substance of research findings may, instead, be an indication of the difficulty of the environment in which they must be implemented. Commonly cited barriers to the use of evidence-based research findings include limited access or difficulty accessing the best evidence and guidelines, as well as a lack of time to search for, appraise, and discuss implications of evidence (e.g., Haynes & Haines, 1998; McColl, Smith, White, & Field, 1998; Straus & McAlister, 2000). These are contextual barriers that can potentially be minimized by environmental adjustments. Thus, consistent with those who have noted the significance of contextualization in research (e.g., Bamberger, 2008; Johns, 2001, 2006; Rousseau & Fried, 2001), we note the importance of context in practitioners' reactions to and adoption of research.

Implications: Potential Solutions to Advance Evidence-Based Management

To this point, we have discussed multiple potential sources of practitioner resistance to research findings. We began with a broad source of resistance to research—distrust of scientists, statistics, and special interests—that would seem to create challenges regardless of the research content. We then presented general types of research findings that practitioners may find difficult to believe or accept: findings that are perceived as threatening, contradictory to personal experience, require change, or are unsupported by context. Consistent with traditional advice in the practice world to "never bring up a problem if you cannot offer a solution," we now turn to a discussion of potential solutions with respect to EBMgt. Given predictable resistance to evidence, what might academics do to promote EBMgt more effectively? In the following sections, we present potential solutions to address these sources of practitioner resistance, although, of course, this is not a comprehensive list (for other solutions to increase practitioners' awareness of, belief in, and implementation of research findings, see Rynes [in press]). For an overview of the solutions presented, see Table 8.1.

Build Trustful Relationships between Academics and Practitioners

One broad source of resistance is practitioners' distrust of academics and scientists themselves. Thus, before we can begin to persuade practitioners to believe our research conclusions and to practice in an evidence-based way, we need to become more trustworthy in their eyes. In the classic *On Rhetoric*, Aristotle (1991) delineated three means of persuasion: *logos*, or appealing to the reason of the audience using logical argument; *ethos*, or emphasizing the credibility of the speaker/writer; and *pathos*, or awakening the emotions of the audience. As others (Bartunek, 2007; Van de Ven, 2007) have pointed out, academics tend to rely almost exclusively on logical argument to the exclusion of *ethos* and *pathos*. Of the three means of persuasion, however, Aristotle regarded *ethos* to be the most important, and becoming more trustworthy in the eyes of practitioners gets directly at the *ethos* aspect of persuasion. Aristotle (1991) conceptualized *ethos* as having three dimensions: intelligence (i.e., knowledge, expertise), character, and goodwill. Once again, academics would seem to concentrate on the first dimension—demonstrating their clear knowledge and expertise on relevant topics—as opposed to the other dimensions. Building trustful relationships with practitioners would help to solidify the dimensions of character and goodwill.

Trust is an integral part of relationships (Pratt & Dirks, 2007), particularly high-quality, positive relationships (i.e., those that are emotionally expressive, resilient, and generative in terms of resources, growth, etc.; Ragins & Dutton, 2007). However, it is difficult to build trust if a relationship does not exist in the first place. In her analysis of the research-practice gap in management, Bartunek (2007) suggested that it is critical to build social relationships between academics and practitioners in order to narrow the gap (see also March, 2005). Her suggestion aligns nicely with our discussion of social identities and the "us-against-them" dynamics they can create (Turner & Haslam, 2001), since individualized relationships are one way in which such intergroup bias can be reduced. Intergroup bias can be lessened to the extent that group membership becomes less salient (i.e., *decategorization* approach; Brewer & Miller, 1984; Gaertner et al., 2000). A key means to reduce group salience is for members of each group to have personalized interactions with one another—in essence, to get to know one another as individuals rather than as members of "the other" group. Pettigrew (1998) cautions, however, that short-term interaction will be minimally effective. There must be sufficient time to allow for close interaction such that individuals begin a process of self-disclosure and friendships form.

One effective way for academics to build trustful relationships with practitioners is to co-produce research with them. Bartunek herself is an excellent role model of building long-term, trustful relationships in this way. For example, between 1988 and 1995, Bartunek (2003) conducted research with the Network Faculty Development Committee (NFDC), a group that designed and implemented an organizational change intervention aimed at empowering teachers. The approach taken was a "joint insider-outsider approach" (Olesen, 1994), in which Bartunek (the "outsider") partnered with the two founders of the group (the "insiders") as co-researchers. Over the course of seven years, Bartunek sat in as a nonparticipant observer of the NFDC. The collaboration and study resulted in multiple publications, some jointly authored and others authored by Bartunek or the insider authors themselves. No doubt it also resulted in individualized relationships that were able to dispel views of one another as a member of "the other" group.

Another excellent example of trustful relationships between academics and practitioners is provided in John Zanardelli's chapter 11 of this volume. Zanardelli is CEO of Asbury Heights, a continuing-care retirement community in Mt. Lebanon, Pennsylvania. He describes in depth his initiatives to ensure both evidence-based medicine

Table 8.1. Proposed Solutions to Address Sources of Practitioner Resistance

Potential Solutions	Sources of Resistance Addressed	Exemplar Medicine	Exemplar Management
❖ Build trustful relationships between academics and practitioners	❖ Distrust of scientists	Zanardelli's (chapter 11 of this volume) collaborative relationships with academic geriatricians and management faculty to ensure evidence-based medical and management approaches	Bartunek's (2003) seven-year, collaborative research study with the Network Faculty Development Committee (NFDC)
❖ Experience the world of practitioners	❖ Distrust of scientists	Taylor's (2006) guide to academic medicine, in which clinical practice is a basic academic skill and academicians maintain direct patient contact	Vermeulen's (2007) interviews and writing of teaching cases; Bartunek's (2003) seven-year, collaborative research study with the NFDC
❖ Help practitioners understand and think critically about research methods and statistics	❖ Distrust of statistics and special interests	"Grading" studies with a "Level of Evidence" designation (Ayres, 2008)	National Council on Public Polls "20 Questions a Journalist Should Ask about Poll Results" (Gawiser & Witt, 2005)
❖ Learn how to tell a good story	❖ Distrust of statistics ❖ Findings contradictory to personal experience	Gawande (2009) and Pronovost & Vohr's (2010) story-filled books to support the use of checklists to improve patient safety	Kotter & Cohen's (2002) and Heath & Heath's (2009) books of stories to illustrate effective change management strategies and tactics
❖ Expand your toolkit	❖ Distrust of scientists	"MacGyver medicine" as illustrated by Dr. Iserson (2009) and Dr. Luckow (2010)	Allen, Bryant, &Vardaman's (2010) article on evidence-based strategies to retain talent; Pearce's (2009) *Organizational Behavior* textbook
❖ Frame EBMgt as a means to alleviate threat and anxiety	❖ Threatening or anxiety-provoking findings	Potential benefits for physicians of adherence to clinical practice guidelines in medical malpractice litigation (Hyams et al., 1995; Mackey & Liang, 2011)	Pfeffer& Sutton's (2006b) presentation of CEOs who did (Cisco's John Chambers) and did not (HP's Carly Fiorina) rely on evidence in decision making regarding mergers
❖ Use knowledge about effective change management	❖ Findings that require change	Berwick 100,000 Lives campaign (Ayres, 2008; Heath & Heath, 2010)	Gerstner's (2002) turnaround of IBM
❖ Provide a social "nudge" toward EBMgt	❖ Findings unsupported by context	Geisinger Health System's 90-day warranty on patient care (Kita, 2010; *PBS Newshour*, 2009); hospital video auditing of hand hygiene (Kita, 2010)	Latham's stories of practicing evidence-based managers (2009a, Ch. 7); Rousseau & McCarthy's evidence-based managers in the classroom (2007)

and management in the operation of his retirement community. He has collaborated with academic geriatricians from the University of Pittsburgh to ensure that his organization employs clinical approaches to medical care that have been "vetted by the latest and best science" (p. 193). He regularly consults with faculty whom he met while enrolled in an executive-education program. He notes that these individuals "became my friends, colleagues, mentors and continue to be my teachers." (p. 192).

Experience the World of Practitioners

As stated earlier, *ethos* consists of the components of intelligence, character, and goodwill of the speaker/writer (Aristotle, 1991). The last component, goodwill, relates to the intention of the communicator toward his or her audience— whether audience members perceive that the communicator is concerned with them, understands them, and has their interests at heart (McCroskey & Teven, 1999). Thus, one way for academics to enhance goodwill would be to demonstrate a genuine interest in understanding practitioners and their work lives. A specific way to accomplish this may be to invest time in experiencing the world of practitioners.

The first author of this chapter spent 10 years in human-resource management in the retail, hospitality, and pharmaceutical industries prior to beginning her PhD. For most of her career, she functioned as a generalist business partner, in which she was assigned to particular business units to help them achieve their strategic and operational objectives through effective management of human resources. Human-resource business partners, like academics, also cannot succeed by *logos* alone. Throughout her career, and particularly at the beginning of an assignment to a new client group, the author would spend significant time working alongside members of her client group. Over the course of her human-resource career, she has waited on retail customers on the sales floor, stocked shelves, cleaned hotel rooms, seated restaurant guests, garnished plates, and washed dishes in restaurant kitchens, participated in "ride-alongs" with pharmaceutical sales representatives, and sat in on many managerial meetings that she would not normally attend. She always considered these efforts to be time extremely well spent. The employees and managers appreciated her efforts to learn about their roles and the challenges inherent in them. It also was an effective way to build rapport with individuals, and emphasized the value

of the skills and talents that everyone contributes to the organization. (The first author learned she is virtually incompetent in forming hospital corners when making hotel-room beds or changing the register tape in a cash register—facts that seemed to serve not only as a source of great amusement to the employees, but also as a sort of "social glue" in her relationships with them going forward). In sum, the first author found that taking the time to experience the world of her client groups allowed her to demonstrate genuine interest, which, in turn, helped her become more effective in her human-resources role. In short, she enhanced *ethos*.

A similar endeavor might be extremely useful for academics. Although some academics have an intimate understanding of the practice world through previous work experience or extensive consulting, many do not. Although such an endeavor might not seem to contribute directly to academics' research and teaching responsibilities, we propose that it would make those efforts more relevant. In a recent analysis of the "implications for practice" sections of journal articles, Bartunek and Rynes (2010) noted that one concern of academics with respect to these sections was their lack of comfort in writing them; as one academic commented, "Unless I'm engaged in the field, what do I say?" (p. 109).

This comment could apply to more than simply "implications-for-practice" sections. Unless academics are engaged in the field, how will they understand the topics most relevant and the challenges most vexing to practitioners? How will they appropriately contextualize their research? How will they link their results to practice? How will they effectively teach current and future practitioners in the classroom? How will they help practitioners to apply evidence-based principles in their organizations? How will they address practitioners' concerns about their ability to do this?

In the field of academic medicine, many individuals who conduct research also stay engaged with practice. For example, Taylor (2006) has written a book to guide clinicians considering careers in academic medicine. He notes that the basic academic skills needed are not only teaching and scholarship but also clinical practice. He observes that the creation of new knowledge (scholarship) is generally more valued than clinical expertise, and cautions prospective academics about the potential atrophy of their clinical skills: "some senior faculty see patients only about 20 percent of the time, and this is not enough direct patient contact to keep up to date..." (p. 114). From the perspective of a management academic, spending 20 percent of one's time in "practice" (or consulting) might leave one susceptible to gripes that he or she has "checked out" or "gone over to the other side."

Although reading results of practitioner surveys or hearing an executive MBA student tell a "practice" story in your classroom allows some insight into the world of practitioners, it is not necessarily the same depth of insight one can experience firsthand (witness the revelations CEOs get from working in entry-level jobs for one week in their own organization in the new United States television series *Undercover Boss*). Vermeulen (2007) advocates communication that focuses on relevance and engages practitioners directly. He argues that what you can learn from sitting in your office is limited and supports instead "regular, direct interaction with practitioners intended to enrich understanding of my research subject. My own way of doing this is to conduct interviews and write teaching cases, although I am sure there are other and perhaps better ways. At this stage, I listen rather than talk" (Vermeulen, 2007, p. 757). Bartunek's (2003) seven-year research experience with the committee of teachers in the midst of a change intervention gave her insight she could not have obtained from her office. Bartunek noted that she was "grateful for what they showed me about the skills and caring involved in teaching" and hoped that her work conveyed the "teachers' vision, spirit, and courage" (p. xiii). In whatever manner individual academics may choose to do it, taking the time to actually experience the world of practitioners can demonstrate goodwill (enhancing *ethos*), build individualized relationships (reducing intergroup bias), and perhaps create an opportunity for practitioners and academics to work together to facilitate EBMgt.

Help Practitioners Understand and Think Critically about Research Methods and Statistics

We presented information about practitioners' distrust of statistics and the scientific method as well as sponsorship and special interests. Helping practitioners to understand and think critically about research methods and statistics can, to some extent, address both issues. A practitioner who understands how to critically evaluate research and its resulting claims can apply these skills to all research and claims, including those that may be biased as a result of sponsorship and special interests. Indeed, developing these skills is vital. Crettaz von Roten (2006) points out that "we live in a statistics-rich society"

(p. 244), with statistics on a variety of content permeating many areas of our lives, including content about health, politics, and work. With respect to critical thinking, Rousseau and McCarthy (2007) refer to this as "perhaps the most crucial capability required in EBMgt" (p. 87).

Rynes (in press) discusses one clear opportunity for academics to facilitate research and statistical understanding as well as critical thinking: make use of our dual role as teachers to help students become more informed consumers of research (e.g., Burke & Rau, 2010; Rousseau & McCarthy, 2007; Trank & Rynes, 2003). Burke and Rau (2010) suggest that such an effort must go beyond stand-alone business statistics or research-methods courses to infuse learning objectives related to research skills across all courses. Recognizing the need to "sell" this idea to students and relevant stakeholders, they also suggest that instructors explicitly make a connection between students' research training, skills, and knowledge and their employability in the workplace (Jenkins & Zetter, 2003), presumably so that students can then effectively "sell" this to employers.

Ideas are available to assist instructors in teaching research and statistical concepts, from Aguinis & Branstetter's (2007) theory-based and empirically supported approach to teaching sampling distribution of the mean to Corner's (2002) presentation of a model for teaching research design with applicable exercises. Rynes (in press) suggests the use of popular press books such as *Super Crunchers* (Ayres, 2008) or *Innumeracy* (Paulos, 2001) in conjunction with more formal statistical references in order to better contextualize and motivate the study of statistics. Leung and Bartunek (chapter 9 of this volume) suggest various tools (e.g., specific skill-building texts) and pedagogical approaches (e.g., case studies) to help managers develop skills in working with evidence. These specific ideas can be supplemented with general tips garnered from other instructors' experience.

For example, Bain (2004) finds that the best college teachers work together with their students on issues and problems that are authentic, that is, that seem important to students and mirror what the students might encounter as professionals in the workplace. In the course of tackling these problems, students are asked not simply to listen and remember, but rather to "understand, apply, analyze, synthesize, and evaluate evidence and conclusions" (p. 115). Bain (2004) contrasts this approach with the "plug-and-chug" approach—memorizing formulas and sticking numbers in equations—that many instructors emphasize and that students then use to make it through mathematical and statistical courses; subsequently, these students are unable to apply the material they have learned to a real-world context.

Markham (1991) offers advice based on teaching research methods within his introductory sociology course for 14 years. He notes that "ideas about variables, hypotheses, and representativeness of samples... represent a completely new way of thinking for the majority of students. A five-minute explanation of what a variable is, with two or three examples, will leave all but the most talented befuddled" (p. 468). (If you have not taught research methods, you may find it difficult to believe students would have trouble understanding the concept of *variable* or *hypotheses*, very basic concepts in research. Such concepts—known as "threshold concepts"—are central to the mastery of a discipline and can transform the way a student thinks about something. However, "threshold concepts" are difficult for students to learn and for teachers to unlearn (Meyer & Land, 2006). As teachers, we suffer from the "curse of knowledge," meaning that once we know something, we cannot imagine not knowing it. In addition, we often struggle in sharing our knowledge with others, because the "curse of knowledge" creates difficulty in taking their perspective and re-creating their state of mind (Heath & Heath, 2006; Heath & Staudenmayer, 2000).) Thus, Markham encourages devoting a significant portion of the course to teaching about research methods, integrating frequent methodological topics with substantive discussions, taking it slow, and using a few extended examples of research studies rather than a great many in passing, among other ideas. Another important notion, given that we are training future business executives rather than professional statisticians, is to teach students to recognize when a situation or issue requires statistical knowledge that is outside their technical expertise and to access experts accordingly (Wild, 1994). Then again, Wild (1994) remarks that many statistical consultants find that their most important skills are those such as asking the right questions, causing others to confront their own assumptions, and problem recognition—in other words, statistical thinking more than technical statistical knowledge.

The classroom is certainly one way to effect a change in practitioners' ability to think critically and use research effectively. However, not every practitioner will find his or her way into a classroom to develop these skills. Thus, another strategy is to

"tweak the environment" (Heath & Heath, 2010), much as Albert Lea, Minnesota did to encourage healthier behavior on the part of its citizens. Remember, "tweaking the environment is about making the right behaviors a little bit easier and the wrong behaviors a little bit harder" (Heath & Heath, 2010, p. 183). It is true that some practitioners may not understand statistics and research at a very high level, but the environment in which they operate can be modified to facilitate appropriate use in spite of this.

For example, Ayres (2008) discusses the practice within medicine of "grading" studies—assigning to each study a "Level of Evidence" designation. According to the "grading system" developed by the Oxford Centre for Evidence Based Medicine (2009), systematic reviews of randomized clinical trials are the highest form of evidence (level 1a), whereas expert opinion without explicit critical appraisal fares the worst (level 5). Such a system— Ayres (2008) characterizes it as perhaps "one of the most important impacts of the evidence-based medicine movement" (p. 102)—allows physicians and other health-care professionals who access the studies to quickly discern their quality, regardless of their personal skill level with research methodology or statistics. In another example, the National Council on Public Polls has published a guide for journalists "20 Questions a Journalist Should Ask about Poll Results" (Gawiser & Witt, 2005) to help educate journalists on the appropriate use of public-opinion polls. Each question is followed by a brief discussion of issues to consider and what the journalists should be looking for to distinguish a well-conducted scientific poll from a poorly conducted or unscientific one. The guide includes such basic questions as: Who paid for the poll and why was it done? How many people were interviewed for the survey? How were those people chosen? (Note that the first question allows the journalist to assess vested interests of the sponsors, a source of distrust for the public). The guide also includes perhaps less obvious questions: Who should have been interviewed and was not? In what order were the questions asked? (Rosenstiel, 2005). This guide is a tool that has made the right behavior—reporting information from only valid and reliable polls in the media—just a little bit easier for journalists. Thus, academics can also help practitioners from outside the classroom. They can provide similar tools, checklists, and decision supports to facilitate practitioner critical thinking and use of high-quality research evidence.

Learn How to Tell a Good Story

We discussed previously the importance of narrative in the human experience (Landau, 1984). People simply prefer stories to statistics (Kida, 2006). Heath and Heath (2008) argue that stories are a necessary component to making ideas "stick," that is, ensuring they are understood, remembered, and impactful in terms of changing an audience's attitudes or behavior. They maintain that stories are powerful because they provide both simulation (knowledge about how to act) and inspiration (motivation to act). Simulation comes from a story's ability to provide context for the abstract. As the authors explain, stories put "knowledge into a framework that is more lifelike, more true to our day-to-day existence" (p. 214).

Stories inspire, often through three basic plots: *challenge* plot, in which a protagonist overcomes a challenge and succeeds; *connection* plot, in which a character develops a relationship that bridges a gap (e.g., racial, religious, demographic, or otherwise); and *creativity* plot, in which a character makes a mental breakthrough or solves a problem in an innovative way. The substantive content of our field—dealing with people and relationships in organizations, management challenges, and problems—would seem to naturally lend itself to these frameworks. Note that the knowledge is *in* the story—that is, the story still contains the core message one is trying to communicate, whether that involves a research-based management principle or the wisdom of adopting EBMgt. The core message is just packaged in such a way that individuals are able to understand, remember, and act on it.

With respect to the Aristotelian framework (i.e., *logos, pathos, ethos*) referenced earlier, stories are particularly effective in fulfilling the function of the *pathos* element of persuasive rhetoric—appealing to the emotions, values, and imagination of the audience; Bartunek (2007) notes that in her conversations with practitioners about what would help management research have a greater impact on practice, practitioners invariably brought up the importance of emotion. They discussed the value of research that "has emotional components, includes narrative, and offers readers the possibility of seeing themselves in the situation described" (p. 1326). In a paper examining the EBMed movement in light of the Aristotelian framework, Van de Ven and Schomaker (2002) argue that EBMed advocates must "understand human emotions so as to better appreciate the beliefs and experiences of others" (p. 91). They note that emphasis on *pathos* is more important the greater the divergence in values, beliefs, and experiences of the various stakeholders of EBMed (e.g., researchers, health-care professionals, patients). Given our earlier discussion about the distinct cultures of academics and practitioners, *pathos* is likely to be particularly important in the EBMgt movement as well.

Other change-management work echoes the *pathos* element of persuasion. Heath and Heath (2010) argue that, for change to happen, we must appeal to both mind and heart. Kotter and Cohen (2002) observe that "the core of the matter is always about changing the behavior of people, and behavior change happens in highly successful situations mostly by speaking to people's feelings" (p. x of preface). It is instructive that Kotter, after publishing his well-known, logos-dominated eight-stage change process in *Leading Change*, followed up with *The Heart of Change* (Kotter & Cohen, 2002), which emphasized emotion ("see, feel, change") rather than logic ("analyze, think, change"). This shift in emphasis was based on large numbers of interviews in which the authors "collected stories that could help people more deeply understand the eight-step formula" (p. x of preface).

Physicians advocating the use of checklists in health care have taken a similar approach. Drs. Peter Pronovost (Pronovost & Vohr, 2010) and Atul Gawande (2009) both promote the use of checklists (based on the most up-to-date research, of course) in order to improve patient care and safety. One cannot help but feel sorrow as Pronovost (Pronovost & Vohr 2010) tells the story of the death of eighteen-month-old Josie King from a catheter-line infection. One cannot help but be persuaded by "feel-good" emotions as both physicians tell the story of Dr. Pronovost's work with over 100 intensive care units (ICUs) in the state of Michigan. He worked with them to implement a checklist for a common ICU procedure: inserting a catheter into a vein just outside the heart for delivery of liquids (the procedure that caused the infection that killed Josie King). In 18 months, the rate of catheter infections had decreased by 66 percent and 1,500 lives had been saved. As Gawande (2009) relays, "Michigan's infection rates fell so low that its average ICU outperformed 90 percent of ICUs nationwide" (p. 44). Illustrative of our earlier point, in these books by Kotter, Pronovost, and Gawande, the same knowledge is still there, just packaged in a more impactful manner.

Expand your Toolkit

Academics' facilitation of EBMgt will require adjustment not only in terms of how research is packaged for practitioners, but also in the nature and breadth of the research that the package contains. Addressing practitioner challenges, which are likely to be multifunctional or multifaceted, will require the use of evidence from different bodies or areas of knowledge. Academics need to be able to package research that addresses organizational issues as they are construed by practitioners; that is, as general problems that need to be solved (e.g., low employee morale, high employee accident rate) rather than as problems labeled by research stream or functional area.

A fitting metaphor is that of Lévi-Strauss' *bricoleur* (1966), or one who engages in *bricolage*. The French word *bricolage* means "to use whatever resources and repertoire one has to perform whatever task one faces" (Weick, 1993, p. 352). Medical professionals have captured the spirit of the bricoleur in their practice of "MacGyver medicine." MacGyver was an American action television series (Winkler, Rich, & Downing, 1985–1992). The main character, MacGyver, was a resourceful secret agent who solved complex problems with whatever materials were at hand, as illustrated by a classic MacGyver quote "If I had some duct tape, I could fix that" (Internet Movie Database, n.d.). Those who practice medicine in remote or chaotic areas are accustomed to such resourcefulness. For example, the annual conference of the Wilderness Medical Society recently featured a session on "MacGyver Medicine: Improvising Patient Care When Other Options Don't Exist," taught by Ken Iserson, MD (2009), Professor Emeritus of Emergency Medicine at University of Arizona—Tucson. The session focused on improvisation and "making do" with the resources one has available.

The field of medicine not only acknowledges and practices such resourcefulness but also attempts to teach it to new physicians. For example, to complete a rotation in the Department of Family Medicine at McGill University, Quebec, Canada, students are required to attend "MacGyver Medicine: Practical Procedures in Family Practice." As instructor Dr. David Luckow (2010) notes, "Sometimes we're not faced with ideal circumstances; we're faced with real circumstances." Hence, he teaches students about "office-based procedures when you are stuck." This practical focus goes beyond the textbook solution to acknowledge the messy reality of practitioners' circumstances. How does the idea of bricolage translate to management?

Weick (1993) and Thayer (1988) have previously characterized organizational actors as bricoleurs who improvise to make creative use of available people, ideas, and resources. Indeed, the challenges that practitioners face in their work often require such improvisation. Schön (1983) described the "changing character of the situations of practice—the complexity, uncertainty, instability, uniqueness, and value conflicts which are increasingly perceived as central to the world of professional practice" (p. 14). He also, however, described a crisis of confidence in the professions—a question about whether professional knowledge is adequate for such situations—and noted that professionals who have thought about the adequacy of professional knowledge tend to conclude that it is "mismatched" (p. 14) to the complexity of the situation. Academics functioning as bricoleurs in the context of EBMgt will need to bring whatever research-based resources are available in order to support practitioners in the complex and ever-changing challenges that they face. Successful bricolage requires "intimate knowledge of resources, careful observation, trust in one's intuition, listening, and confidence that any enacted structure can be self-correcting if one's ego is not invested too heavily in it" (Weick, 1993, p. 353). It is to be expected that successful bricolage in this context will require research from multiple disciplines, perspectives, and methodological approaches in order to "match" the complexity and messiness of the real world.

The breadth required to function as bricoleurs may take academics outside their comfort zone, because studies of management and business researchers show a lack of multidisciplinary or interdisciplinary focus. For example, Agarwal and Hoetker (2007) examined management research over a 25-year period in terms of its relationship with the related disciplines of economics, psychology, and sociology. They noticed a striking negative trend over time in the probability of multiple disciplines being represented in the same research article. The authors conclude that "when management researchers do draw on related disciplines, we seem to do so one discipline at a time" (p. 1317). Biehl, Kim, and Wade (2006) confirm a similar trend on a broader scale. In their study of multiple academic disciplines (e.g., management, finance, operations), they find that "most business academics tend to publish in distinct and mostly non-overlapping disciplines. Akin to Agarwal and Hoetker (2007), Biehl and colleagues (2006) note that "the disciplines' solitude has become more pronounced over time and is counterintuitive" (p. 368) given the emphasis on increasing interdisciplinary research. Both sets of authors express concern about the implications of their results and recommend more interdisciplinary efforts. Agarwal and Hoetker (2007) point out that "such combinations would help address a major critique of management research and education: that it no longer relates to real business problems" (p. 1319). Their calls echo Boyer's (1990) appeal two decades ago for a *scholarship of integration*, whereby scholars give meaning to isolated facts, "putting them into perspective...making connections across disciplines, placing the specialties in larger context, illuminating data in a revealing way, often educating nonspecialists, too" (p. 18).

David Allen and his colleagues (Allen, Bryant, & Vardaman, 2010) provide a recent example of packaging research that addresses an organizational issue—the critical issue of turnover and retaining talent—as it is construed by practitioners. Allen et al. provide guidelines for evidence-based retention management strategies. The breadth of the suggested strategies reflects the fact that retention is a multifaceted challenge. The strategies encompass the areas of recruitment, selection, socialization, training and development, compensation and rewards, supervision, and engagement. Jone Pearce's (2009) *Organizational Behavior* textbook, described in her chapter 21 of this volume, provides another illustration of this principle. Topics are based on the problems with which managers are faced, such as "How to Hire" or "How to Fire and Retain." Pearce notes that she actively resisted adding topics that were interesting but unrelated to addressing managers' problems.

Thus, just as practitioners already function as bricoleurs (Thayer, 1988; Weick, 1993), so must academics do so in order to facilitate practitioners' use of evidence in practice. However, in line with Latham's (2007) advice to "become bilingual" (p. 1029) and communicate in a language practitioners understand, we do not recommend advertising your "bricoleur" status. As one colleague of ours joked about this chapter, "Maybe practitioners would like academics more if they didn't use words like bricolage!" In the practice world, a comparable metaphor might be the idea of expanding one's "toolkit." Like bricoleurs, good practitioners are constantly broadening their repertoire of strategies or tactics for managing and solving problems, even if they do not necessarily have an immediate application. McGrath (2007) points out that a management tool refers to a "framework, practice, or concept that managers use when trying to achieve some result" (p. 1373), and goes on to reassure her academic readers that "a

management tool—although the term might make some academics shudder—is at heart the expression of a theory" (pp. 1373–1374). So whether academics "become bricoleurs" or "expand their toolkits," such an evolution will be necessary to effectively support EBMgt.

Frame EBMgt as a Means to Alleviate Threats and Anxiety

We discussed earlier that threatening or anxiety-provoking research findings will pose a challenge for EBMgt. Indeed, individuals will tend to focus on potentially negative implications of research findings and EBMgt, as research supports the idea that individuals display a negativity bias (Kahneman & Tversky, 1979; Rozin & Royzman, 2001). Baumeister, Bratslavsky, Finkenauer, and Vohs (2001) review a broad range of psychological phenomena—from close relationships and emotions to information processing and memory—and conclude that the principle that "bad is stronger than good" is consistently supported. This principle is particularly true with respect to influencing individuals' psychological reactions (Wang, Galinsky, & Murnighan, 2009).

One way to combat individuals' tendency to focus on how research and EBMgt threaten them may be to encourage their focus on how evidence-based practice can also *alleviate* threat. Such positive reframing of EBMgt may increase use of research findings. Although Wang et al. (2009) did find that the "bad is stronger than good" principle held true with respect to individuals' psychological reactions, they also found that good seems to be stronger than bad in influencing behavior. Helping practitioners to see how research can benefit them may drive behavior.

For example, evidence-based practice provides legitimacy and makes actions more defensible to various stakeholders (Rousseau, 2006). Freidson (1970, 1986) argues that clinical expertise and autonomy have been an important source of power for medical clinicians. He notes that the clinician grows in time to trust his or her own firsthand experience and comes "to rely on the authority of his own senses, independently of the general authority of tradition or science" (Freidson, 1970, p. 170). As Pope (2003) summarizes, however, "there is certain vulnerability in this position at a time when politicians, payers, and the public demand accountability from the professions and medical work is increasingly the subject of external scrutiny. A reliance on tacit, nebulous knowledge means that one cannot use explicit, formally specified knowledge to defend work practices" (p. 277).

This same assessment could be made of the present-day business world. In the wake of the recent Great Recession and its controversial causes and effects—from Wall Street's bundling of subprime mortgages into risky mortgage-backed securities to the federal bailout of companies and industries pronounced "too big to fail"—external scrutiny and demand for accountability are heightened. Indeed, Freidson (1970) points out that a challenge for the expert is "to assure the public that what expertise it does possess will be exercised evenhandedly, with an adequate degree of competence and in the public interest" (p. 338). The use of evidence-based practice can support practitioners in making this assurance.

Faigman and Monahan's (2005) discussion of the Supreme Court's 1993 decision in *Daubert v. Merrell Dow Pharmaceuticals, Inc.* echoes the importance of scientifically defensible practice. They interpret the *Daubert* decision as an assertion that "law must join the scientific age" (p. 635) and note that it "unequivocally endorses 'empirically validated treatments' and 'evidence-based practices'" (p. 656). Judges are now tasked to serve as gatekeepers of evidence, assuring that any evidence that enters into their courtroom is both reliable and valid. Faigman and Monahan (2005) remark, "Fields that operate by consensus rather than through data collection should be expected to have difficulty passing muster" (p. 636). Thus, for practitioners under increased scrutiny by stakeholders or defending themselves in court, the use of evidence-based practice should assuage threat and anxiety.

Indeed, in medicine there is some evidence that physician use of clinical-practice guidelines (CPGs) may be beneficial in malpractice litigation. Hyams and colleagues (Hyams, Brandenburg, Lipsitz, Shapiro, & Brennan, 1995) surveyed 578 malpractice attorneys about the influence of CPGs on their cases. Over one-quarter of the attorneys noted that guidelines had influenced their decision to settle a case; over one-quarter also noted that guidelines caused them to refuse a case (i.e., physician adherence to guidelines would likely exonerate the physician). However, over half the attorneys noted that once a lawsuit is initiated, CPGs are likely to be used to implicate the defendant physician.

Although state evidentiary practices vary with respect to CPGs, "there is a growing trend of CPG admissibility as an affirmative defense in malpractice suits" (Mackey & Liang, 2011, p. 37). Mackey

and Liang (2011) illustrate their point with two cases in which guidelines exonerated the physician. In *Frakes v. Cardiology Consultants, PC*, a cardiologist's decision against hospital admission for a patient who then died within hours was consistent with guidelines created by the American College of Cardiology and the American Heart Association. In *Moore v Baker*, a physician who did not recommend to a patient an alternative treatment—the use of which was not recognized by numerous guidelines as an acceptable treatment for her condition—was affirmed without even going to trial. However, note that the "scope and purpose of CPGs is the subject of some debate" (Recupero, 2008, p. 291), and some states (Maine, Florida, Kentucky, Maryland, Minnesota, and Vermont) have attempted to use CPGs in tort reform and efforts to improve health care to little practical effect (LeCraw, 2007; Recupero, 2008). Thus, although unequivocal conclusions cannot yet be drawn, some evidence does support a protective effect for physicians who use clinical practice guidelines.

In addition to providing legitimacy, the use of evidence-based practice may also contribute to one's power. We discussed how practitioners may perceive the use of research in practice as a threat to their judgment and autonomy, which many practitioners view as their source of power and control (Freidson, 1970, 1986; Pope, 2003). However, we would encourage practitioners to think differently about their source of power. Individuals and departments gain power and influence in organizations to the extent that they are able to reduce uncertainty (e.g., Crozier, 1964; Salancik & Pfeffer, 1977; Salancik, Pfeffer, & Kelly, 1978), particularly if they reduce uncertainty in areas critical to the organization's success and alternative means to reduce the uncertainty are not readily available (Hinings, Hickson, Pennings, & Schneck, 1974). Thus, the use of evidence-based decision making in practice should enhance managers' ability to reduce uncertainty.

For example, imagine that you are the head of the sales organization in your company. Sales revenues are clearly critical to the company, and you are responsible for achieving the company's sales goals. Many factors affect sales results, but a critical component is your sales team. How can you reduce the uncertainty associated with their achievement of performance outcomes and, ultimately, your organization's sales targets? Empirical research offers numerous strategies: select salespeople who are extraverted and conscientious (Vinchur, Schippmann, Switzer, & Roth, 1998); educate your salespeople on how to effectively influence and persuade others (Cialdini, 2009; Petty & Cacioppo, 1996); and motivate your salespeople using specific and challenging goals (Latham, 2009b).

Although these strategies target the individual, research can also provide equally useful strategies at the group or organizational level. For example, research can guide you in designing a structure that facilitates your strategy (Donaldson, 2009) or building a culture of continuous learning to sustain organizational performance (Beer, 2009). To reinforce our earlier point, about the necessity of academics functioning as bricoleurs, it is doubtful that the challenge of meeting sales targets in this scenario is just a "selection issue" or just a "goal setting problem." Management research at the individual, group, and organizational levels will likely be relevant, as will research in the disciplines of marketing as well as, potentially, finance and operations. In short, evidence-based practice may contribute to practitioners' power and control by providing them the tools to reduce uncertainty and giving them the best chance of achieving the results for which they are held accountable.

In this case, it might be useful for proponents of evidence-based practice to also show what can happen when one does *not* rely on evidence. Pfeffer and Sutton (2006b) provide numerous examples in their book on evidence-based management. For example, they discuss research evidence on mergers showing that most mergers "fail to deliver their intended benefits and destroy economic value in the process" (p. 4). They list several CEOs whose careers were effectively ended by poor merger decisions, including Stephen Hilbert of Conseco, Jill Barad of Mattel, and Carly Fiorina of Hewlett-Packard (HP). With respect to the HP case, in which Fiorina oversaw a merger with Compaq, Pfeffer and Sutton (2006b) note that HP had done no research on how consumers viewed Compaq's products until months *after* Fiorina had publicly committed to the merger. Thus, Fiorina dismissed the finding that customers had extraordinarily negative views of Compaq's products and that HP's products were viewed as superior. The subsequent merger, widely viewed as a failure, was impetus for Fiorina's ouster by the board in 2005. Pfeffer and Sutton (2006b) contrast such examples with that of CEO John Chambers of Cisco, whose successful track record with mergers and acquisitions stems from "its systematic examination of evidence about what went right and what went wrong in other companies' mergers, as well as its own" (p. 4). Executives who view evidence as a potential threat to their power would do well to note that use of evidence-based decision making may, rather, allow them to retain it.

Use Knowledge about Effective Change Management

As we discussed, people have a strong affinity for the status quo (Samuelson & Zeckhauser, 1988); unless the incentive to change is compelling, they will tend to persist with what they are currently doing. However, academics have both theory and evidence about how to effectively facilitate change. For example, Kotter (1996) advises the importance of: (1) establishing a sense of urgency by highlighting present and potential crises and opportunities, (2) creating a powerful coalition of individuals who support the change and can persuade others to do so, (3) developing a vision and strategy, (4) communicating the change vision using every vehicle possible, (5), empowering others to act on the vision by changing the environment and culture to facilitate change, (6) generating short-term wins to build momentum for continued change, (7) consolidating gains and continuing to modify unsupportive contextual features so as to produce more change, and (8) institutionalizing the new approaches by connecting the new behaviors to organizational success. Heath and Heath (2010) discuss similar concepts in their research-based guide to successful change. They articulate specific strategies to connect with people's heads (their rational mind) and hearts (their emotional mind) and to alter their environments in order to facilitate change.

Two successful change efforts—one in management and one in medicine—illustrate several of these concepts. Within the field of management, Lou Gerstner's turnaround of IBM in the 1990s is legendary. Gerstner (2002) gives a first-person account of IBM's transformation in his book *Who Says Elephants Can't Dance? Inside IBM's Historic Turnaround*. Business students also study IBM as a model of turnaround in the Harvard Business Case "IBM's Decade of Transformation: Turnaround to Growth" (Applegate, Austin, & Collins, 2008). Gerstner dealt with the most crucial problem first: he stopped the financial bleeding through massive layoffs and the sale of some assets. Since the company was close to being insolvent, Gerstner's actions established a sense of urgency.

In addition, after listening to hundreds of people, Gerstner developed a strategy 180 degrees from the plan in place when he arrived, which was to break up the company into several operating units.

In Gerstner's vision of "One IBM," the company would stay in one piece in order to leverage its hardware, software, and services capabilities to deliver all-encompassing technology solutions to organizational customers (even if that solution included products made by IBM competitors). Inherent in this vision was a strong focus on customers and their needs. Gerstner communicated the vision, including numerous e-mails and "chat" sessions to IBM's employees around the globe. Kotter (1996) points out the importance of communicating such a vision, but he emphasizes that communication needs to be supported by the behavior of important individuals to be credible. Gerstner also embodied his vision in his actions, attending key customer events not historically attended by executives, traveling thousands of miles to visit customers, and holding his senior executives accountable to do the same.

Gerstner also understood Kotter's (1996) advisement to anchor changes firmly in the corporate culture. He writes, "Culture isn't just one aspect of the game—it *is* the game. What does the culture reward and punish—individual achievement or team play, risk taking or consensus building?" (p. 182). Gerstner established eight operating principles, including demonstration of teamwork and acting with a sense of urgency, for doing business as "One IBM," and IBM began rewarding individuals who acted in alignment with these principles. He changed the compensation system to reward on the basis of corporate performance rather than division or unit performance. Employees were required to make personal business commitments related to IBM's broader goals; their performance with respect to those commitments was tied to salary. Criteria for promotions were also revamped. In the end, Gerstner turned around IBM, taking a company from having reported a loss of $8 billion at his arrival to having reported a profit of $8 billion at the end of his tenure.

Both Ayres (2008) and Heath and Heath (2010) share an inspiring story of change within the context of EBMed. It is the story of Don Berwick, MD and the 100,000 Lives Campaign. Berwick, whose quote opened our chapter, is the administrator of the Centers for Medicare and Medicaid Services (CMS) and former CEO of the Institute for Healthcare Improvement. Two events precipitated Berwick's crusade for change. First, the Institute for Healthcare Improvement produced a report documenting the pervasiveness of preventable medical errors in the U.S. health-care system; second, he witnessed these problems firsthand when his wife became ill with a rare autoimmune disorder. In 2004, Berwick launched the 100,000 Lives Campaign. In a speech to a large group of hospital administrators, he set out an ambitious goal: to save 100,000 lives by June 14, 2006 at 9:00 A.M. (18 months from that day). He challenged hospitals to do this by implementing six changes in care to prevent medical errors and, thus, avoidable deaths. Berwick chose the six basic changes—procedures related, for example, to managing patients on ventilators or those with central-line catheters—through analyses of research evidence. For instance, one procedure instructed health-care professionals to elevate patients' heads and clean their mouths regularly while they are on ventilators in order to prevent lung infections.

Berwick did several things during his campaign that made use of what we know about change management. Clearly, he established a sense of urgency and highlighted an opportunity for the hospitals. His organization's report estimated that 98,000 people died each year due to preventable medical errors; however, 25,000 lives would be saved if all hospitals implemented his six recommendations. He appealed to individuals' hearts by having loved ones of patients killed by medical errors participate in his talks. Limiting the campaign to six specific changes was a way to "shrink the change," to use Heath and Heath's (2010) terminology. Large-change efforts—such as the evolution to evidence-based practice—can be overwhelming, but changing six specific procedures was doable and more likely to result in Kotter's (1996) "short-term wins."

He also ensured an environment supportive of the change. Hospital CEOs needed only to sign a one-page form to join the campaign (and Berwick used peer pressure as one strategy to get hospitals to enroll); the hospital then received support from Berwick's organization in the form of research, step-by-step instruction guides, and training. His organization structured opportunities for hospital leaders to talk with one another about challenges and lessons learned, and it paired hospitals further along the implementation curve with those just joining the campaign. In the end, Berwick was able to successfully connect the new behaviors with organizational achievement. More than 3,000 hospitals participated in the campaign (representing approximately 75 percent of U.S. hospital beds) and in the course of 18 months, prevented an estimated 122,300 deaths. Ayres (2008) notes that participating hospitals provided to Berwick's team 18 months of mortality data prior to joining the campaign, as well as monthly updates of number of deaths during the campaign. He acknowledges that a decrease in deaths at one hospital may be just plain luck, but "when the before-and-after results of 3,000 hospitals are crunched, it's possible to come to a much more accurate assessment of the aggregate impact" (p. 93). Ayres (2008) characterizes this effort as a "huge victory for evidence-based medicine" (p. 94).

We tell these stories, not just because they are exciting, but also because they should stimulate us to think about how to apply what we know about effective change management to our EBMgt efforts. Some of our current efforts already reflect such principles. For example, the overarching purpose of the Evidence-Based Management Collaborative (n.d.) is "to design the architecture and support practices for on-line access to best evidence summarized in ways practitioners and educators can readily use"—in other words, to modify the environment to facilitate the change. This *Handbook* represents an effort to further communicate a vision of EBMgt, as well as strategies to achieve that vision. However, other features of effective change management are not so clearly recognizable. What is the inspirational equivalent in management of saving 100,000 lives in medicine? We need to figure this out so that EBMgt efforts appeal to emotions and values as well as minds. Additionally, the overall message of EBMgt—the best available scientific evidence should inform everything you do!—would likely seem overwhelming to even the most enthusiastic practitioner. What can we do to "shrink the change"? Berwick started with six procedures to prevent medical errors. Can we focus our efforts on a small subsection of organizational decisions and practices to make the process more manageable and generate short-term wins? In short, we must ensure we turn to our own evidence in order to facilitate the practice of EBMgt most effectively.

Provide a Social "Nudge" toward Evidence-Based Management

We have discussed the importance of context in both the adoption of and implementation of research findings. Although an unsupportive context can contribute to resistance, a context supportive of EBMgt may contribute to its uptake. As Gladwell (2002) observes, "We are more than just sensitive to changes in context. We're exquisitely sensitive to them" (p. 140). Thaler and Sunstein (2009) use this idea to advocate for *nudges*—contextual features that gently push people toward the best decision without restricting their freedom of choice. An illustration of this idea is provided by organizations that have moved to automatic enrollment (as opposed to nonenrollment) as the default in their defined-contribution retirement plans. This means that employees are enrolled in the retirement plan unless they take explicit action to opt out. Because of individuals' tendency toward inertia (Samuelson & Zeckhauser, 1988), the default option can be a powerful nudge. Indeed, automatic enrollment in defined-contribution plans has been found to be an extremely effective way to boost individuals' savings rates (Choi, Laibson, Madrian, & Metrick, 2002, 2004; Madrian & Shea, 2001).

The popular-press publication *Reader's Digest* recently featured a cover story on hospital errors (Kita, 2010). The feature focused on first-person stories by health-care workers who have made critical errors and profiled innovative ideas to encourage patient safety. It is interesting to note that several of those ideas are essentially contextual features that function as nudges, encouraging people to do the right thing. Pennsylvania's Geisinger Health System offers a "guarantee" that "creates a powerful incentive to do things right the first time" (Kita, 2010, p. 95). Patients pay a flat fee up front for services such as coronary-artery-bypass grafts, childbirth, and hip replacement, and they receive a 90-day warranty whereby they are not billed for treatment for any avoidable complications that develop during that timeframe (*PBS Newshour,* March 2009). The hospital system has a state-of-the-art electronic records system as well as standardized "best practice" action items for the procedures [reminiscent of Gawande's (2009) and Pronovost & Vohr's (2010) checklists] to facilitate health-care staff's ability to provide quality care. Another example is a hospital video auditing system to ensure that health-care workers wash their hands, with performance scores posted on an electronic "scoreboard." Early results show a substantial increase in hand-washing compliance; this increase is promising given our earlier discussion of the abysmal hand-washing rates of health-care employees (Erasmus et al., 2010).

Consistent with our earlier discussion on opinion leaders (Rogers, 2003) and the principle of social proof (Cialdini, 2009), Thaler and Sunstein (2009) argue that one of the best ways to nudge is via social influence because "Humans are easily nudged by other Humans" (p. 55). Thus, one effective way to nudge managers toward evidence-based practice will be to show them other managers who practice in an evidence-based way.

Latham (2009a) applies this principle in chapter 7 of his book, *Becoming the Evidence-based Manager.*

In this chapter, Latham (2009a) presents two case studies of evidence-based managers in action. Not only does this chapter accommodate individual's love of stories, but it also provides information about what other managers are doing—in this case, using evidence-based practices with successful results. In a "live" version of this strategy, Rousseau and McCarthy (2007) note that they bring local executives who practice EBMgt into their classrooms. Scaled-up and expanded versions of Latham's (2009a) and Rousseau and McCarthy's (2007) strategies would become social nudges toward EBMgt.

Given that the present gap between evidence and practice looms large, it is tempting to focus on the problem (particularly given our "bad is stronger than good" bias; Baumeister et al., 2001). Moreover, Rousseau and McCarthy (2007) note that the use of peer pressure may be difficult in EBMgt as compared to EBMed due to the lack of a formal body of shared knowledge among managers. However, Heath and Heath (2010) would encourage a focus on the "bright spots." In other words, concentrate on what is working and discover how that success can be scaled up. Latham (2009a) found two managers effectively practicing EBMgt with newsworthy results. Rousseau and McCarthy (2007) found local evidence-based managers for their classrooms. Advocates of EBMgt need to find others and publicize their successes in order to be able to nudge via social influence.

Conclusion

The movement toward EBMgt is in its early stages. The possibility that research and practice could be closely intertwined is a heady one, and a vision that some academics (e.g., Briner & Rousseau, 2011; Latham, 2009a; Pfeffer & Sutton, 2000, 2006a, 2006b; Rousseau, 2006; Rousseau & McCarthy, 2007; Rynes, 2007; in press) and some practitioners (e.g., Cohen, 2007; Saari, 2007) have worked toward and continue to work to bring to fruition. If EBMgt were to become the norm, we might actually be able to answer Hambrick's (1994) infamous question, "What if the Academy actually mattered?" Certainly it is hoped that, similar to the *British Medical Journal's* (Dickersin et al., 2007) characterization of EBMed, decades from now we will be able to acknowledge EBMgt as one of our most important management milestones.

As we have shown here, however, there will be resistance. Both history (e.g., Johns, 1993; Rogers, 2003) and our examination of EBMed in this chapter strongly suggest that this is to be expected. However, if academics would like their research to be relevant, then they must face the resistance and address it. Marian Wright Edelman, the well-known children's advocate and founder and President of the Children's Defense Fund said, "If you don't like the way the world is, you change it. You have an obligation to change it. You just do it one step at a time" (Traver, 1987, p. 27). There are steps every academic can take to address resistance and to aid the use of research in practice. You just need to start with one: befriend a practitioner, add a story to that journal submission you're writing, or do some reading completely outside your field to expand your toolkit. In this instance, we do agree with one part of Bruce Charlton's opening quote—the time is ripe.

References

Agarwal, R., & Hoetker, G. (2007). A faustian bargain? The growth of management and its relationship with related disciplines. *Academy of Management Journal, 50*, 1304–1322.

Aguinis, H., & Branstetter, S. A. (2007). Teaching the concept of sampling distribution of the mean. *Journal of Management Education, 31*, 467–483.

Allen, D. G., Bryant, P. C., & Vardaman, J. M. (2010). Retaining talent: Replacing misconceptions with evidence-based strategies. *Academy of Management Perspectives, 24*, 48–64.

Allen, M., Preiss, R. W., & Gayle, B. M. (2006). Meta-analytic examination of the base-rate fallacy. *Communication Research Reports, 23*, 45–51.

Allport, G. W. (1955). *Becoming*. New Haven, CT: Yale University Press.

Amason, A. C. (1996). Distinguishing the effects of functional and dysfunctional conflict on strategic decision making: Resolving a paradox for top management groups. *Academy of Management Journal, 39*, 123–148.

Applegate, L. M., Austin, R., & Collins, E. (2008). *IBM's decade of transformation: Turnaround to growth*. Boston, MA: Harvard Business School Publishing.

Ariely, D. (2009). *Predictably irrational: The hidden forces that shape our decisions*. New York: Harper Collins.

Aristotle. (1991). *On rhetoric: A theory of civil discourse*. G. A. Kennedy (Trans.). Oxford, England: Oxford University Press.

Asher, R. (1972). *Richard Asher talking sense*. F. A. Jones, (Ed.). Baltimore, MD: University Park Press.

Ayres, I. (2008). *Supercrunchers: Why thinking-by-numbers is the new way to be smart*. New York: Bantam Books.

Bain, K. (2004). *What the best college teachers do*. Cambridge, MA: Harvard University Press.

Baker, T. B., McFall, R. M., & Shoham, V. (2008). Current status and future prospects of clinical psychology: Toward a scientifically principled approach to mental and behavioral healthcare. *Psychological Science in the Public Interest, 9*, 67–103.

Bamberger, P. (2008). Beyond contextualization: Using context theories to narrow the micro-macro gap in management research. *Academy of Management Journal, 51*, 839–846.

Barley, S. R. (1996). Technicians in the workplace: Ethnographic evidence for bringing work into organization studies. *Administrative Science Quarterly, 41*, 404–441.

Barnes, D. E., & Bero, L. A. (1998). Why review articles on the health effects of passive smoking reach different conclusions. *Journal of the American Medical Association, 279,* 1566–1570.

Bartunek, J. M. (2003). *Organizational and educational change: The life and role of a change agent group.* Mahwah, NJ: Lawrence Erlbaum.

Bartunek, J. M. (2007). Academic-practitioner collaboration need not require joint or relevant research: Toward a relational scholarship of integration. *Academy of Management Journal, 50,* 1323–1333.

Bartunek, J. M., & Rynes, S. L. (2010). The construction and contribution of "implications for practice:" What's in them and what might they offer? *Academy of Management Learning and Education, 9,* 100–117.

Baumeister, R. F., Bratslavsky, E., Finkenauer, C., & Vohs, K. D. (2001). Bad is stronger than good. *Review of General Psychology, 5,* 323–370.

Beer, M. (2009). Sustain organizational performance through continuous learning, change, and realignment. In E. A. Locke (Ed.), *Handbook of principles of organizational behavior: Indispensible knowledge for evidence-based management* (2nd ed., pp. 537–555). Chichester, West Sussex, England: Wiley.

Begley, S. (2009). Ignoring the evidence: Why do psychologists reject science? *Newsweek, 154,* 30.

Begley, S. (2010). Their own worst enemies: Why scientists are losing the PR wars. *Newsweek, 155,* 20.

Bekelman, J. E., Li, Y., & Gross, C. P. (2003). Scope and impact of financial conflicts of interest in biomedical research: A systematic review. *Journal of the American Medical Association, 289,* 454–465.

Bem, D. J. (1972). Self-perception theory. In L. Berkowitz (Ed.), *Advances in experimental social psychology* (Vol. 6, pp. 1–62). San Diego, CA: Academic Press.

Best, J. (2001). *Damned lies and statistics: Untangling numbers from the media, politicians, and activists.* Berkeley, CA: University of California Press.

Biehl, M., Kim, H., & Wade, M. (2006). Relationships among the academic business disciplines: A multi-method citation analysis. *Omega, 34,* 359–371.

Blaine, B., & Crocker, J. (1993). Self-esteem and self-serving biases in reaction to positive and negative events: An integrative review. In R. Baumeister (Ed.), *Self-esteem: The puzzle of low self-regard* (pp. 55–85). New York: Plenum.

Blue Zones. (2010). *The first Blue Zones community.* Retrieved on April 25, 2010 from http:www.bluezones.com/albertlea

Bornstein, B. H. (2004). The impact of different types of expert scientific testimony on mock jurors' liability verdicts. *Psychology, Crime, and Law, 10,* 429–446.

Boyer, E. L. (1990). *Scholarship reconsidered: Priorities of the professoriate.* Princeton, NJ: Carnegie Foundation for the Advancement of Teaching.

Brewer, M. B., & Miller, N. (1984). Beyond the contact hypothesis: Theoretical perspectives on desegregation. In N. Miller & M. B. Brewer (Eds.), *Groups in contact: The psychology of desegregation* (pp. 281–302). Orlando, FL: Academic Press.

Briner, R. B., Denyer, D., & Rousseau, D. M. (2009). Evidence-based management: Concept cleanup time? *Academy of Management Perspectives, 23,* 19–32.

Briner, R. B., & Rousseau, D. M. (2011). Evidence-based I-O psychology: Not there yet. *Industrial and Organizational Psychology, 4,* 3–22.

Brownlee, S. (2007). Newtered. *The Washington Monthly, 39* (10), 27–33.

Buettner, D. (2008). *The Blue Zones: Lessons for living longer from the people who've lived the longest.* Washington, DC: National Geographic Society.

Burke, L. A., & Hutchins, H. M. (2007). Training transfer: An integrative literature review. *Human Resource Development Review, 6,* 263–296.

Burke, L. A., & Rau, B. (2010). The research-teaching gap in management. *Academy of Management Learning and Education, 9,* 132–143.

Caprar, V. D., Rynes, S. L., & Bartunek, J. M. (2010). *Why people believe (or don't believe) our research: The role of self affirmation processes.* Working paper: Sydney, Australia: University of New South Wales.

Centers for Disease Control and Prevention. (September 2009). *Teen vaccination coverage increasing.* Podcast retrieved April 11, 2010 from http://www2c.cdc.gov/podcasts/media/pdf/TeenVaccRatesRising.pdf

Chalmers, I., Enkin, M., & Kierse, M. J. N. C. (1991). *Effective care in pregnancy and childbirth.* New York: Oxford University Press.

Champion, V. L., & Leach, A. (1989). Variables related to research utilization in nursing: An empirical investigation. *Journal of Advanced Nursing, 14,* 705–710.

Charlton, B. G. (1997). [Review of the book *Evidence-based medicine: How to practice and teach EBM* by D. L. Sackett, W. S. Richardson, W. Rosenberg, & R. B. Haynes]. *Journal of Evaluation in Clinical Practice, 3,* 169–172.

Charlton, B. G. (2009). The Zombie science of evidence-based medicine: A personal retrospective. A commentary on Djulbegovic, B., Guyatt, G. H., & Ashcroft, R. E. (2009). *Cancer Control, 16,* 158–168. *Journal of Evaluation in Clinical Practice, 15,* 930–934.

Charlton, B. G., & Miles, A. (1998). The rise and fall of EBM. *QJM: An International Journal of Medicine, 91,* 371–374.

Choi, J. J., Laibson, D., Madrian, B. C., & Metrick, A. (2002). Defined contribution pensions: Plan rules, participant decisions, and the path of least resistance. In J. M. Poterba (Ed.), *Tax policy and the economy* (Vol. 16, pp. 67–113). Cambridge, MA: MIT Press.

Choi, J. J., Laibson, D., Madrian, B. C., & Metrick, A. (2004). For better or for worse: Default effects and 401(k) savings behavior. In D. Wise (Ed.), *Perspectives on the economics of aging* (pp. 81–126). Chicago, IL: University of Chicago Press.

Choudhry, N. K., Stelfox, H. T., & Detsky, A. S. (2002). Relationships between authors of clinical practice guidelines and the pharmaceutical industry. *Journal of the American Medical Association, 287,* 612–617.

Cialdini, R. B. (2009). *Influence: Science and practice* (5th ed.). Boston: Pearson.

Cialdini, R. B., & Trost, M. R. (1998). Social influence: Social norms, conformity, and compliance. In D. T. Gilbert, S. T. Fiske, & G. Lindzey (Eds.), *The handbook of social psychology* (4th ed., Vol. 1, pp. 151–192). New York: Oxford University Press.

Cohen, D. J. (2007). The very separate worlds of academic and practitioner publications in human resource management: Reasons for the divide and concrete solutions for bridging the gap. *Academy of Management Journal, 50,* 1013–1019.

Corner, P. D. (2002). An integrative model for teaching quantitative research design. *Journal of Management Education, 26,* 671–692.

Crettaz von Roten, F. (2006). Do we need a public understanding of statistics? *Public Understanding of Science, 15*, 243–249.

Crozier, M. (1964). *The bureaucratic phenomenon*. Chicago, IL: University of Chicago Press.

D'Aunno, T., & Sutton, R. I. (1992). The responses of drug abuse treatment organizations to financial adversity: A partial test of the threat-rigidity thesis. *Journal of Management, 18*, 117–131.

Dawes, R. M. (1999). A message from psychologists to economists: Mere predictability doesn't matter like it should (without a good store appended to it). *Journal of Economic Behavior and Organization, 39*, 29–40.

DeDreu, C. K. W., & Weingart, L. R. (2003). Task versus relationship conflict, team performance, and team member satisfaction: A meta-analysis. *Journal of Applied Psychology, 88*, 741–749.

Dewey, J. (1922). *Human nature and conduct: An introduction to social psychology*. New York: Henry Holt.

De Wit, J. B. F., Das, E., & Vet, R. (2008). What works best: Objective statistics or a personal testimonial? An assessment of the persuasive effects of different types of message evidence on risk perception. *Health Psychology, 27*, 110–115.

Deyo, R. A., Cherkin, D., Conrad, D., & Volinn, E. (1991). Cost, controversy, crisis: Low back pain and the health of the public. *Annual Review of Public Health, 12*, 141–156.

Deyo, R. A., Nachemson, A., & Mirza, S. K. (2004). Spinal-fusion surgery: The case for restraint. *The New England Journal of Medicine, 350*, 722–726.

Dickersin, K., Straus, S. E., & Bero, L. A. (2007). Evidence-based medicine: Increasing, not dictating, choice. *British Medical Journal, 334* (1), s10. Retrieved April 10, 2010 from http://www.bmj.com/cgi/content/full/334/suppl_1/s10

Donaldson, L. (2009). Design structure to fit strategy. In E. A. Locke (Ed.), *Handbook of principles of organizational behavior: Indispensible knowledge for evidence-based management* (2nd ed., pp. 407–424). Chichester, West Sussex, England: Wiley.

Dopson, S., Fitzgerald, L., Ferlie, E., Gabbay, J., & Locock, L. (2002). No magic targets! Changing clinical practice to become more evidence based. *Healthcare Management Review, 27*, 35–47.

Dopson, S., Locock, L., Gabbay, J., Ferlie, E., & Fitzgerald, L. (2003). Evidence-based medicine and the implementation gap. *Health: An interdisciplinary journal for the social study of health, illness, and medicine, 7*, 311–330.

Doumit, G., Gattellari, M., Grimshaw, J., & O'Brien, M. A. (2009) Local opinion leaders: effects on professional practice and healthcare outcomes. *Cochrane Database of Systematic Reviews, 1*. Art. No.: CD000125. DOI: 10.1002/14651858. CD000125.pub3.

Earle, C. C., & Weeks, J. C. (1999). Evidence-based medicine: A cup half full or half empty? *American Journal of Medicine, 106*, 263–264.

Epstein, S. (1973). The self-concept revisited: Of a theory of a theory. *American Psychologist, 28*, 404–416.

Erasmus, V., Daha, T. J., Brug, H., Richardus, J. H., Behrendt, M. D., Vos, M. C., & Van Beeck, E. F. (2010) Systematic review of studies on compliance with hand hygiene guidelines in hospital care. *Infection Control and Hospital Epidemiology, 31*, 283–294.

Everitt, B. S., & Wessely, S. (2008). *Clinical trials in psychiatry*. Chichester, West Sussex, England: Wiley.

Evidence-Based Management Collaborative. (n.d.) *Credo*. Retrieved May 9, 2010 from https://wpweb2.tepper.cmu.edu/evite/ebm_conf/index.html

Faigman, D. L., & Monahan, J. (2005). Psychological evidence at the dawn of law's scientific age. *Annual Review of Psychology, 56*, 631–659.

Ferlie, W., Fitzgerald, L., Wood, M., & Hawkins, C. (2005). The nonspread of innovations: The mediating role of professionals. *Academy of Management Journal, 48*, 117–134.

Festinger, L. (1957). *A theory of cognitive dissonance*. Evanston, IL: Row Peterson.

Fine, G. A. (1996). Justifying work: Occupational rhetorics as resources in restaurant kitchens. *Administrative Science Quarterly, 41*, 90–115.

Fisher, T. (2004/2005). Architects behaving badly: Ignoring environmental behavior research. *Harvard Design Magazine, 21*, 1–3.

Fiske, S. T., & Taylor, S. T. (1984). *Social cognition*. New York: Random House.

Ford, J. D., Ford, L. W., & D'Amelio, A. (2008). Resistance to change: The rest of the story. *Academy of Management Review, 33*, 362–377.

Forshee, R. A., Anderson, P. A., & Storey, M. L. (2008). Sugar-sweetened beverages and body mass index in children and adolescents: A meta-analysis. *American Journal of Clinical Nutrition, 87*, 1662–1671.

Fowler, P. B. S. (1997). Evidence-based everything. *Journal of Evaluation in Clinical Practice, 3*, 239–243.

Freidson, E. (1970). *Profession of medicine: A study of the sociology of applied knowledge*. New York: Dodd, Mead, & Company.

Freidson, E. (1986). *Professional powers: A study of the institutionalization of formal knowledge*. Chicago, IL: University of Chicago Press.

Gabora, N. J., Spanos, N. P., & Joab, A. (1993). The effects of complainant age and expert psychological testimony in a simulated child sexual abuse trial. *Law and Human Behavior, 17*, 103–119.

Gaertner, S. L., Dovidio, J. F., Banker, B. S., Houlette, M., Johnson, K. M., & McGlynn, E. A. (2000). Reducing intergroup conflict: From superordinate goals to decategorization, recategorization, and mutual differentiation. *Group Dynamics: Theory, Research, and Practice, 4*, 98–114.

Gawande, A. (2009). *The checklist manifesto: How to get things right*. New York: Metropolitan Books, Henry Holt.

Gawiser, S. R., & Witt, G. E. (2005). *20 questions a journalist should ask about poll results* (3rd ed.). Retrieved May 8, 2010 from National Council on Public Poll's Web site: http://www.ncpp.org/?q=node/4

Gerstner, L. V. (2002). *Who says elephants can't dance? Inside IBM's historic turnaround*. New York: Harper Collins.

Gibson, S. (2008). Sugar-sweetened soft drinks and obesity: A systematic review of the evidence from observational studies and interventions. *Nutrition Research Reviews, 21*, 134–147.

Gladwell, M. (2002). *The tipping point: How little things can make a big difference*. Boston, MA: Little, Brown and Company.

Goodman, N. W. (1998). Anaesthesia and evidence-based medicine. *Anaesthesia, 53*, 353–368.

Greenberg, J., & Pyszczynski, T. (1985). Compensatory self-inflation: A response to the threat to self-regard of public failure. *Journal of Personality and Social Psychology, 49*, 273–280.

Greenwald, A. G. (1980). The totalitarian ego: Fabrication and revision of personal history. *American Psychologist, 35*, 603–618.

Griffin, M. A., Tesluk, P. E., & Jacobs, R. R. (1995). Bargaining cycles and work-related attitudes: Evidence for threat-rigidity effects. *Academy of Management Journal, 38,* 1709–1725.

Grol, R. (1997). Beliefs and evidence in changing clinical practice. *British Medical Journal, 315,* 418–421.

Groopman, J. (2002, April 8). A knife in the back: Is surgery the best approach to chronic pain? *The New Yorker,* 66–73.

Grove, W. M., & Meehl, P. E. (1996). Comparative efficiency of informal (subjective, impressionistic) and formal (mechanical, algorithmic) prediction procedures: The clinical-statistical controversy. *Psychology, Public Policy, and Law, 2,* 293–323.

Grove, W. M., Zald, D. H., Lebow, B. S., Snitz, B. E., & Nelson, C. (2000). Clinical versus mechanical prediction: A meta-analysis. *Psychological Assessment, 12,* 19–30.

Hambrick, D. (1994). Presidential address: What if the academy actually mattered? *Academy of Management Review, 19,* 11–16.

Haynes, B., & Haines, A. (1998). Getting research findings into practice: Barriers and bridges to evidence based clinical practice. *British Medical Journal, 317,* 273–276.

Heath, C., & Heath, D. (2006). The curse of knowledge. *Harvard Business Review, 84,* 20–22.

Heath, C., & Heath, D. (2008). *Made to stick: Why some ideas survive and others die.* New York: Random House.

Heath, C., & Heath, D. (2010). *How to change things when change is hard.* New York: Broadway Books.

Heath, C., & Staudenmayer, N. (2000). Coordination neglect: How lay theories of organizing complicate coordination in organizations. *Research in Organizational Behavior, 22,* 155–193.

Highhouse, S. (2008). Stubborn reliance on intuition and subjectivity in employee selection. *Industrial and Organizational Psychology: Perspectives on Science and Practice, 1,* 333–342.

Hinings, C. R., Hickson, D. J., Pennings, J. M., & Schneck, R. E. (1974). Structural conditions of intraorganizational power. *Administrative Science Quarterly, 19,* 22–44.

Hinyard, L. J., & Kreuter, M. W. (2007). Using narrative communication as a tool for health behavior change: A conceptual, theoretical, and empirical overview. *Health Education and Behavior, 34,* 777–792.

Hofstadter, R. (1964). *Anti-intellectualism in American life.* New York: Alfred A. Knopf.

Hyams, A. I., Brandenburg, J. A., Lipsitz, S. R., Shapiro, D. W., & Brennan, T. A. (1995). Practice guidelines and malpractice litigation: A two-way street. *Annals of Internal Medicine, 122,* 450–455.

Internet Movie Database. (n.d.) Retrieved March 6, 2011 from http://www.imdb.com/title/tt0088559/quotes.

Iserson, K. (2009). *MacGyver medicine: Improvising patient care when other options don't exist.* Session presented at the annual conference of the Wilderness Medical Society. Retrieved March 6, 2011 from http://www.wms.org/conferences/Snowmass09/brochure.pdf

Jehn, K. (1995). A multimethod examination of the benefits and detriments of intragroup conflict. *Administrative Science Quarterly, 40,* 256–282.

Jenkins, A., & Zetter, R. (2003). *Linking research and teaching in departments.* Learning and Teaching Support Network (LTSN) Generic Centre. Oxford, England: Oxford Brookes University.

Johns, G. (1993). Constraints on the adoption of psychology-based personnel practices: Lessons from organizational innovation. *Personnel Psychology, 46,* 569–592.

Johns, G. (2001). In praise of context. *Journal of Organizational Behavior, 22,* 31–42.

Johns, G. (2006). The essential impact of context on organizational behavior. *Academy of Management Review, 31,* 386–408.

Judge, T. A., Thoresen, C. J., Pucik, V., & Welbourne, T. M. (1999). Managerial coping with organizational change: A dispositional perspective. *Journal of Applied Psychology, 84,* 107–122.

Kahan, D. (2010). Fixing the communications failure. *Nature, 463,* 296–297.

Kahan, D. M., Braman, D., Cohen, G. L., Solvic, P., & Gastil, J. (2010). Who fears the HPV vaccine, who doesn't, and why? An experimental investigation of the mechanisms of cultural cognition. *Law and Human Behavior, 34,* 501–516.

Kahan, D., Jenkins-Smith, H., & Braman, D. (2011). Cultural cognition of scientific consensus. *Journal of Risk Research, 14,* 147–174.

Kahneman, D., & Tversky, A. (1973). On the psychology of prediction. *Psychological Review, 80,* 237–251.

Kahneman, D., & Tversky, A. (1979). Prospect theory: An analysis of decision under risk. *Econometrica, 47,* 263–291.

Kenny, D. J. (2005). Nurses' use of research in practice at three US Army hospitals. *Nursing Leadership (CJNL), 18,* 45–67.

Kerridge, I. (2010). Ethics and EBM: Acknowledging bias, accepting difference, and embracing politics. *Journal of Evaluation in Clinical Practice, 16,* 365–373.

Kida, T. E. (2006). *Don't believe everything you think: The 6 basic mistakes we make in thinking.* Amherst, NY: Prometheus Books.

Kita, J. (2010). White coat confessions. *Reader's Digest, October,* 86–97. New York: Reader's Digest Association.

Kotter, J. P. (1996). *Leading change.* Boston, MA: Harvard Business School Press.

Kotter, J. P., & Cohen, D. S. (2002). *The heart of change: Real-life stories of how people change their organizations.* Boston, MA: Harvard Business School Press.

Kovera, M. B., Levy, R. J., Borgida, E., & Penrod, S. D. (1994). Expert testimony in child sexual abuse cases: Effects of expert evidence type and cross-examination. *Law and Human Behavior, 18,* 653–674.

Lacey, E. A. (1994). Research utilization in nursing practice—a pilot study. *Journal of Advanced Nursing, 12,* 101–110.

Landau, M. (1984). Human evolution as narrative. *American Scientist, 72,* 262–268.

Lankford, M. G., Zembower, T. R., Trick, W. G., Hacek, D. M., Noskin, G. A., & Peterson, L. R. (2003). Influence of role models and hospital design on hand hygiene of healthcare workers. *Emerging Infectious Diseases, 9,* 217–223.

Latham, G. P. (2007). A speculative perspective on the transfer of behavioral science findings to the workplace: "The times they are a-changin." *Academy of Management Journal, 50,* 1027–1032.

Latham, G. P. (2009a). *Becoming the evidence-based manager: Making the science of management work for you.* Boston, MA: Davies-Black.

Latham, G. P. (2009b). Motivate employee performance through goal setting. In E. A. Locke (Ed.), *Handbook of principles of organizational behavior: Indispensible knowledge for evidence-based management* (2nd ed., pp. 161–178). Chichester, West Sussex, England: Wiley.

Learmonth, M. (2006). "Is there such a thing as 'evidence-based management'?" A commentary on Rousseau's 2005 presidential address. *Academy of Management Review, 31,* 1089–1093.

Learmonth, M. (2009). Rhetoric and evidence: The case of evidence-based management. In D. A. Buchanan & A. Bryman (Eds.), *The SAGE handbook of organizational research methods* (pp. 93–107). Los Angeles, CA: Sage.

Learmonth, M., & Harding, N. (2006). Evidence-based management: The very idea. *Public Administration, 84,* 245–266.

LeCraw, L. L. (2007). Use of clinical practice guidelines in medical malpractice litigation. *Journal of Oncology Practice, 3,* 254.

Leicht, K. T., & Fennell, M. L. (2001). *Professional work: A sociological approach.* San Francisco, CA: Jossey-Bass.

Lévi-Strauss, C. (1966). *The savage mind.* Chicago, IL: University of Chicago Press.

Locock, L., Chambers, D., Surender, R., Dopson, S., & Gabbay, J. (1999). *Evaluation of the Welsh clinical effectiveness initiative national demonstration projects: Final report.* Templeton College, University of Oxford & Wessex Institute for Health Research and Development, University of Southampton.

Locock, L., Dopson, S., Chambers, D., & Gabbay, J. (2001). Understanding the role of opinion leaders in improving clinical effectiveness. *Social Science and Medicine, 53,* 745–757.

Luckow, D. (2010). *MacGyver medicine: Practical procedures in family practice.* McGill University NCS Multimedia presentation. Retrieved March 6, 2011 from http://bcooltv.mcgill.ca/Viewer2/?RecordingID=40693

Luria, A. R. (1976). *Cognitive development: Its cultural and social foundations.* Cambridge, MA: Harvard University Press.

MacCoun, R. J. (1998). Biases in the interpretation and use of research results. *Annual Review of Psychology, 49,* 259–287.

Mackey, T. K., & Liang, B. A. (2011). The role of practice guidelines in medical malpractice litigation. *American Medical Association Journal of Ethics, 13,* 36–41.

Madrian, B. C., & Shea, D. F. (2001). The power of suggestion: Inertia in 401(k) participation and savings behavior. *The Quarterly Journal of Economics, 116,* 1149–1187.

Malik, V. S., Schulze, M. B., & Hu, F. B. (2006). Intake of sugar-sweetened beverages and weight gain: A systematic review. *American Journal of Clinical Nutrition, 84,* 274–288.

Mann, C. (1990). Meta-analysis in the breech. *Science, 249,* 476–480.

March, J. G. (1994). *A primer on decision making: How decisions happen.* New York: Free Press.

March, J. G. (2005). Parochialism in the evolution of a research community: The case of organization studies. *Management and Organization Review, 1,* 5–22.

Markham, W. T. (1991). Research methods in the introductory course: To be or not to be? *Teaching Sociology, 19,* 464–471.

Martin, J., Feldman, M. S., Hatch, M. J., & Sitkin, S. B. (1983). The uniqueness paradox in organizational stories. *Administrative Science Quarterly, 28,* 438–453.

McColl, A., Smith, H., White, P., & Field, J. (1998). General practitioners' perceptions of the route to evidence based medicine: A questionnaire survey. *British Medical Journal, 316,* 361–366.

McCroskey, J. C., & Teven, J. J. (1999). Goodwill: A reexamination of the construct and its measurement. *Communication Monographs, 66,* 90–103.

McGrath, R. G. (2007). No longer a stepchild: How the management field can come into its own. *Academy of Management Journal, 50,* 1365–1378.

McKelvey, B. (2006). Van de Ven and Johnson's "engaged scholarship:" Nice try, but… *Academy of Management Review, 31,* 822–829.

Meyer, J. H. F., & Land, L. (Eds.) (2006). *Overcoming barriers to student understanding: Threshold concepts and troublesome knowledge.* London: Routledge—Taylor & Francis Group.

Miles, A. (2009). Evidence-based medicine: Requiescat in pace? A commentary on Djulbegovic, B., Guyatt, G. H., & Ashcroft, R. E. (2009) *Cancer Control, 16,* 158–168. *Journal of Evaluation in Clinical Practice, 15,* 924–929.

Mink, L. O. (1978). Narrative form as a cognitive instrument. In R. H. Canary & H. Kozicki (Eds.), *The writing of history: Literary form and historical understanding* (pp. 129–149). Madison, WI: University of Wisconsin Press.

Mooney, C. (2005). *The Republican war on science.* New York: Basic Books.

Murphy, K. R., & Sideman, L. (2006). The two EIs. In K. R. Murphy (Ed.), *A critique of emotional intelligence: What are the problems and how can they be fixed?* (pp. 37–58). Mahwah, NJ: Lawrence Erlbaum.

Naylor, C. D. (1995). Grey zones of clinical practice: Some limits to evidence-based medicine. *The Lancet, 345,* 840–842.

Newsweek (October 12, 2009). Member comments regarding S. Begley's "*Ignoring the evidence: Why do psychologists reject science?*" Retrieved on February 13, 2010 from http://www.newsweek.com/id/216506/output/comments/

Newsweek (March 18, 2010). Member comments regarding S. Begley's "*Their own worst enemies: Why scientists are losing the PR wars.*" Retrieved on April 17, 2010 from http://www.newsweek.com/id/235084/output/comments/

Norman, G. R. (1999). Examining the assumptions of evidence-based medicine. *Journal of Evaluation in Clinical Practice, 5,* 139–147.

Olesen, V. (1994). Feminisms and models of qualitative research. In N. K. Denzin & Y. S. Lincoln (Eds.), *The handbook of qualitative research* (pp. 158–174). Thousand Oaks, CA: Sage.

Olson, R. (2009). *Don't be such a scientist: Talking substance in an age of style.* Washington, DC: Island Press.

Oreg, S. (2003). Resistance to change: Developing an individual differences measure. *Journal of Applied Psychology, 88,* 680–693.

Oxford Centre for Evidence Based Medicine. (2009). *Levels of evidence.* Retrieved May 8, 2010 from http://www.cebm.net/?o=1025

Oxford Dictionary (2010). *Resist.* Retrieved August 28, 2010 from http://oxforddictionaries.com/view/entry/m_en_us1284479#m_en_us1284479

Pastor, R. (April 8, 2010). *U.S. sugar group says sugar not to blame for obesity.* Retrieved April 18, 2010 from http://www.reuters.com/assets/print?aid=USTRE6373X920100408

Paulos, J. A. (2001). *Innumeracy: Mathematical illiteracy and its consequences.* New York: Hill & Wang.

PBS Newshour (2009, November 26). *How will proposed healthcare overhaul affect patients?* Retrieved April 8, 2010 from http://www.pbs.org/newshour/bb/health/july-dec09/medicine_11–26.html

PBS Newshour (2009, March 30). *Pennsylvania hospitals test 'warranty' on patient care.* Retrieved February 27, 2011 from http://www.pbs.org/newshour/bb/health/jan-june09/healthwarranty_03–30.html

Pearce, J. L. (2009). *Organizational behavior: Real research for real managers.* Irvine, CA: Melvin & Leigh Publishers.

Pennington, N., & Hastie, R. (1988). Explanation-based decision making: Effects of memory structure on judgment. *Journal of Experimental Psychology: Learning, Memory, and Cognition, 14,* 521–533.

Pettigrew, T. F. (1998). Intergroup contact theory. *Annual Review of Psychology, 49,* 65–85.

Petty, R. E., & Cacioppo, J. T. (1996). *Attitudes and persuasion: Classic and contemporary approaches.* Boulder, CO: Westview.

Pfeffer, J., & Sutton, R. I. (2000). *The knowing-doing gap: How smart companies turn knowledge into action.* Boston, MA: Harvard Business School Press.

Pfeffer, J., & Sutton, R. I. (2006a). Evidence-based management. *Harvard Business Review, 84*(1), 62–74.

Pfeffer, J., & Sutton, R. I. (2006b). *Hard facts, dangerous half-truths & total nonsense: Profiting from evidence-based management.* Boston, MA: Harvard Business School Press.

Piderit, S. K. (2000). Rethinking resistance and recognizing ambivalence: A multidimensional view of attitudes toward an organizational change. *Academy of Management Review, 25,* 783–794.

Pinker, S. (2002). *The blank slate: The modern denial of how the mind works.* New York: Viking.

Pittet, D. (2001). Improving adherence to hand hygiene practice: A multidisciplinary approach. *Emerging Infectious Diseases, 7,* 234–240.

Pittet, D., Mourouga, P., & Perneger, T. V. (1999). Compliance with handwashing in a teaching hospital. *Annals of Internal Medicine, 130,* 126–130.

Pope, C. (2003). Resisting evidence: The study of evidence-based medicine as a contemporary social movement. *Health: An Interdisciplinary Journal for the Social Study of Health, Illness, and Medicine, 7,* 267–282.

Pratt, M. G., & Dirks, K. T. (2007). Rebuilding trust and restoring positive relationships: A commitment-based view of trust. In J. E. Dutton & B. R. Ragins (Eds.), *Exploring positive relationships at work: Building a theoretical and research foundation* (pp. 117–136). New York: Lawrence Erlbaum.

Pronovost, P., & Vohr, E. (2010). *Safe patients, smart hospitals.* New York: Hudson Street Press.

Ragins, B. R., & Dutton, J. E. (2007). Positive relationships at work: An introduction and invitation. In J. E. Dutton & B. R. Ragins (Eds.), *Exploring positive relationships at work: Building a theoretical and research foundation* (pp. 3–25). New York: Lawrence Erlbaum.

Reay, T., Berta, W., & Kohn, M. K. (2009). What's the evidence on evidence-based management? *Academy of Management Perspectives, 23,* 5–18.

Recupero, P. R. (2008). Clinical practice guidelines as learned treatises: Understanding their use as evidence in the courtroom. *Journal of the American Academy of Psychiatry and the Law, 36,* 290–301.

Rogers, E. M. (2003). *The diffusion of innovations.* New York: The Free Press.

Rosenstiel, T. (2005). Political polling and the new media culture: A case of more being less. *Public Opinion Quarterly, 69,* 698–715.

Ross, L. (1977). The intuitive psychologist and his shortcomings: Distortions in the attribution process. In L. Berkowitz (Ed.), *Advances in experimental social psychology* (Vol. 10, pp. 173–220). New York: Academic Press.

Rousseau, D. M. (2006). Is there such a thing as "evidence-based management"? *Academy of Management Review, 31,* 256–269.

Rousseau, D. M., & Fried, Y. (2001). Location, location, location: Contextualizing organizational research. *Journal of Organizational Behavior, 22,* 1–13.

Rousseau, D. M., & McCarthy, S. (2007). Educating managers from an evidence-based perspective. *Academy of Management Learning and Education, 6,* 84–101.

Rozin, P., & Royzman, E. B. (2001). Negativity bias, negativity dominance, and contagion. *Personality and Social Psychology Review, 5,* 296–320.

Rynes, S. L. (Ed.) (2007). The research-practice gap in human resource management [Editor's Forum]. *Academy of Management Journal, 50*(5), 985–1054.

Rynes, S. L. (in press). The research-practice gap in industrial/organzational psychology and related fields: Challenges and potential solutions. In S. Kozlowski (Ed.), *Oxford handbook of industrial and organizational psychology.* Oxford, England: Oxford University Press. Available at SSRN: http://ssrn.com/abstract=1455968

Rynes, S. L., Bartunek, J. M., & Daft, R. L. (2001). Across the great divide: Knowledge creation and transfer between practitioners and academics. *Academy of Management Journal, 44,* 340–355.

Rynes, S. L., Brown, K. G., & Colbert, A. E. (2002). Seven common misconceptions about human resource practices: Research findings versus practitioner beliefs. *Academy of Management Executive, 16,* 92–103.

Rynes, S. L., Colbert, A. E., & Brown, K. G. (2002). HR professionals' beliefs about effective human resource practices: Correspondence between research and practice. *Human Resource Management, 41,* 149–174.

Rynes, S. L., Giluk, T. L., & Brown, K. G. (2007). The very separate worlds of academic and practitioner periodicals in human resource management: Implications for evidence-based management. *Academy of Management Journal, 50,* 987–1008.

Saari, L. (2007). Bridging the worlds. *Academy of Management Journal, 50,* 1043–1045.

Saba, R., Inan, D., Seyman, D., Gül, G., Şenol, Y. Y., Turhan, Ö., & Mamıkoğlu, L. (2005). Hand hygiene compliance in a hematology unit. *Acta Haematologica, 113,* 190–193.

Salancik, G. R., & Pfeffer, J. (1977). Who gets power—and how they hold onto it: A strategic contingency model of power. *Organization Dynamics, Winter,* 3–21.

Salancik, G. R., Pfeffer, J., & Kelly, J. P. (1978). A contingency model of influence in organizational decision-making. *The Pacific Sociological Review, 21,* 239–256.

Samuelson, W., & Zeckhauser, R. (1988). Status quo bias in decision making. *Journal of Risk and Uncertainty, 1,* 7–59.

Schön, D. A. (1971). *Beyond the stable state.* New York: Random House.

Schön, D. A. (1983). *The reflective practitioner: How professionals think in action.* New York: Basic Books.

Schuller, R. A. (1992). The impact of battered woman syndrome evidence on jury decision processes. *Law and Human Behavior, 16,* 597–620.

Shiffrin, R. M., & Schneider, W. (1977). Controlled and automatic human information processing: II. Perceptual learning, automatic attending, and a general theory. *Psychological Review, 84,* 127–190.

Shojania, K. G., Sampson, M., Ansari, M. T., Doucette, S., & Moher, D. (2007). How quickly do systematic reviews go out of date? A survival analysis. *Annals of Internal Medicine, 147,* 224–233.

Slater, M. D., & Rouner, D. (1996). Value-affirmative and value-protective processing of alcohol education messages that include statistical evidence or anecdotes. *Communication Research, 23,* 210–235.

Staw, B. M., Sandelands, L. E., & Dutton, J. E. (1981). Threat-rigidity effects in organizational behavior: A multilevel analysis. *Administrative Science Quarterly, 26,* 501–524.

Steele, C. M. (1988). The psychology of self-affirmation: Sustaining the integrity of the self. In L. Berkowitz (Ed.), *Advances in experimental social psychology* (Vol. 21, pp. 261–302). San Diego, CA: Academic Press.

Stelfox, H. T., Chua, G., O'Rourke, K., & Detsky, A. S. (1998). Conflict of interest in the debate over calcium-channel antagonists. *The New England Journal of Medicine, 338,* 101–106.

Straus, S. E., & McAlister, F. A. (2000). Evidence-based medicine: A commentary on common criticisms. *Canadian Medical Association Journal, 163,* 837–841.

Tajfel, H., Flament, C., Billig, M. G., & Bundy, R. F. (1971). Social categorization and intergroup behavior. *European Journal of Social Psychology, 1,* 149–177.

Taylor, R. B. (2006). *Academic medicine: A guide for clinicians.* New York: Springer.

Thaler, R. H., & Sunstein, C. R. (2009). *Nudge: Improving decisions about health, wealth and happiness.* New York: Penguin.

Thayer, L. (1988). Leadership/communication: A critical review and a modest proposal. In G. M. Goldhaber & G. A. Barnett (Eds.), *Handbook of organizational communication* (pp. 231–263). Norwood, NJ: Ablex Publishing.

Trank, C. Q., & Rynes, S. L. (2003). Who moved our cheese? Reclaiming professionalism in business education. *Academy of Management and Learning Education, 2,* 189–205.

Traver, N. (March 23, 1987). They cannot fend for themselves. *Time, 129* (12), 27.

Turk, D. C., & Salovey, P. (1985). Cognitive structures, cognitive processes, and cognitive-behavior modification: I. Client issues. *Cognitive Therapy and Research, 9,* 1–17.

Turner, J. A., Herron, L., & Deyo, R. A. (1993). Meta-analysis of the results of lumbar spine fusion. *Acta Orthopaedica, 64,* 120–122.

Turner, J. C., & Haslam, S. A. (2001). Social identity, organizations, and leadership. In M. E. Turner (Ed.), *Groups at work: Theory and research* (pp. 25–65). Mahwah, NJ: Lawrence Erlbaum.

U.S. Sugar Association. (2003). *Letter to World Health Organization.* Retrieved April 20, 2010 from http://www.commercialalert.org/sugarthreat.pdf

Van de Ven, A. H. (2007). *Engaged scholarship: A guide for organizational and social research.* Oxford, England: Oxford University Press.

Van de Ven, A. H., & Johnson, P. E. (2006). Knowledge for theory and practice. *Academy of Management Review, 31,* 802–821.

Van de Ven, A. H., & Schomaker, M. S. (2002). Commentary: The rhetoric of evidence-based medicine. *Healthcare Management Review, 27,* 89–91.

Vartanian, L. R., Schwartz, M. B., & Brownell, K. D. (2007). Effects of soft drink consumption on nutrition and health: A systematic review and meta-analysis. *American Journal of Public Health, 97,* 667–675.

Vermeulen, F. (2007). "I shall not remain insignificant": Adding a second loop to matter more. *Academy of Management Journal, 50,* 754–761.

Vinchur, A. J., Schippmann, J. S., Switzer, F. S., & Roth, P. L. (1998). A meta-analytic review of predictors of job performance for salespeople. *Journal of Applied Psychology, 83,* 586–597.

Vrieze, S. I., & Grove, W. M. (2009). Survey on the use of clinical and mechanical prediction methods in clinical psychology. *Professional Psychology: Research and Practice, 40,* 525–531.

Vygotsky, L. S. (1978). *Mind in society: Development of higher psychological processes.* Cambridge, MA: Harvard University Press.

Wanberg, C. R., & Banas, J. T. (2000). Predictors and outcomes of openness to changes in a reorganizing workplace. *Journal of Applied Psychology, 85,* 132–142.

Wang, C., Galinsky, A., & Murnighan, K. (2009). Bad drives psychological reactions, but good propels behavior. *Psychological Science, 20,* 634–644.

Weick, K. E. (1993). Organizational redesign as improvisation. In G. P. Huber & W. H. Glick (Eds.), *Organizational change and redesign: Ideas and insights for improving performance* (pp. 346–379). New York: Oxford University Press.

Wild, C. J. (1994). Embracing the "wider view" of statistics. *The American Statistician, 48,* 163–171.

Willett, W. C., & Underwood, A. (2010). Crimes of the heart. *Newsweek, 155,* 42–43.

Winkler, H., Rich, J., & Downing, S. (Producers). (1985–1992). *MacGyver* [Television series]. Los Angeles; Vancouver: ABC Television.

World Health Organization. (2003). *Diet, nutrition and the prevention of chronic diseases* (Technical report 916). Retrieved April 20, 2010 from http://www.who.int/hpr/NPH/docs/who_fao_expert_report.pdf

Enabling Evidence-Based Management: Bridging the Gap between Academics and Practitioners

Opal Leung *and* Jean M. Bartunek

Abstract

Several barriers, grounded in differences in knowledge, training, skills, and awareness, interfere with academics communicating successfully with practitioners about evidence. We describe several ways to reduce such barriers. These include providing sources that are trustworthy and accessible to managers; developing managerial skill in diagnosis; carrying out evidence-based practice; and communicating evidence in ways that are attractive, understandable, memorable, and actionable through channels that are likely to be noticed. We suggest several means for accomplishing each of these.

Key Words: accessibility, evidence, diagnostic skill, development, barriers to communicating research, evidence channels, memorable evidence, trustworthy sources

The two authors of this chapter illustrate "in practice" what we are writing about "in theory." The first author had supervisory and other practitioner experience prior to beginning a doctoral program. The second author is a long-term academic who is increasingly concerned about links with practice. We put these two sets of experience together to discuss how academics may communicate with practitioners in ways that will foster the application of scholarly evidence.

The expectation of evidence-based management (EBM) is that scholarly evidence, produced from sound academic research, can help managers and their organizations operate more effectively. As Rousseau, Manning, and Denyer (2008), Rousseau and McCarthy (2007), and Briner, Denyer, and Rousseau (2009) and others indicate, using evidence should make it possible for managers to develop and use substantive knowledge as opposed to faddish beliefs, and, thus, be more successful. Even if particular bodies of evidence exist, however, how best can this evidence be conveyed across the "great divide"

(Giluk & Rynes, chapter 8 of this volume; Rynes, Bartunek, & Daft, 2001)—from scholars to managers, from academia to practice—so that it is truly both usable and used?

It has been clear for decades that it is difficult to cross this divide (e.g. Pfeffer & Sutton, 2000; Shrivastava & Mitroff, 1984). Recently, in fact, Kieser and Leiner (2009) have argued, based on Luhmann's (1995) systems theory, that the worlds of academia and management are, by definition, unbridgeable. Although considerable empirical evidence suggests that multiple bridges indeed have been built (e.g., Hodgkinson & Rousseau, 2009), the ongoing dispute reflects the difficulties of finding an appropriate way for scholars to speak to managers (and vice versa) in ways that both can understand.

We are not going to restate all the arguments regarding academic-practitioner relationships; that has been done often (e.g. Bartunek, 2007; Rynes et al., 2001; Shani, Mohrman, Pasmore, Stymne, & Adler, 2008; Shapiro, Kirkman, & Courtney, 2007). Rather, we want to focus on a few arguments pertinent to barriers to the communication of academic evidence to practitioners that we believe are particularly salient and important. Then, based on practitioner as well as academic perspectives, we will suggest some ways that academic evidence might be presented to practitioners in a manner that might garner their interest and positively affect their practice.

An important assumption this chapter makes is that managers are conscientious, able to think critically, and want to perform well for the good of the organization. This means that motives for using (or not using) evidence such as the desire to appear accountable or appearing to have super managerial powers derived from experience, are not considered here. We are aware of political motives that may cause some individuals to ignore evidence (e.g., leading by "gut instinct" is less replicable than leading by evidence). We are also aware that some managers (and some academics) are more adept at critical thinking than others, and that this skill will also affect the capacity to use evidence well (Toulmin, 1984). However, these issues are beyond the scope of this chapter. Potworowski and Green (chapter 16 of this volume) address some of them more fully.

We will begin by focusing on four types of barriers to communication of academic evidence from scholars to practitioners. These have to do with knowledge, training, skills, and awareness. Figure 9.1 shows the barriers.

Barriers to Communication of Academic Evidence

Practitioners' knowledge sources are different from academics'. Management practitioners typically do not read academic journals. They are much more likely to seek out and read trade books, trade journals (especially if they are in technical fields) and periodicals such as the *Harvard Business Review (HBR), California Management Review, Sloan Management Review*, and *Business Horizons*, which are much more readable, accessible and apparently applicable. These also tend to have more novelty. For example, they may have catchier titles such as "Who Moved my Cheese" (Johnson, 1998) and are sometimes written by famous people, e.g., "Trump 101: The Way to Success" (Trump & McIver, 2006).

In addition, there are clear stylistic differences between the ways articles targeted at practitioners and academic journal articles are written (Kelemen & Bansal, 2002). Unfortunately, the style in which journal articles are written tends to alienate most practitioners (Kelemen & Bansal, 2002). Further, although articles in academic journals often include

implications for practice sections, the language used in these sections is typically at a beginning graduate school level (Bartunek & Rynes, 2010), and often includes unfamiliar words and phrases. Measures used to assess the readability of texts focus on the number of syllables in their words and the number of words in their sentences. This does not take into account the fact that many terms used (e.g., variable, log linear) are not familiar to practitioners regardless of the length of the words (cf. Bartunek & Rynes, 2010).

Furthermore, the content of *HBR* and other business periodicals is very different from that of academic journals. The level of abstraction is at a higher level in the latter, and there is a greater emphasis on practice in the former. In terms of Bloom's taxonomy (Bloom, 1956), academic journals tend to focus on evaluation, synthesis, and analysis, whereas practitioners are most helped by application. The implications for practice or application in academic journals are often not the reason for writing the article and are added as an afterthought. In practitioner-oriented publications such as *HBR,* the purpose of the articles is to help practitioners improve their practice, but the analysis and evidence for those practices is often lacking. Further, the time- frame mindset is very different for academics and practitioners. Because academics often are not addressing immediate problems, there is little urgency for journal articles to have relevance to immediate managerial concerns. Scholars are also largely writing for other scholars, with the goal of advancing theory and not necessarily improving practice. The articles that practitioners read, on the other hand, need to be current and relevant.

Even if managers believe in the relevance of EBM in the abstract, academic journals are unlikely to be their primary sources of usable evidence. For example, as a practitioner, the first author was familiar with *HBR.* That was her primary source of management knowledge until she started her PhD program. Even within *HBR,* not all of the issues appeared relevant. She was a supervisor in a music school, and many of the articles were about industries of which she had no knowledge. She didn't know how to bridge gaps across industries, let alone between theory and practice. Further, no one else below the director position, in the school where she worked, read *HBR* (or any other management periodical) on any regular basis. The only way she could learn more about what she was reading about in *HBR* was to attend a night-school management program, which she did—at Harvard—obtaining a masters degree in

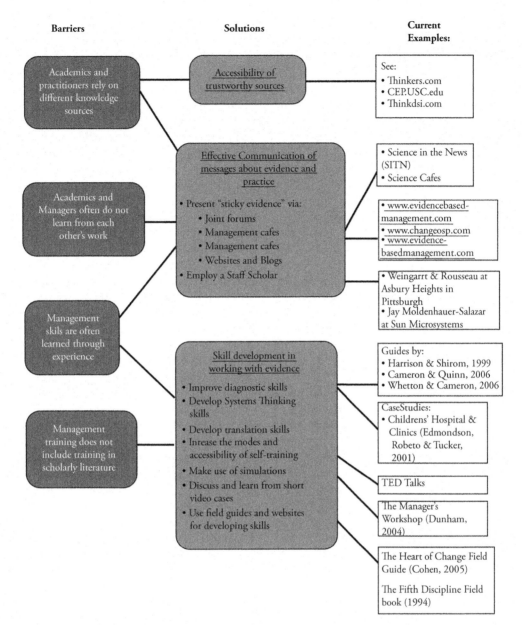

Fig. 9.1. Barriers, Solutions, and Current Examples.

management. Even here, the reading focused almost exclusively on practitioner articles and cases, largely from the Harvard Business School.

Management education doesn't include training in scholarly literature. Business schools are classified as professional schools, just as law schools and medical schools are. However, in their training in medical schools and law schools, potential doctors and potential lawyers read articles from scholarly medical journals and law reviews; they may even write (or review) such articles themselves. As Barends, ten Have, and Huisman (chapter 2 of this volume)

point out, medical researchers and consultants have had clinical experience, and MDs have had training in research methodologies and the scientific method. After MDs complete their training, they continue reading these materials when the articles are pertinent to their work. No one would imagine a doctor learning and advancing in his/her craft primarily by reading popular books written by famous doctors.

Yet, many people who become managers (as was initially the case with the first author) have little or no formal management training on either the graduate or undergraduate level; their becoming a manager is based in part on their technical skills. Further, it is a point of honor for many MBA students, at least in the United States, that they do not read the scholarly literature in management. Even some academics posit that the scholarly literature in management is irrelevant and "deliberately recondite" (Oviatt & Miller, 1989). Some professors feel they need to justify teaching theory (Zell, 2001).

Some of this might be a residual sentiment of the late nineteenth century, when the formation of the first business schools at universities began to be considered. Critics such as Thorstein Veblen thought that business schools did not belong in universities because the purpose of business proficiency was for acquiring "a facile command of the ways and means of private gain" (Veblen, 2009/1918) whereas the purpose of other professional schools was to train people to be proficient at being "serviceable to the community at large" (Veblen, 2009/1918). In other words, from the beginning of their consideration, there has been some discomfort about the appropriateness of business education.

Despite their critics, business schools did attain the status of professional schools. Further, after the scathing criticism of their "trade school" approaches by the Ford and Carnegie foundations (Gordon & Howell, 1959; Pierson, 1959) business schools have moved toward a model in which scholarly research is an expectation of faculty, many of whom are trained in liberal arts disciplines rather than management.

Ironically, this has happened at the same time as there has been an emphasis on making business school curricula more practical (Ball, 2006). For example, starting in the 1980s, business leaders wanted more influence in MBA program curricula (Ball, 2006). *Business Week, U.S. News and World Report,* and similar rankings have also created an environment in which MBA students were becoming more and more like customers and demanding that course material be clearly linked to practice (Zell, 2001). In more recent years, the trend has been to employ more adjunct practitioner faculty, who bring their extensive business experience to the classroom (Ball, 2006). When (as is often the case), these adjunct faculty have MBAs but not PhDs, they are more likely to concentrate on their experiences and not academic research when they teach (Rynes, Giluk, & Brown, 2007). Furthermore, the fact that many adjunct faculty do not have PhDs also means that they are likely to be unfamiliar with scholarly journals. Because their source of business knowledge is likely to be from practitioner literature

such as *HBR* or *Business Horizons,* their syllabi naturally include the same.

Since business schools expect tenure-track and tenured professors to conduct research, why don't management students learn from academic literature as doctors and lawyers do in their training? Rousseau's (2006) point that management is not a real profession suggests one possible reason. Unlike doctors or lawyers, managers do not have to attend professional schools or acquire any kind of license to earn their titles, and they don't have to participate in any continuing education to keep them (Rynes et al., 2007). It is also not clear whether an MBA education makes one more qualified or knowledgeable about management (Pfeffer & Fong, 2002). Barends et al (chapter 2 of this volume) also point out that students have normative beliefs about what they need to learn in their management programs, and as a result, face validity and readability trump scientific rigor. These issues are at the heart of the divide between research and practice—there are no required network, educational, or social links between managers and scholars.

Management skills are often learned primarily through experience. Many managers prefer to rely on their experience or company-based training as a source of learning. After all, what can a bunch of nameless scholars who have never had to meet a payroll tell them about running their business? Implicitly, if not explicitly, many managers believe that it is impossible for professors to know how to teach anyone about management unless they have had experience as executives or high-level managers. To the extent that managers believe this, it is difficult for academics to convince practitioners that EBM is relevant; the "school of hard knocks" trumps academic research.

Law and medical-school faculty, in addition to conducting research, are typically also practitioners in their fields, and, as such, are mentors for their students. It would be difficult to imagine a medical faculty in which members had never treated a patient or a law faculty whose members had never tried a case or met with a client. However, in business schools, "it is possible to find tenured professors of management who have never set foot inside a real business, except as customers" (Bennis & O'Toole, 2005, p. 100).

Although it is not realistic for all professors to have the time to be executives or consultants on the side, there is also little incentive for many academics to contribute to the building of bridges between the academic and practitioner worlds by writing articles that translate scholarly research into practical applications. Professors are typically not rewarded for nonacademic writing (Bennis & O'Toole, 2005). Managers are also not necessarily rewarded for building bridges, especially if the act of asking for help may suggest or signal that they do not know what they are doing. Even in health-care systems, where one would think that evidence-based decision making would be the norm, the search for evidence is often impeded by time pressures and other obstacles (Kovner, chapter 10 of this volume).

Further, practitioners' awareness of research evidence does not necessarily mean that they apply it to their practice (Rynes, Brown, & Colbert, 2002). Organizations have unsystematic ways of making decisions (Yates, 1990), and they are unlikely to change this process without compelling reasons. For example, many business schools only started to take teaching seriously when periodicals such as *Business Week* began including teaching in their ratings; simple generic statements about the value of teaching certainly did not accomplish this on their own.

Academics and managers often don't learn very much from each others' work. Many scholars do not have the time, desire, skill, or obligation to do consulting work or ethnographic research through which they would be able to see better what is happening in many work organizations. Doctoral training in business schools tends to move doctoral students away from concern about practice (Polzer, Gulati, Khurana, & Tushman, 2009). This situation contributes to a knowledge-production problem (Van de Ven, 2007), characterized by practitioners wanting to know one thing and management scholars finding the answers to questions that practitioners do not necessarily see as being relevant (cf. Ekbia & Hara, 2008). But as Pettigrew (2001) points out, "dissemination is too late if the wrong questions have been asked." In chapter 20 of this volume, Salipante and Smith suggest training that links doctoral students more fully with practice, but such training is neither common nor accepted in many esteemed doctoral programs.

Some organizations have research departments or may work with outside consultants that conduct internal research by distributing surveys and collecting data from within the organization. However, the surveys are often not based on academically validated scales, and results are typically not disseminated publicly, let alone to the academic community. Rather, they are often seen as proprietary knowledge. Even within the organization, the results of the surveys might or might not be released to everyone.

There have also been cases of organizations that have attempted to educate their executives but stopped the program due to unexpected results. For example, at Bell Telephone Company in the 1950s, executives were trained at a program established with the University of Pennsylvania. The result was that the young executives started reading more widely after the program and became more confident and intellectually engaged (Davis, 2010). These were positive outcomes. However, the executives also became less interested in prioritizing the company's bottom line ahead of everything else in their lives, an outcome that was not so positive from the company's perspective. Organizational leaders are more likely to see the value of working with academics if they believe that the results serve organizational purposes and do not diminish organizational commitment.

Thus, academics and practitioners both create knowledge. They just don't do so for each other as much as those working with evidence-based management would deem optimal.

Given These Barriers, How Can Academics Foster Evidence-Based Managing

These are formidable barriers to the successful sharing of academic evidence. Some are related to individuals or groups of managers or academics, and some are largely structural, having to do with management learning, education, and taken-for-granted routines. Some have to do with persuasion and some have to do with accessibility. Some have to do with skill level and understanding. Different types of barriers may sometimes be combined.

Although no one approach will succeed in dealing with all the barriers we have described, literature on persuasion offers ways into considering them. This literature (e.g., Johnson, Maio, & Smith-McLallen, 2005; Petty, 1994) provides evidence of a wide array of factors that affect people's attitudes toward something, including, in our case, evidence-based practice.

Applying persuasion literature to the acceptance of EBM and oversimplifying this literature, we suggest that, in order for academic evidence pertaining to management to have impacts on managers' practice, it is important that (1) the sources of such knowledge be trustworthy and accessible to managers, (2) managers receive assistance in developing skill in diagnosing situations well and carrying out evidence-based practice, and (3) evidence be communicated in ways that are attractive, understandable, memorable, actionable, and through channels where they are particularly likely to be noticed. These ways of addressing the barriers and some examples of each are shown in Figure 9.1.

Accessibility of Trustworthy Sources

Literature on persuasion emphasizes the importance of trustworthy sources for messages to be convincing. Although it would be nice to think that a compendium of management evidence along the lines of the Campbell or Cochrane Collaborations would be easily accessible and seen as trustworthy and convincing on their own merits, the chances are good that this would not be the case. Rather, it would likely be more convincing if people who are already credible to managers present the evidence and that they be available for follow-up. Fortunately, there are a number of academics who fit this category.

Thinkers.com, for example, posts an annual listing of "the world's top 50 business thinkers" (http://www.thinkers50.com/gallery; accessed 9/16/2010) based on such criteria as originality and practicality of ideas, presentation style, written communication, and loyalty of followers. Several academics were included among last year's top 10, including Chan Kim, Renee Mauborgne, Philip Kotler, and Gary Hamel. Academics in the top 35 included, among others, Michael Porter, Howard Gardner, Richard D'Aveni, Rosabeth Moss Kanter, Clayton Christensen, Vijay Govindarajan, David Ulrich, and Henry Mintzberg. Presentation of evidence in a convincing manner by academics such as these is likely to be much more impactful than presentation by university professors who are not seen as concerned about practice.

Simple presentations by influential business thinkers, though helpful, are unlikely to be enough to inculcate new practices. Other means that might help are executive development training in settings that are based on serious scholarship and also attuned to practice. A primary exemplar of such a center is the Center for Effective Organizations at the University of Southern California (http://ceo.usc.edu/; accessed 9/16/2010), whose mission is to "improve how effectively organizations are managed." Research scientists there both do research and collaborate with practitioners, and have built up considerable practitioner credibility. Consulting firms that include doctoral-trained senior staff can also be sources of the inculcation of evidence, especially if they were part of scholarly efforts to

develop it. One such exemplar is Decision Strategies International (thinkdsi.com), which sees as its purpose "to help organizations develop a 'strategic compass' to be prepared for whatever unexpected events come their way."

The thinkers.com list is obviously not a complete list of people (including academics) who are trusted to have impacts on business. However, the list does suggest the value of convincing academics about potential values of academic evidence for practice and discussing with them how to convey its value to practitioners (e.g., Bartunek & Rynes, 2010). It also makes clear that academics who wish to be seen as credible to practitioners need to take steps outside the academic community to be known.

Such steps are sometimes taken, and they make a difference. Karl Weick, for example, one of the most renowned theorists in the world, dialogues with practitioners (e.g. Weick & Putnam, 2006), treats them seriously, uses provocative imagery that enables them to link with his work (e.g., O'Leary & Chia, 2007), and sometimes makes presentations at conferences that include practitioners (e.g., http://www.high-reliability.org/Conferences.html, accessed 7/23/2010). Some other scholars do this as well (cf. Bartunek, 2007). If academics assume practitioners' basic intelligence and interest, they are more likely to be able to communicate in a comprehensible and trustworthy manner than if they do not.

Skill Development in Working with Evidence

A feeling of competence in carrying out new behaviors pertinent to working with evidence is very important to willingness to adopt new practices. It is one thing to know about evidence and another to act on it. Thus, we will discuss several aspects of and means of skill development pertinent to evidence-based practice.

Diagnosis

Diagnosis is a critical skill required to use evidence well. One of the principles of EBM (Rousseau & McCarthy, 2007) is that it is important to understand underlying factors associated with a problem being addressed. Otherwise, even sound evidence-based approaches will not be effective because they don't respond to the correct issue(s). For example, Senge (1990) described a systems archetype called "shifting the burden" that we discuss more later. This term refers to managers treating the symptoms of a problem, but not the problem itself. Senge suggests that such action leads to constantly "fighting fires" as core problematic issues remain unaddressed. Without a coach or skills of reflection, it is often difficult to recognize that the repetition of the same issues is just a symptom and not the underlying cause.

In other words, as Briner et al. (2009), Rousseau and McCarthy (2007), and others argue, appropriate diagnosis and skill in carrying it out are key to the proper use of evidence. Symptoms are important because they alert the practitioner that something is amiss, but responding solely to symptoms usually does not solve the underlying problem. For example, abnormally low profits may be a clear symptom, but the underlying cause might be elusive. What can academics do to help managers develop skill in diagnosing situations so that they respond both to symptoms of a problem and their underlying causes?

One means is through book-level guides such as *Developing Management Skills,* 7th ed. (Whetten & Cameron, 2006) and *Organizational Diagnosis: Bridging Theory and Practice* (Harrison & Shirom, 1999) or books that include considerable diagnostic information, such as *Diagnosing and Changing Organizational Culture* (Cameron & Quinn, 2006). These books, all of which are based on sound research, can help practitioners learn how to diagnose organizational issues in more depth. Whetten and Cameron (2006), for example, include skill assessments, discussion questions, and other exercises that could be done individually or in groups, and Harrison and Shirom (1999) include conceptual frameworks that guide managers' approaches to diagnosis. This book revolves around the idea of "sharp-image diagnosis," an approach that helps practitioners "move quickly and decisively from initially stated problems and concerns to the identification of underlying forces that produce ineffective outcomes" (Harrison & Shirom, 1999). Cameron and Quinn (2006) include a conceptual framework based on the competing-values model (Quinn & Rohrbaugh, 1983) and questionnaire measures that can be used to diagnose competing values as they apply in organizations and to individual managers.

Another means academics may use to help managers improve their diagnostic skills is to provide models for them of how managers took steps to understand what was going on beneath the surface of a particular situation and then respond to it. Models can be found in the form of an appropriate case study, a series of steps such as Kotter's (1996) eight steps for organizational change, or a systematic

approach for diagnosing core issues such as Harrison & Shirom's (1999) sharp-image diagnosis.

One common pedagogical tool in business schools is the use of case studies. Many MBA programs revolve around the case method. Using a variety of case studies can help practitioners see the differences and commonalities of using various approaches in different contexts, in order to discern which responses are useful to many contexts and which are limited to certain contexts. Some case studies might even trigger the insight, "That's exactly what's happening in my organization!" Case studies are intended to give the practitioner an arms-length distance to help see situations from a more objective perspective and serve as a form of simulation that can potentially prepare them for the real event.

An illustration of a manager who recognized the need to treat both the symptom and cause of a problem appears in the *HBS* case, "Children's Hospital and Clinics" (Edmondson, Roberto, & Tucker, 2001). In the case, before creating a strategic plan to improve patient safety, the new COO, Julie Morath, employed the principles of EBM. She first made presentations to the hospital staff about research on medical errors. The purpose of this was not only to create buy-in for the organizational change that was to come; the presentations also highlighted the importance of using evidence and research to persuade others that improving an organizational process (i.e., improving patient safety) was necessary. Additionally, she conducted focus groups with employees and parents (of patients) to gather more information to diagnose the possible causes of medical accidents.

This case highlights the point that EBM involves both qualitative and quantitative data (Rousseau et al., 2008; Briner et al; 2009). Although the presentations about medical accidents were from the *Harvard Medical Practice Study (HMPS),* which showed quantitative data such as the percentage of patients that experienced an adverse event, the diagnosis stage involved considerable qualitative data gathering in the form of focus groups and discussions with various members of the hospital community.

One of the concerns that hospital employees had about holding a discussion about patient safety with a group of parents was that it might signal that the hospital was not safe. However, this was based on the assumption that parents were not aware that accidents happened. Morath did not take the assumption as fact, but persisted, eventually succeeding in obtaining permission to talk to the parents, who turned out to be already aware of "near misses" and welcomed the opportunity to contribute their ideas to the new initiative.

If we consider Morath an exemplar of how to use evidence in practice, one of the most important lessons from this case is that practitioners (and scholars) must test assumptions (i.e., engage in "double-loop learning") (Argyris, 1976, 1982) while in the field. Morath might have been the only one to question the assumption because she was a newcomer and might have had the intuition that parents were already aware of "near misses."

COO Morath and CEO Nelson then introduced a new Patient Safety Initiative, which included a new policy of blameless reporting. Rather than assigning blame to people after a medical accident, anyone who was involved in a medical accident could write up the accident anonymously. This was counter-intuitive to many employees because they assumed that staff might act less responsibly if they were not held accountable for their mistakes. However, Morath's goal was to change the organizational culture from one that was described as the "old ABC model of medicine: Accuse, Blame, Criticize," (Edmondson et al., 2005) to one that enabled learning to take place after a medical accident.

This was an excellent example of how an organizational leader used both evidence and diagnostic procedures to understand what was going on beneath the surface of the situation and improve an organizational process. Even if it was not explicitly stated with academic terminology in the case study, Morath diagnosed that, if defensive routines (Argyris, 1990) kicked in, they would lead staff to hide their mistakes and not reveal processes that led to errors. In other words, rather than merely treating the symptom by disciplining employees that made medical errors, blameless reporting enabled everyone who was involved to learn and treat the underlying cause of the medical errors.

At present most teaching cases are not meant to illustrate evidence-based practice. However, the development of more such cases would be particularly useful for training.

Developing Systems Thinking Skills

Managers well versed in systems theory should be more likely to accurately diagnose organizational issues that occur repeatedly because the systems archetypes show the underlying causes that lead problems to recur over and over again. There are multiple approaches that incorporate some type of systems thinking.

First, one of the five disciplines in Senge's (1990) *The Fifth Discipline* is systems thinking. Such thinking is embodied in several archetypes. For example, "shifting the burden" is the archetype that shows how treating a symptom and not the root cause will lead to the problem coming back over time. In the Children's Hospital case, Morath's new Patient Safety Initiative enabled staff to work together in finding the root causes of medical accidents instead of merely treating the symptom by reprimanding those involved in the accidents.

Management schools can offer instruction in this type of systems thinking for managers and management students. The first author included two sessions on systems theory in the undergraduate organizational-behavior course she taught, and the students were able to understand and apply the systems archetypes. For their final projects, many students were able to apply systems thinking to popular movies and television shows. It is conceivable that, combined with situational examples or case studies, systems-thinking skills can arm management students with a powerful set of tools that they can use to analyze organizational events and make better decisions at work or in leadership positions.

There are also consultants who offer training in this approach to systems theory. Consultants affiliated with the Society for Organizational Learning (http://www.solonline.org/; accessed 9/16/2010), in particular, offer programs that foster this type of awareness and skill. There are also several field guides that address management issues from a systems thinking perspective. Those field guides are outlined in a subsequent section.

Second, Goodman's (2000) book, *Missing Organizational Linkages*, describes some ways that systems thinking can be applied to gaps between organizational units and across organizational levels, (e.g., between individual or group performance and organizational performance). It suggests why great individual or group performance does not necessarily lead to great organizational performance; great organizational performance requires an understanding and creation of linkages across levels and units. Goodman provided systems tools that can be used to describe and understand the links among various systems components. These tools, however, are not simple and straightforward for any practitioner to apply; like many pieces of evidence they do not provide "quick fixes" to complicated organizational arrangements.

Third, Cascio and Boudreau's (Cascio & Boudreau, 2008; Cascio & Boudreau, 2011) work suggests ways that many decisions made in organizations can be considered much more systematically than they typically are. Cascio and Boudreau note, for example, that many of the activities associated with staffing, such as recruitment, initial screening, and selection, are typically treated independently, as separate elements. However, by using a metaphor of supply- chain management as a guide, and taking an organizational perspective on what is sometimes seen as solely a human-resources issue, it is possible to understand how decisions such as these are interdependent with each other. The same pattern can be applied to many types of organizational processes, including processes that cut across organizational units (e.g., HR and marketing).

Developing Translation Skills

Students who are studying management in MBA or, perhaps, undergraduate programs, may develop some tools for "translating" academic writing into practitioner writing during their studies, and these skills may help them assimilate academic knowledge more readily later. Such skills may be particularly helpful, for example, in searching out the types of online resources Werner (chapter 15 of this volume) addresses. As one way of how to do this, Professor Deborah Kolb, of Simmons College in Boston, has her MBA-level negotiation students translate an academic article about negotiation into prescriptions that everyday managers can use. The assignment is included in full in Appendix A.

Increasing the Modes and Accessibility of Self-Training

There are many training materials that practitioners can use to help themselves and to enhance their own thought processes when addressing organizational issues. Training in skills related to evidence-based practice does not have to take place only in formal settings.

Videos

One recent trend that is becoming more popular with managers is the TED video series, which is available online (ted.com). According to its URL (http://www.ted.com/pages/view/id/5; accessed 9/16/2010), the creators of this website "believe passionately in the power of ideas to change attitudes, lives and ultimately, the world. So we're building here a clearinghouse that offers free knowledge and inspiration from the world's most inspired thinkers, and also a community of curious souls to engage with ideas and each other."

Especially if some type of index of evidence-related programs is available (and especially, as noted earlier, if these programs are presented by credible sources), managers might find it easier to find relevant information about EBM from web sites like TED or youtube.com than searching through books or periodicals or courses. The Internet is easy to access, and there are filtering mechanisms (tags, search engines, etc.) that make it easier for those who are interested to find what they are looking for. Further, ted.com includes talks on various topics including technology, business, science, global issues, design, and entertainment. Many videos are quite short, making it easy for busy people to watch them and learn in short spurts. Within the business category, there are videos on leadership, motivation, and other related topics.

Many of the videos address ideas that may seem unconventional or counter-intuitive in some way. Speakers often challenge conventional wisdom in ways that may make viewers think differently about the world, and that may foster appreciation of the importance of evidence. Daniel Pink's TED video (http://www.ted.com/talks/dan_pink_on_motivation.html; accessed 9/16/2010), for instance, provides a pertinent example of how standard taken-for-granted assumptions about incentive systems are often wrong. Pink reveals the results of a lab experiment in which people who were financially compensated for the quality of their performance did better than the group not compensated when the task was simple and straightforward. However, when the task involved cognitive skill, the group that was not compensated did better. This is surprising in itself, but what are the implications? Should managers pay creative workers less? Without adequate explanation, it would seem so.

But Pink goes on to emphasize that managers need to make sure that creative workers, and all those not simply carrying out routine tasks, are financially secure, and then provide them with opportunities for intrinsic motivation by means of autonomy, mastery, and purpose. For anyone doing knowledge work, simple if-then rewards destroy creativity. For those who are not doing creative work—but only for these—the "carrot and stick" approach might still be valid.

In other words, Pink is articulating that what often seems like common sense does not really make sense. He is also showing that, in order to know how to act, managers often have to pay attention to contingencies and to think critically about how to respond. Evidence-based approaches do not take the place of serious consideration, and conventional wisdom does not always include contingencies. It should be noted that not everyone agrees with Pink's theorizing as he presents it on the TED video (S. L. Rynes, personal communication, August 8, 2010). Nevertheless, this video does represent a way to go beyond data as given and to attempt to understand its implications more deeply.

The TED video series is just one outlet for both scholars and practitioners to share and disseminate knowledge. Digital technology has spawned several new ways of teaching and training that enable and enrich the more traditional approaches found in classrooms. The following are just a few examples of the various possibilities that have been developed in the recent past.

Managerial Simulation

Dunham's (2004) "The Manager's Workshop 3.0" CD-ROM, (also discussed by Goodman & O'Brien, in chapter 18 of this volume, and available on Amazon.com or through Pearson Higher Education) is an interactive simulation that puts the user in the position of managing five different employees. The home page is a picture of an office with various hyperlinks that take users to the simulation, the employees' personnel files, videos of case studies, explanations of motivation theories, and self-assessment tests. The CD-ROM can be used by individuals or in a classroom or training context.

Individually, managers can take themselves through the scenarios of managing each of the five problem employees. The personnel files give the simulation some realism by giving the manager more information with which to make decisions on how to proceed with each employee. The motivation theory videos can either inform or remind the manager of what the theories were and explain why each decision was more "correct" than others. After each decision is made in the simulation, the next video clip includes feedback on the consequences of that decision. This helps managers see the effects of their decisions.

In the classroom or in training programs, the CD-ROM can be used in a group exercise in which each group talks about the possible courses of action after each video clip in the simulation and have discussions about which choice is the best. Afterwards, the instructor can show the theoretical foundations and evidence that support each decision. Again, students and training participants can see the potential consequences of their choices in each situation. The advantage of the classroom or group setting would be that the consequences could potentially spark an intergroup discussion of how the situation might or might not be generalizable to other situations or organizations, after each group has their own discussion of which choice would be most appropriate. This kind of discussion is made richer when the participants come from different backgrounds and organizations.

In the spirit of EBM, the videos explaining each motivation theory could be used after the group successfully manages each problem employee. This would enable participants to see that the choices made in the simulation were based on evidence and not just other people's experiences. When combined with the experiences of classroom participants, the motivation- theory videos could be powerful learning experiences because participants may be able to clearly see how theory and practice can complement one another.

Short Video Cases

Video cases produced by the Stanford (http://www.leadershipinfocus.net; accessed 9/16/2010) and Harvard (http://harvardbusiness.org/; accessed 9/16/2010) business schools supplement the written cases produced by faculty at each school. Some of the video cases include interviews with key actors in the cases, and others include video clips that illustrate the topic of the case. Additionally, some of the cases are presented entirely on video.

These means of presenting cases can be more engaging than a written case, especially for visual learners. However, the cases need to be presented with a specific learning point that shows how evidence has informed the solution. Otherwise, the case is just another "war story" told by the authors and the protagonist of the case. In other words, the "moral of the story" needs to be made clear and the theories and evidence that support the decisions made by the protagonists in each case need to be discussed in order to illustrate EBM principles in action.

In addition to classroom venues, video cases can be presented to employees at professional development sessions. It is very easy to develop tunnel vision when one has worked in an organization for a long period of time. Watching and discussing a video case about a different setting could inspire people to look beyond their standard boundaries and think about improvements in efficiency or practices. These sessions may be conducted by an outside consultant, but they could also be presented by someone in the HR department who has had experience teaching. If an organization hired a staff scholar (described in a later section in this chapter), who understood the idiosyncrasies of the organization and the current academic research, that person would also be in a good position to present the video cases and help make clear how the case applies to the organization.

Field Guides and Web Sites for Developing Skills

Kotter and Cohen and Senge have supplemented their books, *The Heart of Change* (Kotter & Cohen, 2002) and *The Fifth Discipline* (Senge, 1990), respectively, with field guides in an attempt to help people in organizations apply their principles. Field guides are companion books that help practitioners to apply the principles in the original books. They typically contain activities and concrete steps for the readers to follow and use in their organizations. Kotter's works, *Leading Change* (1996) and (with Cohen) *The Heart of Change* (2002), put forth a model of eight steps for enacting organizational change. The *Heart of Change* is comprised of stories about how organizations have followed the steps and succeeded in enacting change. The *Heart of Change Field Guide* (Cohen, 2005) is user friendly and helps practitioners by giving them frameworks and tools to use in their organizations, including a number of diagnostic tools. There is also a web site, theheartofchange.com (accessed 9/16/2010) that supplements *The Heart of Change*.

Similarly, Senge's work, *The Fifth Discipline* (1990), which introduces systems thinking along with other managerial disciplines, has been supplemented with several field books, which help practitioners apply the principles of the five disciplines in their organizations. In addition to *The Fifth Discipline Fieldbook* (Senge, Kleiner, Roberts, Ross, & Smith, 1994), *Schools that Learn* (Senge et al., 2000), is a field book that is directed at educators and other practitioners who work in the education field. The *Dance of Change* (Senge et al., 1999) is a field book aimed at practitioners embarking on organizational change. All these field books and field guides take the abstract concepts from the books and offer concrete and practical steps that people in organizations can take. The Society for Organizational Learning (SoL) has online resources and networking tools on their web site that help scholars and practitioners exchange ideas. SoL's journal, *Reflections*, is also distributed in pdf format to members who wish to learn more about organizational learning and how other organizations have used organizational learning principles.

How Messages about Evidence and Practice are Communicated

Evidence can be presented in a way that is more or less attractive and memorable. Most academic writing, as we have noted earlier, is neither attractive nor memorable. However, there are ways that it could be made more so. Relationships and communication between academics and practitioners include multiple other components as well.

Sticky Evidence

Heath and Heath (2007) suggested that ideas that "stick" are those that are simple, unexpected, concrete, credible, emotional, and likely to be told in stories, a style of writing that moves readers to feel as the author does (Bartunek, 2007). "Sticky findings" describe "research results that grab attention, gain credibility, and are readily shared" (Rousseau & Boudreau, 2011). The sticky findings can come from many sources, including observing the activities of competing firms, management periodicals, research findings, and popular books.

It is important to note that not all sticky findings are constructive, because theories often depend on assumptions, which may or may not be remembered after the sticky findings spread. For example, the idea of including stock options in management compensation packages is very sticky, but not necessarily good for business (Ghoshal, 2005). The rewarding of stock options is based on the assumption that the shareholder is making a bigger risk than employees, who can leave one job for another if they think that they are not being paid what they are worth. In other words, a perfectly efficient labor market is assumed. However, as Ghoshal (2005) points out, shareholders can sell their shares more easily than an employee can make a job transition. Thus, it is important for academics to develop ways to make sound evidence sticky. Rousseau & Boudreau (2011) offer concrete suggestions on how scholars might do this. The steps academics might take include presenting findings in ways that appear relevant to practice, expressing clear core principles in plain language and familiar analogies, describing the causal processes and mechanisms through which a principle works in plain language and familiar analogies, framing research to the end-users' interests, embedding findings within practitioner decision frameworks, explicating conditions of use, giving users easy access to the research findings and making sure that (local) opinion leaders advocate or attest to use.

Building Relationships

For multiple reasons, as noted earlier, scholars and practitioners often do not interact face-to-face. However, as we have also stated earlier, practitioner understanding of scholarly findings may not be easy, even when findings are presented in a sticky manner. Thus, it is necessary to create other ways for academics and practitioners to create communities of practice that enable opportunities for ongoing information exchange.

Joint Forums

One means of creating communities of practice might be forums, such as those suggested by Bartunek (2007) to flesh out journal articles' implications for practice from both scholarly and practitioner perspectives. Most implications for practice in academic journals are left as more or less free-standing elements, rarely referenced by later work. However, it might be possible for joint researcher/practitioner gatherings (e.g., Academy of Management or SoL conferences) to consider implications for practice from both scholarly and practitioner perspectives. Another means might be forums to discuss topics in which there are shared interests between academics and managers, such as the types of metrics for indicating success. As Bartunek (2007) notes, such efforts extend the types of venues in which managers and academics can get to know each other and each others' concerns. Two examples of such forums are management cafes and online communities.

Management cafes would be similar to the grassroots movement, Science Cafes, to bring science to the public (http://www.sciencecafes.org; accessed 9/16/2010). In Boston, Liz Bromley started a free lecture series called "Science in the News" (SITN) (https://sitn.hms.harvard.edu/; accessed 9/16/2010) at Harvard Medical School when she was a PhD student there. The lectures were aimed at the general public. SITN has now grown to be a more than just a free lecture series held in the fall. Their new offerings also include "Science by the Pint," which is an informal gathering based on the Science Café idea. Typically, a scientist gives a short presentation on a topic at an informal venue, such as a coffee shop or bar, where everyone can have a drink and talk to the scientist about science and technology. The purpose of these gatherings and of everything SITN does is to help people "better distinguish scientific fact from pure speculation" (https://sitn.hms.harvard.edu/about-us/; accessed 9/16/2010). A similar idea can be found in "theology on tap" sessions (http://www.renewtot.org/; accessed 9/16/2010), which aim to help people learn about their religious faith while connecting with friends.

Management scholars could do something similar to the Science Cafes and call them "Management Cafes" or, perhaps, "Managing—100 Proof." This would give management scholars a chance to showcase their work in informal settings. Managers of any level, students, or anyone from the general public could gather together in a coffee shop or bar to discuss particular scholars' work.

Online Communities

Joint forums are not necessarily in person; they can take place online. Indeed, there are also established practitioner online communities in which academics might participate. One example is www.changeosp.com (accessed 9/16/2010), short for the "change management open source project." It includes, among other components, a discussion forum in which practitioners can explore questions with each other and, if they wish, with academics. The second author, for example, participated in a podcast posted on the site on how to measure the success of OD interventions and how vibrant (or not) Organization Development is. Such online communities also offer opportunities for academics to communicate evidence with practitioners, or, at the very least, to hear practitioners' concerns pertinent to evidence and its application.

Web Sites and Blogs

Currently, there is an expanding EBM web site hosted by Carnegie Mellon University (http://evidence-basedmanagement.com; accessed 9/16/2010) that includes blogs, articles, links to other web sites, suggested books, and other materials for anyone interested in learning more about using EBM. Richard Puyt (Vrije Universiteit, Amsterdam) has also created a web site with more materials at: www.evidencebased-management.com (accessed 9/16/2010). The Research and Practice section of this web site lists books and web sites that give the curious EBM practitioner a place to start learning about EBM and how people in various disciplines have used it. For applications of EBM in specific fields, there are links to EBM movement resources in multiple areas, including conservation, criminology, education, government & public policies, librarianship, medicine, social work and software engineering.

Educators can also find useful resources on the EBM web site. In the Teaching Resources section, there are several course syllabi that are either centered on EBM or that have integrated EBM principles into the course. For example, Rousseau's course on Organizational Behavior follows Robbins & Judge's textbook, *Essentials of Organizational Behavior* (2009) but there is a clear emphasis on gathering and using evidence. Instructors can use the posted syllabi as a starting point for including EBM in their own syllabi. If they need more information, there are links to the syllabi creators' web pages.

A Staff Scholar

An organization could hire a "staff scholar." This position would be somewhere between an academic and a Chief Knowledge Officer (CKO), a senior-level executive position that started to gain in popularity after the term, "knowledge management" became popular in the late 1980s (Dalkir, 2005). The role of a CKO is to "drive and co-ordinate knowledge management programs" (Earl & Scott, 2000) and add to knowledge as an important organizational resource (Alavi, 2001). The purpose of a staff scholar would not be to manage the mountains of knowledge in organizations, but to understand and diagnose the (apparently) idiosyncratic issues within an organization, using findings from academic research to inform practice.

The role of staff scholar would also be somewhat like an ombudsperson, who is responsible for resolving conflicts in organizations by being an impartial officer who listens to employee grievances and has the power to investigate them (http://usoa.non-profitsites.biz/en/About_Us/history.cfm; accessed 9/16/2010). However, the staff scholar's job would be to diagnose systemic issues in addition to offering evidence-based solutions to address them.

Sometimes scholars who engage in consulting activities on the side serve in such a capacity in an informal way. For example, due to links that John Zanardelli (chapter 11 of this volume) created with Carnegie Mellon University, CMU Professors Laurie Weingart and Denise Rousseau serve in occasional scholarly roles at a Methodist home for the aged called Asbury Heights in Mt. Lebanon, Pennsylvania. Weingart introduced perspective taking to senior managers there in a way that led to senior managers shadowing each other for a (half) day to get a sense of one anothers' job demands. Rousseau helped the managers there use psychological contracts as a basis for determining the value of rolling out increased co-pay for insurance.

There is also the possibility of a formal staff scholar role. Such a role was enacted by Jay Moldenhauer-Salazar when he directed the human resources lab at Sun Microsystems (Woolcock, 2002). Under the leadership of Crawford Beveridge, Executive Vice President and Chief Human Resources Officer at Sun, and Dee Alcott Rodriguez, Director of HR Strategy and Planning, Moldenhauer-Salazar helped to create and direct an HR lab whose purpose was to find answers to the people-related questions at Sun for which there were no clear answers. He invited academic researchers whose work addressed these issues to come to Sun to collect data and feed them back to Sun and then to publish their findings. For example, Sun conducted a work-from-home pilot program, and wanted to be aware of the implications of working from home, especially in terms of work relationships. Sun's HR lab engaged three external academic researchers to study this, and Beveridge presented the results to senior management. (An executive summary of the academics' report is shown in Corporate Executive Board, 2004). This study and others that were carried out (Woolcock, 2002) were found to be very helpful to Sun, providing very positive returns on investment.

In addition, some university faculty members such as John Boudreau and Morgan McCall served as resident scholars at Sun while on sabbatical from their universities (Boudreau served as a visiting director). Proposals for research were solicited from senior management, in order that the research would meet strategic aims. Multiple HR volunteers aided in data collection for the research, and the scope of the research expanded over time (Woolcock, 2002). HR labs remained an integral part of Sun Microsystems until the company was acquired by Oracle. It clearly proved its worth.

Conclusion

It is one thing for academics to gather and present evidence in ways consistent with common academic communication. It is another thing for practitioners to make use of it successfully. Straightforward presentations of evidence will not accomplish this, no matter how academically convincing the scholarly findings underpinning it are.

In this chapter, we have suggested some important barriers to the adequate communication of academic-based evidence to practitioners. Based in part on insights from scholars who study persuasion, we have tried to suggest means that may reduce these barriers, making it more feasible for evidence to be communicated well and for practitioners to develop skill in carrying out evidence-based practice. We

Table 9.1. Summary of Recommendations

For Academics:
- Participate in management cafes (or start one) or other joint forums.
- Create blogs in your area of expertise to highlight the current research on a particular organizational issue (e.g., motivation, compensation, etc.).
- Contribute to Evidencebased-management.com

For Practitioners:
- Employ a "staff scholar," who is part academic and part organizational member, to advise organizational members on current research.
- Participate in management cafes (or start one) or other joint forums.
- Join an EBMgt web site to keep up to date on current research.

For Educators:
- Introduce systems thinking and encourage students to think about the "big picture" using the principles of systems thinking.
- Assign readings that train students to find and use evidence (e.g., Edmondson et al., 2005 Harrison & Shirom, 1999; Cameron & Quinn, 2006).
- Help students develop skill in translating between academic and practitioner language.
- Use simulations that require students to find and use evidence to solve problems.
- Use short video cases (and written case studies) in class and emphasize the manager's role in gathering and using evidence.

include all of this in our summary of recommendations that we present in Table 9.1.

What we have suggested is not comprehensive. It is, however, a start, one that might lead, with practice, to more effective methods.

Regardless of which means for communicating evidence are adopted, it is clear to us that effective communication will require considerable to attention to trustworthiness, to skill training, to creative presentations of findings, and to the use of a variety of modes of communication, including online ones, that practitioners may be more skilled in than academics are. Their use offers academics the possibility not only of conveying evidence, but of learning skills in communication as they do so.

Appendix A
Negotiation research translation; assignment by Deborah Kolb, Simmons College.

In the field of negotiation, theory and practice are intended to inform each other. Howard Raiffa framed the problem as *asymmetric description prescription*. What he meant was that research in the field *describes* something important that can then be turned into *prescriptive* advice—that is, given to one party (hence the *asymmetric* part) so that they can be more effective negotiators. One of the problems with the aim of description/prescription is that much of the research (*description*) is very technical (and appears in journals that only scholars read) that it is not easy to translate

into *prescriptions* that everyday managers can use. Indeed, one of the comments on the course has been that some of the readings are so technical that they are virtually unintelligible to the average MBA student. One of our colleagues has observed in a similar manner that a search on Amazon.com for a book such as *Getting to YES* (1990) returns 250 results, whereas for a book such as *Barriers to Conflict Resolution* (1995), which contains some significant research on topics such as reactive devaluation, loss aversion, and overconfidence, among other topics, returns 666,000 results! It can be inferred from this that much of the interesting *description* from research does not get translated into *prescriptions* that everyday negotiators can use. Here is a challenge for this paper option— take a new piece of empirical research and write an explanation that makes its findings accessible, relevant, and usable to the average Graduate school of Management student. What that generally means is describing the concepts in everyday language and using common examples from your own experience to ground them in practice.

Select an article. The best journals for finding empirical work on negotiation are *The Journal of Personality and Social Psychology* and *Organization Behavior and Human Decision Processes*. Information from the library about how to access these journals online appears on the eLearning resource page for the course. You do not have to confine yourselves to these two. These journals report primarily the laboratory studies addressed to a scholarly audience. They should be available to you in the library as an online resource. What you have to do is to select an article that has an interesting concept that you think would be helpful for your classmates. If you have a question about the article you want to write about, consult the instructor either in the classroom or via email.

Describe the key concepts and findings in accessible language. Imagine you are writing it for a journal such as *Harvard Business Review, Business Week, Fortune,* or *The Negotiation Newsletter.* Articles in these resources are accessible and they make extensive use of examples to ground the ideas. You do not want to rehash the study, but rather discuss the implications for a negotiator.

What are the key concepts or ideas?

Why are the concepts and findings important?

What are the implications for you as a negotiator, that is, what do you learn about effective practice from the study?

How would you recommend that negotiators make use of the study, that is, what is (are) the prescription(s)?

What is the connection of this work to other concepts and issues in negotiation, that is, how does it extend, confirm, or rebut what you have learned in the course?

Use examples from your own experience. The more you can ground your discussion in specific examples, the easier it will be for the everyday negotiator to grasp the key ideas.

Remember that this is a research translation, not just a description of the article. You need to translate it so that your classmates (and your instructors) would find it useful. The more you can ground your discussion in specific examples, the easier it will be for the everyday negotiator to grasp the key ideas.

References

Alavi, M. L., & Dorothy, E. (2001). Review: Knowledge management and knowledge management systems: Conceptual foundations and research issues. *MIS Quarterly, 25*(1), 107–136.

Argyris, C. (1976). Leadership, learning, and changing the status quo. *Organizational Dynamics, 4*(3), 29–43.

Argyris, C. (1982). *Reasoning, learning, and action: Individual and organizational.* San Francisco, CA: Jossey-Bass.

Argyris, C. (1990). *Overcoming organizational defenses.* Boston, MA: Allyn and Bacon.

Ball, S. R. (2006). Bridging the gap: A model for graduate management education. In C. Wankel & R. DeFillippi (Eds.), *New visions of graduate management education* (pp. 87–106). Charlotte, NC: Information Age Publishing.

Bartunek, J. M. (2007). Academic-practitioner collaboration need not require joint or relevant research: Toward a relational scholarship of integration. *Academy of Management Journal, 50*(6), 1323.

Bartunek, J. M., & Rynes, S. L. (2010). The construction and contributions of implications for practice: What's in them and what might they offer? *Academy of Management Learning and Education, 9*(1), 100–117.

Bennis, W. G., & O'Toole, J. (2005). How business schools lost their way. *Harvard Business Review, 83*(5), 96–104.

Bloom, B. S. (Ed.). (1956). *Taxonomy of educational objectives: The classification of educational goals* (1st ed.). White Plains, NY: Longman.

Briner, R. B., Denyer, D., & Rousseau, D. M. (2009). Evidence-based management: Concept cleanup time? *Academy of Management Perspectives, 23*(4), 19–32.

Cameron, K. S., & Quinn, R. E. (2006). *Diagnosing and changing organizational culture.* San Francisco, CA: Jossey-Bass.

Cascio, W. F., & Boudreau, J. W. (2008). *Investing in people: Financial impact of human resource initiatives.* Upper Saddle River, NJ: Pearson Education.

Cascio, W. F., & Boudreau, J. W. (2011) Utility of selection systems: Supply-chain analysis applied to staffing decisions. In S. Zedeck (Ed.), *APA handbook of industrial and organizational psychology, Vol 2: Selecting and developing members for the organization, APA Handbooks in Psychology* (pp. 421–444). Washington, DC, US: American Psychological Association

Cohen, D. S. (2005). *The heart of change field guide: Tools and tactics for leading change in your organization.* Boston, MA: Harvard Business School Press.

Corporate Executive Board. (2004). *Sun Microsystems: Using an HR research laboratory to support organizational strategy.* Arlington, VA: Corporate Leadership Council.

Dalkir, K. (2005). *Knowledge management in theory and practice.* Burlington, MA: Butterworth-Heinemann.

Davis, W. (2010, June 16). The "Learning Knights" of Bell Telephone. *New York Times,* p. A31.

Dunham, R. (2004). *The manager's workshop 3.0 (CD-ROM).* Upper Saddle River, NJ: Pearson Higher Education.

Earl, M. J., & Scott, I. A. (2000). The role of a chief knowledge officer. In D. A. Marchand, T. H. Davenport, & T. Dickson (Eds.), *Mastering information management.* Financial Times Series, Prentice Hall, pp. 176–181.

Edmondson, A. C., Roberto, M. A., & Tucker, A. L. (2005). *Children's Hospital and clinics.* (Case No. 9–302–050). Boston: Harvard Business School Publishing.

Ekbia, H. R., & Hara, N. (2008). The quality of evidence in knowledge management research: Practitioner versus scholarly literature. *Journal of Information Science, 34*(1), 110.

Ghoshal, S. (2005). Bad management theories are destroying good management practices. *Academy of Management Learning & Education, 4*(1), 75–91.

Goodman, P. S. (2000). *Missing organizational linkages: Tools for cross-level research.* Thousand Oaks, CA: Sage Publications, Inc.

Gordon, R. A., & Howell, J. E. (1959). *Higher education for business.* New York: Columbia University Press.

Harrison, M. I., & Shirom, A. (1999). *Organizational diagnosis and assessment: Bridging theory and practice.* Thousand Oaks, CA: Sage.

Heath, C., & Heath, D. (2007). *Made to stick: Why some ideas survive and others die.* New York: Random House.

Hodgkinson, G. P., & Rousseau, D. M. (2009). Bridging the rigour-relevance gap in management research: It's already happening! *Journal of Management Studies, 46*(3), 534–546.

Johnson, B. T., Maio, G. R., & Smith-McLallen, A. (2005). Communication and attitude change: Causes, processes, and effects. In D. Albarracin, B. T. Johnson, & M. P. Zanna (Eds.), *The handbook of attitudes* (pp. 617- 669). New York: Psychology Press.

Johnson, S. (1998). *Who moved my cheese? An amazing way to deal with change in your work and in your life.* New York: Penguin Putnam.

Kelemen, M., & Bansal, P. (2002). The conventions of management research and their relevance to management practice. *British Journal of Management, 13*(2), 97–108.

Kieser, A., & Leiner, L. (2009). Why the rigour-relevance gap in management research is unbridgeable. *Journal of Management Studies, 46*, 516–533.

Kotter, J. P. (1996). *Leading change.* Boston, MA: Harvard Business Press.

Kotter, J. P., & Cohen, D. S. (2002). *The heart of change: Real-life stories of how people change their organizations.* Boston, MA: Harvard Business Press.

Luhmann, N. (1995). *Social systems.* Stanford, CA: Stanford University Press.

O'Leary, M., & Chia, R. (2007). Epistemes and structures of sensemaking in organizational life. *Journal of Management Inquiry, 16*(4), 392–406.

Oviatt, B. M., & Miller, W. D. (1989). Irrelevance, intransigence, and business professors. *Academy of Management Executive, 3*(4), 304–312.

Pettigrew, A. M. (2001). Management research after modernism. *British Journal of Management, 12,* S61–S70.

Petty, R. E. (1994). Two routes to persuasion: State of the art. *International Perspectives on Psychological Science, 2,* 229–247.

Pfeffer, J. & Fong, C. T. (2002). The end of business schools? Less success than meets the eye. *Academy of Management Learning & Education, 1*(1), 78–95.

Pfeffer, J., & Sutton, R. I. (2000). *The knowing-doing gap: How smart companies turn knowledge into action.* Boston, MA: Harvard Business Press.

Pierson, F. C. (1959). *The education of American businessmen.* New York: McGraw-Hill.

Polzer, J. T., Gulati, R., Khurana, R., & Tushman, M. L. (2009). Crossing boundaries to increase relevance in organizational research. *Journal of Management Inquiry, 18*(4), 280–286.

Quinn, R. E., & Rohrbaugh, J. (1983). A spatial model of effectiveness criteria: *toward* a competing values approach to organizational analysis. *Management Science, 29*(3), 363–377.

Robbins, S. P., & Judge, T. A. (2009). *Essentials of organizational behavior.* Upper Saddle River, NJ: Prentice Hall.

Rousseau, D. M. (2006). Is there such a thing as evidence-based management? *Academy of Management Review, 31*(2), 256–269.

Rousseau, D. M. & Boudreau, J. W. (2011). Sticky findings: Research evidence practitioners find useful. In S. A. Mohrman & E. E. Lawler III (Eds.), *Useful research: Advancing theory and practice* (pp. 269–288). San Francisco: Berrett-Koehler.

Rousseau, D. M., Manning, J., & Denyer, D. (2008). Evidence in management and organizational science: Assembling the field's full weight of scientific knowledge through syntheses. In J. P. Walsh & A. P. Brief (Eds.), *Academy of management annals* (Vol. 2, pp. 475–515). New York: Routledge, Taylor & Francis Group.

Rousseau, D. M., & McCarthy, S. (2007). Educating managers from an evidence-based perspective. *Academy of Management Learning and Education, 6*(1), 84.

Rynes, S. L., Bartunek, J. M., & Daft, R. L. (2001). Across the great divide: Knowledge creation and transfer between practitioners and academics. *Academy of Management Journal, 44*(2), 340–355.

Rynes, S. L., Brown, K. G., & Colbert, A. E. (2002). Seven common misconceptions about human resource practices: Research findings versus practitioner beliefs. *Academy of Management Executive, 16*(3), 92–103.

Rynes, S. L., Giluk, T. L., & Brown, K. G. (2007). The very separate worlds of academic and practitioner periodicals in human resource management: Implications for evidence-based management. *Academy of Management Journal, 50*(5), 987.

Senge, P. M. (1990). *The fifth discipline: The art and science of the learning organization.* New York: Doubleday.

Senge, P. M., Kleiner, A., Roberts, C., Ross, R., & Bryan, S. (1994). *The fifth discipline fieldbook.* New York: Doubleday.

Senge, P. M., Kleiner, A., Roberts, C., Ross, R., Roth, G., & Smith, B. (2000). *Schools that learn: A fifth discipline fieldbook for educators, parents, and everyone who cares about education.* New York: Crown Business.

Senge, P. M., Kleiner, A., Roberts, C., Roth, G., Ross, R., & Smith, B. (1999). *The dance of change: The challenges of sustaining momentum in learning organizations.* New York: Crown Business.

Shani, A. B., Mohrman, S. A., Pasmore, W. H., Stymne, B., & Adler, N. (2008). *Handbook of collaborative management research.* Thousand Oaks, CA: Sage.

Shapiro, D. L., Kirkman, B. L., & Courtney, H. G. (2007). Perceived causes and solutions of the translation problem in management research. *Academy of Management Journal, 50*(2), 249–266.

Shrivastava, P., & Mitroff, II. (1984). Enhancing organizational research utilization: The role of decision makers' assumptions. *Academy of Management Review, 9*(1), 18–26.

Toulmin, S. (1984). *Introduction to reasoning* (2nd ed.). New York: MacMillan.

Trump, D. J., & McIver, M. (2006). *Trump 101: The way to success.* Hoboken, NJ: Wiley.

Van de Ven, A. H. (2007). *Engaged scholarship: A guide for organizational and social research.* New York: Oxford University Press.

Veblen, T. (2009/1918). *The higher learning in America: A memorandum on the conduct of universities by business men.* Ithaca, NY: Cornell University Library.

Weick, K. E., & Putnam, T. (2006). Organizing for mindfulness. *Journal of Management Inquiry, 15*(3), 275–287.

Whetten, D. A., & Cameron, K. S. (2006). *Developing management skills* (7th ed.). Upper Saddle River, NJ: Prentice Hall.

Woolcock, P. (2002). *Sun's HR labs: Driving decisions with data.* Ithaca, NY: Cornell University, School of Industrial and Labor Relations, Center for Advanced Human Resource Studies.

Yates, J. F. (1990). *Judgment and decision making.* Englewood Cliffs, NJ: Prentice Hall.

Zell, D. (2001). The market-driven business school. *Journal of Management Inquiry, 10*(4), 324–338.

PART 3

Practice

Adventures in the Evidence-Based Management Trade

Anthony R. Kovner

Abstract

I have spent more than a decade trying to get managers and those who study management to use an evidence-based process where interventions to improve performance are concerned. This chapter describes my experiences including teaching a graduate capstone course, writing a text on evidence-based management in health-care, decision making as a board member of a large hospital, and attempting to launch evidence-based management research with practitioners.

This chapter describes my experiences and interpretations of early efforts to promote and practice evidence-based management. It includes my personal experiences, tacit knowledge derived from those experiences, the experiences of others in similar situations, expert opinion, case studies and other relevant information.

Key Words: health-care management, best practice, evidence-based management training, teaching evidence-based management, practice-oriented research, consultants

My Background

My careers in health-care management, teaching, and research were not planned in advance. Each choice opened and closed options for me. I pursued a PhD because, with my father's death, the family hospital business was no longer an option for me. Instead, my academic advisors urged me to pursue doctoral studies in management at government expense. One of the faculty members supervising my doctoral thesis subsequently became CEO of a hospital in New York City, and I went to work for him as a manager. His successor fired me, and I then was hired as a manager of a faculty group practice at another university. There I was also involved in starting a master's program in health-care management. When their choice to head that program accepted another position, I was selected as program director. After five years, I withdrew from seeking tenure at the university when I was told that I wouldn't be approved. I then took a position as

senior health consultant for a large industrial union. I next sought a position as rural hospital CEO, was fired, and sought a job as program director and faculty member in health-care administration in my home city of New York. I have worked here for the last 30 years. Because of my work as a rural hospital administrator, while I was a professor, I was chosen, by a large foundation to be part-time national director of a large hospital-demonstration program, a role that has continued with other foundations for which I have run, for example, a demonstration program to train clinicians in management.

My Experiences in Evidence-Based Management

My interest in evidence-based management (EBMgt) began in 1999, 40 years after starting work as a health-care manager. It was occasioned by reading about evidence-based medicine, and resulted in my writing an article with John Billings and Jeff

Elton on "Transforming Health Management: An Evidence-Based Approach (Kovner, Elton & Billings, 2000). The gist of our article is that health-care providers need to make quicker, riskier decisions in a competitive and regulated environment. Leaders tend to make these decisions upon the advice of management consultants. Nonetheless, these leaders generally lack adequate internal support to rigorously evaluate strategic interventions or consultant recommendations. In fact, health-care providers generally underinvest in management support, both in evaluating best practices within the organization and in learning from past strategic interventions. We observed that barriers to improving the quality of management decisions included:

- Little evidence on best practices.
- Available evidence was not widely shared.
- Health-care organizations (HCOs) lacked sufficient size and critical mass to conduct and assess applied research.
- HCO managers focused on operating margins and past budgets rather than on practical managerial questions that research could answer.
- Managers lacked training and experience in use of EBMgt and incentives to practice it.
- Nonprofit organizations like most hospitals tended to lack accountability for performance.

I find that not a great deal has changed over the past 10 years.

Our article suggested forming EBMgt cooperatives (EBMCs) that would bring together managers, consultants, and researchers to improve management, databases, and organizational performance. EBMCs would enhance managerial skills and capacity, improve the availability of information to support better-informed interventions, and lead to better understanding of factors affecting implementation and financing. Resources were required to fund staff and specific research and demonstration projects. In start-up phase, we estimated that an EBMC would require $4–5 million over a four-year period to launch the initiative and provide core support. I spent years, with others, unsuccessfully trying to secure funds to launch this initiative. We were told by health-care managers that the funding of management research was a government or foundation responsibility, and by government and foundation officials that they had other higher priorities. After numerous failed grant proposals, I split our plan into two parts: education and research.

Teaching Evidence-Based Management

NYU/Wagner is a graduate school of public service, one of the smallest of 13 schools at New York University, the nation's largest private university. This school is similar to a school of public administration or public affairs. I am a member of both the School's management and health-services management groups. Most students and faculty are in the School's public and nonprofit management-and-policy group.

My ambition was to integrate evidence-based management into the required curriculum. Along these lines I began by urging faculty to measure the skills and experience of students after admission and again prior to graduation to learn what difference their education made in relation to its cost (and then to improve the educational process if we were not satisfied with the results). EBMgt did not gain school priority either, although I recruited a few faculty converts. One told me "I am completely dedicated to EBMgt and use it as a basis for teaching managing public- service organizations... I don't know what the rest of the management faculty think about it—my hunch is that they don't use it and may not even know what it is." A second faculty member agreed, "I believe EBMgt offers a clear set of steps for practitioners to access and utilize research... it could be a boon to researchers as well, because it can act as a mechanism to have their work actually inform practice."

I decided to demonstrate the benefit of the EBMgt approach by using it in my capstone course. Capstone is one of the required courses at NYU/Wagner, and the School's faculty currently teaches 76 sections. In 2008, I started a new MS program for nursing leaders in which the capstone was required. Based on what I learned in the first year, my revised capstone for 1999–2000 was more focused on (1) the contract between sponsor and team to address answerable research questions rather than management challenges (for example, focusing on the causes of emergency-department waiting rather than on interventions to reduce waiting), (2) carrying student projects through all aspects of the evidence-based management process from working with managers to identify a relevant practice question to helping to design evidence-based interventions, and (3) best practice and the literature in answering research questions rather than on recommendations and their justification. One feature that remained the same to the previous year's capstone was spending sufficient time on documenting problems in current managerial and organizational processes and their causes.

My capstone has had three goals for students: (1) using an evidence-based approach in designing and carrying out management interventions, (2) managing relationships with an external client and various stakeholders, and (3) functioning as members of a client-oriented team. Students learned the following competencies:

• Identifying and carrying out data collection and analytical methods appropriate for a specific project.
• Situating findings in the broad related literature.
• Drawing conclusions warranted by the scientific and organizational data as well as local organizational culture and readiness to change.
• Communicating effectively orally and in writing.
• Working cooperatively with team members on a client-focused project.

Examples of their capstone projects include improving acuity-based nurse staffing, improving the supply procurement process, improving the medication-administration process, increasing nurse volunteering at a local school, and developing system-wide metrics for patient falls/restraints.

Students followed an evidence-based process that included framing the research question(s); finding sources of information; assessing the accuracy, applicability, and actionability of the evidence; and determining the extent to which management has adequate evidence to implement the intervention. This process has now been taken up more broadly at Wagner. One of the elective (now required) courses created for the nursing students was Locating Evidence, developed by NYU librarians, Susan Jacobs and Gretchen Gano. In this course, students frame answerable research questions, select specialized databases, develop effective search strategies, and critically appraise the literature about a management topic (Jacobs, Gano, & Kovner, 2009). NYU/ Wagner's partner in developing the MS (now executive MPA) program for nurse leaders was New York Presbyterian Hospital and Health System (NY/P), one of the largest health systems in the United States. NY/P's chief nursing officer, Wilhelmina Manzano, and her administrator for special projects, Rosemary Sullivan, assisted in teaching and syllabus preparation. They were available to orient and help involve senior managers at NY/P who sponsored capstones, facilitated development of these projects, and facilitated access and support for the student teams with the NY/P sponsors. Student feedback for the course was highly favorable. The course received 5.0 out of a possible 5.0 regarding whether students recommended the course, and 4.9 out of 5.0 regarding whether students recommended the instructor. Capstone sponsors were very satisfied with the students' work and most proposed new capstone projects for the next year as well. Sponsors praised the focusing of research questions, the gathering and assessment of evidence, and the quality of the recommendations informed by high-quality evidence.

I have had some success in launching a variety of evidence-based executive education programs in local health systems. This has included the capstone courses for nurse leaders with NY/P, and executive education courses for managers at Montefiore and for nurse leaders at Memorial Sloan Kettering Cancer Center. I have also been heartened to see the launching of an executive doctoral program at the University of Alabama in Birmingham, where senior managers who are the program's students translate management challenges into research questions. This executive doctoral program uses my book *Evidence-Based Management in Healthcare* as a text. Next, I turn to that text and what we learned about EBMgt practice from writing it.

Developing Text

We decided to develop a textbook (Kovner, Fine, & D'Aquila, 2009) for learning how to practice EBMgt in health-care settings. My co-authors were two distinguished practitioners, Richard D'Aquila, Chief Operating Officer at Yale New Haven Hospital and David J. Fine, Chief Executive Officer of St. Luke's Episcopal Health System in Houston Texas. Originally we wanted the book to serve both student and practitioner audiences. On the publisher's advice, we dropped the practitioner audience, since the publisher saw their primary market for the book to be graduate students in health-care management.

We succeeded in producing a workable text for the capstone course, with these sections: Transformation to EBMgt, Theories and Definitions, Case Studies (which make up most of the text), and Lessons Learned. We also provided a guide to the EBMgt literature and a chapter on search on a particular management topic. (The text also has an instructor's guide.) The Transformation section reviews our experience in organizations where EBMgt was or was not practiced, and the results of a research study on managers in health systems in several cities. Tom Rundall and his colleagues interviewed these managers about why they did not use an evidence-based process in decision making (Rundall et al., 2009). In Theories and Definitions, we reprinted the article by John Hsu and his colleagues on the six steps managers should consider when making a well-informed decision (Hsu et al., 2006). For each step, the authors reviewed background, key points, guides, and checklists. Regarding the ten Case Studies, some followed each step of the EBMgt process, whereas others followed only some of the steps, or failed to report all steps. All the cases illustrated how the EBMgt process could be applied to a set of management challenges, and students can point out where the process was flawed or incomplete. For example, in one case study, an external consulting firm deemed a hospital's palliative-care unit unprofitable and strongly recommended that it be closed (White & Cassell, 2009). Their conclusion that the costs of caring for palliative patients significantly exceeded reimbursement turns out to have been based on a faulty assumption. Because the palliative care program was the last to "touch" these patients, the consultants had assigned the costs of the patients' entire admission to the palliative-care unit. From the hospital data, White and Cassell revealed that about half the palliative care patients had received care on other inpatient units, where the vast majority of costs were incurred. In fact, the palliative care unit was actually running at a profit, and its closure was forestalled.

In Lessons Learned, I concluded that EBMgt was not more widely used because the business case for return on investment had not yet been reliably made. Moreover, widespread use of EBMgt could be seen as shifting power away from senior managers toward better skilled junior managers. Last, lack of regular critical review of the process of organizational decision making by boards and managers meant that neither of these stakeholders was aware of how flawed their decision processes were (Kovner, 2009a). The book has done well on the textbook market and has provided original research to inform the EBMgt movement.

Hospital-Board Decision Making

In 1971, when I started as an academic, my chair advised me to select a small topic and know more about it than anyone. The topic I chose was not-for-profit governance. (I hoped to be a hospital administrator some day, which did happen.). Several years later, I began 26 years as a member of the board of trustees of Lutheran Medical Center, a $2.0 billion health system in southwest Brooklyn, New York.

Soon I was a board member of Augustana (Lutheran's nursing home) and Health Plus (Lutheran's health maintenance organization). I then served as chair of the hospital quality committee and vice-chair of the HMO board.

While a board member (and a professor at NYU) I carried out a research study of four non-profit hospitals in New York City (Kovner, 2001). I examined the information that boards regularly get to carry out their functions. Principal findings were that boards get too little comparative data on performance of similar benchmarked hospitals and that they get too much operational data, that is to say, the same data that management gets. Key recommendations included: (1) the board must take greater responsibility for identifying the information that they get and how they wish to get it; (2) managers must ensure that measureable objectives are used against which organizational performance can be evaluated; (3) the board must get information that is targeted to and supports board functions; (4) managers must develop information sets for main service lines, such as heart and cancer; (5) and the board must get information on the expectations and satisfaction levels of key stakeholders. The study results were shared with Lutheran's CEO and board chair. The only recommendation that was implemented was providing the board with less hospital operating data.

Two other poor decisions at Lutheran illustrate the consequences of not using an evidence-based approach. The first concerned the potential sale of the hospital-owned HMO in 2003. Lutheran needed money. The HMO (for Medicaid patients) had been contributing up to $10 million per year to the hospital's bottom line, although this amount had recently decreased sharply. The primary reason for this decline was an increase in the state's insurance reserve requirements. Hospital operating losses had resulted from poor operating decisions by the board and previous administration. Compounding its financial problems were rising malpractice premiums (the hospital was self-insured) and inadequate pension-fund contributions. Lutheran's top management recommended selling the HMO because, at that time, investor-owned companies were purchasing Medicaid HMOs in other locations for relatively large sums. The board agreed to put the HMO on the market at a price of $300 million and would have accepted considerably less. Three years later, after hundreds of hours of board discussions with various consultant, bankers, and lawyers, the HMO failed to sell. As such, the hospital continued losing money because of questionable management decisions and an unfavorable environment whereas the HMO was making money because of better management decisions and a favorable external environment. At the same time, the HMO was prevented from growing because a large share of its profits was siphoned off by the hospital. The hospital was buffered from facing its operating problems by the subsidies it was getting from the HMO. The board never acknowledged these facts. Nor was the matter ever discussed in terms of improving the health of the people of southwest Brooklyn, which was the mission of the hospital. The board and top management did no long-range planning during a period of 10 or 15 years, although the main facility was obsolete and needed replacement. The CEO framed the management challenge as "How can we balance the budget?" She never raised the issue, "How can we increase revenues in HMO operations?" or "How can we decrease hospital expenditures so that the board can either finance a new hospital or get out of the hospital business?"

A second example concerns presentation of the 2009 hospital budget to the board by the Chief Financial Officer (Kovner, 2009b). The budget was approved as customary with little discussion. I commented and raised some questions at the meeting and in a subsequent e-mail, as follows:

- "You made no report on last year's results as related to what you had forecast.
- There was neither summary nor explanation of variance in the financials presented.
- What are the assumptions on which next year's budget is based?
- How can we increase revenues?
- What are we doing to decrease re-hospitalizations?
- You don't seem to be getting much help from the board on these matters. Is there a problem with the leadership of the finance committee?
- Where is the discussion of how Lutheran will meet its future capital needs?"

Two days later I received an e-mail reply from the CFO indicating (1) the hospital was in the process of refinancing its housing complex and exploring the possibility of moving funds from the HMO to the hospital; and (2) assurance that the finance staff works very closely with management to figure out new ways to fund productive, high-quality programs, and concluding that "I [would] continue to work with the finance committee and the board to make our financial presentations more meaningful."

In both decisions, the management challenge was framed as "How can we balance the budget?" In the matter of the board's rubber stamp of the budget without due consideration of the evidence, the CFO did not examine performance in terms of comparisons with similar hospitals. He did not break the budget down into main lines of business. He did not suggest alternative budgetary approaches, nor did he examine the benefits, costs, and risks of alternative budgets based on evidence gleaned from the literature, best practice, or analysis of this hospital's data.

EB and Related Management Research

I conducted a study designed to identify factors associated with knowledge transfer between researchers and managers in five large health systems (Kovner, 2005). I studied four topic areas: (1) indicators used to identify successful implementation of diabetes management programs, (2) the relationship between budgeting procedures and strategic priorities, (3) the design of managerial dashboards, and (4) the implementation of compensation systems to improve physician performance. Any of these managerial challenges can be translated into a set of research questions (e.g., What triggers changes made in managerial dashboards?), but this was not the purpose of the study. The study methodology included telephone interviews with 64 managers of health systems, 52 of whom were senior and middle managers of five large health systems, which sponsored the research. Another 12 interviews were conducted with senior and middle managers of nonsponsoring health systems.

In these interviews, managers said their health systems placed a high value on evidence-based decision making. They did not mention any financial constraints to obtaining knowledge from external sources. Instead, they indicated that searching for evidence was difficult. Reported difficulties included time pressure, competing priorities, lack of relevant evidence, and difficulties in translating journal findings so that they could be easily applied. Results indicated that few managers had received formal training in seeking and using evidence for decision making. On the other hand, managers reported that external organizations increasingly provided benchmarks and performance targets for health systems. Ironically, managers described the results of these standards as not being sufficiently based on scientific evidence.

Managers studied got most of their evidence from web sites, trade journals, consultants, peer groups, professional meetings, and networking with colleagues, particularly in their own systems, rather than from researchers or research journals. Health systems did not regularly review deliberative processes for making strategic decisions before or after the fact. No manager in any of the participating sites was designated as being responsible and accountable for knowledge transfer or management research, nor were metrics used to assess the benefits of obtaining better evidence for management decision making.

Managers did conduct their own studies, focus groups, and market assessments, but health systems lacked management specialists in knowledge transfer. In my final report, I recommended the following evidence-based management and related strategies for managers in large health-care systems:

- Fund evidence-based management increasingly out of the capital rather than the operating budget.
- Align incentives, such as performance appraisals, to reward evidence-based management.
- Assign responsibility for knowledge transfer.
- Develop metrics to assess the benefits of obtaining better evidence for management decision-making.
- Fix responsibility for review of deliberative processes as part of the regular process of strategic decision-making.
- Examine ways to increase the benefit/cost of current investments in and partnerships for management research.
- Consider new partnership options and funding opportunities for evidence-based management research.
- Develop a priority list of management research opportunities and consider how these may be funded.
- Invest in management research.

Since then, I have been unsuccessful in attempting to launch an evidence-based management- research collaboration with a local large health-care system. The project would consist of: (1) selecting a management challenge that can be translated into a set of research questions; (2) learning what is known and not known in the literature and in best practice on these questions; (3) designing local research studies, as needed, to obtain needed evidence; and then (4) deliberating and choosing among alternative management interventions.

Implications

Arguments that I have read or listened to against using an EBMgt approach have largely focused on excessive time requirements for top managers to collaborate with universities or consultants in applying the EBMgt process. My limited experience also suggests that local health systems are not hastening to fund evidence-based studies, not even accepting opportunities to collaborate at no charge.

My Answers to Recurrent Questions

Basic questions abound regarding evidence-based management. For example, what is the difference between "evidence-based" and "good" management? Aren't effective managers already using an evidence-based approach although they don't refer to it as such? I have observed that most managers do not routinely practice an evidence-based approach, particularly as this involves searching the literature and for best practice, initiating their own research and deliberatively including key stakeholders in decision making.

A second set of issues involves whether methods for developing actionable evidence should be included within academic definitions of "research." The evidence-based-management process is surely not one of developing and testing hypotheses and staging randomized clinical trials. The EBMgt process is one of systematically collecting and analyzing data in ways that reveal trends, patterns, and causal effects. EBMgt uses explicit procedures in a systematic way that enables the findings to be replicated. As Don Berwick (2008), founder of a leading global organization to improve care in hospitals, points out, management interventions are about "leadership and emotion and changing environments and details of implementation and history. It is messy. Complex interventions experience inevitable, complex variation in the detail of its own mechanisms in local settings, that themselves are textured, varying and unstable." As Berwick puts it, "evaluation should retain and share information on both mechanisms (i.e., the ways in which specific social programs actually produce social changes, and contexts (i.e., local conditions that could have influenced the outcomes of interest)." It is possible to rely on methods other than hypothesis testing without sacrificing rigor. Berwick (2008) argues that widespread use of randomized clinical trials for management interventions is largely infeasible for cost and other reasons:

> But the harm is equal if we treat a very complex world as if it were simple, if we treat each other as less than whole people and complex systems as simple and separate from us, and thereby reduce our capacity to learn, to converse, to grow.

Making a Business Case for EBMgt

The elephant in the room is the difficulty of measuring the return on investment from a shift to more EBMgt-related practices. Tom Rundall (2009) takes exception to this notion, asking, Why should ROI be the standard used to evaluate the value of EBMgt? He goes on to say, "what is the ROI for other types of decision- making used in hospitals? Is there a known positive ROI for hierarchical, top-down decision-making? For decision-making by reliance on anecdote and gut reactions?"

I have not been able to make the business case for an investment, say of $100,000, in an evidence-based process, in terms of predictable return on investment, certainly not within one year. I believe that benefits from most evidence-based management studies should be included within the capital rather than operating budgets. I made this case because benefits may be unlikely to show up in 1- to 2-years' time, even as the costs are expended in the first year. Conducting an evidence-based process is certainly not cheap, though I suggest it might be considerably less expensive and more valuable than hiring large consulting firms who don't engage in evidence-based practice.

Rundall (2009) suggests additional criteria need to be used to evaluate modes of decision making. These would include comprehensiveness of alternative actions reviewed, extent of confidence among decision makers that their decision will produce intended results, extent of awareness of possible unintended consequences, acceptable results from most decisions, an extent of understanding of why some decisions failed to produce expected results, and a sense of accountability among the management team for decisions. Rundall argues that EBMgt outperforms all other decision-making modes on all of these criteria.

The Need for Change

Working primarily with larger hospitals, I understand that changing fundamental aspects of manager behavior is difficult, but so much really does need to change. I am not alone in this observation. Toussaint (2009, p. 28) writes, "in our traditional healthcare management world, managers are rewarded for telling their superiors that dysfunctional systems are really fine."

An important reason for implementing EBMgt is the flawed judgments managers make by virtue of the limited information processing capability of human beings. Managers need to reflect upon the biases they bring to the table in seeking and weighing evidence. Groopman (2007) suggests that physicians can easily be led astray by seeing a set of circumstances from only one perspective. He lists the following types of bias:

- Attribution error—discrediting data from a "tainted" source.
- Availability error—basing a decision on the most recent experience.
- Search satisfaction error—stopping the search for an answer as soon as a satisfactory solution is found.
- Confirmation bias—selecting only the parts of the information that confirm an initial judgment.
- Diagnostic momentum—being unable to change one's mind about a diagnosis, despite considerable uncertainty.
- Commission bias—doing something rather than nothing, even if the evidence says sit tight.

Managers are subject to the same biases.

Health-care managers are too comfortable with the way they view the world. If you aren't critical about your own judgment, it is difficult to recognize the need for evidence or additional perspectives. I've learned that health-care managers typically do not research management issues nor do they use research evidence in decision-making. Health-care managers do not generally voice a need for management research in improving hospital and health-system performance. Hospital and health-systems managers, particularly in academic environments, should be more receptive to EBMgt than their business counterparts whose organizations lack an academic mission. On the other hand, as contrasted with large business organizations, particularly in high-tech industries, academic medical centers have never invested much in management development nor in management research.

My Recommendations

I recommend managers apply the six step EBMgt approach of Hsu and his colleagues (2006, see Briner & Denyer, chapter 2 of this volume): (1) formulate the research question; (2) acquire the relevant research findings and other types of evidence; (3) assess the validity, quality, and applicability of the evidence; (4) present the evidence in a way that will make its use in the decision process more likely; (5) apply the evidence in decision making; and (6) then evaluate the results. Although this model appears to move neatly from step to step, this isn't necessarily true in practice. The steps provide a framework for analyzing a proposed management intervention or designing an evaluation. In reality, these steps overlap as managers may have to return to earlier steps or work on several steps simultaneously as the question-answering work unfolds. Flexibility is important. Information gathering occurs in all steps, from framing the question to recommending an intervention. New information may force a manager to reframe the question. Proposed recommendations may prove to be unworkable, requiring decision makers to identify new ones. The EBMgt process is usually not linear. Under certain circumstances, some steps may be combined or abbreviated. EBMgt leaves plenty of room for managerial judgment during and after the process.

A manager reviewing our work said, "I like what you wrote, and I like the idea of EBMgt," but then asked "how much of this should I implement, in what ways, in my organization?" (Rundall & Kovner, 2009). I can not precisely answer this question other than to suggest that managers spend more time reflecting on the strategic decision-making processes of their organization, developing structures that establish transparent accountability for these processes, building a questioning culture, and improving the training of the managerial work force.

References

Berwick, D. (2008). The science of improvement. *Journal of the American Medical Association, 299,* 1182–1184.

Groopman, J. (2007). *How doctors think.* New York: Houghton Mifflin.

Hsu, J., Arroyo, L., Graetz, I., Neuwirth, E. B., Schmittdiel, S., Rundall, T. R., et al. (2006). *Methods for developing actionable evidence for consumers of health services research (match study): A report from organizational decision-maker discussion groups & a toolbox for making informed decisions.* Publication No. 290–00–0015. Rockville MD: U.S. Agency for Healthcare Research and Quality.

Jacobs, S. K., Gano, G., & Kovner, A. R. (2009). *Evidence-based health services management for nurse leaders: An intercampus partnership and curriculum.* Presentation at Positioning the Profession: The Tenth International Congress on Medical Librarianship, Brisbane Australia (1–14), Aug 31-Sept 4, 2009.

Kovner, A. R. (2001). Better information for the board. *Journal of Health care Management, 46*(1), 53–66.

Kovner, A. R. (2005). *Factors associated with use of management research by health systems.* Working Paper. Chicago, IL: Center for Health Management Research.

Kovner, A. R. (2009a). Summing up and lessons learned: Interviews with Richard D'Aquila and David J. Fine with commentary by A R Kovner. In A. R. Kovner, D. J. Fine, & R. D'Aquila (Eds.) *Evidence-based management in health care* (pp. 249–258). Chicago, IL: Health Administration Press.

Kovner, A. R, (2009b). Financial reporting to the board. In A. R. Kovner, A. S. McAlearney, & D. Neuhauser (Eds.), *Health services management: Cases, readings and commentary* (pp. 142–145). Chicago, IL: Health Administration Press.

Kovner, A. R., Elton, J. J., & Billings, J. (2000). Transforming health management: An evidence-based approach. *Frontiers of Health Services Management, 16*(4), 3–24.

Kovner, A. R., Fine, D. J., & D'Aquila, R. (2009). *Evidence-based management in health care.* Chicago, IL: Health Administration Press, 2009.

Rundall, T. R. (2009) Personal communication, November.

Rundall, T. R., Martelli P. F., McCurdy, R., Graetz, I., Arroyo, L., Neuwirth, E. B., et al., (2009). Using research evidence when making decisions: Views of health services managers and policymakers. In A. R. Kovner, D. J. Fine, & R. D'Aquila (Eds.), *Evidence-based management in health care* (pp. 53–78). Chicago, IL: Health Administration Press.

Rundall, T. R., & Kovner, A. R. (2009). Evidence-based management reconsidered: 18 months later. In A. R. Kovner, D. J. Fine, & R. D. Aquila (Eds.), *Evidence-based management in health care* (pp. 79–82). Chicago, IL: Health Administration Press.

Toussaint, J. (2009). Why are we still underperforming? *Frontiers of Health Services Management, 26*(1), 28.

White, J. R., & Cassell, J. B. (2009). The business case for a hospital palliative care unit: Justifying its continued existence. In A. R. Kovner, D. Fine, & R. D'Aquila, *Evidence-based management in health care* (pp. 171–189). Chicago, IL: Health Administration Press.

At the Intersection of the Academy and Practice at Asbury Heights

John Zanardelli

Abstract

As a practicing evidence-based manager over the past two decades, I describe how my use of evidence has been shaped by my professional education and the nature of our organization, a residential care facility for the elderly. Practices I have found particularly valuable in promoting evidence use and good decision making include ongoing management development, regular readings by myself and direct reports of books and articles based on scientific evidence, use of logic models to lay out the critical information and assumptions relevant to managerial decisions, and quality relationships with local universities and their faculty. I also discuss the challenges of making decisions that are evidence based.

Key Words: evidence-based management practice, scientific evidence, logic models; practitioner-academic relationship, evidence-based management culture; leading an evidence-based organization.

At the Intersection of the Academy and Practice at Asbury Heights

This chapter describes my experiences as an organization leader who uses scientific evidence to make both major and everyday decisions. It provides practitioners and scholars with information regarding evidence-based practices that have worked for our organization as well as some of the challenges we have faced in doing so. At the same time, I cannot claim that my ideas and their applications in our organization, Asbury Heights, will work everywhere. Yet through our efforts to use scholarly evidence to help our organization become better and better, I along with our staff, particularly those managers directly reporting to me, have learned a lot.

To shed some light on what evidence-based management (EBMgt) might look like "in the real world" and the factors that influenced our approach, this chapter is divided into three sections. First, I provide background on myself and our organization. Then, I describe the circumstances that led to our conscious adoption of evidence-based management practices. Next, I describe some of the particular

processes, routines, and ongoing practices that have contributed to creating an evidence-based culture at Asbury Heights. Last, I suggest some pointers and opportunities for future evidence-based managers.

Background

Since May 1993, I have been the CEO of Asbury Heights, a continuing-care retirement community located in Mt. Lebanon, Pennsylvania, which is a South Hills suburb of Pittsburgh, Pennsylvania. Asbury provides care and services to a population of primarily frailer older adults in a variety of settings that include independent living, assisted living, specialty care for the cognitively impaired, and long-term and rehabilitation nursing care. These services are provided on a 28-acre parklike and multibuilding campus, as well as one remote location about one mile from the main campus.

Asbury serves almost 500 older adults and generates revenues of approximately $30 million. Revenues are from a variety of sources including receipts from private charges, government sources and insurers. Asbury has a complex debt structure made up of multiple tranches of tax-exempt bonds, some backed by commercial bank letters of credit. Asbury is in an industry that is heavily regulated by government agencies, including the U.S. Centers for Medicare and Medicaid and three State of Pennsylvania Departments: Health, Welfare, and Insurance. Asbury provides over $2 million in charitable services annually and all of its multicorporate entities qualify as tax exempt nonprofits (under IRS Section 501(c)3). Fund raising, therefore, is a major part of my duties. The parent corporation is organized under the Nonprofit Corporation Law of 1988 of the Commonwealth of Pennsylvania and structured as a nonprofit, nonstock corporation with no members. The parent corporation is managed by a board of directors.

Asbury Heights is governed by a 15-member board of directors as voting ex officio members, excluding myself and a representative of the United Methodist Church. Overall, there are 465 employees in classifications ranging from CEO to dietary aides. Asbury has 48 managers of which there is a 7-member senior management team. Of our senior management team, excluding myself, two have Associate degrees, four have Bachelors degrees, including our chief financial officer who is also a CPA, and one has an MBA.

When I arrived, I was the only senior manager who had both formal academic training in management as well as significant experience in health-care delivery organizations as a senior manager. Indeed, prior to my appointment, the organization's leaders were almost all Methodist ministers.

I have a diverse educational and career background that includes a Bachelor's degree in Education, a Masters degree in Public Health, a Post-Masters certificate in the Evaluation of Health Promotion and Health Education Programs, a Post-Bachelors certificate in Accounting, two Associate degrees, one in Liberal Arts and one in Accounting, as well as certificates for the completion of two executive-education programs, one from the Harvard Business School and one from Carnegie Mellon University's (CMU's) Tepper School of Business. My professional work experiences include serving as a research associate in the Graduate School of Public Health, University of Pittsburgh; executive vice president and senior operations officer, Oil City Hospital; executive vice president, Grane Healthcare; administrator, Southwood Psychiatric Hospital; and executive director, Allegheny division, Presbyterian SeniorCare. Since May 1993, I have served as president and CEO of United Methodist

Services for the Aging. I hold an adjunct appointment as associate professor within the Department of Behavioral and Community Health Sciences at the University of Pittsburgh.

Building a Quality Relationship with Carnegie Mellon

I came to be involved with management research and scholarship in the late 1990s when I participated in the Program for Executives (PFE) offered by CMU's Graduate School of Industrial Administration (now renamed to the Tepper School of Business). As a participant in this month-long program, I was introduced to scholars from disciplines such as organizational behavior, financial economics, marketing and operations research, to name but a few.

Participation in the executive program was an eye-opener. I was exposed to research-based frameworks and presented with approaches to the management and leadership challenges contemporary CEOs face. I immediately saw some pretty clear connections to the day-to-day issues I deal with at Asbury. I started doing some more systematic reading in the areas I thought would be most relevant to the challenges I face as Asbury's CEO: organizational behavior, executive communications, and financial economics. I also kept in touch with faculty who ultimately became my friends, colleagues, mentors, and continue to be my teachers. I began adding some new approaches to the decisions I faced based on my PFE experience. Over time, CMU faculty have served as informal consultants to Asbury Heights, as well as instructors providing management training, board members, and research collaborators. Faculty members have been knowledge brokers, providing me, and at times my staff, with leads on useful research and interesting peer-reviewed articles.

Faculty members I met at CMU tell a story about me. Apparently, I am the only person they have ever met who went to the library to read what J. Stacy Adams (1964) had to say on equity theory when trying to decide how to deal with pay raises. It's true.

Being an Evidence-Based Manager Before It had a Name

In point of fact, I have been practicing evidence-based management, without that label, since I became Asbury's CEO. Two initiatives I led demonstrate some of the roots of what today, I believe, is an evidence-based management culture at Asbury Heights. The first is our "systems approach" to improving organizational processes, a practice I introduced at Asbury in an effort to create the desired outputs and outcomes we wished to achieve, and which is now widespread throughout our organization. With the goal to deliver desired results reliably and consistently, our systems approach relies on regular measurement and feedback about intended goals and results. When those results do not meet our expectations, we go back and analyze both the inputs and processes that led to those results in order to identify the root causes of the problem. On discerning the root cause, countermeasures (i.e., interventions) are designed and introduced. Then the process repeats. By measuring the result, we can tell if the countermeasures were successful; then we continue to monitor results to determine if they can be achieved consistently.

In retrospect, I recognize that Asbury's systems approach is an example of using systematic methods to obtain and make decisions on what Rousseau (2006) has called "Little e" evidence, that is, the organization's own metrics and facts, in this case regarding whether we met our desired results. Although I used this systems approach independently of any notion of evidenced-based management, it isn't something we did just by chance. It is most likely attributable to me as CEO and my desire to create an all-encompassing organizational performance model, a sort of algorithm that consistently delivers valid and reliable results.

A second initiative I introduced very early in my tenure as organizational CEO was a collaboration with academic geriatricians from the University of Pittsburgh. These board-certified, fellowship-trained geriatricians brought with them clinical approaches to care for our residents that had been vetted by the latest and best science. It is this fellowship training that makes these physicians so uniquely qualified to take care of older adults. A fellowship is a two- to three-year educational and experiential training program that one goes through after achieving the training and board certification of an internist (internal medicine). Most physicians who complete a fellowship in geriatrics also acquire another advanced degree during the fellowship, in many cases the Master in Public Health degree with a concentration in epidemiology. Additionally, fellowship-trained geriatricians tend to reside within an academic medical center, are involved in research personally, and are well aware of the latest research findings concerning the issues of older adults. In brief, they are highly informed and facile with scientific evidence.

I saw this link with academic geriatricians as a means to promote improved care at Asbury as well as a way to differentiate it from other organizations providing similar services. These fellowship-trained geriatricians have served our resident population since 1996. It is readily apparent to our residents, their family members and friends, and those employees with whom they interact that these fellowship-trained geriatricians used approaches steeped in research-based practices. From my personal observation, when these physicians suggest an approach to a problem, it is usually preceded by them saying "The research suggests that this approach is likely the best," or alternatively, "what the best evidence at this time suggests is..." They link the care they give patients to those practices vetted by science, and they express that fact in their interactions with patients, families, and staff. Along the same lines, the research that motivated the approach these geriatricians advise, what that theory suggested in the clinical setting, and the rigorous measurement of outcome variables are all topics of regular discussion between our geriatricians and the staff with whom they interact.

As in both these initiatives, I began working to establish a culture of science (by which I mean evidence) in the clinical setting from the beginning of my tenure as Asbury CEO. This approach is now part of the knowledge base of a large portion of the Asbury Heights stakeholders from our staff to the board. We characterize it in our discussions, newcomer orientations, and documents as "science-informed care delivered in a heartfelt way." It was not much of a leap from using clinical practices informed by evidence to adopting a more systematic evidence-based approach to management decisions and organizational practices.

My goals in becoming an evidence-based manager were essentially to be a successful organizational leader and to build a successful organization in a valid and reliable way; *valid* referring to working on the "right things" and *reliable* referring to "doing it right" and getting consistent results. Of course, all leaders and managers want to be successful. Success can be defined as the achievement of whatever goals and objectives one sets out to accomplish. It is how they go about this task of attaining organizational goals and objectives that sets apart practitioners who are evidence-driven from those who aren't even evidence-guided. Therefore, other than the observation that evidence-based managers and those who are not act differently, what might be the reasons for the difference in their managerial approach?

For a leader and manager to practice management in a way that utilizes evidence, the first hurdle is to understand what constitutes evidence, where it is found, and how then to apply this evidence in the pursuit of organizational objectives and goals. Understanding what evidence is and finding and using it are not things that managers are trained in. It is not at all obvious at first how to go about finding and using evidence.

My background, along with the fact that I do not have an MBA, has undoubtedly influenced both my becoming an evidence-based manager and the way I practice it. My background and graduate training is in public health. Public health is an offshoot of the field of medicine whose general purpose is to study disease in populations with the ultimate hope of constructing and developing interventions whose purposes are to eliminate disease states in these populations. Public health is grounded in science and uses the scientific method to advance the field's body of knowledge. Statistics and research designs are very much a part of the training of a public-health practitioner. These features in themselves are relevant to the emphasis I have placed on evidence and systematic gathering of organizational facts. However, other practices I have used to apply evidence in making managerial decisions are also tied to my training in public health.

Public health practitioners are trained in a process for solving problems and getting things done. Basically, to understanding the desired end state that is disease elimination, and the process to achieve such a state, public-health practitioners are trained to use a structure, process, and outcomes method, all guided by some "theory of change." That theory of change is the connecting logic, or evidence base, that specifies the mechanisms through which inputs are transformed into outputs. It is the premise or science on which an intervention, managerial decision, or public-health program is based. Ultimately there is always some theory on which one bases the approach used to change something. Managerial evidence and a theory of change can be thought of as describing the same thing. Both represent the knowledge on which your actions are grounded. This is how I was trained. When I participated with CMU's faculty in discussions concerning research findings and their use in management, it was easy to connect using scholarly evidence in making management decisions with my training and experiences working in the field of public health.

What Works for Us at Asbury Heights

At Asbury, reporting to me directly are four senior administrative directors, the chief of staff, the chief financial officer, the senior operations director and a person responsible for sales and our continuous quality-improvement program. We are all located in the same suite of offices, thereby allowing Newcomb's (1961) Law of Propinquity to operate freely. Being in such close physical proximity allows us all to readily interact, both frequently and informally.

A regularly standing senior management team meeting occurs each Thursday morning. Often for the first half of the meeting, we discuss a book or research article that I thought my staff might find informative. Then we spend time on critical strategic issues. We use a formal critical measures dashboard system to track key upstream drivers and lagging downstream performance metrics in the three performance domains we emphasize: economic performance, quality, and customer satisfaction. Our measures include both quantitative and qualitative elements.

At these meetings and other interactions with my closest colleagues we constantly refer to our "three E's." These are evidence, execution, and evaluation. Evidence informs all our organizational actions, and refers to having facts, metrics, and scientific findings that guide our decisions. Execution means that we use a well-delineated process map to guide our actions and analysis. This process map connects inputs, process, and outputs/outcomes. Last, evaluation means that we are constantly measuring our outcomes against our expectations and then feeding this information back in order to create and monitor countermeasures, if warranted, to adjust for those results not up to our expectations.

A framework that I have found most useful in helping our staff base actions at Asbury on a thoughtful theory of change is a logic model. In an advanced academic training program in organizational program evaluation, I was introduced to the logic-model approach described by the Kellogg Foundation (2004). It was developed to guide the implementation of organizational programs and then the evaluation of program performance. In this approach to program evaluation, those programs deemed to have efficacy, that is, they have been shown to work using the scientific method under controlled conditions, were then implemented in organizations. Subsequently they were evaluated to determine if indeed the desired effect was achieved. I regularly use this logic model and have worked with my direct reports to apply it in their own, as well as our joint, decisions.

Here is one application we made at Asbury of the logic model. The Sales Logic Model (Figure 11.1) was developed by our manager of sales, Art Barbus, to figure out how to solve the problem of low sales in our independent-living facility. It includes the evidence on which it is based. Although "expert opinion" is not always considered to be valid evidence by scholars, in practice it is often the most readily available and accessible information. In this particular situation, the expert was an experienced consultant in the area of direct sales—consistent with Herbert Simon's (1991) notion that if a person has 10 or more years of focused experience in a specific area from plumbing to chess, they can indeed have developed valid expert knowledge. Art constructed the logic model based on the expert's data on direct sales, and then ran what amounts to an experiment to see if the model could be used to improve sales. As Art describes it:

> The experiment was conducted in December 2005 when the Asbury Heights Independent Living census was 78.5% against a budget of 91%. Prior to the development of the logic model, the low census was blamed on burned out light bulbs, dirty elevator tracks, and the condition of the front lobby. We even went so far as to hire a cleaning company to clean the elevator tracks on a weekly basis at a cost of several thousand dollars per month. Sales did not increase as a result of clean elevator tracks or all light bulbs illuminated.
>
> Using the logic model I found that the [sales] process can only be as good as the weakest link. Measuring the new inquiries, tours, and sales was the best way to determine where to apply the countermeasures. The numbers pointed me toward the tours.

There were over 30 new inquiries every month. This was a sufficient number to generate sufficient sales to meet the budget.

After meeting with the sales person, I discovered that she needed training on the "follow-up," the action taken after the first initial contact by a new prospect. Sometimes the follow-up call was several days, other times it was several weeks, and if the inquiry was forgotten no follow-up call was made at all. A follow-up protocol was developed and the number of tours increased, which increased sales. At the end of 2006, the Independent Living census reached 91.1%. Through 2007, the Independent Living census continued to track above the 91% budget consistently month after month.

Given that the results achieved were better than in the past, the model's validity was inferred. Those trained in science know that such a leap cannot be made without first, among other things, ruling out other possible causes of increased sales. In practice, however, this example demonstrates how it can be done and, in my opinion, it is a good step on the path to becoming an evidence-based manager.

I have found that in my work as a leader and manager, my colleagues who were otherwise untrained in the scientific method readily grasped the essence of evidence-oriented approaches through use of a logic model. It may be that the logic model helps people understand why a particular scientific finding works, but it also helps them see how to apply it. In some respects, the logic model framework allows people to have the same sort of "aha" moment that scientists experience!

Sales Logic Model

This logic model is based on evidence gathered from several marketing consultants that have worked in the non-profit CCRC business for over 30 years in larger metropolitan areas including Pittsburgh.

To illustrate, we learned that qualified inquiries (age and income appropriate) should lead to tours of the CCRC campus. These tours should lead to sales, unless there are serious issues with product and pricing, which is expressed as "not enough value" by the prospect, or the sales staff is ineffective.

For every 100 new inquiries, at least 30% should be converted to tours. Out of this 30% that toured, 10 to 15% should convert to sales. We also learned that the sales cycle time from the new inquiry's first contact to occupancy can be anywhere from 6 months to a year and a half.

Fig. 11.1.

Ongoing learning is essential to managing based on evidence. I encourage all our managers to participate in continuing education in areas they can use on the job and to develop their career potential. I model and involve them in a robust reading program. In this regard, we have utilized CMU faculty in financial economics, organizational behavior and marketing to name a few, to conduct custom education programs for our management team.

I have come to believe that organizational culture or "what is normative and how it is done here" is the greatest driver of the actions by organizational participants. Further, organizational actions premised on the highest form of available evidence will only be successful to the extent that the organization's participants are helped to understand the evidence and how to apply it in practice.

Close Relationships with Academia and Academics

The management scholars I met at CMU used their research to motivate their class sessions. Utilizing the model that had worked so effectively in our clinical settings (i.e., relationships with fellowship-trained geriatricians), I began to develop closer relationships with some of these scholars with the idea of developing mutual beneficial relationships between the academy and Asbury Heights. Over the last 10–12 years, many successful collaborations have resulted; some of my professors have served on our board and have trained us in their discipline's evidenced-motivated approach. For example, Laurie Weingart advised us on an intervention to reduce conflict and create a shared frame of reference among members of our top management team. Using her research (Cronin & Weingart, 2007), she helped us develop a shadowing process that was used to reduce misunderstandings (i.e., perceptual gaps) between various staff members by opening their eyes to their colleagues' worldviews. The result was more harmonious working relationships among our team. Some faculty conducted executive education classes on site and others have done research with Asbury as a field site. In all, I believe our collaborations have been incredibly mutually beneficial.

Challenges

To be sure, there have been and will continue to be challenges to using evidence to inform leaders' and managers' decisions. One of the first challenges is getting managers to understand, at a well-informed but accessible level, what is meant by "evidence" and how this knowledge might be used in solving organizational problems more reliably. I've found you have to start with a simple approach. Asking our managers to think about the kind of information they actually are basing their actions on can be a good step in itself. Another is to prompt their awareness of evidence by providing them with articles or books that describe management evidence in an interesting readable way. Chapters from Locke's (2009) book with many brief articles on various research findings relevant to practice can be useful here. Getting people used to reading about research to improve their action as managers requires persistence. At Asbury it helps that continuing education is part of our culture. I use our regular management team meetings in part as management development sessions.

It is often challenging when decisions need to be made quickly. In such cases, it may be nearly impossible to find quality evidence in time. By quality evidence I mean that which has been vetted scientifically and addresses organizational problems that are multifaceted and are being written in an accessible format. Organizational leaders are pressed for time. We are not trained as scholars. Instead, we are looking for reasonable solutions for day- to-day organizational problems. In our organization, and I would surmise in others as well, leaders and managers often rise from the ranks. Doing "what comes naturally" and/or makes "common sense" is often the default approach. Constraints of time and training make it challenging to introduce the concept of serious (meaning reliable and valid) evidence that could be used in practice and better achieve the desired outcome. Because of these constraints, it helps to make use of evidence part of everyday life, and not something that is done when a really important decision needs to be made and quickly. Ongoing employee development is also important formally through courses and degree programs as well as in house with managers as coaches and mentors for learning. It is easier to make good decisions quickly if managers are educated and evidence savvy.

Conclusion

I have described an approach to evidence-based management that has worked in my organization. Whether my approach at Asbury can work in other organizations, I cannot say. It's tough for most organization leaders to act on evidence. Most leaders that I am aware of lack the kinds of foundational knowledge about evidence relevant to the problems they face. They are unfamiliar with the scientific facts associated with some of the routine decisions they make, like team building or problem solving. They tend to lack basic understandings regarding what constitutes "scientific evidence."

In education, there is conceptualization of knowledge known as Bloom's (1956) Taxonomy. Its underlying premise is that there must be some basic understanding of the material before students are asked to act on it. I believe this foundation is missing in most organizational leaders and managers with whom I am familiar. Identifying relevant and valid evidence is relatively easy for academics and those who understand scholarship and its creation. It is not so easy for a practitioner who doesn't understand exactly what constitutes reliable and valid information in the first place. That is why readily available pop-management books, what Bob Sutton (2006) has labeled "crap," is so appealing to today's leaders and managers. So what exactly is "crap" and how does a practitioner know it when he or she sees it? Crap, in my view, is the leadership and management information distributed every day in books, magazines, classrooms, and other distribution modes of knowledge to practitioners by those that basically say "do this (fill in the blank here: these seven steps, these ten things, these approaches, etc.) and your outcome will be success!" Usually these suggestions for success are based on someone having tried this approach with apparently the desired results having been achieved. Without the use of any scientific method, these suggestions are then generalized to a larger population. To those not trained in science, especially busy organizational leaders, the 10 suggestions might appear to be just what they are looking for. At last, the answer to all my problems! Whether it is valid and reliably works will most likely never be known, of course, because these purported "theories of change" were never subjected to a rigorous scrutiny. My advice to my fellow managers is pay attention to the logic behind ideas that are proposed to you. Get used to laying out a logic model for your decisions and help your direct reports to do the same. Keep reading and learning so that critical thinking starts to come naturally. And you will have more knowledge of what the evidence says when the need to use it arises. The overarching purpose of management is to see to it that the collective activities of the people who make up our organization achieve desired results. It would seem logical then for those occupying the managerial roles within the organization to premise their actions on the best evidence available that would inform their actions. In this way, there is a better chance that the desired outcome might be achieved.

I would suggest that a good first EBMgt reading is Jeff Pfeffer and Bob Sutton's (2006) book entitled *Hard Facts, Dangerous Half-Truths, and Total Nonsense*. If there is such a thing as one thoroughly researched management book that should be read by anyone seeking to become an evidence-based manager it is Edwin A. Locke's and Gary P. Latham's (1984) *Goal Setting: A Motivational Technique That Works*. It truly is a motivational technique that works from my experience. This book describes effective ways to set goals.

In this chapter, I have described my approach to using evidence as well as ways to inculcate this practice within an organization's culture. This is merely one approach that a manager wanting to become evidence based might wish to consider. I've also suggested some readings that you might wish to consider. I can guarantee you one thing, and that is once you become facile in finding and using quality evidence to inform your managerial actions, you and your organization will be profoundly changed.

References

Adams, J. S. (1963). Towards an understanding of inequity. *The Journal of Abnormal and Social Psychology, 67,* 422–436.

Bloom, B. S. (1956). *Taxonomy of educational objectives, handbook I: The cognitive domain.* New York: David McKay.

Cronin, M., & Weingart, L. (2007). Representational gaps, information processing, and conflict in functionally diverse teams. *Academy of Management Review, 32,* 761–773.

W. K. Kellogg Foundation (2004). *Logic Model Development Guide.* Battle Creek, MI: W.K. Kellogg Foundation.

Locke, E. A. (2009). *Handbook of principles of organizational behavior: Indispensable knowledge for evidence-based management.* Chichester, England: Wiley.

Locke, E. A., & Latham, G. P. (1984). *Goal setting: A motivational technique that works.* Englewood Cliffs, NJ: Prentice-Hall.

Newcomb, T. (1961). *The acquaintance process.* New York: Holt, Rinehart & Winston.

Pfeffer, J., & Sutton, R. I. (2006). *Hard facts, dangerous half-truths, and total nonsense.* Boston, MA: Harvard Business Press.

Rousseau, D. M. (2006). Is there such a thing as evidence-based management? *Academy of Management Review, 31,* 256–269.

Simon, H. A. (1991) Bounded rationality and organizational learning. *Organization Science, 2,* 125–134.

Sutton, B. (2006) Management advice: Which 90% is crap? http://changethis.com/manifesto/show/23.90PercentCrap accessed June 20, 2011.

Evidence-Based *Decision* Management

J. Frank Yates *and* Georges A. Potworowski

Abstract

Decision making is the lifeblood of every organization and the central focus in the practice of evidence-based management (EBMgt). To help guide the practice of EBMgt, this chapter describes fundamental concepts of decision making and decision management. It begins with a discussion of the features that distinguish decision making from other, related concepts, such as more general problem solving and judgment. It then describes how crucial aspects of decision management are approached especially effectively when decision processes are broken down into essential elements. It then describes the theory known as the "cardinal decision issue perspective," and illustrates its use as a decision management tool.

Key Words: decision process, decision quality, decision management, decision appraisal, cardinal decision issues

Picture the following scene at a meeting of the executive board of fictional Northern Manufacturing. The discussion concerns what to do about the Lincoln facility. That installation is relatively new, having opened only a couple of years ago. Part of the problem is that quality is abysmal at Lincoln and costs are high, too. To make matters even worse, demand for the components produced at Lincoln is declining. It is no secret that, if they were to make the decision today instead of four years ago, the executive board would not approve the opening of Lincoln. June Ward, the rapidly rising executive vice president, had been the chair of the committee that recommended building what is now the Lincoln facility. As one might expect, Ms. Ward feels distinctly uncomfortable in this meeting.

The Lincoln scenario illustrates well several ideas and facts about business life. Most prominent is the central role that decisions play in the everyday functioning and welfare of any organization and any manager within that organization. A high percentage of

the Northern executive board's time—including that of June Ward—is spent making decisions. The resulting decisions have great impact on whether Northern and its leaders' careers flourish or, instead, founder. In any organization, it is uncommon for anyone's decisions to be immune to influence by others. Instead, by design or otherwise, and for better or worse, most people's decisions are affected by the actions of numerous other people in that organization. Consider how June Ward's colleagues and superiors on the Northern executive board discuss and respond to the perceived success or failure of the Lincoln decision that had been advocated by Ms. Ward's committee. Those reactions will likely affect not only how Ms. Ward makes decisions in the future but also the decision behavior of everyone who is aware of her experience. Thus, if Ms. Ward's peers and bosses treat her harshly, we should expect more conservative, risk averse decisions in the future (Swalm, 1966). Implicit is the concept of "decision management": the actions a person takes that affect how and how well the people on the scene—subordinates, peers, superiors, and the person him- or herself—make decisions (Yates, 2003). Some decision management effects are inadvertent and even surprising to the manager in question. ("Really? They did that because of something *I* said?") However, this fact simply reinforces the theme of this chapter, that nurturing sound decision management practices is essential to managerial success more generally. This is especially so for those with high standing in an organization. After all, because high-status people control more resources, other people pay more attention to them, are more responsive to their wishes, and are more likely to mimic their behavior.

What are the connections between decision management and evidence-based management (EBMgt)? As noted in Rousseau's chapter 1 in this volume, decision making is at the heart of EBMgt. In particular, EBMgt puts a special emphasis on making decisions that are informed by "the best available scientific findings" (p. 00). Such defensible evidence can have two foci. The first, as Rousseau notes, is on the "content" of the decision problem at hand, for example, rigorously documented facts about the problem faced by the Northern Manufacturing executive board that ultimately resulted in its decision to build the Lincoln facility. The second focus is on the "process" by which a decision is reached, for example, the consistency of the Northern executive board's decision making practices with what valid scientific research has shown to have good chances of contributing to sound decisions. The two foci are clearly related. After all, ideally, a decision process whose elements have been properly validated should (among other things) demand validated facts for every decision. As its earlier definition suggests, in organizational contexts, decision management is largely about the details by which managers' actions—deliberately or inadvertently—affect the processes by which the people in that organization decide. From this perspective, then, decision management is a concrete, primary vehicle through which every manager exercises sound EBMgt principles—or not.

An overarching aim of this chapter is to provide the reader with a practical, working understanding of key decision management ideas, with a special emphasis on the roles of evidence. Among other things, managers should leave the chapter with the ingredients for a checklist of considerations to take into account when attempting to facilitate major decisions in their own organizations. That is, they should have an answer to this kind of question: "How, exactly, can I go about my work such that we decide well, making the best use of evidence-based concepts?" Researchers can expect to gain a clear, functional structure for identifying problems for study that are critical to achieving a deep understanding of fundamental decision principles as well as effective prescriptions for better decision making. Management educators, the essential links between scholarship and practice, can anticipate acquiring an intuitively compelling framework for effectively training the next generation of EBMgt practitioners and researchers.

The plan for the remainder of the chapter is as follows: The next major section describes the decision management portfolio—the major classes of decision management activities that are important to distinguish. The section after that provides requisite clarity about critical decision making essentials, including core concepts such as "decision," "judgment," and "decision quality." The third—and largest—major section of the chapter presents most of the specific, detailed ideas and facts that are essential to high-quality decision making and decision management, within the context of a conceptual theory called the "cardinal decision issue perspective." The final section points toward the next steps that the reader might consider pursuing.

The Decision Management Portfolio

Decision management activities fall into several categories, as summarized in Table 12.1 (Yates, 2003). All managers in charge of an organization have an obligation to carry out these activities to the best of their abilities. After all, if they are performed poorly, the organization's welfare is seriously jeopardized. Table 12.1 can serve as a useful checklist for

Table 12.1. The Portfolio of Decision Management Activities

Making Specific Decisions
• Deciding personally
• Deciding collaboratively
• Leading/facilitating decision making deliberations
• Affecting decisions from a distance
Supervising Decision Making Routines
Shaping Decision Making Practices
Providing Decision Making Resources

the manager to review periodically in her efforts to meet her decision management obligations. ("Am I doing what I'm supposed to be doing? How well am I doing those things?") Let us consider, in turn, what those duties entail:

• *Making Specific Decisions:* This category includes: (1) making decisions personally, as when June Ward exercises her discretion to select her own office staff or to approve purchases below a specified cost level; (2) deciding collaboratively, as when Ms. Ward, as a member of the Northern executive board, voted on whether to approve the construction of the Lincoln facility; (3) leading or facilitating decision making deliberations, as Ms. Ward did for the Lincoln facility committee; and (4) affecting decisions from a distance, as when Ms. Ward lobbied county commissioners, over whom she had no authority whatsoever, for their votes on tax breaks in the county where the Lincoln facility was eventually located.

• *Supervising Decision Routines:* Every organization has routines for making particular recurring decisions. Routines for vetting job applicants and supply vendors are examples. Even when the routines are well established, they do not run themselves. Someone must assure that the people responsible for executing those routines actually fulfill their obligations. Someone must also figure out what to do when odd cases that do not fit the parameters of the established routines come along. These "someones" are the designated supervisors of the company's decision routines.

• *Shaping Decision Practices:* There is seldom a unique, ideal way of making any kind of decision. That is why every organization occasionally tinkers with its decision making practices, often described as making policy changes. Such is the case in universities where the rules for making decisions about promotions from assistant to associate professor are occasionally revised. Someone has to lead the process of making such policy changes. When a new organization is established, someone (perhaps a group) must develop the organization's decision practices from scratch. That is what happened when Charles Jones, the general manager of the new Lincoln facility, was given broad discretion to craft hiring procedures at that unit.

• *Providing Decision Resources:* Decision making is not free. It consumes resources that, depending on the circumstances, can be substantial. And the character and extent of those resources can significantly constrain the quality of the decisions that are made. Thus, a final major decision management responsibility is providing the resources used in making the decisions at hand. For instance, when June Ward led the committee developing plans for the prospective Lincoln facility, she oversaw a sizable committee budget for a host of services, such as site analysis consultations. She expected those services to be essential for informing wise decisions.

When they ponder stories like that of June Ward and the Lincoln facility, practicing managers readily acknowledge that it is important for them to decide well and to somehow induce those around them to do the same. But then comes the hard part: "How can I do that? Do I just need to try harder doing things the way I do them already? Or should I do things differently? And where, exactly, does good evidence enter the picture?" Much of the remainder of this chapter offers paths to answers for questions like these. At the core of the discussion is a particular perspective on the nature of real-life decision processes. These are the mechanisms that produce the decisions in question, by managers themselves and by the people whom managers seek to influence. However, before getting into the details, the meanings of critical concepts must be clarified.

Decision Making Essentials

Decision making is a fundamental human function, on a par with other behaviors such as learning. Everyone does it and seeks to assure that it is done well. Moreover, it is the subject of study in a broad range of disciplines, from psychology to philosophy, economics, strategy, law, engineering, finance, statistics, marketing, and, medicine, to name just a few. This attention is a mixed blessing. On the one hand, it means that when we have questions about how people decide or could decide better, we can draw on an enormously extensive pool of ideas, experiences, and scholarship. On the other hand, among other challenges, the resulting ambiguity about the meanings of common terms can encumber conversation and cripple productive research and development efforts, particularly collaborative ones. To minimize such difficulties, in this section, we describe and define precisely key concepts that are used in the subsequent discussion. These meanings are not arbitrary, however. Instead, they represent the most common (but, of course, not universal), consensus meanings across myriad scholarly and practical decision literatures, particularly the multidisciplinary literature dedicated to fundamentals, which is usually described as being about "judgment and decision making," often called simply "JDM." Specifically, we discuss "decisions," "judgments," "decision parties," and then varieties of decision-related quality.

Decisions

We adopt the following definition of a "decision," which is at the core of ways the term has been used in literatures that address decision making: a commitment to a course of action that is intended to serve the interests and values of particular people (Yates, 2003; Yates & Tschirhart, 2006). We make a distinction between interests and values because they do not always coincide. Consider, for instance, the situation of a cocaine addict. At a particular moment, the addict desperately craves ("values") using the drug, although pursuing that action would be contrary to his long-term interests. Such contradictions implicate a (sometimes philosophical) conundrum that must be worked through in the course of arriving at a decision.

It is useful to acknowledge several varieties of decisions:

• *Choices* are instances in which the decision maker selects a subset from a larger collection of alternatives, for example, Northern Manufacturing's selection of Bartonville over Lexington and New Stanton as the site for the Lincoln facility.

• *Acceptances/rejections* are particular kinds of choices in which the decision maker is presented with a single option and chooses to either pursue it or not, for example, the Northern board's decision to either accept or reject a proposal to acquire its major competitor, Peerless.

• *Evaluations* are special statements of how much some entity is worth. Northern Manufacturing's bid on a contract with Jackson Instruments would be one example. June Ward's performance appraisal of her subordinate, Len Mason, would be another. These statements are special in the sense that the decision maker is willing to back them up with actions commensurate with the magnitudes expressed. For instance, a contract bid of $500,000 indicates the acceptance of an obligation to perform specified actions in return for $500,000 in compensation, no more and no less.

• *Constructions* are the products of decision makers' efforts to create the alternatives they think would be ideal for them, conditional on available resources and constraints, for example, the custom design of Northern Manufacturing's Lincoln facility allowed by the budget allocated for the project.

The various types of decisions described here are useful to recognize because they rest on quite disparate operations and skills. They are also amenable to different kinds of repairs when they go awry. The definitions are important also because they allow for the precision that is demanded of serious scholarship. Consider, for instance, the difference between "decision making" and "problem solving." People are often stumped when asked to discriminate between them. Here, decision making is recognized as a special case of problem solving, one that emphasizes the aim of satisfying the personal interests and values of certain individuals, not people in general. A new Ford Mustang might be the ideal solution to Tom's car-purchase decision problem but totally inadequate for Jim's, who has different transportation needs and esthetic tastes. More generally, the implied highly variable standards of decision adequacy are perhaps the most distinctive and challenging characteristic of decision making, what makes decision problems especially hard to solve.

Judgments

The preferred meaning here for the term *judgment* is an opinion as to what was, is, or will be some decision-significant state of the world (Yates & Chen, 2009). When June Ward's recruiting consultant says that plant manager candidate Dale Laws improved productivity 33 percent at his last job, that is a "was" judgment. A real estate title consultant's assertion that a property being considered as the site for the Lincoln facility is free of liens is an "is" judgment. And the Northern board's expectation that demand for the primary components made at Lincoln "probably" will stay flat for at least 15 months is a "will be" judgment. The kinds of decisions whose wisdom depends on the adequacy of those judgments are easy to envision. It is worth noting that, despite the fact that judgments are "opinions," they do not have to originate with people. Increasingly often these days, devices, such as property-title search algorithms, render judgments. In perhaps the earliest research tradition, the source of a judgment used in making a decision is referred to as the "judge." As the present examples suggest, the judge easily can be different from the decision maker (e.g., a consultant) and does not need to be a human being.

Unfortunately, the expression *judgment* sometimes has different interpretations in decision-related fields. For instance, in law, legal decisions are often referred to as "judgments," as when a court pronounces a "judgment for the plaintiff." In some decision making studies, researchers also sometimes describe evaluation decisions, for example, product or employee performance ratings, as "judgments," to distinguish them from choices (e.g., Sood & Forehand, 2005). The convention described here is older, more common, and, therefore, preferred in the interests of avoiding distracting ambiguity.

To foreshadow later discussions, it is important to highlight the fact that judgments are the primary focus of the "evidence" addressed in evidence-based management discourse. Consider human resources as an example (cf. Boudreau, chapter 13 of this volume). A judgment that drives common and especially important human resources decisions concerns the costs of employee turnover. How do managers arrive at such judgments? How good are they? Are they good enough? How could managers acquire better judgments, perhaps based on better evidence, and at what costs?

Decision Parties

Implicit in the definition of a decision are hints of the fact that, typically, decision episodes in organizations entail more roles than simply "decision maker" and "decision manager." There is good reason to expect that in practice, decision makers (and decision managers) sometimes overlook some of these roles and that that kind of neglect can contribute to decision failures. Table 12.2, which can serve as another practical checklist, summarizes the key players in typical decision making scenarios: decision makers, beneficiaries, decision managers, stakeholders, and bystanders (cf. Yates, 2003):

• *Intended beneficiaries* are the people whose interests and values the decision maker pointedly seeks to serve by the decision in question. Other people might benefit from a decision, too. However, from the decision maker's perspective, this is only

Table 12.2 Common Decision Parties

Intended Beneficiaries
• Immediate
• Distant
Decision Maker(s)
Decision Manager(s)
Stakeholders
Bystanders

coincidental. In organizational settings, it is useful to acknowledge two classes of intended beneficiaries. First are the immediate beneficiaries. These beneficiaries are "immediate" insofar as the desired outcomes of the decision (and often the decision process) would affect them directly. In the Lincoln case, the immediate beneficiaries included the customers, whose needs for high-quality components were intended to be served more quickly and reliably. Workers in the new state-of-the-art facility were among the immediate beneficiaries, too, in that the decision makers hoped that the workers' jobs and working conditions would be improved. Decision makers themselves, such as the Northern Manufacturing executive board members, are almost invariably immediate beneficiaries also. It is hard to imagine nonpathological circumstances in which decision makers deliberately try to make decisions that harm their own personal interests. Then there are the distant beneficiaries. These are people whose improved welfare is sought through the decision, but only indirectly, via the impact of the decision on immediate beneficiaries. In a typical private business, this group includes the owners, such as shareholders. If, for instance, in the Lincoln case, the new facility in fact provides better products and service to Northern's customers, all else being the same, this would result in higher share prices for the owners. Such examples illustrate the fact that "distant" does not mean "unimportant."

• *Decision makers* are the key protagonists in a given decision episode, the ones who make commitments to the courses of action in question. In private life, there is often only one decision maker. However, in organizational life, for high-stakes decisions, there are typically multiple decision makers, as when the Northern Manufacturing executive board voted on building the Lincoln facility. And in bargaining situations, decision scenarios that are part of the very fabric of commerce and politics, there are two or more decision makers who have at least partly opposing interests. A good example, even though many might not normally recognize it as a bargaining situation, is that in which June Ward worked through with her colleagues and superiors the ground rules by which her board subcommittee functioned. Ms. Ward had her own thoughts about what those rules should be and the other board members had different preferences.

• *Decision managers*, whom we discussed already in the context of the decision management portfolio, take actions that affect the processes by which decisions are made, even their own, personal decision processes. A key fact that decision makers and formally acknowledged decision managers are wise to recognize is that in a given situation, there can easily be numerous other decision managers actively attempting to influence how decisions are made, too. For instance, it would not be surprising to learn that a host of nonexecutive board employees at Northern Manufacturing tried to affect the Lincoln facility decision in some fashion or another.

• *Stakeholders* are people who have power and are inclined to apply that power to serve or harm the interests of the decision maker's intended beneficiaries if they are, respectively, either pleased or displeased with the decision in question or, even, how it is reached. A decision maker might sometimes seek to make stakeholders happy, but this is only because doing so might indirectly affect the intended beneficiaries' interests and values. In the Lincoln scenario, government construction inspectors would represent one class of important stakeholders. If they are unhappy about the design or the construction work at the Lincoln facility, they have the power to halt the project until compliance with their regulations is achieved, an action that would frustrate the aims of serving customers and shareholders. The same would be true of powerful local civic leaders.

• *Bystanders* are individuals who are similar to stakeholders except that they can have little or no power, perhaps because they are not organized collectively. Decision makers do not aim to promote bystanders' interests per se. However, perhaps for reasons of ethical concerns or good citizenship, the decision makers seek to assure that their decisions do no harm to those people collaterally. The low-income residents who live close to the Lincoln facility qualify as bystanders. The decision makers on Northern Manufacturing's executive board would hate to see the new unit make the neighbors' lives worse by, for instance, polluting their environment. Thus, the committee members explicitly take that desire into account as they deliberate the facility's design.

It is useful to think of the various roles distinguished here as just that—roles. Accordingly, a given person can assume more than one of them. Thus, June Ward is both a decision manager and a decision maker in executive board meetings. She is one intended beneficiary of her decisions, too. It is also useful to emphasize that failures to recognize almost any of the "players" in a decision episode can have significant adverse consequences. If a powerful stakeholder, say, a local politician, goes unrecognized, then this might be interpreted as a deliberate slight. The result could be the failure to obtain required government permits in a timely fashion, if at all.

Quality

Proponents of evidence-based management contend that it is a sound approach to "making better decisions" in organizations (Rousseau, chapter 1 of this volume, p. 000). Such expectations are at the heart of a surprisingly knotty set of questions about quality, such as, "What, exactly, are 'better decisions?' How can we recognize them when we see them?" Achieving progress toward the goal of making better decisions is exceedingly difficult if we cannot cleanly specify and measure the criteria. Rousseau (chapter 1 of this volume, p. 000) aptly recalls the old business saying that "What gets measured gets managed." The converse almost certainly holds, too: That which is not measured (e.g., decision quality) is done poorly or neglected altogether. After all, if a decision manager cannot tell whether (and how) his efforts have fallen short, how can he make necessary adjustments? So, in this section, we consider, in turn, and describe functional conventions about quality and quality assessment with respect to decisions, judgments, decision makers, and decision processes.

Decision quality: "Is this decision good enough, or do we need to try again?" In everyday conversation, people often speak of a decision as being either "good" or "bad." More than anything else, they mean that a "good" decision is one that has outcomes they like and a "bad" decision is one whose outcomes displease them (Yates, Veinott, & Patalano, 2003). Questions about a decision's quality can have enormous practical significance. Consider, for instance, lawsuits filed against physicians by patients (or their families) when their treatments result in injury, disability, or death. Or take consumer shunning of airlines whose pilots have made decisions leading to fatal crashes. There has been considerable controversy about the legitimate use of the terms *good decision* and *bad decision*. To avoid being unproductively distracted by that controversy, we advocate a characterization of decision quality that follows directly from the previously presented definition of a decision as "a commitment to a course of action that is intended to serve the interests and values of particular people," the intended beneficiaries. Specifically, we recommend avoiding the terms *good decision* and *bad decision* altogether and, instead, speaking

Table 12.3. Decision Effectiveness Dimensions

Overall Effectiveness		
Intended Beneficiary Interests & Values		
Outcomes Per Se	Process Costs & Benefits	
• Aims	Material	Nonmaterial
• Requirements	• Money	• Stress
• Side Effects	• Time	• Discord
• Rival Option Contrasts	• Labor	• Autonomy
…	…	• Learning
…	…	• Bonding
…	…	…

of "effective decisions" as ones that, in fact, serve the interests and values of the intended beneficiaries.

There are many distinct ways in which a decision may (or may not) serve intended beneficiaries' interests and values. It is important for a decision manager to recognize key dimensions along which decision effectiveness can vary. The main reason is that different types of effectiveness tend to result from distinctly different causes. They, therefore, point toward different actions the decision manager should consider to address effectiveness shortfalls.

Table 12.3 summarizes important distinctions among decision making consequences that implicate separate decision effectiveness dimensions. The first distinction turns on whether the consequences in question result from (1) the action that is pursued as a result of the decision—the *outcomes per se*—or, instead, (2) the activities by which the decision was reached—the decision's *process costs and benefits*, irrespective of the effects of the action resulting from that decision.

For the decision to build the Lincoln facility, the outcomes per se included, for instance, the costs of building the facility, the degraded customer satisfaction engendered by the lower-quality components built there, and the increased production costs at that site. As suggested by Table 12.3, outcomes per se come in several varieties. Outcomes that either satisfy or fail to satisfy the decision maker's *aims* are an especially important class; as we shall see, every decision episode begins with such aims, the intended "point" of the decision. Another key category includes outcomes that affect the extent to which the decision meets the beneficiaries' emerging

needs or *requirements*, whether the decision maker deliberately aimed to meet those requirements or not. A concrete example might be the suitability of the Lincoln facility's technology for a newly developed and profitable product line that was never envisioned before the fact. Yet another outcome class encompasses the host of *side effects* or unintended consequences—good and bad—that inevitably accompany every decision. The Lincoln technology applicability just mentioned would be an example. A final noteworthy outcome class consists of contrasts between the outcomes actually experienced as a result of the selected action and the outcomes that would have been experienced had some other, *rival option* been pursued. The regret and other emotions instigated by such counterfactual comparisons are known to influence how people feel about their decisions (e.g., Mellers, Schwartz, Ho, & Ritov, 1997): "We would have been better off if …"

The opposing top-level class of consequences—process costs and benefits—encompasses experiences peculiar to one special category of decision beneficiary: the decision makers themselves. They are the beneficiaries who are directly affected by the decision process. These consequences fall into two categories, *material* and *nonmaterial*, as suggested by Table 12.3. The former include costs and benefits that can be translated more or less directly into money, as in the case of consulting fees and committee members' time and effort spent in meetings. The latter emphasize psychological effects, including process costs such as the personal worry and stress often engendered by the uncertainty inherent to many decision problems. They also include the pain sown by the "fights" that are inevitable in deliberations of decisions that affect the competing interests of different parties. Process benefits are illustrated by the heightened sense of power or autonomy generated by responsibility for a significant decision, the learning gained by the junior members of a decision making group, or the bonding created by committee members' shared experiences when collaborating on a major decision project, such as a search for a new CEO.

"Emergence time," not represented in Table 12.3, is a significant reality that is, oddly, almost never mentioned in discussions about decision quality. Consider outcomes per se. Some outcomes appear immediately after a decision is made. Others, however, can take years to emerge. Moreover, although the outcomes that are experienced during one epoch may be favorable, those experienced at other times could be dreadful. In such instances, according to what principles should the decision be declared effective or ineffective on the whole? Suppose that, during the early stages of his tenure, the Northern Manufacturing CEO clearly performs marvelously but falters badly in later periods. Was his selection an effective or an ineffective decision? (Marriage decisions are a clear parallel in personal life.) To make such questions manageable, it is advisable to condition their discussion on particular periods of time. For example, "Was the CEO decision effective for the first five years of the appointee's tenure?"

Judgment quality: "Would that really *happen?"* Recall that a judgment is an opinion as to what was, is, or will be some decision-significant state of the world. Forecasts of demand for the components slated for production at the Lincoln facility would be a good example. The main quality concept for judgments is "accuracy," the degree of correspondence between the judgments in question and the pertinent true states of the world. Various specific accuracy measures are simply concrete instantiations of this concept. Suppose that consultant A predicted a quarterly demand of 225,000 units, whereas consultant B's prediction was 241,000 units. Suppose that actual quarterly demand was 237,000 units. One commonly used accuracy measure would be the absolute deviation between forecasted and actual demand: 12,000 units for consultant A and 4,000 units for consultant B. So, by that metric, consultant B's judgment was more accurate, and, to the extent that such accuracy differences are reliable, we could expect decisions predicated on consultant B's judgments to be better than those informed by consultant A's opinions. To anticipate later discussions, a judge is said to be accurate to the degree that the judgments produced by that source are accurate. Thus, in the present example, we would describe consultant B as a more accurate judge than consultant A. We can speak of the quality of judgment processes—for example, algorithms within computer programs for diagnosing medical conditions—the same way.

A side note: in some decision making literature, authors occasionally speak of decisions as being "accurate" or "inaccurate." Again, in the interests of avoiding ambiguity, we recommend the more traditional custom of reserving the accuracy term for indications of judgment quality rather than decision quality. As we have seen, decision quality is difficult to assess. Decision beneficiary X, receiving the very same decision outcomes as beneficiary Y, quite legitimately could be considered to have experienced a decision that is either more effective or

less. This can happen because, given their distinct needs and, hence, their distinct interests and values, the personal impacts of those very same outcomes are different. In principle and in practice, things are usually much simpler when assessing judgment quality. That is one reason that judgment problems are as popular among researchers as they are; they are relatively easy to study.

Decision maker quality: "Is she a good enough decision maker, or should we keep looking for someone stronger?" In concept, the notion of decision maker quality is straightforward: A decision maker is good to the extent that the decisions that he or she renders tend to be effective ones. Note that this characterization is statistical—"tends." It assumes representative and sufficient sampling from the universe of the decisions of interest. Suppose that Northern Manufacturing's executive board wants to assess the adequacy of Lincoln general manager candidate Lucy Jackson as a decision maker. Then, ideally, the board should base that assessment on the appraisal of a sizable and representative sample of her decisions in previous similar situations.

Decision process quality: "How good is our process for making these decisions? Is that good enough?" Conceptually, quality considerations for decision processes are the same as those for decision makers: A decision process is a good one to the degree that it has a strong track record of yielding effective decisions, ones that serve the interests and values of the intended beneficiaries.

Practical questions about decision process quality arise in several ways. A particularly straightforward example concerns making large numbers of decisions that are seen as highly similar to one another. Certain kinds of "people decisions" are illustrative. Consider, for instance, processes for making college admissions decisions or those for choosing entry-level employees at large corporations. In such circumstances, evaluators often specify straightforward outcome criteria for the decisions (e.g., freshman-year grade point average (GPA) or supervisor performance ratings). The decision process in question is considered good to the extent that summary criterion measures are favorable (e.g., mean GPAs and performance ratings are high). If the decision making system is maintained by, say, an independent contractor, the decision managers in question could simply replace the current contractor if the process is concluded to be deficient.

Other common situations in which decision process quality assessments are required concern the assignment of responsibility (and liability) for specific, individual decisions—usually blatantly ineffective ones. Take, for example, medical decisions that result in patients being disabled, or investment decisions that result in investors losing their money. Everyone recognizes that there is an element of chance involved in such situations. Thus, it would seem unreasonable to expect every decision made by any given decision maker to be an effective one. On the other hand, it indeed would be reasonable to demand that the decision maker (e.g., a physician or a portfolio manager) decide according to a good process (see, for example, Hammond, Keeney, & Raiffa, 1998). In a very particular way, that is precisely the kind of perspective taken in medical malpractice cases, wherein the issue before the court is articulated something like the following (cf. 'Lectric Law Library, 2010): "Did the physician in question exercise the normal standard of care practiced by a reasonable physician under similar circumstances?"

So how should we draw conclusions about whether the decision maker, in fact, followed a good process when reaching a specific decision? Our notion of decision process quality just described, couched in terms of the rate at which the process yields effective decisions—its "track record"—is fine conceptually. Yet, there are often formidable challenges to our ability to estimate such rates defensibly in given cases. Most of these challenges occur because there are too few cases available to inform sound conclusions about the effectiveness rates of interest. Consider physicians' common contention that, in significant respects, every patient is unique. That is, those patients differ in terms of factors that plausibly can imply different outcomes from the very same treatments. Or consider the task of evaluating the quality of the decision process used by a corporate board of directors. Each of the high-level decisions the board makes is so special—and there are so few—that there is little resemblance among them. Moreover, the pertinent consequences of those decisions often take such a long time to emerge that making process assessments on the basis of outcomes is simply infeasible.

How are these challenges met in practice and how should they be met? Three major approaches all rest on inspection of the decision process in some manner or another:

• *Approach 1: Professional assessment.* Medical malpractice cases exemplify this approach. As suggested previously, in a typical malpractice suit, third-party medical professionals, presumed to be experts, are asked to examine the process by which the physician in question went about deciding what to do, say, through a review of medical charts (see, for instance, Caplan, Posner, & Cheney, 1991). (Some malpractice cases, of course, turn on how well the physician carried out a given treatment, not how that treatment was selected.) The requested assessment is unconstrained in the sense that the professionals who are consulted are not limited or instructed about which aspects of the process they should or should not examine; they can consider any features they personally believe to be appropriate. The consultants then report their own professional opinions about, for instance, the extent to which the physician being sued decided in a manner similar to how typical, well-trained physicians would have decided.

It is of some interest that the U.S. legal system appears reluctant to demand similar concordance with professional consensus for business decisions. For several decades, U.S. legal practice has followed the so-called "business judgment rule." This principle, derived from case law, says that key decision makers in a corporation are immune from liability as long as they make the decisions at issue "in good faith and with reasonable skill and prudence" (West's Encyclopedia of American Law, 2010). Thus, in practice, U.S. courts are disinclined to question the quality of decisions by corporations' board members, officers, and managers, provided that the decision makers had honest intentions and they were diligent.

How likely is it that the professional assessment approach yields "valid" decision process quality assessments? To the best of our knowledge, there have been no studies examining this question in which the ultimate validity criterion has been something obviously akin to the welfare of intended decision beneficiaries, for example, patient health states. However, there is a vast literature documenting an array of specific weaknesses in the human judgment processes on which professional assessment rests (e.g., Gilovich, Griffin, & Kahneman, 2002). There have been a few studies more or less directly indicating that the kinds of substantive professional experts asked to conduct professional assessments are indeed subject to those hazards (e.g., Caplan et al., 1991).

• *Approach 2: Coherence appraisal.* Suppose that a decision maker's behavior is logically inconsistent. For instance, imagine that decision maker 1 (DMR1, for short) prefers shirt A to shirt B, shirt B to shirt C, but shirt C to shirt A. That is, her preferences violate the transitivity principle, which says that, if A > B and B > C, then it must be the case that A > C, too, a principle that DMR1 has said that she would like her preferences to respect. Or consider decision maker 2 (DMR2). He says that it is more likely that both company X and company Y will enter a certain market than simply that company X will do so. That is, DMR2's judgments contradict the conjunction rule of probability theory. This principle, which DMR2 heartily endorses, says that the probability that both event E and event F will occur can be no greater than the probability that event E will occur, that is, $P(E \& F) \leq P(E)$. These are instances of "incoherence" in these people's decision making and judgment behavior. Scholars have long held that coherence is an important standard that decision makers should strive to meet (see discussions by Yates, 1990, chapters 5 and 9). By extension, one reasonable way to evaluate a decision process is to examine it for indications that it protects against incoherence, as in the case of expected utility-based decision analysis (e.g., Vlek, Edwards, Kiss, Majone, & Toda, 1984).

Why would anyone put a premium on coherence in decision making? Three reasons are discussed (see Yates, 1990, chapters 5 and 9). The first is "logical esthetics." As might well have at least partly motivated DMR1 and DMR2, the decision makers involved might simply feel uncomfortable with the very idea that their decisions violate logical principles such as transitivity and the conjunction rule of probability theory. A second potential reason for a desire to honor coherence is an expectation that coherence somehow is likely to pay off materially because the world itself is fundamentally coherent. As an example, a decision maker may cite the fact that relative frequencies of events in the real world must obey the usual rules of probability theory. Therefore, when considering drawing on the services of two potential consultants who might provide judgments to inform decisions, the consultant whose opinions are more coherent somehow should be more accurate in the long run, too. A third common argument for respecting coherence is that it protects the decision maker from being victimized in so-called "Dutch books," which are series of ruinous transactions that exploit instances of incoherence. A fanciful scenario illustrates the idea.

Recall DMR1 from the preceding coherence appraisal example. Suppose that DMR1 buys shirt C and is observed by conspiring exploiters 1 and 2, whom we can just call X1 and X2 for brevity. X1 and X2 are aware of DM1's pattern of intransitive preferences, that is, that she prefers shirt A to shirt B, shirt B to shirt C, but shirt C to shirt A. Realizing that DMR1 likes shirt B more than shirt C, X1 approaches DMR1 and easily persuades her to accept the shirt B he happens to own in exchange for DMR1's shirt C + $1, say. Knowing that DMR1 likes shirt A more than shirt B, X2 then approaches DM1 and has no trouble getting her to take his shirt A in exchange for her shirt B + $1. Next comes X1 again, who, we recall, now owns shirt C. Recognizing that DMR1 prefers shirt C to shirt A, X1 has little difficulty convincing DM1 to take his shirt C in exchange for her shirt A + $1. Note that DMR1 is right back where she was after she bought shirt C for the first time, but is now also $3 poorer. In principle, this clever but cruel cycle of transactions—a Dutch book—could continue indefinitely, with DMR1 playing the role of what is known as a "money pump."

All these arguments for respecting coherence have some appeal to most people. Nevertheless, many practically minded people consider that appeal to be limited. They wonder: "How secure should I feel that assuring coherence will help us greatly in paying the bills?" More specifically, they might well express doubt about how often the real world presents conditions that are equivalent to having exploiters such as X1 and X2 lurking in the background waiting to entangle their companies in Dutch books built on their incoherence. Unfortunately, there has been no research intended to estimate such risks.

• *Approach 3: Decomposition assessment:* Consider the development of a new airplane. How is it determined when a plane is "safe enough" for even its first test flight? Or take the case of constructing a nuclear power plant. How can regulators determine that the chances of a catastrophe are low enough to warrant allowing a reactor to begin operating, even though, in the United States, there has never been a single catastrophic incident, and, thus, track records seem meaningless?

"Probabilistic risk analyses" are an essential tool for solving such problems, and they entail the following basic steps (cf. U.S. Nuclear Regulatory Commission, 2009): First, analysts construct a model of how an event of interest might happen (e.g., life-threatening reactor core damage occurs), identifying all the significant contributors to that event—"components" of the model—and how those contributors relate to one another. Second, they evaluate the risk associated with each of those contributors. Finally, they "insert" those assessments into the model and thereby derive an assessment of the risk of the overall focal event (e.g., core damage). The approach is considered credible because, although there is no track record for the process as a whole (e.g., for a reactor with a new design), there are often extensive track records for the components (e.g., the various parts used in a reactor's construction).

This same kind of logic guides the third approach to assessing decision process quality via inspection, the "decomposition" variety. Such an approach begins with a model of the overall decision process in question. Models of this type amount to empirically documented—evidence-based—claims concerning essential elements of the decision process as a whole. In any given real-life instance, the process evaluator estimates how well each component of the process performs. To the degree that each component is concluded to be sound, the entire decision process is concluded to be sound, too. In probabilistic risk analyses in engineering, as in the design of airplanes or power plants, one of the major payoffs has little to do with overall risk assessments per se. Instead, the value is in isolating specific elements of an entire system that are too risky and thus need special attention for improvement. By analogy, the decomposed models of decision processes presumed in decomposition assessments promise the same advantages. They point toward specific things that decision managers can and should do in order to craft decision process improvements with maximum impact.

For many years, researchers have used the decomposition assessment approach in partially evaluating real-life decision processes, although without using that term. Perhaps the most obvious examples are studies of the validity of tests used in various admissions and job selection procedures (e.g., Powers, 2004). These are only partial instantiations of the approach because few such selection procedures rely solely on test scores; they invariably also involve other elements, too, such as essay reviews and interviews, whose adequacy, in practice, is often unquestioned (van der Zee, Bakker, & Bakker, 2002). Recently, though, Yates and his colleagues (e.g., Yates, 2003; Yates & Tschirhart, 2006) have sought to develop a conceptual theory of how decision making proceeds in virtually any domain, a theory that is intended to be broadly comprehensive and to point toward explanations for the effectiveness of the resulting decisions. Decomposition assessment, according to the constructs of such a theory, in principle should allow for process appraisals that are

highly informative for evaluations as well as other purposes. Most of the remainder of this chapter is devoted to that theory—the "cardinal issue perspective" (CIP) on decision making and its uses.

The Cardinal Issue Perspective on Decision Making

The CIP contends that, in some form or another, every decision problem presents the decision maker with several challenges or "issues." In this view, the decision maker's means for addressing those issues constitute the decision maker's "decision processes." It is worth noting that, sometimes, the decision maker may fail to acknowledge particular issues. In those cases, the issues are resolved by default, according to the circumstances that happen to present themselves.

A core assertion of the CIP is that most, if not all, decision successes and failures can be traced to particulars of how and how effectively the decision maker resolved one or more of the cardinal decision issues. In some respects, the CIP is most useful as a means of organizing one's thinking about decision making and decision scholarship. The latter includes the ever-growing number of specific and detailed theories and findings—"evidence"—about how people decide, which has grown markedly in recent years. The CIP can also serve as a guide for decision makers, decision managers, decision researchers, and decision educators as they go about their work:

• *Appraising decision makers and decision processes:* As just implied, the appraiser starts by determining what each cardinal issue looks like for the decisions in question. The appraiser then characterizes how well the decision maker or the decision process addresses (or addressed) each of those issues. Those elemental assessments constitute the real substance of the appraisal per se, for instance, for a physician's treatment decision or the adequacy of a company's process for choosing suppliers.

• *Guiding major decision making efforts:* When the stakes are high, as were those surrounding the Northern Manufacturing Lincoln facility, it is especially important that decisions be made effectively. Decision managers in such situations do well to guide their efforts according to checklists specialized to the particular decisions at hand. Thus, for example, as in decision process appraisals, such a checklist requires the identification of the form taken by each issue. It then demands that the decision manager assure that measures are taken to make certain that that issue is addressed adequately.

• *Establishing decision research priorities:* A striking and reliable occurrence often occurs as a by-product of systematic decision management efforts, particularly ones guided by the CIP: the limitations of current knowledge about decision making become glaringly obvious. These gaps point directly to research efforts whose products have high practical and purely scholarly impact—something every researcher craves.

Let us turn to details. Figure 12.1 provides a heuristic that makes it easier for practitioners to discuss and use the CIP to manage decisions in an evidence-based way. We will refer to this depiction repeatedly as the occasion requires. A quick overview is useful. The figure's first level highlights the "point" of decision making, as implicit in the definition of a "decision": the welfare ("interests") of the intended beneficiaries of a decision as well as the satisfaction ("values") of those people. Recall that in the case of the Lincoln facility decision problem, the intended beneficiaries included Northern Manufacturing's customers and shareholders as well as the decision makers, including executive vice president June Ward. The next level in the

schematic highlights the fact that the beneficiaries' welfare and satisfaction are products of not only the decision but also "Other Contributors" sometimes considered unrelated to the decision in question, for example, economic conditions for the Lincoln decision. In practice, we normally de-emphasize "Other Contributors," because, typically, one can legitimately argue that other conditions ought to be taken into account in a truly comprehensive and sound decision process. For instance, the Northern Manufacturing executive board arguably could (and should) have factored potentially changing economic conditions into their analysis of the Lincoln decision problem.

The middle portion of Figure 12.1, the "Decision Processes" section, is where the work of arriving at a decision takes place. Observe that the 10 cardinal decision issues are partitioned into three categories. Those categories correspond to phases that occur in every decision episode, in some way or another, whether acknowledged by the decision maker or not. Issues in the "Preliminaries" phase concern preparation for what many consider to be the primary tasks of working through a decision problem. The issues in the "Core" directly concern how those

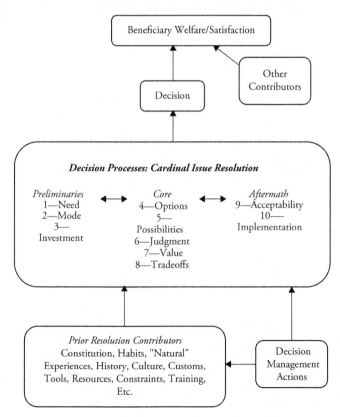

Fig. 12.1. Key elements of the cardinal decision issue perspective.

primary tasks are accomplished. The "Aftermath" issues are about events that normally occur after the decision has been made. The phases are depicted in an orderly sequence: Preliminaries → Core → Aftermath. In real life, however, the activities entailed in those phases can recycle and recur for some time. For instance, implementation difficulties in the aftermath phase might easily induce the decision maker to begin the entire decision process anew, from scratch.

The bottom part of Figure 12.1 highlights the fact that decision processes do not acquire their character arbitrarily. With one exception, "Resolution Contributors" encompass all the current and prior forces that shape the decision processes applied to the problem at hand, for example, the tools available to the decision maker, the decision maker's biological constitution (e.g., temperament or health state), and the decision maker's culture. The exception singled out in this discussion consists of the actions taken by the decision managers on the scene. Observe that some of those actions are directed toward what the decision maker does in the current moment, how the decision maker copes with the cardinal issues as they present themselves "right now." Other decision manager actions are more indirect. That is, they are applied to "Prior Resolution Contributors," which, in turn, help shape how the decision makers deal with various cardinal issues for any number of decision problems that might come along in the future. The provision of tools, resources, and learning experiences is a good example.

In the brief survey that follows, we sketch and discuss each cardinal issue. First, after its label, the focus of that issue is identified. Then the issue is articulated in the voice of a "generic" collective decision maker, such as a committee. We next indicate how that issue translates into specific missions the decision maker and the decision manager might seek to carry out. As the reader will recall from our discussion of the decision manager's portfolio, decision managers exercise their influence in several ways. The specific missions assumed here focus on facilitating the collaborative decision making of a number of people, such as an executive board. We also offer a brief example of the kinds of insights and evidence the literature offers as guidance for principles for how one might proceed with accomplishing those missions. To make things concrete, in every instance we make reference to how things might have appeared in our fictional example of Northern Manufacturing's decision to build its Lincoln facility.

Issues in the Preliminaries
CARDINAL ISSUE 1—"NEED": DETERMINING WHETHER A DECISION EFFORT GETS STARTED

In the Decision Maker's Voice: "Is something happening that merits a decision on our part?" For example, a member of Northern Manufacturing's executive board at some point might well have observed: "For some time now, incoming orders have been growing so large that we've had to run overtime to keep up just halfway. Is that all right, or should we be considering other measures?"

The Decision Maker's Mission: Determine whether current or impending circumstances warrant launching an effort to decide how to deal with those circumstances. Thus, members of the Northern executive board, like the one discussed earlier, sometimes notice situations that seem potentially important to the company's interests—either threats or opportunities. If they are deemed to be real and significant enough, they spur efforts by the committee to make decisions that address them. That is how Northern, in due course, formed the committee chaired by June Ward and eventually launched full-scale deliberations about whether to build a new facility. Suppose that no one on the committee had ever noticed anything suggesting a threat or opportunity that might be addressed by a new-facility decision. Then, there would have been no discussion of such a decision and, of course, no decision to build a new facility, and no new facility.

The Decision Manager's Mission: Somehow assure that the decision makers recognize true threats to the interests and values of the people for whom they are responsible—their "charges" and prospective decision beneficiaries. The same should be done for opportunities, all the while assuring that the decision makers do not make decisions addressing what prove to be illusory—false threats and opportunities. When an organization faces actual threats, it has a "need" to deal with them, and when real opportunities arise, there is a "need" to exploit them, too. In turn, under those conditions, it makes sense to say that the organization has a "need" to make decisions that address those threats or opportunities. On the other hand, when decision makers mistakenly make decisions focusing on misleading "phantom" threats and opportunities, there are several reasons that this is a bad thing, including the fact that it wastes decision making resources. So, at Northern Manufacturing, presumably, some or all the executive board members assume responsibility for discriminating true from false threats and opportunities for the company and inspiring decision making efforts only for the former. Presumably, one or more of those individuals perceived such a threat or opportunity within the repeated large orders the company struggled to meet.

Illustrative Insight and Evidence. Research on "regulatory focus" has shown that there are consistent differences among people in their relative concern with the presence or absence of positive versus negative occurrences (Higgins, 1997). "Promotion-focused" individuals have the former emphasis, whereas "prevention-focused" ones are preoccupied with the latter. It is, therefore, reasonable to expect that promotion-focused people would be particularly sensitive to opportunities that might warrant decision efforts to exploit them. Conversely, prevention-focused people's attention should be especially sensitive to threats that might merit decision making consideration. Studies have also shown that individuals who differ according to regulatory focus also differ in the level of detail at which they examine their surroundings (e.g., Förster & Higgins, 2005). Specifically, there is evidence that people with strong prevention foci are highly sensitive to small details, whereas those who emphasize promotion are more attuned to broad features of their situations—the "big picture," as it were. Findings like these suggest that a decision manager would do well to take regulatory focus into account when seeking to assure that the organization's decision makers adequately address the need issue. Thus, the chair of Northern Manufacturing's executive board would be wise to explicitly solicit board members' observations about impending threats and opportunities to the company. In addition, though, the chair could also profit from a strategy that seeks to recruit a board that includes a mix of individuals who are promotion focused and others who are prevention focused. In addition, the chair should be prepared to develop the facilitation skills that are required to manage meetings among people who have such markedly different perspectives and emphases—meetings that can be highly contentious and unpleasant.

CARDINAL ISSUE 2—"MODE": SETTLING ON WHO (OR WHAT) BECOMES INVOLVED IN MAKING THE DECISION, WHAT THEIR ROLES ARE, AND HOW THEY APPROACH THEIR WORK

In the Decision Maker's Voice: "What 'decision modes' (qualitatively distinct ways of deciding) should we apply in this situation? Specifically, which people (or devices) should we have working on this decision problem? What roles should they play, and what approaches should they employ?" At Northern Manufacturing,

at some point, someone on the executive board asked: "How many board members, and which ones, should we ask to develop recommendations concerning what, if anything, the executive board should do about our difficulties keeping up with the demand for certain components?" The eventual committee chair, executive vice president June Ward, had to consider questions such as the kinds of consultants and analytical tools, including devices such as computer programs, the committee should employ.

The Decision Maker's Mission: Match the vital aspects of the decision problem to the available people or devices that are best equipped to assure that the required tasks are accomplished most effectively. Thus, the Northern Manufacturing executive board had to think through the mode "metadecision" (decision about deciding) of picking a committee to develop proposals for solving the company's component demand problem and then to designate June Ward as that group's leader. The board fulfilled this mission well to the extent that it got every one of the cardinal decision issues "covered" by the right people and the right tools.

The Decision Manager's Mission: Verify that the authorized or assigned parties (people or devices) are capable of rendering a sufficiently high-quality decision solely by themselves. If they are not, then see that the at-risk decision tasks are reassigned such that they can, in fact, be carried out effectively and efficiently. At Northern Manufacturing, ideally someone on the executive board took on the responsibility of determining what capabilities—human and otherwise—were required to achieve reasonable assurance that the component-demand decision problem could be solved well. The appointment of June Ward and the rest of her committee was part of the outcome of that exercise—for better or worse.

Illustrative Insights and Evidence. Alternative decision modes can be distinguished at several levels (Yates, 2003), as suggested by the "mode tree" shown in Figure 12.2. First is the distinction between "individual" and "collective" modes, that is, whether one person or more than one person, such as a committee, has the authority to make a decision. As implied in Figure 12.2, deliberation of the mode issue begins with some prior "history" in which someone designated who has the authority or responsibility for making the decision at hand. At Northern Manufacturing, its founding board of directors might have established that the executive board was responsible for making facilities decisions and the tradition has simply continued. In any given

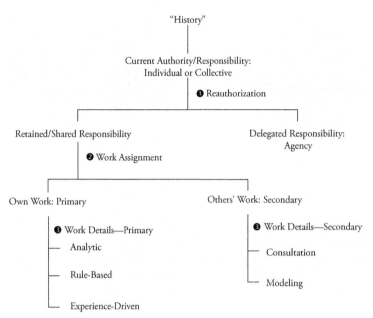

"History"

Current Authority/Responsibility:
Individual or Collective

❶ Reauthorization

Retained/Shared Responsibility

❷ Work Assignment

Delegated Responsibility:
Agency

Own Work: Primary

❸ Work Details—Primary
— Analytic
— Rule-Based
— Experience-Driven

Others' Work: Secondary

❸ Work Details—Secondary
— Consultation
— Modeling

Fig. 12.2. The decision mode tree.

situation, the historically determined authority or responsibility might be changed; hence the first mode choice point, ❶ *Reauthorization*. There, the originally authorized decision makers would retain at least a partial role in the decision making effort—Retained/Shared Responsibility in Figure 12.2—or that responsibility could be "delegated" to someone (or something) else, an "agent." License is granted to a decision agent to decide as the agent sees fit, without involvement or interference from the principal who awarded that agency.

At the second mode choice point, ❷ *Work Assignment*, work required in the decision making effort is either carried out by the authorized or responsible decision maker, in modes described as "Primary," or else they are assigned to other parties, in which cases the modes are referred to as "Secondary." Particular primary decision modes, especially at the individual level, are a major subject of contemporary decision scholarship, and, thus, they deserve special attention.

Three broad classes of primary modes, selected at the ❸ *Work Details—Primary* choice point, can be recognized. First is "Analytic" decision making, in which the decision maker deliberately tries to think through what makes sense to do in the given situation, what most people think of first when they hear the expression *decision making*. A high-stakes, largely unique decision, such as whether Northern Manufacturing should build the Lincoln facility, would certainly be made analytically. The second primary mode consists of "Rule-Based" decision making. This mode entails

rules of the form "If conditions C1, C2,…hold, then take action A." Every organization must solve at least some of its recurring decision problems via such rules; otherwise, it simply could not function. ("Paralysis by analysis," as it is sometimes described, would set in.) Consider, for instance, the criteria that are used by most organizations to winnow down large initial pools of job candidates into smaller pools that are examined more carefully and analytically.

Finally, there is "Experience-Driven" decision making (cf. Klein, 1993). The qualifier "experience" is meant in two distinct but sometimes related senses. The first implies that the decision making in question rests more or less directly on learning. One such example is "automatic" decision making, such as that involved in maneuvering a vehicle into traffic on the highway. Such automaticity evolves gradually, as a result of repetitions, to the point where the decision maker makes the decisions virtually effortlessly, uncontrollably, and outside awareness. The second sense of "experience" implicates the decision maker's reliance on feelings, conscious or otherwise (consider the "somatic marker hypothesis," Bechara, Damasio, Tranel, & Damasio, 1997). So-called intuitive decision making is an illustration (see, for example, Potworowski, 2009). In contemporary scholarship, experience-driven decision making is sometimes characterized as an instance of "System 1" thinking, whereas analytic and rule-based decision making are described as cases of "System 2" thinking (Evans, 2008), with the former being considered more primitive in evolutionary terms.

Primary decision mode distinctions have considerable decision management significance. Suppose, as is common, that assembly line supervisors at Northern Manufacturing assume that, if line employees are making too many operational decision errors, it is because they are not trying hard enough to decide properly. Implicit is the additional assumption that the employees' decisions are being made analytically. Many such decisions are likely to be experience driven, even automatic. If that is, indeed, the case, then exhortations or incentives to work harder at deciding well would be useless. Instead, the first sensible (actually, necessary) task for the supervisors as decision managers would be to disrupt the employees' faulty, uncontrolled decision routines and only *then* to seek to replace them with new, better ones.

Effectively, three varieties of secondary decision making are commonly recognized, too. We have already discussed "Agency," in which the authorized decision maker delegates complete authority and responsibility for the decision problem to the agent. Such would have been the case had the Northern Manufacturing executive board completely relinquished to June Ward's committee its authority to decide what to do about the company's component demand problem. In contrast, in "Consultation," the authorized decision maker retains responsibility for making the ultimate decision. Nevertheless, one or more "consultants" perform some of the work involved in making that decision. This could include arriving at certain essential judgments, such as what future product demand levels will be. Or it could entail making specific recommendations for what the overall decision ought to be, as was the case with June Ward's actual committee. Finally, there is "modeling," whereby the decision maker pursues the same or an analogous course of action that some other decision maker selected in a similar situation, without examining the details carefully. This is common in some cases of casual benchmarking, whereby companies adopt the practices of industry leaders uncritically because they are, after all, the leaders.

It is useful to recognize that, in actual practice, decision makers often use several different decision modes in the same decision episode. In effect, they apply what can be called "hybrid" modes. Such is the case when a decision maker decides mainly analytically but relies on consultants—human and or otherwise—to perform certain elements of the decision work, such as generating alternatives or formulating relevant judgments.

There is considerable current interest in secondary decision modes, such as advice giving and advice taking. A common finding in such research is that advisors often recommend actions for others that are systematically and reliably different from actions they would take themselves. Stone and Allgaier (2008) showed that an important driver of such differences is the nature of social norms in the situation. For instance, if there is a local norm for risk seeking, then advisors will tend to recommend decisions that are riskier than options the advisors themselves would pursue. Suppose that there is such a norm on the Northern Manufacturing executive board. Then we could expect June Ward's committee to recommend component demand proposals that entail more risk than the committee would consider acceptable if they made the final decision on their own. As a good decision manager, therefore, the chair of the executive board would be wise to acknowledge this bias in the recommendations the board receives and to make sure that the board compensates appropriately in making its decisions.

CARDINAL ISSUE 3—"INVESTMENT": GATHERING AND ALLOCATING THE RESOURCES DEVOTED TO THE PROCESS OF MAKING THE DECISION

In the Decision Maker's Voice: "In order to make this decision well, what do we have to spend on the process, and on what, exactly?" Thus, after June Ward was selected to lead the component demand committee of the Northern Manufacturing executive board, her colleagues on the board asked her: "So, what do you need?"

The Decision Maker's Mission: Make sure that the key elements of the decision process receive the resources, material and otherwise, that they require to yield an adequate decision, but no more than that. At Northern Manufacturing, June Ward had to determine what she and her colleagues on the component demand committee needed in order to craft their recommendations to the executive board. At the same time, she also had to assure that their efforts were not overly costly, for instance, undercutting committee members' other responsibilities to the company.

The Decision Manager's Mission: Ensure that the decision makers have the resources—material and otherwise—needed to carry out the tasks required for a sound decision, but that resources beyond that are not wasted. Clearly, this mission speaks most directly to the "Providing Resources" component of the decision management portfolio (Table 12.1) and the

"Process Costs and Benefits" dimension of decision quality (Table 12.3). At Northern Manufacturing, June Ward ideally should develop a plan for assuring that her committee adequately covers every cardinal decision issue when crafting its component demand decision recommendations. She should then determine what is essential for doing that, for example, the minimum number of committee members possessing particular skills and qualities. This is what guides her response to the executive board's question, "What do you need?"

Illustrative Insight and Evidence. People differ in their indecisiveness, that is, whether they tend to decide slowly or are prone to changing their minds (cf. Potworowski, 2010). This has decision process cost implications in several ways. First, by definition, indecisive people take a long time to come to their final decisions, if they get to that point at all, and this translates directly into financial costs (which are often unrecognized). The more time a person devotes to making any one decision, the less time she has to devote to her other duties. The same is true of making decisions and then later changing them. These effects snowball in group decision making, where several people, not just one person, are prevented from getting on with their obligations elsewhere. Moreover, when decisions are part of a sequence of decisions needed to get an organizational initiative underway, indecisiveness ultimately delays the implementation of that initiative. There are nonmaterial costs, too. There are indications that indecisive individuals experience anxiety when making decisions and that decision making is especially unpleasant for them (Potworowski, 2010). Observations such as these imply that a decision manager, such as June Ward at Northern Manufacturing, would do well to take people's apparent indecisiveness into account in assembling decision making groups and in coordinating the activities of those groups.

Issues in the Core
CARDINAL ISSUE 4—"OPTIONS": ASSEMBLING THE POOL OF ALTERNATIVES THAT ARE CONSIDERED

In the Decision Maker's Voice: "What are reasonable alternative actions we should consider as potential solutions to this decision problem we have?" From one perspective, addressing this issue was the Northern Manufacturing executive board's charge to June Ward's committee: "Provide us with recommendations for what we might do to deal with our component demand problem." (The committee was

expected to provide rationales for their recommendations, too.)

The Decision Maker's Mission: Assemble a collection of alternative actions—a "consideration set"—that includes at least one that would be a suitable solution to the decision problem at hand. At the same time, though, constrain the size and character of that collection in order to minimize deliberation costs and risks. Thus, June Ward's committee set out to employ any means at its disposal to bring to mind reasonable approaches to Northern Manufacturing's difficulties keeping up with demand for particular components. Yet, they also sought to avoid being overwhelmed with the task of appraising options that had little chance of being "the one." In the committee's role as consultants, the aim was to resolve the options issue for the executive board as the decision maker. That is, their goal was to provide the board with a set of alternatives that: (1) was small so as to not overburden the board with the chore of appraising the alternatives, (2) consisted of alternatives such that each was likely to yield at least reasonably favorable outcomes, and (3) would not tempt the board to select options that were superficially attractive but were actually "bad news" for the company.

The Decision Manager's Mission: Check and see that the decision makers are employing effective methods for identifying or creating small collections of alternatives, each of which has good odds of adequately solving the decision problem. Ideally, those options should also facilitate the process of appraising all options and should certainly avoid compromising the decision maker's ability to perform such appraisals. Therefore, an important part of June Ward's job as committee chair was to provide committee members with techniques that are known to be effective at producing small but promising option pools for problems similar to Northern Manufacturing's component demand challenge.

Illustrative Insight and Evidence. Many methods for addressing the options issue are discussed these days. The options issue is a popular subject, especially for companies hungry for profitable innovations. Consider, for instance, approaches such as "co-creation" (Ramaswamy & Gouillart, 2010), whereby, in effect, companies and customers collaborate to design products that serve the personal desires of individual consumers. However, almost undoubtedly, brainstorming remains *the* most widely used social technique for generating decision alternatives. The approach retains its popularity despite decades of research contesting its efficacy relative to that of the "nominal group technique" (NGT).

In conventional brainstorming, several people meet face-to-face and work collaboratively to identify or create what are hopefully innovative and viable options for the problem in question. They do so following a small set of simple rules, including a prohibition against criticizing one another's efforts and an appeal to try to "piggyback" or build on others' ideas. If they were applying the NGT, the same individuals would each work alone (and might not even know of one another's existence, thereby constituting a "group" in name only). Each of those individuals would be implored to work hard to try to come up with good ideas. It seems that most people expect that, if brainstorming and the NGT were compared head-to-head, brainstorming would win. However, decades of research (perhaps best illustrated by the classic studies of Diehl & Stroebe, 1987) have demonstrated convincingly the opposite, namely that the NGT tends to yield more and better alternatives. This happens for several reasons. One is that, despite the instructions for participants to avoid being critical of one another, in a brainstorming group, group members are often apprehensive about being seen as stupid. So, it appears that a decision manager seeking lots of creative options would be well advised to suggest that decision makers pursue the NGT approach. It is worth noting, though, that a common result of applying either brainstorming or the NGT is that they typically produce many low-quality options as well as good ones. Thus, if such approaches are adopted, they need to be accompanied by highly efficient screening procedures too.

CARDINAL ISSUE 5—"POSSIBILITIES": IDENTIFYING OBVIOUS AND NONOBVIOUS POTENTIAL OCCURRENCES—ONES THAT MATTER

In the Decision Maker's Voice: "Suppose we were to pursue this course of action. What events—especially nonobvious ones—could occur which, in combination with this action, would result in consequences that are significant for key parties?" June Ward's component demand committee created by the Northern Manufacturing executive board considered a host of alternative actions. It was obvious to the group that future demand for the components in question would matter to just about everyone involved, regardless of the action pursued. However, other, not-so-obvious events could matter, too, and if they were overlooked yet actually materialized, then the company would be caught painfully unawares, "blindsided" by them. Hence the committee's

question to itself: "What specific nonobvious things could happen (or be true) that would affect the wisdom of pursuing each of these courses of action we are pondering?"

The Decision Maker's Mission: Bring to the surface obvious and, most importantly, nonobvious potential occurrences which, if they actually came about, would matter greatly to particular parties, perhaps depending on the course of action pursued. For the Northern Manufacturing component demand committee, the task was to somehow force themselves to see beyond what was immediately apparent to them, to recognize obscure possibilities whose actual occurrences would greatly affect the sensibleness of options, such as building the Lincoln facility. Although that did not actually happen, a competitor's technological breakthrough that renders Northern's components immediately obsolete would be an example of such a possibility.

The Decision Manager's Mission: Assure that the decision makers employ procedures and tools that have good chances of bringing to the surface readily apparent and especially not-so-apparent decision significant potential occurrences. Thus, it was incumbent upon chair June Ward to make certain that her committee members, at minimum, actually *tried* to bring to mind nonobvious potential future events that would affect the wisdom of the alternative actions they considered. In addition, though, it was in her (and, more importantly, the company's) interests to steer them through procedures that reduced the odds of blindsiding. One known contributor to "possibility neglect" is inexperience in the pertinent domain. Recognition of this fact would have led June Ward to make certain that her committee discreetly consulted with a wide spectrum of local people in each of the communities deemed to be serious contenders for a new Northern Manufacturing facility.

Illustrative Insight and Evidence. As suggested earlier, there are myriad reasons that decision makers sometimes overlook significant potential events associated with their options. One is "stress," an unpleasant emotional state instigated by perceived threats to one's welfare (Yates, 1990, p. 376). A long-established, reliable effect of stress on cognition is that it restricts the scope of attention (see Yates, Klatzky, & Young, 1995, for a review, and Booth & Sharma, 2009, for a recent illustration). There have been numerous demonstrations of such effects on people's decision making. One is possibility neglect. That is, stress can be expected to reduce a decision maker's chances of bringing to mind particular nonobvious decision-relevant occurrences, thereby increasing the chances of blindsiding. It is easy to imagine circumstances in which this can happen, as during, say, a catastrophic industrial accident. Any given employee under such conditions is likely to have a significantly narrowed scope of attention. Thus, a good decision manager on the scene would find it beneficial to attempt to counteract such effects by relying more heavily than usual on collaborative deliberation of alternative actions, for example, through structured discussion. That is because, although any single member of the collective has a high probability of overlooking any particular consideration, there should still be a much smaller chance that *every* member will.

CARDINAL ISSUE 6—"JUDGMENT": ARRIVING AT OPINIONS AS TO WHETHER PARTICULAR RELEVANT EVENTS ACTUALLY WOULD OCCUR

In the Decision Maker's Voice: "If this event actually happens, then the action we have chosen would be really good (or bad) for us. But would it happen? What are the chances?" In the Northern Manufacturing case, building the Lincoln facility would be highly beneficial for the company if demand for Northern's components turned out being high enough, more than 100,000 units per month for at least three years. Hence, at the time the decision was being deliberated, the key question was whether demand would be maintained above that critical level.

The Decision Maker's Mission: Formulate or otherwise acquire accurate and inexpensive judgments for the various occurrences that matter to the decision problem on the table. In the current illustration, a most critical task of the decision makers on June Ward's committee was to acquire an accurate prediction—a judgment—of demand for the components that would be produced at the prospective Lincoln facility. If predicted demand were high, the decision makers would be inclined to decide in favor of a new facility to meet that demand, but if that prediction proved to be overly optimistic, then such a decision could prove disastrous.

The Decision Manager's Mission: Appraise the likely accuracy and cost of the requisite judgments currently available to the decision makers. If those judgments appear to be too inaccurate or costly, help the decision makers identify better judgment sources or methods. There are actually many different ways of obtaining judgments to inform decisions, approaches that are sometimes called "judgment modes," in parallel to the broader decision modes discussed in connection with the mode issue, sketched in Figure 12.2 (Yates & Angott, 2009). In one example of a judgment

mode, the decision makers rely on judgments essentially purchased from consultants considered to be experts. In another, companies rely heavily on well-established statistical (e.g., time series) techniques for making demand forecasts from, say, one month to the next (Makridakis, Wheelwright, & Hyndman, 1998). These methods essentially amount to using past occurrences of similar events as predictors of future ones, for example, through extrapolation. Rightly and sometimes wrongly, decision makers often believe that the future will be subject to forces significantly different from previous ones. They, therefore, feel justified in adjusting the statistically derived predictions in the direction of their personal, psychologically driven judgments of what the future holds (Dawes, 1979).

Illustrative Insight and Evidence. More often than many people realize, the judgments people use in arriving at their decisions come from other people—or even devices, such as computer programs—rather than solely from themselves. Thus, when June Ward's committee on the Northern Manufacturing executive board seeks accurate forecasts to inform their decision about whether to recommend building a new facility, we could expect them to go beyond the committee members themselves. Ideally, they should pay attention to the judgments of potential consultants, internal or external, who have good accuracy track records and ignore the assessments of consultants who do not. However, therein lies a significant problem. Studies have shown that people's subjective notions of judgment expertise deviate systematically from what is required by established formal accuracy indicators (Yates, Price, Lee, & Ramirez, 1996). For example, at the expense of other, more defensible, and evidence-based, considerations, decision makers are often inclined to rely on how confident their potential informants appear (Price & Stone, 2004). This suggests that a decision manager, such as June Ward in her role as chair of the component demand committee at Northern Manufacturing, could provide a valuable service by putting in place routines whereby potential judgment consultants' track records are vetted for accuracy per objective methods rather than easily faked mere images of competence.

It is worth noting that the judgment issue is at the core of most calls for evidence-based practice of all kinds. Consider the case of medicine, where such calls sparked the current emphasis on evidence (Sackett, Richardson, Rosenburg, & Haynes, 1997). The impetus for those calls came from instances in which practicing physicians judged that particular treatments were in the best interests of their patients, yet those judgments were contrary to the available or eventually emerging scientific data. Advocates of evidence-based practice in management can similarly point to numerous instances in which managers routinely take actions based on efficacy judgments that are at odds with scientific facts. Continued reliance on unstructured job interviews, mentioned earlier, provides an illustration (van der Zee et al., 2002).

CARDINAL ISSUE 7—"VALUE": ANTICIPATING HOW MUCH KEY PARTIES WOULD LIKE OR DISLIKE VARIOUS OUTCOMES AND OTHER ASPECTS OF THE DECISION SITUATION

In the Decision Maker's Voice: "Would they (and even I) like or dislike that if it actually happened? How much?" At Northern Manufacturing, there were three major alternative locations for a new facility, including Bartonville, the eventual site of the Lincoln facility. In each location, June Ward's committee crafted a request for tax abatements from the local authorities as incentives for Northern to build in that community, with specific job-creation guarantees. In every instance, before proceeding, Ms. Ward and her colleagues asked: "How would they feel about this proposal? Would they welcome it wholeheartedly, or would they be insulted and, therefore, resist further overtures from Northern?"

The Decision Maker's Mission: Make accurate judgments of how key parties to the decision problem— perhaps including the decision makers themselves— would feel about potential outcomes and other facts surrounding the eventual decision. Framed this way, it is apparent that the value issue is a special case of the judgment issue. It is worth distinguishing from the general case because the focus is on what makes decision problems themselves special—the fact that what person X likes, say, a particular color for a house, might easily be abhorred by person Y (perhaps person X's spouse). Valuation judgments are also special because they often are really hard to make accurately, and deceptively so. That is, people frequently think that it is easy to anticipate people's feelings (especially their own) when it can be anything but easy. On June Ward's Northern Manufacturing component demand committee, when they were planning their strategy for negotiating tax abatements, one of the group's chores was anticipating local officials' reactions to alternative proposals the company might offer. Among other reasons, this was a hard problem because none of the committee members knew any of the local officials personally.

The Decision Manager's Mission: As in the case of judgment more generally, anticipate the accuracy and cost of currently used valuation judgment sources and techniques. Then, to the extent that they are deficient, encourage and assist the decision makers in applying better approaches. So, in meetings in which the Northern Manufacturing component demand committee was trying to anticipate local authorities' reactions to tax abatement overtures, June Ward ideally would have first sought to gain a fix on how good the committee itself was at making such assessments, relative to other potential sources. Then, to the extent that there were more accurate and cost-effective alternatives, she would have done well to steer the members in their direction.

Illustrative Insight and Evidence. Consumer-focused marketing research provides excellent illustrations of often well-reasoned approaches to resolving the value issue as it arises in marketing decision problems. Among the most popular methods are various survey techniques and more laboratory-like conjoint analysis methods. It is noteworthy that such methods typically rely heavily on people's assessments of their own values (e.g., "I would really like that product and, therefore, I would buy it"). A popular recent topic in valuation judgment research focuses on "affective forecasting," which addresses people's predictions of their own feelings (Wilson & Gilbert, 2005). A key finding in such work is the "impact bias," the tendency for people to overestimate the intensity and longevity of their emotional reactions to events that occur to them, for example, being promoted or being denied a promotion. To compensate for this bias, it would make sense for a decision manager to moderate actions predicated on people's self-reported expectations of how much they would like or dislike certain experiences, particularly ones for which they have little direct prior familiarity. That is, they would avoid "going out on a limb."

CARDINAL ISSUE 8—"TRADEOFFS": ARRIVING AT A FINAL DECISION, RECOGNIZING THAT EVERY ALTERNATIVE HAS BOTH STRENGTHS AND WEAKNESSES, THEREFORE, APPEARING TO DEMAND TRADEOFFS

In the Decision Maker's Voice: "Every one of our options has drawbacks as well as advantages relative to its competitors. So which of those courses of action should receive our commitment; which should we pursue?" When June Ward was deciding on the last person to invite to join her component demand committee at Northern Manufacturing, she winnowed the options down to two: Joe Wilson and Floyd Chambers. Then, the decision problem got really tough. Wilson was more experienced and broadly knowledgeable than Chambers, but Chambers had the edge in terms of technical expertise. She wondered: "Whom should I pick?"

The Decision Maker's Mission: Determine which alternative course of action should (or at least will) receive the decision maker's commitment despite its comparative weaknesses. For her committee, June Ward's task was to figure out whether it made sense to select Joe Wilson and his experience and broad knowledge while sacrificing Floyd Chambers's technical expertise, or the opposite. Three major classes of tradeoff dilemmas occur. First are *outcome × outcome dilemmas*, as in the case of Wilson versus Chambers. In such instances, in the decision maker's mind, at least, the outcomes in question are known for sure. For example, for June Ward, there was no doubt that Wilson had more experience than Chambers. Then there are *outcome × uncertainty dilemmas*. Eventually, Northern Manufacturing was faced with, in effect, the gamble described in our earlier discussion of the judgment issue. If demand for particular Northern components was sustained above a specified threshold (an uncertain event), then building a new facility would be advantageous for the company (a very favorable outcome), but if that failed to happen (also an uncertain occurrence), then the company's interests would be seriously compromised (an unfavorable outcome). Finally, there are *outcome × time dilemmas*. In a conceptually simple illustration, Judy Jones is confronted with a choice between two assignments in her company. On the one hand, she could accept a moderately attractive assignment that makes good use of her strengths in experience and broad knowledge, right now. On the other, she could take what is essentially a grueling technical training assignment that would shore up her technical capabilities but would pay off only after a couple of years. Typically, decision makers recognize and confront tradeoff dilemmas after they have done all their other thinking about the decision problem at hand, and after resolving these dilemmas, they take the plunge and decide; they commit to one particular course of action.

The Decision Manager's Mission: Ensure that the decision makers are skilled in the use of defensible methods and tools (e.g., software) for resolving tradeoff dilemmas. This includes understanding the methods' rationales and the benefits they can and cannot assure. Tradeoff dilemmas almost certainly have been studied longer and more intensively than any other topic in the history of decision research, and that scholarship has led to numerous tools that are standard fare in business schools and actual business practice. For instance, outcome × outcome tradeoffs are the province of multiple criterion methods, such as multiattribute utility theory (MAUT) procedures (e.g., von Winterfeldt & Edwards, 1988), and also the analytic hierarchy process (AHP) (e.g., Saaty, 1980). Standard expected utility (EU) theory-based forms of decision analysis focus on outcome × uncertainty tradeoffs, as do (implicitly) various portfolio management procedures (e.g., Winston & Albright, 2009). Net present value (NPV) techniques are standard tools for evaluating alternative investment opportunities whose cash flow streams differ—classic outcome × time tradeoff challenges (e.g., Higgins, 1998). Unfortunately, all too often, each of these methods is applied uncritically. This is perhaps because they appear to provide unambiguous and authoritative answers to tough questions, although sometimes they do not. Moreover, the instructions given for the methods rarely even discuss how the decision maker can tell when and whether the needed tradeoffs are being made properly. A good decision manager contributes to the company's welfare by encouraging and guiding the requisite critical thinking.

Illustrative Insight and Evidence. Extensive scholarship on tradeoffs continues. However, it has changed in focus somewhat. One of the most interesting and practically significant areas of work concerns "coherence shifting." MAUT analyses are used in some form or another in many arenas, from product design routines to product recommender systems, such as those at *Consumer Reports,* to employee performance appraisals. The decision maker does the following: (1) Identifies several options, none of which "dominates" any of the others. That is, none is uniformly superior to any of the rest (e.g., Bartonville, Lexington, and New Stanton as potential sites for the prospective Lincoln facility). (2) Specifies the important dimensions that distinguish the alternatives (e.g., distance from major markets, tax rates, employee quality of life). (3) Indicates the relative importance of the dimensions in terms of weights. And (4) assesses the standing of each alternative along each dimension. Every alternative is assigned a score that is the sum of each dimensional assessment for that alternative multiplied by that dimension's importance weight: $S = w_1 \times a_1 + w_2 \times a_2 + \ldots + w_K \times a_K$. The choice rule for MAUT, which implicitly makes the required outcome × outcome tradeoffs, specifies that the alternative that has the best score is the one that should be selected.

It has always been assumed that the decision maker's importance weights and feature assessments are fixed "truths" that are to be discovered during the analysis, thereby pointing toward wise choices. This assumption prohibits the decision maker from any sort of fiddling around with the weights and assessments ("cheating?"). However, for the past several years, there have been persistent indications that, left to their own devices, as their deliberations proceed, decision makers reliably (and perhaps nonconsciously) shift the importance they attach to various dimensions and also their perceptions of the standing of the alternatives along those dimensions (e.g., Simon, Krawczyk, & Holyoak, 2004). Those shifts are "coherent" in a particular way. Suppose that, early in the deliberations, one alternative, say, alternative A, becomes slightly favored over its competitors, even if for arbitrary or chance reasons, for example, alternative A just happens to be seen first. Then, as the deliberations progress, the decision maker comes to feel that the dimensions on which alternative A is strong become more important and those on which it is weak are seen as more trivial. Similar shifts occur with the assessments. Thus, as the deliberations move to the choice point, all considerations become more and more consistent—coherent—with the selection of alternative A.

Exactly why coherence shifting occurs is the subject of current fundamental research, but the practical, including decision management, implications seem apparent. Unless somehow prevented from doing so, decision makers will allow their perceptions of alternatives and their senses of dimensional importance to be co-opted by their initial, possibly ill-founded intuitions. In principle, at least, tools such as formal MAUT procedures, perhaps applied under the guidance of a seasoned decision manager, seem capable of counteracting such effects.

Issues in the Aftermath
CARDINAL ISSUE 9—"ACCEPTABILITY": ACHIEVING KEY PARTIES' ACCEPTANCE OF THE DECISION THAT WAS MADE AS WELL AS THE PROCEDURE USED TO MAKE THAT DECISION

In the Decision Maker's Voice: "How can we cope with or, ideally, preclude negative reactions to our decision—and how we made it—by key parties, especially powerful ones?" Eventually, June Ward and her component demand committee settled on several alternative actions they were prepared to recommend to the entire Northern Manufacturing executive board. One of the committee's greatest fears was that key executive board members would dismiss one or more of the recommendations out of hand and perhaps even ridicule the committee's work. (Such occurrences were not unknown in the company.) The committee, therefore, wondered how it could prevent that from happening.

The Decision Maker's Mission: Make the decision "iron-clad," unlikely to be resisted or sabotaged by key parties because they object to the decision itself or to how it was reached. Thus, June Ward and her colleagues on the component demand committee set out to take actions that would reduce the odds that Northern Manufacturing executive board members would be dissatisfied with the committee's proposals or how they arrived at those proposals.

The Decision Manager's Mission: Check that the decision makers follow procedures that anticipate objections to prospective decisions and how they are crafted. Then, when necessary, assure that the decision makers refine any tentative decision accordingly, before it is finalized. Therefore, in the Northern Manufacturing case, June Ward ideally would have her committee members search for *all* significant parties who might object to prospective decisions, not just executive board objectors. Then, before the committee's proposed actions are finalized, they would be tested and refined according to an acceptability review, perhaps making judicious use of evidence-based persuasion techniques (Cialdini, 2009).

Illustrative Insight and Evidence. An emerging body of research explores connections between decision making and culture (see, for instance, Yates, 2010). A central theme that has emerged in culture research generally cites the distinction between collectivism (sometimes called interdependence) and individualism (sometimes known as independence). Implicit is a recognition that the acceptability issue often arises and is played out differently in collectivistic and individualistic cultures. A study by Briley, Morris, and Simonson (2000) provides a good example. Suppose that product A is highly durable but has an unattractive appearance, whereas product B is the opposite: highly fragile yet beautiful. The "compromise effect" is the phenomenon whereby, when given the choice between options such as products A and B, decision makers seek out and select a less extreme "compromise" alternative, say, product C, which has moderate durability and middling physical appearance. Briley and colleagues found that their East Asian participants were significantly more susceptible to the compromise effect than were their North American participants. This was anticipated on the basis of greater collectivism in East Asia and the fact that seeking compromises (the "Middle Way" in Chinese tradition) is more broadly accepted there. Indeed, Briley and colleagues found some evidence that accepting compromises is actually devalued and discouraged in Western cultures. The more general principle here is that, in today's more culturally interconnected world, decision managers would find it useful to be cognizant that several aspects of their companies' decision procedures are subject to different forces, depending on the decision makers' cultural backgrounds.

CARDINAL ISSUE 10—"IMPLEMENTATION": MAKING CERTAIN THAT SELECTED COURSES OF ACTION CAN BE AND ARE ACTUALLY PURSUED

In the Decision Maker's Voice: "We chose action A. Now, let's get it done—assuming that we can *get it done."* Some decision problems are such that making the decision is tantamount to implementing it. Choosing a shirt to buy at the mall is an example, but other decisions, such as deciding to lose weight, entail executing a project. In those instances, decision implementation can be far from given. Such was the case for Northern Manufacturing's Lincoln facility decision. Even after the executive board decided to proceed with building the facility, any number of things might have prevented it from ever opening, for example, financing falling through. June Ward and her colleagues would hope to prevent such implementation failures.

The Decision Maker's Mission: Make the decision in a fashion such that its implementation is virtually guaranteed. Note that, as with the acceptability issue, the decision maker's focus should be on what happens *before* the decision is reached, not after. That is, the decision maker does not wait until after a possibly ill-conceived decision is made before addressing predictable challenges to its implementation. Thus, during their deliberations, before June Ward and her colleagues on the Northern Manufacturing component demand committee finalize a recommendation to the full executive board, they would first test the ease of implementation and revise their tentative decision such that the significant threats to such implementation are ironed out.

The Decision Manager's Mission: Make certain that the decision makers' procedures for handling "prior" cardinal decision issues (especially the possibilities, judgment, and acceptability issues) are unlikely to result in commitment to an action that contains impediments to its implementation. In the Northern Manufacturing

case, in her role as chair of the component demand committee, Jane Ward had the opportunity to shape the topics and the direction of discussions. In that capacity, it would have been straightforward for her to nudge her colleagues toward more "implementable" decisions (e.g., "Let's spend a little time talking about …").

Illustrative Insight and Evidence. Within the last couple of decades, there has been growing literature on implementation outside what is traditionally considered decision making scholarship per se; for example, there has been considerable work on "action psychology" and medical patient treatment adherence. Regardless of how it has been construed, however, that research has yielded insights that have been shown to improve decision implementation. One of the most robust effects has been that simply explicitly forming implementation plans improves the chances of implementation (e.g., Dholakia, Baggozi, & Gopinath, 2007). Implicit is the conclusion that decisions sometimes fail to be implemented because, when making those decisions, the decision makers failed to craft implementation plans. In effect, they did nothing more than conclude that the aims of the decision (e.g., losing weight) were worthy. Other work has shown that features of the deliberations themselves can significantly affect whether the resulting decisions are actually implemented. One such feature is how effortful those deliberations are: the greater the effort, the greater the chances of implementation (Dholakia & Bagozzi, 2002), perhaps through cognitive consistency mechanisms. ("If I did all that work, it only makes sense for me to follow through.") The decision management prescriptions of such findings are straightforward, for example, make sure that decision makers derive explicit implementation plans and, perhaps surprisingly, that the deliberations do not seem too easy.

Avoiding a Common Misconception: "Paralysis by Analysis"

When many readers first learn about the CIP and its implications for decision aiding and decision management, they often make a false interpretation that leads them to reject the ideas as hopelessly impractical. Specifically, they assume that proponents of the approach, like us, recommend that they replace their current ways of making every decision with a tedious, step-by-step routine for addressing every cardinal decision issue with some science-based prescription. They rightly recognize that such a recommendation would amount to what business people often describe as "paralysis by analysis." Nothing would get done, and, therefore, quite appropriately, potential adoptees of the approach would reject it out of hand. It is important to recognize that we ourselves wholeheartedly reject such a "process replacement" approach. For good reason, similar approaches in the history of decision aiding have failed repeatedly. As we hope was implicit in the preceding, we, instead, advocate an "assessment and tweaking" approach. Thus, for instance, a decision manager should assess how well the decision makers of interest are naturally inclined to address each issue. Only if their approach is clearly likely to lead to significant and costly errors should the decision manager intervene and recommend appropriate adjustments or "tweaks." This strategy is imminently practical and acceptable to most decision makers.

Where to Next?

We have described and concretely illustrated a specific approach to evidence-based management, one that acknowledges the primacy of decision making in managerial practice. It is apparent, though, that true decision management expertise requires much more. Nevertheless, the structure provided by the CIP can serve as a guide for efficiently and effectively developing that expertise. For instance, a manager would do well to pointedly practice facilitating actual major decisions, perhaps using the Northern Manufacturing Lincoln facility illustration as a rough initial model. Ideally, the manager should do this in collaboration with one or more colleagues. An especially attractive feature of this approach is that it highlights the need for specific kinds of evidence, about decision making processes and also about the decision problem at hand. ("How exactly should we be making this decision, and what are the concrete facts that we need to know to make this decision *well*?") The manager and those around him should gradually notice that they have developed a functional common language for addressing decision problems generally and that, at minimum, their decision making proceeds faster and more smoothly than it did before.

In the best of circumstances, based on our experience, the suggested collaboration should extend beyond the manager's organization itself. In particular, when possible, that collaboration should include faculty and students at a nearby university. These "extended" collaborators can provide the organization with direct access to current literature and cutting-edge thinking about decision processes,

decision management, and problem-specific scientific knowledge. In return, the organization provides those collaborators with reality checks that are indispensable for the deep understanding that scholars seek. In addition, as suggested earlier, the collaborations invariably identify gaps in scientific knowledge that provide the focus of scholarship that truly matters. It is a win-win arrangement all around.

References

Bechara, A., Damasio, H., Tranel, D., & Damasio, A. R. (1997). Deciding advantageously before knowing the advantageous strategy. *Science, 275,* 1293–1295.

Booth, R., & Sharma, D. (2009). Stress reduces attention to irrelevant information: Evidence from the Stroop task. *Motivation & Emotion, 33*(4), 412–418.

Briley, D. A., Morris, M. W., & Simonson, I. (2000). Reasons as carriers of culture: Dynamic versus dispositional models of cultural influences on decision making. *Journal of Consumer Research, 27*(2), 157–178.

Caplan, R. A., Posner, K. L., & Cheney, F. W. (1991). Effect of outcome on physician judgments of appropriateness of care. *Journal of the American Medical Association, 265,* 1957–1960.

Cialdini, R. B. (2009). *Influence: Science and practice* (5th ed.). London: Pearson Education.

Dawes, R. M. (1979). The robust beauty of improper linear models in decision making. *American Psychologist, 34,* 571–582.

Dholakia, U. M., & Baggozi, R. P. (2002). Mustering motivation to enact decisions: How decision process characteristics influence goal realization. *Journal of Behavioral Decision Making, 15,* 167–188.

Dholakia, U. M., Baggozi, R. P., & Gopinath, M. (2007). How formulating implementation plans and remembering past actions facilitate the enactment of effortful decisions. *Journal of Behavioral Decision Making, 20,* 343–364.

Diehl, M., & Stroebe, W. (1987). Productivity loss in brainstorming groups: Toward the solution of a riddle. *Journal of Personality and Social Psychology, 53,* 497–509.

Evans, J. St. B. T. (2008). Dual-processing accounts of reasoning, judgment, and social cognition. *Annual Review of Psychology, 59,* 255–278.

Förster, J., & Higgins, E. T. (2005). How global versus local perception fits regulatory focus. *Psychological Science, 16*(8), 631–636.

Gilovich, T., Griffin, D., & Kahneman, D. (Eds.). (2002). *Heuristics and biases: The psychology of intuitive judgment.* New York: Cambridge University Press.

Hammond, J. S., Keeney, R. L., & Raiffa, H. (1998). The hidden traps in decision making. *Harvard Business Review, 76*(5), 47–58.

Higgins, E. T. (1997). Beyond pleasure and pain. *American Psychologist, 52*(12), 1280–1300.

Higgins, R. C. (1998). *Analysis for financial management* (5th ed.). Boston: Irwin McGraw-Hill.

Klein, G. A. (1993). A recognition-primed decision (RPD) model of rapid decision making. In G. A. Klein, J. Orasanu, R. Calderwood, & C. E. Zsambok (Eds.), *Decision making in action: Models and methods* (pp. 138–147). Norwood, NJ: Ablex.

'Lectric Law Library. (2010). Standard of care. Retrieved December 11, 2010, from http://www.lectlaw.com/files/exp24.htm

Makridakis, S., Wheelwright, S. C., & Hyndman, R. J. (1998). *Forecasting: Methods and applications* (3rd ed.). New York: Wiley.

Mellers, B. A., Schwartz, A., Ho, K., & Ritov, I. (1997). Decision affect theory: Emotional reactions to the outcomes of risky options. *Psychological Science, 8*(6), 423–429.

Potworowski, G. (2009). Intuition versus analysis. In M. W. Kattan (Ed.) & M. E. Cowen (Assoc. Ed.), *Encyclopedia of medical decision making* (pp. 638–640). Thousand Oaks, CA: SAGE Publications.

Potworowski, G. A. (2010). *Varieties of indecisive experience: Explaining the tendency to not make timely and stable decisions.* Unpublished Ph.D. dissertation, University of Michigan, Ann Arbor.

Powers, D. E. (2004). Validity of Graduate Record Examinations (GRE) general tests for admissions to colleges of veterinary medicine. *Journal of Applied Psychology, 89*(2), 208–219.

Price, P. C., & Stone, E. R. (2004). Intuitive evaluation of likelihood judgment producers: Evidence for a confidence heuristic. *Journal of Behavioral Decision Making, 17,* 39–57.

Ramaswamy, V., & Gouillart, F. (2010). *The power of co-creation.* New York: Free Press.

Saaty, T. L. (1980). *The analytic hierarchy process.* New York: McGraw-Hill.

Sackett, D.L., Richardson, W.S., Rosenburg, W. & Haynes, R.B. (1997). *Evidence-based medicine: How to practice and teach EBM.* London: Churchill Livingstone.

Simon, D., Krawczyk, D. C., & Holyoak, K. J. (2004). Construction of preferences by constraint satisfaction. *Psychological Science, 15*(5), 331–336.

Sood, S., & Forehand, M. (2005). On self-referencing differences in judgment and choice. *Organizational Behavior and Human Decision Processes, 98*(2), 144–154.

Stone, E. R., & Allgaier, L. (2008). A social values analysis of self-other differences in decision making involving risk. *Basic and Applied Social Psychology, 30*(2), 114–129.

Swalm, R. O. (1966). Utility theory: Insights into risk taking. *Harvard Business Review, 44,* 123–136.

U.S. Nuclear Regulatory Commission. (2009). Fact sheet on probabilistic risk assessment. Retrieved March 10, 2010, from http://www.nrc.gov/reading-rm/doc-collections/fact-sheets/probabilistic-risk-asses.html

van der Zee, K. I., Bakker, A. B., & Bakker, P. (2002). Why are structured interviews so rarely used in personnel selection? *Journal of Applied Psychology, 87*(1), 176–184.

Vlek, C., Edwards, W., Kiss, I., Majone, G., & Toda, M. (1984). What constitutes "a good decision?" *Acta Psychologica, 56,* 5–27.

von Winterfeldt, D., & Edwards, W. (1988). *Decision analysis and behavioral research.* New York: Cambridge University Press.

West's Encyclopedia of American Law (2010). Business judgment rule. Retrieved December 12, 2010, from http://www.answers.com/topic/business-judgment-rule

Wilson, T. D., & Gilbert, D. T. (2005). Affective forecasting: Knowing what to want. *Current Directions in Psychological Science, 14*(3), 131–134.

Winston, W. L., & Albright, S. C. (2009). *Practical management science* (3rd. ed.). Mason, OH: South-Western/Cengage Learning.

Yates, J. F. (1990). *Judgment and decision making.* Englewood Cliffs, NJ: Prentice Hall.

Yates, J. F. (2003). *Decision management.* San Francisco: Jossey-Bass.

Yates, J. F. (2010). Culture and probability judgment. *Social and Personality Psychology Compass, 4*(3), 174–188.

Yates, J. F., & Angott, A. (2009). Judgment modes. In M. W. Kattan (Ed.) & M. E. Cowen (Assoc. Ed.), *Encyclopedia of medical decision making* (pp. 649–655). Thousand Oaks, CA: SAGE Publications.

Yates, J. F., & Chen, L. L. (2009). Judgment. In M. W. Kattan (Ed.) & M. E. Cowen (Assoc. Ed.), *Encyclopedia of medical decision making* (pp. 645–649). Thousand Oaks, CA: SAGE Publications.

Yates, J. F., Klatzky, R. L., & Young, C. A. (1995). Cognitive performance under stress. In R. S. Nickerson (Ed.), *Emerging needs and opportunities for human factors research* (pp. 262–290). Washington, DC: National Academy Press.

Yates, J. F., Price, P. C., Lee, J.-W., & Ramirez, J. (1996). Good probabilistic forecasters: The "consumer's" perspective. *International Journal of Forecasting, 12,* 41–56.

Yates, J. F., & Tschirhart, M. D. (2006). Decision making expertise. In K. A. Ericsson, N. Charness, P. J. Feltovich, & R. R. Hoffman. (Eds.). *Cambridge handbook of expertise and expert performance* (pp. 421–438). New York, NY: Cambridge University Press.

Yates, J. F., Veinott, E. S., & Patalano, A. L. (2003). Hard decisions, bad decisions: On decision quality and decision aiding. In S. L. Schneider & J. C. Shanteau (Eds.), *Emerging perspectives on judgment and decision research* (pp. 13–63). New York: Cambridge University Press.

13

Decision Logic in Evidence-Based Management: Can Logical Models From Other Disciplines Improve Evidence-Based Human-Resource Decisions?

John Boudreau

Abstract

The "mental models" used in organizations often reflect disciplines such as finance, marketing or engineering. Such models can overlook or misinterpret evidence related to human capital, producing poor human-resource (HR) and organizational decisions. Improved evidence-based HR decisions may result from "retooling" HR issues using logic from mental models in other management disciplines. HR researchers and practitioners can tap the power of these well-accepted logic frameworks to "retool" evidence about HR management.

Key Words: mental model, logic model, logic framework, human capital, evidence-based human-resource (HR) management, decisions

In October, 2008, I was a speaker at an event that also included Jack Welch, the former CEO of GE. In the interview, Welch was asked about the growing evidence of an impending downturn, and he acknowledged that he believed the downturn was likely to be more severe than most current leaders had ever encountered. Asked what his most important advice to leaders would be, he chose a human-capital issue. Welch observed that companies would have to make hard choices, and that their top performers were not going to meet the performance targets that would normally have triggered rewards such as bonuses, incentives, and stock-option awards. He admonished leaders to put aside a "bucket of money," to be ready to show the most vital employees how much they are valued, "because your competitors will be at your doorstep waiting for them to become disillusioned and leave you." This remarkable quote vividly shows how business leaders place a priority on talent. Later that day, I was working with a group of top human-resource (HR) leaders who had heard Welch's remarks. I asked, "In your organizations, can your HR and

unit leaders reliably and logically decide which of your employees are vital, and how big that bucket of money will need to be, to retain the vital talent you need?" Only a few hands went up.

The HR leaders at the meeting were members of fine organizations with world-class HR systems to retain and reward their vital talent. However, even with those systems, the HR leaders could not be sure that their counterparts—organization leaders in other functions or business units—possessed mental models that would logically and reliably direct the retention resources to where they would be most vital and most effective.

In contrast, these HR leaders were very certain that their counterparts would use logical and similar models to know where to invest (and cut) scarce resources in technology, manufacturing, and marketing. They admitted that these well-accepted models were not expected to produce perfect decisions, nor were their disciplines (finance, marketing, operations management, etc.) blessed with perfect measures and evidence. Yet, leaders and managers had a consistent and logical way of thinking through difficult questions about these other resources, using principles such as net present value, production optimization, and market segmentation. That kind of consistency and widespread accountability for clear and evidence-based thinking was not as typical when it came to human capital.

These HR leaders were among the best in their field, and they had built and led HR functions that were respected, influential, and award winning. Yet, they recognized the striking contrast between how their leaders approached tough decisions regarding people versus other resources they dealt with. They and their leaders knew these would be vital decisions, such as where to cut talent and where to grow it, how to optimize investments in a reduced array of incentives, and whether to preserve investments in talent-acquisition programs to be prepared for the upturn. Of course, the HR teams and their counterparts would eventually make those decisions, but apparently with frameworks that were far less consistent, logical, and effective, compared with decisions about money, customers, and technology.

Yet, the questions about how to optimize talent-acquisition investments seem remarkably similar to questions about how to optimize acquisition investments for raw materials or assembly components. Questions about where best to apply a limited array of incentives seem similar to questions about where to apply a limited array of financial resources to investment opportunities. Questions about where to grow and where to cut talent seem remarkably similar to questions about where to grow market share and where to allow it to decline.

HR leaders and researchers spend a lot of time trying to learn finance, marketing, and other business disciplines to understand the logic that defines how business leaders think. Yet, HR-related evidence, measurement, information, and reporting systems too often reflect a perspective that is quite foreign to non-HR managers and leaders, even when those HR systems are remarkably sophisticated and data rich. In their zeal to produce ever more sophisticated HR measures, analytics, and scorecards, even the most advanced HR leaders often miss a fundamental point: whatever the outcome of all the number-crunching, it will do little good if it's not used and understood by the key decision makers, and those decision makers are usually not well-versed in HR models, data, or evidence! This chapter proposes that evidence-based HR management will be enhanced by greater focus on the "mental models" that are used to make decisions about human capital. More important, it suggests

that there is a largely untapped opportunity to improve those mental models, by "retooling" traditional HR logic and evidence within the frameworks of well-accepted logical models from other management disciplines.

The chapter first defines the term *mental models,* drawing on a long-standing research stream from organization behavior, marketing, and systems dynamics. Then, it defines the concept of "retooling" HR as the process of reframing HR evidence and decisions using the logical frameworks that leaders already trust and accept—frameworks that are already widely used to make decisions and amass evidence about resources other than human capital. The concept of retooling integrates with vital elements of evidence-based decision frameworks discussed in other chapters in this volume. The chapter describes why mental models matter, describing the evidence that suggests that mental models have significant effects in directing decision-makers' attention; defining what evidence is relevant; and how evidence is amassed, analyzed, and interpreted.

Evidence suggests that leaders know that they are not as adept at decisions about human-capital resources, compared to more traditional or tangible resources, and evidence also suggests that when leaders have a stronger grasp of principles of human behavior, the strategic role of HR is stronger as well (Lawler & Boudreau, 2012). Indeed, even the definition of a decision itself is affected by mental models, which highlights why evidence-based HR decisions may benefit from reframing within more accepted and often more sophisticated management frameworks.

Next, the chapter considers evidence-based HR decisions as a special case of teamwork, with HR leaders and researchers teaming up to work with leaders and researchers in other management disciplines. The research on shared mental models (SMM's) among team members provides a well-developed base of theory and measurement methods for mapping the degree to which leaders in different disciplines develop a common perspective on HR-related evidence and decisions.

Because the question of HR measurement figures so prominently in how leaders approach evidence-based HR decisions, the chapter describes how the "retooling" approach suggests a new perspective on HR measures, and the importance of tapping the right mental models and logic frameworks. The chapter also describes how retooling suggests a different approach to educating decision makers outside the HR profession, and it offers ideas for starting the retooling process in actual organizations. It concludes with implications for research, business education, and practice.

Mental Models of Managers

The "mental model" concept appears in many disciplines, including systems dynamics, education, psychology, and so forth. A review of the definitions used in the literature in systems dynamics produced this definition: "A mental model of a dynamic system is a relatively enduring and accessible, but limited, internal conceptual representation of an external system (historical, existing or projected) whose structure is analogous to the perceived structure of the system" (Doyle & Ford, 1998; 1999).

A more general definition can be found on the web (Answers.com, 2011):

> A mental model is an explanation of someone's thought process about how something works in the real world. It is a representation of the surrounding world, the relationships between its various parts and a person's intuitive perception about their own acts and their consequences. Our mental models help shape our behavior and define our approach to solving problems (akin to a personal algorithm) and carrying out tasks.

This definition arises from mental-model theory that suggests that reasoning depends, not only on objective or logical forms, but on mental models (Johnson-Laird, 1983).

Mental models clearly include schemas that define the structure of perceptions, as well as relationships, including cause and effect, and the ways that evidence and data are incorporated to explain and enhance the schema. The insight that reasoning (and, thus, decision making) depends ultimately on subjective mental models rather than objective logical forms will be fundamental to the dilemmas posed in the introduction to this chapter. Although a great deal of attention in evidence-based management is directed toward developing and amassing more valid and logical relationships, a fruitful avenue for advancing the use of evidence may be to better understand the audience's mental models about that evidence. The mental models of HR leaders, researchers, and practitioners may be very different from the mental models of their constituents. Non-HR leaders' experience and training is often grounded in logical frameworks and tools from disciplines outside the domain of HR, so mental-model theory suggests it may be useful to draw from those other disciplinary frameworks to improve the quality and usefulness of mental models regarding HR decisions.

In the evidence-based management process, mental models can both enhance and hinder the uptake of useful evidence for better decisions. Decision makers certainly have mental models that guide their HR decisions, but they may be less adequate to the task because they are constructed on a less-than-firm foundation. The frameworks of research on HR are less familiar to organization leaders than those for consumer behavior, operations engineering, and finance. Those latter models are likely to be richer and more evidence based if only because leaders use them more or have been trained more deeply in them. Taking elements (e.g., schemas, relationships, evidence connections) from the richer mental models of other disciplines and retooling them to apply to HR decisions may enhance decision makers' HR mental models and their capacity to make use of evidence.

Evidence-based management (EBMgt) is intended to contribute to organizational and management effectiveness. Because mental models influence what evidence receives attention and how it is used, inadequate mental models generally have serious organizational consequences. The unexpected financial market meltdown of 2008 may have been caused in part by organization and regulatory decisions based on mental models inaccurately assuming that certain extreme situations were impossible (i.e., because they had never been experienced by the key decision makers).

There are similar risks to inadequate mental models in the arena of human capital. For example, mental models that view HR mostly as costs can lead to squandering less tangible long-term value in an effort to reduce short-term expenses. Or, mental models that presume it is possible to acquire qualified HR very quickly and at reasonable cost (perhaps because the HR department has always delivered on this promise) can lead to lost opportunities that might arise with better long-term planning and action (Boudreau, 2010b).

Even when inadequate mental models about HR are widely shared (e.g., turnover is bad and should be reduced), their dangers may be avoided by casting them into the light of a superior mental model from another discipline. The evidence of a successful mental-model transformation might be measured by observing how leaders' insights become more sophisticated, such as when "turnover is bad and must be reduced," is replaced with "Employee turnover has benefits and costs just like inventory turnover," or as "staffing means filling my requisitions quickly," becomes "Leaving employee staffing until the last moment is just like leaving decisions about adequate raw materials until the last moment." Mental models focus organization and leader decisions, so enhancing mental models about HR has the potential to improve that focus and, thus, improve how evidence is gathered, analyzed, and used.

Employee turnover is perhaps the most frequently reported statistic about human capital. Virtually every study shows that turnover rates are calculated and reported by the vast majority of organizations. Yet, the mental models used to understand and interpret turnover rates are often rudimentary at best and misleading at worst. Most leaders, when confronted with a turnover rate, have a mental model that clearly sees the costs of replacing the departing employees, and it is often possible to calculate million-dollar savings if turnover can be reduced even a bit (Cascio & Boudreau, 2011). Indeed, when I have posed this question to many groups of business leaders over the years, they almost always initially respond that turnover is costly, and so it should be reduced. This is logical and partially correct, but usually not a complete analysis.

A more appropriate set of questions would ask how much it costs to reduce the turnover, whether those leaving are less qualified or motivated than those that might replace them, whether the cost of replacing the departing employees is a lot less than the cost of what it would take to keep them, and so forth. The turnover rate masks many relevant considerations. Decades of research have shown the importance of understanding functional and dysfunctional turnover and of embedding turnover analysis within a more complete model of the full staffing cycle (Cascio & Boudreau, 2011). Why, then, do smart business leaders so readily ignore these questions and assume that turnover should be minimized to cut costs?

Here's an experiment that I've run that seems to suggest an answer. After I establish that business leaders react to the turnover rate by wanting to reduce it, I follow up with the following question: "Suppose you are a grocer, and I told you that you your spoilage rate of carrots in your warehouse and stores is 44 percent, about industry average, but that there are industries that achieve inventory spoilage rates much lower than that. What would you suggest doing about the spoilage rate for your carrots?"

The answers are remarkably different from the answer about employee turnover. As one would expect, business leaders draw on their knowledge of supply-chain and inventory management. They articulate a logical framework that recognizes that the key outcome is to find an inventory turnover level that optimizes product quality, availability, and cost. So, they ask questions such as, "How much do replacement carrots cost?" "What investment would it take to reduce carrot spoilage?" "How quickly can we replenish the inventory?" "What is the lost margin if we miss a sale of carrots, or if we ask customers to wait until we have more in stock?" The managers implicitly understand that if customers can wait, or margins are slim, or replacement carrots don't cost much, carrot spoilage is not a serious problem.

By now, the managers have recognized that employee turnover and inventory spoilage are remarkably similar. A much more logical approach to evidence-based employee turnover analysis would recognize employee turnover is one element of a larger process of acquiring, retaining, and developing talent. Employee turnover is just like the depletion of inventories. So, the vital outcomes are not limited to turnover rates or costs. Rather, the best decision will strive for the optimum level of talent quality, inventory, and availability, accounting for turnover costs but, also, other costs and the value of that talent. If vacant positions can be covered for a while, or the lost work is not time urgent, or those available to replace the exiting employees are of equal or much better quality, then turnover reduction may not be worth the investment, even if it cuts costs.

According to *Business Week*, "Companies can now model and optimize operations, and can calculate the return on investment on everything from corporate jets to Super Bowl ads. These successes have led to the next math project: the worker. You have to bring the same rigor you bring to operations and finance to the analysis of people, says Rupert Bader, director of workforce planning at Microsoft" (Baker, 2009). That rigor exists, not only in the data of finance and operations, but also and even more fundamentally in the logical tools that guide the data.

Rousseau (chapter 1 of this volume) noted that, in a classic study of functional managers attempting to solve the same business case, financial managers keyed on financing issues, sales managers on marketing matters, and personnel managers on staffing problems: "Presented with a complex stimulus, the subject [the manager] perceives in it what he is 'ready' to perceive; the more complex or ambiguous the stimulus the more the perception is determined by what is already 'in' the subject and less by what is in the stimulus." (Dearborn & Simon 1958). Firms can be viewed as top management mental models (an interpretist view of business) transformed into real organizations (a functional view of business). (Kuhn & Morecroft, 2009).

Non-HR leaders facing decisions about their talent, organization designs, HR practices, or day-to-day employment relationships are certainly confronted with a "complex stimulus." Should it be any surprise if they approach such decisions with models they already understand? Those models are often based on accounting, and they tend to emphasize efficiency, risk reduction, and minimum-cost solutions. Or, they might approach such decisions armed with the latest fad or fashion in "people solutions," such as the HR programs of leading companies (GE was popular to emulate for many years), or the most recent book on leadership.

That managers tend to use their dominant models, even when addressing decisions in areas where the disciplines of those dominant models may not apply, can create significant organizational challenges. A classic mistake is when managers see only the accounting cost elements of human-capital decisions, and they adopt decisions that save money in the short run but create long-term problems (such as downsizing based only on how much money is saved or to minimize disruption, while losing vital talent in the long run). The fact that leaders rely on their dominant models is often presented as evidence that leaders must be enticed—or forced—to learn new frameworks if we hope to get them to incorporate evidence from behavioral science into their decisions about human capital.

However, another interpretation is more optimistic. If managers are already comfortable with dominant logical models from their own disciplines, then using those logical models to convey evidence about human capital may actually accelerate evidence-based HR decisions. These dominant logical models from other disciplines are powerful and untapped platforms on which to build understanding about human-capital issues. It may be better to avoid trying to force leaders to learn new logical models about organizations and human behavior and, instead, to tap the models they already use in other arenas.

Yates and Potworoski (chapter 12 of this volume) suggest that better evidence-based decisions will result from considering the characteristics of the decision, the parties affected, and the ways that decision quality is measured. They note that "cardinal issue resolution" recognizes how decision processes are embedded within prior factors such as habits and experiences, as well as how beneficiaries and welfare are defined. Retooling HR decisions using well-accepted models from other disciplines can better define and explicate these decision elements. For example, employee sourcing might naively be seen as a simple function of filling a position with the most qualified candidate. When retooled within the logical framework of a supply chain, however, it is easier to see that the candidates for any particular position may be a part of a much larger system of jobs, development opportunities, and possible destinations, just as the options for sourcing any organization component are varied. Now, the affected parties to the decision can be seen to include those that supply the candidates (including internal units), and the alternative places the candidate might have been assigned and that might have benefited from hiring that candidate. This is precisely how decisions about sourcing and distribution are made in a supply chain. The logical definition of decision quality now takes on a much broader scope, and it offers the chance to apply evidence and insight from a broader group of constituents.

So, how does the idea of mental models play into the idea of retooling HR? Although the idea of a "talent decision science" has become more accepted, few leaders know how to build and use one (Lawler & Boudreau, 2012). Organization leaders remain stubbornly ignorant of even the basics of human behavior, and they are generally not held accountable for their decision-making quality with regard to people. Rather, they are held accountable for their use of HR programs or workforce characteristics, such as engagement or turnover.

Other disciplines rely more heavily on teaching decision makers their logical frameworks designed to shape mental models. Finance has net present value and portfolio theory. Marketing has customer segmentation and lifetime customer profitability. Operations has supply-chain optimization. Each of these logical frameworks illuminate relationships, such those as between sourcing, manufacturing, and transportation, among other factors. These frameworks also provide evidence-based recommendations about how decisions can optimize the outcomes of those relationships. Manufacturing frameworks integrate throughput, assembly tolerances, and total quality, providing a common logic structure to integrate evidence from materials science, queuing theory, and other disciplines. These mental models are well-understood, commonly taught in management education, and have become an expected capability of virtually all leaders. Leaders, managers, and

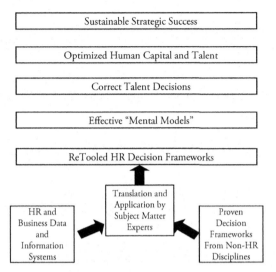

Fig. 13.1. How "ReTooling" HR Builds Strategic Sucess.

employees are already "smart" about risk, return, segmentation, bottlenecks, and tolerances when these ideas are applied to money, customers, and technology. Yet, they don't typically use those ideas when it comes to people.

However, decisions about people are remarkably similar to decisions about inventory, investment risk, materials supply, and customer segments. If key decision makers in organizations already have such well-developed analytical and logical mental models for other resources, why not take advantage of those models to improve decisions about talent and human capital? Table 13.1 shows the idea graphically.

The idea is that all organizations want to achieve greater sustainable strategic success, and they understand that such success is enhanced, or made possible, by optimizing the acquisition, deployment, engagement, and application of human capital or talent. Underlying that optimization are thousands of decisions made by leaders, managers, and employees about their personal human capital and that human capital that is under their stewardship.

The mental models of leaders affect their talent decisions, and more effective mental models likely lead to better decisions. Therefore, a key task for organizations is to enhance their mental models about HR. Mental models for HR are often informed solely by frameworks unique to the HR profession. These are often foreign to leaders, managers, and employees, so these constituents for evidence-based HR will understandably resist requests to learn completely new languages and analytical approaches in order to manage their people. Thus,

traditional HR frameworks, reflected in HR systems, measures, and practices, are often less effective because they are too distant from how business leaders think.

"Retooling HR" is shown at the bottom of the diagram. It means taking proven tools from other disciplines, and translating their principles and logic to apply to decisions and analytics about talent and human capital. Recall the example of turnover analysis at the beginning of this chapter. The "proven decision framework" at the bottom-right of Table 13.1 was the inventory management framework. The "HR and business data and information systems" on the bottom-left of Table 13.1 was the data on turnover rates, performance levels, acquisition costs, quality, and so forth. The middle box reflects reframing the turnover rate as one element of a larger talent inventory concept, and the translation and presentation by HR working with inventory management experts. By reframing, the organization has a "retooled" decision framework for turnover, that is likely to lead to a more logical and complete analysis and, thus, to better decisions.

Retooling HR Is More than Business Partnership or Leader Accountability

Managers within and outside HR can find common ground at the intersection of proven business models and the dilemmas of talent and HR management. It is now a common recommendation for HR leaders to understand the language of business, and for non-HR leaders to become more facile with the principles of human behavior at work, but retooling HR requires more. Retooling requires that HR leaders not only understand the challenges faced by organizations, but also how those challenges are expressed through disciplines like marketing and finance. It also requires that HR leaders and researchers apply the underlying logic of those disciplines to vital human-capital decisions.

Of course, it is important for leaders outside of HR to see human capital as their job and to be held accountable for the quality with which they enact HR programs, but retooling requires more. Retooling requires that leaders outside HR abandon the idea that human capital is totally different from the other resources under their stewardship. It requires that organization leaders apply the logical and analytical mental models they use for traditional resources to their HR. It requires that they unlearn the mental model of HR as an administrative and cost-reducing endeavor, or that HR is largely unpredictable due to the vagaries of human behavior, and instead embrace the idea that risk and optimization are a fundamental part of HR, just like all their other resources.

Retooling HR may be one factor in enhancing the support that organizations provide for field research on human capital and organizational issues such as how HR systems function, which interventions work, and the circumstances that affect them. Research on new products, brands, materials, and technology is supported, in part, because decision makers have rich mental models with which to estimate the potential returns. More accessible HR frameworks, based in part on frameworks leaders already use in other areas, may clarify the value of HR research that "fills in the blanks" of their mental models. For example, organizations engaged in mining, extraction, and exploration invest heavily in large-scale studies to map potential sources of oil, gas, or minerals. They begin the exploration process years or decades before they actually drill or mine. They accept that this is expensive and that most of the exploration does not turn up viable oil fields or ore beds. Yet, it is well worth the investment for the potential payoff.

In the same way, when organizations are embarking on activities in regions with under-developed human-capital infrastructure, early research on issues such as literacy, values, and culture may have large payoffs in terms of insuring an available and ready workforce. I recently worked with a task force for a large global organization, that used this argument to justify spending millions on improved human capital planning. Yet, this type of research is often overlooked, resulting in systems that staff positions at the last minute or produce costly long-term vacancies. Retooling the value of research to improve workforce planning within the framework of prospecting or oil exploration can clarify the value of such research and lead to increased support.

Fitting HR Evidence into Standard Business Logic Models

Table 13.1 provides some initial ideas about where prominent findings from organizational and behavioral science might fit within standard business logic from other disciplines. There are undoubtedly other examples, so the table shows the potential for rethinking how scientific evidence about human capital is conveyed. For each type of human capital evidence on the left, there is a traditional business logic model into which it can be embedded, shown in the middle column. In the right-hand column, the combination of the evidence and the business logic retools the traditional logic. If managers see that "employee recruiting and retention is a lot like customer recruiting and retention," or "building and combining talent assets is a lot like building and combining financial assets," there will be a greater desire and use of evidence from the HR disciplines.

Retooling the "Risk" in HR Using Standard Business Logic

Typical approaches to risk in HR management are often very different from the comparable concerns in other areas. When it comes to HR, the mental models of leaders too often gravitate toward risk-reduction, rather than risk optimization. This is likely due to the important but traditional emphasis of HR on avoiding legal or employment problems, and the greater tangibility of HR costs versus benefits (Boudreau & Ramstad, 2007; Boudreau, 2010b; Cascio & Boudreau, 2011). Each row of Table 13.2 shows how a common HR task or issue can be retooled to reframe a common misconception about risk in HR, using proven business frameworks.

Generally, HR and business leaders approach talent risk with an eye toward reducing or removing it. Yet, a fundamental premise of virtually all other management disciplines is objective evaluation of risk. Evaluating risk objectively commonly entails accepting a certain degree of risk when it makes sense to do so. The figure provides an example of how scholars, teachers, and practitioners might reframe HR-related evidence, to begin the conversation about how to analyze risk in HR to be more similar to the way it is done in other business disciplines.

Retooling HR is consistent with the decision focus and the four elements of EBMgt this handbook specifies. EBMgt aims to enhance decisions. Retooling HR issues using well-accepted logic models is designed to help leaders bring the same decision rigor to HR issues that they bring to more traditional resources, such as money and inventory. Indeed, the well-accepted business frameworks are generally designed as decision support systems, with the frameworks guiding the structure of planning systems, measurement, data, and, ultimately, the definition of optimization (Boudreau & Ramstad, 2007). By fitting HR issues within such frameworks, decision makers are invited to draw upon familiar routines used for decisions about other resources.

Second, retooling HR encourages the use of validated external evidence. Reframing HR issues

Table 13.1. Retooling HR Involves Embedding HR Evidence in Business Logic

Human Capital and Organizational Evidence	Traditional Business Logic	Retooled Business Logic Applied to HR
Policy Capturing c.g., (Karren & Barringer, 2002)	Consumer preference mapping to find customer segments where meeting needs has the greatest payoff at the lowest cost.	Employees or recruits group into "segments," and where providing idiosyncratic "deals" has the greatest payoff at the lowest cost.
Tournament and other models of career progression (Rosenbaum, 1979) Selection validity and meta-analysis	Supply chain analysis can identify optimum sourcing and shipping routes that optimize risk, cost and return	Career paths, recruiting sources and succession plans can be optimized by thinking of them as alternative sources or routes to supply future needed talent.
Employee downsizing, turnover and functional vs. dysfunctional employee separations (Cascio, 2002)	Inventory analysis can identify levels of inventory, shortages and surpluses that optimize cost and risk	Employee turnover, shortages and surpluses can be optimized like inventory, by considering risks and costs of holding versus ordering new inventory
Utility analysis and the standard deviation of performance in dollars, performance management (Cascio & Boudreau, 2011)	Engineering performance tolerance analysis can identify which components of a product or process must be held to tight tolerances and which can be allowed to vary, to optimize risk, cost and return	Performance management and work analysis can be used to identify where variations in employee quality and performance make large vs. small differences, and optimize performance management to focus where the value is highest
Competency and skill development (McCall, 2010)	Financial portfolio analysis can identify the combination of "asset classes" to hold, in order to optimize expected risk and return, considering uncertain future conditions	Competency and skill planning can optimize the types and proportions of skills in the workforce, considering the probability of future scenarios and the correspondence of skills and competencies to those future scenarios

as similar to traditional management issues clarifies the value and need for valid external evidence. For example, lacking a retooled model, how might leaders approach the decision about whether to customize employment "deals" for different employee groups? Leaders unfamiliar with HR evidence might presume that people are so unpredictable and their behavior patterns so obscure that it makes little sense to attempt to systematically optimize how deals are customized to different groups. They might simply offer a similar package of rewards to all, assuming that any further attempts to customize are fruitless. Or, they might agree to individual employee requests for special deals, assuming there is little evidence-based rationale for saying no to some and yes to others.

Yet, there is a great deal of evidence using techniques such as policy capturing to map employee and applicant preferences (e.g., Karren & Barringer, 2002), as well as evidence that matching rewards to employee needs can affect performance, turnover, and engagement. Retooling would recognize that optimally customizing the employment deal is similar to optimizing product and service offerings to customers in the marketing discipline. The marketing discipline brings a wealth of tools to gather evidence from customers, as well as evidence-based frameworks of consumer behavior to help predict where customization will create the greatest response. Retooling the decision customizing the employment deal, using a consumer marketing framework, clarifies the potential value of evaluated

Table 13.2. Retooling HR Involves Rethinking The Idea of Risk in Talent Management

Human Resource Discipline	Traditional HR Risk Framing	Business Tool Applied to HR	Retooled Approach to Talent Risk
Job Analysis	"Top performers in every position, to minimize the risk of bad performance"	Performance tolerance analysis optimizes performance improvement against risks, costs and benefits.	"Minimize risk in risk-averse performance situations, embrace it in risk-loving performance situations, by focusing on return on improved performance (ROIP)"
Talent Planning	"Minimize the risk of talent being unprepared for the future by developing generic competencies that will apply across the board."	Portfolio analysis balances the risks of several uncertain future scenarios against their returns, combining resource investments that fit several future possibilities.	"Balance risk in talent planning, by investing in talent for several future scenarios according to their relative likelihood and risk."
Total Reward and the Employment Deal	"Minimize the risk of employee dissatisfaction by agreeing to customized deals, or minimize the risk of inequity by doing the same thing for everyone"	Customer segmentation optimizes product and service features to customize against market segments, according to their value and cost.	"Balance the risk of dissatisfaction or inequity against the return by customizing where it achieves the greatest return and standardizing where it does not."
Workforce Turnover	"Minimize the risk of employee shortages by filling all requisitions as quickly as possible and keeping turnover to a minimum."	Inventory management optimizes holding costs, ordering costs, and shortage costs by planning for shortages or surpluses.	"Turnover levels and time-to-fill are optimized to create the level of employee shortages or surpluses that best balances risks of surpluses and shortages against costs.
Succession and Career Planning	"Minimize risk by having successors for every position, who have all completed the career development path requirements"	Logistics management optimizes transport patterns to balance the risk of unavailability against the costs and returns to of various supply and demand pathways.	"Optimize the risk and return to succession by balancing the costs, benefits and timing of different career paths."

external evidence on the employment deal question, and suggests new logical frameworks to better use that information. External evidence about employee preferences, demographic segments, and so forth now would have greater meaning.

Third, retooling HR can reveal ways to engage stakeholders and consider their preferences and values. Well-accepted business frameworks are specifically designed to capture and reflect stakeholder preferences and values. Using consumer behavior and marketing frameworks to retool employment customization can reveal methods for tapping and

analyzing employee and leader preferences, often in a more sophisticated way than is typically applied to HR decisions. Retooling HR through supply-chain tools can enhance an organization's ability to transparently communicate with employees about employment and career options, by creating a common language about emerging global work rewards and requirements, as was the case with IBM's global workforce "supply-chain" system (Boudreau, 2010a). Retooling HR also enhances consideration of stakeholder values by specifically engaging experts and leaders from other disciplines, inviting them to bring their professional models to bear on HR decisions. Retooling HR decisions within frameworks such as financial portfolio theory, consumer marketing, engineering, and supply chain creates a natural bridge for experts in those fields to more fully engage and bring their evidence to bear on HR decisions. Indeed, when IBM's HR organization set out to create a talent supply-chain system, they called on one of IBM's highest-ranking supply-chain experts to design and support it.

Fourth, retooling HR reflects the EBMgt principle that systems must incorporate the unique experiences of practitioners to inform the most relevant and effective research questions and designs. Retooling HR increases the relevance and connectivity of HR decisions with stakeholders in non-HR disciplines, so it can increase the amount and diversity of practitioner experience and judgment available to the HR field. For example, a familiar practical issue in optimizing supply chains is that optimizing the whole chain requires sharing decisions across the elements of the chain (e.g., among producers, shippers, retailers, etc.). Yet, each actor in the supply chain may be reluctant to concede decision rights and information to others. If each manufacturer, shipper, warehouse, and supplier chooses to operate without such information sharing, such systems can quickly fall victim to massive and unnecessary excess inventory, as each player mitigates their individual risk by holding buffer inventory levels (Reddy & Reddy, 2001). The solution in operations management, is to develop a common language for the materials and information that flows through the chain, and to allow those with the most current information (usually the retailers at the end of the chain who come into contact with ultimate customers), to drive decisions about how much to produce, store, and ship. It turns out that this practitioner wisdom from operations management is applicable as well to HR management. In particular, when organization can develop a common language to describe jobs, competencies, and development opportunities, they can use it to construct a "supply chain" of talent that is far more transparent and efficient than one based on a multitude of diverse work descriptions and development paths (Boudreau, 2010a).

Finally, retooling HR can address the EBMgt principle that research and practice must appreciate context, organizational actors, and circumstances. Particularly with HR decisions, research and practice often fail to consider the context of the organization and its other systems. Retooling HR decisions using frameworks from other business disciplines creates a natural connection between research and practice in HR with organization actors in other functions. Moreover, as HR researchers and practitioners learn more about accepted business models in other disciplines, they will better understand the logical frameworks and empirical realities of systems from finance, marketing, operations, and others. There is much to be learned by HR researchers and practitioners about these other systems. Equally, however, there are important contributions to these other disciplines that can arise from integrating behavioral considerations into their models and research. Several studies have shown the value of addressing human- behavior consequences of operations-management-design decisions (Boudreau, 2004; Schultz, Juran & Boudreau, 1999).

Mental Models Matter

Organizations miss a significant opportunity to make human-capital decisions more evidence based when they ignore the relevance of business models from other disciplines. Pfeffer (2005) describes the statements of the CEO of American Airlines in the mid-1990s who "wants to see the corpse" of whomever caused a plane to be late, creating a culture of "fear and infighting as people and units tried to pin the blame for problems on others." Pfeffer (2007) notes that, in research on managerial decisions, "practicing managers' responses to scenarios involving various decision dilemmas could be predicted by their different assumptions about human nature, which, in turn, shaped their different philosophies of corporate management and governance. Those assumptions were largely consistent with economics—that is, "the managers assumed that people are self-interested, may engage in self-interest seeking with guile, and are effort averse so that they require incentives and monitoring to ensure performance."

Decades of research suggest such assumptions are likely to lead to poor decisions, increase the risk of losing top talent, reduce the motivation of employees to perform well, and create poorer job attitudes. However, much of that research emanates from psychology and organization behavior, not economics and management. Think how differently leaders might react if their assumptions about people were recast with logic from other business disciplines. For example, "Assuming that your employees require constant monitoring for them to perform is like assuming that the machines in our manufacturing plant need constant monitoring to run well. You waste a lot of time and effort if you try to monitor every aspect of manufacturing, and evidence shows that less monitoring is, often, not that risky and much more productive. You can manage manufacturing by exception. Why, then, do you insist on monitoring your employees so closely, when evidence shows that if you give them more discretion, they will perform better and you will spend less on tracking systems?" Notice how reframing the issue provides a ready metaphor from manufacturing to capture the value and use of evidence about employee monitoring and discretion.

Decision makers use mental models when they confront issues of HR and human behavior at work. Those models determine the evidence they consider relevant and the assumptions they make about evidence that they encounter (Potworowski & Green, chapter 16 of this volume). If they approach decisions about human motivation and performance largely through a logic model that assumes economic self-interest as the exclusive driver, then evidence about trust, commitment, intrinsic loyalty, and nonmonetary needs has little "room" in the model. Reframing within the logic of quality and systems optimization can open the door to evidence about optimum monitoring and risk. Reframing within

the logic of consumer behavior opens the door to consider evidence of intrinsic loyalty, nonmonetary needs, and "trust" in a brand. The catalyst for this might be questions such as, "You know from your background in marketing that our customers are often motivated by product, brand, and social factors that go beyond the simple economic value and price of our offerings. What if that is also true of our employees and their motivation? What evidence might be useful to understand your leadership and employment brand in the eyes of your employees?"

Leaders Know They Are Not Good at Talent Principles

Research conducted at the Center for Effective Organizations suggests that both HR and non-HR leaders know that business leaders have room to improve their sophistication when it comes to principles of human behavior. Table 13.3 shows the results of the Center for Effective Organizations survey of HR and non-HR leaders. We asked both groups to consider whether business leaders use sound principles when they make decisions in several areas of human behavior. We also asked them the same question with regard to several more

Table 13.3. Business Leader Sophistication in Talent Principles Relates Strongly With HR'S Strategic Role

To what extent do business leaders understand and use sound principles when making decisions about ... (1 = little or no extent; 2 = some extent; 3 = moderate extent; 4 = great extent; 5 = very great extent)	Average (HR sample)	Average (Non-HR sample)	Correlation with HR Strategic Role (HR sample	Correlation with HR Strategic Role (Non-HR sample)
Business leaders use of sound principles in human behavior rates lower but relates more to HR's strategic role				
Motivation	2.7	3.0	.31	.40
Devlopment and Learning	2.8	3.0	.27	.48
Labor Markets	2.7	3.1	.18	.33
Culture	2.9	3.1	.21	.32
Organization Design	2.8	3.1	.32	.60
Compated with more "traditional" management disciplines				
Business Strategy	3.6	3.7	.22	.15
Finance	4.0	4.1	.20	−.04
Marketing	3.5	3.2	.22	.25
Technology	3.3	3.3	.22	.25

Adapted from Edward Lawler and John Boudreau Strategic Excellence in Human Resources Management. Palo Alto: Stanford University Press, 2009.

traditional management disciplines including strategy, finance, marketing, and technology.

The first two columns of the table show the average ratings. On average, the use of sound principles in the human capital areas was at or below the midpoint of a five-point scale. Business leaders rated themselves somewhat higher than HR leaders rated them, but both business leaders and HR leaders rated the human-capital disciplines lower than virtually all the more traditional disciplines in the bottom of the table.

When Leaders Are Good at Talent Principles, HR Is a Stronger Strategic Partner

The third and fourth columns show the correlations between a separate question about the strength of HR as a strategic partner, and the ratings of how well business leaders use sound principles. The results show a significant positive association for both samples and for virtually all the human-capital disciplines. The higher the ratings HR or non-HR leaders gave business leaders on using sound human-capital principles, the higher they rated HR's strategic role. Notice that, in the bottom of the figure, this relationship is less pronounced for the traditional business disciplines, suggesting this relationship reflects something specific about human-capital mental models. One might have predicted that weaker business leaders would require a stronger HR strategic partner to make up for their shortcomings, but the results show just the opposite: The stronger business leaders are in sound human-capital principles, the stronger the strategic role of HR.

Retooling and Team-Shared Mental Models

The literature on team mental models and performance offers insights and a research model. If we think of a "team" of HR leaders and their non-HR counterparts, research on how teams benefit from shared mental models (SMMs) is illuminating as a theoretical base for predicting the effects of retooling and reframing HR decisions and evidence using proven business models. An SMM is a team's shared representation, comprising shared knowledge, skill, attitudes, the team's objectives, team processes, teamwork components, communication, coordination, adaptation, roles, behavior patterns, and interactions (Cooke et al., 2003).

Research suggests that SMMs among team members have a number of positive effects (Johnson & O'Connor, 2008):

• Teammates who have similar beliefs and knowledge structure are better able to anticipate their teammates' actions and information needs and to respond effectively (Cannon-Bowers, Salas, & Converse, 1993; Rouse, Cannon-Bowers, & Salas, 1992; Smith-Jentsch, Campbell, Milanovkh, & Reynolds, 2001).

• High levels of SMMs lead to greater team expectations that influence effective team behaviors (Rouse et al., 1992).

• Teams with SMMs require less overt planning because teammates are able to predict what others will expect, thus reducing the need to explicitly communicate (Rouse et al., 1992).

• Teams with SMMs use their shared knowledge to adapt quickly to changing task demands (Cannon-Bowers et al., 1993).

Thus, if retooling HR can contribute to shared mental models (SMMs) among academics in different disciplines, and between HR leaders and non-HR leaders, the SMM evidence suggests untapped opportunities to find common ground and improve performance. However, SMM's seem unlikely to arise solely through the mental models that underpin traditional scholarly research in HR. Rather, it seems more likely that SMMs will be built by first understanding the mental models that ultimate decision makers use, and then tapping those models to reframe human capital decisions and research.

The preceding list of consequences of SMMs would be worthy goals indeed for evidence-based approaches to HR, human capital, and organizational issues. Imagine situations in which the "team" described in the list included scholars, HR leaders and non-HR leaders, and their interactions and performance could be described as having "similar beliefs and knowledge structures," "effective team behaviors," "implicit communication," and "rapid adaptation to changing needs." Many might say that these descriptions seem to be almost the opposite of what is typically observed in "teams" of HR and non-HR leaders, yet such team behaviors describe important underpinnings of a truly effective and evidence-based approach to vital decisions.

How Retooling HR Can Enhance the Elements of SMMs

Research on the composition of SMMs (e.g., Johnson et al., 2007; Mathieu, Heffher, Goodwin, Salas, & Cannon-Bowers, 2000) suggests that they are composed of various categories: team dynamics, such as team members' roles and responsibilities; teammates, including team members' knowledge, skills, abilities, beliefs, preferences, and styles; and task, for instance, cue strategy associations, understanding task procedures, and typical task strategies (Cannon-Bowers & Salas, 2001; Cannon- Bowers, Tannenbaum, Salas, & Volpe, 1995). Let's consider how retooling might affect each of these.

TASK ELEMENTS OF SMMS

Regarding tasks, team SMMs enhance the understanding of facts, concepts, and relations and help in the understanding of the foundation of information needed to perform tasks (Langan-Fox, Anglim, & Wilson, 2004). In addition, sharing knowledge enables teammates to interpret cues in a similar manner, make compatible decisions, and take appropriate action (Klimoski & Mohammed, 1994). Thus, if retooling HR produces SMMs between HR and team members outside HR, the relevant evidence, performance requirements, effectiveness definition, and cues will be interpreted more similarly, leading to more appropriate action.

Consider the decision about whether to customize rewards to individuals or specific groups (such as millenials, developing-market leaders, etc.). When evidence such as differences in needs, total reward elements (such as pay, benefits, development opportunities, flexibility, quality of supervision, etc.), and relationships between rewards and outcomes is framed only within an HR model of compensation structures, expatriation rules, equity theory, and so forth, then non-HR leaders who are neither familiar nor experienced with such frameworks may ignore the evidence or misinterpret it. However, we have seen that, if leaders already understand and accept a logical framework such as customer or market segmentation, then the decision about where and how to customize the employment "deal" may be approached through a mental model similar to the way marketing might examine the decision about where and how to customize the "deal" for consumers. If scholars and leaders within the HR discipline, framed their evidence and arguments using the consumer-customization framework that might create a stronger SMM with their non-HR counterparts. The task of deciding where and when to customize the employment deal now can draw upon shared task knowledge from marketing and consumer research, and it can achieve more of the valued team-based outcomes that research suggests is associated with SMMs.

TEAMMATE ELEMENTS OF SMMS

Teammate elements of SMMs include the shared understanding of team members' knowledge, skills, beliefs, preferences, and styles. Retooling HR seems likely to help clarify the respective relevant expertise of non-HR leaders and HR leaders for human-capital decisions. This is a fundamental problem in evidence-based HR decisions. HR and non-HR leaders are often unaware of existing research knowledge, as many chapters in this volume attest. Non-HR leaders often have no framework for understanding the skills that comprise HR expertise, and the beliefs of HR and non-HR leaders are also often unknown to each other.

For example, non-HR leaders often believe that their knowledge of worker motivation and performance is sufficient for decisions about feedback, goal setting, and performance-based rewards. It is not unusual for them to believe that they should strive to motivate everyone to be a top performer on all elements of the job, and that they should always try to place the best possible candidate in every role. Yet, decades of evidence suggest that the relationship between the quality of employees or job candidates and their contribution to organizational goals can vary. Differences in job performance have very large effects in some roles and much smaller effects in others (Cascio & Boudreau, 2011; Hunter, Schmidt, & Judiesch, 1990). Retooling the job performance question in the framework of engineering performance tolerances reveals that it is a special case of a very typical management question— "Where will improvements in quality or performance make the biggest difference?" Seen through this lens, it is clear that leaders choose where to push for maximum performance or quality, and where to be satisfied with meeting minimum standards, in disciplines such as engineering, operations, and marketing. The same framework applies as well to employee performance (Boudreau 2010b).

Thus, the beliefs of HR leaders and their counterparts about optimal performance can be better aligned when the performance-management question is retooled to resemble engineering and manufacturing tolerance analysis. Moreover, by seeing the question as similar to the performance-value relationship from other management areas the potential contribution of HR research on the relationship between performance and value is clearer.

TEAM DYNAMIC ELEMENTS OF SMMS

A team's SMMs often focus on its members' roles and responsibilities. Retooling HR issues within the frameworks that are well-accepted by constituents can shed light and help align team-member roles. Let us continue with the preceding example involving retooling performance management as a special case of performance tolerances. Typically, a performance-management issue may be seen by line leaders as an opportunity to ask HR to develop a new performance-management system, one that reflects the attributes that are most tangible to the line leader. The leader might want a system that is easier to implement, resembles a system that is used by well-known companies, or one that reduces the need for them to have difficult discussions with poor performers.

Seen through the framework of performance-tolerance models, the relationship of the leader to their HR counterpart is different. When it comes to performance tolerances in other disciplines, a line leader would not ask an engineer or a financial advisor to develop a performance evaluation system simply based on the line leader's specifications, weekend reading, or a desire to avoid facing up to difficult facts. The line leader understands that they certainly must bring their knowledge of their goals and operations, but they also understand that the production engineer will bring many tools for isolating the relative effect of improvements in the quality of different elements of production, and the finance advisor will bring many tools for identifying where investments or better handling of money can make the biggest difference (such as isolating whether improved sales or improved cost control is needed to enhance cash flow).

Armed with this retooled framework for performance management, non-HR leaders may come to understand that their HR counterparts should not just deliver performance processes when asked. Instead, they should bring tools and frameworks for understanding where employee performance and quality make the biggest difference, and how to enhance performance and quality where they matter most. The retooled framework also helps HR leaders understand that their role better. Their task is not to dictate to their non-HR counterparts the "correct" approaches to performance appraisal and rewards, but to work with their counterparts to isolate where such tools are likely to have their greatest effect, and to tailor such systems so that they are simple to use where possible, and have increased detail or complexity when it is clearly worthwhile.

Thus, both HR and non-HR leaders now can proceed from a common understanding that the goal is to optimally match the performance-management

system to the criticality of the performance issue. HR brings evidence to bear where it matters most, but HR is not compelled to create perfectly "valid" systems everywhere. Non-HR leaders realize that although they may have intimate knowledge of their workers and their business goals, they should no more adopt a performance-management system without consulting their HR counterparts than they would adopt a cash-flow or production system without consulting their financial or operations-engineering experts.

Measuring the Mental Models of HR and Its Counterparts

Research on team mental models suggests intriguing methods for measuring the effects of retooling HR on SMMs. Kang, Yang, and Rowley (2006) noted that SMM measurement has focused on both the similarity of knowledge structure and knowledge content. Cannon-Bowers and Salas (2001) identify three approaches to measuring knowledge structure. The first concentrates on the "pathfinder" that calculates the psychological distance between constructs. The second, the "concept map," depicts the structure of individual beliefs in a particular domain. The third checks the similarities of cards chosen as the "reflective measure" of psychological similarities or diversity.

These all focus on measuring knowledge structure rather than knowledge content contained within it (Kang, Yang, & Rowley, 2006). Is it enough that the mental models be shared, or should the models themselves also be consistent with evidence-based knowledge? HR leaders and their counterparts can probably achieve SMMs by adopting shared models that may not fully use evidence-based knowledge. A typical model might focus on "efficiency," or achieving the lowest-cost HR activities. For example, it might dictate that the correct way to implement layoffs would be to cut across the board to meet necessary cost levels. Both HR and their line counterparts might have very aligned mental models regarding their roles, expertise, and objectives, yet, evidence suggests that such approaches may be harmful to long-term organization success and employee well being (Cascio, 2002). Thus, the measure of the quality of SMMs should not simply be based on alignment and effective team functioning but also on whether the mental models themselves are evidence based. Again, retooling HR using logical frameworks from other well-accepted disciplines may address this; as in many other disciplines there is an explicit framework for considering distinctions between short- and long-run consequences, and between cost reduction and value creation.

Imperatives for Improving Team Mental Models, and the Role of Retooling

Arthur, Maes and Bratton-Jeffrey (2005) summarized five imperatives for improving team effectiveness through shared mental models. They suggest several ways that retooling HR with accepted logical frameworks from other disciplines can contribute to each imperative.

Imperative 1: Clarification of Team Objectives, Tasks, Environment, and Variables. Retooling clarifies objectives by suggesting new measures of success, such as the difference between minimizing turnover and optimizing it, the difference between insuring that competencies are useful in all future situations versus optimizing a portfolio of competencies. Retooling redefines how the group considers the relevant variables and environmental factors, such as by redefining the relevant data as comparative turnover rates to instead be the business risk associated with vacancies, and the "ordering" and "holding" costs of staffing.

Imperative 2: Establishing Roles and Responsibilities. Traditional role assumptions might hold that HR addresses talent issues at the request of line leaders, that the "business" models apply to nontalent issues and that "HR" models apply to talent. Retooling suggests that non-HR leaders may bring useful logical models to the talent arena, and that HR leaders are expected to shape solutions by considering options that arise from understanding talent value, cost, and risk.

Imperative 3: Information Processing, Communication, and Collaborative Modeling Rules and Procedures. Retooling suggests new frameworks for information processing, communication, and collaboration. Reframing talent issues within logic that is accepted by line leaders causes data such as turnover rates, engagement scores, competency levels, and so forth to be processed differently. It opens up new ways to communicate about those ideas. It heightens collaboration because the new model examines what we can learn about talent by applying proven logical models wherever they exist, rather than seeing the talent decisions as distinct from the dominant logical models of other disciplines.

Imperative 4: Knowledge of Team Members' Backgrounds and Styles. Although it is often quite apparent that different decision makers have expertise in their different functions, retooling provides a means for discussion about those boundaries and distinctions. For example, retooling workforce strategy and competency planning within the framework of portfolio theory shows that workforce competencies can be optimized against an uncertain future, using tools similar to those that optimize financial portfolios (Boudreau, 2010b). This perspective reveals the value in solving HR planning issues with team members who have backgrounds in portfolio risk.

Imperative 5: Collaborative Modeling Scheme. Retooling suggests that new collaborative models will arise when HR and non-HR leaders agree in principle to pool their resources, by using proven business logic to reframe and inform talent analytics and decisions. Collaboration is not limited simply to identifying talent needs and then relying on an HR process model to meet them. Instead, it begins earlier as talent issues are considered more collaboratively through the lens of proven business logic.

Mental Models May Be More Vital Than Comprehensive HR Measures

A common belief is that, if HR measured itself in ways more similar to areas such as finance and marketing, the improved measures would enhance HR's strategic role and the sophistication and quality of the decisions that non-HR leaders and employees make about the human capital under their stewardship. Typically, such competencies seem to reflect HR's ability to gather, summarize, and analyze data, often using statistical approaches from the disciplines that are already foundations of HR management, such as industrial psychology. HR analytics and evidence-based HR is often synonymous with statistically proving the causal relationships between HR investments and organizational financial outcomes (Gates, 2004).

Yet, without clear logical frameworks for using data, even such causal measurements can be dangerously misinterpreted or ignored. Evidence-based decisions not only require measures, but also sound logic (Boudreau & Ramstad, 2007; Cascio & Boudreau, 2011). More measures don't necessarily improve the logic. Indeed, trying to foist complex statistical analyses on business leaders is a recipe for frustration and resistance. For example, HR might be able to show the causal relationship between organizational outcomes and such things as employee engagement, turnover, performance, or training prowess. Nonetheless, this finding still begs the question of how much should be invested in each of these things to optimally improve organization performance. Even if HR can use sophisticated data-mining techniques to predict which employees are likely to leave or join the organization, that still begs the question of how to use that knowledge to optimally invest in the right levels of employee retention and acquisition. A fundamental pillar of EBMgt is identifying the relevant scientific evidence on which to base organizational actions. Better mental models are a precursor for organizational decision makers to know when and how to use HR research.

The paradox is that HR is based on some of the most rigorous and analytically sophisticated analysis methods in the social sciences, but these findings and methods are simply not in the lexicon of the leaders that make most of the decisions about people. Decades of research by psychologists, sociologists, and others has produced statistical tools that can unearth important insights and an array of well-documented tools to track things like turnover, engagement, performance, capability, skills, and commitment, as several chapters in this volume describe. Too often, however, these tools and analysis frameworks are the sole purview of HR professionals, or the purview of those PhD analysts in the HR function. Why are such potent tools more widely used by leaders outside of HR? This has been a perennial question at professional meetings of industrial psychologists, researchers in HR, and HR professional societies for decades.

The answer may lie partly in the realization that we must consider not just the sophistication of the frameworks used within the HR profession, but rather their accessibility to leaders and employees outside HR. It requires considering how to connect HR analysis frameworks to the logical mental models that leaders already know, use, and trust. This is far different from convincing leaders they should attend to measures, analysis, and findings that are couched exclusively in the lexicon of HR.

There is a growing emphasis on evidence-based approaches to talent management, inspired in part by the "evidence-based medicine" movement. The idea of evidence-based medicine is that doctors, nurses, and other clinical decision makers will draw upon the best possible evidence in making their choices. Yet, studies of how doctors really made decisions suggest that much clinical practice is not based on the latest scientific information but, rather, on such things as textbooks, obsolete premises, untrustworthy research, unendorsed reviews, and anecdotes or personal experiences. They may rely too heavily on what professors told them, rather than more recent or comprehensive evidence. Even in medicine, clinicians often do not believe that results observed in trials can be directly translated into clinical practice (Rodrigues, 2000).

Create HR Measurement Systems That Make It Easy to Use Evidence

A key element of evidence-based medicine is getting evidence used. That requires changing the way clinicians think about how they approach their work, and the role of evidence within it. Evidence must fit with the way clinicians do their work. It needs to be more naturally embedded in the way they actually encounter patient problems, and it needs to be appropriate to the particular questions they need to address. Clinicians want fast, up-to-date and concise responses to their queries. They need the body of scientific evidence organized into "systematic reviews" that answer a specific clinical question by using rules that capture, appraise, and synthesize the information in the most relevant ways (Briner and Denyer, chapter 7 of this volume).

In the same way, an overlooked key to greater analytical and evidence-based sophistication in talent management may be that the information is not organized and presented in ways that managers can use in making their decisions. Far too many HR information systems were designed to be efficient and accurate sources of information to satisfy the compliance or financial reporting needs of the organization. A compliance-based design seldom makes it easy to discern the most vital trends, relationships, and factors affecting key decisions.

The Conference Board research on evidence-based HR management reported that in 2004, it was still difficult to establish causal relationships between human capital metrics and business outcomes, despite the fact that about half the respondents reported active collaboration between HR managers and those in other business disciplines (Gates, 2004). The answer may be to connect the data to different frameworks that are more familiar and more useful to those that make the vital human-capital decisions. It seems unlikely that much progress will be made by insisting that leaders become adept at the disciplines that underlie HR, such as psychology, organizational behavior, and behavioral decision making. Decades of research in these areas do not seem to have produced deep penetration into leadership mental models or training. Something different is needed to bridge the gap.

Educate Non-HR Leaders

It has often been suggested that improved decisions about human capital and greater credibility for the HR profession requires that HR professionals become more familiar with "the business," meaning the operational, financial, and strategic goals and logic of their organizations. Anthony Rucci, EVP at Cardinal Health and a key opinion leader on using HR measurements to connect people and business outcomes, stated, "Business acumen is the single biggest factor that HR professionals in the U.S. lack today" (Gibbons, 2009). This gap is typically addressed by increasing the development and training of HR professionals in disciplines such as finance, marketing, and operations. It is also the reason many organizations place leaders from outside the HR profession in leadership positions within HR.

However, it's also possible that fostering a connection between HR and business expertise misses a crucial point. No matter how well HR understands the business, a key to better decisions is in the mental models of those outside HR. In particular, a significant limitation may be the sophistication with which non-HR leaders approach decisions about human capital and talent. An HR industry survey found that 39 percent of HR leaders rated "understanding how to align with business leaders" as a most needed competency (Bersin, 2009). Alignment requires more than being right or even "knowing the business." It is much more about educating non-HR leaders, and a vital element of that education is the mental models that business leaders use.

Yet, non-HR leaders are seldom informed of these principles. The standard curricula for organization and business leaders rarely require as much training in human behavior, as it does in the behavior of money markets, customers or supply chains (Colbert, Rynes, & Brown, 2005). Although no organization allows anyone to run a significant operating unit without demonstrating a basic understanding of these traditional management disciplines, many organizations allow leaders to pursue entire careers without ever assessing whether they are remotely familiar with sound principles in human capital areas. It seems likely that it will be some time before non-HR general managers become sophisticated in the standard paradigms that define human capital research and evidence. The path toward greater sophistication regarding talent issues, among non-HR leaders, is not navigated simply by providing analysis and insights that reflect the traditional mental models of the HR profession. The first steps must likely be taken by meeting leaders at least halfway. To advance evidence-based HR management requires translating the valuable insights that reside in HR data, systems, and processes in a way that leaders can comfortably digest.

Avoid Opacity

The frameworks and systems that HR provides are often based on disciplines that non-HR leaders don't understand, use jargon that is exclusively understood only by those in the HR "club," and require decision makers outside HR to be counseled and even overseen by certified HR professionals. It is tempting to see this opacity as giving the HR discipline exclusivity and power. There is certainly a place for controls in certain areas of HR, to maintain legal compliance, for example. However, if carried too far, the use of frameworks, data, and principles that are foreign to those outside the profession can shut out managers who would like to better understand HR issues such as attraction, retention, and performance, but are discouraged by the tendency for these things to be addressed in very arcane ways. If your club is so exclusive that your key constituent can't join, you can't very well influence those who are excluded!

More mature professions like finance and marketing have distilled a set of principles that not only invite those outside their profession to use their frameworks, they actually often require that the basic principles be understood, as a prerequisite to a managerial or leadership role. The analysis systems of finance, marketing, operations and manufacturing actually teach these fundamental principles as users interact with the system (Boudreau & Ramstad, 2007). For example, in finance, the formula for return on equity (ROI) is well-known to managers in every discipline. It provides a useful and consistent starting point for understanding where the effects of operating and financial decisions may impact financial returns. There is a deep underlying set of measures, principles, and calculations supporting this concept, and the finance profession requires at least a basic understanding of this formula for virtually any competent business leader (Boudreau & Ramstad, 2007). With this consistent and valid framework, finance and accounting professionals can be much more effective at helping all organization members to think clearly about the financial implications of their decisions.

When it comes to talent decisions, such broad principles are often more obscure. For example, it is not unusual for HR to present its measurements in the form of a vast array of indicators, sometimes organized into categories based on a scorecard or portal. Yet, it is often quite difficult for leaders to know where to look to understand the overall pattern. This is often the basis for managers' requests that HR simply provide three to five measures for leaders to track. The problem is that the three or five most available measures may not be very informative regarding underlying relationships between human capital and organizational outcomes. For example, every set of such measures includes turnover rates, but as we saw, turnover rates have very different implications depending on the situation.

Finance, Marketing, and Operations Are More Systematic—and More Transparent

Improving the quality of HR activities like staffing, training, succession planning, and compensation is valuable and important, but such sophisticated practices can only go so far, in the hands of employees and leaders who are not equipped to think clearly and logically about the underlying issues. Well-meaning leaders and employees will dutifully implement HR practices or attend to HR measures, such as turnover and engagement, but often without a logical framework that helps them understand how these things relate to the organization's ultimate success.

Managers are also held accountable for outcomes such as cash flow and market share, but here they often have a far better idea about why these things are connected to strategic success. This is because of a subtle difference between the way organizations approach their competition in the market for talent and the way they approach decisions in the markets for money and customers. Finance frameworks create organizational value by enhancing decisions that depend on or impact financial resources. Marketing frameworks create organizational value by enhancing decisions that depend on or impact customer or product resources. Finance and marketing provide reliable and deeply logical frameworks that connect financial and customer capital to the organization's sustainable strategic success. Strategic decisions must go beyond generic "best practices" to create a unique and sustainable competitive position for the organization (Porter, 1996).

In the same way, an important element of the evolution of talent management and HR will be the development of a decision science that provides principles to guide decisions in the market for human capital or talent (Boudreau & Ramstad, 2007). The power of more evolved disciplines isn't merely that finance, marketing, and operations are necessarily more logical, analytical, or even more precisely measured. After all, there is plenty of available logic, analysis, and measurement to help leaders make better decisions about people. However, unlike the other disciplines, HR has not yet developed a decision science that is understood and used by leaders outside the profession.

Decision sciences like finance and marketing have developed a body of principles that are commonly understood by those outside the profession. One might think that if everyone understands the body of principles, the profession will be diminished because everyone will think they can do it as well as the experts. However, in the case of finance and marketing, widespread knowledge of the basic principles does not detract from the credibility of the profession; quite the opposite. By making the profession's principles more transparent, such basic principles actually foster greater understanding and respect for the more nuanced underlying principles on which they are based. Recall the findings in Figure 13.3. Business leaders savvier about human-capital principles were more—not less—likely to perceive HR as a strong strategic partner. Connecting the considerations in the world of talent and human capital to these already-trusted frameworks, can enhance understanding and, ultimately, respect for the systematic principles that underlie the HR and talent discipline.

Getting Started—Unlearning, A-B-C Priorities, and Rapid Prototyping

How to begin? Three perspectives, themselves long recognized by other disciplines but not as often applied to changes in HR, may provide some clues about where to begin. They might be called "unlearning," "A-B-C priorities," and "rapid prototyping." Let's examine each of them.

Unlearning to Make Room for Learning

Rousseau (chapter 1 of this volume) suggests that EBMgt may require building "scaffolding" between the dominant mental models of leaders and the logical models required to make better decisions based on evidence. This requires that managers be induced to think about their thinking, specifically to think about what is their dominant mental framework, and to shore up weak spots or to connect to other disciplines. In order to motivate meta-cognition about HR decisions, it may be necessary to frame them in terms of more familiar models, precisely to provide a framework for meta-cognition among leaders unaccustomed to human-behavior principles.

Rousseau (chapter 1 of this volume) also notes the reluctance of leaders to gather and confront organizational facts, citing the leader who asked not to be given evidence because, "if you give me data I have to act on it." The idea of retooling HR evidence is in many ways a proposal to confront managers with their blind spots, by showing how differently they approach human-capital decisions from other decisions, and then to invite them to build scaffolding between their more standard and rigorous decision models and the human-capital decisions they face.

C.K. Prahalad, writing about how leaders must rethink their ideas of "competition," suggests that organizations must unlearn in order to learn (Gibson, 2010, p.1) He says,

> Companies are going to have to unlearn a lot of their past—and also to forget it! The future will not be an extrapolation of the past. Like a space rocket on the way to the moon, a company has to be willing to jettison the parts of its past which no longer contain fuel for the journey and which are becoming, in effect, excess baggage. That is particularly difficult for the senior managers—those who actually built the past, and who still have a lot of emotional equity invested in it. If you want to escape the gravitational pull of the past, you have to be willing to challenge your own orthodoxies, to regenerate your core strategies and rethink your most fundamental assumptions about how you are going to compete.

A great deal of evidence suggests that everyone from leaders to military strategists to scientists tend to become attached to the mental frameworks they have used, particularly when they helped to build them. For example, the idea that ancient "land bridges" allowed animals to migrate across the oceans between continents like North America and Africa had to be unlearned in order for the theory of continental drift to offer what turned out to be the more correct explanation for the dispersion of species and geological formations across the continents.

What are the conditions that foster unlearning? Starbuck (1996) suggests the following premises that often drive recognition of the need to unlearn past logical frameworks (Starbuck, 1996):

1. Welcome the realization that things are not good enough. Dissatisfaction with the outcomes being achieved is an obvious reason to consider unlearning. Unfortunately, because mental models are often very entrenched, it often takes very serious

problems or disappointments to support fundamental unlearning. Still, HR leaders can be alert to situations in which results have been disappointing for a long time. For example, in the arena of talent development, it is not unusual for leaders to recognize that, despite a belief that identifying and listing successors for future positions should be a useful way to guard against top-level vacancies, the succession chart is too often not the place from which future leaders emerge. In particular, with the broad recognition of the top-level shortages potentially driven by an aging workforce, it may be possible for HR leaders to use their dissatisfaction with the standard approaches to succession and development to suggest how those approaches might benefit from the perspective of logistics and risk optimization. Evidence about the patterns of career progress, the determinants of career success and satisfaction (Judge, Cable, Boudreau, & Bretz, 1995), and factors that accelerate learning and experience (McCall, 2010) may be more useful and compelling when portrayed within such goals.

2. Frame the unlearning as an experiment. If leaders see themselves as experimenting, and not abandoning long-held approaches, they may be more willing to test and question their assumptions. Experiments provide opportunities to create surprises in controlled situations that may become the evidence that leaders need to rethink their existing models, unlearn them, and apply other models instead. For example, it's not necessary to apply preference mapping to the entire workforce to identify the preference patterns and talent segments for total rewards. Many organizations begin such applications by focusing on a particular group of employees, in which there is obviously high potential value for innovative reward policies. Such experiments often occur when the organization is having a hard time attracting new people or when it is losing valued players. The idea is to try it out, understanding that it might not work, but focus on the learning, rather than setting up failure by claiming that the new approach will certainly produce a better outcome.

3. Use surprises as question marks. Surprises are often dismissed as simple anomalies, random effects that don't identify anything significant. However, surprises can foster unlearning when they are reframed as opportunities to question the existing paradigms. Starbuck (1996) notes an episode in World War I in which the prevailing mind-set was that tanks moved too slowly to support infantry, but when a tank commander surprisingly charged a

German enemy line with three tanks and routed the enemy and destroyed their cannon, General Patton used the episode to rethink the value of tanks as advance reconnaissance. For HR leaders, the moral of the story is not to hide or avoid surprises but to use them as valuable tools. For example, leaders are often surprised to find that younger workers and managers simply do not want to pursue career advancement with the same dogged determination and sacrifice of time with family that older leaders did. One can frame this simply as an anomaly of aging, a short-run result of young people who just haven't matured enough to understand the value of hard work. Or, one can suggest that if this pattern continues, the entire basis on which many career-development and succession programs are built may be threatened. Seen in this way, it is natural to consider how alternative "paths" might be identified using logistics and planning tools, or how to better get ahead of changes in talent segment preferences using conjoint analysis or preference mapping as done with product consumers.

4. Take dissents and warnings seriously. In an era in which innovation has been elevated to a mantra, and some of the seemingly craziest ideas have disrupted long-standing principles about markets, customers, and economic progress, it hardly seems necessary to mention the danger of hastily rejecting outwardly weird dissents. Unlearning suggests that such dissents should at first be seen as reminders that existing approaches might be wrong or obsolete. Starbuck (1996) goes as far as to suggest that organizations take all dissents and warnings as at least partially valid, look for evidence about the odds that they might be correct, evaluate the potential consequences if the dissent turns out to be right, and find ways to test those dissents that have the greatest capacity for significant costs or benefits. Organization leaders need look no further than the economic turmoil of 2008 and 2009. There are many examples of individuals calling attention to the dangers of collateralized debt, even referring to such instruments as the "weapons of mass destruction" in the financial system. Yet, many warnings went unheeded because the sort of financial meltdown these ideas predicted had not happened in recent memory. Scenario analysis often requires decision makers to break out of typical decision patterns and consider strange possibilities. Evidence about HR can be connected to such scenario analysis by retooling the workforce questions as an application of portfolio theory. The question might be framed as, "How prepared would our talent be for all the different future scenarios that might occur, and how can we hedge our bets?" Portfolio theory is a systematic way to do precisely what Starbuck (1996) recommends, carefully considering the likelihood, costs, and benefits of unusual or novel situations. The financial crisis may have provided leaders with an unprecedented opportunity to use disruptive ideas as a way to encourage evidence-based talent planning, even for unlikely scenarios. When seen within the framework of financial portfolio theory, the payoffs to such evidence and research are much clearer.

Seen in this context, evidence regarding traits that affect performance more generally (intelligence, personality, etc.) can be framed as "assets" that are likely to be useful in any future situation, versus those that are more situation-specific (skills, experience, emotions). Such evidence now becomes similar to what an investment analyst would gather to evaluate different asset classes in constructing a portfolio. Reframing talent scenario analysis within portfolio theory logic is also an opportunity to use risk optimization as a framework for meta-cognition, identifying potential biases regarding assumptions about human capital and its adaptability.

5. Contrary beliefs may not necessarily be contradictions. Sometimes, what appear to be clear contradictions may actually reflect underlying consistencies, if we can unlearn our old way of thinking and make room for a new way. Is it possible that a work element can be highly important, yet improving performance in that area does not produce significant returns? This seems to be impossible, until we unlearn the tendency to think of things that are important as necessarily pivotal. In fact, this is true about many aspects of work, including performance of commercial pilots. Being at the (very high) standard of acceptable performance is the key, and there is not much difference between the best and the moderate performing pilot in the cockpit, precisely because such positions are too important to allow for performance risk. Understanding the difference between a work element that is important and not pivotal, and other work elements that are pivotal, may help better frame evidence regarding performance management and performance improvement. For example, it makes little sense to encourage strong performance differentiation for work elements that offer little difference between "good enough" and "great." The literature on utility analysis in selection, training, and compensation (Cascio & Boudreau, 2011; Sturman, Trevor, Boudreau, & Gerhart, 2003) would likely make more sense to managers when couched in the more familiar terms of performance tolerances. When beliefs seem contrary, but are held strongly by reliable and credible sources, it's a clue that perhaps we need to unlearn old models to resolve the controversy.

6. What a stranger thinks to be strange may be a good question. This means that "strangers" to the established way of thinking will often ask what appear to be naïve questions, or pose perspectives that seem less "expert" than those familiar with the dominant way of thinking. Yet, when the "strange" thoughts of a stranger are given some credence, what was naïve may seem profound. Starbuck (1996) notes the example of the Sony Walkman, which originated as a failed stereo tape recorder, because the tape-recorder division could fit stereo playback components but not stereo recording components into the unit. The received wisdom was that, if it could not record and it required an external speaker, it could not be a successful product. Sony's founder, Masaru Ibuka, while touring the factories, realized that by attaching headphones to the unit, there would be no need for speakers, and the unit could play back recorded music for one person. The Sony Walkman was born.

The fundamental theme of "retooling HR" is to create opportunities for "strangers" to share their ideas. Well-understood by management disciplines and functions provide valuable logical models to reframe evidence about work behavior. There are smart, well-meaning, and motivated experts in HR and in functions like operations, supply chain, finance, and marketing. As we've seen, some things in HR will seem very strange to an engineer or to a financial risk expert or to a supply-chain analyst. They may well wonder why HR maintains rules such as "minimize talent shortages everywhere," "top performers in every role" or "four successors for every leadership position," when such rules so clearly run counter to standard logic models in the other functional areas. Leaders within and outside HR need to listen more carefully to what appears strange to each of them, and find new insights by reconciling their perspectives.

One specific implication of this idea is that researchers and practitioners in HR seek out their counterparts in other disciplines in reconciliation conferences, to share their respective professional logical models and dilemmas. Rather than defending their respective frameworks, the idea would be to invite criticism and to have all sides articulate things that seem "strange" to them. Indeed, drawing on the earlier discussion, the techniques developed to measure, articulate, and resolve team mental models may well prove quite valuable as a means to study such reconciliation encounters in the field. The result may be more widely shared logic frameworks that integrate HR with diverse disciplines, and a much deeper understanding of what characteristics of the logic models are easy or difficult to reconcile.

The philosopher, George Hegel, advocated dialectical reasoning, which involves taking one proposition, stating its converse, and then considering whether both might be valid (Miller, 1969). The original proposition is called the thesis, the converse is the antithesis, and the union of the two is called a synthesis. Such reasoning contributes to unlearning, by questioning the theses that we come to accept out of habit, and looking for novel syntheses with their antithesis.

For example, the thesis that "better job performance is always valuable" may seem unquestionable, until one considers the antithesis "better job performance can be less valuable, if good enough is as valuable as great performance." The same thing shows up with the thesis "more valid employee selection is good," and the antithesis that "more valid employee selection is bad." The synthesis is that valid selection adds value only under certain conditions in the talent acquisition supply chain, and it is considering the rest of the supply chain that shows us when it is worth the investment and when it is better to forego greater validity to maximize other supply-chain elements.

The thesis "employee turnover is bad" and its antithesis "employee turnover is good," finds synthesis in an approach to turnover more clearly based on optimizing the inventory of employees, the costs of that inventory, and actually planning for strategic employee shortages and surpluses. The thesis that "Developing talent that may not suit future conditions is bad," matches with the antithesis, "developing talent that may not suit future conditions is good." The synthesis is that it may be best to develop separate talent pools suited to different future conditions, because that's the only way to take advantage of the power of diversification to optimize risk and return.

Focus Where It Matters—The A-B-C's of Setting Talent Priorities

Organization leaders can be more systematic in setting HR priorities, and those priorities provide clues to using evidence most productively. There is a concept in inventory management called ABC analysis. Simply put, some types of inventory deserve much greater attention and control than others. For example,

> ABC analysis consists of separating the inventory items into three groupings, according to their annual cost volume usage (unit cost × annual usage). These groups are: A, items having a high dollar usage; B, items having an intermediate dollar usage; and C, items having a low dollar usage. While percentages vary from firm to firm, it's common to find a small percentage of the items accounting for a large percentage of the annual cost volume usage. ABC analysis provides a tool for identifying those items that will make the largest impact on the firm's overall inventory cost performance when improved inventory control procedures are implemented.
> ABC analysis helps focus management attention on what is really important.
> (Volimann, Berry, Whybark, & Jacobs, 2004).

Leaders must make choices, and evidence should be framed within those choices. Improved performance is not equally vital or valuable everywhere. Attention to employee shortages and surpluses is not equally vital in every position. Certain career and development paths may be much more vital to future workforce preparedness than others. Certain future scenarios hold much greater implications for talent investments than others.

When HR leaders overlook this principle, they find themselves recommending blanket policies such as reduced turnover, increased engagement, or enhanced innovation, across the board, in a kind of "peanut butter" approach to HR (Boudreau & Ramstad, 2007), spreading a good thing equally all across the organization. Those outside HR, who are familiar with even the rudiments of ABC analysis, will rightly see that this is not how other management disciplines work. Their discomfort with a blanket HR policy may be deeply rooted in their experience of ABC analysis applied to inventory or other areas. A first step in retooling may be simply to start engaging the conversation about which elements of talent strategy and investments are probably "A," "B," or "C."

Innovation, Serious Play, and Rapid Prototyping

How many individuals would associate the words "innovation," "play" and "rapid prototyping" with HR management? Not many. Yet, retooling HR requires just such perspectives. The frameworks suggested here embody a paradox: The business models have been around for decades, and have a large and well-developed array of specifications and logical rules. Applying them to the arena of HR is largely new, and certainly not widely accepted. These approaches are foreign to most organization leaders, and today's HR system specifications are seldom compatible with the logical frameworks described here. How will one measure the "holding costs" of an employee "inventory?" How will one map the paths through the career pipeline, and assign values to them that allow optimizing the flow of talent? How can we measure the performance-value curves for different roles, jobs, and competencies, when our existing systems rely so heavily on job descriptions?

Of course, these are all legitimate concerns, but in some ways they fail to recognize the innovation path toward the retooled HR of the future. In most disciplines it was the logic that preceded the systems and the measurement. Today's well-developed supply-chain, market research, finance, and operations-management systems did not emerge first, and then become infused with logical models like portfolio theory, linear programming, and conjoint analysis. Rather, the concepts of risk return, logistics optimization, and market segmentation came first. Those concepts were tested and applied, usually imperfectly, using existing systems and data, and a good deal of speculation and estimation. However, as the power of the logic became apparent, it also revealed how to advance the systems and measures to support the new tools.

This brings us back to "innovation," "play" and "rapid prototyping." Michael Schrage's book *Serious Play* (Schrage, 2000), chronicling how companies innovate successfully, makes the point well.

> The essence of serious play is the challenge and thrill of confronting uncertainties. Whether uncertainties are obstacles or allies depends on how you play. The challenge of converting uncertainty into manageable risks or opportunities explains why serious play is often the most rational behavior for innovators. Serious play is about improvising with the unanticipated in ways that create new value. Any tools, technologies, techniques or toys that let people improve how they play seriously with uncertainty is guaranteed to improve the quality of innovation. (Schrage, 2000).

Traditional HR tends to be "specification driven," meaning that it operates from a desire to give careful consideration to all the necessary elements, develops a specification that is well vetted and seems to encompass all the needs of the various clients, and implements the system based on that specification. As Schrage points out, this is in stark contrast to a "prototype-driven" approach, in which the goal is to get quickly to a working, and imperfect, prototype that clients can see and use. It means accepting the inevitable result that clients will probably reject and wish to modify the prototype in ways that they themselves did not anticipate when they provided the original specifications. In a specification-driven approach, this is a failure—the client rejected the carefully designed system. In a prototype-driven approach, this is a success—the prototype facilitated a quicker and much deeper understanding of the clients' requirements, and can now be modified more accurately to fit them.

Schrage notes how powerful the idea of rapid prototyping can be for innovation, and how important it is to understand the distinction between pursuing specifications as if they were fixed and pursuing specifications for the purpose of developing prototypes whose rejection is an expected part of the process. For example, (Schrage, 2000) notes the common problem that "at least one-quarter of internal software-development initiatives are cancelled outright and written off as total losses." He suggests that this is caused by the tendency for software-development groups to follow procedures eerily similar to today's HR organizations: The developers, in a sincere effort to be responsive, perform extensive requirements analysis for weeks, results are circulated for approval, modifications are made, and clients are required to sign off on the requirements analysis before work is started. Then, the development team takes weeks to construct a prototype designed to meet all of the specifications and presents it to the client expecting to be praised for the careful design, but the client says, "it's almost right, but now that we see it, we realize we need something different." The design team is disappointed, the client is surprised that the design team doesn't welcome the feedback, and far more resources have been spent than needed. Schrage suggests an alternative approach in which the goal is to identify the few most important initial design criteria and create a "quick and dirty" prototype specifically designed to be rejected. Such prototypes are treated as vehicles for further conversation and development (Schrage, 2000). This is the essence of the contrast between being "specification driven" and "prototype driven."

This goes directly to the EBMgt pillar of stakeholder concerns, and applies it to evidence-based HR. Too often, HR professionals see their role as delivering programs and services that are fully developed and finished. Evidence is seen as something one gathers prior to design and implementation, in an effort to make sure the final product is satisfactory to as many stakeholders as possible, and as empirically and logically defensible as possible. Yet, when HR "products" are reframed within the accepted logic of software or product development, it is apparent that, often, the right approach will be actually to strive for fast but imperfect, and use field evidence to modify accordingly. Theresa Welbourne coined the term "Fast HR" to express this idea (Welbourne, 2010). Fast HR reframes HR program development using logical principles from the discipline of "extreme programming" (Lindstrom & Jeffries, 2004), which is an accepted logical framework in the discipline of information systems and software development.

Embedding HR and organizational behavior evidence within trusted and familiar business logic will require recognition that imperfection is not a reason to wait. Yes, the evolution described here is significant, but it also has the potential to create significantly greater common ground between HR leaders and their clients and counterparts. It has the advantage of starting with logical frameworks that are already familiar to organization leaders and, thus, don't require them to learn an entirely new language. In many cases, the new tools can be built initially on existing measurements and data systems, even if they require some additional speculation or simulation.

Thus, the conditions for rapid prototyping are abundant, but organizational leaders will need to adopt a very "non-HR" mind-set to engage the process. HR has made great progress, and created immense value, by becoming very good at ensuring compliance with vital rules, avoiding risk, and delivering programs and services only after very careful design and analysis. Yet, the rest of the organizational world is shifting toward a fast-changing environment that requires more attention to innovation and rapid response. By starting with tools that already have proven business value, the necessary rapid prototyping for the retooled HR is partially underway. It is much easier for leaders outside HR to envision new HR tools, when they can use as their template the tools they already use quite easily. HR leaders must resist the temptation to impose their own logical frameworks, and embrace the chance to connect to tools that already exist.

So, HR leaders should invite an open-minded counterpart to "play" with one of the ideas in this handbook's chapters: "What if we thought of turnover as inventory depletion. How would that change the way we look at it?" "What if we mapped the flow of employees through our organization and got those engineers that do pipeline and logistics analysis to help us understand them?" "What if we drew a few performance-value curves for some of the jobs in which performance issues seem to be most troublesome?" This is the kind of "serious play" that has revolutionized management disciplines in the past and has the potential to do so for HR.

Implications for Scholarly Research**

This chapter has noted many potential research questions about how evidence is used, the development of shared mental models, and how more traditional business concepts such as risk and performance tolerances apply to HR. Generally, future research might use retooled frameworks to guide how evidence about HR is gathered, and it might study mental models to better understand how evidence is and might better be used.

Regarding how evidence is gathered, the analogies described in this chapter may suggest how to extend or deepen research in areas such as performance management, turnover, leadership development, and employment arrangements. For example, approaching performance-management research within the framework of performance-tolerance analysis suggests that techniques from engineering and product design might be used to map performance curves (Pritchard & Roth, 1991), rather than assuming a strictly linear relationship between performance changes and organizational value. Can the tools that engineers use to estimate performance curves for product features be applied to assist leaders in mapping such relationships with work performance?

The metaphor of inventory and supply-chain optimization applied to turnover and employee staffing suggests that future research in these areas might draw on data about costs and risks more fully. Although utility analysis models incorporate these variables (see Cascio & Boudreau, 2011), research on turnover and staffing often focuses on predicting turnover itself or enhancing the validity of staffing systems. When seen through an optimization lens, research could focus on the possibility that turnover may be higher (lower) in some situations precisely because employees and leaders sense or understand that this is more optimal, based on the costs and benefits they perceive. Similarly, research on staffing systems might incorporate operations concepts

such as the return on better quality control, to explain why the optimal validity may be lower or higher in some situations, rather than focusing only on how to enhance validity. Approaching questions about customizing employment arrangements through the lens of consumer behavior opens the research to tools from marketing to study such issues as anticipated emotions (Patrick, MacInnis, & Park, 2007).

Regarding the second issue, retooling HR research suggests the possibility of better understanding the mental models that govern how evidence is used. Earlier, this chapter described how theories and techniques from the field of team-shared mental models (SMMs) might be used to better understand the mental models used by HR leaders and their counterparts, as a special case of team effectiveness. In addition, mapping the mental models that HR leaders and others bring to questions of motivation, learning, and engagement may explain the patterns of how evidence is used or not used.

For example, when studying how leaders use performance-management systems, the engineering concept that performance-value functions may be nonlinear might explain why some managers welcome, and others resist, systems that encourage significant differentiation in performance ratings. Where performance differences have little significance, it is quite logical for a leader to resist investing time and effort in mapping those differences, despite the fact that such mapping creates a more useful criterion for selection, training, and so forth. Similarly, using a supply-chain or inventory metaphor to understand employee staffing may help explain why leaders are eager to better understand evidence about selection validity or turnover in some situations but not others. Such evidence is less useful where the return or risk-reduction of better selection or reduced turnover is lower, but to study that question requires a framework for measuring how those potential returns are perceived by different constituents.

In essence, it may be quite logical for decision makers to forego the effort to understand and incorporate better evidence in some situations. Assuming that such behavior is always a mistake or limitation may limit our understanding of how evidence is actually used. Finally, bringing accepted management logic models to bear on HR issues may reveal ways to "hook" evidence into frameworks that leaders already understand, and thus better articulate its significance, as the examples in this chapter have shown. Future research might study the difference in evidence use when it is presented in a traditional HR-centric way as compared to when it is embedded in mental models that leaders already accept from other disciplines.

Implications for Business Education and Management Practice

An overarching theme of retooling HR practice and research is the value of creating cross-discipline connections. The premise is that greater integration between the explicit and implicit logic models of disciplines outside and inside HR and organization behavior will lead to greater insight, easier use of untapped evidence, better decisions about employment and management, and, ultimately, more successful and humane organizations.

For HR practitioners, the implication is to learn the logic models of the organization and apply them to HR issues, in addition to the more traditional admonishment to learn how human capital might affect outcomes that are measured using those models. It means that HR education might benefit from using logic models from other disciplines to reframe common topics such as total rewards, staffing, turnover, learning, and workforce planning. This seems particularly important when HR education is targeted to future leaders who will not be HR professionals, because it may enhance their understanding and motivation to learn these topics. However, it is also important for future HR professionals to understand how to retool these HR topics through better-accepted business lenses, so that they can deepen their understanding about those processes and better engage with their non-HR counterparts as practitioners.

In my own MBA classes on HR, I increasingly introduce topics such as rewards, turnover, staffing, and workforce planning by having my MBAs first recall their logic models from consumer behavior, inventory, supply chain, and portfolio risk, and then develop analogies to these HR issues. I find that this engages them to better understand the importance of HR decisions, but also to ask deeper and more sophisticated questions.

Ultimately, one might envision collaborative HR classes that would actually engage instructors or professionals who are experts in business models from other disciplines, work with them to translate those models for application to vital HR issues, and then challenge students to apply the analysis tools and metrics from those well-established disciplines to common HR decisions they must make as future leaders. The objective is not to create technical HR experts, but to create savvy collaborators with future HR professionals.

References

Answers.com. Mental Model. Retrieved , 2011 from http://www.answers.com/topic/mental-model#cite_note-0

Arthur, J. B., Maes, J. D., & Bratton-Jeffery, M. F. (2005). Improving team decision-making performance with collaborative modeling. *Team Performance Management, 11*(1/2), 40–50.

Baker, S. (2009). Data mining moves to human resources. *Business Week*. Retrieved from http://www.businessweek.com/magazine/content/09_12/b4124046224092.htm?chan=top+news_top+news+index+-+temp_top+story

Bersin, J. (2009). *The career factbook for HR and learning professionals*. San Francisco, CA: Bersin and Associates.

Boudreau, J. W. (2004). Organizational behavior, strategy, performance and design in management science. *Management Science, 50*(11), 1463–1476.

Boudreau, J. W. (2010a). *IBM's global workforce initiative*. Washington, DC: Society for Human Resource Management.

Boudreau, J. W. (2010b). *Retooling HR*. Boston, MA: Harvard Business Publishing.

Boudreau, J. W., & Ramstad, P. (2007). *Beyond HR: The new science of human capital*. Boston, MA: Harvard Business Publishing.

Cannon-Bowers, J. A., & Salas, E. (2001). Reflections on shared cognition. *Journal of Organizational Behavior, 22,* 195–202.

Cannon-Bowers, J. A., Salas, E., & Converse, S. A. (1993). Shared mental models in expert decision making teams. In N. J. Castellan Jr. (Ed.), *Current issues in individual and group decision making* (pp. 221–246). Mahwah, NJ: Erlbaum.

Cannon-Bowers, J. A., Tannenbaum, S. L, Salas, E., & Volpe, C. E. (1995). Defining team competencies: Implications for training requirements and strategies. In R.A. Guzzo & E. Salas (Eds.), *Team effectiveness and decision-making in organizations* (pp. 333–380). San Francisco, CA: Jossey-Bass.

Cascio, W. F. (2002). *Responsible restructuring*. San Francisco, CA: Berrett-Koehler.

Cascio, W. F., & Boudreau, J. W. (2011). *Investing in People* (2nd ed.). Upper Saddle River, NJ: Pearson Education.

Colbert, A., Rynes, S. L., & Brown, K. G. (2005). Who believes us? Understanding managers' agreement with human resource research findings. *Journal of Applied Behavioral Science, 41*(3), 304–225.

Cooke, N. J., Kiekel, P. A., Salas, E., Stout, R., Bowers, C. A., & Cannon-Bowers, J. A. (2003). Measuring team knowledge. *Group Dynamics: Theory, Research, and Practice, 7*(3), 179–199.

Dearborn, D. C., & Simon, H. A. (1958). Selective perception: A note on the departmental identification of executives. *Sociometry, 21,* 140–148.

Doyle, J. K., & Ford, D. N. (1998). Mental models concepts for system dynamics research. *System Dynamics Review, 14*(1), 3–29.

Doyle, J. K., & Ford, D. N. (1999). Mental models concepts revisited: Some clarifications and a reply to Lane. *System Dynamics Review, 15*(4), 411–415.

Gates, S. (2004). *Measuring more than efficiency: The new role of human capital metrics*. Conference Board Research Report 1356.

Gibbons, J. (2009). *Evidence-based HR practitioners guide.* Conference Board Research Report R-1427–09-RR.

Gibson, R. (2010). A tribute to C.K. Prahalad. *Blogging Innovation* Retrieved from http://www.business-strategy innovation.com/2010/04/tribute-to-ck-prahalad.html

Hunter, J. E., Schmidt, F. L., & Judiesch, M. K. (1990). Individual differences in output variability as a function of job complexity. *Journal of Applied Psychology, 75,* 28–42.

Johnson, T. E., Lee, Y., Lee, M., O'Connor, D. L, Khalil, M. K., & Huang, X. (2007). Measuring sharedness of team-related knowledge: Design and validation of a shared mental model instrument. *Human Resource Development International, 10*(A), 437–454.

Johnson, E. T., & O'Connor, L. D. (2008). Measuring team shared understanding using the analysis-constructed shared mental model methodology. *Performance Improvement Quarterly, 21*(3), 113–134.

Johnson-Laird, P. N. (1983). *Mental models: Towards a cognitive science of language, inference, and consciousness.* Cambridge, MA: Cambridge University Press.

Judge, T. J., Cable, D. M., Boudreau, J. W., & Bretz, R. D. (1995). An empirical investigation of the determinants of executive career success. *Personnel Psychology, 48,* 485–519.

Kang, K., Yang, H., & Rowley, C. (2006). Factors in team effectiveness: Cognitive and demographic similarities of software development team members. *Human Relations, 59*(12), 1681–1630.

Karren, R. J., & Barringer, M. W. (2002). A review and analysis of the policy-capturing methodology in organizational research: Guidelines for research and practice. *Organizational Research Methods, 5*(4), 337–387.

Klimoski, R., & Mohammed, S. (1994). Team mental model: Construct or metaphor? *Journal of Management, 20*(2), 403–437.

Kuhn, M. H., & Morecroft, J. D. W. (2009, February). *Journal of the Operational Research Society, 60*(2), 191–200.

Langan-Fox, J., Anglim, J., & Wilson, J. R. (2004). Mental models, team mental models and performance: Process, development and future directions. *Human Factors and Ergonomics in Manufacturing, 14*(4), 331–352.

Lawler, E. E., & Boudreau, J. W. (2012). *Achieving excellence in HR management.* Stanford, CA: Stanford University Press.

Lindstrom, L., & Jeffries, R. (2004). Extreme programming and agile software development methodologies. *Information Systems Management, 21*(3), 41–52.

Mathieu, J. E., Heffner, T. S., Goodwin, G. F., Salas, E., & Cannon-Bowers, J. A. (2000). The influence of shared mental models on team process and performance. *Journal of Applied Psychology, 85*(2), 273–283.

McCall, M. W. (2010). Recasting leadership development. *Industrial and Organizational Psychology, 3*(1), 3–19.

Miller, A. V. (1969). *Hegel's science of logic.* Amherst, NY: Humanity Books.

Patrick, V. M., MacInnis, D. J., & Park, C. W. (2007). Not as happy as I thought I'd be: Affective misforecasting and product evaluations. *Journal of Consumer Research, 33*(4), 479–490.

Pfeffer, J. (2005). Changing mental models: HR's most important task. *Human Resource Management, 44*(2), 123–128.

Pfeffer, J. (2007). Human resources from an organizational behavior perspective: Some paradoxes explained. *Journal of Economic Perspectives, 22*(4), 115–134.

Porter, M. E. (1996). What is strategy? *Harvard Business Review, 74,* 61–78.

Pritchard, R. D., & Roth, P. G. (1991). Accounting for nonlinear utility functions in composite measures of productivity and performance. *Organizational Behavior and Human Decision Processes, 50*(2), 341–359.

Reddy, R. & Reddy, S. (2001). *Supply chains to virtual integration.* New York, NY: McGraw-Hill Companies.

Rodrigues, R. (2000). Information systems: The key to evidence-based health practice. *Bulletin of the World Health Organization, 78*(1), 1344–1351.

Rosenbaum, J. E. (1979). Tournament mobility: Career patterns in a corporation. *Administrative Science Quarterly, 24*(2), 220–241.

Rouse, W. B., Cannon-Bowers, J. A., & Salas, E. (1992). The role of mental models in team performance in complex systems. *IEEE Transactions on Systems, Man, and Cybernetics, 22,* 1296–1308.

Schrage, M. (2000). *Serious play.* Boston, MA: Harvard Business School Press.

Schultz, K., Juran, D., & Boudreau, J. W. (1999). The effects of low inventory on the development of productivity norms. *Management Science, 45*(12), 1664–1678.

Smith-Jentsch, K. A., Campbell, G. E., Milanovkh, D. M., & Reynolds, A. Mt. (2001). Measuring teamwork mental models to support training needs assessment, development, and evaluation: Two empirical studies. *Journal of Organizational Behavior, 22,* 179–194.

Starbuck, W. (1996). Unlearning ineffective or obsolete technologies. *International Journal of Technology Management, 11*(7), 725–737. A working paper version of the article is available at http://pages.stern.nyu.edu/~wstarbuc/unlearn.html

Sturman, M. C., Trevor, C. O., Boudreau, J. W., & Gerhart, B. (2003). Is it worth it to win the talent war? Evaluating the utility of performance-based pay. *Personnel Psychology, 56*(4), 997–1035.

Volimann, T. E., Berry, W. L., Whybark, D. C., & Jacobs, F. R. (2004). *Manufacturing planning and control systems for supply chain management.* New York: McGraw-Hill.

Welbourne, T. M. (2010). *Fast HR.* Retrieved from http://eepulse.net/documents/pdfs/Fast.HR.FINAL.pdf

Evidence-Based Management (EBMgt) Using Organizational Facts

Lex Donaldson

Abstract

Managers using evidence-based management (EBMgt) use data that exist in their organization to draw inferences and make decisions. This process is prone to a number of errors, including the small-numbers problem, measurement unreliability, range restriction, and confounding. This chapter makes recommendations about how managers can minimize these errors and make better-informed decision. Recommended procedures include statistical corrections and computation methods that make data more interpretable as well as changes in the way data are reported and aggregated within organizations.

Key Words: organizational facts, organizational data, meta-analysis, small-numbers problem, aggregation, reliability

A long time ago (when I was young!) there was a popular television show called *Dragnet*. This was a drama about police in the United States. The detective hero, a hard-boiled type, would interrupt weeping witnesses to curtly say: "Just give me the facts, Ma'am." This became a catch phrase: "Just give me the *facts*." EBMgt seeks to have managers make judgments based on facts by analyzing facts appropriately to make these judgments better. These goals are difficult to achieve. What seem like facts in many organizations may be misleading or easy to misinterpret. However, methods for reporting and analyzing data in academic research can help managers overcome these problems in using organizational data. By identifying critical errors in use of data and ways to avoid them, this chapter seeks to assist management in organizations to become more soundly evidence based.

This chapter is informed by a theory of organizations that I developed: statistico-organizational theory (Donaldson, 2007, 2008, 2010). Other organizational theories draw on economics (Williamson,

1975) or biology (Hannan & Freeman, 1989) as their foundations. Statistico-organizational theory draws on statistics and other methodological principles as ideas on which to build a new theory of management. Statistics and methodological principles provide insights about what errors can occur in academic research. Many are errors inherent in making inferences from numerical data. These same errors occur when managers look at organizational data. Statistics and methodology offer academic researchers guidance about when the errors will be most egregious and how to avoid them. Similarly, statistico-organizational theory uses statistics and methodology to foresee what errors managers may make in drawing inferences from their data.

In particular, statistico-organizational theory uses the principles that small samples lead to random errors, range restrictions and measurement errors lead to understated correlations, and confounds introduce spurious correlations. Although statistics and methodology identify factors that make these errors larger or smaller, statistico-organizational theory identifies the corresponding situational variables that lead managers to make larger or smaller errors in making inferences from their organization's data. For instance, a smaller organization tends to have smaller numbers of observations and so figures derived from its data tend to contain more random error.

Importantly, but more tentatively, statistico-organizational theory offers managers advice on how to avoid or minimize making errors in drawing inferences from numerical data. Of course, not all organizational decision making is, or should be, based solely on numerical data. Some of the evidence used in organizations will be qualitative, but it is the quantitative data that are the focus of statistico-organizational theory and of this chapter.

Modern organizations generate numerical data on many different variables, such as sales, quality, customer satisfaction, and so on. These data are held inside the organization, often across units of varying sizes, hierarchical levels, tasks, and metrics. They can be about the organization, for example, the costs of each of its departments. Or they can be about the organization's environment, for example, the percentage share the company holds of the market. The data could be generated internally, for example, the costs of its departments. Data could come from outside, for example, data from a market-research firm about customer perceptions of the firm's products. Once gaining access to these numbers, managers seeking to make inferences from them are prey to certain problems, as predicted by statistico-organizational theory. Statistico-organizational theory focuses on four sources of error in organizational data: small numbers, measurement error, range restriction, and confounding. We will discuss each error in turn and identify how managers may reduce them.

Four Sources of Error
Small Numbers

Definition: Smaller samples have more sampling error than do larger samples. When organizational data are based on a small number of observations, then any statistic calculated from them can contain random error (Moore, McCabe, Duckworth, & Alwan, 2009). Thus, the true value of that statistic can vary above or below the value calculated from the data. This error can arise whenever a sample is taken from a population or universe. The smaller the sample, the larger the sampling error will tend to be in the sample figure (Moore et al., 2009). Often managers look at a figure not as a mere description

but rather as an estimate of some larger population or universe.

In statistics, sampling error has known characteristics. For example, sampling error decreases as the number of observations increases (N) (Moore et al., 2009). This knowledge may be used to identify where in the organization management will face a sampling error problem. A figure based on only a small number of observations can contain considerable sampling error, causing the observed figure to vary randomly about the true figure. Given the prevalence of situations in which managers face data based on small numbers of observations, sampling error is likely to exist frequently, rendering figures misleading.

EXAMPLES

For instance, an automobile dealership may calculate the average number of sales of automobiles by its salespersons over the last year. However, this is in order to forecast what next year's average will be. Thus, the average is being used to convey information, not just about this year's sales and this year's customers, but also about the future, such as next year's sales and next year's customers, few of whom will be this year's customers. Hence, a figure about this year is being used as information about the future (Ehrenberg, 1975). Last year's sales were by last year's salespersons, but next year's may be by a different set of salespersons. Yet the average from last year may be used to try to predict how many extra sales would be obtained by adding, say, three additional salespersons. Thus, last year's figure is being used to generalize about the future and for different customers and salespersons.

This is often the case in management because managers look at figures (e.g., averages) from the past to predict the future. The reason is that managers are trying to decide what actions to take in the future. The action-orientation of managers means that they are using the data to estimate a population or universe that is wider than those cases actually studied. Hence, managers are often involved in sampling from a population or universe (e.g., all the present and future customers and salespersons), and so their data are samples and are subject to sampling error.

Problem: The small-numbers problem is commonplace. The potential problem of small numbers of observations (N) occurs in any organizational characteristic that draws on only a small number of cases. Even a large company may make a small number of products (e.g., heavy industrial machinery) or have just, say, five different information-technology systems; therefore, any analysis of these variables will tend to be beset by the problem of small numbers. A small company, if defined as having a small number of employees, will face the small-numbers problem in any analysis of its employees, for example, mean job satisfaction, absenteeism, quitting rates, and so forth. Countries with small populations (e.g., New Zealand) tend to have smaller organizations and, therefore, are prone to the small-numbers problem in their analyses. Even a large organization in a large country, with many employees, can fall into the small- numbers problem if it conducts analyses of, say, employees in one small branch.

Recommendation: The best solution to the problem of small numbers is to avoid it by having larger numbers of observations. Larger organizations have this large number of observations for numbers of employees and related variables. However, for this to hold, the large organization has to aggregate its data rather than leaving them disaggregated in the parts of the organization, such as its branches, departments, or divisions. Large organizations that do aggregate their data can calculate statistics fairly free of sampling error. Also, organizations have to aggregate their data over time, such as accumulating sales for the year, or monthly, rather than daily. However, if they have sufficient sample sizes, for example, as a result of being a large organization, they can use data that are somewhat temporally disaggregated, such as by month, to spot trends over time. This ability of large organizations to make superior inferences from data is an "inference advantage," giving them a comparative advantage over smaller, rival firms.

A small or medium-sized organization could gain this inference advantage by merging with another organization to form a larger organization. The data from the various business units can be aggregated together in the head office. In this way a parent company could bestow a "parenting advantage" (Goold, Campbell, & Alexander, 1994) of superior inference on its "children" (i.e., subsidiaries). Although firms may not merge for this reason, when they do so the inference advantage can be part of the economies of scale frequently sought in mergers.

There are other creative tactics for data combination in smaller settings. A small organization that remains independent can gain access to data based on larger numbers of observations by pooling data with other firms, in a strategic collaboration or through an industry association, government bureau, consulting company, or other means.

Similarly, organizations in a small country may gain access to data based on larger numbers of observations through international organizations, for example, UNESCO, or by being subsidiaries of large multinational organizations.

Historically, U.S. organizations have had an inference advantage in that their size could be large by world standards because the United States was larger than most other countries. For instance, it could be easier for a U.S. company to spot trends because of its larger size. However, the integration of countries into the European Union and the economic rise of more populous countries such as China and India are reducing the U.S. inference advantage.

If a large number of observations is not available to managers through these various stratagems, their data will be infected with random error. Managers and staff analysts need to recognize this explicitly. Calculating the confidence intervals around the statistic, such as mean or correlation coefficient, may do this. Hence, instead of the single figure that emerges from the calculation, there is a range of figures, so that the true statistic is acknowledged as lying within a possible range. For instance, sales figures being looked at by managers in an organization could have their confidence intervals routinely supplied by the organization's IT system. Alternatively, managers or their staff analysts could use personal computers to calculate the sampling error around figures of interest to them.

Since managers at higher levels will tend to look at aggregate data, they will tend to make superior data-based inferences than those at lower levels. Looking at such aggregate data requires a centralized collection of organizational information. It also requires use of standard definitions for the particular type of data throughout the organization. Furthermore, it implies that there are routine operations of recording and collating data. Moreover, there will need to be organization-wide rules, such as that all branches report their week's total sales to head office by 4 P.M. on Saturday, so that some increased formalization is also required. In these ways, for an organization to benefit from better inferences based on its data, some degree of centralization, standardization, and formalization of data collection is needed. Therefore, for upper-level management to have the benefit of aggregate data, incremental increases are required in the levels of the structural variables of centralization, standardization, and formalization (Pugh, Hickson, Hinings, & Turner, 1968).

In theory, data can be brought together in data-banks used by lower-level managers, in order to gain the benefits of aggregate data without centralizing decision making. However, lower-level managers will tend to focus on "my figures," that is information from their own unit. Such feelings are prompted by a sense of responsibility and accountability, as well as by personal identification with one's immediate work setting.

Aggregating data at higher organization levels reduces sampling error, thus eliminating the spurious variation in figures endemic to the data analyzed at lower levels in the organization. However, not all the variation is necessarily spurious. There may be some true difference in figures about lower-level subunits, such as geographic regions. Aggregate data better display these true differences. For instance, the mean sales figures differ by region and these differences are true, rather than being spurious. Such real differences may then be a basis on which the organization delegates decentralized authority down to those subunits. For example, in a national retail chain, winter clothing could differ between California and the midwest regions so that those regions are given autonomy to select their own winter clothing. However, such decentralization is only valid if derived from aggregate statistical analyses that show true differences between California and the midwest regions. Therefore, decentralization of decision making that reflects real differences between parts of the organization is only valid when made after centralized data analysis, because that aggregate data will have larger numbers of observations and so avoid much of the random error from small numbers of observations. Thus, such centralization should precede decentralization. This is a sounder managerial strategy than assuming *a priori* the existence of differences between parts of an organization that are based on commonsense or myths that may merely appear to be borne out by the spurious differences from sampling error.

Measurement Error

Definition: Whenever something is observed and measured, from profit to intelligence, its score is likely to deviate somewhat from its true score. This deviation is measurement error. This is also known as unreliability (Cohen, Cohen, West, & Aiken, 2003). Nothing is measured perfectly whether it be accident rates or customer sales. Having some measurement error is unavoidable. Research methodology offers guidance as to where measurement error will be most egregious and how to reduce it.

Measurement error tends to be greater where the variable is a difference score, meaning that it is one variable minus another. In psychology, this is well understood to occur when measuring, say, the difference between desired pay and actual pay. Psychometrically, the difference score has lower reliability than the two variables that compose it (e.g., desired pay and actual pay) when those two variables are positively correlated (Johns, 1981). The higher the positive correlation between them, the lower the reliability of the difference score (Johns, 1981). It is possible for the two variables to be highly reliably measured and yet for their difference score to be low in reliability. In other words, two variables that are measured with very little error can be the origins of a variable with great measurement error that is formed by simply taking their difference.

Examples: Profit is widely used to measure the financial performance of companies and often their constituent business units and subsidiaries. Yet profit is a difference score: sales minus costs. This allows profit to be unreliable. There can be much measurement error in profit, even if sales and costs are both measured with very little error.

For instance, the Walt Disney Company reports financial data for 2002 for its four business segments. Sales and costs are highly, positively correlated, 0.981, which implies that sales and costs must be measured quite reliably (otherwise their correlation would be attenuated to be much less than 1.0). The most conservative estimate of the reliability of sales and costs is that they are both 0.981 (for details of calculations see Donaldson, 2010, pp. 109–110). Despite this very high reliability of sales and costs, the reliability of profit can be as low as 0.22 (see Donaldson, 2010, pp. 107–110). Thus, although little measurement error may exist in sales and cost measures, there can be much measurement error in profit. The average error in the profits of the business segments could be 91 percent. For instance, the reported profit of the Media Networks business segment of $986 million could truly be only $229 million, an overstatement error of $757 million (Donaldson, 2010, p. 90).

Problem: Measurement error, that is, unreliability, of a variable reduces its potential correlation with another, a condition referred to as attenuation (Hunter and Schmidt, 2004). When two variables are correlated, the lower their reliability, the more that the observed correlation understates their true correlation. For instance, if training of business unit employees truly correlates 0.3 with business unit profit, but profit has reliability of only 0.22, then the observed correlation is only 0.14. Such a small correlation could easily be dismissed by managers as "too small to bother with," or "nonsignificant." Thus, the policy implication drawn could be that training is ineffectual and training budgets should be cut or not increased, whereas the sounder policy would be to maintain or increase training because it is effective.

Recommendation: Measurement error can be reduced by using multiple indicators and combining their scores. There could be multiple measures of financial performance such as profit, sales growth, and so forth. Performance could be broadened, so that to financial performance variables are added measures of consumer satisfaction, quality, innovativeness, and other aspects of organizational performance, such as a balanced scorecard (Kaplan & Norton, 1996).

Consider the correlation between an independent variable (that is, the presumed cause), say business-unit employee training, and a dependent variable (the presumed effect), say, business-unit profit. The problem of the unreliability of profit could be avoided in the following way. Rather than conducting a single regression with profit as the dependent variable, two regressions would be conducted: a regression with sales as the dependent variable and a regression with costs as the dependent variable. If training correlates positively with profit, then training will have a positive relationship with sales in the first regression, and training will have a negative relationship with sales in the second regression. Further, if the beneficial effects of training on sales and costs come from the beneficial effects of training on profit, then the sizes of the regression coefficients of sales and costs will be equal. In this case, the standardized regression coefficients of sales and costs will be the correlation between training and profit. For instance, if the regression of sales on training is +0.4 and the regression of costs on training is −0.4, then the correlation between training and profit is +0.4.

This correlation is attenuated far less than if only profit were used in the regression, because sales and costs are usually measured far more reliably than profit because of its being a difference score. To return to the example above, if the true training-profit correlation is +0.3, if sales are measured with reliability of 0.981 then the observed correlation is 0.297. Hence, the attenuation (i.e., reduction) in correlation due to the error in measuring sales is only 0.003, which is trivial. The same applies to costs. Thus, using sales and costs to estimate effects on profits allows use of variables that avoid most of the measurement error of profit and the attenuation

of correlation that comes from it. The results more accurately answer the question of the true correlation between an independent variable and profit, providing a higher correlation. Thereby, managers can appreciate the full merit of a practice, such as employee training, and make more optimal decisions about allocating resources and support to those practices.

Where, nevertheless, the manager's analyses include a correlation involving profit (or other variable with considerable measurement error) a correction formula can be applied (Hunter and Schmidt, 2004, p. 97):

$$r_t = \frac{r_o}{\sqrt{r_{xx}}}$$

Where r_t is the true correlation, r_o is the observed correlation, and r_{xx} is the reliability of profit. For instance, returning to the preceding example, if the observed correlation between the training of business-unit employees and business-unit profit is 0.14, and the reliability of profit is only 0.22, then the true correlation is 0.14 divided by 0.47 (the square root of 0.22), which is 0.3. Thus, the correlation can be corrected to give an estimate of the true correlation without the measurement error. A method to estimate the reliability of profit in a data set is given in Donaldson (2010, p. 107). The reliability of the variable that is being correlated with profit is also needed. Then, the correction formula from Hunter and Schmidt (2004, p. 97) can be applied to turn the observed into the estimated true correlation. A staff analyst could readily perform these steps. The resulting higher correlation would give the manager a truer sense of the amount of effect training has on profit. The correction formula for providing a truer estimate of a correlation could be utilized on any correlation for which the reliability of one or both of the variables is not high. The method for obtaining the reliability of a difference score can be applied to any difference score variable (Donaldson, 2010, p. 219), for example, pay disparity defined as desired pay less actual pay.

We have focused here on the measurement error in profit that arises from it being a difference score. Often financial performance is a ratio, but the ratio involves profit, for example, the ratio of profit-to-sales, so that the same problem of potentially high measurement error exists, because profit is still a difference score (sales minus costs). Also, many other financial performance variables are difference scores and so they are prey to the same high degree of measurement error. For instance, sales growth is the difference between sales in one time period and sales in the preceding time period. More generally, any growth rate is the difference between a variable in one time period and that variable in the preceding time period (Donaldson, 2010, p. 97), for example, growth in capacity, so the problem of difference scores producing unreliability can occur in more than just financial-performance variables.

Range Restriction

Definition: Range restriction occurs when a variable in the data has less than the range it possesses in the population or universe (Hunter & Schmidt, 2004). Such range restriction reduces any potential correlation between that variable and another. Range restriction can occur unwittingly through limiting the range in the data that are gathered. For example, if data are gathered in a factory that has all low-skill employees, then any positive effect of job skill on job satisfaction will be severely attenuated and thus understated. Managers interested in such a relationship would do well to ensure that they draw data from across their organization to obtain the true range of skill among its employees, which will yield a higher, truer correlation.

Example: Range restriction can occur in an organization though organizational learning and adaptation. Suppose that the Acme Corporation has poor safety. It starts training employees in safety, conducting courses in some of its branches and not in others. At this time, safety training is found to correlate considerably with safety (lack of accidents). Therefore, Acme mandates that all its employees receive safety training. Now the correlation between training and safety decreases to about zero. Managers draw the lesson that safety training no longer works, and they discontinue it. In reality, the safety training still works very well. All employees score high on amount of safety training leading to range restriction in that variable. This, in turn, attenuates the correlation between training and safety causing it to decrease to near zero. Managers need to ensure that any study using correlations or other methods of association has enough variance in the variables to reveal their true correlation.

Lack of variation can occur within an organization through its subunits following a standard approach through, say, training or mimicry (DiMaggio & Powell, 1983). The managers of the subunits may wish to vary from each other but lack the power and autonomous decision making authority to do so. Again, organizations may be required to follow

a standard template by powerful outside organizations, such as funding agencies or governments (DiMaggio & Powell, 1983). Or organizations may be required to follow a standard template by professional service firms, such as auditors (DiMaggio & Powell, 1983). Any of these mechanisms will reduce variation and restrict range leading to attenuation of correlations. Managers may need to look at the scientific evidence to better observe effects of these practices or to aggregated data from industries or larger firms besides their own.

Range restriction can occur in an organization through differential survival. Suppose that a government department for small business conducts a study of success factors in small retail shops in a shopping mall. It studies 10 shops and finds that overstocking has very little correlation with success measured as profit. However, over the past 10 years 50 such shops have opened and 40 have failed (Aldrich, 1979) so that they are not in the study. Across the 50 shops there is a strong negative correlation between overstocking and profit, so that overstocking is a major cause of failure in these shops. However, to see that, a manager needs to look at data that captures the variation that exists over time but is missing from cross-sectional data. Hence, the governmental officials and their staff need to conduct longitudinal studies that include those businesses that exit from the population.

Problem: The preceding example essentially explains that a true correlation can be reduced toward zero. Denrell (2005) has cogently argued that a true negative correlation can falsely appear positive through what is here termed range restriction. Projects vary in risk, with low-risk projects having outcomes that vary only from slightly positive to slightly negative, whereas high-risk projects have outcomes that vary considerably from highly positive to highly negative. However, the projects with negative outcomes are discontinued, so that a cross-sectional study finds only the survivors, which have positive outcomes. Among the survivors, the average outcome is higher for the more-risky than for the less-risky projects. Hence the study concludes that risk leads to higher outcomes. However, this is false, because, if the discontinued projects are included, the relationship is much less positive and can actually be negative. Once again, managers need to conduct inquiries that are not limited to survivors.

There is another possible problem about range and that is range extension. Range extension is the opposite of range restriction. Range extension occurs when a variable in a data set has more than the range it possesses in the population or universe. Such range restriction overstates any correlation between that variable and another. Range restriction can occur unwittingly through taking just extreme cases. For example, suppose management want to investigate the relationship between personality and performance of its salespersons. Out of 50 salespersons, they took the top three performances and the bottom three and correlated their extraversion scores with their performances. The correlation is +0.6, leading the managers to conclude that "success as a salesperson is really mostly due to having the right personality," so they select on extraversion.

Taking only the highest and lowest performers, however, produces range extension, so that the correlation is exaggeratedly high. In a correlation coefficient, cases distant from the mean have more leverage and so produce higher correlations than cases nearer the mean. Hence, excluding the middling cases produces an exaggeratedly high correlation. Returning to the example, the 44 middling performing salespersons would have had a lower correlation, for example, +0.2. If all 50 salespersons had been used in the correlation, the true, lower correlation of (say) +0.3 would have been found. If the management had seen this true correlation, they might have correctly concluded that extraversion was a factor in performance, but only *one* of a number. This might have led them to seek other factors that affect the performance of salespersons, such as mental ability—so that it is not just "having the right personality."

Recommendations: Range extension can be avoided by managers by not just taking extreme cases for analysis but rather studying all the cases or a representative sample. In practice, managers need to avoid focusing solely on the "winners and losers" when they are seeking to find associations that will inform them about the true effects of drivers of outcomes.

The best way to avoid both range restriction and range extension is to use a set of observations that captures the actual range in the relevant population. Capturing the range in one variable will usually also capture the range in any other variable with which it is being correlated, so that range problems are avoided simultaneously on both the independent and dependent variables. Hence, getting the right data to use in the analysis is the preferred approach.

Nevertheless, if the right data aren't available and yet a correlation has been obtained from data that are afflicted by either range restriction or range extension, a correction formula may be applied to obtain an estimate of the truer correlation (Hunter & Schmidt, 2004, pp. 107–8):

$$r_t = \frac{Ur_d}{\sqrt{(U^2 - 1)r_d^2 + 1}}$$

Where r_p is the correlation in the population (that is, the organization), U is the ratio of the standard deviation of the population divided by the standard deviation of the data, and r_d is the correlation in the data. For instance, returning to the Acme Corporation example, suppose that standard deviation in the data was half that in Acme overall and that the correlation between training and safety in Acme's data was only 0.2. Then, the population correlation would be 0.38. Thus, the considerable restriction in range of the data relative to the population leads to the correlation in the data understating the population correlation by about half. However, by using the formula, the population correlation can readily be found. The correlation for Acme overall gives a truer picture to the manager of the effect that increasing training will have on safety in Acme. This formula will increase the value of a correlation that has range restriction and decrease a correlation that has range extension.

The correction formula just given could readily be used by a staff analyst. The key would be to determine the range of the relevant population. Acme conducted a study of the relationship between training and safety in only one plant in the organization. This plant had less range of training than Acme as a whole, so that the observed training-safety correlation understates the true relationship. The range of training may be known in organizational records and so can be used in the preceding formula to correct the correlation in the data so that it is increased up to its truer value. Alternately, the range of the safety variable, if it is known, can be used to make the correction. This corrected correlation gives the managers a truer picture of the strength of the association between training and safety in their organization.

Confounds

Definitions: A confound occurs when the true relationship between two variables is obscured because of some contaminating effect. Usually in social science this is considered to be due to the influence of a third variable or some unmeasured factor common to both variables. We will discuss this case before turning to two other ways in which confounding can occur in numerical analyses: confounding due to definition and confounding due to reverse causality.

Problem: Suppose training all employees has a beneficial effect on organizational effectiveness of correlation +0.4. This could be obscured by confounding by spurious correlations such that the observed correlation between employee training and organizational effectiveness was zero, so that the training budget was not increased or cut. This confounding could occur in three ways.

The first way is confounding due to a third variable correlated with both employee training and organizational effectiveness. Employee mental ability also positively affects organizational effectiveness, but those divisions recruiting persons high on mental ability do not feel it necessary to train them, whereas those divisions recruiting persons low on mental ability do feel it necessary to train them. Therefore, there is a negative correlation between employee mental ability and employee training. Given that employee mental ability is positively correlated with organizational effectiveness, there is a spurious negative correlation between employee training and organizational effectiveness that is due to employee mental ability. This masks the relationship between employee training and organizational effectiveness and could reduce it from +0.4 to zero.

The second way to have confounding is due to definition. If organizational effectiveness is measured by profit, then by its definition, profit is positively correlated with sales and negatively correlated with costs. Suppose that sales are negatively correlated with employee training because managers of high-sales divisions judge that training is not needed. Then, there is a spurious negative correlation between employee training and profit. Or suppose that costs are positively correlated with employee training because managers of high-cost divisions judge that employee training *is* needed, then, again, there is a spurious negative correlation between employee training and profit. These spurious negative correlations between employee training and profit mask the relationship between employee training and organizational effectiveness and could reduce it from +0.4 to zero.

The third way to have confounding is due to reverse causality. For a firm, having a structure that fits its strategy positively affects firm performance, but firms tend not to adopt a fitting structure until their performance is poor, so performance negatively affects fit. Therefore, in a cross-sectional correlation,

the positive correlation of fit with performance is masked by the negative correlation of performance with fit. The result could be an observed correlation of zero.

CONFOUNDING BY A THIRD VARIABLE

The true effect of X on Y can be obscured by a third variable, Z, that is correlated with both X and Y. Z leads the observed correlation between X and Y to be greater or smaller than its true value. In social science, this is often dealt with by including Z into the analysis and conducting a multivariate analysis that gives the relation between X and Y, controlling for Z. Managers can also do this in their analyses inside their organizations.

Example: To continue the earlier example, having discovered that across all 50 salespersons extraversion correlates +0.3 with performance, when they go on to study the effect of mental ability on performance they could control for extraversion by including it in a multivariate analysis. If extraversion happens to correlate with mental ability, given its correlation with performance, extraversion will introduce a spurious correlation into the observed correlation between mental ability and performance. Including extraversion in the multivariate analysis essentially removes this spurious effect, rendering the observed correlation the same as the true correlation (ignoring sampling error, etc.).

Recommendation: There could be numerous control variables included into the multivariate analysis to control for them. However, to control a confounding variable by inclusion into a multivariate analysis, the analyst has to know that a variable is a confound. Thus, the analyst has to identify all the variables that confound a relationship. This can be a tall order. In practice many multivariate analyses explain much less than all the variance in the dependent variable (e.g., the performance of salespersons). This leaves open the possibility that there are some other variables that are correlated with both the dependent and independent variables and so confound the focal relationship.

Some social scientists who are worried about the possibility of such unidentified confounds use experimental methods with a control group. In the experiment the subjects are isolated from the effects of all other variables except the independent variable. The corresponding changes in the dependent variable are the true effects of the independent variable on the dependent variable. However, in organizational research, it is hard to prevent all other variables from affecting the experimental subjects, in part because, once again, not all the other variables may be known. Therefore, experimentalists often make use of having a control group, which registers the effects on the experimental subjects of all other variables that affect the dependent variable. The effect in the control group can be measured and subtracted from the effect in the experimental group, yielding the true effect of the independent variable on the dependent variable. This is a very attractive approach, because the control group registers the effects of *all* the other variables that affect the dependent variable without the analyst needing to identify *what those other variables are*.

Ideally a control group needs to be identical to the experimental group in every respect, including type of person. This may be facilitated in university laboratories by random assignment of subjects to the experimental and control groups. Experiments in organizations may adopt the somewhat weaker approach of trying to have the control group be as similar as possible. To do so, they may use formal groupings of the organization as control groups, such as members of two plants that are manufacturing the same product, so that they have similar technology, routines, employee skills, and so forth. The treatment is then introduced into one plant, the experimental group, but not the other, the control group.

However, having two near-identical organizational subunits would be unlikely in a small organization (i.e., with few employees) and is more likely in a large organization. The reason is that size positively affects structural differentiation (Blau and Schoneherr, 1971). Similarly, formal structuring of activity through rules that are in common between the two plants provides standardization between the two plants, but it is more likely in large than small organizations, because size positively affects bureaucratic standardization (Pugh, Hickson, Hinings, & Turner, 1969). Again, measurement of dependent variables in organizational experiments often relies on the formal control systems to measure productivity, absenteeism, costs, and so forth, but these are more likely in large organization (Pugh et al., 1969). Therefore, although organizational experiments are an attractive idea, they may be infeasible in small and medium-sized organizations, and feasible only in large organizations (see Donaldson, 2010, pp. 171–173). Thus, managers in many smaller organizations may find that they cannot use experiments in their organizations to control for confounds.

Although this seems to leave organizational experiments as a viable option for managers in large organizations, this could be beguiling. In a large organization having a subunit use a new approach (the experimental group) while another subunit uses the old approach (the control group) is facilitated where opinion is divided among its managers about the efficacy of the new approach. This leads to the philosophy of "trying a little as an 'experiment.'" The new approach may be championed only by staff personnel (e.g., human resources), or by a local manager who allows his or her plant to be used as the site of the experiment (Rodgers & Hunter, 1991). Top managers may be skeptical or hostile about the new approach.

Yet, in research on the effectiveness of management by objectives, top management support has been shown to be a strong moderator interacting with the management technique to impact its effectiveness. High top-management support produced high performance outcomes whereas low top-management support produced only low performance outcomes (Rodgers & Hunter, 1991). Moreover, it was in organizations with low top-management support that experiments could be run because there were simultaneously organizational subunits using the new technique (the experimental groups) alongside organizational subunits not using the new technique (the control groups). In contrast, if there is high top-management support for a technique, it is likely to have been adopted organization-wide so that there are no organizational subunits that are not using it and, hence, no control group, so that an organizational experiment with control groups cannot be run in that organization.

Thus, organizational experiments that utilize control groups can unwittingly introduce conservative bias (Donaldson, 2010, pp. 173–176). Managers looking at the only modest benefits shown by the experiment may wrongly conclude that the technique is ineffective in their organization. Initial skepticism may be reinforced. Initial skepticism leads to "let's try an experiment to see if it works in our organization," which concludes that the initial skepticism was justified. Thus, there can be a self-fulfilling prophecy in that the initial skepticism leads to running an organizational experiment, which inherently will tend to show only modest benefits, confirming the initial skepticism, so that the innovation is never adopted organization-wide Thus, organizational experiments unwittingly lead to dysfunctional conservatism in that innovations that would be highly beneficial if adopted organization-wide and implemented in a full-bodied way are not.

Aggregation of data sets can eliminate confounding. The confounding variable may introduce a spurious correlation that is positive in one data set, but negative in another data set. If the two data sets are aggregated together, then the two spurious correlations will offset each other so that the net confounding effect may move toward zero. If the confounding variable is genuinely independent of the independent variable, then there will be no correlation between them. Then, any correlation between the confounding variable and independent variable in a data set will be wholly spurious and specific to that data set. Combining such data sets will tend toward a zero correlation between the confounding and independent variables, thereby eliminating the confounding element from the combined data set (Donaldson, 2010, pp. 177–197).

Moreover, random variation from data set to data set in the confounding spurious correlation is eliminated by the aggregation of data sets, so that false inferences are avoided about the focal relationship being stronger in some situations than others. Aggregation of data sets is essentially similar to averaging the results of data sets. The aggregate figure provides a better estimate of the general effect across the multiple situations than do the disaggregate figures that display a lot of variation, some of which is actually spurious due to variations in idiosyncratic confounding from situation to situation. Where there is a confound existing in a population, aggregation will not eliminate it, but it will still eliminate the specious variations across situations.

Similarly, in an organization, the data from each subunit are prey to spurious effects from confounding that are idiosyncratic to that data set. As data go up the organizational hierarchy, they become aggregated. For example, the sales of salespersons become sales of the branch. In turn, branch sales are aggregated into area sales, then territory sales, regional sales, and company sales. At every level in the hierarchy, the combination of data can lead to the offsetting of spurious confounds in one direction (e.g., positive) by spurious confounds in the opposite direction (e.g., negative). Therefore, the more aggregate data typically found at higher levels in organization will tend to be less infected by confounding. Hence, organizational data at higher levels in the hierarchy will give a truer picture than data at lower levels.

If the confound is real, so that it exists even in aggregate data, it may still be small (e.g., a correlation of +0.1) so that the aggregate figure is substantially valid. Only if the confound is high, relative to the relationship between the independent and the dependent variable, will the confounding still be substantial after data aggregation. For the true confound to be high relative to that relationship, there must be correlations between both those variables and the confound that are both greater than the relationship between the independent and the dependent variable.

Example: For example, if X and Y correlate +0.5, then, for the confound Z to completely obscure the XY relationship, the correlations between X and Z, and between Y and Z must both be at least 0.7, with one positive and the other negative, because the confound is the product of their correlations, $-.49$ (= 0.7 x –0.7). Only then will the confounded correlation between X and Y appear, wrongly, to be near-zero, +0.01 (= 0.50 –0.49). This kind of strong confounding is unlikely, because the confounding variable (Z) rarely will be strongly correlated with *both* the dependent and the independent variables. Partial confounding is more feasible.

Continuing the example, if correlations between X and Z and between Y and Z were both 0.4, with one positive and the other negative, then the confounding of XY by Z would be –0.16 (= 0.4 x –0.4), so that a true XY correlation of +0.5 would appear to be lesser at +0.34 (0.5 –0.16). Managerially, partial confounding only matters if it is strong enough to cause managers to make the wrong decision, for example, not implementing a new technique because it wrongly appears not to be beneficial.

Aggregation of data sets reduces confounding more, the greater the number of data sets aggregated, but at a decreasing rate (see Donaldson, 2010, p. 190). Thus, the big decreases in confounding come from aggregating the first few data sets, so that even modest aggregation of data can help considerably to reduce the confounding problem. Therefore, managers would be well advised to use aggregation of data in their organization to reduce confounding.

This benefit from reducing confounding is independent from the benefit of reducing sampling error (Donaldson, 2010, p. 195). Thus, data aggregation benefits inference making in two ways: reducing confounding and reducing random error from sampling. This gives managers two reasons why they should aggregate their organizational data.

CONFOUNDING DUE TO DEFINITION OF A VARIABLE

Definition of this type of confounding: Some variables are difference scores, meaning that the variable is defined as being the difference between the level of one variable and the level of some other variable. For example, profit is sales *less* costs. These definitional connections between the difference score variable and the variables from which it is composed lead to associations among them.

Example: For instance, by definition, profit is positively correlated with sales and negatively correlated with costs. Therefore, if sales happen to be positively correlated with some other variable, there will be a spurious positive correlation between that variable and profit. This would confound any true relationship between that variable and profit. Similarly, confounding can arise from costs, and it could reinforce confounding from sales.

Recommendation: The way to control for these confounds is to enter both sales and costs into any analysis of the relationship between some variable and profit. Thus, a multivariate analysis is required in which sales and costs are present as control variables. A manager interested in the causes of profit could have a staff analyst use a personal computer to conduct such a multivariate analysis.

CONFOUNDING DUE TO REVERSE CAUSALITY

Definition: When the presumed cause is in actuality the result of the presumed effect, reverse causality exists. In this case, observed relationships can be misinterpreted.

Example: Managers are perennially interested in their organization's performance and that of their rivals. They conduct analyses to pinpoint the causes of organizational performance. However, performance levels often feed back to produce changes in the organization. In particular, low performance can be the crisis that triggers changes in the organization's structure, strategy, or leadership (Chandler, 1962). Thus, although some organizational characteristic, such as organizational structure, may positively affect organizational performance, organizational performance can also negatively affect that same organizational characteristic (e.g., organizational structure). Hence, a true positive effect on organizational performance can be masked by a negative effect of organizational performance. If the positive effect on performance was of the same degree of correlation as the negative effect from performance, then the observed correlation would appear to be zero. This would give the false message that the organizational characteristic (e.g., structure) has no effect on performance when it actually has a beneficial effect. A manager might conclude that it is best not to increase the level of that organizational

characteristic when actually such an increase would be beneficial for the organization. Similarly, successful firms may invest more in R and D, confounding the effect of R and D on firm performance.

Recommendation: The solution is to conduct a study over time so that organizational performance is measured after the organizational characteristic (e.g., structure). In some academic studies, an appropriate time lag between the organizational characteristic and organizational performance is two years (Donaldson, 1987; Rogers, 2006). This means waiting two years to see the performance effects of some organizational characteristic. Some managers may resist such delay, being impatient to know the results of the analysis so that they can take action. Delay may seem irresponsible to the manager. By the time the lagged effect of the organizational characteristic on organizational performance is known, it may appear to the manager to be "merely academic," because it addresses the past rather than the present. However, managers would be well advised to curb any such natural impatience and use studies with substantial time lags to avoid confounding by reverse causality and the false lessons it teaches.

Conclusions

Evidence-based approach entails using data to inform decisions. However, data contain errors that can mislead anyone looking at them. Numerical data—which have been the focus of this chapter—risk particular kinds of errors. Small numbers of observations lead to random error around the true value. This is best avoided by aggregating the observations in an organization, which involves some centralization, standardization, and formalization of the structure that collates and analyses the data. For a small organization, its managers can seek to obtain data that aggregate across numerous organizations, such as from a parent company, market research firms, or governmental bureaus.

Measurement error occurs in organizational variables, especially profit, even if there is little measurement error in the sales and costs figures from which profit is derived. A solution is for staff analysts interested in profit to conduct separate analyses for sales and costs, and then combine their results. Also, the understated profit correlations can be corrected upward by use of the formula given in this chapter.

Range restriction leads to observed correlations that understate the true correlations. The solution is for staff analysts to obtain the full range of the variables of interest, or to correct the correlations

Table 14.1 Summary of Sources of Errors and Recommendations

Source of Error	Error	Recommendation
Small numbers of observations	Random error	Aggregate organizational data through centralization, standardization, and formalization
Measurement error	Unreliability of profit	Make both sales *and* costs analyses
	Understatement of correlation	Correct correlation upward by use of a formula
Range restriction	Understatement of correlation	Use full range of the variable in the organization in analysis
		Correct correlation upward by use of a formula
Confounding by a third variable	Misleading correlation	Aggregate organizational data through centralization, standardization, and formalization
Confounding due to the definition of a variable	Misleading correlation	Include constituent variables in analysis, e.g., for profit analysis include also sales and costs
Confounding due to reverse causality	Misleading correlation	Measure effects *after* causes

upward in value using the formula given in this chapter.

How best to deal with confoundings depends on the kind of confounding in the data. Confounding by a third variable is best dealt with by aggregating the organizational data. (Thus, data aggregation has the twin benefits of reducing the error from this confounding and from small numbers of observations.) Confounding due to the definition of a variable can be avoided by including in the analysis the constituent variables, for example, sales and costs in an analysis of profit. Confounding due to reverse causality can be reduced by measuring the effects *after* the causes.

In these ways, these major sources of error in numerical data can be avoided by managers and their staffs. Table 13.1 gives a summary of the errors and the recommendations for reducing them. Other errors made by managers who are seeking to make evidence-based decisions may be reduced by the use of the techniques of qualitative academic social research, and scholars other than the present author would be better able to identify these.

Hence, managers seeking to best use their organization's data to make evidence-based decisions can adopt ways to help attain this goal through structural arrangements or use of analytic approaches.

Aggregation of data will minimize random errors in the figures inferred from the data, and such aggregation is facilitated by centralizing, standardizing, and formalizing the data-handling procedures in the organization, to produce a big N from which to compute the statistics of interest to managers, for example, sales trends. This data aggregation will also reduce confounds and their misleading effects. Problems introduced by the use of profit can be ameliorated by using sales and costs in regressions conducted to identify profit drivers. Under-stated correlations involving profit can also be corrected upwards to their true value by use of a formula. And understated correlations due to range restriction may be corrected upward by another formula—though the more enlightened analysts will avoid the problem by capturing the full range of a variable in the organization in their studies.

Through this combination of structural and analytic approaches managers can extract the most information value from the data their organizations possess. In this way, managers may make sound inferences and our organizations will better attain what may be termed "inference security." Such organizations will realize their potential inference advantage, so that the benefits of EBMgt will come to be more fully realized.

References

Aldrich, H. E. (1979). *Organizations and environments.* Englewood Cliffs, NJ: Prentice Hall.

Blau, P. M., & Schoenherr, R. A. (1971). *The structure of organizations.* New York: Basic Books.

Chandler, A. D., Jr. (1962). *Strategy and structure: Chapters in the history of the industrial enterprise.* Cambridge, MA: MIT Press.

Cohen, J., Cohen, P., West, S. G., & Aiken, L. S. (2003). *Applied multiple regression/correlation analysis for the behavioral sciences* (3rd ed.). Mahwah, NJ: Lawrence Erlbaum.

Denrell, J. (2005). Selection bias and the perils of benchmarking. *Harvard Business Review, April,* 114–119.

DiMaggio, P. J., & Powell, W. W. (1983). The iron cage revisited: Institutional isomorphism and collective rationality in organization fields. *American Sociological Review, 48(2),* 147–160.

Donaldson, L. (January 1987). Strategy and structural adjustment to regain fit and performance: In defence of contingency theory. *Journal of Management Studies, 24*(1), 1–24.

Donaldson, L. (2007). Statistico-organizational theory: A new theory of organizations. In G. M. Schwarz, S. Clegg, T. G. Cummings, L. Donaldson, & J. B. Miner (Eds.), *We see dead people? The state of organization science. Journal of Management Inquiry, 16*(4), 300–317.

Donaldson, L. (2008). Statistico-organizational theory: Creating organizational management theory from methodological principles. In D. Barry & H. Hensen (Eds.), *The SAGE handbook of new approaches to management and organization* (pp. 135–145). London: SAGE Publications.

Donaldson, L. (2010) *The meta-analytic organization: Introducing statistico-organizational theory.* Armonk, NY: M.E. Sharpe.

Ehrenberg, A. S. C. (1975). *Data reduction: Analysing and interpreting statistical data.* London: John Wiley.

Goold, M., Campbell, A., & Alexander, M. (1994), *Corporate-level strategy: Creating value in the multibusiness company.* New York: John Wiley.

Hannan, M. T., & Freeman, J. (1989). *Organizational ecology.* Cambridge, MA: Harvard University Press.

Hunter, J. E., & Schmidt, F. L. (2004). *Methods of meta-analysis: Correcting error and bias in research findings* (2nd ed.). Thousand Oaks, CA: Sage.

Johns, G. (1981). Difference score measures of organizational behavior variables: A critique. *Organizational Behavior and Human Performance, 27*(3), 443–463.

Kaplan, R. S., & Norton, D. P. (1996). *The balanced scorecard: Translating strategy into action.* Boston, MA: Harvard Business School Press.

Moore, D. S., McCabe, G. P., Duckworth, W. M., & Alwan, L. C. (2009). *The practice of business statistics* (2nd ed.). New York: W. H. Freeman.

Pugh, D. S., Hickson, D. J., Hinings, C. R., & Turner, C. (1968). Dimensions of organization structure. *Administrative Science Quarterly, 13*(1), 65–105.

Pugh, D. S., Hickson, D. J., Hinings, C. R., & Turner, C. (1969). The context of organization structures. *Administrative Science Quarterly, 14*(1), 91–114.

Rodgers, R. C., & Hunter, J. E. (1991). Impact of management by objectives on organizational productivity. *Journal of Applied Psychology, 76* (2), 322–336.

Rogers, M. (2006). Contingent corporate governance: A challenge to universal theories of board structure. PhD thesis, University of New South Wales, Sydney, Australia.

Williamson, O. E. (1975). *Markets and hierarchies: Analysis and antitrust implications.* New York: Free Press.

Buried Treasure: A Business Librarian's Insights on Finding the Evidence

Roye Werner

Abstract

This chapter offers my perspective as a professional librarian and former manager on accessing the research evidence in the business and management fields. I describe the barriers faced by managers, students, and scholars in locating and reading the peer-reviewed literature: its scattered placement, varying formats, controlled access, and swiftly changing environment. I explore how those roadblocks are being overcome, and I offer practical recommendations for both managers and researchers on what they can do today to bring that evidence to light.

Key Words: peer-review; academic journals; electronic, on-line sources; evidence ; search; libraries; databases

The following is a true story:

Congratulations—you've just been promoted to manager. After years of hard work, you're now the department head. People report to you. You have products and services to deliver and customers to satisfy. How do you learn to manage all this, day-to-day and for the long term? With luck, you've had some training. You might find yourself a good mentor or two, and perhaps someday you'll get a chance to enroll in executive education at the local business school. However, those are future, and only partial solutions. Wait a minute! There must be a multitude of answers and good advice available in the thousands of business books and articles published each year. Don't forget the assault of blogs, wikis, web sites, even twitter feeds. How do you find those answers? Once you do, can you actually get hold of and understand them? And most importantly, how do you know what is good?

This was the situation I found myself in when, in 1998, after eight years as a business librarian, I became the head of my department: the branch of Pittsburgh's public library that provides business- and finance-related information to residents, employees, and companies in Allegheny County, Pennsylvania. Suddenly in charge of 20 staff members (professional librarians as well as library assistants and clerks,) a budget, planning, customer service—I needed to study up on how to be the person in charge, and fast.

You would think that as a business librarian—surrounded by books, journals, and computers all filled with the works of experts, much of which I and my staff had selected and organized—I would know just what to do. However, amid the pressing demands of proposals, interviews, meetings, reports, forms, assessments, conflict resolutions, and so on—finding just the right coaching at the right time was as overwhelming for me as for any new manager. Given the time pressure, what drew me most strongly were book titles. I succumbed to the appeal of the *One-Minute Manager* (Blanchard and Johnson, 1982)—though I put it down again pretty quickly. It's also how I found *First, Break All the Rules* (Buckingham and Coffman, 1999)—a book from the Gallup Organization whose findings

I ultimately came to trust and use, not least because the first chapter describes the large amount of evidence behind them. In all honesty, it never occurred to me to search for research articles, let al.ne meta-analyses on specific topics. If this is what it was like for me, then how is it for other managers?

This chapter offers my perspective as a professional librarian on accessing the research evidence related to business and management. I describe the roadblocks that the layperson and typical manager would commonly face in trying to answer a practice question using this evidence, and also the challenges that even students and scholars confront in locating this research. I then discuss ways to surmount those roadblocks in the short term, and what might be done to reduce them further on. As my experience and research has been Western-focused, this will cover the situation as I see it in the English-speaking and European world; certainly similar situations exist in Asia, South America, and Africa, but that coverage awaits another author.

Roadblocks

It wasn't until I became a librarian at a university that I discovered the range, promise, and complexity of scholarly research and recommendations on management issues. The density of language in that research, and its sometimes tenuous relation to the problems managers face, has been discussed in numerous articles (Cascio, 2008; Markides, 2007; Sutton, 2004; Vermeulen, 2007). Those problems aside, there is another formidable obstacle to contend with: the complex configuration (primarily in cyberspace) of that body of knowledge—how it is stored, how to identify what is relevant to a particular question, and who can get to it. As healthcare manager John Zanardelli says in his chapter in this handbook, "It is often challenging and may be near impossible to find quality evidence." Here I'll attempt to explain why that is by describing those barriers, after which I'll explore the ways they can be circumvented, more of which are opening up each day as a result of new technologies, attitudes, and initiatives.

As a nod to all those practitioner-aimed books that flow into public libraries and airport bookstores, let's examine the three roadblocks to finding the evidence.

Roadblock 1: Chaos

The first roadblock to finding the evidence is the way it is currently located and configured. At the moment, the peer-reviewed research articles and books that could form the basis for evidence-based decision-making are scattered over a diverse and disordered universe of publications. These articles and books are in numerous formats: print, microfilm and microfiche, CD-ROMs, and on the Internet.

In the past, of course, the printed and bound academic journals and books that contained all scholarly knowledge were kept and accessed exclusively in research libraries and in the private collections of individual subscribers. To find articles on a particular topic, the only tools available were print indexes, also only in libraries; in the case of business literature, those were the *Industrial Arts Index (1913–1957)*, *Business Periodicals Index (1958 - present)*, and starting in 1972, the *Social Sciences Citation Index*. Those collections and indexes still exist, in print, in microforms, and even in electronic storage devices like floppy discs or CD-ROMs, though they are rapidly moving to off-site storage. (These facilities are now sometimes euphemistically called the "heritage collection.")

However, with warp speed once we entered the Internet Age, the great majority of those articles, past and present, leaped into cyberspace, along with a much smaller but increasing number of books. They now have extraordinary reach through their potential availability over any Internet line. That reach is compromised by a mix of controls, costs, and compartmentalization. For instance, there are 89 academic journals specializing in management research listed in the "management" category in ISI Web of Knowledge, a database containing citations for most international scholarly literature. (This is in addition to many other academic journals in marketing, leadership, strategy, etc.) The articles in those journals are made available over the Internet in various ways. One way, of course, is by direct subscription—a costly and time-consuming arrangement, for both individuals and libraries. It is also rare that all articles of interest will be contained in a few publications, and no person or library can subscribe to everything. Most of the significant business and management scholarly journals have been acquired by a small group of publishers, of which the principal ones are: Elsevier (Science Direct,) Wiley-Blackwell (Wiley Interscience,) Emerald, and SAGE. This can be helpful in terms of consolidation and standardization, since they provide across-the-board searching systems (though only for titles they own and via web sites that they control.) However, the bad news, for libraries at least, is that the dwindling competition gives these publishers more monopolistic pricing power.

A more efficient way to access these articles is through subscription-based databases, which have contracts with the journals' publishers. These databases also offer searching systems that can locate articles on a particular topic. The most widely used are: ABI/INFORM (from ProQuest); Academic Source Premier/Complete and Business Source Premier/Complete (from EBSCO); Academic OneFile, General Businessfile and Business & Company Resource Center (from Gale/Cengage); and JSTOR (from ITHAKA). The holdings within these databases differ widely—there is much unique but also overlapping coverage. They also often contain a mix of practitioner, mainstream, and academic publications (though most make some effort to distinguish which is which). Furthermore, the holdings are a moving target: titles are constantly dropped and added, dates are expanded and cut back. Some of these databases have exclusive contracts with high-demand publications—for instance, EBSCO currently has a lock on the *Harvard Business Review*. Many journals are not fully available in any database, and must be subscribed to directly. Added to this, the entire publishing industry is undergoing a radical transformation, making the entire situation temporary and unstable.

Poised on the outer edge of the world of official refereed publications, there are other sources for reputable research output in the management field. Working papers and other forms of prepublication efforts are made available on the web through sites such as the Social Science Research Network (www.ssrn.com) and Research Papers in Economics (repec.org), and increasingly through authors' websites and institutional repositories. There are also research and professional organizations that publish their own books and journals—both academic, like the Academy of Management, INFORMS, Cornell's International Labor Relations School, the Academy of Human Resource Development; and practitioner-oriented, like the Conference Board, the American Management Association, and the Society for Human Resource Management. Abroad, there are the Advanced Institute of Management Research (UK) and the European Foundation for Management Development (Belgium). Finally, there are management-oriented consulting firms, like McKinsey, Gartner, and Bain & Co. The output of these organizations is readily accessible to members or clients, but for nonmembers they are often exorbitantly expensive and sometimes unavailable at any price.

Books are the other important repository of management research and knowledge, and their landscape is quite different from that of journal publishing. First, the electronic availability of academic books is proceeding more slowly than that of journal articles (Housewright & Schonfeld, 2008). In academic libraries, the books that tend to be acquired as e-books are not research monographs, but textbooks, reference works, multimedia, and out-of-print books (Tedd, 2005). Publishers, also, are still issuing their scholarly books primarily in print form. A look at the book purchasing options from Baker & Taylor's YBP Library Services—a major purchasing service for academic libraries—shows that of 371 titles classified both as "advanced academic" and "management" published between 2008 and 2010, only 64 were available as e-books as of this writing. Even at Amazon, which has put a supreme effort into supplying e-books for its Kindle book reader, its "Management Science" category—admittedly mixing the practitioner books with scholarly ones—offers over 9,400 printed titles compared to 936 Kindle titles. Thus, the primary place at the moment to get hold of book content is not over the Internet, as in articles, but still in libraries and in bookstores (or purchased over the Internet, but still in a physical package). Although, with the milestone recently reached at Amazon, where by July of 2010 more electronic books were being sold than print ones (Miller, 2010), this situation is quickly evolving.

Second, although there is a recognizable group of book publishers that reliably submit their books to the peer review process, notably university presses and others such as Routledge, SAGE, Blackwell, and Palgrave Macmillan, the boundaries are becoming blurred. Some professors go commercial, availing themselves of the greater marketing power of publishers like Penguin or HarperCollins. This would make it difficult for a random reader to know in which corner—popular or scholarly—a particular book stands, unless that reader has learned how to detect the signs of a solid underpinning of research, such as scholarly citations, academic credentials for the author, and the use of scientifically determined evidence. At the same time, university presses, under increasing financial pressure, must base decisions on what is viable in the marketplace, and so a greater number of well-researched manuscripts never see the light of day (Wilbourne, 2001).

Roadblock 2: Invisibility

The second roadblock consists of difficulties in locating research relevant to your needs in this confusing landscape. The first thing to consider is how to even learn of its existence. This trove of carefully researched, compiled and vetted knowledge is largely invisible to varying degrees, depending on whether you are a manager, a student, or a professor.

It seems almost hopeless for the byzantine and unadvertised research landscape described earlier to compete with the marketing juggernaut that ubiquitously offers up the likes of *Who Moved My Cheese?* (Johnson, 1998) and *Fast Company* magazine, particularly for managers. The diffusion of business books and magazines is a big industry, as is clearly seen in the thriving "business" sections in airport and other bookstores (Furnham, 2000,) not to mention public libraries. Amazon has almost 340,000 books in its "Management & Leadership" category, and *The Five Dysfunctions of a Team* (Lencioni, 2002), literally a fable, is currently at the top of its "Management Science" list. For executives who need help wading through all those titles, several online services like 800ceoread.com and Soundview Executive Book Summaries (summary.com) have sprung up to deliver commentary, podcasts, summaries, and selections. The FT Press, a unit of the *Financial Times*, now presents "insights from great business minds" in e-snippets that are so short they can be read in 10 minutes on a cell phone and are priced under $3 (Rich, 2010). Any Google search will turn up a veritable Babel of practitioner-oriented magazines, reports, and newsletters. Small wonder that multiple studies have shown that managers read little academic research (Terpstra & Rozell, 1997; Kay, 2001; Rynes, Colbert, & Brown, 2002; Case, 2008). For evidence-based management to find some visibility among all that glitz will be a daunting challenge. This is not to say that all of popularly available management advice is, to quote Bob Sutton, "crap" (Sutton, 2006), but that it's hard for the nonacademic to distinguish opinion from science unless they know to look for citations to scientific research.

Students and professors make use of the scholarly literature at their disposal in varying degrees. Professional journals in academic librarianship are filled with laments about how few campus denizens use databases as opposed to the open web (Cason & Van Scoyoc, 2006; Griffiths & Brophy, 2005), inspiring a campaign led by academic libraries to promote "information literacy" (more on this below). When I give lectures on business information resources to both undergraduate and MBA students, their surprise and even wonder at what has been for years right under their noses shows that mere availability is not enough. Guidance and promotion are also needed, if students are to "search for the best available evidence," a key component of evidence-based teaching (Rousseau & McCarthy, 2007). Professors, however, especially junior faculty, are gradually making the transition from their traditional methods—scouring journals and keeping in touch with collegial networks—to a dependence on electronic information resources (Shen, 2007; Housewright & Schonfeld, 2008).

Even for those aware of the great body of research that exists, there is the challenge of learning to search through terabytes of electronic text. The other evidence-based fields of medicine and education have a much easier time, since each has its research consolidated in one dedicated overarching database: PubMed and ERIC, respectively (both funded by the government). In those cases, there is only one system to learn, and one route to finding the material. However, in the case of business research, every database and most of the publishers described earlier provide their own searching and retrieval systems, which are maddeningly unique and often opaque. Even seasoned scholars report significant frustration and difficulty when trying to navigate through these systems (Institute for the Future, 2002). Most universities have tried to address this problem of multiple search environments by purchasing and providing a "federated search" application, with names like MetaLib and WebFeat—systems that can search through multiple commercial databases as well as other text-based digital collections and catalogs simultaneously. These, however, are far from perfect and suffer from numerous usability problems (Gibson, Goddard, and Gordon, 2009. The database ISI Web of Knowledge, though not a federated searching product, provides essentially the same function for scholarly literature, as it searches through and delivers citations from over 12,000 academic publications. Using it is so complicated that it offers lengthy online tutorials. More recently, libraries have been acquiring newly developed "discovery services," such as Summon and Worldcat Local, which create Google-like search engines for all library-provided content.

Google is addressing this difficulty with characteristic aplomb. Google Scholar (scholar.google.com) is, in fact, a free federated searching tool, available to anyone with an Internet connection; it looks through the contents of thousands of scholarly journals, papers, and books. (It has recently added patents and legal documents.) As one might expect, it is far more intuitive and easier to use than the commercial products. It provides, for the most part, only access to citations, linking to a publisher's site where the content can be purchased. (There are two exceptions to this. One is that, for anyone attached to a university, Google Scholar is usually linked to the subscriptions that the university has paid for, and so there is a seamless connection to the full content for those who are on campus or who are using the off-campus Internet access application. Another is that Google—in its customary magical way—can occasionally find a link to content even when it is protected, such as to a prepublication document, to a research repository, or to a professor's personal web site.)

Roadblock 3: Inaccessibility

The third obstacle is actually getting hold of the articles and books themselves. Savvy and determined managers (or those who have read this chapter) might use Google Scholar to find exactly the right article—even a meta-analysis or systematic review—to address a particular management problem. Will those managers be able to get their hands on it? Databases are like gated communities; access to the full text of all of these articles is severely limited by ownership rights, subscription or pay-per-view systems, and intellectual property controls.

For individual managers, the barrier is significant. Although larger corporations in the past had their own corporate libraries, those have been disappearing for decades (Matarazzo & Pearlstein, 2007; Housewright, 2009). The cost of databases and subscriptions to individuals and small businesses can be prohibitive; for instance, the *Journal of Organizational Behavior* costs $363 yearly for individual subscribers, who can only get it in print. Single articles can be purchased from most publications, but that cost is also a deterrent—$31.50 per article from Science Direct, for example. Databases cost tens of thousands of dollars. The relation of scholarly research to practitioner publications has been compared to haute couture vs. prêt-a-porter (Alvarez & Mazza, 1998)—elite and expensive on the one hand, accessible and affordable on the other. Studies showing that managers value "ease of use and general accessibility" in their information sources (Terpstra & Rozell, 1997) reveal that these obstacles can be fatal to hopes of scholars reaching practitioners.

For students and professors, who have campus connections, university libraries have undertaken the role of acquiring and managing these subscriptions, but, especially lately, they are under severe budgetary pressure to cut back, even as costs increase

each year (Oder, 2009). Furthermore, the databases provide far from unlimited access to begin with, often enforcing "embargoes"—meaning that a certain number of months or years of current content is blocked. Online subscriptions to individual titles do provide current content, but exact heavy extra costs for early issues. Only the most well-endowed university libraries can afford to provide unfettered immediate access to all management publications. (Although for those willing to wait, the interlibrary loan system can usually deliver a needed article or book.)

New Forms of Access

Roadblocks can be overcome, so let's look at the ways that we—students, researchers, managers, and librarians—can now or in the near future get our hands on good, solid evidence in books and journals, in meta-analyses and systematic reviews, and in handbooks and encyclopedias. We hope for a quick evolution of handy and authoritative tools emerging from an EBMgt collaborative (Rousseau, 2007), but even in an optimistic scenario, those will probably be a few years in the making. In the meantime, we are not without resources.

Where you are—working in a large corporation, affiliated with a university, starting up your own business, even what city you live in—makes a difference in your access rights. For those affiliated with universities, access to subscription journals and databases is generally a given. However, those who are not might be surprised to find that a free library card from their local public library will give them online access to some of the better business and management databases. Major cities have multiple offerings, but even smaller cities, such as Hartford, Birmingham, Worcester, and Cincinnati, provide at least one of the major business research databases (although, sadly, the recent financial crisis is causing some libraries to cancel those subscriptions.) In addition, alumni offices are starting to provide similar access to their university's graduates; a 2006 report showed that 18 percent of 102 top universities surveyed already offered this (Wells, 2006,) and if queries by the MBA students that I see are any indication, there is a growing demand for this service.

As mentioned earlier, Google is working on this as well, and since that is where most people go for information online today (Marshall, 2009), this is a good thing. Google Scholar (scholar.google.com) and Google Books (books.google.com) are not the whole answer, but as meta-searching tools, they are immediately accessible, simple to use and constantly evolving. A simple search: "meta-analysis pay for performance" in Google Scholar turns up a number of good peer-reviewed possibilities. For those not university related, of course, it will not lead to the article itself, but the abstract, readily available, may be almost enough. The same search in Google Books also provides some excellent sources, one of which is the *Blackwell Handbook of the Principles of Organizational Behavior*, edited by Edwin Locke (2000). My search led directly to the chapter "Pay for Performance" by Cathy Durham and Kathryn Bartol (both management professors,) and provided the scanned entire text of that chapter, references and all (Durham & Bartol, 2004). Due to copyright restrictions, the texts available from Google Books will be missing numerous pages, and the results of searches like this will be serendipitous and changeable from day to day, but they will certainly provide something of substance. By 2009, Google Books offered the searchable contents of over 10,000,000 entire books, and is making plans to provide "free access to full texts at a kiosk in every public library in the United States." (Brin, 2009).

Two recent movements spearheaded by university libraries are attempting to have some impact on some of these issues. First, the growing "information literacy" movement is aimed at teaching students at all levels (Bennett, 2007), not only about "the practical skills involved in effective use of information technology," but also about "the nature of information itself, its technical infrastructure and its social, cultural, and even philosophical context and impact." (Shapiro & Hughes, 1996). This will hopefully address both the "difficult to search" and "not knowing what exists" problems, in that students who go on to the business world will have an educated sense of what information has true value, where it is, and how to get to it. Hopefully, this will instill in students the motivation and skills they need to look for and find useful evidence in their post-graduate careers.

Second, the "Open Access" movement encourages the authors of scholarly research to make their work freely accessible to the public, eliminating the stranglehold that scholarly publishers have on the kind of management articles discussed here (Suber, 2007). In 2008, in the biomedical field, this was given a boost by the National Institutes of Health policy requiring any research that is NIH-funded to be freely available—and so liberating a large quantity of those articles from fee-based status. Now the Federal Research Public Access Act of 2009

(H.R.5253, S.1373), requiring all government-funded research to follow the same requirements, is being considered in Congress, and holds promise for liberating many more publications in all fields. Entire journals are being born as peer-reviewed open-access publications; an example in the business field is *BuR-Business Research* (www.business-research.org/) that was begun in 2008 by the German Academic Association for Business Research. This migration to unrestricted online access will probably grow as scholars see the advantages of vastly increased exposure of and citations to their writings as a result (Odlyzko, 2002) and develop their bargaining power in establishing contracts with the publishing industry. If this phenomenon becomes more standard for academic publications, the restrictions on access will lessen considerably. In the meantime, many organizations are moving ahead in the race to provide informational guidance on management issues.

The effort to gather, consolidate, and compress research-based management knowledge on specific topics into readable and authoritative form is proceeding on numerous fronts, some profit-oriented and some not, and with varying degrees of accessibility and trustworthiness. For instance, the Society for Human Resource Management now offers 11 reports that are "effective practice guidelines," which present "important research findings in a condensed, easy-to-use format for busy HR professionals" (www.shrm.org). These are handy, attractive, and quickly downloadable booklets of around 50 pages, covering topics like "Recruiting and Attracting Talent," "Employee Engagement and Commitment," and "Performance Management" performance management—and free to anyone with a computer.

There is also a growing number of handbooks and encyclopedias on business and management. These are works that strive to present concepts and findings in a concise and authoritative way; some of them have been published in print form for years, but their recent electronic publication and corresponding publicity blitz makes them far more visible, though with price tags that would generally limit their reach. Scholarly publishers Oxford University Press (Oxford Handbooks Online—Business & Management), Wiley/Blackwell (Blackwell Reference Online—Business and Management), and SAGE (various business e-encyclopedias) attempt to do this based on academic research. The more commercially oriented and relatively inexpensive *Business: The Ultimate Resource*, in its 2nd edition from British publisher A.C. Black is a hefty, mixed mélange of solutions, recommendations, and best practices "from the world's top practitioners, thought leaders, and academics." (A new edition is scheduled for 2011.)

Long-time academic publisher Emerald—www.emeraldinsight.com—which claims to be the "world's leading publisher in management research," has initiated an ambitious foray into resolving the research-practice gap. As they clearly state on their web site: "To make the world better managed means a bridging of the gap between the world of research and the world of application. Emerald's mission is to make this a reality" (first.emeraldinsight.com/about/philosophy.htm). They have developed a number of information packages specifically targeted at business students, teachers, and managers. These include: "Emerald Management Reviews," abstracting articles (both their own and other publishers') from what they describe as "the top 300 management publications worldwide, as selected by an independent accreditation board of industry experts;" a "Literature Review" search of the journals in their collection, which turns up meta-analyses and systematic reviews, the abstracts of which neatly outline the purpose, methodology, and findings in each article; and the "Emerald Management First" selection aimed at managers. Their statement that "successful managers recognize the value of quality research and know that actions based on sound evidence beat those based on suspect intuition every time" sounds as though it comes directly from the EBMgt movement! However, since the content they provide is basically limited to their own publications, which do not include many important management research sources, this is not only an inadequate solution, it's a misleading one because there is little hint of what is missing. However, the format and the intent—providing a link between managers and researchers—are definitely on the right track.

Internet developments over the last few years, such as social networking, collaborative online projects, self-publishing, and OpenCourseWare, have not been ignored by businesspeople trying to share important information, or those trying to reach them. Witness: HRM Today (network.hrmtoday.com) a social networking site for human resources managers begun in 2008, with over 2000 members; HRSpace on Twitter (twitter.com/HRSpace) with over 5,400 followers; portal hr.com, offering links to its own articles, case studies, whitepapers, wikis, forums, polls and blogs; WikiProject Business where volunteer editors assess and improve on the 18,000 Wikipedia articles related to business. (The large majority rate C or below.) There is a vast and wide range of bloggers—from serious scholars to consultants and CEOs to everyman and everywoman, viz. www.hrworld.com/features/top-100-management-blogs-061008/, www.mbaexplorer.com/blog/2008/08/top-50-business-professor-blogs/, and blogs.hbr.org. Finally, universities and business schools are beginning to broadcast their lectures, and even entire courses, for free; MIT Sloan School of Management is the pioneer, with over 50 graduate courses available.

Another future consideration is the information-seeking behavior of the next decade's managers and faculty, as well as that of current students. A number of studies (Connaway, Radford, Dickey, De Angelis Williams, & Confer, 2008; Rainie, 2006) have looked at the habits of "digital natives," as they enter the workplace and the academy, and who would be ready to enter management and scholarly ranks in 2016. This paradigm-shifting experience, of having grown up online, will impact all aspects of management practice and theory, but it will also affect how future generations look for, evaluate, and even create evidence. Rainie sees video games, for instance, which are played by virtually all college students today, as "the 'training program' for young workers that helps form their attitudes about the way the work-world operates—a world full of data streams, where analysis and decisions come at twitch speed, where failure at first is the norm, where the game player is the hero, and where learning takes place informally." How this will play out vis-à-vis the world of academic publishing in management—where recommendations are carefully considered and investigated, where success is what is aimed for, where the work of many is compared and consolidated, and where discourse is formulaic and codified—is something to think about.

Recommendations Until the Future Arrives

So in hindsight, having learned, since my days as a middle manager, about the utility and availability of scientifically based management advice, what could I have done—and what can other enlightened managers do now—to avail ourselves of it?

There are several ways that managers can find published research in articles and books. One is to ask your friendly local librarian for advice. Some excellent business libraries in the United States are public—namely the James J. Hill library in St. Paul, MN (www.jjhill.org/), New York Public Library's SIBL (www.nypl.org/locations/sibl),

Boston's Kirstein Business Branch (www.bpl.org/research/kbb/kbbhome.htm), the Library of Congress' Business Reference Service (www.loc.gov/rr/business/), and Brooklyn's Business Library (www.brooklynpubliclibrary.org/business/)—and many more cities in the United States and Canada have large sections of their public libraries devoted to business, entrepreneurship, and management. The British Library has a Business & IP Centre in London, and has just launched an impressive Management and Business Library Portal (www.mbsportal.bl.uk) to "support the impact of research by making the findings of management research—from various sources—more readily available to working managers." Many university or community college libraries also keep their libraries open to everyone, with access to databases generally allowable from within the buildings. For small business owners in the United States, there are over 1,000 government-funded Small Business Development Centers (www.asbdc-us.org,) which are often connected to universities or business schools and can make use of their resources.

Taking this one step further, managers could, possibly through their professional associations, work with those libraries, universities, and business development organizations in their communities to enhance, support, and publicize those resources. This would work two ways: promoting the collections of research that exist to those who can make use of them, and providing some much-needed outside support to develop them further (or at least keep them from disappearing through today's imminent budget cuts.) This would also identify them as stakeholders in the advancement and dissemination of management science, further tying practitioners to research and its production.

Another way of finding published research would be to join forces with other managers, researchers, professors, and students locally and globally—in investigative and publishing collaborations, in executive training programs, in communities of practice, and even in social gatherings (Rynes, 2009). Taking advantage of burgeoning social networking technologies to do this would be a good way to connect and to leap over geographical boundaries. (Join the EBMgt Facebook page!) Participating in organizations dedicated to furthering management knowledge, such as the Academy of Management, SHRM, or, ideally, an EBMgt collaborative (Rousseau, 2007) will also provide both a forum for communication and a source of continued learning.

What can educators and researchers do to increase the visibility and accessibility of their research findings? For the former, professors can, as Giluk and Rynes say in their chapter 8 of this handbook, "help students become more informed consumers of research" with the intent that it will carry over into their lives as managers. In doing so, they can enlist the skills of their university librarians, information professionals who are immersed in how scholarly literature is organized and who regularly teach people to navigate it. (Speaking from personal experience, we are glad to be invited into the classroom.) They can also take advantage of the many suggestions offered in Leung & Bartunek's chapter 9 of this volume, which enumerates many new communication tools available due to evolving new technologies.

To improve accessibility, researchers can also enlist in the "Open Access" movement by maintaining their right to self-archive their own work on their own web sites or in their university repositories, thus making it freely available despite being published in a subscription-based journal. This is done by selecting a journal for publishing one's work that makes this option contractually available. The SHERPA-RoMEO consortium, based at the University of Nottingham, keeps track of scholarly publishers' copyright policies; according to their data, out of 799 academic publishers, "63%...formally allow some form of self-archiving." (SHERPA-RoMEO, 2010.) A list of those is available on its web site, www.sherpa.ac.uk. Visibility is also enhanced in the process, as search engines such as Google Scholar readily locate and provide the articles in these archives. In fact, numerous studies "point to open access papers' being cited and consulted more often than toll-access work," which incidentally also serves promotion requirements for academics. (Willinsky, 2006.) Even better than simply participating would be to actively endorse and support this movement, in one's own university, in professional associations, and with colleagues. Federal legislation will push this substantially further, so all interested parties should voice support for the Federal Research Public Access Act of 2009.

The roadblock of "chaos" discussed earlier could be overcome by an organization taking on the responsibility of providing a single access route to reputable business research; this has been done in medicine with PubMed, in education with ERIC, and in psychology with PsycInfo, all of which are administered as not-for-profit enterprises by the National Library of Medicine, the U.S. Dept.

of Education, and the American Psychological Association, respectively.

Libraries and librarians can help in various ways. Most academic libraries already champion Open Access, and many actively participate by undertaking the task of handling their university's repositories for faculty research. Academic librarians can contact management professors in their schools to offer their services as guides to finding research and developing search strategies—either by giving a class lecture, by being "embedded" in a course (as an on-call information expert), by creating online resource guides, or by offering a course like the Finding Evidence course developed by NYU librarians, described by Anthony Kovner in his chapter 10 of this volume. Public libraries for their part need to publicize their resources for businesses much more than they currently do, in order to increase their visibility, perhaps even engendering some corporate support for their continued existence.

The pace of change in the information industry is so breathtakingly fast that by the time this handbook is in print, much of this terrain will look different. This argues powerfully for speedy and resolute action on a major project to consolidate, clarify, publicize, and provide easy access to the valuable findings that are now buried in this hidden and costly avalanche of research. When that future does arrive, with roadblocks gone, our managers, students, and scholars alike will cruise down the evidence-based highway.

References

Alvarez, J. L., & Mazza, C. (1998). Haute couture or pret-a-porter: Creating and diffusing management practices through the popular press. *IESE Research Papers D/368*. Retrieved from http://ideas.repec.org/p/ebg/iesewp/d-0368.html

Bennett, S. (2007). Campus cultures fostering information literacy. *portal: Libraries and the Academy, 7*(2), 147–167. doi:10.1353/pla.2007.0013

Blanchard, K. H., & Johnson, S. (1982). *The one minute manager*. New York: Morrow.

Brin, Sergey. (2009). Official Google blog: The 2008 founders' letter. Retrieved March 1, 2011 from http://googleblog.blogspot.com/2009/05/2008-founders-letter.html

Buckingham, M., & Coffman, C. (1999). *First, break all the rules: What the world's greatest managers do differently*. New York: Simon and Schuster.

Cascio, W. F. (2008). To prosper, organizational psychology should bridge application and scholarship. *Journal of Organizational Behavior, 29*(4), 455.

Case, D. O. (2008). *Looking for information: A survey of research on information seeking, needs, and behavior* (2nd ed.). London: Emerald Group Publishing.

Cason, C., & Van Scoyoc, A. M. (2006). The electronic academic library: Undergraduate research behavior in a library without books. *Portal: Libraries and the Academy, 6*(1), 47–58. doi:10.1353/pla.2006.0012

Connaway, L. S., Radford, M. L., Dickey, T. J., De Angelis Williams, J., & Confer, P. (2008). Sense-making and synchronicity: Information-seeking behaviors of millennials and baby boomers. *Libri, 58*(2), 123–135.

Durham, C. C., & Bartol, K. M. (2004). Pay for performance. In E.A. Locke (Ed.), *The Blackwell handbook of principles of organizational behavior* (pp. 150–165). Malden, MA: Blackwell. Retrieved from http://books.google.com/

Furnham, A. (2000). Secrets of success from the Heathrow School of Management. *Business Strategy Review, 11*(3), 61–67.

Gibson, I., Goddard, L., & Gordon, S. (2009). One box to search them all: Implementing federated search at an academic library. *Library Hi Tech, 27*(1), 118–133. doi:10.1108/07378830910942973

Griffiths, J. R., & Brophy, P. (2005). Student searching behavior and the web: Use of academic resources and Google. *Library Trends, 53*(4), 539.

Housewright, R. (2009). Themes of change in corporate libraries: Considerations for academic libraries. *portal: Libraries and the Academy, 9*(2). Retrieved from http://muse.jhu.edu/journals/portal_libraries_and_the_academy/v009/9.2.housewright.pdf

Housewright, R., & Schonfeld, R. (2008). *Ithaka's 2006 studies of key stakeholders in the digital transformation in higher education*. Retrieved from http://www.ithaka.org/research/Ithakas%202006%20Studies%20of%20Key%20Stakeholders%20in%20the%20Digital%20Transformation%20in%20Higher%20Education.pdf

Institute for the Future. (2002). *Final synthesis report of the e-journal user study*. Retrieved from http://ejust.stanford.edu/SR-786.ejustfinal.html

Johnson, S. (1998). *Who moved my cheese? An amazing way to deal with change in your work and in your life*. New York: Putnam.

Kay, C. (2001). What do managers read? A survey of journals and periodicals used by lodging managers in the hospitality industry. *Journal of Hospitality and Tourism Education, 13*(3/4), 76–86.

Lencioni, P. (2002). *The five dysfunctions of a team: A leadership fable*. San Francisco, CA: Jossey-Bass.

Markides, C. (2007). In search of ambidextrous professors. *Academy of Management Journal, 50*(4), 762–768.

Marshall, J. (2009). Yahoo and Bing lose U.S. search share in November. *ClickZ*. Retrieved from http://www.clickz.com/3635900

Matarazzo, J., & Pearlstein, T. (2007). Marrying two expert tools will help you sustain your corporate library. *Library Journal Academic Newswire*. Retrieved from http://www.libraryjournal.com/article/CA6407767.html

Miller, C. C. (2010). Amazon says e-books now top hardcover sales. *The New York Times*. Retrieved from http://www.nytimes.com/2010/07/20/technology/20kindle.html?_r=1

Oder, N. (2009). ARL budget roundup: Large academic libraries face cuts in collections, staff, hours. *Library Journal Academic Newswire*. Retrieved from http://www.libraryjournal.com/article/CA6655234.html

Odlyzko, A. (2002). The rapid evolution of scholarly communication. *Learned Publishing, 15*(1), 7–19.

Rainie, L. (2006). Digital natives invade the workplace. *Pew Internet & American Life Project*. Retrieved from http://pewresearch.org/pubs/70/digital-natives-invade-the-workplace

Rich, M. (2010). Kindle books in snack sizes. *New York Times*. Retrieved from http://www.nytimes.com/2010/02/08/business/media/08condense.html

Rousseau, D. M. (2007). A sticky, leveraging, and scalable strategy for high-quality connections between organizational practice and science. *Academy of Management Journal, 50*(5), 1037–1042.

Rousseau, D. M., & McCarthy, S. (2007). Educating managers from an evidence-based perspective. *Academy of Management Learning and Education, 6*(1), 84–101.

Rynes, S. (2009). The research-practice gap in industrial-organizational psychology and related fields: Challenges and potential solutions. In S. Kozlowski (Ed.), *Oxford handbook of industrial-organizational psychology*. New York: Oxford University Press. Retrieved from http://papers.ssrn.com/sol3/papers.cfm?abstract_id=1455968

Rynes, S. L., Colbert, A. E., & Brown, K. G. (2002). HR professionals' beliefs about effective human resource practices: Correspondence between research and practice. *Human Resource Management, 41*(2), 149–174.

Shapiro, J. J., & Hughes, S. K. (1996). Information literacy as a liberal art? *Educom Review, 31,* 31–35.

Shen, Y. (2007). Information seeking in academic research: A study of the sociology faculty at the University of Wisconsin-Madison. *Information Technology and Libraries, 26*(1), 4.

SHERPA. (2010). Statistics on publishers' copyright policies & self-archiving. Retrieved from http://www.sherpa.ac.uk/romeo/statistics.php

Suber, P. (2007). *Open access overview*. Retrieved from http://www.earlham.edu/~peters/fos/overview.htm

Sutton, R. I. (2004). Prospecting for valuable evidence: Why scholarly research can be a goldmine for managers. *Strategy & Leadership, 32*(1), 27.

Sutton, R. I. (2006). Management advice: Which 90% is crap? *Change This*. Retrieved from http://changethis.com/manifesto/show/23.90PercentCrap

Tedd, L. A. (2005). E-books in academic libraries: An international overview. *New Review of Academic Librarianship, 11*(1), 57–79.

Terpstra, D. E., & Rozell, E. J. (1997). Sources of human resource information and the link to organizational profitability. *The Journal of Applied Behavioral Science, 33*(1), 66.

Vermeulen, F. (2007). "I shall not remain insignificant": Adding a second loop to matter more. *Academy of Management Journal, 50*(4), 754–761.

Wells, C. (2006). Alumni access to research databases: The time is now. *College & Research Libraries News, 67*(7), 413–416.

Wilbourne, S. (2001). The expanding ocean of difference between academic research and book publishing. *Publishing Research Quarterly, 17*(3), 29–32. doi:10.1007/s12109-001-0030-3

Willinsky, J. (2006). *The access principle: The case for open access to research and scholarship*. Cambridge, MA: MIT Press.

Culture and Evidence-Based Management

Georges A. Potworowski *and* Lee A. Green

Abstract

This chapter explicates the role that organizational culture plays in the ways that evidence is used to inform management practice. Both culture and the process of making management practice evidence-based are multifaceted. Drawing on various literatures, we offer a cultural framework to help one assess how and why evidence-based management (EBMgt) is or is not used in a particular organization. We characterize culture as a complex, but only partly coherent, set of patterns shared by a group, where a pattern consists of mutually supporting beliefs, values, and practices. Patterns vary in what they are about, how broad, connected, and coherent they are, as well as how important they are to a given culture. Each of these factors affects how easy it is to change a pattern and change culture. We frame EBMgt as a pattern, outline its core beliefs, values, and practices, and then explain which cultural patterns are necessary in an organization if the EBMgt pattern is to take root. We go on to identify eight ways in which culture and EBMgt affect each other, and conclude by suggesting steps to implement EBMgt in organizations, research programs, and classrooms.

Key Words: culture; evidence-based practice, belief justification, mental models, evidence-based organizations

Every day, organizations use evidence to guide decisions about how to manage their operations. They differ in what evidence they use, how and where they use it, and why. A key driver of these differences is culture. Consider, for example, how the cultures of organizations as different as a Fortune 500 company, a nonprofit startup, a manufacturing plant, a consulting firm, and the military might affect the evidence they use to improve their respective management and organizational practices (hereafter referred to as management practices). The underlying premise of this handbook is that the management practices in organizations such as these would be more effective if they were more systematically informed by current scientific evidence. The focus of this chapter is to help explain the role that culture plays in this process.

The reader may hope to find in this chapter some insight into what a culture must be like to support evidence-based management (EBMgt). Because

both culture and the process of making practice evidence based are multifaceted and involve complex interactions, we felt it was not sufficiently helpful to summarize existing suggestions about what cultural characteristics support EBMg. Rather, this chapter frames both culture and EBMgt as being composed of patterns of beliefs, values, and practices. The pattern framework provides a structured way to understand the mechanisms of how different cultures and EBMgt interact, and to meaningfully integrate insights from other scholars. Finally, the framework is theoretically grounded, but not overburdened, allowing it to help generate testable hypotheses and be actionable in organizations and management classrooms.

The chapter consists of four sections. In the first, we draw on theories and concepts of culture to characterize it as a complex, but only partly coherent, set of patterns shared by a group. Each of its patterns consists of mutually supporting beliefs, values, and practices. Patterns vary in what they are about, how broadly they are construed, and how coherent, interconnected, and influential they are in a given culture. We then explain how organizations do not have one culture, but rather exist in an ecology of cultures with interacting elements and patterns.

In the second section, we elaborate on the components of EBMgt, then use a dimensional model of culture to characterize EBMgt as a pattern with specific beliefs, values, and practices. In the third section, we bring culture and EBMgt together by identifying eight ways in which they affect one another, and argue what three cultural dimensions must look like in an organization for EBMgt to take root. Where appropriate, we tie in other scholars' important suggestions about what an EBMgt culture demands. In the final section, we describe strategies to implement EBMgt, and conclude by suggesting future steps for scholars, practitioners, and educators.

Our goal is for all readers to gain a clearer understanding of culture, EBMgt, and how the two are related. The practitioner should develop sufficient understanding to assess how evidence is currently viewed and used in her organization. She should also be able to identify existing cultural patterns in the organization that have synergies with EBMgt that can be leveraged, and patterns that conflict with EBMgt and need to be addressed. Scholars should gain insight into how different cultural dimensions are related to EBMgt, and we expect them to find interesting gaps in our description worthy of empirical investigation and theoretical development. The educator will gain a framework to help students think systematically and practically about culture and its effect on using evidence to improve management practice. The framework can inform case analyses and field exercises by helping students assess an organization's cultural ecology, and how it affects its current and potential use of management-related evidence. Finally, it can help the educator assess the impact that the cultural ecology in her own classroom has on students' receptivity to different forms of evidence.

Culture

There are many different approaches to understanding culture, from the thick descriptions of anthropological ethnographies (e.g., Martin, 1992; Trice & Beyer, 1993), to typologies (e.g., Quinn & Rohrbaugh, 1983), hierarchical models (e.g., Schein, 2010), and dimensional conceptualizations (e.g., Dennison & Mishra, 1995). In this chapter, we adopt Detert, Schroeder, and Mauriel's (2000) dimensional framework, which is a synthesis of 25 established

models of culture, and we supplement it with a few additional cultural concepts. This hybrid framework helps characterize culture, if imperfectly and incompletely, and enables the management practitioner, scholar, and educator to better understand the ways in which culture and EBMgt affect one another.

We propose, as others have, that culture can be thought of as a complex system of elements—language, symbols, stories, myths, heroes, artifacts, norms, beliefs, values, and practices—that are shared by and shape the identity of a group of people. These elements coalesce and mutually support each other in meaningful patterns. In the following pages, we describe in more detail what patterns are and some of their key characteristics and mechanisms.

Cultural Patterns

Cultural patterns guide people in making sense of, organizing, and acting in the world. They vary in what they are about, how broadly they are construed, and how coherent, connected, and influential they are within and across cultures. For simplicity's sake, we limit our characterization of cultural patterns to the interactions among their three most important elements—beliefs, values, and practices.

A "belief" is a truth claim about the past, present, or possible future state of the world: It is a claim about what was, is, or will be the case. The degree to which a given belief is justified depends on what theory of justification one explicitly or implicitly appeals to: foundationalist, coherentist, or correspondence (though variations and mixes of these exist). The differences between these theories are important because a belief that is justified using one theory may not be justified using another.

Briefly, foundationalist theories hold certain beliefs as given (i.e., first principles or self-evident truths), which act as the basis for the justification of all other beliefs. Coherentist theories hold that the justification of a given belief is contingent on its compatibility with the other beliefs one holds. Finally, in correspondence theories, a belief is justified to the extent that it accurately describes or predicts a state of the world. That said, our understanding of the world does not consist of disconnected beliefs. We construct sets of mutually supporting beliefs into patterns, sometimes called "mental models" (Gentner & Stevens, 1983), and both theories of justification and mental models are patterns integral to a culture: They shape and are shaped by culture (Hirschfeld & Gelman, 1994).

A "value" is a specific type of belief—one about how things *ought* to be (or *ought* to have been)—given beliefs about how things *can* possibly be (or *could* have been) (Schwartz, 1992; Rokeach, 1973). Values can be especially challenging to identify accurately because what one claims to value—say, in a mission statement or press release (i.e., one's "espoused value")—may not necessarily be consistent with what one's behaviors suggest about what one values (i.e., one's "enacted value"; Argyris & Schön, 1978). Common expressions, such as "putting your money where your mouth is," address the alignment between espoused values and enacted values, or "behavioral integrity" (Simons, 1999).

Finally, we depart from most theories of culture by considering management practice, instead of behavior, as an important element of culture. Our principal reason is that practices, and not merely behaviors, are what EBMgt aims to improve. We adopt Cook and Brown's (1999) definition of practice as "the coordinated activities of individuals and groups in doing their 'real work' as it is informed by a particular organizational or group context" (pp. 386–387). A management practice, then, is a special kind of behavior that is characterized, not only by having a specific meaning, but also by having meaning that is drawn from, contributes to, and can be evaluated against a shared body of knowledge.

Which beliefs, values, and practices make up a given pattern depend on what the pattern is about and how specific it is. Although cultural patterns exist on a continuum of specificity, for pragmatic reasons we categorize them in this chapter as broad patterns and narrow patterns. Thus, each pattern is about *something* that can be as broad as "human motivation" or as narrow as "employee compensation."

Broad Patterns: Cultural Dimensions

The broadest type of cultural pattern is arguably the cultural dimension. Various scholars have taken a dimensional approach to characterizing and comparing cultures (e.g., Dennison & Mishra, 1995; Smith, Dugan, & Trompenaars, 1996), in which each dimension consists of the beliefs and values on a basic characteristic of culture. (When dimensions do not explicitly include values or practices, they have implications for values and practices.) Detert, Schroeder, and Mauriel (2000) synthesized over 25 prominent theories of organizational culture and found the following eight general, recurring cultural dimensions:

1. *The basis of truth and rationality* concerns ideas about what is real, what one can know about what is real, and the means to do so.

2. *The nature of time and time horizon* concerns whether planning and goal setting tend to focus more on the long or short term.

3. *Motivation* involves ideas about the nature of what drives people to act, what parts are endogenous and exogenous, and what can be done to influence those drives.

4. *Stability versus change, innovation, and personal growth* includes beliefs about people's desire and propensity for stability or change, their openness to change, and their beliefs about whether there is always room for improvement.

5. *Orientation to work, task, and co-workers* distinguishes between work as a production activity versus social activity, a means to an end versus an end in itself, and a results focus versus process focus.

6. *Isolation versus collaboration and cooperation* speaks to beliefs about the relative effectiveness, efficiency, and effects on individual autonomy of working alone or in groups.

7. *Control, coordination, and responsibility* refers to how centralized, controlled, formal, and rule-based goals, decision making, and work are versus how decentralized, flexible, shared, and autonomous they are and should be.

8. *Internal and/or external orientation and focus* refer to where an organization looks for a way to improve its standards for performance and its sources of ideas and leadership.

Cultures vary in what specific beliefs, values, and practices make up each of these distinct, but interconnected patterns. Taken together, the eight dimensions are an informative, high-level, but incomplete way to characterize and compare cultures. These dimensions interact and play out in narrower patterns, which consist of proportionally more specific beliefs, values, and practices. Cultural beliefs about the motivations of individuals (dimension 3), for example, are central to narrower cultural patterns about effective sales, marketing, and negotiation. Beliefs about motivation combined with beliefs and values about orientation to work (dimension 5) and collaboration (dimension 6) shape the narrow patterns of employee incentives, recruitment, labor relations, and change leadership.

Narrow Patterns: Daily Management Practices

If broad patterns are useful to get a "big bucket" sense of a culture's beliefs, values, and practices, narrow patterns are more directly useful in assessing, comparing, and improving day-to-day management practices. For example, Rasmussen, Sieck, & Smart (2009) compared the shared mental models of good project planning of British and American military officers. Using a technique called "cultural network analysis" (CNA), they mapped out the chains of beliefs, values, and resulting planning practices and found several insightful cultural differences. British military planning, for instance, emphasizes communicating the plan's intent to those who will execute it so that it can be flexibly implemented in the field. In contrast, American military planning aims to reduce the number of decisions in the field by providing a step-by-step action "roadmap" with several contingencies. Thus, CNA revealed that important differences in military planning were rooted in cultural differences on the control, coordination, and responsibility dimension (dimension 7).

Significant differences between the mental models of planning in the two military cultures had affected their ability to effectively conduct joint planning operations. The concrete understanding of the differences and similarities in beliefs, values, and practices between the British and American planning models eventually allowed for the strategic integration of members from both military cultures into synergistic and effective planning teams.

Core and Peripheral Elements and Patterns

A key characteristic of patterns and elements in a given culture is how important or "core" they are to that culture. Extending Lachman, Nedd, and Hinings' (1994) distinction between core and peripheral values, core patterns and elements are those that are more strongly held by more people in a culture, exert a stronger influence on other patterns in the culture, and play a greater role in shaping the identity of cultural members. Although the idea of core and peripheral patterns and elements suggests a stable hierarchy, how core a pattern or element is to a culture can change. On the one hand, the relative importance of cultural values (and by extension, patterns) can shift temporarily depending on context in a process Osland and Bird (2000) call "value trumping." On the other hand, successful cultural change initiatives can alter, add, remove, or replace one or more core elements or patterns.

Pattern Coherence

Just as a pattern's importance in a culture can shift, so too can its coherence. Not only do patterns vary in how coherent they are, but the system of patterns that makes up cultures are themselves typically not entirely coherent (Alvesson, 2002; Hitlin & Piliavin, 2004). There are contradictions, tensions, ambiguities, and gaps within any culture: "Coherence is at most a characteristic of part not the 'whole' of culture" (McSweeney, 2009, p. 24). To understand and make practical use of the concept of culture, it is important to consider what makes (and keeps) those parts coherent. There are two levels at which to characterize a culture's coherence—within patterns and among patterns. Both levels are addressed next.

How patterns emerge, are sustained, strained, changed, or broken, begins with how the elements within a pattern interact. So-called "onion" models of culture (e.g., Schein, 2010) generally place hidden assumptions (i.e., tacit beliefs) at the center of culture, and the effects of hidden assumptions radiate outward to the subsequent "layers" of values, then behaviors (or practices), and so on. The chain of effect has beliefs setting the boundary conditions for values, which are then enacted in practices. There is considerable evidence, however, that beliefs, values, and practices influence one another reflexively. The outcome of attempting a new practice can increase or decrease both one's perception of the practice's effectiveness and beliefs in one's own efficacy. Similarly, feedback or reflection on a practice can reveal one's beliefs about that practice to be inaccurate. For example, one of the first lessons learned in a typical negotiation class is that not all negotiations are completely zero-sum interactions: One can get a better deal if one first tries to discover and increase how much is negotiable.

Whether one notices, accepts, and acts on such lessons and feedback can depend on one's wishful thinking and hopes—ways in which what one values (i.e., prefers to be true) can influence what one believes is possible or true (e.g., Bastardi, Uhlmann, & Ross, 2011). Practice also influences the formation and transformation of values through various mechanisms, from enacted values that are role modeled during professional socialization (White, Kumagai, Ross, & Fantone, 2009) to small acts of corruption that are rationalized and incrementally increased until corruption in the organization becomes normal (Ashforth & Anand, 2003).

An actual pattern exists (or emerges) when a set of beliefs, values, and practices is sufficiently mutually reinforcing to result in stable interactions. As an illustration, consider what elements make up the pattern for employee compensation. A widely shared element in most compensation patterns is the value that people ought to be rewarded for the work they do. When one looks more closely at forms of compensation, however, differences in specific values and beliefs begin to emerge. Some patterns value compensation based on status (e.g., seniority), whereas other patterns value compensation based on the work done. The latter group can value compensation based on services rendered (e.g., piece work, billable hours, fee-for-service), on outcomes (e.g., commission, contingent fee, pay for performance) or some combination of the two (e.g., stock options). Compensation can be standards-based or not, it can be individual or collective, and it can include a variety of nonmonetary incentives (e.g., corner office, fancier job title, protected time for pet projects).

Beliefs, values, and practices begin to cohere in a pattern through various mechanisms, including logical entailment, belief justification, consistency with other mental models, and the desire for behavioral integrity. Each enactment of the pattern's practice(s) refines and reinforces its supporting beliefs and values, and, thus, the pattern itself. In this way, the pattern becomes more coherent and potentially more connected through the enactment of its practice(s).

Pattern Connectedness

The second way in which cultures are coherent is through the connectedness of their patterns. Patterns are connected to each other within a culture through shared elements that act as "nodes," and cultures are connected to each other through shared patterns that act as nodes. The core value in compensation—that "people ought to be rewarded for the work they do"—is an example of a value node. Another example of a node is the core value in the "democracy" pattern, namely, that rule ought to be by the people. Yet, despite this core value node, democracy takes many different forms. Each form has its distinct, narrow pattern of values, beliefs, and practices, and what might appear as a small difference among patterns can be very meaningful (e.g., appointed senate, state rights, vetoes).

Not One Culture, but a Cultural Ecology

Up to now, we have discussed culture (and will continue to do so) as if organizations had one culture. This was for simplicity's sake. In reality, each organization exists at the intersection of various cultures. An organization's own culture is embedded in its industry culture, and in or across national and regional cultures. Depending on an organization's size and mission, it can contain various subcultures and countercultures, based on division, department, location, and profession or trade (Martin & Siehl, 1983). Moreover, each employee, partner, supplier, and client has overlapping memberships in different cultures: ethnic, national, professional, recreational, and so on. To a greater or lesser extent, each of these cultures shapes a member's identity, what she values and believes, and how she acts. With increasing globalization and the ubiquity of multidisciplinary teamwork, how evidence is perceived and used in an organization will be affected not by one, but by several cultures.

To systematically address how interacting cultures affect the adoption and implementation of EBMgt, we adopt Baba's (1995) view that an organization is best construed as existing in a cultural ecology. A cultural ecology approach involves taking a systems perspective on the effects of an organization's multiple interacting cultures, patterns, and elements. It acknowledges that the ecology is in constant flux and is affected by changes in everything from organizational structure and leadership, to markets, laws, industry regulations, and the sudden emergence of risky opportunities.

Why does this matter? Because understanding an organization in terms of interacting cultures composed of interacting patterns composed of interacting elements allows one to better appreciate the challenges of assessing how receptive a given organization might be to a particular change such as EBMgt, and where, by whom, and why that change might be well (or poorly) received. To prepare the reader to better anticipate and monitor the effects of introducing the EBMgt pattern into a cultural ecology, we turn our attention to the dynamics of pattern change.

Pattern Change

The mutual reinforcement among elements in a pattern implies that a change in one element can have repercussions on the elements connected to it. Consider the common belief that employees perform better when they are offered greater monetary incentive. New evidence is emerging suggesting that, at a certain point, intrinsic motivation improves performance on cognitive tasks more than does extrinsic motivation (e.g., Ariely, Gneezy, Loewenstein, & Mazar, 2009). If this evidence were to lead one to change one's beliefs about motivation (dimension 3), it would entail, among other things, that one's employee compensation practice incorporate intrinsically motivating incentives and not strictly monetary compensation.

A change in a pattern comes about when one of two inconsistencies arises. Inconsistencies in coherence occur when some beliefs, values, and practices within a pattern (or between existing patterns) change and become inconsistent with the others.

Inconsistencies in correspondence occur when a pattern fails to explain or predict experiences that it was expected to explain or predict. Both forms of inconsistency create pattern instability, which can lead to confusion, anxiety, and even identity crisis. Instability itself, however, is neither bad nor good. It can linger and cause enduring harm, just as it can lead to learning, growth, and more stable and beneficial patterns than existed previously. In more extreme cases, instability can spread through nodes and cascade across patterns to destabilize the culture itself. History is replete with social and political upheavals that have some pattern inconsistency at their core.

To address the potential effects of pattern inconsistency, two sets of cognitive and sociocultural mechanisms act in opposing ways: One set aims to prevent and minimize inconsistencies, and the other aims to resolve them. The first set of mechanisms maintains a pattern's stability (i.e., its coherence). At the individual level, stability mechanisms include our tendency to seek and interpret experiences in a way that is congruent with existing patterns (e.g., "confirmation bias," Lord, Ross, & Lepper, 1979; Nickerson, 1998) and to privilege sources, forms, and standards of evidence that support existing patterns over those that challenge them (e.g., "disconfirmation bias," Taber & Lodge, 2006). Stability mechanisms at the cultural level include dogma, moral codes, social norms, taboos, rules, punishments, myths, heroes, and other mechanisms that encourage conformity.

The competing set of mechanisms improves the accuracy of patterns, that is, their ability to explain and predict experiences. Accuracy mechanisms at the individual level include our disposition to look for better or new patterns by learning, creating, improving, and innovating. Our intolerance of excessive or prolonged ambiguity and conflicting accounts of the world, or our inability to predict and control our environment to our satisfaction can also push us to look for better or new patterns.

At a cultural level, accuracy mechanisms include social norms, rules, practices, myths, and heroes. Consider the example of modern science, whose norms and practices (or methods) aim to improve the validity and reliability of our understanding of the natural world. Science does so in a collective cycle of systematically building, questioning, refining, and replacing our existing beliefs and mental models (or theories). Accuracy mechanisms exist within organizations as well. Process improvement practices, such as General Electric's "workout sessions" (Potts, 1992) and the Toyota Production System's concept of *kaikaku* or radical improvement (Womack & Jones, 2003), incorporate and publicly support an environment that encourages participants to voice questions and concerns about long-held beliefs and accepted wisdom when doing so might lead to improvement.

Which of the two sets of mechanisms prevails when a pattern becomes unstable depends on the circumstances and on the personal and cultural beliefs about knowledge and knowing of those interpreting the experiences (i.e., cultural dimension dimension 1). After all, two individuals, just as two groups, often interpret the same event or phenomenon very differently. Some are open to being changed by the event, and others less so.

Just as a change in an element destabilizes a pattern, so, too, can a change in one pattern affect the stability of the patterns connected to it. Each pattern and each node connected in the node-pattern structure reinforces and stabilizes the structure. The more stable the structure, the harder it is to change a node or pattern in that structure. Following this logic, any successful change to a node can have broader repercussions, as the effects of the change ripple across any patterns the node is connected to, any other nodes in those patterns, and so on.

Using the analogy of a web of beliefs, Quine and Ullian (1978) argued that those beliefs at the center (i.e., core beliefs) are connected to many other beliefs and so are more stable, whereas those beliefs at the edge of the web are not as interconnected and, therefore, are more easily changed. In this spirit, Sieck, Rasmussen, and Smart (2010) propose that an explicit cultural mental model can help in strategically structuring messages to affect "the values [or other elements] of the most vulnerable concept…(i.e., those for which there is the least consensus) which then propagate across perceived influences to affect the values of other concepts" (p. 17).

In sum, a number of factors affect the stability of patterns, and consequently how easily they come apart, get reconfigured, or change altogether. A pattern that is more internally coherent, more core to the culture, plays a larger role in defining cultural identity, or a pattern that is more integrated with other patterns is more stable and thus harder to change (see Chi, 2008 for an analogous description of degrees of conceptual change).

In this section, we described what cultural patterns are and several ways in which they differ from one another, including what they are about, how broad or narrow they are, and how core they are to a culture. We also argued that patterns vary in in their coherence, which is a function of how mutually supporting their elements are and how connected they are to other patterns. Finally, patterns differ in how shared they are across a cultural ecology. To more easily explain how EBMgt and culture are related, we first characterize EBMgt as a pattern and delineate its core beliefs, values, and practices.

Evidence-Based Management

The EBMgt decision-making process is a pattern with component patterns, beliefs, values, and practices. Although the peripheral patterns and elements to EBMgt will vary from one instantiation to the next, for a decision process to be considered EBMgt it must possess certain core beliefs, values and practices. Som of these appear in Briner, Denyer, and Rousseau's (2009) definition of EBMgt (which is derived from Sackett, Rosenberg, Gray, Haynes, & Richardson's 1996 definition of evidence-based medicine):

> Evidence-based management is about making decisions through the conscientious, explicit, and judicious use of four sources of information: practitioner expertise and judgment, evidence from the local context, a critical evaluation of the best available research evidence, and the perspectives of those people who might be affected by the decision.
>
> *(Briner, Denyer, & Rousseau, 2009, p. 19)*

This definition reveals three characteristics of EBMgt. First, the core practice of EBMgt is making management decisions. Second, EBMgt decisions need to be based on evidence from four sources of information. Third, EBMgt decisions need to be made in a conscientious, explicit, and judicious manner. To gain a more concrete sense of the EBMgt pattern that emerges when these three characteristics come together requires looking more closely at the component beliefs, values, and practices of each characteristic.

The Core Practices of EBMgt

The core practice of "making management decisions" can be broken down into component practices at different levels of specificity. A common way of characterizing any decision-making process is in terms of three phases: (1) the *acquisition* of information (or evidence); (2) its *interpretation,* which culminates in a decision; and (3) the subsequent *implementation* of that decision. Nested within these three phases are even more specific ways of characterizing the component practices of the EBMgt decision process. Yates and Potworowski (chapter 12 of this volume), for example, present a relatively

comprehensive, intermediate-level characterization of these component decision practices in the form of 10 "cardinal issues." Some cardinal issues apply across all three phases, such as what resources are expended (i.e., investment), who does the deciding and how (i.e., mode), and whether the decision process and outcomes are satisfactory (i.e., acceptability). Other cardinal issues are more specific to one or two phases, such as the generation of alternatives (i.e., options) and their potential outcomes (i.e., possibilities) during the acquisition and interpretation phases.

By delving into each cardinal issue, one can get concrete enough to ask four questions to identify the component decision-making practices and assess how evidence based they are: (a) What measurable, decision-making component practices are in place, if any? (b) How effective are they? (c) How conscientiously, explicitly, and judiciously is evidence used in these practices? and (d) To what degree are the practices based on evidence? This means that it is neither very meaningful nor helpful to try to characterize an organization's management-decision-making process as simply evidence based or not. Rather, by asking the four questions of specific decision practices, one can begin to systematically and meaningfully assess what parts of an organization's decision-making process can be made more evidence-based. Addressing these four questions allows the practitioner to undertake more informed and targeted practice- change initiatives, the scholar to generate more specific organizational research hypotheses, and the educator to create more effective EBMgt education exercises.

The Core Beliefs and Values of EBMgt

EBMgt, like evidence-based medicine (EBM), serves as a means to achieving intrinsically valued outcomes. In EBM, the goal is to maximize patient health in a way that integrates individual patient values. In EBMgt, the goal is to identify practices that maximize any combination of organizational outcomes. Which outcomes should be valued (and why) by any given organization falls outside the purview of EBMgt, but typically they include combinations of such goals as profitability, growth, efficiency, quality, safety, customer value, and employee satisfaction. Rather, the core values and beliefs of EBMgt concern the best means to identify the management practices that maximize an organization's valued outcomes. Specifically, they concern principles of belief justification and the integrity of the decision process.

People appeal to a mix of principles to tacitly or explicitly justify a belief in the efficacy of an existing or proposed management practice. As an illustration, consider the different ways in which the following sentence can be completed: "This is the way we hire people in this organization because…" The "way we hire" refers to the current hiring practice. What follows "because" is a justification for the hiring practice, and different kinds of justifications exist: authority, tradition, consistency, status quo, experience, faith, intuition, advice, expertise, empirical results, consensus, convenience, cost, efficiency, speed, and so forth.

On closer inspection, one can see that these justifications try to do one of two things. Process-centered justifications such as intuition, expert advice, consensus, and empirical results, speak to *how* one ought to form beliefs about the quality of management practices. Outcome-centered justifications make claims about *what* attributes of candidate practices are desirable. By signaling that attributes such as low cost, efficiency, and speed are priorities, outcome-centered justifications serve as guides for making trade-offs among practices. A third group of justifications, which includes authority, faith, and tradition, does not separate process from outcomes. In the end, the specific justifications to which people are receptive vary by context and culture.

Some of these principles of justification may seem more compelling than do others, but none, arguably, go as deep as the two principles of justification at the core of EBMgt pattern: reliability and effectiveness. The primary aim of the EBMgt process is to identify the management practices that most effectively and reliably achieve intrinsically valued management outcomes. Any given EBMgt process is, of course, imperfect and can be improved. To better achieve its primary aim over time, the EBMgt process has as its secondary aim to improve its own effectiveness and reliability by using evidence to *transform itself*. The capacity for reflexive self-improvement is what gives the EBMgt process the greatest potential for effectively and reliably identifying effective and reliable management practices. At the risk of belaboring the point, *the success of EBMgt in an organization rests on the degree to which that organization values and uses empirically demonstrated effectiveness and reliability, above all other principles of justification, as the basis for choosing its management practices.*

Pfeffer and Sutton (2006) address the issue of alternative principles of process justification in their description of how an EBMgt mindset clashes with how managers and organizations typically operate. They explicitly warn against continuing to base management decisions on strongly held but untested beliefs (e.g., intuition), the status quo, casual benchmarking of successful organizations' practices, and what was done in the past. Interestingly, and perhaps more controversially, they also suggest adopting a "neutral stance toward ideologies and theories" (p. 71). Adopting a neutral, if not skeptical, stance towards a new theory is consistent with EBMgt principles. Sustaining a completely neutral stance toward a theory would be inconsistent with EBMgt principles if, after sufficient testing, that theory explained and predicted phenomena more effectively and reliably than did competing theories. To be fair, Pfeffer and Sutton's warning was likely against protecting pet or popular theories from disconfirming evidence. Such protection can manifest itself as a failure to conscientiously collect disconfirming evidence or a failure to judiciously give that disconfirming evidence its due weight. In this respect, we fully endorse their warning.

Adopting a neutral stance toward ideologies is a potentially more complicated matter because ideology and culture have much in common and can overlap. We take ideology to mean a collection of patterns that fundamentally shapes a group's *sociopolitical* understanding, perceptions, and identity. Pfeffer and Sutton (2006) warn against ideologies because many of them, if not most, adopt a strong foundationalist principle of belief justification. In an ideology, the core beliefs, values, and practices are taken as given (i.e., self-evident truths) and then act as the basis for other beliefs, values, and practices. Ideologies tend to have strong stability mechanisms (e.g., dogma and social norms) and weak accuracy mechanisms. In contrast, EBMgt is a pattern that acts as an accuracy mechanism—one so strong that can be self-correcting. When an ideology drives decision-making about management practices for which empirical evidence exists, that ideology risks blinding the deciders to whatever evidence is inconsistent with or threatening to its foundational values, beliefs, and practices. This suggests that ideologies are not simply incompatible with the EBMgt process, they tend to be antithetical and even hostile to it.

In addition to the principle of justification, EBMgt is defined by its core process beliefs and values that spell out the means of achieving an effective and reliable EBMgt decision process. Process beliefs center on four sources of information and the unique type of evidence each provides. To benefit from all four types of evidence requires that one conduct the EBMgt process in accordance with three process values. We now turn to describing the four types of evidence and the three process values in EBMgt.

Four Types of Evidence in EBMgt

Why does EBMgt draw on four sources of information for evidence? The simple answer is the belief that each of the four sources contributes unique and valuable evidence to identify the most effective and reliable, locally adapted management practices. This implies that using three or fewer of these sources of information, or including alternative sources of information (e.g., advice from popular management books at face value), will reduce one's chances of finding the most effective and reliable management practices (cf. Green & Yates, 1995 on "pseudodiagnosticity").

The belief that each type of information contributes something unique and valuable can itself be broken down into two component beliefs: (a) that each source provides a different kind of evidence that helps ensure the identification of effective and reliable management practices, and (b) that partly by virtue of its kind, each source of evidence has its strengths and weaknesses. Taken together, the four sources cover the necessary types of evidence, and their strengths at least partly compensate for each other's weaknesses. Each type of evidence, which cultures value differently, is described in more detail below.

PRACTITIONER EXPERTISE AND JUDGMENT

Who is an expert? The debate about how one should identify experts is ongoing. On the one hand, some have argued that experts can be identified by peer nomination, experience, or position (Shanteau, 1992a; Wood, 1999). Others have argued that experts are those capable of demonstrating reproducible superior performance on a representative task (Ericsson & Smith, 1991). Although peer nomination, experience, and position are often related to a track record of performance, they are by no means a guarantee of it. In fact, relying on the judgment of a so-called expert purely on the basis of peer nomination, her experience, or her position amounts to justifying a belief on the basis of authority. In contrast, the yardstick of reproducible superior performance is tied directly to the justificatory principles of reliability and effectiveness, and as such is consistent with EBMgt. The lesson here is that, before accepting that a given individual is an expert, one ought to first conduct due diligence on the basis of that expertise.

Even experts who demonstrate reproducible superior performance have strengths and weaknesses that are important to consider if one is to judiciously assess the evidence those experts provide (see Chi, 2006 for a brief review). Experts tend to make more accurate judgments and more accurate assessments of the contextual relevance of evidence. They also identify exceptions to a rule more easily than do nonexperts because experts ignore less relevant surface features, conceptualize problems in terms of their deep structure, and identify what key information is missing (Sackett, 1997; Shanteau, 1992b). As a result, experts are in a unique position to help acquire and evaluate the four sources of evidence (including practitioner expertise).

Perhaps not surprisingly, practitioner expertise tends to be the most highly valued of the four sources of evidence, especially by the experts themselves (Highhouse, 2008; Wyszewianski & Green, 2000). Tellingly, one of the main sources of resistance to EBM lies in the perception by some clinicians that systematic reviews and practice guidelines are restrictive "cookbook medicine" impositions on clinician intuition (see Potworowski, 2009 for a summary of the debate). When so-called experts object to (sources of) evidence that challenge their "expert" intuition, one should examine their track record of superior performance. For despite their strengths, even experts have shortcomings for which other sources of information and a robust EBMgt process can compensate. Experts tend to be overconfident, bound by their disciplinary training when diagnosing problems and offering solutions, and not as flexible and adaptable as one might expect (Chi, 2006). In addition, experts often disagree with one another, do not tend to exhibit superior judgments in certain domains (Shanteau, 1992a), and have personal motives (e.g., professional advancement, financial, ideological) that may not align with those of the organization employing them. Finally, the knowledge and processes that lead to expert judgment are difficult and expensive to make explicit with fidelity (although Crandall, Klein, & Hoffmann, 2006 offer ways to do so).

EVIDENCE FROM THE LOCAL CONTEXT

There are at least two forms of information from the local context that yield evidence relevant to EBMgt. The first is an existing understanding of the local context that helps one to assess the relevance of practitioner expertise, stakeholder perspectives, research evidence, or evidence from another organization. The second is data from a local sample, which can be gathered independently (e.g., data mining) or to test and customize management practices. Pfeffer and Sutton (2006) address both forms of evidence from the local context. They explicitly warn against the uncritical adoption of practices from outside, or "casual benchmarking," because what works in one context may not work easily in one's own, and they extol the virtues of constant local experimentation and learning by doing.

Both forms of local evidence are critical in helping assess whether and how a given management practice can be (made more) effective and reliable in a given organization, but each has its weaknesses. For one, those who do the work do not always know it best. Employees and management often hold inaccurate and counterproductive beliefs about their context, or profess beliefs that are smokescreens for their disinclination to change or be held accountable. The danger, to echo Pfeffer and Sutton (2006), is when these beliefs go unexamined (e.g., "Our context is unique, so external evidence Y does not apply").

Similarly, collecting local evidence is no guarantee that it will be good evidence. Although no organization is too small to collect formal, local evidence, many organizations are poorly equipped to do so with sufficient rigor and sophistication. Small sample sizes, lack of methodological expertise, poor theoretical grounding, and no independent review can each threaten the validity, reliability, and meaningfulness of local evidence. Still, these threats can, to some extent, be mitigated if one draws on the other forms of evidence to guide *what* local evidence one acquires and interprets and *how* one does so.

CRITICAL EVALUATIONS OF THE BEST AVAILABLE RESEARCH EVIDENCE

The best available research evidence has several advantages tied directly to the core EBMgt values of effectiveness and reliability. When scientific evidence is gathered together in a critical evaluation such as a systematic review (see Briner & Denyer, chapter 7 of this volume), the goal is to identify and evaluate studies on the effectiveness and reliability of a particular practice. A systematic review is the most reliable (though by no means infallible) of the four sources of evidence because it uses a rigorous methodology explicitly aimed at eliminating various threats to reliability (e.g., biases). It reduces bias is by comparing results from multiple independent studies, and increases its reliability by its transparency: The component studies are identified, the inclusion criteria for the studies in the evaluation are stated *a priori*, each component study has a methods section that facilitates independent verification (i.e., replication) and manipulation, and the assessment of the strength of the evidence and corresponding practice suggestions are proportional and explicitly stated. This allows readers to reevaluate

the same evidence themselves if they so choose. The key weakness of the best available research evidence is that it does not always generalize (completely) to the local context.

STAKEHOLDER PERSPECTIVES

The fourth source of evidence, the perspectives of people who might be affected by the decision, is considerably different from the other three sources. The analog for these people, or "stakeholders," in EBM is the patient. The critical difference between EBM and EBMgt, however, is that a single EBMgt decision usually affects many stakeholders, both inside and outside the organization.

There are at least three justifications for considering stakeholder perspectives when making EBMgt decisions. First, stakeholders can be experts or have unique knowledge of the local context, and, as such, can serve as a valuable source of evidence about, among other things, the feasibility of a particular practice under consideration. Second, they may have power over the successful implementation of whatever decision is ultimately made, which means there is a pragmatic rationale for getting their input and buy-in into the decision process (see "acceptability" in Yates and Potworowski, chapter 12 of this volume). Finally, depending on the stakeholder, one can argue that there is an ethical rationale—their values *ought* to be considered because they will be affected by the decision.

Although stakeholder perspectives are a valid source of information, they may not be as reliable as one expects. People are surprisingly inaccurate when anticipating how events will make them feel in the future (Wilson & Gilbert, 2005): Values are labile, beliefs are sometimes updated, and perspectives are affected by how situations are framed. As a result, stakeholders may not know how they feel about potential management practices, or they may be ambivalent and later change their minds. People's perspectives can be affected (or manipulated) by any number of cognitive biases (e.g., framing) and social phenomena (e.g. peer pressure). For this reason, considerable effort has been invested in helping patients better understand their situations so that they can make choices with which they will be happy and not later regret (Peters, Hibbard, Slovic, & Dieckmann 2007).

Using stakeholder perspectives (conscientiously and judiciously) in EBMgt involves meeting three major challenges. The first, as has just been shown, is gathering "accurate" stakeholder perspectives, to the extent that this is possible. The second is understanding the different cultural memberships of stakeholders to better appreciate and respect the beliefs and values that shape their perspectives. The third challenge is identifying and strategically balancing the perspectives of all stakeholders given the heterogeneity of beliefs, values, and hence perspectives in a cultural ecology.

Integrity of the EBMgt Decision Process

Drawing on these four sources of evidence is necessary but not sufficient for a robust EBMgt process. Decision making is susceptible to both intentional manipulation and a wide range of cognitive and social biases inherent in acquiring, interpreting, and implementing evidence—biases that people tend not to be aware of (see MacCoun, 1998 for a review). Research has consistently found, for example, that individuals and groups tend to seek and interpret evidence that fits with their prior beliefs (Ditto & Lopez, 1992; Lord, Ross, & Lepper, 1979).

For this reason, the definition of EBMgt stipulates that to protect the integrity of the process, evidence needs to be acquired, interpreted, and implemented in a contentiousness, explicitness, and judiciousness manner. Without a clear understanding of how to apply these three core values to the decision-making process, EBMgt is vulnerable to manipulation and risks losing its effectiveness, reliability, and credibility. The patterns for each of these core values are described next.

A CONSCIENTIOUS EBMGT PROCESS

The conscientious use of the four sources of information means that an EBMgt approach involves paying careful and sustained attention to sources of what can be potentially different, conflicting, and sometimes difficult-to-interpret information. (p. 7, Briner & Rousseau, 2011)

The three beliefs that help make an EBMgt process more conscientious are that different, conflicting, and difficult-to-interpret information (a) should be expected and sought, (b) can to some degree be resolved, and (c) is ultimately beneficial. Pfeffer and Sutton (2006) speak to the these points implicitly and explicitly by repeatedly emphasizing the importance of being committed to "fact-based" decision making, where that commitment involves (conscientiously) facing the "hard facts" by encouraging truth telling, however unpleasant it might be.

Being genuinely open to, let alone seeking, conflicting (and disconfirming) information can be difficult, uncomfortable, and counterintuitive. However, knowing that people tend to place greater value on information that is congruent with current beliefs (i.e., myside bias), seek information that supports their current beliefs (i.e., confirmation bias), and seek the company of others with similar beliefs allows one to address those tendencies by putting in place organizational practices that act as strategic countermeasures (Heath, Larrick, & Klayman, 1998). Examples of such countermeasures include installing routines to actively seek disconfirming information and identify counterfactuals (Wong, Galinsky & Kray, 2009), and assigning someone to play the devil's advocate (Schwenk, 1990).

AN EXPLICIT EBMGT PROCESS

Being explicit means using information from each source in a clear, conscious, and methodical way such that the roles played by all the information in the final decision are understood. (p. 7, Briner & Rousseau, 2011)

Although explicit process documentation can be expensive if done from scratch each time, documenting the EBMgt decision process clearly and methodically has several advantages. First, when a process is recorded, it becomes open to scrutiny, which makes the decision makers more accountable (Lerner & Tetlock, 1999) for having conducted it conscientiously and judiciously. As a result, the process is harder to covertly manipulate and, in turn, more credible to those affected (see process acceptability, Yates & Potworowski, chapter 12 of this volume). A second advantage is that having an explicit account of the original decision can make it easier and cheaper to re-consider and improve that decision, especially in light of new evidence or a significant change in context or values. One potential benefit to the organization is that extant policies and practices whose rationales have been lost or forgotten can slowly be reconsidered and replaced with ones whose rationales, contingencies, and alternatives are recorded. Finally, being explicit is essential for the knowledge management of the EBMgt process and practices, which facilitates the comparison of results from different local experiments and bringing pilot projects successfully to scale by sharing lessons learned.

A JUDICIOUS EBMGT PROCESS

Being judicious involves using reflective judgment to evaluate the validity and relevance of the information from each source. Evidence and information is critically evaluated in relation to the practice context and problem. (p. 7, Briner & Rousseau, 2011)

The meaning of "judicious evaluation" hinges on the criteria for validity and relevance and the role of "reflective judgment." What counts as valid and relevant information, and thus evidence, is perhaps the most central question of EBMgt. Misunderstanding what is meant by valid and relevant evidence in EBMgt will inevitably lead to a flawed understanding of EBMgt itself, which can result in its being misrepresented, misapplied, and eventually abandoned. The misunderstanding of EBM should serve as a lesson: A nontrivial proportion of healthcare workers hold an overly narrow understanding of what EBM considers to be evidence and how it proposes that such evidence be used. This has led them to label EBM as "cookbook medicine" and fueled suspicions that EBM is nothing more than a managerialist justification for cost reduction with little actual concern for quality. Proponents of EBMgt have already tried to clear up early misunderstandings (see Briner, Denyer, & Rousseau, 2009), but what counts as valid and relevant evidence is both epistemically and politically contentious in evidence-based fields as diverse as EBM (Rycroft-Malone et al., 2004), social work (Witkin & Harrison, 2001), public policy (Marston & Watts, 2003), and education (Ingram, Louis, & Schroeder, 2004; Slavin, 2002).

What counts as "evidence" is epistemically contentious because people (Kuhn, Cheney, & Weinstock, 2000; Perry, 1970; Wyszewianski & Green, 2000), organizations (Von Krogh, Roos, & Slocum, 1994), and cultures (Tabak & Weinstock, 2008) vary in what they consider to be legitimate principles of belief justification. Consider, for example, ethical review boards, whose purpose is to assess whether research proposals comply with the ethical principles (e.g., participant rights) set forth by funding agencies, professional associations, and the institution that the review board represents. Different research methods carry different ethical risks, so ideally such boards should have a sophisticated and unbiased method for assessing the appropriateness of research methods and the types of evidence they produce, given a proposal's research questions. There is evidence, however, that medical review boards are often ill-equipped to evaluate, and are prejudiced against, qualitative methods (American Association of University Professors, 2000; Tod, Nicolson, & Allmark, 2002). Still, qualitative methods are the most appropriate means of producing evidence on questions such as the range of patient values about chronic disease management. The quantitative bias of medical review boards' epistemic beliefs narrows

what they consider valid and relevant evidence and the appropriate means to obtain it. This, in turn, affects what gets studied and how, what new evidence is generated, and consequently what practices have a chance of being evaluated and improved.

The term *evidence* is politically contentious because the quality of the outcomes of evidence-based decisions is limited by the quality of the mix of evidence that is considered and how it is considered, both of which can be manipulated for political reasons. Without effective organizational (dis)incentives, checks, and balances, the evidence supporting an outcome that is a priori desired by an influential party can be emphasized or exaggerated, whereas evidence against the desired outcome can be played down, obfuscated, or suppressed. It is telling that the English-language edition of Huff's classic book from 1954, *How to Lie with Statistics,* has sold over 1,500,000 copies—more than any other statistical book (Steele, 2005). This leads to the question of how reflective judgment makes the EBMgt process judicious.

Over the last 25 years, psychologists Patricia King and Karen Kitchener have developed a concrete, developmental model of reflective judgment (see King & Kitchener, 2002 for a review). The seven stages in their model fall into three broader clusters, each representing a more sophisticated form of reflective judgment than the last: pre-reflective reasoning (stages 1–3), quasi-reflective reasoning (stages 4 and 5), and reflective reasoning (stages 6 and 7). The stage at which a person is reflecting is determined by his or her beliefs about how knowledge is gained (or the basis of knowledge), about how certain that knowledge *can* be, and whether problems have a "right" answer. By extension, each stage entails a distinct principle of belief justification.

In pre-reflective reasoning, one accepts beliefs as justified if they come from one of two sources of knowledge: a respected authority (e.g., community leaders, texts, traditions) and direct experience. All problems are believed to be solvable and to have a right answer, and so knowledge claims are either correct or incorrect. In quasi-reflective reasoning, knowledge claims are believed to be uncertain because one believes that information is incomplete and the methods of getting that information are imperfect. At this stage, individuals do not grasp how it is possible for evidence to entail certain conclusions but not prove them definitively. As a result, they believe knowledge claims to be subjective. Finally, in reflective reasoning, knowledge claims are assumed to be tentative and vary in how reasonable they can be. The reasonableness of a knowledge claim is believed to be based on context and on what data is available, both of which can change. Consequently, at the reflective reasoning stage, it is epistemically justifiable to reconsider accepted claims (or theories) in light of changed circumstances, new evidence, or an improved method of acquiring or evaluating evidence.

Pfeffer and Sutton (2006) advocate several concrete strategies that are consistent with the reflective reasoning stage of assessing the reasonableness of knowledge claims. These include being suspicious of "breakthrough" ideas and (single) studies, emphasizing the drawbacks (e.g., risks) and virtues of different options, carefully examining the logic of the evidence (i.e., gaps, inferences, incentives), and recognizing the limits of what one knows (which they call the "attitude of wisdom").

Three Levels of Evidence Use

Now that we have described the decision-making process of EBMgt, we turn to the question, "Decisions about what?" We propose that in EBMgt one can use evidence to inform, reform, or transform management decision-making. These represent increasingly higher levels of evidence use, which address higher orders of effectiveness and reliability. Thus, applying evidence to reform management practices and transform the EBMgt process results in the most effective and reliable outcomes.

EVIDENCE USED TO INFORM

Evidence is said to inform a decision using an existing management practice when it is used as input for a discrete decision. Imagine a company that wants to hire a new manager and is considering two candidates. It uses a mix of organizational needs assessments, questionnaires, tests, and interviews in its current hiring process, and it relies on the judgment of its seasoned HR manager to make the final hiring decision. The evidence from each of these sources is combined to determine which of the two candidates will turn out to be the more suitable employee, and thus it is used to inform the hiring decision. When evidence is used to inform whom to hire, the question that is ultimately asked is "who do our results suggest is the better candidate?"

In this example, the needs assessments draws on the local context to some extent, stakeholder perspectives are considered insofar as area managers participate in the interviewing process, and "expert" judgment plays a role because a trained and experienced HR manager has input. What is not specified is whether the best available research evidence was used in this decision, and whether evidence was gathered, interpreted, and applied in a conscientious, judicious, and explicit manner. For example, one could ask what checks and balances are in place to ensure that both candidates were given a fair chance.

EVIDENCE USED TO REFORM

At the next level, evidence is used to reform an existing management practice. The focus of the decision is on identifying and implementing management practices that are the best suited to the context. When evidence is used to reform how a company hires managers, the question becomes: "On what bases should we be making hiring decisions?" or "What evidence supports how we use the Myers-Briggs inventory in hiring managers?" As this level of EBMgt becomes standard practice, one develops a continual improvement process and becomes a learning organization (Argyris & Schön, 1978; Garvin, Edmondson, & Gino, 2008; Senge, 1990).

EVIDENCE USED TO TRANSFORM

The third and highest level of evidence use is transformational, whereby the EBMgt process is self-reflexive. At this level, the focus is on improving the EBMgt decision process itself by addressing how the acquisition, interpretation, or application of evidence can be made more conscientious, judicious, or explicit. The use of evidence to transform can also aim to make the organizational context more conducive for EBMgt. The hiring experience might lead to process transformation questions such as: "What can we do to better interpret conflicting evidence about desirable job candidate characteristics when what our HR manager believes conflicts with what the HRM literature claims?" or "What would it take to demonstrate to the skeptics in our organization that an explicit EBMgt process will improve how well we hire?"

In summary, breaking down one's EBMgt process into its specific, measurable, component practices can facilitate the systematic identification of opportunities and use of evidence to improve them. Such improvement can focus on informing discrete management decisions, reforming specific managerial practices, or transforming the EBMgt process itself. Having considered both culture and EBMgt as patterns of beliefs, values, and practices, we can now turn to how the two are related.

Culture and Evidence-Based Management

The successful adoption of an EBMgt process is both contingent on and designed to transform existing cultural and personal management beliefs, values, and practices. The adoption of specific evidence-based practices is also contingent on and can transform the cultural ecology. Understanding the dynamics of how both the EBMgt process and EBMgt practices are implemented can help an organization strategically navigate potential cultural pitfalls and leverage cultural synergies. We propose eight ways in which an organizational culture (or a cultural ecology) and EBMgt interact—four of which involve the EBMgt process and four of which involve the practices that emerge from the EBMgt process.

1. Culture affects whether the EBMgt process gets adopted.
2. Culture shapes the EBMgt process.
3. The EBMgt process changes the culture.
4. The EBMgt process draws on parts of culture as information.
5. Culture affects which practices are subjected to the EBMgt process.
6. Culture affects what EBMgt practices are adopted.
7. Culture shapes EBMgt practices.
8. New EBMgt practices change culture.

How the EBMgt process draws on parts of a culture as information (dimension 4)—including stakeholder values, practitioner beliefs, and local practices—was addressed in our section describing the EBMgt process. We, therefore, turn to the seven remaining forms of interaction.

Culture Affects Whether the EBMgt Process Gets Adopted

Detert et al. (2000) point out that contingency theory (Lawrence & Lorch, 1967) predicts that not all eight dimensions of culture would be equally important for every change implemented in an organization. Detert and colleagues then suggest that more research is needed to

> …identify the cultural configurations of successful adoption of specific innovations, including the internal patterning of these cultures… [especially] the interplay between enhancing subcultures (those that particularly embrace the new initiative) and countercultures (those that actively oppose it) in order to understand why some cultural conflicts end with real changes and others with a return to the status quo. (p. 858)

In this spirit, this section proposes which cultural beliefs, values, and practices are necessary to support the implementation of EBMgt by framing the core patterns and elements of EBMgt in terms of Detert and colleagues' (2000) cultural dimensions. The result is an account of EBMgt-culture fit with both normative and contingent facets. We first describe the normative facet by identifying on which three cultural dimensions the cultural ecology of *any* organization *must* align with EBMgt if it is to successfully adopt and institutionalize even the most basic EBMgt process. We then describe how, if a cultural ecology meets these minimum requirements, the shape that EBMgt takes is contingent on what that ecology is like on the remaining five dimensions. We only offer a couple of examples, because not all combinations of dimensions and their effects on EBMgt are presently understood. For this reason, we echo Detert and colleagues' call for more study of the effect of cultural differences on the adoption of innovations, and specifically on the adoption and implementation of EBMgt.

Incorporating EBMgt into one's organization can be an especially challenging cultural change. It involves changing the very process by which management decisions are made, which, in turn, entails adopting the management practices identified by the new decision process. Although EBMgt as a pattern has core elements that define it, its more peripheral elements can vary. Exactly what configuration of EBMgt core and peripheral beliefs, values, and practices will "stick" (Szulanski, 1996) in a given organization depends on the "internal patterning" of that organization's cultural ecology. Improving the chances of implementing EBMgt into an organization's cultural ecology can itself be an evidence-based endeavor—one best undertaken with an understanding of both the EBMgt pattern and the patterns of that cultural ecology.

Adopting EBMgt is exceedingly difficult if an organization's cultural ecology does not have compatible core beliefs, values, and practices. We propose that a promising way to assess that compatibility is by mapping the core elements of the EBMgt pattern onto Detert and colleagues' (2000) eight culture dimensions. Specifically, we argue that three of the eight dimensions are core to EBMgt: (a) Beliefs about the basis of truth and rationality in the organization, (b) orientation toward stability versus change, innovation, and personal growth, and (c) internal and/or external orientation and focus.

BELIEFS ABOUT TRUTH AND RATIONALITY

Central to EBMgt is the belief that to identify the most effective and reliable management practices requires a decision-making process that draws on four types of evidence and enacts three values to help ensure process integrity. This involves specific beliefs about what constitutes evidence and how that evidence justifies (beliefs about) what is an effective and reliable management practice. It also entails beliefs about the value, strengths, and weaknesses of each of the four types of evidence. Finally, it entails a cluster of beliefs about threats to the integrity of the EBMgt process and how conscientious, explicit, and judicious practices address those threats. Taken together, these beliefs are "epistemic"—that is, they are about the nature of knowledge and knowing. In Detert and colleagues' (2000) terms, they are beliefs about the basis of truth and rationality.

In EBM, these beliefs manifest themselves in principles that are explicitly embodied in the hierarchy of scientific evidence (see Guyatt, Rennie, Meade, & Cook, 2007). In this hierarchy, formally collected evidence is valued over subjectively interpreted uncontrolled experience, and within formal evidence, more rigorous study designs are valued over less rigorous ones. The epistemic rationale is that valid and reliable measurement of the effects of interventions on health outcomes is paramount. The hierarchy arises because formally collected data are much less affected by the biases that affect human judgment than are subjectively interpreted experiences and opinions, and among formal studies, some designs control potential biases and confounders better than do others. However, the epistemology of EBM is inextricably linked with sample size and subject matter; the kinds of evidence it prioritizes require that interventions be implemented and measured hundreds or thousands of times, that many other variables be controlled, and that the relationship between intervention and outcome can be modeled by linear or other straightforward models (i.e., not by complex nonlinear dynamics). These particular requirements are often not possible or applicable to management practices. Nevertheless, EBMgt does hold the same epistemic beliefs that hold formally evaluated experience to be more reliable than subjectively interpreted experience and requires explicit consideration of context.

CHANGE VERSUS STABILITY

That EBMgt aims to improve, and, therefore, change, management practice is, at this point, obvious. What may be less obvious is that EBMgt can be meaningfully thought of as a form of continuous improvement for at least two reasons. One is its core belief that management practices can always be improved. The second is that EBMgt aims to identify

superior management practices based on four, constantly evolving types of evidence: Practitioners refine their expertise, the realities of the local context shift, external science advances, and stakeholders and their values change. That EBMgt is fundamentally oriented to change, process innovation, and the personal growth of an organization's members (i.e., dimension 4) should, therefore, also be obvious.

That said, organizations are not simply open or closed to change, but rather differ in what practices they are (potentially) willing and able to change, in what ways, and by how much. This leaves us with several theoretically interesting and practically important questions. When does (or should) an organization change its beliefs about stability? How do an organization's epistemic beliefs affect which management practices it believes *can* be improved using an EBMgt process? How does an organization's cultural ecology affect its openness to the progressively greater degrees of change entailed by informative, reformative, and transformative evidence use?

INTERNAL VERSUS EXTERNAL FOCUS

The third cultural dimension from Detert and colleagues (2000) that bears on a culture's compatibility with EBMgt is where the organization looks for its new ideas and standards of performance: internally, externally, or both. On the one hand, EBMgt is internally focused in that it draws on evidence from the local context. On the other hand, EBMgt is externally focused in that it considers the best available scientific evidence. When it comes to practitioner expertise and stakeholder values, EBMgt can look internally, externally, or both. For this reason, we argue that a judicious EBMgt process involves finding the right balance between internal and external orientations such that the strengths of the internal sources of evidence can compensate for the weaknesses of the external sources of evidence, and vice versa. Moreover, the "right" balance can change from one decision to the next, depending on the availability, reliability, and relevance of the evidence from each of the four sources. Consequently, to the degree that an organizational culture holds beliefs about, values, and acts on one orientation (internal or external) to the exclusion of the other, it cannot implement EBMgt completely. A more subtle point is that the extent to which a culture restricts an organization's ability to adjust appropriately when the evidence suggests a different balance, that culture impedes the judicious use of internal or external evidence.

In summary, for an organization to adopt and institutionalize the most basic level of EBMgt, it must (a) have compatible epistemic beliefs, (b) be oriented toward change, and (c) adaptively balance its internal and external focus. Although these are the necessary conditions for its cultural ecology to support an EBMgt process, they do not guarantee its adoption. Although what an organization looks like on the remaining five cultural dimensions is less critical to whether EBMgt is adopted, it can still affect what shape the EBMgt process will ultimately take in the organization.

Culture Shapes the EBMgt Process

We began the chapter by raising the question of how the cultural environments of organizations as different as a Fortune 500 company, a nonprofit startup, a manufacturing plant, a consulting firm, and the military might affect how and what evidence is used to inform and improve their respective management practices. We can now look to differences on Detert and colleagues' (2000) cultural dimensions to ask more focused questions about how culture can shape the EBMgt process in an organization. For example, how might the time horizons of a mature Fortune 500 company, a manufacturing plant, and a startup affect the types of practices they would consider changing, how much they invest in identifying a given evidence-based practice, and the duration of their EBMgt decision cycles? How do differences in the intrinsic motivations of people who join organizations such as the military, a nonprofit, or a consulting firm bear on their motivation to use EBMgt to learn and change? How does the nature of teamwork in the military and in consulting firms, or even among different branches of the military and different consulting firms, affect who is involved in the EBMgt process? How do differences in how flat or hierarchical these organizations are affect the control, coordination, and responsibility dynamics involved in the EBMgt process? Note that each of these questions addresses one effect of one dimension. In reality, these dimensions can be expected to interact, and so we advocate taking a systems approach to understand how specific configurations will affect who is involved in the EBMgt process and how they might implement an effective and culturally adapted version.

The EBMgt Process Changes the Culture

The EBMgt process has both direct and indirect effects on the culture into which it is adopted. The main direct effect is that it changes the way decisions about management practice are made. How great this change is depends on how (and how consistently) a

given organization was making management decisions before adopting EBMgt. Making explicit (i.e., transparent) how the new EBMgt process needs to be conscientious and judicious, as well as the beliefs and values underpinning the EBMgt process, could affect the cultural ecology in a number of ways.

First, the implementation and visible use of EBMgt by leadership is an endorsement of its core beliefs and values, and such an endorsement can reinforce or call into question the beliefs, values, and practices of other patterns in the cultural ecology. For example, it could affect what information, evidence, and suggestions are sought by and provided to the decision makers (e.g., increases in employee voice and truth telling). Second, to the extent that the EBMgt process is made explicit and transparent, it can increase the accountability of the deciders. A change in accountability can, in turn, affect a variety of cultural norms, including increasing the pressure for behavioral integrity (i.e., the correspondence between espoused and enacted values).

The EBMgt process has an indirect effect on a culture through the management practices that it identifies. With each EBMgt practice that succeeds, the chance increases for the EBMgt process to be given some of the credit. As the EBMgt process gains credibility, it may be afforded a greater role in shaping other management practices. As the scope of EBMgt expands in an organization, it becomes a more prominent means to achieve the organization's ends, slowly replacing alternative methods that identify so-called "best practices." Its success may also lead to a recognition of its current limitations and precipitate the realization that transformative evidence use is critical to maximize the potential of the EBMgt process. Ultimately, as EBMgt grows in influence, it not only changes the culture, but slowly *becomes* part of culture—a core pattern with its own nodes.

Depending on the original cultural ecology into which the EBMgt process is introduced, and how the successes of EBMgt practices affect the different cultures in that ecology, EBMgt could become a core *intercultural* pattern. A shared (explicit and transparent) decision-making process has the potential to increase the voice and buy-in of organizational members (e.g., as experts and stakeholders) in the EBMgt process. There is a danger, however, that the successes of EBMgt practices could be viewed as a threat to authority or autonomy, and exacerbate existing differences and tensions within the ecology. A longitudinal investigation of the diffusion of EBMgt adoption would prove insightful in this regard.

Culture Affects Which Practices Are Subjected to the EBMgt Process

Although an organization might use EBMgt, it may have strong cultural beliefs and values about certain management practices. In principle, the more core these beliefs, values, and practices are to the culture, the less likely they are to be subjected to the EBMgt process. After all, any practice subjected to the EBMgt process runs the risk of being improved by being modified or replaced. Still, even apparently core practices can be changed. Consider, the U.S. military, which spends millions of research and development dollars each year to improve its management practices. Which management practices the military is willing to consider changing and which it is not is an interesting question, and the answer might be surprising. For instance, the military chain of command, which falls under Detert and colleagues' (2000) cultural dimension of control, coordination, and responsibility, is core to military culture. As such, one might expect the chain of command to be off limits to EBMgt. However, circumstances can arise where two or more core cultural values conflict, and sticking with the status quo will not lead to the best outcome. This is precisely the situation the U.S. military faced recently in Iraq and Afghanistan.

The "military decision-making process" (MDMP) is the traditional process of bringing information from the field up the chain of command for a strategic decision, and then sent back down to the field to be implemented. The MDMP was found to be too slow and unreliable because of the fast-pace and spotty communication channels in the Iraqi and Afghan theaters. Troops in the field were less responsive to changing and unexpected conditions, which threatened their safety and effectiveness. The military decided that troop safety and effectiveness were a higher priority than preserving the MDMP, and so it began experimenting with the more nimble "tactical problem-solving process" (TPSP) (see Winkler & Russell, 2010 for a description of how TPSP was learned).

TPSP empowers lower-level field officers to make decisions for which they would have previously needed authorization. To work, TPSP provides officers with added decision-making training and a more complete understanding of strategic goals. The adoption of TPSP has resulted in faster, more adaptive decision making in the field. Interestingly, the TPSP pattern is strikingly similar to that of British military planning. It is plausible, therefore, that the transition to TPSP changed the American military

planning pattern through changes in shared belief nodes (e.g., degree of soldier autonomy). Thus, when one alters one pattern, the connected patterns are affected, which can lead to shifts in broader cultural patterns (e.g., control, coordination, and responsibility). When the inter-pattern structure and hierarchy change, it effectively "resets" the universe of patterns that the culture might be open to reconsidering.

This example illustrates that even practices one thinks are core to an organization may be less important than competing intrinsic values when push comes to shove. When circumstances bring important cultural values, beliefs, and practices into conflict with each other, they force leaders to reexamine their priorities and how best to achieve them. What worked in the past will not necessarily work going forward. What works in another organization will not necessarily work in one's own organization. In deciding how to resolve these conflicts, leaders often need to propose courses of action that call into question cultural patterns. Although such high level conflicts may not be common, the military's adoption of TPSP demonstrates that even some degree of EBMgt can help navigate critical management problems.

Culture Affects Which EBMgt Practices Are Adopted

Building on the previous example, when an organization adopts a new EBMgt practice, its culture will have influenced that adoption at two or three points in the process. First, when a need arises in the organization for a new practice, either because no practice exists or the current practice is called into question, a limited set of alternative practices is considered. Culture affects how the problem is framed and what options are identified because culture shapes both internal stakeholder perspectives and information from the local context. Second, culture can also affect the evaluation of candidate practices through the same two mechanisms. Finally, an EBMgt practice is chosen because it fits or can be adapted to fit into the existing cultural ecology (see Ansari, Fiss, & Zajac, 2010 for a review of how elements and patterns in the ecology can be tweaked to accommodate an EBMgt practice).

Culture Shapes EBMgt Practices

Just as culture can shape the form that the EBMgt process takes, it can shape the form that new EBMgt practices take. In deciding who in the organization performs the new practice (see "Mode,"

Yates & Potworowski, chapter 12 of this volume), a culture that values isolation will likely favor a different solution than would a culture that values collaboration. The same two cultures might use different incentive structures to get their members to perform the new EBMgt practice (e.g., individual versus team performance bonuses). Organizations that differ in how centralized their power is, differ in their short or long term focus, or in their beliefs about motivation (e.g., carrot versus stick), could arrive at different solutions. These examples illustrate that the cultural patterns that influence which specific evidence-based practice is most locally suitable also influence the specifics of how it will be implemented. Consequently, when evaluating the potential effectiveness and reliability of EBMgt practices for a given organization, it stands to reason that one should reflect on the configuration of the eight dimensions in the cultural ecology, and how it bears on the form that practice should take.

New EBMgt Practices Change Culture

Although evidence-based practices are chosen because of their anticipated results, they may well have unanticipated positive or negative effects as they interact with other patterns in the cultural ecology (Harris & Ogbonna, 2002). The adoption of after-action reviews, for instance, can have ripple effects on the willingness of subordinates to voice problems to their bosses and to acknowledge failure. Similarly, the shift from relying on individual changes to using a systems-reengineering approach to improve health-care delivery in organizations has led to role changes affecting health-care professionals' beliefs, values, practices, and identities.

New practices, from when they are proposed to when they are implemented, can also call into question the beliefs, values, and practices in that culture's other dimensions. For example, a new EBMgt practice may have unanticipated short or long-terms effects, may not respond well to the incentive structure initially coupled to it, may be more effective if done individually (or collaboratively), or may better meet local needs if the balance in how standardized and tailored it is were changed. These unexpected results are an important form of local evidence that, in EBMgt, are fed back into the decision process to further improve how the practice is implemented. In this cyclical process, each iteration and tweak can have new implications for connected beliefs, values, and practices.

When a new (tweak to an) EBMgt practice calls into question existing beliefs, values, or other practices, it can force a pattern, and that pattern's relative importance in the culture, to be reexamined. Reexamining a pattern can result in changes in that pattern or its coherence, changes to connected patterns, and even shifts in the culture and cultural ecology. On the one hand, clarifying and reexamining values, beliefs, and practices can reduce cultural fragmentation and bring about greater integration with every culture in the ecology that embraces the new EBMgt practice. On the other hand, it can result in greater fragmentation and differentiation if cultures in the ecology disagree about the new practice (Martin, 1992). Either way, the reexamination of a pattern affects the culture. In fact, the very consideration of practice options can plant the seed of a discussion and reexamination of cultural beliefs and values—what they are, whether they are shared and by whom, how important they are relative to other values, and so forth.

In summary, to the extent that a change to a practice (and its associated values and beliefs) is closer to the core of that culture, the more that new practice will affect the character of the organizational culture—both directly and through the radiating effect on the patterns connected to its nodes. The U.S. military's adoption of TPSP resulted from a clarification of the relative importance of existing beliefs, values, and practices. When TPSP proved successful, it changed the beliefs, values, and practices concerning field-officer decision autonomy (e.g., "Decentralized command and control can work!"). Whenever a cultural shift occurs as a result of a change to a pattern, it changes which practices will be subsequently open to scrutiny by the EBMgt process.

Summary and Next Steps

The aim of this chapter was to offer a framework that would equip the practitioner, scholar, and educator with an actionable understanding of how culture and EBMgt are related. We began by describing culture as being only partly coherent, and proposed that its coherence stems from the connections between shared patterns. A pattern is a set of mutually reinforcing beliefs, values, and practices about something, and it is itself as coherent as the ties among these elements and its degree of connection to other patterns through nodes. We showed how patterns can be construed broadly as cultural dimensions (e.g., cooperation versus competition), or more narrowly based on specific practices (e.g., strategic planning). We distinguished core from peripheral patterns, with the former defined as shared by more members of a culture, more closely tied to the culture's identity, and more connected to other patterns in that culture. For these reasons, core patterns are harder to change. We argued that when a change is attempted in a pattern, the coherence mechanisms act to prevent that change. Finally, we explained the importance of thinking about an organization's culture in terms of its cultural ecology.

We then described EBMgt as a pattern, and identified its core practice, values, and beliefs. The core practice of EBMgt is making management decisions, its core values are reliability and effectiveness, and its core beliefs are that the decision-making process needs to draw on four sources of evidence and ensure process integrity to succeed. We pointed to the cardinal issues discussed by Yates and Potworowski (chapter 12 of this volume) as a tool to help systematically evaluate whether one's specific, measurable decision-making practices are evidence based. Three levels of EBMgt were then proposed in which evidence is used to inform one-off management decisions, to reform existing management practices, and to transform the EBMgt process itself. Finally, we discussed eight distinct ways in which culture and EBMgt affect each other.

The framework was meant to help practitioners assess where, to what extent, and how their organizations are prepared to adopt the EBMgt process and EBMgt practices. Practitioners can start by identifying local practices perceived to be ineffective, and then begin searching for evidence-based alternatives (see Pearce, 2009 for some examples). They can then narrow the list of candidate EBMgt practices by drawing on evidence from the other sources to conduct a rough cost-benefit analysis. For example, using Rogers' (2003) criteria for the diffusion of innovations, a short list of EBMgt practices would include those whose benefits would be significant, immediate, and measurable, and that would be relatively cheap, easy, and low risk to test.

At one or more points in this decision-making process, candidate EBMgt practices would be vetted, more or less extensively, for their cultural fit. A more thorough assessment of fit might involve conducting cultural network analyses to identify the key beliefs and values tied to the current management practice and compare them to those implicit in the short-listed EBMgt practices. This would help identify which EBMgt practices would most easily fit in the cultural ecology, and idenitfy implementation barriers and leverage points. Each EBMgt practice that is implemented and produces results provides

the EBMgt process with a "small win" (Weick, 1984) that offers proof—or evidence—of concept. This further establishes the credibility of EBMgt as the decision process of choice to identify locally effective and reliable management practices.

Scholars reading this chapter may have identified gaps in our descriptions of culture, EBMgt, and how the two are related that need to be addressed. They may have found theoretical questions worthy of empirical investigation, or have generated ideas about how to approach the questions we raised. Our hope is that they react to, test, and further our understanding of the relationship between culture and EBMgt.

The educator can use the framework to help students think systematically and practically about how culture affects evidence-based management decisions. Ideally, the educator has also come away with novel ideas for exercises and projects, and a basis for investigating the often tacit beliefs, values, and practices interacting in the multi-cultural classroom.

This chapter would have its greatest impact, however, if practitioners, scholars, and educators recognize and embrace the key roles each plays in making EBMgt a reality (Potworowski & Green, 2011). To that end, the framework can serve to advance the discussion of how EBMgt might become a shared pattern across the cultures of industry, scholarship, and education, and in so doing benefit all who are involved in and affected by management decisions.

References

Alvesson, M. (2002). *Understanding organizational culture.* Thousand Oaks, CA: Sage.

American Association of University Professors. (2000). *Protecting human beings: Institutional review boards and social science research.* Washington, DC: Author.

Ansari, S. M., Fiss, P. C., & Zajac, E. J. (2010). Made to fit: How practices vary as they diffuse. *Academy of Management Review, 35,* 67–92.

Ariely, D., Gneezy, U., Loewenstein, G., & Mazar, N. (2009). Large stakes and big mistakes. *Review of Economic Studies, 76,* 451–469.

Argyris, C., & Schön, D. (1978). *Organizational learning: A theory of action perspective.* Reading, MA: Addison Wesley.

Ashforth, B. E., & Anand, V. (2003). The normalization of corruption in organizations. In R. M. Kramer & B. M. Staw (Eds.), *Research in organizational behavior* (Vol. 25, pp. 1–52). Amsterdam, Netherlands: Elsevier.

Baba, M. L. (1995). The cultural ecology of the corporation: Explaining diversity in work group responses to organizational transformation. *Journal of Applied Behavioral Science, 31,* 202–233.

Bastardi, A., Uhlmann, E. L., & Ross, L. (2011). Wishful thinking: Belief, desire, and the motivated evaluation of scientific evidence. *Psychological Science, 22,* 731–732.

Briner R. B., Denyer, D., & Rousseau D. M. (2009). Evidence-based management: Concept cleanup time. *Academy of Management Perspectives, 23*, 19–32.

Briner, R. B., & Rousseau, D. M. (2011). Evidence-based I-O psychology: Not there yet. *Industrial and Organizational Psychology: Perspectives on Science and Practice, 4*, 3–22.

Chi, M. T. H. (2006). Two approaches to the study of experts' characteristics. In K. A. Ericsson, N. Charness, P. J. Feltovich, & R. R. Hoffman (Eds.), *The Cambridge handbook of expertise and expert performance* (pp. 21–30). Cambridge, England: Cambridge University Press.

Chi, M. T. H. (2008). Three types of conceptual change: Belief revision, mental model transformation, and categorical shift. In S. Vosniadou (Ed.), *Handbook of research on conceptual change* (pp. 61–82). Hillsdale, NJ: Erlbaum.

Cook, S. N., & Brown, J. S. (1999). Bridging epistemologies: The generative dance between organizational knowledge and organizational knowing. *Organization Science, 10*, 382–400.

Crandall, B., Klein, G., & Hoffman, R. R. (2006). *Working minds: A practitioner's guide to cognitive task analysis*. Cambridge, MA: MIT Press.

Dension, D. R., & Mishra, A. (1995). Toward a theory of organizational culture and effectiveness. *Organizational Science, 6*, 204–223.

Detert, J. R., Schroeder, R. G., & Mauriel, J. L., (2000). A framework for linking culture and improvement initiatives in organizations. *Academy of Management Review, 25*, 850–863.

Ditto, P. H., & Lopez, D. F. (1992). Motivated skepticism: Use of differential decision criteria for preferred and nonpreferred conclusions. *Journal of Personality and Social Psychology, 63*, 568–584.

Ericsson, K. A., & Smith, J. (1991). Prospects and limits of the empirical study of expertise. An introduction. In K. A. Ericsson & J. Smith (Eds.), *Toward a general theory of expertise*. New York: Cambridge Press.

Garvin, D. A., Edmondson, A. C., & Gino, F. (2008). Is yours a learning organization? *Harvard Business Review, 86*, 109–116.

Gentner, D., & Stevens, A. L. (Eds.). (1983). *Mental Models*. Hillsdale, NJ: Erlbaum.

Green, L. A., & Yates, J. F. (1995). Influence of pseudodiagnostic information on the evaluation of ischemic cardiac disease. *Annals of Emergency Medicine, 25*, 451–457.

Guyatt, G., Rennie, D., Meade, M. O., & Cook, D. J. (2007). *Users' guide to the medical literature: Essentials of evidence-based clinical practice* (2nd ed.). New York: McGraw-Hill.

Harris, L. C., & Ogbonna, E. (2002). The unintended consequences of culture interventions: A study of unexpected outcomes. *British Journal of Management, 13*, 31–49.

Heath, C., Larrick, R. P., & Klayman, J. (1998). Cognitive repairs: How organizational practices can compensate for individual shortcomings. *Review of Organizational Behavior, 20*, 1–38.

Highhouse, S. (2008). Stubborn reliance on intuition and subjectivity in employee selection. *Industrial and Organizational Psychology: Perspectives on Science and Practice, 1*, 333–342.

Hirschfeld, L., & Gelman, S. (Eds.). (1994). *Mapping the mind: Domain specificity in cognition and culture*. New York: Cambridge University.

Hitlin, S., & Piliavin, J. A. (2004). Values: Reviving a dormant concept. *Annual Review of Sociology, 30*, 359–393.

Ingram, D., Louis, K. S., & Schroeder, R. G. (2004). Accountability policies and teacher decision making: Barriers to the use of data to improve practice. *Teachers College Record, 106*, 1258–1287.

King, P. M., & Kitchener, K. S. (2002). The reflective judgment model: Twenty years of research on epistemic cognition. In B. K. Hofer & P. R. Pintrich (Eds.), *Personal epistemology: The psychology of beliefs about knowledge and knowing* (pp. 37–61). Mahway, NJ: Erlbaum.

Kuhn, D., Cheney, R., & Weinstock, M. (2000). The development of epistemological understanding. *Cognitive Development, 15*, 309–328.

Lachman, R., Nedd, A., & Hinings, B. (1994). Analyzing cross-national management and organizations: A theoretical framework. *Management Science, 10*, 40–55.

Lawrence, P., & Lorsch, J. (1967). *Organization and environment*. Boston, MA: Harvard University Press.

Lerner, J., & Tetlock, P. E. (1999). Accounting for the effects of accountability. *Psychological Bulletin, 125*, 255–275.

Lord, C. G., Ross, L., & Lepper, M. R. (1979). Biased assimilation and attitude polarization: The effects of prior theories on subsequently considered evidence. *Journal of Personality and Social Psychology, 37*, 2098–2109.

Maccoun, R. J. (1998). Biases in the interpretation and use of research results. *Annual Review of Psychology, 49*, 259–287.

Marston G., & Watts, R. (2003). Tampering with the evidence: A critical appraisal of evidence-based policy making. *The drawing board: An Australian review of public affairs, 3*, 143–163.

Martin, J. (1992). *Cultures in organizations: Three perspectives*. New York: Oxford University Press.

Martin, J., & Siehl, C. (1983). Organizational culture and counterculture: An uneasy symbiosis. *Organizational Dynamics, 122*, 52–65.

McSweeney, B. (2009). Incoherent culture. *European Journal of Cross-Cultural Competence and Management, 1*, 22–27.

Nickerson, R. S. (1998). Confirmation bias: A ubiquitous phenomenon in many guises. *Review of General Psychology, 2*, 175–220.

Osland, J., & Bird, A. (2000). Beyond sophisticated stereotyping: Cultural sensemaking in context. *Academy of Management Executive, 14*, 65–77.

Pearce, J. L. (2009) *Organizational behavior real research for real managers.* (2nd ed.) Irvine, CA: Melvin & Leigh.

Perry, W. G. (1970). *Forms of intellectual and ethical development in the college years: A scheme.* New York: Holt, Rinehart & Winston.

Peters, E., Hibbard, J., Slovic, P., & Dieckmann N. (2007). Numeracy skill and the communication, comprehension, and use of risk-benefit information. *Health Affairs, 26*, 741–748.

Pfeffer, J., & Sutton, R. I. (2006). Evidence-based management. *Harvard Business Review, 84*, 63–74.

Potts, M. (1992). Toward a boundary-less firm at General Electric. In R. M. Kanter, B. A. Stein, and T. D. Jick (Eds.), *The challenge of organizational change* (pp. 450–455). New York: The Free Press.

Potworowski, G. (2009). Intuition versus analysis. In M. W. Kattan (Ed.) & M. E. Cowen (Assoc. Ed.). *Encyclopedia of medical decision making* (pp. 638–640). Thousand Oaks, CA: SAGE Publications.

Potworowski, G., & Green, L. A. (2011). Assessing the uptake of evidence-based management: A systems approach. *Industrial and Organizational Psychology: Perspectives on Science and Practice, 4*, 54–56.

Quine, W. V., & Ullian, J. S. (1978). *The web of belief* (2nd ed.). New York: Random House.

Quinn, R. E., & Rohrbaugh, J. (1983). A spatial model of effectiveness criteria: Towards a competing values approach to organizational analysis. *Management Science, 29,* 363–377.

Rasmussen, L. J., Sieck, W. R., & Smart, P. R. (2009). What is a good plan? Cultural variations in expert planners' concepts of plan quality. *Journal of Cognitive Engineering & Decision Making,3,* 228–249.

Rogers, E. M. (2003). *Diffusion of innovations* (5th ed.). New York: Free Press.

Rokeach, J. (1973). *The nature of human values.* New York: Free Press.

Rycroft-Malone, J., Seers, K., Titchen, A., Harvey, G., Kitson, A., & McCormack, B. (2004). What counts as evidence in evidence-based practice. *Journal of Advanced Nursing, 47,* 81–90.

Sackett, D. L. (1997). Evidence-based medicine. *Seminars in Perinatology, 21,* 3–5.

Sackett, D. L., Rosenberg, W. M. C., Gray, J. A. M., Haynes, R. B., & Richardson, W. S. (1996). Evidence-based medicine: What it is and what it is not. *British Medical Journal, 312,* 71–72.

Schein, E. (2010) *Organizational culture and leadership* (4th ed.). San Francisco, CA: Jossey-Bass.

Schwartz, S. H. (1992). Universals in the content and structure of values: Theoretical advances and empirical tests in 20 countries. *Advances in Experimental Social Psychology, 25,* 1–65.

Schwenk, C. R. (1990). Effects of devil's advocacyand dialectical inquiry on decisionmaking: A meta-analysis. *Organizational Behavior and Human Decision Processes,47,* 161–176.

Senge, P. M. (1990). *The fifth discipline.* London: Century Business.

Shanteau, J. (1992a). Competence in experts: The role of task characteristics. *Organizational Behavior and Human Decision Processes, 53,* 252–266.

Shanteau, J. (1992b). How much information does an expert use? Is it relevant? *Acta Psychologica, 81,* 75–86.

Sieck, W. R., Rasmussen, L. J., & Smart, P. (2010). Cultural network analysis: A cognitive approach to cultural modeling. In D. Verma (Ed.), *Network science for military coalition operations: Information extraction and interaction* (pp. 237–255). Hershey, PA: IGI Global.

Simons, T. (1999). Behavioral integrity as a critical ingredient for transformational leadership. *Journal of Organizational Change Management, 12,* 89–104.

Slavin, R. E. (2002). Evidence-based education policies: Transforming educational practice and research. *Educational Researcher, 31,* 15–21.

Smith, P. B., Dugan, S., & Trompenaars, E. (1996). National culture and the values of organizational employees: A dimensional analysis across 43 nations. *Journal of Cross-Cultural Psychology, 27,* 231–264.

Steele, J. M. (2005). Darrell Huff and fifty years of how to lie with statistics. *Statistical Science, 20,* 205–209.

Szulanski, G. (1996). Exploring internal stickiness: Impediments to the transfer of best practice within the firm. *Strategic Management Journal, 17,* 27–44.

Tabak, I., & Weinstock, M. (2008). A sociocultural exploration of epistemological beliefs. In M. S. Khine (Ed.), *Knowing, knowledge and beliefs: Epistemological studies across diverse cultures* (pp. 177–195). Amsterdam, Netherlands: Springer.

Taber, C. S., & Lodge, M. (2006). Motivated skepticism in the evaluation of political beliefs. *American Journal of Political Science, 50,* 755–769.

Tod, A. M., Nicolson, P., & Allmark, P. (2002). Ethical review of health service research in the UK: Implications for nursing. *Journal of Advanced Nursing, 40,* 379–386.

Trice, H., & Beyer, J. (1993). *The cultures of work organizations.* Englewood Cliffs, NJ: Prentice-Hall.

Von Krogh, G., Roos, J., & Slocum, K. (1994). An essay on corporate epistemology. *Strategic Management Journal, 15,* 53–71.

Weick, K. E. (1984). Small wins: Redefining the scale of social problems. *American Psychologist, 39,* 40–49.

White, C. B., Kumagai, A. K., Ross, P. T., & Fantone, J. C. (2009). A qualitative exploration of how the conflict between the formal and informal curriculum influences student values and behaviors. *Academic Medicine, 84,* 597–603.

Wilson, T. D., & Gilbert, D. T. (2005). Affective forecasting: Knowing what to want. *Current Directions in Psychological Science, 14,* 131–134.

Winkler, C., & Russell, C. T. (2010). *Measuring organizational learning: A preliminary progress report* (Contract No. W91WAW-07-C-0074). Arlington, VA: United States Army Research Institute for the Behavioral and Social Sciences.

Witkin, S. L., & Harrison, W. D. (2001). Editorial: Whose evidence and for what purpose? *Social Work, 46,* 293–296.

Womack, J. P., & Jones, D. T. (2003). *Lean Thinking: Banish waste and create wealth in your corporation.* New York: Free Press.

Wong, E. M., Galinsky, A. D., & Kray, L. J. (2009). The counterfactual mind-set: A decade of research. In K. Markman, W. Klein, & J. Suhr (Eds.), *The handbook of imagination and mental simulation* (pp. 161–174). New York: Psychology Press.

Wood, B. (1999). Visual expertise. *Radiology, 211,* 1–3.

Wyszewianski, L., & Green, L. A. (2000). Strategies for changing clinician's practice patterns: A new perspective. *Journal of Family Practice, 49,* 461–464.

Designing Strategies for the Implementation of EBMgt among Senior Management, Middle Management, and Supervisors

Jayne Speicher-Bocija *and* Richard Adams

Abstract

Proponents of evidence-based management (EBMgt) point to a range of benefits accruing to users, including more effective decision making through exploitation of the science base. Despite this lure, incorporating research evidence findings is relatively new to much management practice. In this chapter, EBMgt is conceived of as a technological innovation, and we draw on diffusion-of-innovation theory and the transtheoretical stages-of-change model to explore some individual and organizational factors impacting the adoption of EBMgt at different levels of management. In light of this analysis, a number of strategies and initiatives to accelerate the adoption of EBMgt are proposed.

Key Words: levels of management, executives, middle managers, supervisors, diffusion of innovation, transtheoretical stages of change, evidence-based practice

Although the concept of evidence- based management (EBMgt) is relatively new, some confusion has developed around precisely what it means. At its core, EBMgt is about managers making decisions "through the conscientious, explicit, and judicious use of four sources of information: practitioner expertise and judgment, evidence from the local context, a critical evaluation of the best available research evidence, and the perspectives of those people who might be affected by the decision" (Briner, Denyer, & Rousseau, 2009).

In fields in which the notion of evidence-based practice has been established longer than in management, observers have noted its mixed reception, even among professionals who are neither stupid nor hostile to science and rigor. Among medical practitioners, for instance, a range of possible reasons for mixed uptake have been posited, these include: the argument that professional practice is as much art as science and is not algorithmic (formulas cannot account for all possible cases); a lack of faith regarding the scientific process (witness recent debates on

the causes of climate change); and, an absence of convincing evidence that dogmatic adherence to the application of research evidence necessarily results in better performance than the judicious application of the professional's own understanding, experience, and judgment (Lewis, 2007).

Although some of these issues may be analogous to EBMgt, the unique characteristics of the practice of management demand that, if EBMgt is to be more widely promulgated, managers must pay special attention to encouraging its diffusion and adoption. One outcome of EBMgt, it is argued, can be more effective decision making (Briner, Denyer, & Rousseau, 2009). To make EBMgt a reality, managers must put it into use in organizations. EBMgt requires educators, researchers, and managers to develop processes and practices designed to facilitate its uptake. Managers vary in their training, backgrounds, experience, and attitudes. Their decision-making responsibilities vary by level in the organization. Across many fields of endeavor evidence-based practices have achieved uptake through diffusion, dissemination, and implementation processes. Diffusion processes naturally occur through existing social networks, dissemination processes facilitate intentional distribution of research findings, and implementation processes assist their ongoing active use.

The focal issues of this chapter are conceptualizing EBMgt as a technological innovation and its diffusion and adoption among mangers. Specifically, it addresses the question of how proponents of EBMgt can design processes to promote EBMgt practices: What factors must be taken into account? Which strategies from diffusion, dissemination, and implementation should be utilized at each level of the organization to maximize uptake? The literature on EB evidence-based practice, drawn predominantly from health-care and social-service settings, is used to inform the design of such strategies since EBMgt is still new to business organizations. This chapter looks at the factors that influence uptake, focuses on their impact by level, and discusses design elements of processes and practices to infuse EBMgt into day-to-day organizational decision making.

The Challenge Facing EBMgt

It would be incorrect to suggest that managers do not use evidence in their day-to-day decision making. Managers are well disposed to the use of evidence: they draw heavily on their own experiences, take cues from their local operating environment, and the more attuned may take readings from those who might be affected by the decision. On this basis, and with particular reference to managers' expertise and judgment, evidence is already widely incorporated into decision practices, though perhaps not always consciously or explicitly.

However, evidence from the research base is less readily incorporated into decision-making processes. Pfeffer and Fong (2002) found little evidence that business school research is influential on management practice. Other studies support this view (e.g., Johnstone & Lacey, 2002), further showing that research findings have little chance of being implemented without at least being strong, compelling, and suitably adapted for local conditions, and implemented in a climate characterized by supportive opinion leaders and conducive organizational conditions (Dopson, Locock, Chambers, & Gabbay, 2001).

The issue, then, about the practice of EBMgt is not so much that managers do not undertake or value *evidence*, but they appear not well oriented to turning to the academic community for support in the resolution of challenges to which research evidence can contribute.

Changing practitioner behavior is difficult, even where there is rigorous evidence to suggest that change would be beneficial (Kitson, Harvey, & McCormack, 1998). Often, demonstrably efficacious innovations are met with stubborn resistance to adoption either within populations of potential adopters or across the whole population of potential adopters (e.g. David, 1985). Innovation efficacy is not of itself sufficient for adoption to occur (Adams & Bessant, 2008).

Clearly, managers seem to be coping, to an extent, without much recourse to research evidence. The argument in favor of EBMgt is that managers could cope much better and that the quality of decision making would be less grounded in dogma, hype, personal marketing or the "mindless mimicry of top performers" (Pfeffer & Sutton, 2006).

Apart from its putative utility, managers are also subject to other forces that may be encouraging greater use of the research evidence. In addition to the contemporary challenging economic environment requiring more effective management decision making, there are pressures, at least in some quarters, for the practice of management to be more accountable and evidence based. In the wake of recent financial crises and organizational malpractice (the credit crunch, Enron, WorldCom, etc.), there is increasing pressure for transparency in organizational affairs.

No form of evidence can offer guarantees of effectiveness, always to improve and not sometimes to worsen practice. However, research evidence provides another and different sort of evidence for the practitioners' armamentarium, which can be drawn upon (like other forms of evidence) and assessed in the context of a specific problem through the filter of judgment and experience in support of decision making.

In spite of the potential benefits of an evidence-based orientation to management, its practice has been slow to diffuse through the business community. A number of factors influence its rate of progress, two of which—individual characteristics and organizational culture—are considered in the following section. Understanding these factors and their interaction at different management levels provide insight on the design of strategies and initiatives to influence uptake.

Factors Impacting the Adoption of EBMgt
Individual Characteristics

In examining the individual characteristics that impact evidence-based practice uptake, Aarons (2004) found that social-service-agency providers, with higher educational attainment, and interns displayed positive attitudes toward adoption of evidence-based practices. Aarons developed the Evidence-Based Practice Attitude Scale (EBPAS) to measure four domains of provider attitudes toward adoption of evidence-based practices: appeal, requirements, openness to change, and divergence. The attitudinal factor of appeal measures intuitive appeal of the practice, specifically whether the provider believes the practice can be used correctly and is being used by colleagues who endorse the practice. The requirement factor measures the person's attitude toward evidence-based practices that are mandated by superiors, the organization, or an accrediting body. The third factor, openness to change, is the individual's general responsiveness to innovation and new learning. The final factor, divergence, assesses the extent to which providers perceive evidence-based practices to be a departure from their own experience. Aaron's findings are consistent with Shortell, Rundell, & Hsu's (2007) conclusions that preference for personal experiences and perceived threats to autonomy are factors that hinder the use of EBMgt practices.

Another important factor related to EBMgt adoption, at least in health care, is the training model of the practitioner (Miller, Sorenson, Selzer, & Brigham, 2006). Miller distinguished between two training models: the craft model and the scientific model. Miller and his colleagues suggest that those whose training experience is from a craft model are encouraged to learn by observing and emulating the behavior of master practitioners. Analysis and criticism of the training master's methods and assumptions is discouraged. The craft model promotes loyalty to the mentor and fidelity to his or her methods. Conversely, persons who are trained in the scientific model are encouraged to be skeptical and to demand evidence or proof of efficacy. Scientific training encourages independent analysis and critical thinking skills. According to Miller et. al., people trained under a craft model are less open to alternate views and innovations and are less likely to take a questioning stance toward their own assumptions or approaches, even when presented with evidence that disputes the efficacy of them. Thus, the craft model of training impedes the uptake of evidence-based practices. In the business world, management training generally bears greater resemblance to a craft model than a scientific model. Executives value learning derived from on-the-job experiences (McCall, 2010), and they encourage managers to observe

and model behavior after successful leaders in the workplace. There is often modest, if any, exposure to a critical analysis of management styles or the efficacy of one leadership approach in comparison to another. The lessons drawn from on-the-job experience are rarely reflected on and, as Jackson and Lindsay (2010) describe, can be "guided by opinions and biases" rather than informed by evidence or data.

Organizational Culture

Research evidence strongly indicates the influencing power of organizational culture in promoting or hindering the adoption of innovations. A number of authors have shown the adoption of novel practices to be greatly facilitated by supportive cultures (e.g. Anderson & West, 1996), the same has been found to apply in the case of EBMgt. Kovner and Rundall (2006) assert that "a questioning organizational culture," one that encourages questioning behavior among its managers and analysis of decisions in the light of research findings, facilitates EBMgt.

Aarons and Sawitzky (2006) assessed attitudes toward evidence-based practice in two kinds of organizational cultures: constructive cultures and defensive cultures. Constructive cultures are those that value norms of achievement and motivation, individualism, self-actualization, supportive and encouraging interactions with others. Constructive organizational culture led to more positive attitudes toward adoption of evidence-based practice. In contrast, defensive cultures promote approval seeking and consensus, conformity, and dependence. Such cultures imbue more negative attitudes toward adoption of EBMgt. In these cultures, asking questions and bringing forward research evidence to challenge decisions can be viewed as threatening.

These factors are summarized below:

Individual Characteristics

- Professional training—Apprentice versus scientific model.
- Experience.
- Education.
- Intuitive appeal (alignment with preexisting values).
- Attitude toward requirement from authority.
- Openness to change.
- Divergence (tolerance for deviation from current practice).

Organizational Culture

- Constructive and questioning.
- Defensive and negative.

In order to design processes and practices that facilitate EBMgt uptake, a managers' level within the organization must be taken into account in addition to the factors already described. Different levels within an organization present opportunities and challenges to deploy EBMgt in decision making. Three general levels may be considered: senior managers, middle managers, and supervisors. Within each level, four specific aspects are examined: the manager's main focus, sphere of influence, accountability timeframes, and decision-making capacity. Each level's interaction with organizational culture and individual characteristics are explored.

Senior Managers

Senior managers within an organization have strategy setting as a principal focus. They enjoy a broad sphere of influence both within their organization and with other organizations. Shareholders and boards of directors hold senior executives responsible for the performance of the company. Senior managers' accountability for outcomes is generally assessed quarterly to multiyear for some initiatives. Their decision-making capacity is broad and filters throughout the organization. Adopting EBMgt, like other organizational initiatives, is heavily impacted by senior managers' priorities and preferences.

Given the prominence of senior executives in the organization, they have the greatest ability to influence the development of a constructive and questioning culture. The senior managers can set the tone for creating a culture where questioning is encouraged and attention paid to interactions occurring in a supportive environment. Likewise, senior managers can discourage overly conventional and conforming actions and attitudes that would discourage innovations such as the practice of EBMgt. However, despite their influential impact on culture, senior executives are likely to experience resistance in shifting a culture from defensive to constructive. In defensive cultures, managers are likely to feel threatened by having decisions questioned or evaluated for effectiveness and predictably will react negatively if EBMgt practice is pushed out without first attention being given to influencing current cultural norms. Of primary importance is establishing a supportive environment where mistakes are assessed as part of the organization's learning process and not used to denigrate those involved in the decision.

With regard to personal factors, senior managers present some challenges. Generally, senior executives are highly experienced in their roles. Research shows that length of experience is inversely related to openness to evidence-based practice. The longer one's experience in a role, the less favorable their attitudes to evidence-based practice and the more disposed they are to favor their own judgments (Aarons, 2004). Senior managers are likely to place a high value on their experience. As one consultant to managers said when queried about barriers to uptake on EBMgt,

> Executives' first response will be, the decisions I've made up until now are what has gotten me where I am at, why should I change what has worked so well for me?

Indeed, managerial judgment is highly valued in most business settings. This is despite the social-science evidence that suggests that experience in a role does not necessarily translate into effectiveness in that role and that generally people are over-confident about their own judgments. Explanations that cast doubt about managerial decision-making are not likely to influence senior managers' opinion. A more effective route to the design of EBMgt is to encourage senior managers' uptake by characterizing it as a technical innovation that enhances managerial decision making and demonstrating its uptake offers potential competitive advantages in a global economy, akin to other technological advances senior managers may have promoted.

Another individual factor that has the potential to positively impact senior managers' uptake is higher educational attainment and science training. Industries vary in the frequency by which executives have advanced degrees. Many executives do not have degrees above an MBA, and despite the general acceptance of an MBA as a requirement for an executive position, individual executives continue to have a mixed response on the necessity of an MBA for effectiveness in a role. The strong emphasis placed on experience often reduces the value placed on attaining advanced degrees. There is also lack of consistency in MBA programs' expectations that students understand and directly interact with social-science research. As a result, executives with MBAs may hold less favorable attitudes toward evidence-based practices than those with advanced degrees in other fields.

Although some senior executives have science training, science training in and of itself is not a guarantee that executives will value EBMgt. In industries with physical-science-trained executives, there can be a devaluing of social-science and management research. As an internal consultant who works with executives with backgrounds in engineering stated,

> They are the hardest. They won't accept any management research as valid and they expect people to behave according to black and white decision rules.

The expectation that EBMgt is able to deliver simple decision rules or straightforward equations with one consistent answer can lead to frustration for physical science trained managers when they are confronted with the contextualized, parsed, and fractious research from the social sciences and management literature in particular. The frustration can result in suspicion of the utility of social-science research and a consequent disinclination to adopt.

An important factor contributing to the uptake of EBMgt is appeal. For the senior executive, an EBMgt design must possess intuitive appeal, be capable of being implemented correctly, and have a track record with colleagues who have been happy with the results. To achieve intuitive appeal, EBMgt must resonate with already held beliefs and attitudes. For example, practices that can be shown to relate to positive ROI and carry a competitive advantage are likely to have appeal. Even with strong intuitive appeal, senior executives are unlikely to adopt EBMgt practices unless they are confident that they can be implemented effectively throughout the organization. Design of EBMgt within an organization must be structured in a way that can be reproduced systematically or scaled up. Zanardelli (chapter 11 of this volume) regularly invokes the three Es to his senior executives: evidence, execution, and evaluation. Tying the use of evidence with well-delineated processes to carry out any evidence-based practice reliably is likely to increase adoption. Finally, uptake by senior managers is likely to accelerate if other similar executives have adopted the practice of EBMgt and are satisfied with their results. Ideally EBMgt practices should be shared widely between executive team members to enhance uptake of those less open to change.

The senior manager's attitude toward a requirement to employ EBMgt that comes from another entity is likely to depend on the perceived business need to meet the requirement. Senior executives are likely to be responsive to mandates that have an effect on the bottom line but their attitude toward requirements from sources that do not offer a financial incentive may be ignored. Kovner

and Rundall (2006) cite external accountability as likely to increase the uptake and implementation of EBMgt practices. Large implosions, such as Enron and Lehman Brothers along with the 2008 financial crisis, has led to increased scrutiny of organizational actions by stockholders, institutional investors, and the general public. Some have begun to question and examine current organizational decision processes. Thus, if shareholders, customers, or government authorities place demands on an organization to engage in EBMgt for decision making, senior managers' attitude toward uptake is likely to increase. Within this environment senior executives who adopt EBMgt processes may be perceived to be taking steps toward assuring due diligence and proper risk-management practices.

Another individual factor that influences evidence-based uptake across settings is openness to new experiences. This is likely to be true for senior managers as well. Before implementing an EBMgt process, a useful first step is to assess executive team members to learn which are more open to new experiences in general and more likely to try different approaches. For example, a COO familiar with business process-improvement strategies may be more open to EBMgt than a CFO who may place a higher value on consistency and stability. Implementing the EBMgt process first in operations may have a greater likelihood of uptake and implementation. Lastly, the divergence between current practice and a proposed evidence-based practice impact uptake can also differentially affect senior managers. A chief marketing officer may view EBMgt as similar to conducting measurements in marketing research whereas a CEO with a background in sales may find EBMgt practices quite divergent from the rapid, fluid, and intuitive decision-making found in sales negotiations. The opinion that EBMgt diverges widely from current practice may hinder adoption.

Middle Managers

The primary focus of middle managers is tactical execution. As compared to senior managers and executives, their sphere of influence is bounded within the organization and their accountability for outcomes is more near term with close evaluation of month-end outcomes through quarterly outcomes. Middle managers are held accountable for ensuring activities that support the strategic goals of the organization are taking place. They have influence on the supervisors who report to them and can engage in managing upward activities to influence the senior managers. Middle managers gain recognition and are rewarded for showing solid managerial judgment, seeing that initiatives are carried out, and ensuring strategic objectives are reached. Decision making often occurs under significant time pressures. As senior leaders often put it to middle managers, "I am looking at my watch and not the calendar (for results)."

The organizational context of the middle manager, whether embedded in a constructive, questioning culture versus a negative, defensive culture, affects his or her readiness to implement EBMgt. Middle managers in constructive cultures who feel supported to try out new approaches and assess outcomes without fear of retribution are most likely to experiment with EBMgt. Those in defensive and negative cultures are at greater personal risk for attempting something different and are likely to perceive minimal pay off from implementing an EBMgt approach. Additionally, due to the close scrutiny of near term outcomes middle managers may perceive that EBMgt processes will reveal their misjudgments and errors. This level of transparency leaves middle managers particularly vulnerable in defensive cultures. As Kovner (chapter 10 of this volume) indicates, reflection on strategic decisions, transparent accountability, building a questioning culture, and improving how managers are trained are key steps to implementing EBMgt. Each step is particularly necessary to support middle management adoption of EBMgt.

Taking into account the personal demographic factors of experience and education, middle managers may have somewhat less experience than senior managers and as a result be more receptive to EBMgt. However, middle managers can also be long-tenured employees who view their current status as a result of exercising judgment and making decisions without the support of EBMgt and question its utility. Educational background is again likely to be mixed in middle management levels with fewer advanced degrees, which could limit interest in applying EBMgt practices. In some environments, middle managers have advanced technical and science degrees, and this generally portends a positive influence on EBMgt uptake. However, the same caveat about unrealistic expectations of being able to obtain concrete answers from social science research still applies. The nature of social-science research findings may alienate those with a physical-science research model of achieving definitive outcomes.

The individual attitudinal aspects of EBMgt (appeal, requirements, and openness to new experience, and divergence from current practices) are likely to have different meaning among middle managers compared to senior managers. Middle managers need EBMgt processes that are designed to be intuitively appealing at a pragmatic level. In these situations, adoption is likely to be increased if EBMgt practice meets an identified need (Wejnert, 2002). Middle managers are not interested in whether a practice is empirically efficacious if there is no proof of effectiveness in their environment. According to Meyer & Goes (1988) innovations viewed as feasible, workable, and easy to use are adopted more readily. Middle managers will not be convinced to employ EBMgt processes unless their teams are able to implement the processes effectively.

The individual characteristic "attitude toward requirement" will vary with middle managers, depending on the source of the requirement. If the requirement is coming from senior leaders or an outside accrediting body, which is necessary to attain International Organization for Standardization (ISO) certification, uptake is likely to be enhanced. Middle managers, by virtue of their role within an organization, are likely to comply rather than resist such requirements. Openness to change can be variable within the middle management ranks. Managers in divisions such as IT, where innovation is the norm, may be more accepting of new approaches. Conversely managers in divisions that operate at a currently successful steady state may be less open to adopting new practices. Again, knowing which middle managers are more open to new experiences can be useful in determining where to first initiate EBMgt practices. Any divergence between current practice and EBMgt is likely to have a large impact on middle managers. These managers must shepherd initiatives through lower levels and ensure accurate execution. New practices that appear to diverge strongly from current practice carry with them potential complications for effective execution. However, if EBMgt processes can be presented as similar to, yet a refinement of, current decision making and one that can facilitate effective execution, uptake is enhanced. Indeed in some situations middle managers may welcome research evidence to assist them in challenging current practices that are not effective.

Supervisors

The primary focus of supervisors is to implement processes directly through individual contributors and teams. Their sphere of influence is quite narrow, generally having the greatest impact on direct reports and some persuasion over peers. Managing upward can occur in limited situations. Supervisors are held accountable for outcomes as immediate as end of day or end of shift in manufacturing environments. As such, they are concerned with consistency and repeatability. Day-to-day decision making often requires immediate solutions or end-of-day recommendations, and time pressures are acute.

First-line supervisors in constructive cultures may be more open to experimentation when supported by superiors. Encouragement to ask questions may also embolden early career supervisors to critique standard practice. In constructive cultures, EBMgt offers first line supervisors the time to learn what works for their area and to implement new practices with evidence of effectiveness. As one health-care supervisor explained, "awareness and support" were necessary to use data-driven processes because they can be both "painful and illuminating." Defensive cultures are likely to represent a strong barrier for supervisors to implement EBMgt practices. The values of being conforming and subservient are antithetical to adopting EBMgt practices. Front-line supervisors have little autonomy in most circumstances and implementing actions that are contradictory to current practice, regardless of how well supported by the research, are likely to result in negative appraisals by superiors. Supervisors in defensive cultures are aware of their place within the organization structure and unwilling to risk their position by violating cultural norms.

With regard to the demographic factors that affect evidence-based uptake, first line supervisors are the least likely to have advanced degrees, which may limit the value they place on research data. However, they also are likely to have the least experience in the managerial role and less experience in a role is associated with more positive attitudes toward EB uptake. Particularly for those new to a supervisory role, EBMgt may offer reassurance that they are implementing sound processes and processes that are most effective at achieving their immediate outcomes. Additionally, having their perceptions validated or refined by evidence gives new supervisors greater confidence in their skills.

The other personal factors under consideration in regards to first line supervisors are appeal, requirements, openness to change, and divergence. EBMgt's appeal to supervisors may be in the credibility it gives to their decision making in situations. When supervisors can show good cause for their decision and that their choice has outcome data behind it, that can bolster the chances of the decision being accepted by both those who work for them and those above them. Supervisors, like other managers, find word-of-mouth reports that confirm satisfaction with a practice as highly motivating to accept the practice. Like other levels of management, receiving communication about the benefits of EBMgt from peers and superiors drives its appeal and uptake. Organizational requirements to include EBMgt as a necessary part of decision making are also likely to increase uptake at this level.

Knowing that senior leaders, their managers, or outside groups expect the use of EBMgt is likely to increase compliance among supervisors. The personal characteristic of openness to change will vary at this level as at other levels in the organization. Again, for organizations that want to increase uptake of EBMgt, identifying those supervisors who show openness to change offers insight into where EBMgt pilot projects should be housed. Starting initiatives with supervisors who display positive attitudes toward change is likely to accelerate adoption across work teams. Finally, the characteristic of attitude toward divergence has the potential to cut both ways with supervisors. Supervisors could perceive EBMgt to diverge widely from current decision-making practice and consequently impede their ability to hit objectives. This would produce strong negative attitudes toward uptake. Alternatively, supervisors could perceive EBMgt as similar to their current decision making processes and potentially beneficial in meeting expectations by improving accuracy. EBMgt processes must be developed with modest divergence from current practice and reveal direct benefit.

Designing Strategies to Promote the Adoption of EBMgt

The concept of EBMgt may be relatively new, but the desire to reduce the research-practice gap is decades old. Calls to close the gap recur frequently in the academic literature, yet tend not to be heeded by managers or by educators. Johns (1993) found that managers often view research-based personnel practices as administrative innovations rather than technical innovations and consider administrative innovations simply a matter of managerial operating style. This is analogous to educators' concept of their teaching style, and likewise their disinclination to engage in research-based teaching practices that do not comport with their adopted teaching style. Consequently, when research-based practice findings are viewed as a matter of style and the findings do not comport with current perceived operating styles, they are less likely to be incorporated into day-to-day practice. As a result, the impact of research-based practices can be minimized. Technical innovations are frequently viewed as independent of operating style, and technical innovations are more likely to be implemented based on perceived benefit to the organization. To enhance the impact of EBMgt and facilitate uptake by managers and educators, academic research findings should be presented as part of a knowledge production process that drives innovation and positive outcomes. Thus, EBMgt would benefit from being viewed as a technical innovation that has the capacity to enhance decision-making accuracy. Just as in information technology, engineering, or the pharmaceutical industry, where basic research leads to innovation, so, too, can management research be viewed as a driver of decision-making innovation in organizations. Characterizing EBMgt as a decision-making innovation also eliminates the concerns expressed over contradictory findings or research recommendations that change over time. People expect innovations to continually transform, and a static state is not desired. As an example, it is reasonable to anticipate that current goal-setting theory and research (Locke & Latham, 2009) will be refined and modified with additional research and implementation in different settings with different people. New findings should be expected and welcomed as advances in understanding management activities, which continue to inform practice. By defining EBMgt as a technical innovation to improve decision-making accuracy, its proponents might draw on innovation theory to encourage uptake through the design of diffusion, dissemination, and implementation strategies.

To design effective processes and practices, EBMgt proponents should employ processes that enhance diffusion, dissemination, and implementation. Diffusion is the naturalistic process by which innovations become known and are eventually adopted. Dissemination is formal and planned communication about an innovation (Greenhalgh, Robert, Macfarlane, Bate, & Kyriakidou, 2004). It is distinct from diffusion processes because dissemination is intentional and includes targeted distribution of information and intervention materials to a specific audience (Proctor et al., 2009). Implementation occurs when innovations are put into active use, ultimately becoming taken for granted. Successful implementation strategies require knowledge of the factors that facilitate uptake and barriers that derail it. See Table 17.1.

Innovation Attributes

Innovation attributes are people's subjective impressions of an innovation, impressions that powerfully impact individuals' adoption decisions (Moore & Benbasat, 1991) and should be considered in the design of EBMgt processes and practices. Rogers (2003) identified five attributes that enhance the adoption of innovations: relative advantage, compatibility, low complexity, trialability, and observability, each of which is briefly considered next.

The *Relative Advantage* of EBMgt, the extent to which an innovation is perceived as being better than the idea it supersedes, must be established by

Table 17.1. Strategies to enhance EBMgt uptake

Innovation Attributes	Dissemination Strategies	Implementation & Stages of Change
Relative advantage	Popular media marketing Generate exemplars	*Precontemplation* knowledge
Compatibility	Opinion leaders Authority figures Management CPD	*Contemplation* persuasion
Complexity	Presentations & consultants	*Preparation* decision
Trialabilty	Manuals & decision trees	*Action* implementation
Observability	Business intelligence & knowledge management	*Maintenance* confirmation

demonstrating that EBMgt is an improvement over current decision-making processes and one that leads to greater accuracy and clearly better results. Generally, the advantage must be conceived and presented in terms of some technical superiority or economic benefit: usefulness, in which the potential user positively assesses the contribution of the innovation to increasing job performance within a given organizational context, must be demonstrated.

One strategy would be to link relevant research evidence to a specific business need and demonstrate the advantage of EBMgt decision making over current standard practice. For example, placing the concept of EBMgt decision making within risk management and identifying the practice as a better tool to assess the risk versus rewards of endeavors can show its relative advantage over intuitive decision making. Another example is to identify EBMgt as helping managers develop broad cross-cultural knowledge required to thrive in global competition. Including research evidence gathered in international contexts increases corporations' skill in negotiations and business development. Particularly at the senior-managerial level, EBMgt must be seen as an innovation that results in competitive advantage.

However, the benefits of incorporating the research evidence into decision making are still only speculative. Even in more established fields of practice, there is little solid empirical evidence of its unique contribution. This is a significant gap and, if the use of research evidence in decision making is to be effectively promoted, credible evidence demonstrating its beneficial impact must be made available. There is an urgent requirement for future studies to address this challenge.

Innovations that are compatible with adopters' values, norms, and needs are more readily adopted. Recent work has refined compatibility's conceptualization to include four distinct aspects: compatibility with (1) previous experience, (2) with preferred working style, (3) with values, and (4) with existing working practices (Karahanna, Agarwal, & Angst, 2006) and, in empirical applications of Rogers's framework, compatibility has consistently been shown to be positively associated with adoption. This, then, is a critical area on which to focus.

Making certain that the recommended practice is consistent with the end user's current frame of reference is necessary to facilitate uptake, for example, by aligning EBMgt with current work practices focused on contemporary management concepts and practices such as knowledge management,

business intelligence, and business process re-engineering The greater the divergence of a new practice from the current one, the worse the manager's attitude toward adopting it is likely to be. Initially EBMgt may best be introduced within an organization as a methodology similar to Six-Sigma or Lean Engineering to maintain familiarity and enhance uptake.

However, promoting compatibility with previous experience, preferred working style, and values are more challenging tasks in a context that has little tradition of connecting with the research base. In this case, longer-term strategies must be considered, including: researchers undertaking more collaborative research that addresses the real-world problems managers face, and, in the design of training program, ensuring that managers are versed in research methods, means, purposes, and outputs, so that they can reasonably assess the quality of a piece of work on which they might base a decision.

Innovations that are perceived as simple to use are more easily adopted. Complex innovations place extra demands on the learning capacity of individuals and firms because they are required to take on new knowledge and skills to assimilate the innovation effectively. Management and organization studies are characterized by a diversity of modes of knowledge production, and ontological and epistemological positions. One of the principal artifacts of EBMgt is the systematic review, a rigorous scientific investigation of the literature generating a synthesis of individual studies by means of an explicit analytic framework defined by clear and precise aims, objectives, and methodological criteria (Tranfield, Denyer, & Smart, 2003) Although systematic reviews usefully synthesize the research evidence, they are complex studies in their own right, and further translational efforts are necessary to ensure important messages are appropriately communicated.

In spite of recent methodological developments that have increased the opportunity to synthesize the diversity of primary studies, the use among the research community (by and large the producers of syntheses of the evidence) to utilize these methods is in the earliest stages of adoption. Greater efforts must be made by the research community and more incentives must be made available to promote the use of these methods widely.

Ease of use and simplicity are necessary design elements to drive uptake. The principles and practices of EBMgt must be phrased in nontechnical, jargon-free language. Senior managers expect concise executive summaries and bulleted presentations. Extensive research bodies must first be synthesized through systematic reviews and then further pared as narrowly as possible to express the core concepts, recommendations, and caveats. Middle managers and supervisors are impacted by complexity as well. Those responsible for execution and implementation in organizations are slow to adopt practices that require extensive retraining or added steps.

Trialability refers to the opportunity to test out innovations without needing to make a commitment to fully adopt, implying a risk-free exploration of the innovation prior to committing to sustained usage. When designing EBMgt practices in organizations, starting with pilot projects or beginning in one manufacturing cell can facilitate diffusion more effectively than system-wide implementation. Piecemeal implementation has drawbacks, but given that organization-wide change processes tend to occur in fits and starts and are generally uneven, initially limiting EBMgt practice is preferable. As discussed earlier identifying those managers with attitudes most open to change and most likely to find EBMgt methods appealing are strong starting points for EBMgt implementation. Uptake is enhanced as managers adapt and customize EBMgt processes to their unique circumstances.

Lastly, greater *observabililty*, defined as the opportunity to directly and easily observe the benefits of an innovation, can facilitate diffusion. Arguably, the use of scientific evidence in managerial decision-making should have a positive impact on the users' careers and in their organizations. Lack of observability of the benefits of EBMgt can be a challenge in organizations. It is difficult to observe the direct outcomes of management decisions since their impact unfolds over time in changing economic circumstances. Furthermore there may be modest interest in collecting or analyzing data on the efficacy of management decisions. However, linking managerial decisions to business outcomes and revealing choice points that can produce stronger results are likely to be appreciated and replicated within the organization. Processes should be designed so results are reported and widely distributed across the organization. The improved decision-making accuracy that results from EBMgt must be made visible across levels and divisions.

Dissemination Strategies

Effective dissemination of EBMgt requires communicating through multiple channels within organizations and those available outside organizations. Dissemination in the design of EBMgt processes and practices is important. The number of managers using EBMgt in their decision making is, by any accounting, extremely small, so dissemination is necessary to increase awareness and knowledge.

There is a variety of dissemination channels that can be used to facilitate the transfer of research evidence from the academic community to practice, including publication in peer-reviewed and practitioner journals, teaching from undergraduates to executives, attending conferences, contract research programs, sharing facilities, adopting roles in industry, personnel exchange, and so forth. It appears, though, that academics have their preferred methods and that these do not always overlap with those preferred by managers (D'Este and Patel 2007), thus limiting opportunities to trial. The academic community needs to become better at getting close enough to managers in order that they can be clearer about the specific problems for which solutions are required.

Providing information through channels that managers currently access is more effective than expecting managers to access research journals. Salas and Kosarzycki (2003) suggest that nontechnical, jargon-free writing must appear in outlets such as trade magazines, *Harvard Business Review, Business Week,* and the *Wall Street Journal* to directly reach managers and facilitate uptake of research findings. Additionally the media, as another driver of dissemination (Rabin, Brownso, Kerner, & Glasgow, 2006), should be enlisted in articulating relevant and compelling stories of the effectiveness of EBMgt in enhancing organizational decision making. Recently, social networking tools have been used to disseminate research information to practitioners and create connections between the academic community. Web sites, blogs, podcasts, RSS feeds, and other communication pathways should be employed.

Some scholars have been writing systematic reviews with the express purpose of summarizing the state of current knowledge relating to a phenomenon with practitioner purposes in mind. However, these are still few in number, expensive to produce, and often in a format that does not provide rapid, accessible, and digestible summaries of key points.

Within an organization, dissemination through multiple communication processes is necessary to facilitate adoption. Disseminating information related to EBMgt decision making should include executive summaries, internal newsletters, intranet postings, webinars, staff presentations with Q & A and ongoing requests for feedback, and suggestions for refinement or customization. Dissemination alone has a modest impact on uptake of evidence-based practices. Implementation strategies are required for the EBMgt process to be accepted as a standard practice.

Implementation and Stages of Change

Implementation and adoption requires both organizational and individual change processes. At the organizational level, establishing a questioning and constructive culture is necessary. Development of a constructive culture must overcome significant barriers. People in organizations often gain status from, and are rewarded for exercising managerial judgment and for executing others' decisions without consideration of their outcomes. Allowing others to have input into decision making can reduce the perceived status of many decision makers.

Making statements like "the research says" tends to reduce, not enhance, how others perceive a manager's confidence and competence. Perceived confidence, stature, and competence are strong currencies that managers trade in to be successful in their role and gain further promotions. In defensive cultures questioning decision-making processes, identifying faulty assumptions, or bringing up countervailing viewpoints is seen as exhibiting resistance and being an obstructionist. As Kovner and Rundall (2006) state, "challenging decisions and introducing research evidence into problem-solving discussions can cause anxiety among managers, creating a sense that managerial judgment and expertise is perceived by colleagues as inadequate or not trustworthy."

These are difficult emotions to override and require thoughtful action to ameliorate their impact. Leaders of the organization have the greatest influence on creating a constructive culture. Characterizing the adoption of EBMgt as a sign of organizational and personal achievement (i.e., black belt in Six-Sigma), such that its implementation means that the company and its managers are innovators and on the leading edge, can quell anxiety and encourage motivation for adoption. Additional practices, identified to encourage the development of a questioning and constructive organizational culture, include sharing research journals and articles among managers, leaders making an EBMgt approach to decision making a requirement, manager development and training in EBMgt processes, and directly linking compensation to acquiring metrics and using relevant evidence in decision making (Kovner & Rundall, 2006).

For implementation to occur, individuals must adopt an innovation. Rogers identified five steps in adoption: knowledge, persuasion, decision, implementation, and confirmation. Managers learn about the practice of using EBMgt in decision making (knowledge) and receive confirmatory information that it is useful (persuasion). Managers become convinced of its effectiveness and make a choice to try it (decision). They actively engage in using EBMgt in decision making (implementation), and they obtain feedback that they are achieving stronger results (confirmation). These roughly parallel the stages-of-change model of Prochaska and DiClemente (1982). An advantage of using Prochaska and DiClemente's transtheoretical model is that it offers specific interventions to facilitate progress through the implementation steps. These interventions can guide the design of processes and practices to enhance EBMgt adoption.

As EBMgt is in its infancy (perhaps more accurately described as embryonic), the majority of managers are in a *precontemplation* stage with regards to changing their decision- making approach to include EBMgt. The precontemplation stage is one in which a person is not considering change and has a paucity of knowledge about the benefits of changing. This is a main reason why dissemination through multiple outlets is necessary. Dissemination needs to include emotional arousal that stirs the person toward the needed change, or away from the old behavior. This can result from sharing compelling stories of improved productivity, retention, engagement or profitability from using an EBMgt approach. Conversely the tales could be cautionary about the losses, cost overruns, and employee dissatisfaction incurred from not using EBMgt in decision making. Raising awareness is one method of advancing people from the precontemplation to the *contemplation* stage of change.

People in the contemplation stage are aware of the need for change, but not convinced the benefits outweigh the costs. Managers at this stage require persuasion to propel them forward. People tend to overestimate the costs of change and underestimate the benefits. The literature on implementation of evidence-based practice finds lack of access, lack of time, preference for peer viewpoints and preference for personal experience as common impediments to action. Two drawbacks to making the change to EBMgt are time pressures and effort required. Intuitive decisions are emotionally appealing and quicker than well-vetted, reflective decisions. Past experience is regarded as reliable and less effortful than disciplined, rigorous thinking. Another common rationale for not making changes is that someone else may not like it. Managers who contemplate reducing their reliance on peers' managerial viewpoints in favor of research-supported findings may fear being less regarded or supported by colleagues.

Making a convincing case for the benefits of change can overcome personal anxiety and put the costs of change in a more realistic perspective. The benefits must be identified in ways that are meaningful to managers, for example, pointing to return on investment from EBMgt. Despite time pressures, if front-line managers are assured that acting on research data is likely to improve their metrics, they are willing to sacrifice time to achieve better outcomes. As a front-line manager in a health-care setting explained, he would rather take the time to collect and analyze data-driven information that shows a clear advantage of one method over another than act quickly without it. Demonstration projects on the benefits of EBMgt or interactions with other similar organizations that have successfully implemented EBMgt can be effective in motivating managers to move from the contemplation stage to *preparation*. Likewise, recruiting authority figures, opinion leaders, and EBMgt champions within an organization to disseminate information and influence peers (Dearing, Mailbach, & Buller, 2006) can move people and organizations closer to the preparation stage.

Preparation is the step at which plans are made to adopt new behavior. A strong plan enhances the likelihood of successful adoption and sustained use for both the individual and the organization. Most managers have experienced change processes that lasted for a few months or years, only to be dropped in favor of previous practices or another fad. Solid preparation includes gathering information, training, consulting with those experienced in EBMgt and planning for impediments. Failure to develop processes that offer multiple routes to attaining the best available evidence in a rapid and simple manner, such as via web sites and intranets, are unlikely to succeed. Preparation is the step at which all processes must be reviewed for ease of use and speed of results. As one internal human-resources consultant inside a large academic research institution explained, "managers must find something useful in less than 5 to 7 minutes when they access an online database," Successful implementation requires making the organizational environment as conducive as possible for EBMgt practices. An important preparatory step is for organizations to assign opinion leaders to push out and monitor the uptake of EBMgt. For interactive networks to develop and successfully spread interest in EBMgt, directors of EBMgt must be distributed across different functional areas, not housed in a center or within a staff department. This also provides a framework for different areas to work together to achieve implementation. A plan of action to move forward employing EBMgt in decision making requires recursive iterations between proponents and skeptics. Responding to skeptics' questions and criticisms improves organizational preparation and gradually brings skeptics into alignment with EBMgt uptake. Moving too quickly through the preparation stage reduces successful implementation, but companies should also avoid preparation fatigue while awaiting total acceptance because it is both unlikely and unnecessary in this stage.

With adequate preparation, taking *action* to implement is the next step. This is when people put EBMgt into use in making organizational decisions. It is important to distinguish between core principles of EBMgt that should not be altered and more peripheral aspects that can be tailored to the specific environment. One core principle is that organizations and managers should exhibit a strong preference for well-vetted evidence over opinion. Involving managers in ongoing research stimulates interest, sustains behavior change, and produces constructive and effective reinventions of EBMgt processes.

Partnerships between academic institutions and organizations can be pathways to continued adoption activity. Many organizations fund university institutes to produce research on topics that are relevant to their business. Executives, housed within the institute, become adept in research methodology. The resultant research is first disseminated directly to the funding organization, and then moves into the academic publication stream for general distribution. Dearing and colleagues (2006) explain that organizations must continue to support new practices in order to sustain their ongoing use and encourage adaptations to their unique circumstances. Stakeholders who take a long-term view to implementing EBMgt into organizational decision making achieve greater success. Supportive actions are needed until the practice becomes part of the institutional fabric or simply the way decisions are made.

The final implementation process is confirmation, whereby the decision to put an innovation into practice is affirmed by satisfaction with outcomes.

This is necessary to sustain use of the practice over the long term. The stages-of-change model describes this as maintenance. By this point, users feel confident that they are able to continue the practice on an ongoing basis with little risk of failure. Transparent appraisal processes verifying the positive outcomes obtained by including relevant research create motivation to continue its practice. Demonstrating that EBMgt can be applied reliably throughout the organization builds user confidence and reduces the chance of falling back into past practices.

Future Directions

EBMgt is a means for managers to increase the accuracy and effectiveness of the day-to-day decisions they make in organizations. Evidence-based practices are encouraged across medicine, education, and social services. The research on diffusion, dissemination, and implementation in these other areas is a practical starting point for the design of EBMgt processes and practices. The major stakeholders—researchers, educators, and managers—all have a role in advancing the science of EBMgt. As follows:

Scholars and Researchers

- Conduct systematic reviews.
- Disseminate systematic review findings.
- Use social media to report immediate results.
- Produce appealing executive summaries.
- Publish in mass-media outlets.
- Create research-institute partnerships with organizations and maintain ongoing dialogue.
- Understand the influencing strategies that work within each organization that are key to getting messages heard.
- Understand that evidence needs to be presented in a timely manner.
- Be honest about the limitation of evidence— do not promise answers where none can be delivered.

Educators and Consultants

- Teach social-science research methodology.
- Teach systematic review findings to students.
- Maintain web sites that catalogue research results.
- Use social media to link students/managers/researchers.
- Cast EBMgt as an innovation in decision-making accuracy.

- Construct EBMgt procedures compatible with past practices.
- Generate EBMgt podcasts, webinars, and presentations.
- Develop conferences for EBMgt managers to interact.

Organizations and Managers

- Create constructive and questioning cultures.
- Fund systematic reviews in relevant areas of interest.
- Develop quick access points to relevant research.
- Establish research-findings reading groups.
- Use social media to link managers with researchers.
- Maintain an intranet site of relevant research results.
- Assess managers for openness to change.
- Offer EBMgt training and skill development.
- House executives in research institutes to learn methods.
- Pilot EBMgt in receptive areas of the organization.
- Disseminate results widely and request feedback.
- Name directors of EBMgt to remove uptake barriers.
- Require EBMgt in organizational decision making.
- Link compensation with use of EBMgt in decision making.
- Teach managers to be sensitive to their context and develop the skill of applying the findings of research to the demands of day-to-day management practice.
- Develop critical and evaluative skills for managers so that they can assess the evidence for themselves.
- Employ EBMgt knowledge-management systems and maintain outcomes as business intelligence.

Conclusion

EBMgt is done by managers; it cannot be imposed on them by researchers, educators, or consultants (Briner et. al., 2009). Proponents of EBMgt are faced with the task of designing processes that appeal to senior managers, executives, middle managers, and front-line supervisors. A starting point is to understand the factors that have driven evidence-based uptake in health care and social services. In these settings, manager characteristics (training type, educational attainment, experience, attitudes toward evidence-based practice) and organizational factors (constructive or defensive) affect uptake of evidence-based processes. Principles derived from diffusion of innovations (Rogers, 2003) and the transtheoretical stages-of-change model (Prochaska & DiClemente, 1982) offer guidance on accelerating EBMgt adoption.

References

Aarons, G. A. (2004). Mental health provider attitudes toward adoption of evidence-based practice: The evidence-based practice attitude scale (EBPAS). *Mental Health Services Research, 6,* 61–73.

Aarons, G. A., & Sawitzky, A. C. (2006). Organizational culture and climate and mental health provider attitudes toward evidence-based practice. *Psychological Services, 3,* 61–72.

Adams, R., & Bessant, J. (2008). Accelerating diffusion among slow adopters. In J. Bessant & T. Venables (Eds.), *Creating wealth from knowledge: Meeting the innovation challenge* (pp. 227–250). Cheltenham, England: Edward Elgar.

Anderson, N., & West, M. A. (1996). The team climate inventory: Development of the TCI and its applications in team-building for innovativeness. *European Journal of Work and Organizational Psychology, 5,* 53–66.

Briner, R. B., Denyer, D., & Rousseau, D. M. (2009). Evidence-based management: Concept clean-up time? *Academy of Management Perspectives, 23,* 19–32.

David, P. A. (1985). Clio and the economics of QWERTY. *Economic History, 75*(2), 332–337.

Dearing, J. W., Maibach, E. W., & Buller, D. B. (2006). A convergent diffusion and social marketing approach for disseminating proven approaches to physical activity promotion. *American Journal of Preventive Medicine, 31,* 11–23.

D'Este, P. D., & Patel, P. (2007). University–industry linkages in the UK: What are the factors underlying the variety of interactions with industry? *Research Policy, 36,* 1295–1313.

Dopson, S., Locock, L., Chambers, D., & Gabbay, J. (2001). Implementation of evidence-based medicine: Evaluation of the promoting action on clinical effectiveness programme. *Journal of Health Services Research and policy, 6* (1), 23–31.

Greenhalgh, T., Robert, G., Macfarlane, F., Bate, P., & Kyriakidou, O. (2004). Diffusion of innovations in service organizations: Systematic review and recommendations. *The Milbank Quarterly, 82,* 581–629.

Jackson, R. J., & Lindsay, D. R. (2010). Lessons for experience: Why wait? *Industrial and Organizational Psychology, 3,* 48–51.

Johns, G. (1993). Constraints on the adoption of psychology-based personnel practices: Lessons from organizational innovation. *Personnel Psychology, 46,* 569–592.

Johnstone, P., & Lacey, P. (2002). Are decisions by purchasers in an English health district evidence-based? *Journal of Health Services Research and Policy, 67*(3), 166–169.

Karahanna, E., Agarwal, R., & Angst, C. M. (2006). Reconceptualizing compatibility beliefs in technology acceptance research. *MIS Quarterly, 30*(4), 781–804.

Kitson, A., Harvey, G., & McCormack, B. (1998). Enabling the implementation of evidence-based practice: A conceptual framework. *Quality in Healthcare, 7,* 149–158.

Kovner, A. R., & Rundall, T. G. (2006). Evidence-based management reconsidered. *Frontiers of Health Services Management, 22,* 3–22.

Lewis, S. (2007). Toward a general theory of indifference to research-based evidence. *Journal of Health Services Research and Policy, 12*(3), 166–172.

Locke, E. A., & Latham, G. P. (2009). Has goal setting gone wild, or have its attackers abandoned good scholarship? *Academy of Management Perspectives, 23,* 17–23.

McCall, M. W. (2010). Recasting leadership development. *Industrial and Organizational Psychology, 3,* 3–19.

Meyer, A. D., & Goes, J. B. (1988). Organizational assimilation of innovations: A multi-level contextual analysis. *Academy of Management Journal, 31,* 897–923.

Miller, W. R., Sorensen, J. L., Selzer, J. A., & Brigham, G. S. (2006). Disseminating evidence-based practices in substance abuse treatment: A review with suggestions. *Journal of Substance Abuse Treatment, 31,* 25–39.

Moore, G. C., & Benbasat, I. (1991). Development of an instrument to measure the perceptions of adopting an information technology innovation. *Information Systems Research, 3*(3), 192–222.

Pfeffer, J., & Fong, C. T. (2002). The end of business schools? Less success than meets the eye. *Academy of Management Learning and Education, 1*(1), 78–95.

Pfeffer, J., & Sutton, R. I. (2006). Evidence-based management. *Harvard Business Review, 84*(1), 62–74.

Prochaska, J. O., & DiClemente, C. C. (1982). Transtheoretical therapy: Toward a more integrative model of change. *Psychotherapy, Theory, Research and Practice, 19,* 276–288.

Proctor, E. K., Landsverk, J., Aarons, G., Chambers, D., Gilson, C., & Mittman, B. (2009). Implementation research in mental health services: An emerging science with conceptual, methodological, and training challenges. *Administrative Policy Mental Health, 36,* 24–34.

Rabin, B. A., Brownson, R. C., Kerner, J. F., & Glasgow, R. E. (2006). Methodological challenges in disseminating evidence-based interventions to promote physical activity. *American Journal of Preventive Medicine, 31,* 24–34.

Rogers, E. M. (2003). *Diffusion of innovations.* New York: Free Press.

Salas, E., & Kosarzycki, M. P. (2003). Why don't organizations pay attention to (and use) findings from the science of training? *Human Resource Development Quarterly, 14,* 487–491.

Shortell, S. M., Rundall, T. G., & Hsu, J. (2007). Improving patient care by linking evidence-based medicine and evidence based management. *Journal of the American Medical Association, 298*(6), 673–676.

Tranfield, D., Denyer, D., & Smart, P. (2003). Towards a methodology for developing evidence-informed management knowledge by means of systematic review. *British Journal of Management, 14,* 207–222.

Wejnert, B. (2002). Integrating models of diffusions of innovations: A conceptual framework. *Annual Review of Sociology, 28,* 297–326.

PART 4

Education

Teaching and Learning Using Evidence-Based Principles

Jodi S. Goodman *and* James O'Brien

Abstract

In this chapter, we present several cognitive learning theories relevant for novice, expert, and advanced learning, and we discuss their implications for the instructional design and delivery of university management courses. We describe how evidence-based instructional strategies can be derived from cognitive learning theories, and then we apply the strategies to commonly used teaching practices in management courses. We also address a number of challenges that we believe have impeded evidence-based teaching practice.

Key Words: evidence-based teaching, cognitive learning theory, instructional strategies, cognitive load, learning, scaffolding, feedback, meta-cognition, critical thinking, expertise, adaptive expertise

Many common teaching strategies contradict scientific evidence about how people learn, to the detriment of student learning. Consider these taken-for-granted strategies, widely used in business-school classrooms and beyond:

• Making things less cognitively demanding for learners by simplifying content and tasks.
• Assigning activities because they are enjoyable, without assessing their learning outcomes.
• Providing more feedback and guidance than is truly needed, which can impair learning, even as it benefits immediate performance.

This chapter will provide evidence that the preceding strategies are actually counterproductive to learning. In contrast, evidence-based teaching strategies like introducing complexity early on and helping students to learn to deal with the complexity, while providing only the necessary guidance, are more likely to benefit learning. The latter teaching strategies are less pleasant. They can even impair

performance in the short term, as students struggle with complexity. However, scientific evidence on learning indicates that such demanding strategies ultimately better prepare students for the future.

Recent comments from our colleagues reflect conventional wisdom about teaching and illustrate certain challenges in promoting an evidence-based approach to management teaching:

Us:	"I'm working on a chapter on teaching management in evidence-based ways."
Colleague 1:	"I do that already...and besides, my evaluations are excellent!"
Colleague 2:	"I don't do that. I prefer to use the case method."
Colleague 3:	"Hey, it'll take the fun out of class *and* ruin my evaluations."

In our responses to these colleagues, we point out that student course evaluations are deficient measures of teaching quality and learning, and cases and other interactive tools are not antithetical to taking an evidence-based approach to teaching. Cases, exercises, and other common teaching practices can be employed in evidence-based ways.

This chapter represents our joint response to skeptical colleagues who tend to think of the problem this chapter addresses as a nonissue. It responds to the blind faith instructors in business schools place in commonly used teaching practices—unsupported by research evidence. Our purpose is to clarify what an evidence-based approach to teaching is, to present the scientific evidence on which it is based, and to describe its application to management education. Ultimately, we hope to advance the practice of evidence-based teaching in management education.

We would also like to highlight two distinguishing features of our chapter. Most of this handbook is about evidence-based management (EBMgt), which involves combining the best research evidence with professional judgment and local evidence. Some chapters address what our students need to learn to become evidence-based managers (e.g., the application of research evidence to practice, Salipante & Smith, chapter 20 of this volume) and the resources required to support efforts to practice EBMgt (Briner & Denyer, chapter 7 of this volume ; Pearce, chapter 21 of this volume; Werner, chapter 15 of this volume). Although we touch on these issues and our context is management education, our primary focus is on evidence-based teaching as a necessary condition for learning and practicing EBMgt. Additionally, in essence, our chapter is an illustration of evidence-based practice. We provide a model for how educators can use the best available evidence about learning and instruction to take an evidence-based approach in their practice of teaching.

This chapter begins with our explanations of several relevant cognitive learning theories. It describes how evidence-based instructional strategies can be derived from the cognitive learning theories and identifies effective methods of instruction to promote knowledge and skill acquisition and the transfer of learning to actual practice. Next, it applies evidence-based instructional strategies in discussing common management teaching practices, including lecture, discussion, experiential exercises, cases and the case teaching method, and group projects. It addresses the appropriate use and potential misuse of evidence-based learning principles, as well as problems created by relying on teaching approaches that contradict the evidence. Finally, the chapter

confronts the individual and institutional challenges that can impede implementation of EBMgt teaching and learning and recommends responses to these challenges.

Our Thesis

We contend that instructional methods in management should be thoroughly grounded in scientific evidence about how people learn. Cognitive and instructional psychology and education theory and research should be used to develop evidence-based instructional methods. Evidence-based teaching fosters the intellectual skills required to engage in EBMgt. These skills will enable our students to apply course content to the workplace and prepare them for the life-long learning that the practice of management requires.

Teaching strategies that support real learning demonstrate substantial transfer of knowledge and skills to various tasks and contexts. In contrast, many commonly used strategies (e.g., task simplification; specific, immediate, and frequent feedback; specific goals) have been found to result in increased training performance, *at the expense of transfer*. Common teaching practices, such as cases and experiential exercises, also can be (mis-) applied in ways that lead to lively discussion and interesting ideas, but do not support transfer. The confusion of means with ends common in management education reflects a lack of familiarity with the learning literatures. Widespread ignorance regarding the body of evidence on teaching and learning gets in the way of identifying and then using effective educational strategies. Consistent with the principle of rewarding A while hoping for B (Kerr, 1995), a good deal of management education focuses attention away from learning outcomes toward more general self-reports of learning and affective outcomes captured in the fundamentally flawed course evaluations (Armstrong, 1998) our institutions typically use.

Clear goals need to be specified for management education, particularly in terms of the learning outcomes that we seek to achieve. If we think of managerial performance on a continuum from novice to expert performance, the goal of our efforts should be to move our students further along this continuum and help prepare them for future learning, whether they are undergraduates or experienced executives. The management domain contains both well- and ill-defined problems, and no one can fully anticipate the problems our students will face as practitioners. It is imperative that management educators cultivate students' abilities to continue to learn and adapt to new, unexpected, and complex problems. This cultivation requires critical thinking, reflection, and other meta-cognitive habits of mind, developed in the context of acquiring and applying concepts, models, and theories to management practice. Instruction needs to expand habits of mind to allow learners to disentangle personal beliefs from what the evidence actually says. Overall, we endeavor to have our students learn to identify problems, engage in evidence-based causal analysis, and develop analysis-based solutions, consistent with the practice of EBMgt. These aspirations necessitate active and informed engagement in the learning process by both learners and instructors.

Cognitive Theories of Learning and Associated Instructional Strategies

The learning research in cognitive and instructional psychology and education varies in its depth and specificity. Research streams differ in their theoretical development, subjects' levels of expertise, task domains, attention to learning processes and strategies, relative emphasis on automatic and controlled cognitive processes, and assumptions made about working memory's scope and structure. Yet, all streams agree that learners must deploy active cognitive processes, such as meta-cognition, critical reasoning, and hypothesis generation and testing to truly learn, and that instructional conditions must be structured to support these cognitive activities.

Our detailed analysis starts with learning theories that address short and long-term memory and the processes of information encoding and schema construction in novices, experts, and advanced learners. We connect these to other relevant theories and perspectives to inform our discussion of specific management-education practices.

Cognitive Load Theory

Cognitive load theory (CLT) builds on knowledge of human cognitive architecture to address the mental processes in which learners engage in response to information presented during instruction (Pollock, Chandler, & Sweller, 2002). CLT assumes that working memory holds only a small number of elements at one time, and that knowledge stored in unlimited long-term memory can overcome the limits of working memory (Pollock et al., 2002). Human cognitive architecture is hierarchically organized: Individual bits or elements of information are combined into organized cognitive structures or schemata, and less complex schemata are combined to form more complex schemata. Schemata are stored in long-term memory and called into short-term working memory when needed. These bigger chunks of information are treated as individual elements in working memory and, therefore, require less working memory capacity than the set of individual elements that comprise them (Pollock et al., 2002; Sweller, van Merriënboer, & Paas, 1998). With sufficient practice and memorization, schemata are processed automatically, further decreasing their demands on working memory and freeing up its capacity (Sweller et al., 1998).

Information received during instruction imposes cognitive load on the working memory of the learner. According to CLT, total cognitive load is the sum of intrinsic, extraneous, and germane load. Intrinsic load is imposed by task complexity, increasing with the number of information elements in the task and the extent to which these elements interact. For example, the task of memorizing the definitions of fairly isolated concepts has low element interactivity. Alternatively, the task of understanding a complex model or theory that contains a set of interrelated and causally connected concepts is high in element interactivity, and thus imposes higher intrinsic cognitive load. Extraneous and germane extrinsic cognitive load are imposed by the way instructional information is presented and the learning activities the instructional design requires. Germane load comes from information and activities that contribute to schema construction and automation, whereas the information and activities that produce extraneous load do not promote these processes. Following our earlier example, having students learn the theory in the context of applying it to an organizational problem increases germane cognitive load because this activity can support the construction of knowledge structures for understanding and using the theory. Extraneous cognitive load may be imposed, for example, by prematurely focusing students' attention on generating problem solutions, grades, or other outcomes that could detract from schema construction. The learner's current knowledge impacts both the intrinsic cognitive load experienced and whether learners experience instructional information and activities as extraneous or germane load (Paas, Renkl, & Sweller, 2004).

CLT researchers have observed that novice problem-solvers tend to use goal-directed, means-end analysis (Sweller, 1988). This strategy involves working backward from a goal to try to bring the current state of the problem (e.g., a/b − c x d = e) progressively closer to the goal state (e.g., b =?) by recognizing differences between the current and goal states and identifying and progressively implementing problem-solving operators (e.g., rules of algebra) to move closer to the goal (Sweller et al., 1998). As the problem-solver gets closer to the goal, previous actions and strategies can be ignored, because the focus is on reducing the distance between the goal and the most recent current state. This strategy can benefit performance (i.e., the problem is solved), but it increases extraneous cognitive load (Sweller et al., 1998), and thereby impedes learning by inhibiting the construction of appropriate schemata for the problem (Sweller, 1988). Alternatively, more experienced problem-solvers tend to use history-cued strategies in which they work forward from previous moves and develop and test hypotheses to identify subsequent moves. Working forward through a problem supports schema construction, rule induction, and transfer (Sweller, Mawer, & Howe, 1982).

CLT suggests that learning is best facilitated when the conditions of learning are aligned with human cognitive architecture (Paas et al., 2004). Research in this area has resulted in a number of instructional methods designed to optimize cognitive load in order to facilitate the construction and automation of schemata. Methods such as introducing variability in worked examples and practice problems and requiring learners to provide self-explanations attempt to decrease extraneous and increase germane cognitive load (Pass et al., 2004; Renkl, Atkinson, & Grobe, 2004; Sweller, 2004; Sweller et al., 1998). These instructional methods have been examined with novice learners in primary and secondary school to train discrete problem-solving skills in mathematics and science domains (e.g., Gerjets, Scheiter, & Catrambone, 2004; Renkl & Atkinson, 2003; Renkl et al., 2004; Sweller, 1998, Schwonke et al., 2009) and with college students and vocational and professional trainees on computer programming, troubleshooting and equipment testing, concept mapping, and simulated decision making tasks (Hilbert & Renkl, 2009; Moreno, 2004, Pollock et al., 2002; van Gog, Paas, & van Merriënboer, 2006; van Merriënboer, Schuurman, Crook, & Paas, 2002).

For instance, the "worked example effect" has received a great deal of research support (e.g., Hilbert & Renkl, 2009; Renkl et al., 2004; Schwonke et al.,

2009). At the beginning of instruction, learners are provided and work through a complete model protocol showing the steps taken to complete a problem, along with the final solution. Critical features are annotated to show what the steps are intended to illustrate. Providing worked examples imposes less extraneous cognitive load than conventional problems, for which students are presented with whole problems to solve and tend to use means-end strategies. Worked examples free cognitive resources for schema building around understanding and learning all of the procedural steps involved in a task.

After the complete worked example has been studied, the solved steps are sequentially removed or faded, either backward or forward, in subsequent worked examples to progressively give the learner additional responsibility for problem-solving. After all of the worked steps have been faded, learners are responsible for solving problems in their entirety. Fading out the worked examples as learning progresses helps students to experience impasses on those parts of the problem they work out themselves (Renkl et al., 2004). This approach is particularly effective when learners are prompted to engage in self-explanation (Hilbert & Renkl, 2009).

Providing nonspecific goals is also a recommended strategy for decreasing the use of means-end strategies and promoting schema construction. For example, in a physics problem, instead of assigning the specific goal of solving for particular variables, such as velocity, students would be instructed to find as many variables as possible (Sweller, et al., 1998). In the context of management education, students could be given a case or simulation and instructed to identify problems and the causes of problems using relevant theories. They would not be told what the end state should be (e.g., sales or other performance goals), as this may limit their search for problems and causes.

Interestingly, general goals have been found to be more supportive of learning processes and transfer than specific goals (e.g., Burns & Vollmeyer, 2002; Vollmeyer & Burns, 2002; Vollmeyer, Burns, & Holyoak, 1996). General goals promote the systematic development and testing of hypotheses, which supports rule induction (Klahr & Dunbar, 1988; Simon & Lea, 1974). Alternatively, specific goals tend to focus learners' attention on the goal itself, which decreases systematic exploration (Burns & Vollmeyer, 2002; Vollmeyer & Burns, 2002). Management goal-setting researchers also recognize the disadvantages of specific performance outcome goals in situations that require learning. They suggest that instructors assign or encourage learners to set learning goals for discovering the steps and strategies for effective task execution (Latham & Locke, 2007; Latham & Pinder, 2005). Setting or assigning learning goals or providing general goals may not be sufficient for grade-obsessed students, but combined with other evidence-based teaching strategies, these types of goals can support learning and transfer.

Expertise/Expert Performance

CLT and theories of expertise and expert performance are similarly based on memory processes, with some important differences. First, contrary to CLT, expertise scholars assume that working- memory capacity can be expanded with the acquisition of long-term working memory. Experts develop cognitive schemata for knowledge and procedures by using a variety of elaborate encoding processes to store information in long-term memory. Long-term working memory is a mechanism that allows for the rapid and efficient retrieval and temporary storage of information encoded in long-term memory when such information is needed for task performance (Ericsson & Delaney, 1999; Ericsson & Kintsch, 1995). The shift in view from limited to unlimited working memory capacity has implications in the design of instruction for advanced learners who possess more of the necessary schemata (van Gog, Ericsson, Rikers, & Paas, 2005).

In addition, CLT places significant emphasis on schema automization, which is consistent with theories of skill acquisition (e.g., ACT-R, Anderson, Bothell, Byrne, Douglass, Lebiere, & Qin, 2004). Alternatively, although many knowledge and skill structures become automated, expertise researchers maintain that the essential aspects of expert performance remain under the control of the performer (van Gog et al., 2005). The flexible representation of information in long-term working memory supports explicit cognitive processes such as planning, reasoning, anticipating, and self-monitoring. In turn, these explicit processes facilitate current task performance, adaptation, and further performance improvement (Ericsson & Delaney, 1999; Ericsson & Lehmann, 1996).

Expert performance is characterized by "superior reproducible performances of representative tasks [that] capture the essence" of a performance domain (Ericsson, 2006a, p. 3). The amount of accumulated experience is not sufficient to develop expertise.

Rather, expertise is acquired through deliberate practice, over a period of at least ten years, which may seem like a lifetime to undergraduate and MBA students. Deliberate practice activities are those that are specifically designed with the intention of acquiring and improving particular skills. The types of activities will vary, depending on the performance domain and the current knowledge and skills of the performer. However, across domains and skill levels, expertise researchers advocate highly structured deliberate practice activities that involve extensive, repetitive engagement with the same or similar tasks and immediate feedback on performance. Activities are designed to address specific weaknesses, and performance is closely monitored to provide cues for how to improve. Deliberate practice is typically scheduled for a limited time each day, because of the focused effort involved. It is also not inherently enjoyable or rewarding. Motivation must come from incremental performance improvements and the prospect of improved performance over time (Ericsson, Krampe, & Tesch-Romer, 1993).

Deliberate practice activities initially are designed and supervised by instructors and coaches, with additional rehearsal of the activities between instructional sessions (Ericsson et al., 1993). Effective instruction is designed to guide practice in self-monitoring, self-assessment, and the use of feedback (Glaser, 1996). As expertise develops over time, the responsibility for designing deliberate practice activities and the regulation of learning and performance transitions from external scaffolding (i.e., supports) to the learner. Instructors decrease the instructional scaffolding to promote self-regulatory activities such as planning, self-instruction, self-monitoring, generating feedback, self-evaluation, and seeking assistance when needed (Zimmerman, 2002; Glaser, 1996).

Teaching learners to use feedback and to become self-regulating are particularly important in light of research showing negative effects of immediate, frequent feedback on transfer (Bjork, 1994; Schmidt & Bjork, 1992) and of specific feedback on exploration (Goodman et al., 2004; Goodman & Wood, 2004), stimulus variability (Goodman & Wood, 2004; 2009), and explicit cognitive processes (Goodman, Wood, & Chen, 2011) that support transfer. Left to their own devices, learners tend to passively follow the advice feedback provides, which interferes with learning processes. Most of the research examining the effects of feedback on transfer suggests that limiting feedback during training aids effective learning and the transfer of the skills required to deal with errors, crises, malfunctions, and other difficulties that may present themselves.

Despite evidence to the contrary, "the more feedback, the better the learning" has become conventional wisdom. Prescriptions for frequent, immediate, specific performance feedback are found in edited academic volumes, journal articles, and textbooks. Some recommendations are inappropriately derived from research showing the positive effects of feedback on performance, although positive performance effects are by no means guaranteed (Kluger & DeNisi, 1996). Prescriptions typically lack detail on what immediate, frequent, and specific feedback look like in practice. Recommendations also are not qualified by conditions, such as cognitive load or learners' processing capabilities, and they do not consider potential negative effects on transfer-appropriate information-processing activities. In the expertise literature, the effects of the various components of deliberate practice have not been isolated, and, therefore, recommendations for providing immediate feedback must be qualified. As a rule, when learning is involved, feedback interventions should be designed to promote the cognitive activities that are needed for transfer. Determining the precise content, timing, and frequency of feedback that will promote transfer-appropriate processing will require professional judgment on the part of the instructor. Alternatively, once a skill is acquired, immediate and continuous feedback is useful in fine-tuning expert performance or preparing for presentations, competitions, or other activities that require maximum performance (Bjork, 2009).

Returning to the topic of expertise in general, the research focuses on the cognitive and performance activities of adult experts, the acquisition of expertise through deliberate practice, and comparisons of novices and experts in well-defined domains such as chess, typing, specific sports, military tasks, and medical diagnosis in specific specialties (Ericsson, Charness, Feltovich, & Hoffman, 2006). The research has expanded recently into the more varied work domains of insurance agents (Sonnentag & Kleine, 2000) and small business owners (Unger, Keith, Hilling, Gielnik & Frese, 2009).

The objectives of deliberate practice are the same across work settings and the well-defined domains expertise research typically examines. Nonetheless, deliberate practice activities in work settings differ because of the nature of the work (Sonnentag & Kleine, 2000; Unger et al., 2009). For example,

small-business management involves a diverse set of tasks, with little opportunity for repetition (Unger et al., 2009), which may not lend itself to the repeated practice of distinct tasks (Sonnentag & Kleine, 2000). Deliberate practice in work settings has been found to involve activities such as preparing for task completion; seeking feedback and other information from clients, colleagues, and domain experts; attending formal training sessions; engaging in self-instruction through reading; and tracking data (e.g., sales, inventory), errors, and employee performance (Sonnentag & Kleine, 2000; Unger et al., 2009). Knowledge of the types of deliberate practice activities that take place in organizations can help us to prepare our students for generating and engaging in those experiences themselves when they enter or reenter the work world.

Adaptive Expertise

Researchers specifically interested in adaptive expertise distinguish routine from adaptive expertise, based on the work of Hatano and colleagues (Hatano & Inagaki, 1986; Hatano & Ouro, 2003). Routine expertise is characterized by the fast, accurate, automatic, efficient application of highly developed knowledge and procedures to problem-solving (Hatano & Ouro, 2003). People expert in routine situations are highly successful with standard problems, but run into difficulties with those that are nonroutine. They dismiss or otherwise fail to take into account distinctive features of problems that do not fit their existing understanding, and apply existing knowledge and procedures to problems to which they do not apply (Crawford & Brophy, 2006). In other words, discriminant learning suffers, and people overgeneralize the application of their strategies (Anderson, 1982). For example, in a study of radiologists, Raufaste, Eyrolle, and Marine (1998), found that experts who used deliberate, explicit reasoning to make diagnoses from X-ray images performed better than experts who relied on automatic processes. The distinguishing feature between these two groups of expert radiologists was that the latter were full-time practicing radiologists, whereas the former were not only practicing radiologists but also academic researchers and teachers, whose work regularly involved explicit cognitive processing.

The efficient use of highly developed schemata is necessary for expert performance. However, innovation is also essential, and adaptive expertise requires balancing efficiency and innovation (Schwartz, Bransford, & Sears, 2005). Adaptive experts rely on heuristics and routines when appropriate, but recognize when to let go of them, expand their knowledge, and develop and apply new approaches to novel or more complex problems and situations (Crawford & Brophy, 2006; Klein, 2009). Adaptive expertise entails continuous learning through the act of problem-solving (Wineburg, 1998). Alternatively, in crisis situations, such as emergency medicine, adaptive experts make fast judgments in real-time based on routine expertise, then reflect on and learn from the experience later in meetings with colleagues (Patel, Kaufman, & Magder, 1996). This type of analysis is also a significant component of the U.S. Army's After Action Reviews following unit-training exercises (Fletcher, 2009), a process that institutionalizes learning from experience. Adaptive experts use metacognition, self-regulation, and reasoning to recognize current knowledge limitations, detect important differences between problems, and develop and test hypotheses to identify when current knowledge does and does not apply and to adapt strategies as needed. Adaptive experts perform better than routine experts on complex tasks, such as medical diagnosis, technical troubleshooting, and the avoidance of workplace errors, and they have been found to exhibit superior cognitive flexibility (Crawford & Brophy, 2006).

A number of instructional principles emerge from research in adaptive expertise. Still, research is needed to develop specific guidelines for the application of this body of knowledge (Crawford & Brophy, 2006). Preparing learners for future learning (Bransford & Schwartz, 1999) entails embedding opportunities for learners to build and adapt their knowledge and skills throughout their learning experiences. Instruction should be structured so that domain knowledge and efficient routines are developed in conjunction with innovation skills. This can be done by providing opportunities for iterative problem-solving, by which students work through assignments in which they engage a task, get or generate feedback, and try again (Crawford & Brophy, 2006). This strategy is consistent with dual space theories of problem-solving, which emphasize the role of learners' coordinated efforts for generating and testing hypotheses in fostering rule induction (Klahr & Dunbar, 1988; Simon & Lea, 1974).

For assignments to be effective, learners need to engage in deliberate, explicit reasoning and metacognitive strategies. To this end, learners need training in how to effectively use feedback, to counteract the tendency to passively follow the feedback provided. Adaptive expertise research also supports introducing experiences with variability in tasks and conditions, including nonroutine problems that require gaining new knowledge and developing and applying new solutions. The innovation skills required for adaptive expertise can also be fostered through interactions with others. For example, medical students accompanying physicians on rounds are asked a number of medical and diagnostic questions that require them to reason independently and listen to and learn from one another (Crawford & Brophy, 2006).

Expert performance tends to be domain-specific (Chi, 2006), although some experts are able to apply their knowledge and skills across domains (Kimball & Holyoak, 2000; Hatano & Ouro, 2003). For example, Barnett and Koslowski (2002) compared the performance of strategic business consultants and restaurant owners on novel problems related to restaurant management. The consultants outperformed the restaurant owners, despite their lack of restaurant experience. Analyses suggested that consultants engaged in more theoretical reasoning, which was enabled by the variety of experiences those consultants had in their work.

Meta-cognitive skills, abstract general reasoning, and critical reasoning are likely influences of within and cross-domain transfer of expertise (Billing, 2007; Kimball & Holyoak, 2000). Reviewing the cognitive psychology literature, Billing (2007) found considerable evidence that instructional design affects skill transfer in higher education. Billing provided a series of instructional strategies to support transfer, which are too numerous to repeat here, but they are easily accessible in his article and overlap substantially with the strategies we include in the Appendix to this chapter.

Despite the primary focus on experts, adaptive expertise researchers emphasize that adaptability can be displayed at any stage of skill development, from novices, to advanced learners, to experts. Adaptability is not a matter of the quantity or quality of knowledge acquired, but rather how that knowledge is used to support high-level reasoning processes and problem-solving strategies (Crawford & Brophy, 2006). Moving along the continuum toward adaptive expertise is an effortful process that can lead to increased errors and decreased performance during transitional periods occurring throughout learning processes. It is, therefore, important to foster an innovation mindset early on and adopt the view that errors are beneficial for learning (Bransford & Schwartz, 1999; Keith & Frese, 2008).

Advanced Learning

As noted earlier, CLT research focuses on the early skill acquisition of novice learners, whereas the study of highly skilled expert performers is the focus of expertise research. A recent attempt to connect the CLT and expertise literatures (van Gog, et al., 2005) was prompted by CLT findings that instructional methods suitable for novices can be less effective or even dysfunctional for advanced learners (expert reversal effect; Kalyuga, Ayres, Chandler, & Sweller, 2003). However, CLT methods can, in some cases, be appropriately modified for use with more advanced learners, for example, by instructing learners to engage in self-explanation and envision their next steps (van Gog et al., 2005).

Advanced learners, whose skills fall somewhere between novices and experts, are the subjects of instructional research with medical students (Feltovich, Spiro, & Coulson, 1993). The goals of advanced knowledge acquisition are the deep understanding of complex information and the ability to apply this knowledge to new situations. The flexible use of knowledge requires deep understanding, which is particularly important for applying knowledge in ill-structured domains (Feltovich et al., 1993), such as medicine and management. Educational methods commonly used with novices can impede later advanced learning, partially by reinforcing learners' misconceptions that come from their inclinations to oversimplify complex material. For example, Feltovich and colleagues (Feltovich et al., 1993) found that simplifying strategies, such as teaching topics in isolation, presenting common scenarios but not exceptions, and testing for rote memory, interfere with advanced learning. This conclusion is consistent with the body of learning research on cognitive and motor skills that has found that conditions of practice that present difficulties for learners can decrease performance during and immediately following training while benefiting retention and transfer. These "desirable difficulties" (Bjork, 2009, p. 314) include providing less specific (Goodman & Wood, 2004; 2009), delayed, infrequent, or summarized feedback; introducing variability by providing experience with a representative sample of tasks and task conditions; randomizing the order of tasks and topics instead of presenting them in a blocked fashion; and spacing over time rather than massing training sessions (Bjork, 1994; Schmidt & Bjork, 1992).

Scaffolding researchers also emphasize the importance of striking a balance between providing supportive structure and "problematizing," by guiding learners into complexities and difficulties that will benefit learning. Supportive structure should provide only enough guidance to avoid undue frustration and confusion and a total lack of progress. Scaffolding should be used to support performance processes that would not be possible without assistance (Reiser, 2004). However, many tutors and instructors do not necessarily provide scaffolding in a way that optimizes independent performance (Merrill, Reiser, Merrill, & Landes, 1995; VanLehn, Siler, Murray, Yamauchi, & Baggett, 2003). Although most learning occurs when learners experience impasses, tutors often provide guidance and modeling that prevents impasses. When learners make errors, tutors tend to identify them immediately and demonstrate how to correct errors, without giving learners the chance to try to correct the errors themselves (Merrill et al., 1995; VanLehn et al., 2003).

VanLehn et al. (2003) concluded that the most effective tutors create opportunities for learners to make errors. They identify errors if learners do not detect them themselves, but allow learners to figure out how to recover from and correct their errors. Effective tutors also prompt learners to explain their errors and identify corrections, and only provide explanations when learners are unable to do so (VanLehn et al., 2003). The conclusions from this research concur with error management training research demonstrating the positive effects of communicating the benefits of errors to learners and providing active exploration training on transfer (Keith & Frese, 2008). The scaffolding literature affirms an important point: instructors often have difficulty stopping themselves from correcting learners' errors.

Contrary to the scaffolding literature and research on advanced learners, the results of some CLT research suggests advantages to decreasing intrinsic cognitive load by beginning instruction with simplified tasks, and then increasing task complexity after isolated concepts have been acquired (isolated–interacting-elements approach, Pollock et al., 2002; van Merriënboer, Kester, & Paas, 2006). However, CLT researchers recognize the potential for compromised understanding that can result from task simplification (Pollock et al., 2002). The evidence in favor of integrated instruction (e.g., Feltovich et al., 1993) leads us to suspect that the results of studies of the isolated–interacting elements approach may be limited to novice learners, and that early simplification could have delayed negative effects on subsequent advanced learning.

Feltovich et al. (1993) presented a series of strategies derived from learning theories and their research that are consistent with the integration of "desirable difficulties" (Bjork, 2009, p. 314) into instructional design. For example, they recommended providing direct challenges to students' misconceptions, clustering related concepts together rather than teaching each in isolation, helping students cope with complexity instead of simplifying material, and engaging students in active cognitive processing. They also provided a number of recommendations for the use of cases, which are particularly relevant for management education. According to Feltovich and colleagues (1993), cases should be used to integrate the learning of knowledge and its application to support the development of reasoning skills. Notably, this type of integrated instruction challenges conventional wisdom that acquiring declarative knowledge precedes procedural knowledge. Feltovich et al. (1993) also recommended using multiple cases and scenarios that differ in their surface structures (cover stories) and deep structures (applicable concepts, rules, procedures), and emphasizing the relationships among the cases.

Application to Management Education Practices

We now turn to the matter of applying the preceding evidence to commonly used practices in management education. Our goal is to provide a model for evidence-based teaching practice. In doing so, we hope to inspire the management education community to bring its practice into closer alignment with learning theory and research.

Many commonly used instructional methods in management and business schools were developed and implemented for practical reasons, like efficient delivery of instruction to large groups. Others may have appeared to promote learning but may have drifted away from this focus over time as attention shifted to teaching ratings and school rankings (Khurana, 2007). Others were driven by an objective to promote the active engagement of students in the learning process. This is an admirable objective that is supported by evidence, but whether active engagement moves students along the path to adaptive expertise and supports transfer depends on the design and implementation of specific teaching practices. Unfortunately, many common practices

appear to have been designed around fragmented, casual knowledge of how people learn, promoted by teaching lore with a hint of evidence built in.

We would like to emphasize at the outset that teaching methods are not inherently evidence-based (or evidence deficient), *per se*. Rather, whether the practices are consistent with the evidence depends on how instructors design and implement them. For example, the case teaching method can be applied either in an evidence-based fashion that promotes learning and transfer or in a way that is merely engaging and interesting, but does not develop valuable or enduring capabilities. We wholeheartedly agree that, "a challenge facing educational researchers is to discover instructional methods that promote appropriate processing in learners rather than methods that promote hands-on activity or group discussion as ends in themselves" (Mayer, 2004, p. 14). With this goal of promoting transfer-appropriate cognitive processing firmly in mind, we now turn to consideration of widely used management education practices.

Lecture

Lecturing is a customary and enduring form of instructional delivery in higher education. Perhaps the major problem with the lecture is that it consigns the learner to a fairly passive role as a member of an audience. This method has the added deficiency of providing little feedback to the instructor about student understanding. Bligh (2000) cites evidence that the lecture is comparable to other methods for conveying information, but it is relatively ineffective for changing attitudes and teaching behavioral skills.

In addition, the exclusive use of lecturing or the sequencing of lectures followed by more engaging activities contradicts evidence that an integrated approach to instruction early on supports more advanced, later learning and fosters transfer (Crawford & Brophy, 2006; Feltovich et al., 1993). Therefore, we recommend that lectures be combined with other teaching methods in a way that integrates content learning with its application. Short, minilectures can be interspersed with cases or other activities. Students' direct questions about course material they read or otherwise encountered, as well as students' misconceptions, identified during activities and discussions, may also suggest impromptu minilectures. This type of lecturing can provide an opportunity to model problem-solving processes, akin to a verbal worked example (Renkl et al., 2004) or walk-through, and consistent with social learning theory (Bandura, 1986). We view lecturing as a type of scaffolding that should be used when students have tried and are unable to understand or apply material on their own (Reiser, 2004).

The cognitive load imposed by the content of lectures is a concern. Consistent with CLT, carefully designed verbal or written worked examples increase germane cognitive load, however, digressions or excessive detail often distract learners and increase extraneous load. In general, we tend to convey too much detail in lectures. This particular error echoes Rousseau's admonition (2009, personal communication) that, in the management classroom, we perhaps ought to seek to teach less material in better, more skillful ways.

Class Discussion

Discussion is a useful complement to lecture, as it can promote increased engagement among learners while providing feedback on class and individual learning to instructors. It also represents a potentially more open, democratic approach to learning than the lecture, which harnesses the social context of the class to help meet learning goals. Managing discussion can be challenging, because learners may be reluctant to contribute or may engage in hard-to-integrate digressions. There is a body of literature on techniques for leading discussion, asking questions in ways that promote deeper discussions, and increasing student contribution (e.g., Hill, 1977). For some instructors, it may be difficult to give up apparent control of the learning environment (Tompkins, 1990), out of fear that anarchy will ensue or that learning objectives will be missed.

The value of skillfully facilitated class discussions rests in its encouragement of errors and acceptance of misapprehensions as opportunities for learning and development. This calls for courage on the part of learners, in the face of anxiety about performance and perceived loss of face that many assume accompanies "being wrong." In management education, neutralizing the fear of contributing to class discussion is an important objective. This allows discussion to serve as an opportunity for risk-taking and the testing of new ideas in a critical but supportive environment.

From an evidence-informed perspective, management educators should ask questions that will allow misconceptions to emerge in discussion and confront them directly and nonpunitively, in a way that encourages learning from errors (Crawford & Brophy, 2006; Feltovich, et al., 1993). Further,

discussion leaders can contribute to the development of reasoning skills typical of good social science practice by modeling these skills during discussions. They can probe unclear or incomplete responses or contributions, ask for summarizing and integrative comments, provide or prompt for alternative explanations, and expose and address flaws and errors in logic. This kind of active, reflective responding in class can be valuable for creating self-directed learning strategies. These, in turn, may endure and support future learning, consistent with the principles of developing adaptive expertise (Bransford & Schwartz, 1999; Hatano & Ouro, 2003). Over time, it is probably also appropriate to fade the scaffolding that instructors provide to class discussions, to transition the responsibility to students (Reiser, 2004; Sherin, Reiser, & Edelson, 2004) for initiating the elaboration of points and the productive critique of peer comments.

Thus far, our treatment of discussion practice has focused on matters of form for class discussion. Next, we turn to the activities that provide the context and substance for discussion, because discussion is integral to the administration of experiential exercises and case teaching.

Experiential Exercises

Experiential exercises are popular management education activities that involve role-playing, problem-solving, or other hands-on activities (e.g., puzzles, building towers). They are readily available commercially (e.g., Dispute Resolution Research Center (DRRC), Kellogg School of Management), featured to varying degrees in textbooks, and published in peer-reviewed sources like the *Journal of Management Education*.

Experiential exercises vary in the degree to which they are grounded in management theory and research. For example, the exercises published by the DRRC tend to be based on negotiation and decision-making research, which facilitates the integrative application of theory and research findings in the execution and debriefing of the exercises. However, like anything else, it comes down to how individual instructors use the exercises. For example, the Carter Racing exercise (Brittain & Sitkin, 1986) was designed to expose a number of common decision-making process errors (e.g., sampling on the dependent variable, framing decisions as a choice between two losses, escalation of commitment). It was also developed as a context in which learners can practice and develop skills, such as effective decision framing, accurate computation of expected values, and prediction, using historical data. However, some instructors simplify the exercise to address only one or a small number of the issues (e.g., groupthink) that are represented in this exercise. We see this oversimplification as a missed opportunity to help students learn to deal with the realistic complexity afforded by the Carter Racing exercise. Other exercises and role-plays similarly can be oversimplified, decreasing their value for learning and transfer.

Simplicity is a deliberate feature of other popular exercises, including survival exercises (e.g., Desert Survival) and those involving puzzles or building with children's toys. These types of exercises typically are designed to highlight just one or a small number of points about difficulties coordinating group activities or biases that may occur in team decision making. Although these exercises may address validated concepts, they do not conform to many of the evidence-based teaching principles listed in the Appendix. They present concepts in an isolated manner and often require no more than cursory application of content knowledge to complete the exercise. In addition, the application often comes after the exercise, and is not integrated into the activity itself. These types of activities may be fun and engaging for (some) students. They may also help students to encode a small number of fairly isolated concepts. However, given the class time and effort they require, it is unlikely that they do enough to support complex schema development and to help prepare students for the complex problems they are likely to encounter in later learning or during their organizational lives.

Some popular self-assessment exercises, like the MBTI, color-coded teamwork styles, and learning styles assessments have received conflicting or no support from the research literature (McCrae & Costa, 1989; Pittenger, 1993; Pashler, McDaniel, Rohrer, & Bjork, 2009). Instructors may justify using these self-assessments because of students' immediate, positive affective responses to them or because they believe they facilitate growth in self-awareness. This may be true, but it is not at all clear to us how an unsubstantiated approach could support the instructional goals we have laid out in this chapter.

We recommend that more complex exercises be used and that their complexity be preserved, as in our preceding Carter Racing example. In addition, using a series of exercises or an exercise with multiple phases can further promote learning and transfer of domain and meta-cognitive skills. For example, a series of negotiation role-play exercises could be used that require students to iteratively apply overlapping sets of evidence-based negotiation concepts and practices. Between exercises, students should be coached to engage in self-reflection and self-evaluation of their role-play performance, including how well they applied negotiation concepts and practices and what they need to learn and do to improve their application in future role-plays. They should also be required to do an evidence-based analysis of the causes of the conflicts written into the exercise instructions and experienced during the role-plays. These activities can help to maximize the impact of the exercise on learner meta-cognition, setting the stage for future learning and practice.

If properly designed and implemented, exercises also afford the opportunity to explicitly teach learners how to collect and interpret feedback from multiple sources, including observations of themselves and peers during the exercise itself and after-action feedback from peers and instructors. To promote schema development, exercises should be set up and debriefed to capture and contextualize learning and identify problems and unresolved issues. Instructors should also seek to collect and analyze data to validate what was learned and support evidence-based refinement of exercises over successive administrations. These supporting structures for exercises can promote deeper, more mindful engagement with the exercises on the part of both learners and instructors.

Our recommendations are consistent with deliberate practice activities (Ericsson et al., 1993) in that they are structured, monitored, and involve repeated engagement with similar tasks. However, the limited time and other resources typical of educational settings often restrict the ability to provide the individualized design and guidance, intensity of practice, and amount of repetition recommended by Ericsson and colleagues (1993).

Cases and the Case Teaching Method

Cases typically describe a real or realistic organizational situation, from the point of view of a particular manager, other employee, or set of actors. The business cases typically used in management education usually include problems that need to be solved and decisions that need to be made. Cases can take several forms including written accounts, video depictions, computerized interactive simulations, and multimedia formats. We typically think of written cases as being fairly long, like those published by Harvard, Ivey, Darden, and others. However, broadly conceived, cases also include short scenarios that are readily available in textbooks or may be written by instructors for specific purposes.

The appeal of cases for management education may rest in part on their narrative structure, as well as the knowledge that cases often are drawn from actual managerial practice "in the wild," frequently including recognizable companies and products. Yet, from an EBMgt perspective, cases may also be exemplary platforms for the discussion of the judgment and expertise of practicing managers and the integrative application of management theories and concepts.

The case teaching method is an overarching strategy for management education originally based on practice at Northwestern University's Kellogg School of Management and the Harvard Business School. This method of instruction relies on the use of cases in class settings in which learners discuss the elements of the case to develop a recommended course of action for the decision-makers depicted in the case. In the Harvard Business School construal of the case method, instructor intervention is minimized and limited to discussion facilitation. There are a number of sources that address strategies for teaching written cases along these lines (Mauffette-Leenders, Erskine, & Leenders, 2003), as well as materials for students on how to learn from cases under this approach (Ellet, 2007). The authors have experience with this approach from the perspective of having attended the case discussion leadership workshop at Harvard Business School and the case teaching workshop at the Ivey School of Business.

The traditional case teaching method has both advocates (Christensen & Carlile, 2009) and critics (Shugan, 2006; Chipman, 2009). Shugan (2006) asserts that, "… the traditional case method of teaching often ignores important research findings…. Students lose the benefit of important research findings while leaving the classroom with false confidence about what they know" (p. 109). In contrast, Mauffette-Leenders, Erskine, and Leenders, (2003) are quite clear about the central role of relevant theories and concepts to the case method of teaching. To this end, case teaching notes

often contain relevant references, and students may be assigned supplementary readings in parallel with cases. In practice, this may be a matter of execution, because instructors vary in the emphasis they place on theory. Although neglect of theory is a potential pitfall of the case teaching method, it is not necessarily a property of the method *per se*. In addition, Shugan (2006) cites Argyris (1980) in arguing that it may be more accurate to describe case teaching methods, rather than method, because there is variance in case teaching practice across and even within individual instructors and universities.

Like experiential exercises, cases vary in the extent to which their design supports the application of management theory and research to practical problems. We regularly have to read through dozens of commercially available cases before finding one that is consistent with this criterion. In addition, cases tend to be written in a way that encourages a bias toward action, which may support learners' tendencies to engage in superficial causal analysis in favor of reaching the specific goal of quickly choosing a solution. Also, few cases implicitly favor a solution that defers action, argues for more time for the situation to develop, or requires more or better data, despite the consideration that these responses may be legitimate under particular circumstances.

USING CASES TO INTEGRATE THEORY AND PRACTICE

Some cases lend themselves very well to integrating the acquisition of evidence-based knowledge and its application to practice. For example, Vista-Sci Healthcare Inc. (Gandz, 2004) provides the opportunity to apply evidence about person-job fit, in terms of personality, values, and competencies, in the context of a personnel promotion decision. The *Rogers Cable: First Time Right Program* (Martens, 2007) case lends itself to evidence-based causal analysis about performance problems, as well as the development of evidence-based solutions for job design and reward systems. The *Overhead Reduction Taskforce* (Wageman & Hackman, 1999) case combines written background information with a video case that depicts a team running into a number of difficulties as they work on a two-week project. The case was designed around recommendations for the effective design and leadership of teams derived primarily from Hackman and colleagues' program of research. During class, the video is stopped at various critical points in the team's work, and analysis centers on evaluating the team processes and performance, diagnosing the causes of the problems experienced, and developing recommendations for solving and preventing problems. The case has many evidence-based practical lessons for learners to use in their course project teams and other current and future teams, such as agreeing to ground rules early in the team's development and engaging in team reflection and self-assessment during and following teamwork. The case is also useful for creating an appreciation for the need for team contracts, which student project teams can prepare after the case.

USING CASES TO PROMOTE EVIDENCE-BASED CAUSAL ANALYSIS

The use of cases can be enhanced further by designing instructions and case preparation questions that focus on evidence-based causal analysis prior to solution generation and leading case discussion and simulation execution along these lines. This approach is consistent with the recommendation to provide nonspecific goals (i.e., figure out the causes), which promotes working forward through the case, instead of backward from a specific goal (i.e., identifying a solution), in support of schema construction and transfer (Sweller, Mawer, & Howe, 1982).

For example, *The Managers Workshop* (Dunham, 2004) is an interactive computer simulation that provides the opportunity to increase understanding of motivation (e.g., expectancy, equity) and attribution theories in the context of managing five poorly performing sales representatives. On the surface, the five employees have similar performance problems, but the underlying causes are different. Students have a tendency to make their management decisions based on "common sense" or trial-and-error and then working backward to figure out what went wrong. To counteract this tendency and support schema construction and transfer, instructors should assign the nonspecific goal of determining the causes of the performance problems and basing managerial actions on those causes, while steering students away from outcome goals (e.g., to reach sales goals, to solve the problem by firing or otherwise punishing an employee) they may set for themselves. In addition, monitoring and guidance are needed to prompt students to choose managerial actions on the basis of the relevant theories as they interact with the simulation. This will help students learn to correctly interpret the reactions of the sales representatives (i.e., feedback) to their management decisions. This is consistent with guided-exploration strategies advocated in the organizational literature (e.g., Debowski, Wood, & Bandura, 2001). The guidance should be faded as learners begin to monitor and manage their own performance strategies (Reiser, 2004) by keeping track of their own performance processes, engaging in self-evaluation, carefully interpreting the feedback from the simulation, and planning and responding in more mindful, evidence-informed ways. Through the repeated use of this simulation, we have observed that students have an easier time managing the employees when they do the extensive cognitive work involved in engaging in evidence-based causal analysis in the process of working through the simulation. This may decrease the extraneous cognitive load associated with the trial and error approach and increase the germane load associated with using productive strategies (Sweller et al., 1998). It also represents the coordinated efforts between hypothesis development and testing that supports rule induction (Klahr & Dunbar, 1988; Simon & Lea, 1974).

USING SHORT OR MINIMAL CASES

Transfer-appropriate processes also can be supported with short case scenarios that depict problem situations. For example, textbooks and other sources often include a series of conflict scenarios (as well as scenarios on decision making, leadership, and other topics) that vary in length from a few sentences to a couple of paragraphs. All the scenarios incorporate some sort of organizational conflict, but they differ in terms of the circumstances and parties involved and the underlying causes of the conflict. Using an assortment of brief scenarios that vary in their surface features and deep structures can be useful for learning to distinguish important from irrelevant features of problems. This sort of stimulus variability supports discriminant learning of the circumstances under which different responses apply and do not apply (Anderson, 1982) and the development of, "more elaborate and flexible mental representations" (Ghodsian, Bjork, & Benjamin, 1997, p. 83) characteristic of adaptive expertise (Crawford & Brophy, 2006; Feltovich et al., 1993). It is also consistent with recommendations for engaging in deliberate practice to support the development of expertise (Ericsson et al., 1993). Explicit discussion and acknowledgment of similarities and differences in surface and deep structures of problems would further support the learning process.

No matter what case formats we choose, we ought to use cases that illustrate exceptions as well as those that are prototypical, in the interests of promoting deeper reasoning and less reliance on superficial or commonsensical strategies for problem-solving. We should also emphasize relations across cases, as well as other examples that were given by the instructor and students over the course of the semester, to promote connections across course topics, the development of more-elaborated schemata, and deep learning (Feltovich et al. 1993).

CALL FOR ADDITIONAL CASES

Overall, we recommend that case writers, course developers, and instructors explore ways to better integrate theory and practice in the cases they construct and adopt. In addition, it would be valuable to have some exemplary cases that depict managers using the same analytic processes we seek to instill in our students. These could serve as worked examples or models of expert practice. For example, the *Gary Loveman and Harrah's Entertainment* (Chang & Pfeffer, 2003) case provides a model of a manager using data to make decisions, which is consistent with the principles of EBMgt. These types of cases can be further enhanced by depicting managers applying and integrating relevant organizational research into their decision-making processes.

The development of such cases would facilitate the fading of worked examples, with each successive case requiring more analysis on the part of the student. For example, a complete exemplar could be provided with the first case, including problem identification and representation, causal analysis, and analysis-based solutions. The second case would provide a model for problem identification and causal analysis, but leave the analysis-based solution identification to the students. The third case would provide a partial model of the causal analysis, and so forth.

Projects

Projects, especially team projects, are commonly assigned in management courses. The same types of instructional practices we have been describing all along can be applied in the design of projects. Students can be assigned to choose a company to work with or a situation presented in the business press, identify and define problems, engage in evidence-based analysis of the causes of problems, and develop analysis-based, practical solutions. As with formal cases, the causal analysis would rely on evidence from organizational theory and research. This could be supplemented with data collection, when students are working with companies on current problems. Instruction, feedback, and other guidance provided to learners over the course of their projects should be designed to encourage deep cognitive processing relative to the company's problems and self-monitoring, self-evaluation, and self-instruction on the part of the learners. Projects can also be used to support iterative problem-solving, by which students perform part of the project, receive appropriate feedback, and make revisions before moving on to the next part of the project. Instructor-provided feedback should require reflective action on the part of the learner, and students should be required to use the feedback for continuous learning and project development.

Consecutive projects or the use of cases followed by projects can be used to fade scaffolding. For example, in the *Manager's Workshop* (Dunham, 2004) simulation, students could be told which theories and concepts apply to the management of the sales representatives. In a subsequent project, students could be required to identify applicable theories and concepts on their own, with appropriate guidance only when necessary.

Group projects also present an opportunity for students to learn to work in and manage teams. In organizational behavior courses, students can directly integrate what they are learning about research on team processes with the application of this research to their current project teams. For example, the *Overhead Reduction Taskforce* (Wageman & Hackman, 1999) case, discussed earlier, along with relevant assigned readings (e.g., Hackman & Wageman, 2006; Wageman, Fisher, & Hackman, 2009) are useful for introducing teams research, demonstrating the importance of effective team design and management, and encouraging students to manage their teams in accordance with lessons from teams research. In future courses, instructors can remind students of the lessons learned from teams research and reinforce application of these lessons in new project teams.

Challenges Associated with Evidence-Based Teaching

The challenges associated with the successful implementation of evidence-based teaching come from the nature of our subject matter, the institutions and systems in which we work, our students and colleagues, and finally ourselves. Misconceptions and partial understandings about learning processes and effective teaching practices present significant challenges. They may be the result of inadequate teaching training available for doctoral students and faculty, and may be reinforced by the resources commonly used for information on teaching strategies and classroom activities. "Teaching tips" of dubious value may be handed down through generations of faculty, published in newsletters or online, or presented by well-meaning colleagues whose teaching is highly rated by students or by those who have authored popular textbooks. The tendency to rely on such sources is exacerbated by those who see teaching activity as a trade-off against time that could be spent engaged in research. Unfortunately, some of these erroneous beliefs are reinforced in the academic and practitioner literatures. For example, the provision of performance feedback (Goodman & Wood, 2004; 2009) and setting of performance goals (Burns & Vollmeyer, 2002; Vollmeyer & Burns, 2002) are two significant areas in which common misconceptions can give rise to ineffective teaching strategies.

Even armed with accurate information, faculty members may be reluctant or unwilling to incorporate "desirable difficulties" and other lessons from the learning literatures because of direct and indirect, real and perceived pressures from their universities and students. It is common practice to use student course evaluations as the sole measure of teaching effectiveness and for the results of these assessments to be used for raise, promotion, and tenure decisions. Unreasonable demands from students for limiting ambiguity, decreasing their workload, making assignments and exams easier, and giving them high grades are often hard to resist, even for those of us who know better. The situation is further complicated by evidence that some instructional strategies that support transfer are likely to have a negative impact on proximal performance (Bjork, 1994; Schmidt & Bjork, 1992), and instructors are likely to encounter resistance from students whose grades suffer. These and other pressures likely contribute to too much "hand holding" in the form of overly structured assignments and providing detailed PowerPoint slides, notes, and study guides that decrease the cognitive burden on students, while simultaneously limiting their learning and preparation for future learning. Even without student pressures, it is difficult to withhold

immediate responses to errors and consistently promote students' deep cognitive processing, as the scaffolding literature has demonstrated (Merrill et al., 1995; VanLehn et al., 2003).

Many of these pressures could be alleviated with cross-curriculum coordination. Ideally this would involve all university courses, within and outside of management, adopting evidence-based teaching strategies and focusing efforts on building general cognitive capabilities, such as meta-cognitive and critical-reasoning skills, in the contexts of their fields. It would also require professors from various disciplines to learn about other disciplines and emphasize to their students the similar problem-solving skills and processes that are applicable across disciplines. There is precedent for this in the communications field, where "writing across the curriculum," an approach that considers the importance and value of effective writing across disciplines, has informed thinking and practice in undergraduate education and curriculum development (Cosgrove & Barta-Smith, 2004).

Another challenge stems from a belief among some management researchers that they do not have much to contribute to practice. The consequence of this mistaken belief is that instructors may elevate applied experiences and the views of executives above research-based knowledge, rather than taking advantage of the benefits of careful integration of knowledge from these sources. Instructors may treat theories and their associated research results as information students need to "know," rather than something they ought to understand deeply and learn to apply. We believe these approaches undervalue the applicability of management theories and research, oversimplify complex information and processes, and reinforce the instructional separation of more complex domain knowledge from practical skills. Management academics should be heartened by findings like those of Raufaste et al. (1998) that demonstrate that the deliberate, explicit reasoning that academics commonly use in their work is beneficial when applied to organizational practice.

Textbooks that include discrete "theory" chapters and "practice" chapters also exacerbate this separation of research from practice. For example, the topic of motivation is often presented in two separate chapters, with one chapter including expectancy, equity, and other theories of motivation, and another chapter covering options for reward systems, job design, and other techniques. The latter are typically based on research, but an artificial distinction is made between foundational theories and applied research and practice. This disjunction does little to facilitate the skilled application of theories and gives the false impression that theory-based research and practice are distinct concerns for distinct constituencies. Also, questions identified as "application" items in test banks often have little to do with the application of theory. Instead, they tend to assess rote memorization of terms associated with particular techniques and questions about the effectiveness of the techniques as drivers of performance, motivation, and job attitudes. This supports the partial and rather superficial integration of the acquisition of domain knowledge with its application. In keeping with the learning literatures, we urge a more comprehensive and deeper integration.

The content and structure of textbooks, especially for survey courses, may contribute to an apparent tendency to cover a large number of topics and a large number of concepts, theories, and practices, within each topic. In addition to a sizable amount of evidence-based information, textbooks also typically include popular, but unsupported theories (e.g., Maslow's needs hierarchy, situational leadership theory), concepts (e.g., Goleman's version of emotional intelligence), and assessment instruments (e.g., MBTI). (See Pearce, chapter 21 of this volume.) These are occasionally treated as though they are evidence-based or presented as useful despite the acknowledged lack of evidentiary support. In other cases, the lack of research support is pointed out to students, but students often miss the point. Reaching our instructional goals may require paring down the number of topics, concepts, theories, and practical applications to better balance depth of learning and breath of coverage, manage cognitive load, and ultimately support transfer.

Our goals of preparing students for future learning and promoting the transfer of skills to their future work environments are likely impeded by common instructor and course assessment practices. The assessment of educational achievement tends to occur during and immediately following a course, which can confound transient effects of instruction with more permanent learning effects (Schmidt & Bjork, 1992; Wulf & Schmidt, 1994). Transient effects are sustained by the supports provided during instruction. They do not persist with the removal of supports and do not transfer across time or changing task and contextual conditions. True learning effects are more enduring and resistant to the removal of supports and changes in context and task characteristics (Christina & Bjork, 1991; Schmidt & Bjork, 1992).

Assessing former students' use of course material in their jobs presents obvious practical difficulties in terms of assigning grades upon course completion, accessing job performance data, and validly assessing relevant job performance. Nonetheless, our assessments of student learning need to be improved to better support our educational goals. First, instead of separate tests or test items that assess the retention of declarative knowledge, we can give assessments (i.e., exams, case write-ups, simulations, projects) that evaluate the ability to apply knowledge to real or realistic organizational problems. Correct responses would be indicative of a combination of knowledge acquisition and the ability to apply the knowledge, which is consistent with recommendations for integrated instruction (Crawford & Brophy, 2006; Feltovich et al. 1993; Reiser, 2004; Simon & Lea, 1974). For example, students could be given scenarios and asked to make evidence-based judgments about the causes of problems, and then to identify suitable solutions given those causes. The scenarios would be designed to differ from one another and from those presented during instruction in terms of both surface and deep structures. Learning would be assessed on tasks that differ from those encountered during formal instruction, with minimal guidance, and, if possible, separated in time from initial instruction (e.g., later in the semester, during finals week). However, the time between instruction and assessment may be more important for retention tests than for assessments of transfer to modified tasks (Ghodsian, Bjork, & Benjamin, 1997).

A shift in focus from summative (i.e., grades) to formative assessment with purely developmental purposes would also support reaching our instructional goals. This shift could facilitate refocusing students from outcome goals (e.g., "I want to get an A.") to the processes of learning (e.g., "I want to understand and develop adaptive skills."), which could benefit transfer. Of course, the prospect of eliminating formal grades is unrealistic at most universities. Nevertheless, simulations and projects that allow for experimentation and revision, with suitable levels of guidance and developmental feedback, could be incorporated into the design of courses. However, there are continuing concerns for the time required to evaluate and reevaluate students' work, a lack of help from qualified (or any) teaching assistants, and the possibility that many students will persist in their focus on grades.

An additional challenge is the fact that the management domain is not clearly defined. This may be due to the domain's permeable and fuzzy boundaries. Much of the expertise research is done in complex, but well-defined domains, with clear boundaries, such as chess and sports. In addition, management is not a profession in the same sense as medicine or accounting. There is no formal set of professional standards or comprehensive set of identifiable responsibilities. At this point, we do not know what a true management expert looks like, and there are currently no objective ways of identifying management experts. The field would benefit from identifying management experts and using knowledge elicitation methods (Ericsson, 2006b; Hoffman, Crandall, & Shadbolt, 1998) to study their knowledge and skills. The processes involved in the development of management expertise also should be examined, including the deliberate practice and other instructional strategies used as learners progress from novices to advanced learners to experts. Information about the domain knowledge needed by management experts and effective (and ineffective) developmental methods and processes would be valuable input for instructional design.

Finally, it is unrealistic to expect business students to search through, read, understand, and apply the academic management literature at the same level as academics who regularly consume and perform research. (See Werner, chapter 15 of this volume.) In addition, many universities withdraw library privileges upon graduation, so even if graduates had the skill and motivation to search and use the literature, access would be an issue. Having a large body of systematic reviews, available free of charge in accessible online locations, would certainly be advantageous (Briner, Denyer & Rousseau, 2009). In the meantime, we can use evidence-based teaching principles to help our students gain content knowledge from imperfect textbooks and other sources, to evaluate the merits of this knowledge, and to develop their problem-solving, critical reasoning, and meta-cognitive skills in the context of applying the knowledge to management problems. Along the way, we can help them gain an appreciation for systematic thinking about management

problems and for the applicability of management research to management practice. We can require students to use some academic research articles in their practical research projects, providing guidance as needed. We can also encourage them to practice their skills in their work, school, and volunteer activities; show them how to distinguish between resources that are largely opinion based and those that are primarily evidence-based (e.g., academically oriented books, journals, and annual review journals; the more evidence-based practitioner journals), and point them to some evidence-informed resources that may be helpful to them in the future.

Conclusion

Theory and research findings from cognitive and instructional psychology and education can help us develop evidenced-based instructional strategies for management education. We refer readers to the Appendix for descriptions of a number of instructional strategies derived from these theories.

Evidence-based teaching has the potential to promote processing in learners that leads to better transfer of skills and knowledge to the workplace and contributes to the emergence of adaptive expertise. We also anticipate possible supplemental effects, along the following lines. When future and current managers observe and experience the consistent modeling of evidence-based teaching practices in their professional education, they will be well positioned to adopt and adapt those practices in support of the learning and development of others. In this way, the evidence-based teaching practices we use may have indirect benefits for other organizational members, above and beyond the principal benefits for instructors and learners that we address in this chapter.

If you seek to adopt evidence-based teaching strategies in your own practice, the chapter and Appendix suggest a myriad of things you can do, right now. Foremost among these may be recognizing that this path will likely be difficult, because of various current institutional arrangements, as well as the fact that much of what we suggest here calls for a trade-off of short-term advantages for the benefits of deeper learning, improved transfer of training, better preparation for practice (including future learning), and improvements in skills related to meta-cognition and critical thinking.

Appendix Overview of Evidence-Based Instructional Strategies

Instructional strategy	Description	Mechanisms	Literature sources & implementation issues
1. Fading worked examples	• Model protocol shows the steps taken to complete a problem. • Critical features are annotated to show what the steps are intended to illustrate. • Start with complete worked example (including the final solution), then sequentially remove solved steps (backward or forward) in subsequent worked examples to progressively give the learner responsibility for problem-solving. • Later problems are solved by learners in their entirety.	• Decreases extraneous cognitive load compared to conventional problems (where students start out solving whole problems, and use means-end strategies) to free resources for schema building around understanding and learning procedural steps, in the context of the whole task. • Fading helps students to experience impasses on parts of problem they work out themselves, and prompts self-explanations. • Additional prompting or instruction on self-explanation may be needed to ensure that freed cognitive resources are being used to promote understanding. Fading helps this, but also needs to make sure the worked parts of the example are being properly studied.	**Literature source** • CLT (worked example and completion effects) **Issues and proposals** • Possible issues with generalizability from the task domains examined (e.g., algebra, statistics, computer programming). • Calls for a library of examples, annotations, and protocols. • Takes time to administer this approach. • Instructors need to ensure that freed-up cognitive resources are applied to understanding. • Can give students a scenario and model (verbal, written, demonstration) how it should be solved (where and how to gather information for causal analysis, how to draw conclusions, how to develop cause-based recommendations). With successive scenarios, give students responsibility for performing more and more steps.
2. Non-specific goals	• Provide a general goal for a problem (e.g., identify causes of problem, find as many variables as possible, etc.) instead of describing the desired end-AU:state/specific goal (e.g., reach a specific performance level, solve for X, etc.).	• Novices use means-end analysis to solve problems because they do not have the schemata needed to work forward. • Specific outcome goals increase the use of means-end strategies. Means-end is an efficient strategy for reaching a solution, but it does not promote schema construction. • Providing a general goal decreases the cognitive load associated with means-end strategy, freeing resources for schema construction as learners focus on the problem states and the processes that move them forward.	**Literature sources** • CLT (goal-free effect) • Dual space theory for rule induction • Educational psychology **Issues and proposals** • Generalizability from task domains studied may be an issue. • In management education, can ask open-ended questions; avoid setting page limits; use ambiguity strategically to promote exploration of problem space, consideration of assumptions, and creative responding.

(Continued)

		• Less specific goals also support systematic exploration, but some learners also need direct instruction for how to systematically test hypotheses.	• Students may become anxious about performance when expectations are not directly and unambiguously described. • It may be helpful to adopt a managerial frame of reference, telling students that managers proactively identify and solve problems without explicit direction or supervision.
3. Interacting elements	• When concepts are interdependent, teach them together. • Emphasize their connections, interdependence, and variance in how they interact across contexts. • Instead of simplifying material, help learners to cope with complexity.	• Focusing on concepts in isolation gives the false impression that they are independent and facilitates learners' tendency toward oversimplification. • Integrated instruction promotes understanding of individual concepts and how they interact. • Task simplification that benefits novices' learning initially can hurt them later, during more advanced learning.	**Literature sources** • Advanced knowledge acquisition. • Adaptive expertise. **Issues and proposals** • This strategy imposes high cognitive load. • Novices and possibly advanced learners will likely need support for coping with the complexity. Strategies such as providing written and modeled worked examples may provide the support needed for schema development for complex tasks. • Further research may be required in the management domain, where multivariate interactions are a likely domain property.
4. Deliberate practice	• Design tasks for practicing the essential skills needed in performance domains that address the specific weaknesses of the learner. • Activities are highly structured and closely monitored and involve extensive, repetitive engagement with the same or similar tasks, and immediate feedback on performance. • Promote meta-cognition and self-regulation by guiding practice in self-monitoring, self-assessment, the	• Increases long-term working-memory capacity, supports the acquisition of structures for domain knowledge and procedures, promotes flexible performance within a domain, and supports the meta-cognition and self-regulation needed for independent performance. • Expertise research does not address feedback's mechanisms, possible negative effects on transfer, differential effects of various sources (coach vs. naturally occurring feedback), or different needs for different levels of expertise. The immediate feedback recommendation needs to be qualified.	**Literature source** • Expertise/expert performance. **Issues and proposals** • The issue of immediacy of feedback is important. There is a distinction to be made between preparing for a situation requiring maximal performance or refining existing skills vs. acquiring a skill in the first place. • Expertise requires skill in interpreting one's own performance and integrating feedback from multiple sources.

Appendix (Continued)

Instructional strategy	Description	Mechanisms	Literature sources & implementation issues
	use of feedback, the self-generation of feedback for self-evaluation, planning, self-instruction, and seeking assistance when needed. • Instructional scaffolding is decreased over time.	• Increases long-term working-memory capacity, supports the acquisition of structures for domain knowledge and procedures, promotes flexible performance within a domain, and supports the meta-cognition and self-regulation needed for independent performance. • Expertise research does not address feedback's mechanisms, possible negative effects on transfer, differential effects of various sources (coach vs. naturally occurring feedback), or different needs for different levels of expertise. The immediate feedback recommendation needs to be qualified.	• Expert performance is a long-range objective, and management education typically does not have the resources to implement this approach fully. • However, some elements can be applied, particularly the purposeful development of activities to promote learning and independent performance and guidance for developing self-regulatory skills.
5. Performance feedback	• Provide less specific, delayed, infrequent, and/or summarized feedback.	• Limited feedback tends to decrease performance during and following training, but promotes long-term retention and transfer. • Prepares learners for independent performance, without the aid of instructional supports. • Provides opportunities to make errors and to learn to recover from and to prevent errors. • Less specific feedback promotes exploration, explicit cognitive processes, and stimulus variability.	**Literature sources** • Cognitive and motor skills learning. • Organizational behavior. **Issues and proposals** • This is a substantive issue in management education, where much of learner performance on reports and exams is evaluated and detailed feedback may be provided, without the opportunity for learners to revise their work and demonstrate that they have reacted appropriately to feedback. • There are motivational overtones here, including the problem of feedback-seekers' expectations for uniformly positive feedback and reinforcement. • There is a need to make sure learners can handle the "desirable difficulties" from feedback or other sources, or this strategy may backfire.

6. Training scheduling	• Space practice sessions our instead of having massed, bunched training sessions.	**Literature sources** • Cognitive and motor skills learning. **Issues and proposals** • Suggests that class preparation might be best done earlier than immediately before the relevant class. • Instructors can use "forcing devices" like required submission of intermediate products and peer review to prevent cramming and last-minute work.
	• Provides more opportunities for elaboration and schema construction.	
7. Stimulus variability	• Design training tasks to provide experience with a representative sample of tasks, task conditions, and analogies.	**Literature sources** • CLT. • Associative and discriminant learning. • Cognitive and motor skills learning literatures. • Organizational behavior. • Advanced knowledge acquisition. **Issues and proposals** • Addresses problem of students anchoring on single, vivid examples, or seizing on the surface features of an example. • This approach might seem repetitive, but it likely will deepen understanding. • Supports consideration of exceptions and atypical circumstances as well, which may reflect deep principles (e.g., Manager's workshop discussion in the text).
	• Introduce variability in problem/task dimensions by varying the features of the task itself (e.g., complexity, underlying rules/structure, surface features, routine and nonroutine problems), how the task is presented, and the context in which the task is performed.	
	• Assists with schema construction because it gives learners opportunities to identify similar features and distinguish relevant from irrelevant features.	
	• Increases germane cognitive load, and has positive effects on transfer to novel problems not encountered before.	
	• If extraneous load is high, it should be decreased because variability adds to the total load.	
	• Tends to decrease performance during and following training, but promotes long-term retention and transfer.	
	• Prepares learners for independent performance, without the aid of instructional supports.	
	• Promotes elaboration, explicit cognitive processes, and discriminant learning.	
	• Provides opportunities to: ○ make errors and to learn to recover from and prevent future errors. ○ experience and distinguish problems that differ in terms of their surface and deep structures. ○ experience various aspects of a concept to limit misconceptions.	

(Continued)

Appendix (Continued)

Instructional strategy	Description	Mechanisms	Literature sources & implementation issues
8. Task sequencing	• Randomize the order of various tasks and topics instead of presenting them in a blocked fashion where one skill or topic is presented before moving onto the next.	• Tends to decrease performance during and following training, but promotes long-term retention and transfer. • Prepares learners for independent performance, without the aid of instructional supports. • Provides opportunities to make errors and to learn to recover from and prevent future errors. • Promotes elaboration, explicit cognitive processes, and discriminant learning.	**Literature sources** • Cognitive and motor skills learning. • Advanced knowledge acquisition. **Issues and proposals** • On the surface, this would be challenging to implement, as normative expectations for task learning are linear over time, and disrupting sequences is "heavy lifting," cognitively speaking. Worked examples, scenarios, and cases that begin in the middle of a process and require learners to proceed iteratively can take advantage of the principle.
9. Address learners' misconceptions	• Determine what misconceptions learners have or typically have in the domain (diagnostic component) and directly challenge them (prescriptive component). • Also, have students provide self-explanation and focus on trying to reconcile conflicting information.	• Directly addresses incorrect mental models that are often implicit, including private theories about how the world works. • Makes mental models explicit and encourages students to think about their knowledge and what they may have to unlearn.	**Literature sources** • Advanced knowledge acquisition. • Educational psychology. **Issues and proposals** • Test preexisting beliefs about counterintuitive management issues using instruments designed for this purpose in the management/organizational behavior domain (e.g., McShane & Von Glinow, 2010; Rynes, Colbert & Brown, 2002) • Expose implicit theories and invite learners to test them in light of observed facts. • Consider how faulty or deficient theories emerge and are propagated, and the perils of commonsensical approaches to management analysis and social scientific reasoning (Stanovich, 2007).

| 10. Integrate the acquisition of content (declarative) and procedural knowledge (application) | • Design instruction to engage learners in acquiring declarative knowledge (the what) simultaneously with procedural knowledge (the how) by integrating instruction on concepts with their applications.
• Provide examples that couple abstract principles with applications. | • Integration promotes the development of reasoning skills and deeper understanding.
• It also provides opportunities to actively engage learners earlier in the learning process. Integration supports rule induction by promoting the coordinated movement back and forth between generating and testing hypotheses about concepts, processes, and cause-effect relationships. Separating skill acquisition into declarative and procedural stages can limit more advanced learning. | **Literature sources**
• Advanced knowledge acquisition.
• Adaptive expertise.
• Dual space theories of rule induction.
• Scaffolding.
Issues and proposals
• This principle is applicable to various case formats and projects. Students would be required to identify and define problems, engage in evidence-based causal analysis (using evidence from organizational theory and research), and develop analysis-based, practical solutions.
• Media sources could be used to demonstrate abstract principles in organizational contexts.
• Systematic rule induction and reasoning principles may impose less cognitive load for management students when embedded in work and organizational problems. |
| 11. Articulation and reflection | • Design activities that require students to reflect on and articulate how they performed a task, what they learned, opportunities for future learning, and strategies for correcting errors.
• Have students articulate their misunderstandings and engage in self-explanation. | • Promotes meta-cognitive processing, self-monitoring (e.g., of misconceptions, comprehension), self-evaluation, and planning. | **Literature sources**
• Adaptive expertise.
• Scaffolding.
Issues and proposals
• Articulation and reflection may be naturally difficult for students, and they may need to be taught how do perform these tasks in productive ways.
• One way to do this might be to have the students interview each other about an activity or experience, using probes to elicit more elaborated, reflective responding. There is some skill-based discussion of this in Whetten and Cameron (2007). |

(Continued)

Appendix (Continued)

Instructional strategy	Description	Mechanisms	Literature sources & implementation issues
12. Interactions with others	• Design activities that require learners to work with one another on interdependent tasks or assist one another on individual tasks. • However, just putting people together does not guarantee learning. Activities need to be structured, for example, by assigning discussion questions and requiring students to share their products with the class. • Students can easily get off track and discuss unrelated things. • Students also need instruction and other guidance for managing team processes and coordinating teamwork.	• Promotes reasoning and adaptation of knowledge and skills.	**Literature source** • Adaptive expertise. **Issues and proposals** • This principle is a good fit for organizational behavior or courses that cover team processes. • Explicit discussion and cases that demonstrate the common pitfalls of teamwork (e.g., free-riding, conflict) can be used. Student project teams can be required develop of preventive measures (e.g., team contracts, enabling team structures) and remedies (e.g., social accountability, rules for norm enforcement). • Instructors can model appropriate behaviors and help set appropriate norms for the class.
13. Scaffolding and fading scaffolding	• Decrease the support provided to learners as they develop the capability to perform various aspects of the task on their own.	• The initial scaffolding supports performance processes that would not be possible without assistance. • Scaffolding can be used for actual task performance and to provide an organizing structure for planning and monitoring, which can be difficult for students. • Fading promotes gradual independence, based on the readiness of the learner.	**Literature source** • Scaffolding. **Issues and proposals** • Fading is important, because learners may become dependent on the scaffolding. • This may be most applicable to one-on-one instruction, or during meetings with individual students or teams, because it requires diagnosis of current knowledge and skills, which would be difficult in the classroom in real-time. • Fading can be used with a sequence of cases or projects in which students are given increasing responsibility for each case or project in the sequence. • In addition, structured formats can be provided for early assignments, which incorporate planning and self-monitoring tasks. This scaffolding can be decreased on subsequent assignments, so that students are expected to plan on their own and self-monitor. • The risk here is that some students will not be ready for or will resist taking on the additional responsibility.

| 14. Guided exploration/ discovery | • Systematic guidance is provided to support constructive cognitive activity, with enough freedom for the learner to actively engage in the sense-making process.
• There are many different options that are often combined in studies, so it is not possible to isolate their effects. E.g., Provide an organizing structure for the task, a general task strategy (leaving learner to figure out specific actions), hints, direction, coaching, modeling, and reminders to keep the learner on track.
• Provide meta-cognitive instructions that prompt learners to articulate goals, generate and elaborate on ideas, and strive for mastery and deep understanding. | • Pure discovery, with no guidance, can lead to impasses that novice learners cannot get past. Also, learners may not gain experience with important concepts and rules, because what learners come into contact with depends on how they explore.
• Alternatively, providing too much instruction can hurt adaptive transfer.
• Limited guidance helps to focus cognition and task behaviors and develop meta-cognitive skills. | **Literature sources**
• Educational psychology.
• Organizational behavior.

Issues and proposals
• This approach requires students to assume responsibility for their learning, which among novice learners, may call for some persuasion or "selling" on the part of the instructor.
• Students who are naturally or have been conditioned to be intolerant of ambiguity will likely struggle.
• These manifestations of resistance may be useful in themselves, in that they provide opportunities to link this instructional practice with managerial work. There is actually quite good alignment between this instructional practice and management work, as it occurs naturally. |

References

Anderson, J. R. (1982). Acquisition of cognitive skill. *Psychological Review, 89,* 369–406.

Anderson, J. R., Bothell, D., Byrne, M., Douglass, S., Lebiere, C., & Qin, Y. (2004). An integrated theory of cognition. *Psychological Review, 111,* 1036–1060.

Argyris, C. (1980). Some limitations of the case method: Experiences in a management development program. *Academy of Management Review, 5*(2), 291–298.

Armstrong, S. (1998). Are student ratings of instruction useful? *American Psychologist, 53,* 1223–1224.

Bandura, A. (1986). *Social foundations of thought and action: A social cognitive theory.* Englewood Cliffs, NJ: Prentice-Hall.

Barnett, S., & Koslowski, B. (2002). Adaptive expertise: Effects of type of experience and the level of theoretical understanding it generates. *Thinking and Reasoning, 8,* 237–267.

Billing, D. (2007). Teaching for transfer of core/key skills in higher education: Cognitive skills. *Higher Education, 53,* 483–516.

Bjork, R. (2009). Structuring conditions of training to achieve elite performance: Reflections on elite training programs and related themes in Chapters 10–13. In K. Anders Ericsson (Ed.), *Development of professional expertise: Toward measurement of expert performance and design of optimal learning environments* (pp. 312–329). Cambridge, UK : Cambridge University Press.

Bjork, R. A. (1994). Memory and metamemory considerations in the training of human beings. In J. Metcalfe & A. P. Shimamura (Eds.), *Metacognition: Knowing about knowing* (pp. 185–205). Cambridge, MA: MIT Press.

Bligh, D. (2000). *What's the use of lectures?* New York: Jossey-Bass.

Bransford, J. D., & Schwartz, D. L. (1999). Rethinking transfer: A simple proposal with multiple implications. *Review of Research in Education, 24,* 61–100.

Briner, R. B., Denyer, D., & Rousseau, D. M. (2009). Evidence-based management: Construct clean-up time? *Academy of Management Perspectives, 23*(4), 19–32.

Brittain, J. & Sitkin, S. (1986). Carter Racing. Evanston, IL: Dispute Resolution Research Center, Kellogg School of Management, Northwestern University.

Burns, B. D., & Vollmeyer, R. (2002). Goal specificity effects on hypothesis testing in problem solving. *The Quarterly Journal of Experimental Psychology, 55A,* 241–261.

Chang, V., & Pfeffer, J. (2003). *Cary Loveman and Harrah's entertainment.* Stanford, CA: Stanford Graduate School of Business.

Chi, M. T. H. (2006). Two approaches to the study of experts' characteristics. In A. K. Ericsson, N. Charness, P. J. Feltovich, & R. R. Hoffman (Eds.), *The Cambridge handbook of expertise and expert performance* (pp. 21–30). Cambridge, UK : Cambridge University Press.

Chipman, S. (2009). Expertise in the management of people: A new frontier for research on expert performance. In K. Ericsson (Ed.), *Development of professional expertise* (pp. 470–473). Cambridge, UK: Cambridge University Press.

Christensen, C., & Carlile, P. (2009). Course research: Using the case method to build and teach management theory. *The Academy of Management Learning and Education, 8*(2), 240–251.

Christina, R. W., & Bjork, R. A. (1991). Optimizing long-term retention and transfer. In D. Druckman & R. A. Bjork (Eds.), *In the mind's eye: Enhancing human performance* (pp. 13–32). Washington, DC: National Academy Press.

Cosgrove, C., & Barta-Smith, N. (2004). *In search of eloquence: Cross-disciplinary conversations on the role of writing in undergraduate education.* Cresskill, NJ: Hampton Press. Inc.

Crawford, V. M., & Brophy, S. (2006). Adaptive expertise: theory, methods, findings, and emerging issues. Symposium Report. Menlo Park, CA: SRI International.

Debowski, S. J., Wood, R. E., & Bandura, A. (2001). Impact of guided mastery and enactive exploration on self-regulatory mechanisms and knowledge construction through electronic inquiry. *Journal of Applied Psychology, 86*(6), 1129–1141.

Dunham. R. (2004). *The managers workshop.* Upper Saddle River, NJ: Prentice Hall.

Ellet, W. (2007). *The case study handbook.* Boston: Harvard Business School Publishing.

Ericsson, K. A. (2006a). An introduction to Cambridge Handbook of Expertise and Expert Performance: Its development, organization, and context. In A. K. Ericsson, N. Charness, P. J. Feltovich, & R, R. Hoffman (Eds.), *The Cambridge handbook of expertise and expert performance* (pp. 3–19). Cambridge, UK : Cambridge University Press.

Ericsson, K. A. (2006b). Protocol analysis and expert thought: Concurrent verbalizations of thinking during experts' performance on representative tasks. In A. K. Ericsson, N. Charness, P. J. Feltovich, & R. R. Hoffman (Eds.), *The Cambridge handbook of expertise and expert performance* (pp. 223–241). Cambridge, UK : Cambridge University Press.

Ericsson, K. A., Charness, N., Feltovich, P. J., & Hoffman, R. R. (2006). *The Cambridge handbook of expertise and expert performance.* Cambridge, UK : Cambridge University Press.

Ericsson, K. A., & Delaney, P. F. (1999). Long-term working memory as an alternative to capacity models of working memory in everyday skilled performance. In A. Miyake & P. Shah (Eds.), *Models of working memory mechanisms of active maintenance and executive. control* (pp. 257–297). Cambridge, UK : Cambridge University Press.

Ericsson, K. A., & Kintsch, W. (1995). Long-term working memory. *Psychological Review, 102,* 211–245.

Ericsson, K. A., Krampe, R. Th., & Tesch-Romer, C. (1993). The role of deliberate practice in the acquisition of expert performance. *Psychological Review, 100,* 363–406.

Ericsson, K. A., & Lehmann, A. C. (1996). Expert and exceptional performance: Evidence for maximal adaptations to task constraints. *Annual Review of Psychology, 47,* 273–305.

Feltovich, P. J., Spiro, R. J., & Coulson, R. L. (1993). Learning, teaching, and testing for complex conceptual understanding. In N. Frederiksen, R. J. Mislevy, & I. I. Bejar (Eds.), *Test theory for a new generation of tests.* Hillsdale, NJ: Lawrence Erlbaum Associates.

Fletcher, J. D. (2009). The value of expertise and expert performance: A review of evidence from the military. In K. A. Ericsson (Ed.), *Development of professional expertise: Toward measurement of expert performance and design of optimal learning environments* (pp. 449–469). Cambridge, UK : Cambridge University Press.

Gandz, J. (2004). *Vista-Sci Health Care Inc.* London, Ontario: Richard Ivey School of Business.

Gerjets, P., Scheiter, K., & Catrambone, R. (2004). Designing instructional examples to reduce intrinsic cognitive load: Molar versus modular presentation of solution procedures. *Instructional Science, 32,* 33–58.

Ghodsian, D., Bjork, R. A., & Benjamin, A. S. (1997). Evaluating training during training: Obstacles and opportunities. In M. A. Quinones & A. Ehrenstein (Ed.), *Training for a rapidly* changing workplace: *Applications of psychological research* (pp. 201–222). Washington, DC: American Psychological Association.

Glaser, R. (1996). Changing the agency for learning: Acquiring adaptive performance. In K. A. Ericsson (Ed.), *The road to excellence: The acquisition of expert performance in the arts and sciences, sports, and games* (pp. 303–311). Mahwah, NJ: Lawrence Erlbaum Associates.

Goodman, J. S., & Wood, R. E. (2004). Feedback specificity, learning opportunities, and learning. *Journal of Applied Psychology, 89,* 809–821.

Goodman, J. S., & Wood, R. E. (2009). Faded versus increasing feedback, task variability trajectories, and transfer of training. *Human Performance, 22,* 64–85.

Goodman, J. S., Wood, R. E., & Chen, Z. (2011). Feedback specificity, information processing, and transfer of training. *Organizational Behavior and Human Decision Processes, 115,* 253–267.

Goodman, J. S., Wood, R. E., & Hendrickx, M. (2004). Feedback specificity, exploration, and learning. *Journal of Applied Psychology, 89,* 248–262.

Hackman, J. R., & Wageman, R. (2009). Foster team effectiveness by fulfilling key leadership functions. In E. A. Locke (Ed.), *Handbook of principles of organizational behavior* (2nd ed., pp. 275–293). New York: Wiley-Blackwell.

Hatano, G., & Inagaki, K. (1986). Two courses of expertise. In H. Stevenson, H. Azuma, & K. Hakuta (Eds.), *Child development and education in Japan* (pp. 262–272). New York: W. H. Freeman and Company.

Hatano, G., & Ouro, Y. (2003). Commentary: Reconceptualizing school learning using insight from expertise research. *Educational Researcher, 32*(8), 26–29.

Hilbert, T.S. & Renkl, A. (2009). Learning how to use a computer-based concept-mapping tool: Self-explaining examples helps. *Computers in Human Behavior, 25,* 267–274.

Hill, W. F. (1977). *Learning through discussion.* Beverly Hills, CA: Sage.

Hoffman, R. R., Crandall, B., & Shadbolt, N. (1998). Use of the critical decision method to elicit expert knowledge: A case study in the methodology of cognitive task analysis. *Human Factors, 40*(2), 254–277.

Kalyuga, S., Ayres, P., Chandler, P., & Sweller, J. (2003). The expertise reversal effect. *Educational Psychologist, 38,* 23–31.

Keith, N., & Frese, M. (2008). Effectiveness of error management training: A meta-analysis. *Journal of Applied Psychology, 93,* 59–69.

Kerr, S. (1995), On the folly of rewarding A, while hoping for B. *Academy of Management Executive, 9,* 7–14.

Khurana, R. (2007). *From higher aims to hired hands: The social transformation of American business schools and the unfulfilled promise of management as a profession.* Princeton NJ: Princeton University Press.

Kimball, D. R., & Holyoak, K. J. (2000). Transfer and expertise. In E. Tulving & F. I. M. Craik (Eds.), *The Oxford handbook of memory* (pp. 109–122). New York: Oxford University Press.

Klahr, D., & Dunbar, K. (1988). Dual space search during scientific reasoning. *Cognitive Science. 12,* 1–48.

Klein, G. (2009). *Streetlights and shadows: Searching for keys to adaptive decision making.* Cambridge, MA: MIT Press.

Kluger, A. N., & DeNisi, A. (1996). The effects of feedback interventions on performance: A historical review, a meta-analysis, and a preliminary feedback intervention theory. *Psychological Bulletin, 119,* 254–284.

Latham, G. P., & Locke, E. A. (2007). New developments in and directions for goal-setting research. *European Psychologist, 12,* 290–300.

Latham, G. P., & Pinder, C. C. (2005). Work motivation theory and research at the dawn of the twenty-first century. *Annual Review of Psychology, 56,* 1–32.

Martens, J. (2007). *Rogers cable: First time right program.* London, Ontario: Richard Ivey School of Business.

Mauffette-Leenders, L.A. Erskine, J.A., & Leenders, M.R. (2003). Learning with Cases (3rd. Edition). London, ON: Ivey Publishing.

Mayer, R. E. (2004). Should there be a three-strikes rule against pure discovery learning? The case for guided methods of instruction. *American Psychologist, 59,* 14–19.

Merrill, D. C., Reiser, B. J., Merrill, S. K., & Landes, S. (1995). Tutoring: Guided learning by doing. *Cognition and Instruction, 13,* 315–372.

Moreno, R. (2004). Decreasing cognitive load for novice students: Effects of explanatory versus corrective feedback in discovery-based multimedia. *Instructional Science, 32,* 99–113.

McCrae, R., & Costa, P. (1989). Reinterpreting the Myers-Briggs type indicator from the perspective of the five-factor model of personality. *Journal of Personality, 57*(1), 17–40.

McShane, S. L., & Von Glinow, M. (2010). *Organizational behavior: Emerging realities for the workplace revolution* (5th ed.). Boston: McGraw-Hill Publishing.

Pashler, H., McDaniel, M., Rohrer, D., & Bjork, R. (2009). Learning styles concepts and evidence. *Psychological Science in the Public Interest, 9,* 105–119.

Pass, F., Renkl, A., & Sweller, J. (2004). Cognitive load theory: Instructional implications of the interaction between information structures and cognitive architecture. *Instructional Science, 32,* 1–8.

Patel, V. L., Kaufman, D. R., & Magder, S. (1996). The acquisition of medical expertise in complex dynamic environments. In A. Ericsson (Ed.), *The road to excellence: The acquisition of expert performance in the arts and sciences, sports and games* (pp. 127–165). Hillsdale, NJ: Lawrence Erlbaum Publishers.

Pittenger, D. (1993). The utility of the Myers-Briggs type indicator. *Review of Educational Research, 63*(4), 467–488.

Pollock, E., Chandler, P., & Sweller, J. (2002). Assimilating complex information, *Learning and Instruction, 12,* 61–86.

Reiser, B. J. (2004). Scaffolding complex learning: The mechanisms of structuring and problematizing student work. *The Journal of the Learning Sciences, 13,* 273–304.

Renkl, A., & Atkinson, R. K. (2003). Structuring the transition from example study to problem solving in cognitive skills acquisition: A cognitive load perspective, *Educational Psychologist, 38,* 15–22.

Renkl. A., Atkinson. R. K., Grobe. C. S. (2004). How fading worked solution steps works - A cognitive load perspective. *Instructional Science, 32,* 59–82.

Raufaste, E., Eyrolle, H., & Marine, C. (1998). Pertinence generation in radiological diagnosis: Spreading activation and the nature of expertise. *Cognitive Science 22,* 517–546.

Rynes, S. L., Colbert, A. E., & Brown, K. G. (2002). HR professionals' beliefs about effective human resource practices: Correspondence between research and practice. *Human Resource Management , 41,* 149–174.

Schmidt, R. A., & Bjork, R. A. (1992). New conceptualizations of practice: Common principles in three paradigms suggest new concepts for training. *Psychological Science, 3,* 207–217.

Schwartz, D. L., Bransford, J. D., & Sears, D. (2005). Efficiency and innovation in transfer. In J. Mestre (Ed.), *Transfer of learning: research and perspectives* (pp. 1–51). Greenwich, CT: Information Age Publishing Inc.

Schwonke, R., Renkl, A., Krieg, C., Wittwer, J., Aleven, V., & Salden, R. (2009). The worked-example effect: Not an artifact of lousy control conditions. *Computers in Human Behavior, 25*, 258–266.

Sherin, B., Reiser, B. J., & Edelson, D. (2004). Scaffolding analysis: Extending the scaffolding metaphor to learning artifacts. *The Journal of the Learning Sciences, 13*, 387–421.

Shugan, S. M. 2006. Editorial: save research—abandon the case method of teaching. *Marketing Science, 25*(2) , 109–115.

Simon, H. A., & Lea, G. (1974). Problem solving and rule induction: A unified view. In L. W. Gregg (Ed.), *Knowledge and cognition* (pp. 105–127). Maryland: Lawrence Erlbaum Associates.

Sonnentag, S., & Kleine, B. M. (2000). Deliberate practice at work: A study with insurance agents. *Journal of Occupational and Organizational Psychology, 73*, 87–102.

Stanovich, K. E. (2007). *How to think straight about psychology* (8th ed.). Boston: Allyn and Bacon/Pearson Education, Inc.

Sweller, J. (1988). Cognitive load during problem solving: Effects on learning. *Cognitive Science, 12*, 257–285.

Sweller, J. (2004). Instructional design consequences of an analogy between evolution by natural selection and human cognitive architecture. *Instructional Science, 32*, 9–31.

Sweller, J., Mawer, R. F., & Howe, W. (1982). Consequences of history-cued and means-end strategies in problem solving. *American Journal of Psychology, 95*, 455–483.

Sweller, J., van Merrienboer, J., & Paas, F. (1998). Cognitive architecture and instructional design. *Educational Psychology Review, 10*, 251–296.

Tompkins, J. (1990). Pedagogy of the distressed. *College English, 52*(6), 653–660.

Unger, J. M., Keith, N., Hilling, C., Gielnik, M. M., Frese, M. (2009). Deliberate practice among South African small business owners: Relationships with education, cognitive ability, knowledge, and success, *Journal of Occupational and Organizational Psychology, 82*, 21–44.

VanLehn, K., Siler, S., Murray, C., Yamauchi, T., & Baggett, W. B. (2003). Why do only some events cause learning during human tutoring? *Cognition and Instruction, 21*, 209–249.

Van Gog, T., Ericsson, K. A., Rikers, R. M. J. P., & Paas, F. (2005). Instructional design for advanced learners: Establishing connections between the theoretical frameworks of cognitive load and deliberate practice. *Educational Technology Research and Development, 53*, 73–81.

Van Gog, T., Paas, F., van Merrienboer, J. J. G. (2006). Effects of process-oriented worked examples on troubleshooting transfer performance. *Learning and Instruction, 16*, 154–164.

Van Merriënboer, J., Kester, L., & Paas, P. (2006). Teaching complex rather than simple tasks: Balancing intrinsic and germane load to enhance transfer of learning. *Applied Cognitive Psychology, 20*, 343–352.

Van Merriënboer, J., Schuurman, J., de Croock, M., & Paas, F. (2002). Redirecting learner's attention during training: Effects on cognitive load, transfer test performance and training efficiency, *Learning and Instruction 12*, 11–37.

Vollmeyer, R., & Burns, B. D. (2002). Goal specificity and learning with a hypermedia program. *Experimental Psychology, 49*, 98–108.

Vollmeyer, R., Burns, B. D., & Holyoak, K. J. (1996). The impact of goal specificity on strategy use and the acquisition of problem structure. *Cognitive Science, 20*, 75–100.

Wageman, R., Fisher, C. M., & Hackman, J. R. (2009). Leading teams when the time is right: Finding the best moments to act. *Organizational Dynamics, 38*, 192–203.

Wageman, R., & Hackman, J. R. (1999). *The overhead reduction task force*. Cambridge, MA: Harvard Business School Press.

Whetten, D., & Cameron, K. (2007). *Developing management skills* (7th ed.). Upper Saddle River, NJ: Prentice-Hall.

Wineburg, S. (1998). Reading Abraham Lincoln: An expert/expert study in the interpretation of historical texts. *Cognitive Science, 22*, 319–346.

Wulf, G., & Schmidt, R. A. (1994). Feedback-induced variability and the learning of generalized motor programs. *Journal of Motor Behavior, 26*, 348–361.

Zimmerman, B. J. (2002). Achieving academic excellence: A self-regulatory perspective. In M. Ferrari (Ed.), *The pursuit of excellence through education* (pp. 85–110). Mahwah, NJ: Lawrence Erlbaum Associates.

Reflections on Teaching
Evidence-Based Management

R. Blake Jelley, Wendy R. Carroll, *and* Denise M. Rousseau

Abstract

Educators have begun developing courses and curricula to help managers cultivate an evidence-based mindset and acquire relevant knowledge and skills. This chapter describes what three evidence-based management (EBMgt) educators have learned in the process of creating relevant courses and curricula. It presents the learning objectives that their teaching has promoted along with the frameworks, content, and exercises used to realize them. It also describes specific assignments and activities to encourage EBMgt teaching and provide a basis for further adaptation and innovation by educators seeking to prepare learners to practice EBMgt.

Key Words: critical thinking, finding evidence, practice for learning, EBMgt curriculum, EBMgt course, EBMgt teaching, reviews

"Guiding students through a process of conceptual change takes time, patience, and creativity."
—Ambrose, Bridges, DiPietro, Lovett, & Norman (2010)

"Don't confuse me with the facts." That quote from an organizational decision maker seems to represent an all-too-common mindset that may help explain "the apparent lack of demand" for an evidence-based approach to managing organizations (Briner & Rousseau, 2011, p. 18). Evidence-based management (EBMgt) is fundamentally "a way of thinking" (Pfeffer, 2007, p. 12) about organizational decisions in a systematic manner; with due consideration for stakeholder concerns, practitioner expertise and judgment, local evidence, and evidence from formal research (Briner, Denyer, & Rousseau, 2009). Instead of balanced consideration of those four EBMgt elements, managers tend to base decisions on personal experience, their strengths and preferences, hype and fads, uncritical benchmarking of others' practices, or ideology (Pfeffer & Sutton, 2006a). Scholars have argued that an EBMgt

approach has the potential to enhance the productivity of organizations and the well being of their members (Pfeffer & Sutton, 2006; 2007). Realizing EBMgt's potential requires changes in how managers think and act. To that end, fundamental shifts in management education are called for to forge closer links among teaching, research, and practice (e.g., Burke & Rau, 2010; Rousseau & McCarthy, 2007).

Management educators are beginning to adopt an EBMgt perspective in their teaching (Briner et al., 2009). Yet the fact remains that MBAs and other management students are not typically taught to know or use research evidence in their decision making (Graen, 2009; Rousseau, 2006; Rousseau & McCarthy, 2007). Educators who do incorporate scientific evidence in their classes, even if not teaching EBMgt per se, know well the resistance students can demonstrate when their assumptions and beliefs are challenged. In teaching EBMgt, these challenges are amplified. Educators need to give attention to both evidence and assumptions in teaching EBMgt, in that major barriers to its uptake lie in the tendency of individuals to reject evidence at odds with a heartfelt opinion or preferred course of action. Further barriers stem from the limited capacity of human beings to systematically process information, including evidence. In educating students about both evidence and assumptions, we have sought to promote among our Masters-level students greater ability and motivation to consider evidence with respect to practical questions and decisions.

The present chapter focuses on our experiences teaching EBMgt and, in particular, things we have done to support our students' learning. We begin by offering a few stories about our students to set the stage for our own stories. Next, we introduce the contexts in which we teach and approaches we use. We distinguish between stand-alone EBMgt-titled courses and a more integrated approach in which EBMgt ideas are woven through several elements of a graduate business program. Last, we provide a more detailed account of our teaching methods.

Stories to Set the Stage

Not all students have been equally receptive to or successful in grasping EBMgt and supporting concepts. Nevertheless, we have had sufficient positive experiences to reinforce our efforts. For example, we have seen executive MBA students interrogate, in a most impressive way, a guest speaker about a field experiment published in the *Journal of Applied Psychology* (i.e., Barling, Weber, & Kelloway, 1996):

> Frankly I was astounded at both the motivation and knowledge of the students. Not only had they read the published research that formed the basis of my presentation, they had clearly thought about the issues in considerable depth. My presentation quickly turned into a question and answer session during which the students probed every potential weakness of the research designs and in several cases suggested potential "fixes" for future research or extensions to the research questions that I had not previously considered. The level of discussion was far beyond that of a first year EMBA class – indeed I would be pleased to have this type of discussion in my PhD research seminars.
>
> (Dr. Kevin Kelloway, Canada Research Chair, Saint Mary's University, personal communication, 2009)

At the same time, consciousness-raising about evidence and its implications for the individual manager is a major focus in our teaching. Carnegie Mellon MBA students have peppered the placement office with questions about whether its resume-writing advice and interview training is evidence based. In addition, students report, "I go for pizza with a classmate, something comes up and I wonder, 'where's the evidence'?" And when their own heartfelt beliefs are tested, students experience the same resistance we need to help them overcome from others when they take a job and try to practice EBMgt. As one student noted in his reading log:

> It was interesting to me, especially in light of my [learning goal *to be able to motivate others to use evidence-based techniques*], to see how resistant I was to the *That's Incredible* article [Highhouse (2008), addressing why use of tests and systematic methods are superior in selection to managerial judgment]. At first I liked it, because I like using better information and better methods to do what I have to do better. Who doesn't want to be the best at their job? But as it kept going, it began to undermine what I saw as one of my strengths, which is my ability to read people. And then I started to get a little less receptive to the article's findings. Evidence won't be accepted if it makes people feel less competent or deprives them of a cherished activity without replacing it with something they find meaningful.
>
> After denial ("This guy is just wrong. He doesn't understand people.") came bargaining ("My intuitive judgments aren't really that intuitive. I'm reading into signals. I'm collecting another kind of evidence!") This was the mindset I was bringing in to class, at least. The discussion there was more helpful. I realized one of my biggest problems with the evidence-based approach to hiring was that I didn't trust tests to make good choices, and I felt like it was easier to deal with people who make hiring mistakes than tests that lead to hiring mistakes. But you made a valid point that it can be easier to fix a test and adapt it to the needs of an organization than it is to change people. And that is something I agree with. Tests can't get testy when you change them.
>
> I think this was a good week for EBMgt, since I got to watch the same process happen to me that goes through some people when they are told that what they're doing is not good enough, and there's a way to make it better.

Our teaching has generated many more stories, as graduates take what they have learned into the workplace. Former students contact us about a current work challenge after they have already reviewed the evaluated research evidence to discuss possible implications for their decisions. We are heartened by the strong demand from our graduating students to retain access to academic databases as a critical source of evidence on the job. Alumni remain in close contact with us and some have expressed great interest in developing a collaborative EBMgt group as a way of staying connected, knowledgeable, and involved with research. We do not pretend that our courses have imparted all our students' critical thinking skills. We do believe that we have sparked an appetite for critically considering and using evidence.

At this point, the quality of evidence we can provide about changes in students' knowledge, skills, attitudes, and behavior is somewhat limited. (Self-rated changes by students are reported later.) We recognize that EBMgt proponents face heightened calls to produce high-quality evidence for their own positions and programs (e.g., Briner et al., 2009; Reay, Berta, & Kohn, 2009; Rynes, Trank, Lawson, & Ilies, 2003) and we encourage rigorous evaluations of EBMgt education and implementation. Indeed, more rigorous research is needed for management education, generally (Rynes et al., 2003). Examples of systematic reviews of EB-related education initiatives are emerging in other evidence-based practice domains such as education and medicine, although the amount and quality of evidence tends to be low, even in more established professions (Parkes, Hyde, Deeks, & Milne, 2001). We take solace in the argument that "using evidence does not mean slavishly following it, acting only when there is good evidence or doing nothing if there is none" (Briner & Rousseau, 2011, p. 6). An evidence-based approach to teaching does not mean that educators must or should delay action pending the results of a systematic review of randomized control trials of EBMgt teaching strategies. Like EBMgt, EB teaching is action-oriented, reflective, and receptive to better information as it becomes available. We concur with our counterparts in other evidence-based practice domains (e.g., Murad et al., 2009; Wyer et al., 2004) that it is valuable for educators to share information about their instructional approaches. We encourage educators to consider, reflect critically on, and experiment with insights (formally or informally) about teaching EBMgt. Resources for teaching EBMgt have appeared online (e.g., evidencebased-management.com and its associated Google group). Readers are encouraged to contribute. Importantly, there is considerable research on education, generating teaching and learning principles that figure prominently in how we have developed our teaching. In that regard, Goodman and O'Brien (chapter 18 of this volume) summarize important principles to support EB teaching.

Our Contexts and Approaches

Management educators face numerous decisions about how best to bring new concepts, knowledge, and skills into program curricula. For example, approaches for bringing ethics and entrepreneurship knowledge to students have been debated by faculty members in business schools. Some faculty think the best approach is to deliver stand-alone course(s) concentrating on the central elements, whereas others suggest that integrating a focal topic across all courses increases knowledge transfer. Although it appears that integration is seen as valuable to enhance learning and transfer, there is a risk that integration may only pay lip service to the topic. Both approaches have strengths and weaknesses and we can find no clear synthesis of evidence to suggest that one is better. Developing EBMgt awareness, knowledge, and skills can be debated along these same lines. Although there is no one best answer, we can share our experiences from both a course-based and integrated curriculum approach.

A Course-Based Approach

Carnegie Mellon has two schools of "management," the Tepper School of Business and Heinz College of Public Policy, Information, and Management. Both are strongly research focused, with Tepper having begun as a PhD program before adding a Masters program for managers. The first EBMgt course was launched in Tepper in 2008 and is now taught in both programs. It is basically the same course in both, but the teaching and student experience differ in several respects. The majority of Heinz Master of Science in Public Policy and Management (MSPPM) students have social-science backgrounds whereas Tepper students tend more toward engineering, physics, and math. Students in both programs are in their mid-twenties. Tepper students tend to have five-plus years of experience working in industry whereas Heinz students have worked in government in the United States or elsewhere, nongovernmental organizations (NGOs), education, or the Peace Corps. In Tepper, the course is classified as an elective in organizational behavior (one elective is required for graduation) and at Heinz it is a management elective. Heinz students typically take the course in the second (final) year whereas Tepper students tend to take it in the first year following the required organizational-behavior course.

The same syllabus, readings, and assignments are followed in both courses. It focuses on evidence-based ways to make decisions using business/local data and scientific knowledge, and ways to reduce bias and judgment errors in gathering and interpreting information. As the syllabus describes,

> EBMgt means making decisions based on scientific evidence and organizational facts. These decisions rely on judgment processes that reduce bias and judgment errors and give due consideration to stakeholder interests. This mini course promotes your understanding and use of the principles of EBMgt. It also guides you in developing the skills and knowledge needed to identify, access, and use quality evidence from science and practice in making better decisions.
>
> This course addresses both the content and process of evidence-informed organizational decisions. Your instructor is also committed to pursuing an evidence-based approach to the course itself. Scientific evidence strongly supports the effectiveness of promoting student responsibility for learning. This approach is sometimes referred to as natural or student-centric learning based on active participation in learning activities. It is the opposite of conventional teacher-centric learning....

The flow of the course starts with an introduction and overview and drills down into understanding what "best available evidence" means. Concurrently, we address the role that cognitive biases play in failing to use or misusing evidence. The goal is to help students recognize the effects of bounded rationality and bias in their thinking. Then, we work on learning to think more critically about both their experiences and responses to scientific evidence. The course then provides repeated practice at finding and interpreting scientific evidence. Repeating this process of gathering evidence has the advantage of helping students make their tacit learning more explicit. This allows in-class sharing of how well various search strategies have worked. Subsequent classes present different types of decisions practitioners face in context beginning with basic, routine, and recurring issues (e.g., selection, people management) for which there is evidence. Here we introduce the notion of procedural knowledge, that is, how to convert well-established evidence into implementable ways to solve practical problems and make decisions. This set of classes on decision making for which there is evidence also covers designing solutions as well as managing the implementation and politics of evidence. We

then address how to make decisions by making the best use of available organizational facts, developing points raised in Pfeffer and Sutton's (2006a, 2006b) treatment of EBMgt. Ways to improve the reliability and meaningfulness of data (Donaldson, chapter 14 of this volume) are presented— what we call turning data into information. Then, we address the most difficult decisions managers are likely to face, responding to unforeseen events. This calls attention to the next theme in the course, evidence-based processes. Emphasis is placed on the value of process (decision steps and practices; e.g., Weick & Sutcliffe, 2007) when neither experience nor evidence can inform the content of the decision, as in the case when unforeseeable disasters coincide with economic downturns. Last, the course foreshadows the experiences students are likely to have upon graduating, addressing how to practice EBMgt in organizations where evidence is not understood or valued. This module promotes student planning to help them transfer learning as they prepare to move along the novice-to-expert pathway in practicing EBMgt.

From the course's outset, students are told that they are guinea pigs. That is, EBMgt is a very new concept, established in other professions, but novel in management. The course addresses EBMgt 1.0. As the students' own professional practice develops, they can help develop its 1.n, 2.0 versions, and beyond. For this reason, the course focuses on basic principles that can be adapted over time as students' learning deepens and they find ways of integrating EBMgt practice with their other learning from the graduate curriculum and elsewhere.

The primary learning in this class comes from a series of exercises and projects for which class time is used to prepare and debrief. These include having students examine popular business books to determine whether they make use of scientific evidence (not so much) and working in groups to get evidence on practical questions (e.g., Do credit checks improve workforce quality? Can virtual teams perform as well as face-to-face teams? How to hire (or reward) good performers in a start-up firm? Can a hospital acquisition succeed financially when the firms have different cultures?). Having a reference librarian advise students on how to search proves to be very important since most Internet-savvy students believe themselves to be great searchers (though many have not used Google Scholar before this class). Repeating the process of asking a question, searching for and interpreting evidence turns out to be critical to what students learn. Students are hungry for cases and real-life illustrations of managers using evidence. John Zanardelli (chapter 11 of this volume), a local executive and long-time evidence-based management practitioner, has related first-hand experience that students enjoy querying. He has followed this up by having his direct reports come to class to share their experiences, reactions to EBMgt practices, and their own personal applications of EB approaches like using logic models and searching for evidence. A variety of EBMgt cases have now been written and, as the practice evolves, more will be, which is a very important development for both credibility and learning among business students.

Students at Tepper are more heterogeneous in their responses to EBMgt than at Heinz. As policy students, most participants from Heinz have written research reports in the past, think research is important because of its policy role, and are more familiar with the jargon and methods of scholarship (e.g., hierarchical regression, panel analysis, scale development). Some of the business students are restive when it comes to writing up research findings (e.g., "feels like a PhD class"). Basic principles of management-research design and assessment are also sometimes at odds with marketing-research practices at Tepper (e.g., single-item scales). On the other hand, Tepper students tend to take their future role as decision makers very seriously and bring a good deal of experience in making decisions and implementation. They tend to be quite animated by the difference between using evidence in structured and recurrent decisions as opposed to novel and unforeseen ones. In the course, we focus on using scientific evidence in two ways: as information to inform decisions, and as science-based practices for improving the decision process itself. Business and public policy and management students resonate with the notion of developing different approaches to various kinds of decisions.

An Integrated Approach

The University of Prince Edward Island (UPEI) is a primarily undergraduate teaching institution that has made notable advances in research and graduate programs in recent years. Among Canadian universities, UPEI had the largest percent gain in research income between 1999 and 2009 (Re$earch-Infosource, 2010).

It has also introduced new graduate programs, including an executive MBA program in the fall of 2008. The EMBA program was designed to meet the needs of people who are working full-time but

wish to return to university to pursue graduate-level studies. The EMBA program provides flexibility to mature students through course scheduling outside the traditional workday and flexibility of program completion between two and four years (maximum six years). Degree requirements consist of 14 courses, including a signature project (equivalent to two courses) that involves research or consultancy with an organization.

The average age of UPEI EMBA students who have participated in our courses to date was 38 years, with an average of 14 years of work experience. Approximately 55 percent of students worked in the private sector and 60 percent were men. As with many MBA and EMBA programs, students varied considerably in terms of their fields (e.g., arts, business, culinary, engineering, sciences) and levels of previous education. A few had PhDs and some had no undergraduate degree, but were admitted based on extensive experience, professional credentials, or other qualifications.

Starting a new program, such as an EMBA, comes with both opportunities and challenges for faculty and administrators. The opportunity within this context was presented because two UPEI faculty members (Jelley & Carroll) are both interested in promoting EBMgt to enhance students' development and, ultimately, better outcomes for organizations and their stakeholders. We seek to provide students with the skills, tools, and knowledge required to critically assess academic literature, integrate this knowledge with other sources of information, and apply such learning in practice back in their workplaces. In short, our overarching goals are to turn students on to research, make them savvy consumers of it, and help them use it in meaningful ways to foster improved decisions and actions in practice.

The UPEI EMBA approach to develop EBMgt awareness and education is to integrate EBMgt knowledge and skills throughout various aspects of the program. We first introduce EBMgt and relevant skills as part of the program orientation for students. Our most recent orientations have included a day, prior to beginning the first EMBA course, in which students are exposed to the landscape of academic literature and the ways in which it can be accessed efficiently and effectively. First, students are provided with a broad understanding of business and management research. After an overview of EBMgt, we explain to students the differences among journals (such as academic, bridge, and popular press). Second, our librarian or a faculty member conducts a session with students to show them how to find and use online databases to locate literature. This hands-on session provides students with the basics on the types of databases available to them and effective literature search methods. We encourage students during this session to think about a problem at their workplace that they want to know more about. The student then searches a database to locate articles of possible interest. Thereafter, we have woven EBMgt into required courses we were assigned to teach.

The students' first course after orientation is Managing People and Organizations, which focuses on management and strategic human-resource-management content. Importantly, the management course provides opportunities for students to practice skills learned during orientation to access existing literature on topical issues. This course is an ideal start to the program, given the centrality of the content to managers and because, in many instances, EMBA students *think* they are already well informed about management practices. As a result, it provides rich grounds to "myth bust" and question assumptions. Throughout this course, students develop skills in focusing research questions, gathering literature related to management and workplace problems, synthesizing and summarizing the results from their searches, integrating other sources of information with the research evidence, and assessing the practical implications of the knowledge. Students develop a familiarity and comfort with accessing and reading academic literature and begin the process of using the research evidence as one source of information to help guide decision-making in practice.

Subsequently, students take a Business Research Methods course, which further elaborates EBMgt and provides more practice opportunities with respect to gathering and appraising evidence and ideas. The EBMgt perspective seems to make research-methods content (reasonably) palatable to pragmatic students, and the research-methods content provides more of the knowledge and skill required to move students beyond a basic awareness of EBMgt. That is, research-methods content provides students with perspectives and tools (e.g., checklists) to improve critical thinking about the nature of evidence. Students are also encouraged to be appreciative of research as both a rigorous and a creative process. As well, some appreciation of difficulties inherent in designing and conducting research should be gained. The broad goals of this course are to provide students with essential grounding in methodology to help them evaluate evidence from formal studies or local investigations in a critical, yet constructive manner, and to prepare them to conduct or collaborate in original research and abbreviated versions of systematic reviews.

The three initial components of the UPEI EMBA program build a foundation to develop EBMgt as, hopefully, a viable approach for practitioners. Further opportunities for students to practice and refine these skills are available in some other courses (e.g., Innovative Leadership and Cultures). In addition, students are also required to complete a signature project in the form of a business plan, applied research project, or systematic review, providing another more in-depth opportunity to apply and refine EBMgt knowledge and skills. Some students have presented findings from their signature project research at academic conferences and in practitioner forums, and have also impacted change within their organizations. This level of post-program engagement shows promising signs of facilitating knowledge transfer beyond the classroom environment.

We cannot claim that the EBMgt perspective has been fully integrated within all UPEI EMBA courses. However, we have shared basic information about EBMgt with our colleagues and EBMgt seems to be emerging as a feature of our EMBA program. Our undergraduate programs represent further opportunities for the future of EBMgt. We will continue to reflect on, adapt, and share our efforts to teach EBMgt within and beyond our respective institutions.

What and How We Teach (So Far)

Now let us turn to more specific descriptions of teaching strategies we have tried. Goodman and O'Brien (chapter 18 of this volume) review distinct research streams from cognitive psychology, instructional psychology, and education. They note that, despite diversity in focus and assumptions, "all streams agree that learners must deploy active cognitive processes, such as meta-cognition, critical reasoning, and hypothesis generation and testing to truly learn, and that instructional conditions must be structured to support these cognitive activities" (p. 311). We now describe our efforts to engage students with EBMgt and promote their active learning in the fashion Goodman and O'Brien describe. Although we deal both with the "what" and "how" aspects of our EBMgt teaching, our emphasis here is on the exercises and assignments used ("how") in our different courses.

This section follows a structure developed for EBMgt by Barends (2010), based on EB steps outlined in health domains (e.g., Hadley, Davis, & Khan, 2007; Thomas, Saroyan, & Dauphinee, 2011). The educational elements our courses use to support EBMgt target (1) developing basic awareness of evidence and evidence-based practice, (2) learning to ask the right questions, (3) obtaining the best available evidence, (4) critically appraising the evidence, (5) integrating EBMgt elements in support of organizational decisions and actions, and (6) evaluating the process. None of us has used all the exercises, assignments, or substantive content discussed below in any one course; nor is the material presented in terms of a particular sequence for suggested use. Certain assignments require students to engage in multiple EBMgt steps in support of their deeper learning (i.e., interacting elements; Goodman & O'Brien, chapter 18 of this volume). For this chapter, we have categorized each exercise or assignment in terms of the step it most directly serves.

Basic Awareness of EBMgt

During introductory sessions on EBMgt with students, faculty, or professional audiences, we have conducted informal polls with respect to familiarity with EBMgt or evidence-based practice in other domains (e.g., education, medicine, and other health professions). Previous familiarity with the term *evidence-based management* has been low, although some people profess familiarity with evidence-based practice in other fields. Showing links to other evidence-based-practice movements conveys that respected professions have adopted a similar perspective (e.g., evidence-based medicine; Pfeffer & Sutton, 2006a; Rousseau, 2006). Highlighting relevant champions and authors draws attention to the fact that other respected people are concerned with evidence. For example, we have provided examples of other faculty from leading business schools on our course syllabi or during introduction to EBMgt presentations. Quotable endorsements from well-known and respected executive champions would likely be helpful to add. The EBMgt Collaborative credo has appeared on some of our course syllabi to signal that a community of people are promoting and practicing EBMgt. The credo presents a definition of EBMgt (https://wpweb2.tepper.cmu.edu/evite/ebm_conf/index.html).

Discussing EBMgt definitions and descriptions is important for creating basic awareness. Drawing on Briner et al. (2009), Pfeffer (2007), Pfeffer

and Sutton (2006a, 2006b; 2007), and Rousseau (2006), we have described EBMgt as a way of thinking about organizational decisions in a systematic manner, gathering and translating both scientific evidence (i.e., Big "E" Evidence) and local data (i.e., little "e" evidence) to inform decision making, and learning systematically about human behavior to improve management practice. The "concept cleanup" offered by Briner et al. is helpful both in terms of the EBMgt definition provided, as well as clarification of what EBMgt is and is not (see their Table 1, p. 21). An important aspect of this concept clarification is that students become familiar with the notion that EBMgt uses scientific evidence in two ways: both as content to inform decisions and through the processes whereby these are made—related but distinct approaches.

To highlight the importance of being familiar with evidence-based content, consider the following argument: if you (allegedly) have no time to search and evaluate evidence, then you will be acting on the information you have. How have you prepared yourself to be ready? No time, know answers. We have used Rynes, Colbert, and Brown's (2002) human-resource-management knowledge quiz as an example of the extent to which EBMgt content is known. Rynes et al.'s results demonstrate that established research findings are not well known among human resource (HR) managers. When administered to students, this quiz serves to highlight their awareness of evidence-based content in HR management and as a basis for discussing limits in the dissemination of that knowledge. [Rynes offered a note of caution in that regard via evidence-based-management@googlegroups.com (May 25, 2011). Some instructors have encountered very negative student reactions such as defensiveness from students feeling exposed as "uninformed." Educators must use caution to ensure students do not feel distanced from an evidence-based perspective as a result of this or any assignment or exercise.] As noted by Goodman and O'Brien (chapter 18 of this volume), this type of pretesting helps instructors identify and address some learner misconceptions. Armstrong and Green's (2011) adprin.com web site has an online "test your advertising IQ" quiz that could be used similarly in that domain. Also, Cialdini's (2011) influenceatwork.com web site provides a 10-item quiz based on work-related influence scenarios appropriate for testing current knowledge. Having small groups discuss their implicit theories related to quiz items may make use of other learning principles summarized by Goodman and O'Brien such as interactions with others, articulation of their perspectives, and delayed feedback (i.e., if quiz results are not made available immediately). Based on our own limited trials, it appears that EMBA students take considerably longer to discuss their answers to quiz items than do senior undergraduates, possibly reflecting EMBA students' more elaborated mental models about management.

The Self-Guided Field Trip is a simple assignment to encourage critical thinking about common sources of business prescriptions, which may contribute to students' mental models. Students are asked to visit the business section of a bookstore, look through four or five business books, and prepare a one-page report in which they describe what the authors' bases of "evidence" appear to be. What types of sources are cited? Approximately what proportion of sources appear to be (1) personal or anecdotal, (2) based on so-called "best practices" or benchmarking of other companies, (3) other business books or publications, or (4) scientific evidence? Students are also asked to identify the book that appears most useful and explain their perception of what makes it most useful. Does evidence-based affect perceived usefulness? Having students go and look at the actual shelves of a bookstore seems to work well. Discussion of the Self-Guided Field Trip also allows the instructor to suggest that students start building their own professional research library for evidence-based knowledge related to their practice.

A lack of knowledge is not the only or even the biggest barrier facing would-be evidence-based managers. "It ain't what you don't know that gets you into trouble. It's what you know for sure that just ain't so" (Mark Twain; Will Rogers offered a similar observation). Misconceptions revealed via an evidence-based-content quiz provide a starting point for learners to address their own false beliefs (Goodman & O'Brien, chapter 18 of this volume). Discussions of quiz results can also be useful to examine others' claims critically. Student questions about the evidence underlying the scoring key or research designs to probe alternative interpretations are opportunities to promote critical thinking. If such questions and challenges do not emerge spontaneously the instructor can point out that raising questions about research findings and their implications for practice is central to EBMgt. As instructors in EBMgt, it is important that we model receptivity to constructive challenges. For example, questions like "What's the evidence on evidence-based management?" (Reay et al., 2009) provide great opportunities to welcome discussion and make the point

that EBMgt education is about helping students develop as critical thinkers, not to create disciples.

The process aspect of EBMgt refers to the use of practices of known effectiveness in making decisions and improving the quality of the information used in decision making. Processes refer to the routines EBMgt practitioners must learn if they are to overcome the inherent cognitive limitations of human beings and to create procedures that effectively act on evidence. Based on the idea of cognitive repair (Heath, Larrick, & Klayman, 1998), we explore the routines, heuristics, and management practices that can help people be "smarter" than we otherwise are when we make decisions or act without aids. Asking students to describe all the information and decision aids they use in their lives (from shopping lists to goals on posted notes) introduces the broad utility of information and decision aids. This sets the stage for subsequent discussions of how scientific findings can be organized into procedures, checklists, and other artifacts that ease their practical use (e.g., Yates & Potwoworski, chapter 12 of this volume).

EBMgt instructors may also wish to consider presenting ideas like the attitude of wisdom (Pfeffer & Sutton, 2007) and the set of steps to becoming an evidence-based manager (Rousseau & Barends, 2011) as part of creating basic awareness. Together, those sources encourage managers to think about decisions explicitly, ask for and seek out evidence, and use the best available knowledge. Note that the best available knowledge at a given point in time may be incomplete and is prone to obsolescence. Thus, evidence-based managers must be open to learn and adapt management practices in light of better evidence (Pfeffer & Sutton, 2007). Revisiting explicitly the four facets of EBMgt outlined by Rousseau (chapter 1 of this volume) is another way to reinforce the dynamic nature of EBMgt; it is a decision-making process in which evidence from formal research is considered in conjunction with evidence from the local context, stakeholder perspectives and preferences, and practitioner judgment and expertise. This overview material can be presented as a stand-alone, in a brief workshop at orientation, or at a lunch discussion to get students thinking about EBMgt's four facets. Consider having students ask questions about a management problem by using each EBMgt element as a perspective to consider.

Asking the Right Questions

To use evidence, people must be aware of the decisions they are making (including decisions to take no action). The EBMgt process starts with the problem, question, or issue facing a manager or other practitioner (Briner et al., 2009). One way to emphasize the point that EBMgt is an inquiry-based approach is to engage students early in their education in developing a questioning mindset. For example, during EMBA orientation, we have used an exercise in which students are asked to diagnose an attendance problem using the four elements of EBMgt, building on Briner and Rousseau's scenario (2011, Table 1). The scenario presented is brief: "Senior managers in your large firm believe the organization has high absenteeism and want something done to fix it." Students' task is to think of questions from each of the four EBMgt sources that could prove relevant to understanding the problem and what, if anything, should be done to fix it. Students are given time (e.g., 5 min) to work on the task individually before discussing it in small groups (e.g., 15 min). A plenary discussion of students' work precedes consideration of questions adapted from Briner and Rousseau's Table 1. EMBA students seem to do quite well on this exercise, collectively. The main objective of this Absenteeism Diagnosis exercise is to jumpstart students' integrative thinking about the types of questions and evidence that may be brought to bear on a problem. The problem used, allegedly high absenteeism, is one any organization may encounter. Importantly, this exercise highlights that all four EBMgt elements deserve consideration. The present version of the exercise is focused at the question development stage. It can be amended to be a more integrated assignment in which students also engage in subsequent stages of EBMgt (e.g., getting and evaluating evidence as the basis for action planning). Note this adaptation might require a more elaborate case.

We try to demonstrate links between EBMgt teaching and students' professional lives. Other exercises and assignments can help students identify issues and topics to investigate on their own or with instructor or peer support. An out-of-class assignment that may be used to provide a richer and more personally motivating practice experience is the Burning Question assignment. Based on discussions in class and through individual interactions with students, the instructor develops a list of possible topics that may be used for the assignment. (In instances where less support is appropriate, students could be given complete responsibility for topic identification). Students are expected to take an EBMgt approach to this assignment and a rubric is provided to assist students with their understanding of the assignment. Graduate business students

reasonably want to think in terms of "big picture" issues and often struggle to specify their question sufficiently. Students learn to "pull the thread" as a first step in learning to develop and focus their questions. In other words, as students migrate to broad areas of interest, we work with them to refine their question to the specific issue or challenge they find problematic in their organizations or in business in general (e.g., interventions such as selection, mentoring). The identification of a broad-interest area is like selecting a book you find interesting and pulling the thread means that students decide on a specific quote, passage or theme of the book that is of most interest (e.g., types of interviews, formal versus informal mentorship, or gender differences in mentorship). More generally, students are guided by the FINER (feasible, interesting, novel, ethical, and relevant) principles of research question development (Littell, Corcoran, & Pillai, 2008) and pulling the thread is a first step to help students focus and create a specific research question to examine in a meaningful way. Often, working with students one-on-one to help decide on a topic, narrow the question to something specific, and understand peer-reviewed research evidence can facilitate learning about numerous steps in the EBMgt process. Students have examined specific topics such as barriers to women's advancement in leadership positions, fairness of chief executive officers' (CEOs') compensation, and the effectiveness of downsizing. After conducting a rapid evidence assessment and synthesis of the relevant research evidence, students are often surprised to find that the answer is not exactly as they thought or the issue is not as straightforward as they expected.

Other assignments, discussed in subsequent sections, build on student-identified and articulated questions, as well as more refined uses of other EBMgt skills. For example, a Persuasive Paper assignment is meant to replicate an authentic, real-world task in which the student attempts to convince his or her (real or hypothetical) manager to take a particular "evidence-informed" action, related to a substantive topic from class. That assignment requires students to apply various EBMgt steps and is more fully discussed later.

A Preliminary Research Proposal is another assignment in which identifying a good, researchable question relevant to practice is the central challenge. It is the final deliverable for an EMBA business-research-methods course. Broadly, it is an opportunity for students to apply methods content to a substantive issue of their choosing. Students may use the preliminary proposal as a basis for their EMBA signature project, but that is not required. The proposal is meant to be a brief sketch of a problem; relevant background information; specific research questions or hypotheses; and a basic design, measurement, and analysis plan. The instructor explains how brief, preliminary proposals can be used in applied settings to get agreement in principle from decision makers before going forward with more detailed submissions for formal approval (i.e., it is not only an academic exercise). Students are instructed to think of this assignment as an opportunity to prepare a succinct, well-written description of their plans for a busy executive with neither time nor patience to read a long proposal.

Before students develop their own proposals, the instructor gives a mini-lecture outlining considerations and examples of real projects to show how general topics were refined into more specific research questions or hypotheses. Examples provided include real applied and academic projects that run the gamut from experimental, relational, and descriptive research. General aspects of design, measurement, and analysis considerations for those projects are also explained. This mini-lecture and the project examples are provided early in the EMBA research methods course, along with a workshop opportunity for students to start thinking about their own interests and research questions. Students are encouraged to think about the guiding question, "What don't we know that matters?" (Locke, Spirduso, & Silverman, 2007, p. 44). Then they work to find an angle that transforms a general topic into a researchable question. Characteristics of good, researchable questions are discussed in terms of being: right for you, right for your audience, acceptable, well articulated, and practical (O'Leary, 2004).

Clear and explicit statement of the question or problem is crucial for EBMgt (Briner et al., 2009), as is true for research questions more generally. A well-designed question points to the relevant theory and literature to be reviewed, the data pertinent to answering it, and how those data should be collected and analyzed (O'Leary, 2004). Systematic literature reviews that integrate and interpret pertinent evidence are seen as central for moving EBMgt forward (Briner et al., 2009; Rousseau, Manning, & Denyer, 2008). Adapting the PICO (Patient, Intervention, Comparison, Outcomes) framework for systematic EB medicine reviews, advocates of systematic EBMgt reviews have suggested use of the CIMO (Context, Intervention, Mechanisms,

and Outcomes) framework (Briner et al., 2009; Denyer & Tranfield, 2009). The CIMO framework seems useful to help specify both review and primary research questions. It helps students formulate their self-directed projects, including research studies or mini-systematic reviews (Critically Appraised Topics, Barends, 2010; Rapid Evidence Assessments, Briner et al., 2009).

A smaller-scale Question Specification exercise can be done in class or online to provide students with deliberate practice using CIMO to refine a question. For example, Denyer and Briner (2010) asked participants in their Academy of Management systematic review workshop to make more specific the question, "Does team-building work?" Following that lead, we have used a similar, in-class exercise wherein students are asked to use CIMO to make the team-building effectiveness question more specific.

Surfacing Assumptions complements learning to formulate useful questions. This technique can be used in a variety of ways. To help students identify uncritical assumptions, have them read a pop-management-magazine article (e.g., *Working for Boomers*, Filipczak, 1993), one that is full of unsupported assumptions, and let them have at it. An alternative involves pre-class online discussions (e.g., twitter) of a different popular-press article each week. In one example, pre-class discussions were held on twitter with students in a management course, five leading HR practitioners, and the instructor. The article was initially tweeted, and students and practitioners exchanged reactions and ideas about the article. Students examined the article for strengths and weaknesses based on the content material for the upcoming class, and they related evaluated research evidence they could find. An in-class session reviewed the article in depth, including all four facets of evidence. This exercise helps students critically assess popular press articles and understand the limitations of the information provided.

Getting the Best Available Evidence

The Surface Assumptions exercise highlights that readers must be wary of their sources and mindful of Rousseau's rule 1 (from her course syllabus): Never trust truth claims made without references! It leads directly to Rule 1.1, Do your due diligence: Check (at least a sample of) those references. Similar warnings (i.e., "reader beware") have been conveyed in lecture materials by drawing on Rynes et al.'s (2002) points regarding an *HR Magazine* article on graphology.

Explaining the business research landscape to students exposes them to different disciplines and paradigms as well as types of sources (e.g., academic, crossover, and practitioner journals). It helps them make sense of the variety of perspectives and quality of information they encounter as they search for the best available evidence. Instructors can provide students with examples of highly-respected peer-reviewed journals as part of familiarizing them with original sources of management and social-science research.

To support students in the development of their practice as evidence-based managers, we have partnered with librarians at our respective institutions to provide students with specific instruction on literature searching (Literature Search Workshops), a partnership strongly encouraged by proponents of systematic reviews (see, for example, Littell et al., 2008). Briefly, keyword searching, reference and citation searching, and pointer knowledge (key informants) are taught. Search instruction is covered in more detail elsewhere (Werner, chapter 15 of this volume), but there are a few points worth noting here. Both our experiences and principles of learning (Goodman & O'Brien, chapter 18 of this volume) suggest that guided exploration/discovery and opportunities for deliberate, distributed practice are important for supporting search-skill acquisition. As noted earlier, the UPEI EMBA program includes a structured library-skills session as part of program orientation. Students are then expected to practice those skills as part of personally relevant assignments, such as the Burning Question assignment discussed earlier. In the subsequent research-methods course, an "advanced" session is held with the librarian wherein search strategies are revisited and elaborated, and additional resources are revealed. Most recently, students in the advanced session have been given a topic to search consistent with that investigated in an existing systematic review (i.e., Joyce, Pabayo, Critchley, & Bambra, 2010). The Joyce et al. study serves as an example of an elaborate search strategy (see their Appendix 1) and presentation of results from a systematic review. Students are encouraged to come to the advanced search session prepared with questions and challenges they have encountered, as well as successful tips to offer others. We advocate a similar session for faculty members.

Insofar as the volume of articles, books, and online entries continues to grow, the task of finding relevant, high-quality evidence is challenging, especially for time-constrained managers. Summaries or reviews of the literature *should be* helpful to distill theories and evidence pertinent to one's research questions. However, too many such reviews are ad hoc. It is important to contrast traditional narrative reviews with systematic reviews, including but not limited to meta-analyses, to help students find appropriate syntheses of the best available research evidence.

Despite the questionable evidentiary value of traditional literature reviews, those works and other opinion pieces (e.g., this chapter) may be useful for sharing ideas, perspectives, and propositions. Literature reviews also provide contextual information for a study, be it primary research or a systematic review. Drawing on Easterby-Smith, Thorpe, and Jackson (2008) and O'Leary (2004), we have explained that literature reviews are used to educate the author; inform readers [*cf.* Campion (1997), for a dissenting guideline]; establish author credibility; argue for and position the study in a wider context; and describe and critically evaluate others' perspectives, methods, and findings. We believe it is also important to provide graduate business students with guidance for using and managing references, given the wide range of students' prior preparation and possibly years (or decades) since they participated in formal education. Campion's (1997) survey of journal reviewers identified guidelines for referencing that are especially helpful in that regard. Reference management and write-and-cite software that may be available to students can also be introduced.

The paucity of systematic reviews on management questions means that evidence-based managers may have to gather and synthesize existing research themselves, typically using a more expedient form rather than a full-scale systematic review (e.g., Critically Appraised Topic; Barends, 2010; Rapid Evidence Assessment, Briner et al., 2009). Various assignments such as Get the Evidence, Myth Busting, and the Snake Oil Symposium have provided practice opportunities in this regard. As an example, the Snake Oil Symposium (thanks to Dr. Kevin Kelloway for the name) involves groups of students completing a rapid evidence assessment of a management fad, program, or practice to evaluate its validity and strength of research evidence. Students prepare a plain-language translation and summary for managers in the form of a comprehensive, yet concise (2,000 word) paper and a 15–20 min presentation. Supplementary materials include an appendix outlining the specifics of the literature search strategy (e.g., databases and keywords searched) and results (e.g., number of relevant studies). More elaborate systematic reviews are possibilities for students' EMBA signature projects.

The EMBA Signature Project can include the collection of primary data for applied research or consulting purposes and provides students a deeper application of using an EBMgt approach. Research involving data existing within organizations or other sources of secondary data are also possibilities for signature projects. Projects involving local data are examples of "little e" evidence (Rousseau, 2006). To this point, our discussion of the search for the best available evidence has focused on "Big E" evidence (Rousseau, 2006) derived from formal research. However, it is important not to overlook evidence from the local context. Readings emphasizing local experimentation (e.g., Davenport, 2009; Pfeffer & Sutton, 2006a) and use of organizational data (e.g., Donaldson, chapter 14 of this volume) can be assigned to support this perspective.

Instruction on how to design, conduct, and interpret formal research fits within the mandate of a business-research-methods course, yet it is challenging to incorporate any array of practice opportunities within any single course. The Preliminary Research Proposal is one reasonably integrated opportunity to think about primary research, and some of those projects could provide local-context evidence. More limited exercises have also been conducted to give students practice with Semi-Structured Interviewing and Statistical Analysis of existing data sets. Data sets could come from an instructor's previous research studies or may be packaged with textbooks (e.g., Hair, Celsi, Money, Samouel, & Page, 2011), if quality or logistic concerns preclude class-originated data collection and analysis. An Online Questionnaire Development workshop has also been used to demonstrate available technology in that regard. Becoming a proficient producer of research requires much more instruction and deliberate practice than can be offered in a single course. Nevertheless, introductory background in research methods may promote willingness and perceived capability to collaborate in research, appreciation for difficulties inherent in conducting research, and ability to critically appraise research.

Critically Appraising the Evidence

"Critical appraisal is the process of assessing and interpreting evidence by systematically considering its validity, results and relevance to an individual's work" (Parkes et al., 2001, p. 1), and is argued to be central to evidence-based practice

(Norman & Shannon, 1998). Thoughtful criticisms of the EBMgt movement (e.g., Learmonth, 2008; Learmonth & Harding, 2006) reinforce the careful and inclusive explication of what constitutes evidence in management and organizational science (e.g., Rousseau et al., 2008). We have introduced students, albeit briefly, to philosophical issues regarding the nature of knowledge, and different ontological and epistemological perspectives (e.g., Easterby-Smith et al., 2008; Rousseau et al., 2008; Shadish, Cook, & Campbell, 2002). Even brief introductions alert students to the idea that they may encounter different, valuable perspectives during their searches for the best available evidence. We also let students know where we are coming from. Our perspective is that reality exists independent of our efforts to understand it; and that observations, facts, and concepts (our lay term for "constructs") are subjective and value laden, but not completely fallible (Rousseau et al., 2008; Shadish et al., 2002). We differentiate between meta-analyses and other forms of systematic reviews as examples of high-quality evidence, and opinion-pieces (expert or nonexpert) as examples of weak evidence. However, evidence hierarchies, if presented, are inclusive of research designs (e.g., case studies; descriptive research; quasi-experimental investigations) that may be applicable for some questions, entities, or stages of knowledge development. Triangulation across methods and theoretical pluralism are valued, consistent with a critical realist perspective (Rousseau et al., 2008).

Learning to plan one's own research and critically appraise others' research are complementary learning experiences. We encourage critical appraisal of evidence from all four EBMgt elements (Briner et al., 2009). We describe to students various ways of acquiring knowledge (e.g., personal experience, tradition, authority, formal research) and associated strengths and limitations. Whereas personal experience is valuable and will inform managerial decision-making, an EBMgt perspective requires critical reflection upon that source, as well as the others. For example, the Absenteeism Diagnosis exercise, discussed previously, includes questions adapted from Briner and Rousseau (2011) such as, "What are my beliefs about the causes of absence?" and "How relevant and applicable is my experience?" Such questions are designed to encourage critical appraisal of personal experience. An additional question, "Have I developed an 'expert's intuition' (versus a 'gut feel')?" has been used in debriefings of the Absenteeism Diagnosis exercise to encourage students to appreciate expert-level insights developed over years of education and deliberate, reflective practice (Thomas et al., 2011). Instead of "research versus experience" we believe an EBMgt perspective fosters careful consideration of research *and* experience. Nevertheless, limitations of personal experience are important to highlight with students. Limited sample size of experiences, perceptual biases, and our tendency to underestimate the role of chance factors (randomness) place limits on the quality of evidence we can gather solely from our personal experiences (March, 2010). These problems can be used to help explain why formal research is also needed to obtain high-quality evidence (E and e; Rousseau, 2006). By formal research we mean the systematic gathering, analysis, and interpretation of information to describe, predict, explain, and/or manage a phenomenon of interest. The critical appraisal of formal research is a central focus of EBMgt education.

Instruction in research fundamentals should be included in EBMgt-related education, although the exact form likely depends on the nature of the course (e.g., substantive versus methods focus) and the students' prior training. Fundamental considerations include things like types of variables such as independent and predictor, dependent and criterion, mediator and mechanism, and moderator and contingency. Students can be given examples of each type and asked to work in groups to generate their own Variable Type and Hypothesis Example as an in-class exercise. Although a seemingly simple exercise, it provides opportunities for discussion and clarification of concepts both in working with small groups and in plenary discussion of groups' examples. Other fundamental considerations include control and validity (see, for example, Pedhazur & Schmelkin, 1991). We also discuss threats to validity and threats to legitimacy of findings. The latter includes the perspectives of stakeholders that might not have been accounted for in the way a study was framed. Such might be the case in research on high-commitment work systems, which tend to emphasize benefits to the firm in terms of productivity and a motivated workforce but ignore its potential impacts on employee health or work-family balance.

The research trinity, the elements design, measurement, and analysis, defines the core of empirical research (Kline, 2009; Pedhazur & Schmelkin, 1991). The trinity elements are covered more explicitly in a business-research-methods course than, for example, in a substantive course on management.

Covering these elements aids in critical appraisal of research reports as well as helping students plan their own projects (e.g., Preliminary Research Proposal). Integrated coverage of the research trinity is recommended to "foster a sense of how each of design, measurement, and analysis gives context and meaning to the others" (Kline, 2009, p. 39) and provide a foundation for more advanced learning (i.e., interacting elements; see Goodman & O'Brien, chapter 18 of this volume). Coverage of the research trinity may be constrained in any single course. Still, an integrated framework accommodates some coverage of measurement and statistics as well as qualitative approaches to data collection, analysis, and interpretation. More advanced content related to the research trinity can be supplemented by later courses or independent studies.

Although the multidisciplinary nature of business research makes it difficult to identify universal evaluation criteria, O'Leary (2004) provided a set of indicators of good research that are useful for judging the credibility of research conducted from various perspectives. Research credibility is higher to the extent that subjectivities are managed, methods are approached with consistency, the "true essence" has been captured, findings are applicable beyond the immediate context, and the research can be verified. These indicators can be used to foster critical engagement with others' research as well as serving as goals for one's own research (O'Leary, 2004). We have also provided students with other readings or summaries of criteria for appraising research and research reports. Rousseau et al. (2008) outlined six criteria for evaluating evidence which are especially applicable to a synthesis of a body of knowledge. Other indicators of good research come in the form of criteria for evaluating a research report, such as reviewer's checklists (e.g., Colquitt & Ireland, 2009; Derosiers et al., 2002). Such checklists can provide advanced frameworks to help students organize incoming knowledge about critical appraisal and possibly be used as aids for practicing EBMgt.

To provide a practice opportunity in critical appraisal, a Favorite Article Review assignment asks students to appraise highly-respected articles from prestigious peer-reviewed journals using indicators of good research. The objective is to help students articulate what they find particularly compelling about their chosen article while providing multiple (e.g., three) models of good research and writing for students. Students recognize that even highly-acclaimed studies are imperfect, yet the Favorite Article Review assignment is meant to be relatively inspirational. Its purpose is to foster a mindset that is critical, constructive, and appreciative of well-executed research.

We have tried a couple of variations of the Favorite Article Review assignment. In one version, students prepare papers of up to six double-spaced pages wherein they discuss the compelling features (e.g., exposition, design, measurement, analysis, interpretation, and implications) of their favorite of the target articles. They are asked to assume they are writing an award nomination for that article. They are also asked to identify areas in which their favorite article is deficient and suggest ways that future research could remedy those deficiencies. Brief descriptions of the other target articles can be included, but detailed review of all three articles is not required. Another version of this assignment asks students for a shorter write-up of the pros and cons of the target articles (e.g., one page) in terms of usefulness to practice, along with a stated choice and rationale for the one they see as most useful to practice. The pros and cons of each paper are subsequently discussed in class and the class votes on the most useful paper in terms of informing management practice. Different instructors have also varied somewhat in terms of the target readings assigned. To date, three of the following articles have been used for this assignment, which also goes by the name Fun with Evidence or Award Winning and Otherwise Famous Studies: Audia, Locke, and Smith (2000); Frese, Garstf, and Fay (2007); Margolis and Molinsky (2008); and Sutton and Rafaeli (1988). Instructors should be aware that some resourceful students have used their literature search skills and found Frost and Stablein's (1992) book, *Doing Exemplary Research*, in which the Sutton and Rafaeli paper is featured. Use of the commentaries within that source, with appropriate citations, may not be a problem, depending on the instructor's perspective. Nevertheless, the availability of external commentary on award-winning articles is something to consider.

Critical thinking about claims made by authorities is important to encourage. One assignment in that regard is the Myth of Market Share reflective paper. The assigned reading is Armstrong's (2007), "The 'Myth of Market Share': Can Focusing Too Much on the Competition Harm Profitability?" (cf. Armstrong & Collopy, 1996; Armstrong & Green, 2007). Students are assigned to write a brief (one page) paper reflecting upon how market share has been treated in their business school and university education more broadly. Students are also asked to

consider any evidence they have that market-share-related course content has been evidence based. (At Carnegie Mellon, our finance faculty does a good job of debunking students' beliefs about market share's importance. This assignment has become more focused on how to convince others in a company to be less competition oriented and focus instead on business and profitability improvement). Providing "reader beware" examples of EBMgt proponents' contrasting positions is another way to encourage students to reflect carefully on authorities' claims. For example, as noted by Rousseau et al. (2008), whether incentive pay is deemed to be an effective motivator may depend on which EBMgt proponent you ask (cf. Pfeffer, 1998; Rynes, Gerhart, & Parks, 2005). Topics such as pay for performance can be investigated in more depth as part of students' assignments wherein they refine one or more questions, seek relevant evidence (as well as theories and opinions), and critically appraise the information they obtained. Titles and details of the assignments of this genre may differ, but all have students get and critically appraise practice-relevant evidence.

Working in groups, students select a business problem within one of their organizations or develop another practice-related question to examine. Past groups have chosen to examine the construct of employee engagement, the role of personality testing in hiring, and some of the barriers to women's advancement such as the glass cliff (see, for example, Ryan & Haslam, 2005; 2007). Other specific questions might look like these: When are distributed teams more likely to perform effectively? Would pay for performance work in our company? When is investing in workforce training most likely to be financially beneficial? Students consult with the instructor about their topics and specific questions. Students are required to use an EBMgt approach to examine the fad or phenomena they have selected. The group reviews the literature to examine the topic and includes information from other sources, such as the local context. Their task is to evaluate the literature and marshal the best available management and social science research to answer their question. Deliverables for assignments like these include papers (of lengths varying from 2–3 to 6–8 pages) and presentations. An instructor may require an annotated appendix to describe the search process the group employed to identify their sources. Often, students discover that the evaluated research evidence does not support the management practice that is commonly used in business. After reviewing and evaluating the literature, the group may be required specifically to address the "so what" question to determine the practical implications for managers in the workplace, examining ways in which we can meaningfully incorporate evidence (rigor) into practice (relevance). One important learning point for the students is to construct a table describing each study's quality, context, variables, and findings. Without a table, students tend to interpret each study separately and have difficulty integrating the studies. With a table, patterns and trends become more apparent. By doing an assignment like Myth Busting or Get the Evidence twice in a term, students recognize what and how much they have learned. This experience reinforces the value of having opportunities to practice the kinds of behaviors and techniques we seek to help transfer to students' work lives.

Integrating EBMgt Elements to Support Decisions and Actions

We emphasize the four EBMgt facets (Briner et al., 2009) through various exercises and assignments discussed in the previous steps. Classroom-based education, like ours, may foster knowledge about evidence-based practices, whereas evidence-based education that is more closely integrated to practice settings seems to result in improved skills, attitudes, and behaviors (Coomarasamy & Khan, 2004). Moreover, "it may be unrealistic to expect university students to reach expert performance levels in EBP [evidence-based practice] by the end of their educational experience" (Thomas et al., 2011, p. 262). Those insights on evidenced-based education in health domains are important to consider. Classroom-based interventions may not be as powerful as practice-integrated evidence-based education in affecting all relevant outcomes (e.g., attitudes, skills, behavior). Nevertheless, classroom teaching can incorporate cases and projects, including those dealing with real and current problems, to augment the authenticity of learning (Coomarasamy & Khan, 2004; Thomas et al., 2011) and provide a foundation for longer-term development.

Other assignments, though contrived, afford students opportunities to practice anticipating and planning for the challenges they may face in applying EBMgt. That's Incredible! is one such assignment. The content deals with employee selection, perhaps the most thoroughly researched management practice organizations use. Employers recruiting, screening, and hiring new employees can draw on 100 years of systematic research. Nonetheless, the vast majority of employers, even large corporations,

use selection practices known to be invalid. For this assignment, students are asked to read Highhouse's (2008), "Stubborn Reliance on Intuition and Subjectivity in Employee Selection." In two or three pages, students are asked to (1) summarize the gist of the findings from selection research; (2) explain in their own words (a) why companies fail to act on these findings, and (b) what makes the findings difficult to act on; and (3) suggest two or three ways to overcome the problems of (2) to help companies apply the beneficial findings from selection research. Guidance about ways to overcome problems is offered in the form of "sticky evidence" considerations (Rousseau & Boudreau, 2011).

A more context-specific assignment is the Persuasive Paper. Students prepare a short (2–3 page double-spaced) paper in which they attempt to convince their (hypothetical or real) manager to take a particular "evidence-informed" action, using evidence and organization-related facts. A few of these have been written up as dialogues between themselves and their boss, sometimes in dialect. Topics for the Persuasive Paper relate to substantive issues discussed in class (e.g., whether to outsource the firm's HR function, use team-based rewards, or pursue a merger with another firm). Students are cautioned that many bosses have little professional management training and even less knowledge of social science. Criteria for evaluating papers consist of (1) how effectively the student marshals the best scientific evidence to make the case; (2) the extent to which the student has made the case in a strong, truthful, and convincing manner; and (3) how well the student used facts about the particular organization (again, real or hypothetical) to help make his or her case "sticky" (Rousseau & Boudreau, 2011).

A similar context-specific assignment is also used in a second-year EMBA course. Students are engaged in The Great Debate assignment to encourage critical appraisal of all four sources of evidence and to use the evidence to develop a compelling argument to support their case. The instructor assigns sets of three students to work independently on a specific debate topic. For each topic, there is a person to take each of the two sides of the debate and one moderator. Two participants in the debate taking a specific side must develop their position and argument using an EBMgt perspective and incorporating all four sources of evidence (Briner et al., 2009); and the moderator becomes familiar with both sides of the debate and develops questions to highlight the key issues. Debate topics in the past have included "Is EBMgt a fad?" "Are MBA programs contributing to a leadership crisis?" and "Should organizational leaders assume responsibility for employee health and wellness in the workplace?" The debates are held in class and provide a rich platform to stimulate further discussion.

Encouraging students to reflect, self-monitor, and engage in meta-cognitive processing should help them develop adaptive expertise for dealing with new and complex problems inherent in the practice of management (Goodman & O'Brien, chapter 18 of this volume). De Dea Roglio and Light (2009), in a study of EMBA students, developed a model of the "reflective executive," offering insights to scholars and educators about ways to bridge the rigor-relevance gap. The concept of the reflective executive focuses on the convergence of connective, critical, and personal thinking. For the EMBA student to experience this convergence, the learning environment must be structured around adult learning principles, with an instructor acting as a model and guide to prompt open dialogue and reflection.

Reflection and self-awareness is the goal of having each student complete a Learning Diary, log, or blog as part of course requirements (*Learning How to Study Again*, Dawson, 2004). Students are encouraged to make regular entries and instructors provide examples of ideas to help students get started. Learning Diaries are to go beyond a descriptive record of what students have done, read, or noted in class. Instead, they are encouraged to reflect on course readings, class discussions, group work, what they have learned, what they have found difficult, and what they need to learn more about. Students are also asked to note demonstrated applications of course learning to practice (e.g., raising the issue "what's the evidence" outside class). To date, a variety of diary formats have been used (hard copy, word processing files, web based, e.g., google.docs). Sometimes diaries have been reviewed only on completion of the course. Or the instructor may review diary entries and engage with students as the course proceeds. Pragmatic versions of the latter are likely more valuable to students and instructors. Through diary assignments, we hope to develop conscious, reflective habits among students, as well as help them to be more effective learners. Studies show that "good" learners organize their learning, set their own goals, seek practice opportunities, and monitor and evaluate themselves effectively (Ambrose, Bridges, DiPietro, Lovett, & Norman, 2010). Diary keeping not only encourages reflection and preserves valuable insights, but may also reveal attitudes and beliefs hindering learning. Students receive support and feedback to encourage authentic reflections on their personal learning experiences. Entries can transition over time from being descriptive to being analytical, from accepting to questioning, from doing to thinking, and ultimately to doing while being reflective and self-aware.

Instructors can further encourage students to plan to apply and continue their learning through a Letter to Self, which students complete as an in-class exercise in one of the final class meetings. This letter can be posted to www.futureme.org to be automatically sent to the student six months (or several times) after course completion. Relapse prevention is a concern in promoting knowledge transfer. It is an important concern in EBMgt given that learners will work in settings not necessarily supportive of integrating evidence into decisions.

Evaluating the Process

The final step in the EBMgt process we adopted involves evaluating the process in terms of efficiency and effectiveness with respect to the previous steps (Barends, 2010; Thomas et al., 2011). The evaluation phase involves reflection on the EBMgt process as applied to a practical opportunity or problem. Reflective evaluation is an opportunity to use systematic approaches to gather evaluation-relevant local evidence and stakeholder perspectives. One approach we have taught in class to support students' EBMgt practice can actually be used to evaluate the progress made and needed improvements within EBMgt courses. Modeled after the After Action Review (AAR) used in the U.S. Army (Garvin, 2000), it reflects the process-improvement approach investigated in project research (Cho & Egan, 2010; Darling & Parry, 2000). After discussing the evidence on the importance of task and process feedback, we show the Harvard film (*Put the Learning Organization to Work: Learning After Doing*) and then use it to engage in a mini-after- action review midway through the course. Students form small groups to identify features of the class that should be continued, in which they recommend change or improvement, and lessons learned (in this case, about effective learning processes for EBMgt). Groups then report through a spokesperson to provide psychological safety in voicing criticisms. Following the next group assignment, students participate in an AAR in their study groups during class time and then share their lessons learned with the class. At the end of the class, we do a full-blown AAR. One major idea from final

AARs to date is the importance of more cases and more explicit framework for organizing evidence and business information.

At the last class, students also complete an assessment (now also given as a pretest on the first day of class) to indicate how they rate themselves on specific skills the class intended to address and on meeting their learning goals. These have included either initial goal choices identified by the instructor or a set of learning goals collected from students in the first week of the course, and students are asked the extent to which each of the goals was met during the course (1–3 scale: not at all, somewhat, substantially). Goals include such dimensions as "Find evidence," "Use evidence to make better decisions," "Persuade others with evidence," "Define problems in my work environment that can be addressed with EBMgt," and "Show others how to practice EBMgt." Finally, students are asked to rate their "current level of expertise regarding evidence-based management" from (1) novice, (2) between novice and intermediate, (3) intermediate, (4) between intermediate and expert, and (5) expert. It is perhaps a comment on the success of the class that ratings on day 1 usually turn up a couple of students who rate themselves EBMgt "experts," whereas there are no self-rated experts on the posttest. The vast majority of students judge themselves to be either novices or between novice and intermediate at time 1, increasing at time 2 to between novice and intermediate or intermediate, an outcome consistent with expectations. The last class (prior to the final AAR) is dedicated to the topic "next steps on the road to mastering EBMgt" to help students envision how they might continue to develop themselves as professional evidence-based managers postgraduation.

The effectiveness of EBMgt teaching lies ultimately in whether it transfers to the workplace. In particular, EBMgt's focus is improved quality of managerial decisions and organizational practices. Because all forms of education increasingly emphasize assessment and accountability, evaluation of the effects of EBMgt teaching will be closely linked to the effects of EBMgt itself (Reay et al., 2009).

Conclusion

Teaching EBMgt is a work in progress. It is increasingly prominent in executive management programs and executive doctoral programs (Salipante & Smith, chapter 20 of this volume). Textbooks (Pearce, chapter 21 of this volume) and cases (Kovner, Fine, & D'Aquila, 2009) are appearing and ease the transition to this innovative form of management education. In its EBMgt 1.0 phase, educators have the opportunity to apply evidence-based principles of learning in novel and creative ways. Further, integration of the EBMgt perspective and skills into other courses provides students with more opportunities to refine their skills and helps make searching for the best available evidence a habitual response. We enjoy the challenge that teaching EBMgt poses and invite you to join in.

References

Ambrose, S. A., Bridges, M. W., DiPietro, M., Lovett, M. C., & Norman, M. K. (2010). *How learning works: Seven research-based principles for smart teaching*. San Francisco, CA: Jossey-Bass.

Armstrong, J. S. (2007). The 'myth of market share': Can focusing too much on the competition harm profitability? *Knowledge @ Wharton*. Retrieved from http://knowledge.wharton.upenn.edu/article.cfm?articleid=1645

Armstrong, J. S., & Collopy, F. (1996). Competitor orientation: Effects of objectives and information on managerial decisions and profitability. *Journal of Marketing Research, 33*(2), 188–199.

Armstrong, J. S., & Green, K. C. (2007). Competitor-oriented objectives: The myth of market share. *International Journal of Business, 12*(1), 117–136.

Armstrong, J. S., & Green, K. C. (2011). Advertising principles: Evidence-based knowledge on persuasion through advertising. Retrieved from http://advertisingprinciples.com/ (accessed November 16, 2011)

Audia, P. G., Locke, E. A., & Smith, K. G. (2000). The paradox of success: An archival and a laboratory study of strategic persistence following radical environmental change. *Academy of Management Journal, 43*(5), 837–853.

Barends, E. G. R. (2010). A post graduate course on evidence-based management. In E. Barends & R. B. Briner (Eds.), *Evidence-based management: A new approach to teaching the practice of management. Professional development workshop*. Montreal, Canada: Academy of Management.

Barling, J., Weber, T., & Kelloway, E. K. (1996). Effects of transformational leadership training on attitudinal and financial outcomes: A field experiment. *Journal of Applied Psychology, 81*, 827–832.

Briner, R. B., Denyer, D., & Rousseau, D. M. (2009). Evidence-based management: Concept cleanup time? *Academy of Management Perspectives, 23*, 19–32.

Briner, R. B., & Rousseau, D. M. (2011). Evidence-based I-O psychology: Not there yet. *Industrial and Organizational Psychology, 4*(1), 3–22.

Burke, L. A., & Rau, B. (2010). The research-teaching gap in management. *Academy of Management Learning & Education, 9*(1), 132–143.

Campion, M. (1997). Rules for references: Suggested guidelines for choosing literary citations for research articles in applied psychology. *Personnel Psychology, 50*, 165–167.

Cho, Y., & Egan, T. M. (2010). The state of the art of action learning research. *Advances in Developing Human Resources, 12*(2), 163–180.

Cialdini, R. (2011). *Influence at work*. Retrieved from http://www.influenceatwork.com/ (accessed November 16, 2011)

Colquitt, J. A., & Ireland, R. D. (2009). From the editors: Taking the mystery out of AMJ's reviewer evaluation form. *Academy of Management Journal, 52*(2), 224–228.

Coomarasamy, A., & Khan, K. S. (2004). What is the evidence that postgraduate teaching in evidence based medicine changes anything? A systematic review. *British Medical Journal, 329,* 1017–1019.

Darling, M., & Parry, C. (2000). *From post-mortem to living practice: The evolution of the after action review.* Boston, MA: SR&C Publications.

Davenport, T. H. (2009). How to design smart business experiments. *Harvard Business Review, 87*(2), 68–76.

Dawson, C. (2004). *Learning how to study again: A practical guide to study skills for mature students returning to education or distance learning.* Oxford, England: How To Books.

De Dea Roglio, K., & Light, G. (2009). Executive MBA programs: The development of the reflective executive. *Academy of Management Learning & Education, 8,* 156–173.

Denyer, D., & Briner, R. B. (2010). *Systematic review and research synthesis. Professional development workshop.* Montreal, Canada: Academy of Management.

Denyer, D., & Tranfield, D. (2009). Producing a systematic review. In D. A. Buchanan & A. Bryman (Eds.), *The Sage handbook of organizational research methods* (pp. 671–689). Thousand Oaks, CA: Sage.

Derosiers, E. I., Sherony, K., Barros, E., Ballinger, G. A., Senol, S., & Campion, M. A. (2002). Writing research articles: Update on the article review checklist. In S. G. Rogelberg (Ed.), *Handbook of research methods in industrial and organizational psychology* (pp. 459–478). Malden, MA: Blackwell.

Easterby-Smith, M. P. V., Thorpe, R., & Jackson, P. (2008). *Management research* (3rd ed.). Thousand Oaks, CA: Sage.

Filipczak, B. (1993). Working for boomers. *Training, 30*(1), 8.

Frese, M., Garst, H., & Fay, D. (2007). Making things happen: Reciprocal relationships between work characteristics and personal initiative in a four-wave longitudinal structural equation model. *Journal of Applied Psychology, 92*(4), 1084–1102.

Frost, P. J., & Stablein, R. E. (1992). Introductory remarks: Journey four. In P. J. Frost & R. E. Stablein (Eds.), *Doing exemplary research* (pp. 113–128). Newbury Park, CA: Sage.

Garvin, D. A. (2000). *Learning in action, a guide to putting the learning organization to work.* Boston, MA: Harvard Business School Press.

Graen, G. B. (2009). Educating new management specialists from an evidence-based perspective: A proposal. *Academy of Management Learning & Education, 8,* 255–258.

Hadley, J. A., Davis, J., & Khan, K. S. (2007). Teaching and learning evidence-based medicine in complementary, allied, and alternative healthcare: An integrated tailor-made course. *The Journal of Alternative and Complementary Medicine, 13*(10), 1151–1155.

Hair, J. F., Jr., Celsi, M. W., Money, A. H., Samouel, P., & Page, M. J. (2011). *Essentials of business research methods* (2nd ed.). Armonk, NY: M. E. Sharpe.

Heath, C., Larrick, R. P., & Klayman, J. (1998). Cognitive repairs: How organizational practices can compensate for individual shortcomings. *Research in Organizational Behavior, 20,* 1–37.

Highhouse, S. (2008). Stubborn reliance on intuition and subjectivity in employee selection. *Industrial and Organizational Psychology, 1*(3), 333–342.

Joyce, K., Pabayo, R., Critchley, J. A., & Bambra, C. (2010). Flexible working conditions and their effects on employee health and wellbeing. *Cochrane Database of Systematic Reviews*, CD008009.

Kline, R. B. (2009). *Becoming a behavioral science researcher: A guide to producing research that matters.* New York: Guilford Press.

Kovner, A. R., Fine, D. J., & D'Aquila, R. (2009). *Evidence-based management in healthcare.* Chicago, IL: Healthcare Administration Press.

Learmonth, M. (2008). Evidence-based management: A backlash against pluralism in organizational studies? *Organization, 15,* 283–291.

Learmonth, M., & Harding, N. (2006). Evidence-based management: The very idea. *Public Administration, 84,* 245–266.

Littell, J. H., Corcoran, J., & Pillai, V. K. (2008). *Systematic reviews and meta-analysis.* New York: Oxford University Press.

Locke, L. F., Spirduso, W. W., & Silverman, S. J. (2007). *Proposals that work: A guide for planning dissertations and grant proposals* (5th ed.). Thousand Oaks, CA: Sage.

March, J. G. (2010). *Ambiguities of experience.* Ithaca, NY: Cornell University Press.

Margolis, J. D., & Molinsky, A. (2008). Navigating the bind of necessary evils: Psychological engagement and the production of interpersonally sensitive behavior. *Academy of Management Journal, 51*(5), 847–872.

Murad, M. H., Montori, V. M., Kunz, R., Letelier, L. M., Keitz, S. A., Dans, A. L., Silva, S. A., & Guyatt, G. H. (2009). How to teach evidence based medicine to teachers: Reflections from a workshop experience. *Journal of Evaluation in Clinical Practice, 15,* 1205–1207.

Norman, G. R., & Shannon, S. I. (1998). Effectiveness of instruction in critical appraisal (evidence-based medicine) skills: A critical appraisal. *Canadian Medical Association Journal, 158*(2), 177.

O'Leary, Z. (2004). *The essential guide to doing research.* Thousand Oaks, CA: Sage.

Parkes, J., Hyde, C., Deeks, J., & Milne, R. (2001). Teaching critical appraisal skills in healthcare settings. *Cochrane Database of Systematic Reviews*, CD001270.

Pedhazur, E. J., & Schmelkin, L. (1991). *Measurement, design and analysis: An integrated approach.* Hillsdale, NJ: Lawrence Erlbaum.

Pfeffer, J. (1998). Six dangerous myths about pay. *Harvard Business Review, May-June,* 108–119.

Pfeffer, J. (2007). Evidence-based management in industrial and organizational psychology: A celebration of accomplishments and some aspirations for the future. *The Industrial-Organizational Psychologist, 45*(1), 11–15.

Pfeffer, J., & Sutton, R. I. (2006a). Evidence-based management. *Harvard Business Review, January,* 1–11.

Pfeffer, J., & Sutton, R. I. (2006b). *Hard facts, dangerous half-truths, and total nonsense.* Boston, MA: Harvard Business School Press.

Pfeffer, J., & Sutton, R. I. (2007). Suppose we took evidence-based management seriously: Implications for reading and writing management. *Academy of Management Learning & Education, 6*(1), 153–155.

Reay, T., Berta, W., & Kohn, M. K. (2009). What's the evidence on evidence-based management? *Academy of Management Perspectives, 23,* 5–18.

Re$earch-Infosource. (2010). Spotlight - Decade in review. Retrieved from http://www.researchinfosource.com/media/Spotlight

2010WinnersCircleWebVersion.pdf (accessed November 16, 2011)

Rogers, W. (n.d.). BrainyQuote.com. Retrieved from BrainyQuote.com web site: http://www.brainyquote.com/quotes/quotes/w/willrogers385286.html (accessed November 16, 2011)

Rousseau, D. M. (2006). Is there such a thing as "evidence-based management"? *Academy of Management Review, 31,* 256–269.

Rousseau, D. M., & Barends, E. G. R. (2011). Becoming an evidence-based HR practitioner. *Human Resource Management Journal, 21*(3), 221–235.

Rousseau, D. M., & Boudreau, J. W. (2011). Sticky findings: Research evidence practitioners find useful. In S. A. Mohrman & E. E. Lawler (Eds.), Useful Research: Advancing Theory and Practice. San Francisco, CA: Berrett-Koehler.

Rousseau, D. M., Manning, J., & Denyer, D. (2008). Evidence in management and organizational science: Assembling the field's full weight of scientific knowledge through syntheses. *Academy of Management Annals, 2*(1), 475–515.

Rousseau, D. M., & McCarthy, S. (2007). Educating managers from an evidence-based perspective. *Academy of Management Learning & Education, 6,* 84–101.

Ryan, M. K., & Haslam, S. A. (2005). The glass cliff: Evidence that women are over represented in precarious leadership positions. *British Journal of Management, 16*(2), 81–90.

Ryan, M. K., & Haslam, S. A. (2007). The glass cliff: Exploring the dynamics surrounding the appointment of women to precarious leadership positions. *The Academy of Management Review, 32*(2), 549–572.

Rynes, S. L., Colbert, A. E., & Brown, K. G. (2002). HR professionals' beliefs about effective human resource practices: Correspondence between research and practice. *Human Resource Management, 41*(2), 149–174.

Rynes, S. L., Gerhart, B., & Parks, L. (2005). Personnel psychology: Performance evaluation and pay for performance. *Annual Review of Psychology, 56,* 571–600.

Rynes, S. L., Trank, C. Q., Lawson, A. M., & Ilies, R. (2003). Behavioral coursework in business education: Growing evidence of a legitimacy crisis. *Academy of Management Learning & Education, 2*(3), 269–283.

Shadish, W. R., Cook, T. D., & Campbell, D. T. (2002). *Experimental and quasi-experimental designs for generalized causal inference.* Boston, MA: Houghton, Mifflin.

Sutton, R. I., & Rafaeli, A. (1988). Untangling the relationship between displayed emotions and organizational sales: The case of convenience stores. *Academy of Management Journal, 31*(3), 461–487.

Thomas, A., Saroyan, A., & Dauphinee, W. D. (2011). Evidence-based practice: A review of theoretical assumptions and effectiveness of teaching and assessment interventions in health professions. *Advances in Health Sciences Education, 16*(2), 253–276.

Twain, M. (n.d.). BrainyQuote.com. Retrieved from BrainyQuote.com web site: http://www.brainyquote.com/quotes/quotes/m/marktwain109624.html

Weick, K., & Sutcliffe, K. (2007). *Managing the unexpected: Resilient performance in an age of uncertainty* (rev. ed.). New York: Wiley and Sons.

Wyer, P. C., Keitz, S., Hatala, R., Hayward, R., Barratt, A., Montori, V., & Guyatt, G. (2004). Tips for learning and teaching evidence-based medicine: Introduction to the series. *Canadian Medical Association Journal, 171*(4), 347–348.

From the 3 Rs to the 4 Rs: Toward Doctoral Education that Encourages Evidence-Based Management through Problem-Focused Research

Paul Salipante *and* Ann Kowal Smith

Abstract

To make evidence-based management (EBMgt) commonplace and effective, senior managers and academics must develop the capabilities that problem-focused research requires. Drawing lessons from alternative doctoral programs and problem-focused research, this chapter offers its readers concrete ways to support EBMgt in their educational, research, and senior management activities. It covers three related developments: (1) alternative doctoral-education programs producing a community of managerially experienced practitioner-scholars, that fosters EBMgt by bridging managerial and academic practice; (2) problem-focused research, providing a new model of research for more effective EBMgt, refined in alternative doctoral programs; and (3) overcoming barriers to EBMgt, new educational pedagogies and problem-focused research via relevance, respect, resourcefulness and reframing, or "the 4Rs." This chapter presents these developments as exemplified through an alternative doctoral program's 15-year evolution.

Key Words: review synthesis, alternative doctoral programs, executive doctoral programs, problem-oriented research, practice-oriented research

"Profound differences in theory are never gratuitous or invented. They grow out of conflicting elements in a genuine problem..."
John Dewey, The Child and the Curriculum, 1902

This chapter demonstrates that a powerful step toward encouraging senior managers to apply research evidence is to engage them in becoming practitioner-scholars: generators as well as consumers of the evidence they need. Managers must find the evidence and its foundational theories not only to be relevant and accessible, but *respectable* too. Managers and practitioners often remain skeptical about theoretical contributions to a particular problem, fearing that a theoretical focus supplants practical, demonstrably usable suggestions in a world too fast-paced for debate. The push to "do" trumps the mandate to "consider." Issues of relevance have been recognized

and seriously addressed in scholarly literature (c.f., Schon, 1995; Huff, 2000; Van de Ven, 2007). However, the skepticism and even disrespect for both research and the scholars who produce it tend to go unrecognized and unexplored. Fulfilling the mandate for relevance, rigor, and respectability requires a change, not only in managerial outlook, but also in the fundamental development in the knowledge generation and educational practices of academics.

Alternative doctoral programs created since the mid-1990s attempt to produce doctoral graduates whose scholarship optimizes relevance and rigor. Based on the authors' personal experiences (one as professor, the other as a graduate student and research fellow) with Case Western Reserve University's Weatherhead School of Management Doctor of Management (DM) program (hereafter, DM Program), we propose that the lessons from these programs for evidence-based management (EBMgt) can be applied as meaningfully to traditional doctoral programs and to management education and research efforts generally. Indeed, expanding management inquiry from problems of theory to problems of practice bridges the divide between producers and consumers of knowledge, a divide both unnecessary and damaging to both scholars and practitioners.

Senior manager practitioner-scholars can become ambassadors linking research and practice. As such they are a critical resources for EBMgt, affecting both the respect manager's place on research-based evidence and the academy's capacity to generate relevant research. This bridging role is not without its challenges but, given their organizational and community stature, these practitioner-scholars have the advantage of implementing and modeling the use of EBMgt for their senior management peers and for lower levels of managers. Of, perhaps, greater importance for managerial practice, they participate in normative networks to inform (Gill & Hoppe, 2009, p. 48) senior managers elsewhere about the use of research in practice. In their teaching and consulting endeavors, practitioner-scholars argue far more persuasively for EBMgt's efficacy than traditionally trained scholars can. The academy has as much to learn from practitioner-scholars, too. In their quest for doctoral credentials, practitioner-scholars model a different approach to articulating and solving practical problems, bringing theory to bear on problems, rather than using problems as anecdotes in support of theory. This shift in knowledge generation requires the academy to use new and different muscles as well; by engaging all sides in the "debate," we believe that more practical, relevant, and rigorous outcomes will ensue. By creating a vibrant, sustainable community of hybrid scholars, we will better link two worlds too often divided by prejudices, misunderstandings and miscommunications.

We first present an overview of alternative doctoral education and the practitioner-scholar movement it supports, then the structure of the DM Program from which this chapter's illustrations are taken. Next, we consider developments positive for EBMgt, in particular problem-focused research, which enhances research's managerial *relevance*. We examine what this research reveals about the knowledge needs of senior managers and how those needs can be framed as problems of practice and research questions to guide systematic inquiry. Turning to the "dark side" of our experiences, we then analyze two barriers to EBMgt that stem from lack of *respect*—specifically,

skepticism manifested by senior managers about research-based evidence and the active disrespect that practitioner-scholars experience from some of their managerial peers. Overcoming these barriers involves changes in motivations and skills, requiring *resourcefulness* by academics as well as managers. We then return to positive developments, describing pedagogies used in alternative doctoral education that offer promise for producing such resourcefulness. We close by describing ways that practitioner-scholars are spreading problem-focused research, stimulating cadres of managers and academics to *Reframe* their work in ways that favor and honor EBMgt.

Doctoral Education of Practitioner-Scholars: A "Case" Study

"Alternative" doctoral education complements EBMgt in that it promotes empirical research combining rigor with relevance. It produces expert managers who apply scholarly skills in their practice, as well as managerially experienced educators. Our DM Program was one of the first in a growing number of programs educating senior managers with high levels of experience. Some programs offer DBA degrees, some PhDs, and others executive doctorates. Gill and Hoppe (2009) provide a compendium of such degree programs in the United Kingdom, the United States, and in Europe. They find that the programs fit the characterization of "professional doctorates" (Bourner, Bowden & Laing, 2001), including a focus on research into issues of concern to practice and a part-time format that sustains the candidates' managerial identities.

The learning contract (Goodman & Beenen, 2008) in alternative doctoral programs imposes obligations on both students and faculty. Programs are committed to their candidates' personal growth and transformation by developing their skills of scholarship while maintaining skills for practice. In return, the candidates contribute to the institution's mission and stature by producing and disseminating scholarly research and by carrying out their managerial work in ways that advance theory, while serving as thought leaders among their managerial peers. Because the DM Program's members see it as innovative and frequently discuss its distinctive characteristics, mention of their own unique obligations under the learning contract is frequent and explicit. In our experience, both students and faculty see themselves as part of a movement to reduce the gap between the academy and managerial practice. The formation, in 2010, of the Professional Doctorate in Business Council, an international council of leading programs, and the earlier creation of the Executive Doctor Consortia within the Organization Development and Change Division of the Academy of Management (Spreitzer & Shwartz, 2004), give credence to the growing appeal of this movement. So, too, does the promoting of "professional" doctorate programs by the accrediting body for business schools, the Association to Advance Collegiate Schools of Business (AACSB) (Gill & Hoppe, 2009). As a community of practice (Wenger, 1998), faculty, students, and graduates of alternative doctoral programs are developing their own epistemologies, epistemologies that favor the generation of research useful to managers.

What motivates a faculty to create an alternative doctoral program? At the Weatherhead School, faculty from various disciplines came together out of a desire to attend to the needs of advanced, executive-level professionals encountering vexing problems at high organizational levels. For many senior faculty members, teaching lower-level managers in the school's masters degree programs, these advanced professionals and their complex problems held a different appeal. The DM Program's journey has challenged its faculty, graduates, and students. With much reflection and more than a little angst, program members sought, made, and endured frequent curricular and pedagogical revisions aimed at continuous improvement and production of scholars who would remain in, and transform, managerial practice.

The DM Program is as research intensive as it is practice oriented. Each fall its 20–25 new students start their research fieldwork as early as their first semester coursework. The program is designed as a lock-step three-year program, with a total of 54 credit hours including 32 research credit hours logged over a series of three- to four-day residencies in six semesters and two summers. The timeframe is ambitious and the curriculum demanding; after 15 years of experience, we find that approximately 65 percent of enrolling students are able to complete the program in their first three years. The program has developed an option for a fourth year of discipline-based study, culminating in a traditional PhD degree. This option was designed to satisfy some candidates' desires for entry to faculty positions at conventional management schools that question alternative degrees.

A common view among academics, even reflected in the AACSB's own prioritizing of doctoral programs (Gill & Hoppe, 2009), in fact, is that practice-oriented doctorates are of lower quality than traditional, disciplinary-focused doctorates. To counter this perspective, the DM Program is as concerned with rigor as it is with relevance. It measures its success in producing rigorous research by the high acceptance rates of its students' research at the Academy of Management's (AOM's) annual conferences and other academic conferences, and by the receipt of several AOM awards and nominations. Table 20.1 lists the presentations made and awards received in one calendar year by 27 members of the second- and third-year classes.

Somewhat to our surprise, we have discovered that the problem-focused research pursued in the program not only produces relevant knowledge but advances theory, too. We hope that this palpable contribution to managerial theory will ultimately cause a reexamination of the underlying assumptions in the academy about the value of these alternative programs, putting them deservedly on par with traditional disciplinary-focused doctoral programs. By virtue of their contributions to theory and research, elements of alternative doctoral education's purposes and pedagogies can enhance the education of traditional doctoral candidates, to further the progress of EBMgt.

Achieving Managerial Relevance through Problem-Focused Research

Differentiating itself from discipline-based research driven by theory, practice-relevant research starts and ends by focusing on *problems of practice*. The goal of such research, and of evidence-based management, is to produce knowledge that is *used* by managers to address their problems, rather than knowledge that academics deem *usable* but few managers actually use.

The DM Program's research requirements, outlined in Table 20.2, present the stages of problem-focused research. In the program's first year, the candidate specifies a problem of practice and a conceptually informed research question. In the second year, the candidate investigates this question empirically and develops grounded theory, developing insights via descriptive fieldwork and qualitative methods. Re-conceptualizing the problem of practice in light of this qualitative inquiry, the candidate then specifies a research question to be pursued via quantitative inquiry. During their final semester, students integrate their qualitative and quantitative findings and begin disseminating their findings to groups of managers, primarily in their own organizations and industry associations, who are facing a comparable problem of practice.

Table 20.1 Academic Conference Presentations and Awards in One Calendar Year DM Program

Awards

Academy of Management Annual Conference, Montreal

    Kathleen Buse, nominee, William H. Newman Award

        "Why they stay: The ideal selves of persistent women engineers."

    Kathleen Roche, Best Paper Proceedings

        "Managing the mission through times of adversity: What leads to reliable nonprofit performance?"

    Ann Kowal Smith, finalist, TIM Division, Best Student Paper

        "The 'where' and 'how' of explore and exploit: Balancing leadership to drive innovation and performance."

    Sridhar Seshadri, HCM Division, Best Paper Proceedings

        "How many minds does a team have? Contextual ambidexterity and goal harmony in healthcare."

Academy of Financial Services Annual Conference, Denver

    Jill McCullough, Best Doctoral Student Paper

        "The influence of positive psychological factors on small business owners' retirement planning activities."

Academic Conference Presentations—Multiple

Academy of Management, Montreal	20 presentations
Association for Research on Nonprofit Organizations & Voluntary Action, Washington, DC	8 presentations
Decision Sciences Institute, San Diego	4 presentations
Pierre Belzier and Machine Tools Symposium, Society for the History of Technology, Paris	2 presentations

Other Academic and Conference Presentations

Academy of Financial Services, Denver

European and Global Pricing Conference, Brussels

International Conference on Information Systems, St. Louis

International Council for Small Business, Cincinnati

Midwest Academy of Management

Pricing Capabilities and Pricing Strategies Workshop, Lund School of Economics and Management, Lund, Sweden

Society of Women Engineers, Orlando

The choice of problem in the research process just described belongs to the student, not the faculty, and is typically based on the candidate's own substantial managerial experience and vexations. The candidate performs direct inquiry into the chosen problem of practice, carrying out semistructured interviews with managers and a review of popular management literature to create an initial specification of the problem. The candidate then combines this specification with a multitheoretical, often multilevel conceptualization, producing a model of the problem and its associated managerial, organizational, and institutional processes. In this way, the research is both problem driven and theoretically informed (Salipante & Aram, 2004). From the model, the doctoral researcher specifies an overarching research question that is both problem and context specific, and then investigates it through the sequence of qualitative and quantitative inquiries as described earlier.

Qualitative and Quantitative Methods for Inquiring into Managers' Problems of Practice

Through hard experience, the DM Program faculty has learned to limit the forms of qualitative and quantitative methods used by candidates. One reason is to provide efficiency in training candidates in rigorous methods, conserving faculty resources for guiding candidates to completion within the contracted time frame of the program. Of equal importance, particular qualitative and quantitative methods have proved better than others at facilitating a continuing connection with practice and enabling the researcher to address the complexity of senior management problems. This narrowing is consistent with Briner, Denyer, and Rousseau's (2009) call for evidence to be created with methods that are appropriate to the questions being asked. Through choices of appropriate methods, and specifications grounded in both managers' own constructions of a problem and its context, the findings from problem-focused research are more meaningful and actionable for managers than is often the case with traditional, theory-driven doctoral research.

The DM Program has evolved to rely more heavily on interpretive methods where qualitative research is concerned. Candidates develop grounded theory reflecting practitioners' realities (Glaser & Strauss, 1999) and focusing on processes that senior managers can influence. Students are trained in ethnographic methods, including phenomenological interviewing (Spradley, 1979; Kvale & Brinkmann, 2009) and naturalistic data analysis (Lincoln & Guba, 1985; Emerson, Fretz & Shaw, 1995; Strauss & Corbin, 2008). In the initial stage of their research, undertaken in the first months of doctoral study, students apply these methods in small sample studies of expert practitioners who are living the researchers' focal problems. This immediately inserts the budding practitioner-scholars into the field to discern how other managers are framing and experiencing their chosen problem. Importantly, this grounding in practice is consistent with the attributes of practice-oriented research in other evidence-based fields—it investigates the conditions of practice and the actual experiences of practitioners (Rousseau, chapter 4 of this volume). In parallel, the nascent researchers receive in-depth instruction in information literacy, enabling search for a range of relevant scholarly literatures to inform and conceptualize the problem (Werner, chapter 15 of this volume).

Ethnographic and grounded-theory research methods enable problem-focused researchers to better understand the lived worlds of managers, and such methods are likely to be valuable in practice-oriented research more generally. We found that students' qualitative inquiry yielded insights into the nature of the problems that senior manager practitioner-scholars failed to see when they were operating in their everyday managerial mode. Consistent with studies finding that organizational members lack an ability to specify key features of their own organizational culture (cf. Capelli & Crocker-Hefter, 1996), managers can find it difficult to objectively identify and analyze key features of the problems they confront. Stepping back to systematically and qualitatively observe a phenomenon provides insights otherwise overlooked during business as usual. Not only is it difficult for managers to recognize and appreciate the key features of a particular problem "in the trenches," but also the pace of activity and pressure for rapid action can impede the reflection time necessary to process those problems in a meaningful way.

What is it about phenomenological interviews that led candidates to revise the framing of their problems of practice? Ethnographic interviewing differs from structured interviewing by not relying on respondents' assessments and analyses. Rather, it collects their descriptions of events and social interactions related to the problem. When analyzed by the practitioner-scholar researcher, these descriptions inevitably provided insights into the problem's underlying issues. We learned the value of these expert practitioner interviews by accident. Initially, faculty simply suggested to students that they engage in one or two interviews with managers experienced with the problem. Students found these interviews useful and conducted additional interviews on their own. Doing so helped to build skills used in the many phenomenological interviews required for their subsequent qualitative research projects.

Besides helping to identify the evidence needs of managers, ethnographic interviews may offer an additional possibility for fostering EBMgt. When subjects describe their experiences in ethnographic interviews, they have an opportunity to ponder their own "evidence" for making decisions. Managerial informants often thank students for the interviews, expressing appreciation that the time and method involved permitted valuable reflection and insight. Many requested further information about the research, eager to learn new ideas and practices. Such comments indicate that an ethnographic interview based on a problem of practice in itself can be a valuable tool for opening respondent-managers to the consideration of research-based evidence and knowledge.

Table 20.2 Research Requirements and Deliverables Doctor of Management Program

The inquiry courses in the first three semesters focus on identifying and conceptualizing one's topic of interest, and designing and collecting structured qualitative information to refine and contextualize one's conceptual method. The sequence in the fourth and fifth semesters addresses survey research and quantitative methods in the testing of hypotheses embedded in the conceptual model.

Conceptual Paper – Due in May, Academic Year 1

This qualitative research proposal frames the research problem and question. It synthesizes a substantial body of scholarly literature (theoretical and empirical) into a conceptual framework and model that provides insight into a significant problem of practice reflecting the lived worlds of a specified body of practitioners. The paper produces a "grand tour" research question to guide the qualitative research project and specifies a design for the fieldwork to be carried out in the qualitative research project. To produce this paper, candidates develop and apply skills of conceptualizing (including modeling), creating ethnographic/phenomenological interview protocols, conducting phenomenological interviews, and interpretively analyzing qualitative interview data.

Qualitative Research Report – Due in December, Academic Year 2

The Qualitative Research Report presents findings and explanatory concepts from the qualitative fieldwork project. It identifies and frames a potent "phenomenological practice gap" wherein current practitioner and academic knowledge is lacking in guiding effective practice. By understanding ethnographic observation and field notes, and the development of grounded theory, candidates formally and rigorously analyze qualitative data in an interpretive fashion. The research synthesizes findings and significant scholarly literature into a coherent conceptual framework and an understandable model of relationships among theoretical constructs, presenting a logical flow of well-supported arguments.

Capstone – Due in July, Academic Year 2

The Capstone integrates the analytical approaches the student has learned in EDMP 643, Foundations of Quantitative Research Design, and EDMP 649, Model Building & Validation. The Capstone exercise allows candidates to demonstrate their independent competence in quantitative inquiry skills and, based on a satisfactory assessment, to progress toward the completion of the quantitative inquiry project.

Quantitative Research Paper – Due in December, Academic Year 3

The objective of the quantitative inquiry project is to generate a rigorous and valid quantitative empirical study that is guided by a sound conceptual model of the candidate's phenomenon of interest. The study is positioned with respect to the theoretical and research literature of the topic. It utilizes a robust research design to collect credible data that mitigates biases, reflects systematic and rigorous quantitative analysis indicative of material covered in the quantitative inquiry courses, and meets high scholarly standards to merit publication in top-rated journals and outlets.

Doctor of Management Dissertation – Due in April, Academic Year 3

As a final requirement, each candidate writes an overview statement introducing and synthesizing their conceptual, qualitative, and quantitative research reports, making substantive observations and conclusions about each project, and presenting a personal reflective statement about its significance to the author. This overview statement and the three approved research reports serve as the dissertation requirement of the DM Program.

In the quantitative research phase of the DM Program, a parallel evolution resulted in the use of structural equation modeling to analyze constructs based on candidates' collected survey data. Students are directed to find and customize validated scales that reflect important phenomena identified in their qualitative research. Often, students also construct and validate their own scales, if they have identified concepts that have received little or no prior research. We have found that methods of structural equation modeling, by enabling the simultaneous analysis of differing constructs, capture sufficient conceptual complexity to match the most important features of a problem of practice. In addition, because structural equation modeling is not uniformly used or even understood in practice, it permits students to explore the possibility of deeper, more complex quantitative relationships than they may have previously considered.

Broadening the Adoption of Problem-Focused Research

The problem-oriented style of research described in the previous section, with its constant attention to managerial practice, can be understood as corresponding to key elements of EBMgt defined and conceptualized by Briner et al. (2009). Their definition of EBMgt as combining the use of particular sources of information – practitioner expertise and judgment, evidence from the local context, critical evaluation of best available research evidence, and the perspectives of people affected by the manager's decision—focuses on the particular, the specifics of problem and context that the manager confronts. Correspondingly, problem-focused research attends directly to a particular problem situation that confronts managers. In seeking to discover involved managers' understandings and perspectives on the problem, including their constraints and their knowledge of the problem's context, it addresses Briner et al.s fundamental claims about the nature of EBMgt—it represents what managers (not scholars) do, concerns managerial practice, involves managers generating their own knowledge, and requires getting research out to managers.

Problem-focused research has evolved sufficiently that its key features have been tested in various doctoral education and research settings. For more in-depth discussions, we suggest two references. As introduction, see Salipante and Aram's (2003) overview of practitioner-scholarship, based on the doctoral education of advanced practitioners in the DM Program. For greater detail and a broader targeting of doctoral students and faculty studying organizations, see Van de Ven's *Engaged Scholarship* (2007). The two approaches are highly complementary. Combining their stated characteristics, as in Table 20.3, provides a concise summary of elements of problem-focused research that can be pursued by students and faculty in both alternative and traditional doctoral programs. The reader is invited to note differences from theory-driven research and consider their consequences, as we do next.

By conducting research that engages managers in a systematic inquiry into problems of practice rather than problems of theory, a researcher avoids framing a challenge and its associated phenomena in their own construction of reality. Highly lauded scholars have learned the value of focusing on reality as experienced by practice. In his work on the effect of automation on the skill requirements of industrial jobs, Michael Piore framed a problem and survey in conjunction with John T. Dunlop, one of the most renowned labor economists and labor-relations experts in the United States and a former Secretary of Labor. Yet Piore (1979) reported that his respondents steered him away from this academically driven framing as disconnected from their realities. Similarly, Sutton and Rafaeli's (1988)

exemplary research turned to participant observation and semistructured interviewing in order to comprehend their subjects' realities, when their theory-driven research produced unexpected and unexplainable results (Frost & Stablein, 1992).

Problem-focused knowledge production is not a novel idea, even if infrequently used in formal management research. It is an everyday practice among managers, since they continually generate their own practical knowledge in a manner consistent with Dewey's (1929) work on pragmatism (Aram & Salipante, 2003). This knowledge always arises from a practical, real-world problem. Gibbons and associates (1994) differentiate two modes of knowledge production, with mode 1 being the traditional academic model. Mode 2, knowledge generation, occurs more naturally among people in practice, starting and ending with a relatively short-term problem. Knowledge to solve the problem is generated by drawing together, often across the boundaries of organizations and occupations, the specialized expertise of a variety of individuals. The analog in problem-focused research is drawing together, often across disciplinary boundaries, multiple informative theories and bodies of empirical studies. The criterion for successful knowledge generation in mode 2 is a practical solution to the problem, in the form of a process, product, or service. Due to that criterion, participants in the knowledge generation are socially accountable for their efforts in the short term, in a manner that academics are not. Once the problem is solved, it is rarely codified, and there is little attention to generalizing the practical knowledge beyond the particular situation in which it was generated. The knowledge is typically not spread through publication but, rather, through individuals moving from one project or employment context to another.

Those concerned with the limited application of mode-1 produced knowledge by practitioners have proposed that the academy meld some elements of mode-2 knowledge production into its research efforts. Most specifically, Huff (2000) has proposed a mode 1.5 synthesis. This synthesis is more demanding than modes 1 and 2, requiring the meeting of additional criteria beyond that of either mode alone. As the characteristics of Van de Ven's engaged scholarship outlined in Table 3 suggest, mode 1.5 requires that participants in the knowledge-production process engage with people in practice and address their issues, while continuing to strive for abstraction and generality.

To more fully realize EBMgt, the academy must expand Huff's (2000) mode 1.5 idea considerably.

Table 20.3 Characteristics of Problem-Focused Research

	Practitioner-Scholarship (Aram & Salipante, 2003)	Engaged Scholarship (Van de Ven, 2007)
Reason for lack of use of management research	A knowledge *production* problem.	
Problem Specification	Initiate research with problem, including own and others' personal experiences.	Engage those experiencing and knowing the problem.
	Center on practitioner audience; Limit scope to one audience as research clients.	As criterion, use relevance.
	Address a knowledge deficiency inhibiting practice.	Ground & diagnose problem from close and afar.
Theory Construction	Identify multiple context-near and context-far concepts.	Use abduction, induction, & deduction to create theory.
	Use problem to integrate theories.	Engage knowledge experts from disciplines and functions.
		As criterion, use validity.
Methods/Design	Be epistemologically open to people providing access.	Engage methods experts and
	Sequence induction and deduction, interpretation, and empirical testing.	Develop variance or process model.
	Attend to validity, being reflexive about design and findings from different methods.	As criterion, use truth (verisimilitude).
Dissemination for Use	Be reflexive about match with practitioners' interpretations.	Communicate, interpret & negotiate findings with intended audience.
	As criterion, judge expansion of practitioners' theories in use.	As criterion, use impact.
	Disseminate to practitioners via publications and presentations.	Engage intended audience to interpret uses.
	Apply to own practice.	

Rather than melding the nature of the knowledge production in which practitioners and scholars engage to create a hybrid, we assert that new forms of scholarly inquiry be considered. Specifically, problem-focused research should be recognized as a model of knowledge generation with its own epistemology and methods, prizing and producing both particularized and generalized knowledge (Aram & Salipante, 2003) by synthesizing relevant theories around a reality-framed problem of practice. In the following sections, we develop the claim that, although rich scholarly traditions have been built on exploring problems of theory and should be continued, only inquiries into problems of practice (with their amorphous, transdisciplinary, and sometimes baffling dimensions) will yield evidence-based solutions that match senior managers' needs. This form of engagement with the research ultimately creates more ambidextrous managers, equally at home with intuition and with evidence while integrating the two. By reframing scholarly inquiry to include knowledge generation driven by the problems of practice, we lever the power of alternative doctoral programs, institutionalizing their processes and creating more opportunities for EBMgt to find its way into classrooms and managerial practice.

Increasing Relevance through Synthesis of Theories

Although problem-focused research starts and ends with a problem of practice, it is not atheoretical. Quite the contrary, as noted earlier, problems of practice should be informed by not one but several theories. In the DM Program we have relied on a premise that has been repeatedly confirmed:

> Rarely, if ever, does a single body of evidence or theory sufficiently inform a problem of practice.

Accordingly, each candidate is guided by several advisors to search for evidence and theory that lend insight into phenomena associated with a problem of practice. Relevant literature is often located in diverse disciplines, requiring access to advisors from a variety of disciplinary backgrounds. In this regard, problem-focused inquiry diverges sharply from theory-based inquiry that observes disciplinary bounds, and even from research that is interdisciplinary in a limited fashion. An active search process is necessary to identify scholarly literatures that offer promise for remedying the problem. This process is inevitably inefficient; false starts are common. It is also conceptually demanding, since the candidate must integrate a range of evidence and concepts from different scholarly literatures.

As noted in Table 20.3, the need to integrate multiple theories is characteristic of problem-focused research into senior-management problems. This characteristic is both a critique of and significant challenge to EBMgt, because management research and education are typically segmented by disciplines (e.g., applied psychology) and functions (e.g., accountancy). Integration of multiple bodies of research-based knowledge does not fit neatly into either normal or revolutionary science (Kuhn, 1962). Rather, it is a *synthetic science* that requires substantial creativity (Gardner, 1988) in order to select and integrate disparate concepts and evidence. It is demanding of nascent scholars and, for that matter, traditionally trained academics. Methods of conceptual integration across disparate bodies of literature are not formally developed in academia. Few faculty are expert in them, since the scholarship of integration (Boyer, 1990) has been slow to gain acceptance in traditional academia (Dauphinee & Martin, 2000), despite calls for more interdisciplinary studies.

A consequence of this dearth of integration across disciplines in the academy is that many members of the DM Program have experienced a significant challenge in using multiple theories, a challenge that might be termed *conceptual reductionism*. When initially developing a conceptual model to address a problem of practice, a candidate is sometimes pushed by a faculty advisor to narrow the conceptual focus to a single theory with which the advisor is most familiar. This is a natural often-unconscious process, since many academics make their contributions by dedicating themselves to one body of theory. Conceptual reductionism also occurs when designing the conceptual model that guides the quantitative phase of the research, this time due to methodological considerations rather than theoretical commitments. The temptation at this stage is to narrow the focus to those constructs that have been well researched quantitatively, offering validated instruments to the researcher.

We would like to claim that skills of integration are taught formally in our DM Program. They are not. Rather, candidates are pushed by the faculty that teach their research methods courses to identify, explore, select, and synthesize evidence and concepts from a range of literatures. As problem-focused researchers, practitioner-scholars must be willing to hold their ground with discipline-based scholars concerning the importance of being synthetic. Faculty who teach the methods courses in the DM Program attempt to be the watchdogs for reductionism. In pushing our candidates, we not only encourage them to bridge the divide across disciplines to develop effective evidence-based insights to address their problems of practice, we also encourage our faculty colleagues to think more broadly about their own fields, enriching their experiences, and creating yet another "hybrid" group of scholars with a focus on practical relevance. Both faculty and students are on an important journey, as we strive to maintain the multidisciplinary nature of problem-focused inquiry.

Synthesizing Concepts, Near and Far

In quantitative research, transporting findings from one setting to another raises questions about external validity, calling for field research to test the application. In problem-focused inquiry, however, findings and concepts from other contexts are seen as potentially informative. From an interpretive research perspective, the issue is whether a particular concept developed in one context can be transported to another to aid in thickly describing phenomena in one's focal context:

> Theoretical ideas are not created wholly anew in each study; . . . they are adopted from other, related studies, and, refined in the process, applied to new interpretive problems. If they cease being useful with respect to such problems, they tend to stop being used and are more or less abandoned. If they continue being useful, throwing up new understandings, they are further elaborated and go on being used. (Geertz, 2003, p. 192.)

For problem-focused research, identifying several concepts that can be usefully transported to the focal managerial context is a way of responding to the complexity of the problem of practice. Drawing from anthropology, we have described this transporting process in terms parallel to those of *-emic* and *-etic* knowledge. Theory that is developed in a particular context and that reflects members' understandings can be understood as "experience-near" (Geertz, 1974) to a particular field of practice. In our program we apply this idea to theory that is specific to a given context, terming it *concept-near*. An example is agency theory in the field of corporate governance. In contrast, *concept-far* refers to theory that has been developed in other contexts, including other industries. Often, concepts-far are at a higher level of abstraction with potential application in a wide range of managerial situations. Examples include structuration theory, complexity theory, and theories of collective action. Each of these theories provides a broad integration framework that enables the researcher to incorporate several otherwise disparate concepts. Such theories are not often taught in management programs, but senior managers in the DM Program find them to be powerful conceptual resources for examining their problems.

As Geertz suggests in the preceding quotation, attempts to transport concepts and findings from concept-far literatures are valuable for theory development. They provide a test of the theories' utility, in particular managerial contexts, and they provide an opportunity to refine the theories. In this fashion, problem-focused inquiry can make two contributions that support the generation and application of evidence-based knowledge:

1. Problem-focused inquiry can further the development of practice-relevant theory by academics.

2. Problem-focused inquiry can identify broader bodies of evidence and theory that senior managers would find useful in addressing their problems.

The first of these points suggests that it is realistic to ask management academics to engage in problem-focused research, particularly in partnership with colleagues from other disciplines, since it leads to theory development. The second point indicates that engaging in such research would increase the relevance of research findings for senior managers, expanding their use of research. Taken together, these points suggest that the problem-focused research developed in alternative doctoral programs could be exercised by many management

academics and become integral to the development and dissemination of EBMgt in practice. As we reconsider the nature of the problems we address, we bring the academy's scholarly contributions closer to the real-world problems found in twenty-first-century management, a point that we attempt to develop next.

The Revealed Nature of Senior Managers' Problems

What are the characteristics of twenty-first-century management problems? Put another way, what are managers' knowledge needs? Madhavan and Mahoney (chapter 5 of this volume) note the challenges that EBMgt encounters in addressing "macro" issues that managers face, such as those in strategic management. Similarly, we have found that senior-manager practitioner scholars focus on problems of practice at the macrolevel. These problems differ in scale and scope from those encountered at lower managerial levels, the levels typically considered as targets for EBMgt.

Proper framing of a problem of practice is essential to producing managerially useful knowledge. The goal of problem framing is to identify puzzling or challenging aspects hindering effective outcomes. For instance, one DM student was concerned about misguided technology-investment decisions in medicine. He eventually framed his problem as involving surgeons' rejection of new clinical technologies, which led his inquiry to ask, "How do surgeons make decisions to adopt or reject clinical technologies?" Although at first blush this may seem like a theoretical inquiry, for practitioners developing and disseminating new innovative medical technologies, this decision-making process on the part of users was the critical puzzle to unravel. Because of the myriad directions in which any research project might proceed, effectively pinpointing the challenging aspects of the problem identifies the particular types of research-based knowledge that managers need.

To better understand senior managers' knowledge needs as they search for information relevant to solving macrolevel problems, we reviewed the problems of practice and related research questions that recent graduates of the DM Program have addressed. Analyzing these problems of practice led us to several tentative, but interesting, interpretations. First, the time horizon of these questions is quite long, in contrast to Gibbons et al.'s (1994) specification of mode 2, practitioner inquiry. Second, the questions are complex, tending to operate at multiple structural and theoretical levels. Third, they vary broadly in scope, raising interesting insights about the generalized nature of their outcomes. The following paragraphs illustrate each of these in turn.

Long Time Horizon

The problems of practice represented in practitioner scholar research are persistent and vexing. They reflect the knowledge needs of senior managers concerned with guiding their organizations in a strategic fashion, rather than smaller, short-range problems faced in day-to-day managerial life, even though the insights they generate contribute to the daily routine. As a result, these problems of practice have long time horizons, or they might even be viewed as time-neutral. For example, one student chose to explore the role of governance and leadership in interorganizational collaborations, seeking to better understand how to make these collaborations more effective over time (Brennan, 2010). Another sought to understand how for-profit executives fare when migrating into leadership positions in the nonprofit world (La Belle, 2010). A third student looked deeply at how companies might repair trust at times when loyalty and customer confidence have been severely damaged by company or industry actions (Talton, 2010). The context in which these questions arise is timely and very current. Experience in the intuitive world of practitioners provides unsatisfactory answers to these broad questions.

Practice-oriented research generates new avenues for thinking about these critical and persistent challenges. The combination of the timely nature of the context of the challenge, together with the extended, nearly time-neutral nature of the inquiry, suggests that EBMgt may be well positioned to tackle the "wicked" problems (Rittel & Webber, 1973) of managerial and organizational life. These wicked problems of practice are ones in which the nature of the problems that practitioners face are not satisfactorily answered in the practitioner literature, do not lend themselves to a "silver bullet" response, or are not answered by a single body of research-based evidence.

Structural and Theoretical Complexity

Nearly all the enumerated problems of practice we reviewed represent complex problems that can be explored on multiple levels—structurally and theoretically. La Belle's (2010) work with crossover CEOs (as described earlier) has application at the sectoral level (for nonprofit sector leaders concerned about mission dilution), the organizational level (for organizations seeking effective leaders), the personal

level (for current and future nonprofit leaders), and at the team level (for boards and search committees seeking to better understand the process to select and develop effective leaders). La Belle (2010) drew from several theories, from upper-echelon theory to socialization theory to leadership theories of behavioral complexity, creating a platform that addressed the issues unique to her inquiry.

The work of a fourth student, Teague (2010), similarly captures structural complexity by drawing on multiple theories. Seeking to understand how to drive employee volunteerism, Teague (2010) searched for academic literature to frame the problem. Drawing on four different academic theories, he created a frame of reference for potential volunteers, for corporations seeking to encourage volunteerism and for nonprofits looking to corporations to help them recruit people to assist in their causes.

Finally, marrying structural as well as theoretical complexity, the research of a fifth student investigated the role of leadership and organizational learning in creating effective innovative outcomes (Smith, 2010). Her initial problem of practice sought to understand how leaders use conversation to drive learning and innovative co-creation of solutions to organizational challenges. As her work proceeded, she examined her findings at an organizational level, asking whether certain types of balanced leadership led to more effective innovation and ultimately to better company-level financial performance. In each of these cases, the theories and sources that formed the foundation of her work shifted with the unit of analysis. The findings were highly consistent across both structures—individuals assessing their teams and their own behaviors and individuals assessing their organizations—but the sources and methods differed. The former drew on adult learning theories, discourse analysis, motivation, and absorptive capacity, whereas the latter applied multifactor leadership theory and ambidextrous innovation theories. In fact, although the two sections of Smith's (2010) work provided a consistent set of insights about organizational leadership and innovation, her qualitative work was accepted for presentation at the Annual Meeting of the Academy of Management by the Managerial and Organizational Cognition Division, and her quantitative work was accepted the following year by the Technology and Innovation Management Division of the same body. Her multifaceted problem of practice led to application of multiple theories from different academic fields, and to contributions to those fields' theories.

Variations in Scope

Problems differ in their scope, some applying to single industries, others to multiple; some to single societies, and others to a range of geographical or cultural settings. These differences have implications for the generalizability of the knowledge needed, raising issues of external validity (for quantitative evidence) and concept transportability (for qualitative evidence).

Our student Adelegan's (2009) work was very specific to Nigerian pulp and paper companies, as he sought to understand the drivers of adoption of eco-innovation. Finding a strong link between the adoption of cleaner technologies and higher firm performance, Adelegan used his research to make a case for a particular course of action by these companies. Might this apply more broadly in other developing countries or in other industries? Perhaps his findings may be generalized, but the research scope was quite limited to a particular, highly localized challenge.

Another student sought to understand the drivers of performance in academic medical centers, in particular the role of organizational sensemaking among the sponsors, designers, and implementers of change (Seshadri, 2010). Although Seshadri's (2010) work was context-specific, looking into the role of doctors and other important stakeholders, his insights on the role of the team in implementing change has important applicability to complex organizations broadly.

How Senior Managers' Problems of Practice Evolve

Earlier, we noted that the stated problems of practice evolve as the problem-focused researcher proceeds through key phases of their multimethod project. Here we consider how that happens, and what this portends for senior managers' use of EBMgt. Fundamentally, conceptions of a problem of practice evolve as practical realities and theory interact. As Talton (2010) reflected:

> I came in wanting to help a company become more beloved, developing loyalty through an emotional connection with stakeholders. But this seemed to be too big a problem. I realized that any emotional connection, or even transactional loyalty starts with trust. Trust became my focus while the economy was tanking and trust was being violated all over (leaders, bankers, priests). This led me to ask, how can we repair trust when it's broken?

Talton's (2010) stated problem evolved in practice as she was looking to shape its parameters.

External factors, which were further evidence of the timely nature of the stated problems, necessitated a flexibility that might not have occurred were her work a problem of theory.

Fisk (2010) reported a similar experience to us: "I came in to study enterprise integration assuming that the answer would be technological. But the literature took me down a social processes path." And Seshadri (2010) agreed: "I started thinking about the technology of change (like Six-Sigma and other similar processes) only to discover that it's less about that than about how incompletely we have studied teams. Sense making came out of my concept paper process." With a theory and a new perspective to shape his thinking, Seshadri (2010) observed that he had started with a quite narrow focus, switched paradigms, widened his scope, shifted and ultimately found a very different set of insights than he expected to find. Both Fisk (2010) and Seshadri (2010) developed critical insights that might not have developed had they not begun a deep literature search; the academic literature held insights that not only surprised them but helped them to shape fundamentally better questions.

Finally, Oliver (2010) started with a broader problem of practice as he sought to better understand the financial impact of microfinance in emerging economies. Over time, his focus narrowed considerably as he looked at the effect of microcredit on poverty in a single African country, using an established database to provide a wealth of information.

In every case we examined, however, the doctoral students were seeking insights that extended beyond their own felt challenges—even the relatively narrow questions resulted in broadly stated descriptions of their own scholarly identity. Clearly, they all sought to bring a range of new conceptual tools to their multilevel, complex problems and perceived their own journeys as "proof" that research-based evidence provides insights to persistent problems. We asked one cohort of graduating DM students to write statements of their scholarly identity. The resulting statements mitigate any concern that engaging in problem-focused research would lead scholars away from theory. We suggest again that EBMgt provides an important avenue to permit practitioners to reflect on their own contributions to problem-focused practice. As more practitioners are trained in its use and more academics adopt a problem-focused approach, EBMgt's value to practitioners will be recognized and will proliferate.

In sum, problem-focused research seems to lend itself to addressing the macrochallenges senior managers face in guiding their firm's strategic, operational, and functional direction. The scope and timelessness of the questions practitioner-scholars ask suggests that EBMgt value may be most evident to senior level managers, since they tackle complex, multilevel problems that have eluded solution for years.

Senior Managers' Problems Call for a New Mode of EBMgt Problem Framing

To respond effectively to the knowledge needs outlined directly in the preceding section, EBMgt must provide senior managers with theory and evidence that reflect the same holistic and strategic perspective that these managers apply to their complex problems. In chapter 7 of this handbook, Rob Briner and David Denyer discuss the proper framing of questions in systematic reviews of empirical research that will be effective for EBMgt. They present examples of questions "that require much greater specificity." Because systematic reviews must identify extant bodies of empirical literature from which to synthesize evidence, and because those bodies of research are narrowly focused, a review question must itself be narrow. Nearly always, a selected body of such research deals with a single phenomenon, requiring a narrowing of the problem to that phenomenon. This narrowing is not only necessary but also effective at providing evidence useful in particular managerial decisions, as Briner and Denyer illustrate. However, this very narrowing is ill-suited to many types of problem statements that our senior manager scholars frame.

Consider Briner and Denyer's example of a question requiring greater specificity for a systematic review: "How is trust between organizations broken and repaired?" This question is exactly of the complexity that senior managers face, as discussed earlier—long in time horizon, broad in scope, and involving multiple levels. Note that Talton's (2010) problem of practice, discussed earlier, was of a remarkably similar focus and breadth to the cited example—namely, the breakdown of trust. For Talton (2010), the context was trust between organizations and their consumers. The breaking of bonds of customer loyalty led her and other senior managers to have a strong concern with broken trust. Her problem's breadth was maintained at that managerially relevant scope throughout her research by framing her research question as, "How can organizations repair trust when it is broken?" In her inquiry, this breadth was maintained first by synthesizing two bodies of theory to address both

micro- and meso-level phenomena, and then by conducting field research directly tied to the stated problem of practice. Achieving this breadth is not easy. In each research project, the problem-focused researcher faces the daunting task of framing the problem and research question in a way that retains managerial relevance, yet still makes the question researchable.

If senior managers are to find EBMgt relevant, narrowing each problem so it matches an extant body of research will reduce their view of its relevance. Problem-focused research can be contrasted with applied research, with the latter understood as the application of a particular theory or evidence to a problem. Applied research requires a narrower framing of the problem to match an extant body of research. However, when EBMgt proceeds this way with a complex problem, senior managers will reduce their assessment of EBMgt's relevance. In contrast, relevance can be maintained through the methods of problem-focused research discussed earlier, particularly the synthesis of multiple bodies of academic knowledge, specification of a research question that targets the key managerial puzzles and knowledge deficiencies, and research design that addresses the broad problem in a specified managerial context. These methods enable EBMgt to address the complex problems that senior managers face.

Lack of Respect for Management Research and Researchers

So far, this chapter offers positive developments concerning EBMgt; however, there is a "dark-side." Strong forces operate against senior managers' adoption of EBMgt. We turn to those here. Certain experiences in the DM Program indicate severe challenges for EBMgt's goals of getting research out to practitioners for their use.

The "Will" and the "Skill" for EBMgt

The most significant managerial challenges to EBMgt we believe center on two elements: managerial dispositions toward research-based evidence, and managerial skills for locating and critically interpreting such evidence for use in their decision making. In the practical world, these concepts might be described simply as "will" and "skill." The prototypical candidate in our program is an executive, typically 40- or 50-something in age, with substantial experience at high levels of for-profit, nonprofit, or public-sector organizations. These senior managers have self-selected into doctoral education and, accordingly, should be more inclined toward using scholarly products than their peer managers—that is, they have higher EBMgt "will" than their managerial brethren. Our general experience, however, is that even senior managers who self-select to pursue scholarly work are largely unaware of research-based evidence. They are neither disposed toward, nor skilled in, reading empirical research and reviews of such studies. We have discovered that our senior managers' doctoral education must include features that change their dispositions toward research and provide them with skills in locating scholarly literature and critically interpreting it. A particular challenge in developing senior managers into practitioner-scholars is to change their mindsets such that, rather than being committed to a particular problem solution or a theory promising such a solution, they become committed to pursuing a research question that will yield empirically based knowledge. Often, this can be accomplished in a single semester with, as we will discuss in the "Overcoming Barriers" section later, instruction and tasks that develop skill in locating and deconstructing empirical research studies. Similar student tasks might be applicable to masters-level education, in order to provide a larger cadre of managers with EBMgt-relevant dispositions and skills.

As with senior manager doctoral candidates, faculty in the DM Program also face challenges of dispositions and skills in problem-focused research. Regarding will, we faculty have found that we must often bend on our disciplinary commitments to particular theories in order to guide candidates toward other theories that might better inform their problems of practice. We have discovered that we lack skill and methods for synthesizing multiple theories, as problem-focused research requires. Also, we have found that we are now more critical and reflective about our own research and its practical impact or lack thereof. These are important issues because the dispositions and skills of faculty as well as senior managers bear heavily on the possibilities for more widespread adoption of EBMgt.

Skepticism Regarding Research-Based Evidence

Other contributors to this handbook, particularly Kovner (chapter10) and Leung and Bartunek (chapter 9), address lack of managerial receptivity to EBMgt. This barrier has a weak and a strong form. The weak form involves a bias against empirical research and its tendency toward descriptive analysis of small slivers of a particular theory and toward the prescriptions of management gurus. The strong

form is manifest by an active disrespect for doctorally trained academics, seen as possessing slowly derived, theory-driven knowledge that is out of touch with practical realities.

Doctoral candidates can be expected to be well-read with an appreciation for scholarly thought, consistent with EBMgt's call for managers to incorporate research-based evidence in their decisions. Indeed, we have found that participants in our alternative doctoral program were active consumers of "new thinking" prior to entering our program. They sought to stay abreast of knowledge in the management field by reading sophisticated analyses in places such as *The Economist* and books by popular management authors. In this regard, they likely distinguished themselves from their managerial colleagues, betraying their interest in advanced graduate education and willingness to commit significant time to learning the craft of empirical research. Once in their doctoral studies, they were encouraged by their instructors to locate and read academic literature relevant to their individually chosen problems of practice. Depending on their specific educational and professional backgrounds, some were able to locate and master empirical work from respected academic journals, while others experienced great difficulty in doing so. Some individuals in the latter group searched for writings by management gurus known to them. These writings were not empirical research reports but, rather, prescriptions based on the scholar's accumulated work and wisdom. When one student was encouraged to search for the empirical research that a particular scholar had produced and that underlay the scholar's claims, the candidate reported that he could not locate such work. The good news is that these senior managers were willing to incorporate thinking from the academy in their decision making. The bad news is that their will and skill in reading and incorporating managerially focused literature does not always transfer to will and skill in locating and consuming empirical research.

Another form of skepticism derives from unfamiliarity with statistics and quantitative research methods. In the first months of their doctoral studies, some students report that they simply skipped the methods and results sections of articles. By so doing, they were expressing their discomfort with the most uniquely scholarly sections of quantitative empirical research, those requiring the most critical reading to assess the work's rigor. These omissions speak to the research's relevance to these managers. However, as one student reflected upon completing the program, "I now realize the importance of being able to understand all of the analysis myself and being able to access knowledge that I didn't previously understand."

Additionally, some candidates lack experience in synthesizing qualitative findings to develop meaningful, thoughtful observations. The bullet-point presentation styles that managers widely use can impede the ability to inquire, analyze, synthesize, and report in clear, well-articulated prose. These underused skills can create obstacles in writing, as well as critically reading texts whose insights would contribute to the shape and outcomes of their research. In fact, each year, a few new candidates drop out because of the program's critical reading and writing demands. In addition, formulaic approaches to classic management dilemmas presented in the practical literature do not always transition effectively to evidence-based inquiry; as a result, students often find that relearning methods for crafting an inquiry and stating a problem is as hard as developing the evidence to inform a solution. Finally, to be successful, managerial students must commit themselves to inquiry and not rush to demonstrate a proposition. These factors, as well as time challenges and life interruptions, drive the lion's share of the dropout rate in the program. This suggests that there may be a reasonable proportion of senior managers that will struggle with evidence-based management, no matter how compelling its contributions.

Finally, problem-focused research demands that its pursuers develop the skill of moving across levels of abstraction, from the particular to the general, and back again. Many of our doctoral candidates initially experienced difficulty in finding research relevant to their problem of practice. The difficulty arises when a student looks solely for concept-near studies, only to discover a lack of empirical research on the particular topic and in the specific setting of interest to the student. For example, La Belle's (2010) empirical work on CEOs crossing over to the nonprofit sector was a first in its field. Her research necessitated significant extrapolation from other areas of leadership research, including studies of managerial transitions and leader competencies conducted in various for-profit settings. Eventually, with assistance from their instructors and reference librarians, candidates discover that they can build their conceptual models by transporting to their focal settings concepts and research from other settings. They learn that their problems of practice and research questions need to be restated at higher levels of abstraction, in order to identify and apply research-based knowledge that was concept-far. Managers searching for research-based guidance will likely encounter similar difficulty, and

thus benefit from specific research training not currently in the typical manager's tool-set.

Past education plays a role in how practitioner-scholar doctoral candidates approach the research literature. Engineers have less difficulty in coping with the methods and results sections of quantitative research. Professionals from fields such as law regularly use scholarly literature, making them more at ease with empirical management research.

Is skepticism about research-based evidence common among managers? The revealed preferences of some among our scholarly leaning students—namely, favoring popular management literature and avoiding empirical research—suggests that a broad cross-section of senior managers are unwilling or unable to access research-based literature directly. We consider antidotes to this skepticism, after discussing the stronger form of managerial unwillingness.

Active Disrespect of Research-Based Evidence

Most DM Program graduates remain in managerial practice during and after their doctoral studies. In surveys of graduates, a small but significant number reported that they had encountered active disrespect for their doctorates among some clients. This disrespect was sufficiently strong and frequent that the graduates had learned, in certain situations, not to disclose their doctorate.

Others experience a misfit between their positions and their newly acquired scholarly skills. Some have been told by their peers that they had changed, and not necessarily for the better. Many practitioners unaccustomed to academic theory do not favorably regard the word "theory"—the moniker "theoretical" is often likened to "abstract" or "irrelevant to everyday practice." These candidates frequently sought new positions where they could express their scholarly skills. In contrast, other graduates successfully continued in their current organizations, applying their research findings and scholarly skills in such settings as medical centers where education and research are valued.

One DM candidate investigated the use of research-based evidence in decision-making bodies charged with policy formulation (Walker, 2009). She found major differences across institutions, with some highly politicized bodies neither seeking nor using such evidence in any systematic fashion. A common belief in such politicized bodies was that research-based evidence is not definitive. Rather, members saw it as marshaled by parties on both sides of an argument to support their particular positions.

That such a jaundiced perspective would exist among managerial decision makers would be disheartening enough, but these findings provide even more cause for pessimism since the subjects of the research were themselves academics—specifically, educators from community colleges. If significant numbers of educators disrespect empirical research as irrelevant to their own decision making, and if few among us practice in our educator roles the type of evidence-based teaching discussed by Goodman & O'Brien's (chapter 18 of this volume) should we be surprised that some managers actively disrespect empirical research and the academics who produce it?

The claim here is not that active disrespect permeates all managerial settings. Rather, the indication is that settings vary dramatically in their receptivity for research-based evidence. Settings in which receptivity might be expected, such as educational settings, are not always characterized by evidence-based decision making. Consequently, those training doctoral candidates, and proponents of EBMgt, should be realistic about the prospects for active consumption of practice-relevant research. The implication is that initial EBMgt efforts should be targeted, and DM Programs interested in promoting EBMgt might best orient themselves toward those organizations and managerial functions that favor the application of research-based knowledge. Indeed, as one first-year student reported, as soon as her colleagues in the organization's HR function heard of her doctoral studies, they asked her to partner in several publishing endeavors.

Overcoming Barriers to EBMgt through Pedagogy and Reframing

Although simply training a cohort of practitioner-scholars goes some distance toward demonstrating the value that exists at the intersection of practice and the academy, sensitivity to the particular challenges suggests that further efforts are required. In particular, how might we create antidotes to skepticism and disrespect for empirical research? From observing the journey of DM Program candidates, we offer several suggestions.

To mitigate skepticism of academic research, we suggest the following:

1. Programs that purport to address practitioner-scholar research must stay scrupulously focused on rigor and relevance. This means continually shifting between rigorous academic process and very practically focused and well-articulated problems of practice. As referenced earlier, pursuing relevance and rigor provides an ever-present challenge not only for the student but also for the members of the faculty advising and engaging them. This process of learning enriches and expands the skill sets of each. Clearly, the academy must not view practitioner-scholar programs—doctoral or otherwise—merely as opportunities to indoctrinate the uninitiated.

2. Practitioners seeking evidence-based insights need significant time and instruction to learn, appreciate, and adapt to the style of academic research. It is key that they develop skill in critically assessing the quality of scholarship. Toward this end, in the DM Program, two instructional approaches have proved critically important. The first type of assignment requires students to *deconstruct* the structure of empirical research articles. Over the course of one semester, each student searches for and deconstructs approximately 20 empirical studies relevant to that student's particular problem of practice. With assistance from reference librarians and scholarly online search tools, students become skilled at finding relevant empirical literature. In their initial searches, it is critical that they use Google Scholar rather than standard academic bibliographic databases, because it has familiar features. Once they look beyond concept-near to concept-far literature, students are surprised at the amount of research relevant to their problem. Although some are challenged by their initially meager knowledge of statistics, repeated deconstruction of articles' structure enabled students to become comfortable with digesting empirical studies within a few months of entering doctoral studies.

Part way through their first semester, an additional requirement is added to the deconstruction assignments: to analyze the author's *line of argument*. Toulmin's (2003) framework for deconstructing arguments is a valuable tool for this purpose. His framework of claims, grounds, warrants, backing, and qualifications (Toulmin, Rieke & Janik, 1984) alerts students to weakly versus strongly supported claims, and enables them to identify the various bases on which a claim could be supported. It provides students with a conceptual tool for knowledgeably critiquing an article's quality and for constructing their own scholarly work. In addition, this deconstruction enhances our nascent practitioner-scholars' respect for well-supported arguments and rigorous empirical work. It gives them the skill and confidence to tackle scholarly literature. Their skills and respect are deepened by contrasting exemplary scholarly work with popular management pieces, leading them to become highly critical of less careful, poorly supported work on both sides of the aisle.

3. DM Program members—faculty and students alike—must reframe the meaning of the word *theory*. Faculty can reframe theory beyond simple unitary models to include transdisciplinary syntheses that better match the complexity of many managerial problems. Managers can reframe their mindsets to understand that a theory is not, by definition, an ivory-tower concept, and that good theories are built on empirical testing. Similar to the function of a systematic review for EBMgt, a well-tested theory represents knowledge based on a body of empirical research. "There is nothing as practical as a good theory" sounds silly on its face, but is far more meaningful than it seems. All managers and leaders have a set of beliefs, or "implicit theories" that guide them, consciously or not, in their judgments and decisions (Levy, Stroessner and Dweck, 1998). By better understanding implicit theories that guide managerial decision making and their role in determining ultimate outcomes, there is potential to reframe an important element of managerial skepticism in a manner that supports evidence-based inquiry. Although our doctoral cohort may represent the "converted," many express a newfound appreciation for theory. As one student commented, "I find myself now looking to the literature not for answers but for theories."

To mitigate the disrespect some of our doctoral candidates experience from their colleagues, we suggest the following:

1. Engage industry associations as research partners and disseminators. Such associations often have educational missions and can reach industry members who appreciate research-based knowledge. The associations add legitimacy to the knowledge and reframe it in ways relevant to their members.

2. Require presentations of research-based evidence by practitioner-scholar doctoral candidates to their managerial peers. These should be presentations that explore with those peers the incorporation of the research in their practice. For instance, several of our doctoral candidates presented their research and their findings within their own organizations and the settings in which they collected data, with joint discussion of how the research might directly benefit the organization. Other candidates presented their findings in small colloquia in which the audience consisted of managers and academics from the region. Prominent expert practitioners served as discussants on the candidates' research papers, assessing their relevance and stimulating discussion. These

discussants and the general managerial and academic participants were enthusiastic about these experiences and encouraged the program to create more exchanges around research and practice, although discussants often remarked that they had to read a paper three times before they caught its meaning.

Leung and Bartunek (chapter 9 of this volume) offer additional ideas for creating forums for interchange, and they note the importance of clear communication. Indeed, after being immersed in academic terminology for several years, our soon-to-graduate scholars rediscovered the necessity of paying careful attention to the language used to describe their research and its findings. They put special effort into translating their findings and methodologies, making them more familiar and less intimidating. For example, practitioners are not well versed in structural equation modeling. Our students work to explain findings in metaphors, managerial terms, and plain language to make their value clear without requiring statistical knowledge.

3. Exploring new formats for disseminating practitioner-scholar research, including online forums and blogs, connecting research-based knowledge to the direct experiences commonly reported in such forums. For instance, one graduate responded to a blog posted by a consultant on an industrial marketing forum. His response drew on theories of trust and findings from his own research to challenge the consultant's statements. Exploring new outlets, such as hybrid journals and books, might also aid in the dissemination of problem-focused research.

Reframing among Doctoral Faculty

The preceding six strategies for overcoming managerial skepticism and disrespect are designed to produce, among managers, a positive reframing among managers of both research and researchers. However, as we have noted, making EBMgt attractive to senior managers also requires reframing efforts by faculty themselves about the production and dissemination of knowledge. Ideally, from an EBMgt perspective, faculty engaged in doctoral education would devote some of their own research efforts toward problem-focused research, producing the kinds of rigorous and relevant knowledge that they are asking of their doctoral candidates and engaging with managers concerning the relevance of their research questions and findings. At a minimum, when guiding the focus and design of their candidates' research, doctoral faculty concerned with the dearth of EBMgt must be sensitive to helping their doctoral candidates bridge the practice-theory divide. For instance, they must encourage dissemination not only through interaction with academic communities but also managerial communities. The latter requires that faculty be open to their candidates writing in a style that translates evidence-based insights into practitioner language. In many ways, an EBMgt-supportive reframing by doctoral faculty requires that they be reflexive regarding their own natural, often unconscious, inclinations to (re)produce theory-focused, discipline-based scholars such as themselves.

Do practitioners and academics need to compromise their identities in order to reframe their perspectives in ways that support the spread of EBMgt? For instance, should traditional PhD programs give less attention to developing disciplinary depth? We believe the answer to be a resounding no. Regarding managerial identities, consider that Briner et al.'s (2009) definition of EBMgt roots the use of research-based evidence in the everyday managerial practice of information-based decision making. Doing so enables EBMgt to be an extension, rather than a departure, from managerial practice and identity. It brings EBMgt into line with Gibbons et al.'s (1994) mode 2 analyses describing how practitioners generate usable knowledge. Similarly, academic researchers can take a lesson from practitioner-scholars' research. Discipline-based academics can at least occasionally pursue problem-focused research, knowing that this style of research produces contributions to theory and, sometimes, identifies new conceptual domains or syntheses with powerful concepts from other disciplines. Problem-focused research can be understood as "discipline-based *plus*," where academics access, appreciate, and import concepts from other disciplines. Similarly, there is no need to provide candidates in traditional doctoral programs with less disciplinary training. For them, learning methods of problem-focused research will build on their disciplinary bases, enabling them to partner effectively with academics from other disciplines and with senior managers.

Conclusions: Sustaining and Leveraging a Field of Practitioner Scholarship

This chapter addresses the emergence of a field of scholarship—practitioner-scholarship—that offers significant opportunities for the advancement and spread of EBMgt. The contemporary community of practitioner-scholars is generating knowledge explicitly designed to optimize rigor and managerial relevance. This community models EBMgt managerial practice and credibly informs communities of managerial practitioner peers. The significance

of the field of practitioner-scholarship for EBMgt, then, can be at least partially understood as involving knowledge production, research dissemination, and the institutional spread of EBMgt. In terms that run through this chapter, these issues take the form of the 4Rs: relevance, respect, resourcefulness, and reframing. Reflections on our pursuit of an engaged, problem-focused style of research in an alternative doctoral program lead us to several conclusions about these 4Rs., reflected in the following list and in Figure 20.1.

1. Relevance: When armed with the proper scholarly skills, experienced senior managers who are doctoral candidates find academic research and theory to be relevant to their problems of practice. This experience indicates that, in the right circumstances, their peers could become similarly disposed to using research-based evidence in EBMgt. Analyzing the senior-management problems studied by candidates in the DM Program at Case reveals that such problems are typically complex, long-term, broad in scope, and across multiple levels. They call for a style of research—termed *engaged* or *problem-focused research*—that responds to these characteristics. These problems also require EBMgt supporters to develop new methods for transforming academic knowledge into managerial knowledge; in addition to systematic reviews, methods are required that synthesize multiple bodies of theory and empirical research. Alternative doctoral programs, such as the DM Program at Case, are in the process of refining such methods of problem-focused research, educating practitioner-scholars in their use, and informing faculty elsewhere about these methods and pedagogies.

2. Respect: Significant challenges to EBMgt reside in the differing responsibilities (Speicher & Adams, chapter 17 of this volume), perspectives (Leung & Bartunek,chapter 9 of this volume), and views of evidence (Potoworski & Green, chapter 16 of this volume) of academics and managers. Experiences with senior managers in our DM Program indicate that such high-level managers tend to be skeptical about academic theories and research. Part of this skepticism resides in their lack of experience and skill in using academic research. The skepticism is not as severe a problem as is the active disrespect for scholars that some practitioner-scholar graduates have experienced. Some organizations and functional areas are more inclined toward research and researchers, suggesting that EBMgt efforts be initially directed toward

	Relevance	Respect	Resourcefulness	Reframing
Senior Managers	Managers must explore real problems of practice to create evident-based research projects whose outcomes relate meaningfully to practice	Managers must combat skepticism and disrespect for the scholarly process (e.g., disdain for the "theoretical") as these perspectives impede the effective dissemination of evidence-based research	Managers must develop both the will and the skill for scholarly work and embrace the challenge of bridging two divergent approaches	Managers must model and embrace practitioner-scholarship when working with other managers and the Academy to create and effective bridge between two "worlds"
Management Faculty	Faculty must embrace multi-theoretical, multi-level research inquiries because problems of practice rarely fit within a single theory	Faculty must model respect for alternative doctoral programs and be willing to produce graduates "not in their own image"	Faculty must accept new approaches inherent with problem-focused research and embrace alternative skills	Faculty must accept and embrace a new epistemology and actively nurture a community of practitioner-scholars
What's required?	*New Muscles*	*New Mindsets*	*New Skills*	*New Identities*

Fig. 20.1. Future Implications for the Four R's.

managerial fields that respect rigorously produced evidence.

3. Resourcefulness: Senior managers' skepticism about use of academic theories and research-based evidence can be overcome through particular educational efforts and pedagogies discussed in this chapter. These provide advanced managers with the opportunities and skills for locating and critically interpreting academically produced knowledge. Making these educational efforts requires resourcefulness on the part of management education programs and senior managers. Programs must devote resources to making these opportunities available for managers at all levels of education. Senior managers need both the will and time to develop these skills themselves and to provide opportunities for lower-level managers to do so.

4. Reframing: It is easy for members of the academy to recognize the need for managers to reframe their perspectives, if EBMgt is to be more broadly applied. However, issues of respect and reframing cut both ways. Management researchers and educators

must respect managers' problem perspectives, contexts, and capabilities in developing and applying knowledge. Challenges lie, not only in the dissemination of research-based evidence, but also in the production of research by the academy. New ways for academics and managers to engage each other, and for the hybrid practitioner-scholars to pursue both practice and research, ultimately rest on the willingness of various practitioner and academic communities to reframe particular perspectives that they hold. This reframing need not challenge their identities but, rather, add new elements to expand them.

Supporting EBMgt

Individuals serving in many roles can support EBMgt by helping to develop and sustain a community of practitioner-scholars and by participating in problem-focused research. Educators in research-intensive institutions can consider the initiating of an alternative doctoral program to train practitioner-scholars, or add to their traditional doctoral programs training in problem-focused research. Similarly, academic researchers can stretch beyond their theory-driven research to engage with managers and carry out problem-focused research. On their side, managers can provide access to themselves and their peers for problem-focused research. They can help to shape new research questions and research applications by creating joint manager-academic forums in which managerial problems and the managerial interpretations of findings from problem-focused research projects are discussed.

However, this paper's main contention is that practitioner-scholars are in the most potent positions to support EBMgt, not only by continuing to produce and disseminate research that connects with managers' problems of practice, but also in modeling their application of research-based knowledge in practice. Interviews with DM Program graduates conducted and analyzed by Adjunct Professor Nicholas Berente indicate that practitioner-scholars pursue issues in their managerial practice in greater depth, assessing those issues and using information in a more disciplined way:

moving beyond *"Power Point slides and three paragraph notes... [to] get the chance to make arguments"*

"to look at things in a deeper way"

"to stop, think, look around and ask questions"

"to reframe how you view problems"

"think about things in a much more analytical way."

Practitioner-scholars use their own and others' research-based knowledge in their daily practice:

"on a professional level it helped me look at issues in a way... an evidence-based approach."

"There are things that I learned about building trust that I employ everyday... I'm living the research that I conducted."

Not only can practitioner-scholars model such EBMgt-supportive behavior for others, they can be more explicit in informing and guiding others:

"Still making presentations around the world on my research."

"Now I dedicate every ounce of free time to teaching and mentoring others at my company."

"As a result of my analysis we actually revised company policy... It is the first leading indicator ever created in our industry and it is being published as a best practice."

The training of doctoral graduates who possess the desire and skills required to actively bridge between the academy and practice is well under way. Expanding the community of practitioner-scholars will require the commitment of yet more management academics to producing scholars in other than their image.

In this chapter we have discussed a number of concrete practices that have proven useful in educating practitioner-scholars. We have proposed that these practices can be used not only in alternative doctoral programs but also in traditional doctoral education, to the benefit of EBMgt. However, is it sufficient to educate only doctoral students to inhabit the intersection between practice and scholarship? We assert that it is not. Kovner (chapter 10 of this volume) identifies graduate education as the one venue where EBMgt initiatives are well accepted and where protracted efforts, such as Pearce's (chapter 21 of this volume) EBMgt textbooks and Rousseau's (chapter 19 of this volume) EBMgt courses to MBAs, can be crafted to encourage and develop the will and skill among managers and managers to be.

Our experience suggests that the community of practitioner-scholars is well positioned to contribute both to practice and the academy. Nonetheless, inserting EBMgt approaches in traditional management education may further enhance the ability to effectively meld two seemingly diverse approaches and styles. In short, we assert that these alternative doctoral programs represent the tip of the proverbial iceberg—that problem-focused empirical research can be spread through an enlarging community of practitioner-scholars and adopted by many discipline-based academics, and that this style of research may prove to play a critical role in the evolution of management practice. How exciting to think of a future in which these ideas have become so prevalent in management education that the alternative doctoral programs need no longer be described as "alternative"!

References

Adelegan, J. A. (2009). *Environmentally benign technologies and financial performance: Evidence from the pulp and paper industry in Nigeria.* EDM Research Archive. Retrieved from http://library.case.edu/digitalcase/SearchResults.aspx?q=%28Adelegan%29+AND+%28%28collection%3A%22ksl.edm%22%29%29&extra=Adelegan

Aram, J. D., & Salipante, P. (2003). Bridging scholarship in management: Epistemological reflections. *British Journal of Management, 14,* 189–205.

Bourner, T., Bowden, R., & Laing, S. (2001). Professional Doctorates in England. *Studies in Higher Education, 26*(1), 65–83.

Boyer, E. L. (1990). *Scholarship reconsidered: Priorities of the professoriate.* Princeton, NJ: Princeton University Press.

Brennan, N. (2010). *Exploring sustained collaborations: Activities and behaviors that make a difference.* Unpublished doctoral dissertation, Case Western Reserve University, Weatherhead School of Management, Cleveland, Ohio.

Briner, R. B., Denyer, D., & Rousseau, D.M. (2009). Evidence-based management: Concept clean-up time? *Academy of Management Perspectives ARCHIVES, 23*(4), 19-32.

Capelli, P., & Crocker-Hefter, A. (1996). Distinctive human resources are firms' core competencies. *Organizational Dynamics, 24*(3), 7–22.

Dauphinee, F., & Martin, J. B. (2000). Breaking down the walls: Thoughts on the scholarship of integration. *Academic Medicine, 75*(9), 881–886.

Dewey, J. (1902). *The child and the curriculum.* University of Chicago Press.

Dewey, J. (1929). *The quest for certainty: A study of the relation of knowledge and action.* New York: Minton, Balch & Co.

Emerson, R. M., Fretz, R. I., & Shaw, L. L. (1995). *Writing ethnographic fieldnotes.* Chicago, IL: University of Chicago Press.

Fisk, A. G. D. (2010). *The effect of social factors on project success within enterprise-class system development.* Unpublished doctoral dissertation, Case Western Reserve University, Weatherhead School of Management, Cleveland, Ohio.

Frost, P. J., & Stablein, R. E. (Eds.) (1992). *Doing exemplary research.* Newbury Park, CA: Sage.

Gardner, H. (1988). Creative lives and creative works: A synthetic scientific approach. In R.J. Sternberg (Ed.), *The nature of creativity: Contemporary psychological perspectives* (pp. 298–321). Cambridge, England: Cambridge University Press.

Geertz, C. (1974). "From the native's point of view": On the nature of anthropological understanding. *Bulletin of the American Academy of Arts and Sciences, 28*(1), 26–45.

Geertz, C. (2003). Thick description: Toward an interpretive theory of culture. In C. Jenks (Ed.), *Culture: Critical concepts in sociology* (pp. 173–196). London: Routledge.

Gibbons, M., Limoges, C., Nowotny, H., Schwartzman, S., Scott, P., & Trow, M. (1994). *The new production of knowledge: The dynamics of science and research in contemporary societies.* London: Sage.

Gill, T. G., & Hoppe, U. (2009). The business professional doctorate as an informing channel: A survey and analysis. *International Journal of Doctoral Studies, 4,* 27–57.

Glaser, B. G., & Strauss, A. L. (1967/1999). *The discovery of grounded theory: Strategies for qualitative research.* New York: Aldine de Gruyter.

Goodman, P. S., & Beenen, G. (2008). Organizational learning contracts and management education. *Academy of Management Learning and Education, 7*(4), 521–534.

Huff, A. S. (2000). Changes in organizational knowledge production. *Academy of Management Review, 25,* 288–293.

Kuhn, T. S. (1962). *The structure of scientific revolutions.* Chicago, IL: University of Chicago Press.

Kvale, S., & Brinkmann, S. (2009). *InterViews.* Thousand Oaks, CA: Sage Publications.

La Belle, A. (2010). *Nonprofit leaders and their organizations: Routes to and repertoires for effectiveness.* Unpublished doctoral dissertation, Case Western Reserve University, Weatherhead School of Management, Cleveland, Ohio.

Levy, S. R., Stroessner, S. J., & Dweck, C. S. (1998). Stereotype formation and endorsement: The role of implicit theories. *Journal of Personality and Social Psychology, 74*(6), 1421–1436.

Lincoln, Y. S., & Guba, E. G. (1985). *Naturalistic inquiry.* Thousand Oaks, CA: Sage Publications.

Oliver, W. J. (2010). *Improving the effectiveness of microfinance in reducing household poverty.* Unpublished doctoral dissertation, Case Western Reserve University, Weatherhead School of Management, Cleveland, Ohio.

Piore, M. J. (1979). Qualitative research techniques in economics. *Administrative Science Quarterly, 24*(4), 560–569.

Rittel, H. W. J., & Webber, M. W. (1973). Dilemmas in a general theory of planning. *Policy Sciences, 4*(2), 155–169.

Salipante, P., & Aram, J. D. (2003). Managers as knowledge generators: The nature of practitioner-scholar research in the nonprofit sector. *Nonprofit Management & Leadership, 14*(2), 129–150.

Seshadri, S. B. (2010). *How many hands does a team have? Developing ambidextrous in academic medical centers.* Unpublished doctoral dissertation, Case Western Reserve University, Weatherhead School of Management, Cleveland, Ohio.

Schon, D. A. (1995). The new scholarship requires a new epistemology. *Change, Nov.-Dec.,* 27–34.

Smith, A. K. (2010). *The delicate balance of organizational leadership: Encouraging learning and driving successful innovation.* Unpublished doctoral dissertation, Case Western Reserve University, Weatherhead School of Management, Cleveland, Ohio.

Spradley, J. (1979). *The ethnographic interview.* New York: Holt, Rinehart & Winston.

Spreitzer, G. M., & Schwarz, G. M. (2004). Report to the Academy Professional Division Review Committee: Organizational Development and Change Division, 1999–2003. Retrieved from http://www.google.com/url?sa=t&source=web&ct=res&cd=2&ved=0CBUQFjAB&url=http%3A%2F%2Fdivision.aomonline.org%2Fodc%2Findex.php%3Foption%3Dcom_docman%26task%3Ddoc_download%26gid%3D7%26%26Itemid%3D73&ei=EGztS-yqJI6yNv3ZveoL&usg=AFQjCNFG4T84S0QRzS7ZsSVKjK4Cq_oGuQ

Strauss, A., & Corbin, J. (2008). *Basics of qualitative research.* Thousand Oaks, CA: Sage Publications.

Sutton, R. I., & Rafaeli, A. (1988). Untangling the relationship between displayed emotions and organizational sales: The case of convenience stores. *Academy of Management Journal, 31*(3), 461–487.

Talton, R.Y. (2010). *Dare to restore trust and drive loyalty in distrust-dominated environments: A stakeholder perspective.* Unpublished doctoral dissertation, Case Western Reserve University, Weatherhead School of Management, Cleveland, Ohio.

Teague, D. E. (2010). *The effect of charisma on employee volunteer programs.* Unpublished doctoral dissertation, Case Western Reserve University, Weatherhead School of Management, Cleveland, Ohio.

Toulmin, S. E. (2003). *The uses of argument.* Cambridge, England: Cambridge University Press.

Toulmin, S. E., Rieke, R. D., & Janik, A. (1984). *An introduction to reasoning.* Upper Saddle River, NJ: Prentice-Hall.

Van de Ven, A. H. (2007). *Engaged scholarship: A guide for organizational and social research.* Oxford, England: Oxford University Press.

Walker, A. J. (2009). The *paradox of evidence-based management in higher education.* EDM Research Archive. Retrieved from http://weatherhead.case.edu/academics/doctorate/management/research/details.cfm?id=13136&topic=23

Wenger, E. (1998). *Communities of practice: Learning, meaning and identity.* Cambridge, England: Cambridge University Press.

Creating Evidence-Based Management Textbooks

Jone L. Pearce

Abstract

A close look at textbooks helps to illustrate that we do not now translate research into practice in our teaching. There are two areas in which our textbooks fail: by too often reporting as research evidence information for which there is no reliable supporting scholarship, and by undermining the field by persisting in wasting scarce space (and students' attention) on theories that have long been debunked by rigorous research. Why textbooks too often fail to accurately present research and what the chapter author has done to make her teaching more evidence based are described.

Key Words: textbooks, debunked theories, EBMgt (EBMgt) teaching, executive education, systematic review, MBAs

Evidence-based management (EBMgt) seeks to help managers more easily draw on research evidence for information to support their policies and practices. One of its central purposes is developing decision supports that aid managers to be informed by the best evidence available (Rousseau, 2006; 2012). That is, EBMgt seeks to facilitate integrating research evidence into organizational decisions and practices. Many in our scholarly field who struggle with the idea of EBMgt believe that it is not new, but something that we are already doing in our professional work as scholars and teachers. One approach to fostering evidence-based practice is in the formal communication of what our research says for practice through our textbooks. After all, textbooks are the most common way that those who are now or who hope to practice management learn how research can inform their decisions. This chapter asks, How well do management textbooks facilitate the use of evidence in management practice? I will focus on introductory textbooks in organizational behavior, a required course in most business programs, and one that is often found in public administration,

education, and other programs intending to train managers. I contend that a review of introductory-organizational-behavior textbooks suggests we are not now doing a good job of basing our teaching on the research evidence. Taking a close look at our textbooks helps to illustrate that our translation of research into actionable practice does not live up to our assumptions about it.

If we assume that an important purpose of organizational-behavior textbooks is to introduce the best available scientific evidence about the behavior of individuals and teams doing organizational work, textbooks should accurately present the most up-to-date research-based knowledge, should refrain from presenting ideas that have never been examined or have been debunked by research, and should help all readers distinguish between what we can confidently conclude from research and reasonable practical implications that can be generalized from that research. That is, you might assume that introductory-organizational-behavior textbooks are in the business of translating and communicating scholarly research that can inform practice, but most do not. Too often, textbooks in management and organizational behavior misrepresent what research does show, they persist in reporting theories that have long been debunked, and they do not distinguish between what the research demonstrates and commonsense advice for action. I will lay out the case for these strong claims and then describe how I took action to try to create an organizational-behavior textbook that was more evidence based.

Are Our Textbooks Really Reporting Research Evidence?

There are two areas in which our textbooks fail. First, too often they report as research evidence information for which there is no reliable supporting scholarship. I will provide an example of this failure from one area, where I conduct my own research. Second, too many textbooks persist in wasting valuable space (and students' cognitive capacity) on theories that have long been debunked by rigorous research. The database for these two inquiries consists of eight organizational-behavior textbooks, including the most popular textbooks (Robbins & Judge, 2011, and Schermerhorn, Hunt, & Osborn, 2010), the top sellers according to www.amazon. com, and the ones on my shelves (the other six are George & Jones, 2008; Greenberg & Baron, 2008; Hellriegel & Slocum, 2007; Nelson & Quick, 2009; Osland, Kolb, Rubin & Turner, 2007; Tenbrunsel & Messick, 1999). This is a convenience sample; however, the books on my shelves were not selected with this small inquiry in mind but, rather, arrived based on decisions made by publishers' salespeople who sent unsolicited copies of these books. I can think of no reason why these textbooks would not be representative of the textbooks presenting organizational behavior to students.

I first reviewed these books for the accuracy of their representation of what research says about what causes interpersonal trust, or the relative trust one individual might have in another. This is an area in which I had systematically collected research data from the fields of management, decision sciences, sociology, and psychology for my own research. The importance of trust in one another among those who must work together is a constant theme repeated by advice-giving practitioners. All the surveyed textbooks note the value of interpersonal trust for actions such as citizenship behavior, innovation, team performance, as well as the organizational costs of employee distrust. These statements of the importance of workplace interpersonal trust beg an important question: What leads someone to be more likely to trust someone else? If it is important to me that my clients, subordinates, peers, and bosses trust me, how can I gain that trust?

There might be many other ways that textbooks can facilitate evidence-based action by their readers. For example, they might assist the readers in how to diagnose and categorize issues, so they know where to look for the relevant evidence, or they might organize the material into holistic systems that might help readers to organize and make sense of the material. For this brief discussion, I am only focusing on whether the introductory textbooks accurately present research evidence for a selection of topics, as one necessary but not sufficient requirement to help our textbooks facilitate EBMgt.

Here I consider systematic research on interpersonal trust to be a study that has established that the factor purported to cause trust really is causal, either through the use of experiments (in which the factor was manipulated and the level of interpersonal trust assessed as the dependent variable) or through longitudinal field studies in which causal direction could be tested. I eliminated the large number of one-shot correlational studies in which trust was correlated with other variables, because we cannot confidently conclude that trust was caused by or caused the factor, or that it was caused by an unmeasured factor in such studies. Because virtually every introductory methods course warns that one-shot correlations cannot be confidently interpreted as supporting causality, I do not think I was being overly strict in eliminating these reports. However, I note that these correlational studies, with confident conclusions about what causes interpersonal trust, dominate the organizational-behavior literature, and this may be a reason for the textbook representations reported later.

Two of the sampled textbooks noted the importance of interpersonal trust but did address the causes of trust (Nelson & Quick, 2009; Schermerhorn, et al., 2010). This is reasonable: all textbook authors face space constraints and must make decisions about what to include and exclude. No textbook author should be faulted for excluding someone else's favorite topic.

Five of the textbooks did report what leads others to trust someone else at work; their statements and whether there is solid research evidence supporting these statements are provided in Table 21.1, with an illustrative research citation supporting (or debunking) the statement provided. We can see that no textbook reported causes of interpersonal trust that were supported in full by the research

Table 21.1 Comparison of Textbook Statements on Causes of Trust with Systematic Research

George and Jones (2008, pp. 83–84)

Share personal values and goals.	No research
Share important values.	No research
Other is in a good mood.	Yes–Dunn and Schweitzer (2005)

Greenberg and Baron (2008, pp. 431–432)

Propensity to trust.	Yes–Parks and Hulbert (1995)
Reputation for trustworthiness.	Yes–Polzer (2004)
Meet deadlines.	No research
Follow through as promised.	No research

Hellriegel and Slocum (2007, p. 243)

Encourage two-way communication.	No research
Share critical information.	Yes–Tenbrunsel and Messick (1999)
Reveal their perceptions and feelings.	No research

Osland, et. al (2007, pp. 3–5)

Share information.	Yes–Tenbrunsel and Messick (1999)
Accessibility.	No research
Answer hard questions.	No research
Deliver on promises.	No research
Recognize and appreciate.	No research
Show personal concern.	No research

Robbins and Judge (2011, pp. 395–396)

Honesty.	No research
Integrity.	No research
Benevolence.	Not, if "nice" Komorita, Hilty, & Parks (1991)
Ability.	No research
Trust propensity.	Yes–Parks and Hulbert (1995)
Time	Yes–Sniezek and Van Swol (2001)
Avoided Opportunism	Yes–Tenbrunsel and Messick (1999)
Competence	Yes–Butler and Cantrell (1984)

evidence. The best performers are Greenberg and Baum (2008) and Robbins and Judge (2011) with 50 percent of their claims supported by the empirical evidence. Unfortunately, best-selling Robbins and Judge's (2011) comparatively positive record is undermined by the figure they report on p. 396, which lists only integrity, benevolence, ability, and propensity to trust as causing trust, whereas only one of these (propensity to trust) enjoys empirical support as a cause of trust. It is unclear why the claims unsupported by research evidence are given this visual prominence when those that are supported by research evidence do not appear in a figure. Other textbooks range from only one out of six of the reported causes of trust supported by systematic research (Osland et al., 2007) to one-third (George & Jones, 2008; Hellriegel & Slocum, 2007) of the claims supported. Thus, in this sample of the best-selling organizational-behavior textbooks, the majority of statements about what leads someone to trust another at work are not supported by empirical research.

Second, our textbooks undermine the field by persisting in wasting scarce space (and students' attention) on theories that have long been debunked by rigorous research. All seven of these textbooks devoted substantial space (much, much more space than they devoted to all discussions of trust combined) to Herzberg's (1987/1959) two-factor theory and Maslow's (1970) need hierarchy of motivation. I need not remind the readers of this chapter that these theories were roundly and confidently disproved over 40 years ago (see, King, 1970; Hall & Nougaim, 1968; Goodman, 1968). Any organizational-behavior doctoral students making the claims for Herzberg's and Maslow's theories reported in these textbooks would be summarily failed out of their doctoral programs. Many (but not all) of these textbook authors state that there are controversies about these theories, and that their claims may not apply in all circumstances. However, there are no real controversies here. There is simply no evidence whatsoever that some workplace incentives serve as hygiene factors whereas others are motivators (does anyone doubt the power of money to motivate investment bankers?), or that, after employees have had their esteem needs gratified at work, they automatically begin to desire self-actualization. No one who knows the organizational-behavior research would make these claims, yet they appear in every single one of these seven prominent textbooks. What is worse, these disproven theories are given a great deal of space, usually with multicolor graphic illustrations. In short, a lot of textbook space is devoted to ideas these textbook authors surely know are not consistent with the research evidence.

To be fair, apparently, this isn't only a problem in organizational-behavior textbooks. Recently, Tavris and Wade, in an interview in the Association for Psychological Science's Newsletter (Changes in Psychological Science, 2010) note that one of their challenges in updating their introductory psychology textbook (Tavris & Wade, 2010) is how to include

"material that 'has always been there' even if it is now outdated," implying that they are expected to do so. In the same article, Susan Nolen-Hoeksema says that many psychology instructors now (but apparently not before) want theories that have not been empirically verified to be excluded from their introductory-psychology textbooks (Nolen-Hoeksema, Fredrickson, Loftus, & Wagenaar, 2009).

Are these examples of statements not supported by empirical research in organizational behavior textbooks isolated incidents? I did not conduct the same review of every statement made in these textbooks that I did for the causes of interpersonal trust. I am sure that there are many, many statements in these textbooks that are based on the best research evidence available. However, it is incontrovertible that not all claims in our most prominent organizational-behavior textbooks are based on research evidence, and that decades of disconfirming research evidence have not dislodged favored theories from their featured places in our textbooks. Taken as a whole, we certainly cannot claim that our textbooks, and, therefore, what we are teaching our students, is evidence-based organizational behavior.

Why Our Textbooks Have Strayed so Far from the Research Evidence

How could this have happened? There seem to be two primary reasons that I will address in turn: consensus on what constitutes evidence in the field, and the pressures of the textbook marketplace to be all things to as many people as possible.

Inconsistent Use of Evidence

First, not all textbooks claim to be basing their statements on the research evidence. For example, Osland, et al. (2007) are explicit that their listed causes of interpersonal trust are not research-evidence based, quoting a list of causes developed by the consultant Robert Levering (Levering, 2004). Certainly, we do not have systematic research on every practical concern that textbook authors wish to address. However, these textbooks do claim to report evidence from a scholarly field, and, therefore, such mixing of personal advice, experience-based hunches, common sense, and research evidence threatens to undermine the field's claims to being a social science.

Second, as noted earlier, much of the research on the question of the causes of workplace interpersonal trust in the field of organizational behavior consists of correlational reports in which trust is found to correlate with a factor that common sense suggests should probably cause people to trust some-one else. It is not clear who is at fault here. Textbook authors might reasonably conclude that they do not have the time to investigate the scholarly rigor of so many different studies on the hundreds of different topics they must address. If the paper appears in a respected scholarly journal in their field, perhaps they feel it is not their responsibility to second-guess these journal editors' and reviewers' standards. It is a case of the scholarly field not taking care to follow sound methodological practices for confident causal claims, and the textbooks simply reflect a "weak field." This takes us to a core debate within EBMgt about what counts as evidence, and this is addressed in other chapters in this volume.

The Textbook Marketplace

Textbooks are published by businesses seeking to make profits, and there are many, many organizational-behavior textbooks competing in that marketplace. This means that textbook authors must respond to market pressures, and so we need to understand the market pressures on our textbook authors. The textbook market is complex, consisting of the publishers who bring the books to market, the instructors who decide whether to adopt the book, and the students who purchase the books and provide the instructor evaluations.

The publishers are the ones who make decisions to publish (commission, produce, market, and deliver) textbooks. Publishers are businesses, and people in business need to worry about the bottom line. Large textbook publishers have high fixed costs and many have judged that those costs can only be covered with large-volume sales. So textbook publishers are very much concerned with volume; they have to be. That is, the more instructors who adopt their textbooks, the more sales. Further, the more large classes in large schools that use their textbooks, the more sales. Who are the instructors who teach those large-volume introductory courses in large schools? The instructors are often doctoral students or lecturers who may not have been trained in organizational behavior or scholarship. This means that publishers feel they need to include a great deal of ancillary materials to support new instructors, and those with no scholarly training in the subject matter. Publishers do not worry about the content of what goes in textbooks, this is the author's responsibility not theirs. They are not subject-matter experts and are in no position to review their textbooks for the quality of the research presented. It is their job to know what will sell.

Further challenges are created because textbook sales are not driven by the students who pay for the books but by the instructor who adopts the textbook for a course. This means that textbook sales are most dependent on decisions by adopting instructors (and their textbook committees for those schools that make department-wide adoption decisions for their courses). What criteria do they use to make these decisions? No doubt they want books that are clearly written and appealing to the particular students in their courses. However, they also want to make sure that the books include every topic they personally think is important. And in a field as eclectic as organizational behavior, with instructors with widely diverse interests and trained in the full range of the social sciences, this means that authors are under pressure to include every conceivable topic. Because instructors will not adopt textbooks if they do not cover their own personal topic of interest, authors are advised by publishers to include everything. This is why textbooks look like endless lists of so many topics. Textbook authors cannot possibly know the systematic research on all of them.

What is more, too many instructors of introductory courses do not themselves respect or value research evidence. Either they were not trained in rigorous research or they do not value it for other reasons. There really are instructors out there who will not adopt a book if it does not discuss Maslow's hierarchy of needs. They see this theory as foundational and really do not care what the research evidence says. For all these reasons, there is not much pressure from adopting instructors to rely exclusively on what the research evidence says.

Finally, students also are important players in the textbook market. Although students are not as important as adopting instructors, their voices do matter. Students complete teacher evaluations and no instructor wants to get a poor evaluation because students did not like the assigned readings. So, what do students like? Students taking organizational behavior courses differ in what they want—the 18-year old freshman wants something different than the 40-year old middle manager in an executive MBA program.

We already know that the publishers target the students in large introductory courses because that is where the volume is. Young, inexperienced students like lots of examples, and they want those examples to be up to date; they want to learn about the latest and most trendy companies. They like glossaries with vocabulary lists they can quickly memorize the night before the test instead of reading the entire book. Finally, they want lots of interesting gee-whiz stories and tips for action. Students in large introductory courses do not know what research is and have not yet been trained in the limitations of common sense, bias, and wishful thinking. I think I can be confident in my belief that no student in an introductory-organizational-behavior class has ever complained that a textbook was not sufficiently based on research.

In summary, textbook authors have to meet a lot of demands—large-volume sales, demands for books that are easy to read, inclusion of all possible topics that adopting instructors from a very heterogeneous field might want to cover, lots of material to support inexperienced teachers and student exam preparation, and numerous current examples and engaging graphics. The principle players in the textbook marketplace do not insist that textbook claims be based on research, but isn't that because they assume their textbooks are based on research? These players may not all be trained in rigorous research, but if you asked publishers, introductory-course instructors, or students, wouldn't most say that they assume that the statements and conclusions in their organizational-behavior textbooks are based on research? That they are not is a dirty little secret that we all should hope does not get out.

What I Did about This Problem

Like all academics, I began by putting my complaints into writing (Pearce, 2004). However, I decided that it was not enough to complain; if I really thought this was a problem, I should do something about it. What I did was to start from scratch to write a textbook that would be based on research evidence. However, this undertaking required several preliminary decisions.

Which Market?

Because I was teaching executive MBAs and was dissatisfied with textbooks aimed at teenagers, I decided that my target market would be experienced MBA students. Instructors of experienced students have long recognized that textbooks do not address their students' needs. These students want practical help, are better able to recognize nonsense, and do not want to be treated like teenagers. How have instructors for these students coped? By using articles from various sources—good summaries of research for practice like Locke's (2000), but also practitioner articles and popular books. These readings focus on these students' needs for clarity and practicality, but they are not always (or even often)

based on rigorous research. I decided to keep the focal audience clear: experienced MBA students taking an introductory organizational behavior course.

What Content and Format?

I needed to address both main market players: experienced students and adopting instructors. I decided to place the students first. The first problem I had to confront in making the book attractive to students was how to select topics that they would find useful and interesting. I decided not to try to engage their interest through trendy examples and stories about popular organizations. Rather, I sought to engage their interests by addressing their own problems and concerns—relying on them, experienced managers, to select the topics from organizational behavior that best addressed their own challenges. The textbook was not going to be a history of the field of organizational behavior (covering topics with no practical relevance to them, or those that had been debunked decades ago) but a compilation of what systematic research could tell them about their own most pressing practical problems today.

What topics would experienced MBA students find the most useful? Because I had been teaching these students for years, I thought I knew what they wanted. I had been gathering their "important organizational-behavior problems" for years. At the beginning of each class, these executive MBA students had been asked to write down "what their most important organizational problems were." In preparing class sessions, I would review their problems in order to expand and contract material in the course. For the textbook, I took the past several years of these expressed most-important problems and grouped them into topics. Examples included, "giving performance feedback," "getting the corporate office to realize that our customers here in California need to be handled differently," and so forth.

However, I was concerned that our particular population of experienced MBA students might be a skewed sample—they come primarily from small and medium-sized high technology, design, and health-care companies. Their organizational problems could be quite different from those of managers in other industries. Because I wanted to be sure that I had collected as many of the problems that experienced students faced as I could, I decided to also gather practical problems from the shelves of my local bookstore. I reasoned that the books sold in bookstores to practicing managers needed to appeal to the purchaser (unlike text-books, which are intended to primarily appeal to adopting instructors). Such books must address managers' challenges or they would not sell and, therefore, would not be able to command valuable shelf space in a bookstore. Therefore, I spent several weeks systematically going through the books in the management and leadership sections of my local bookstore and writing down the problems such books addressed either explicitly or implicitly. I then added these topics to the ones from my own students, and worked to address these problem-based topics and to resist adding topics from the field that I thought interesting but that did not address their problems.

In addition to selecting those topics from organizational behavior that would be most interesting to these experienced MBA students, I also wanted to develop a way of presenting the material that would seize and hold their interest. I decided to make use of true-false questions around common misconceptions. I am a fan of Davis's (1971) argument about what makes a theory interesting. He proposes that the important theories in the social sciences are not the ones that are true, but the ones that question their readers' assumptions about what is true. So, for example, Sigmund Freud's theories became important not because it is true that human psyches are composed of an ego, super ego, and id, but because he made claims that questioned readers' assumptions at that time—assumptions like Freud's assertion that the behavior of children, primitives, neurotics, and adults in crowds, as well as dreams, jokes, and slips of the tongue and pen, which were considered at the time he wrote to be unrelated, are, in fact, all various manifestations of the same instinctual drives. In my teaching, like many instructors, I had been explaining how research debunks the usual practitioners' commonsense assumptions, such as "happy workers are more productive workers." So, I decided to expand that approach throughout the book, drawing on the many commonsense assumptions and claims that were not supported by research taken from those practical management and leadership books from the bookstore shelves. These popular books turned out to be a rich source of nostrums that were only rarely supported by research; examples include, "Having employees engage in self-evaluation makes performance appraisals more democratic," and "The most effective organizations have strong corporate cultures."

So, I thought I knew how to address the needs and desires of experienced MBA students in their introductory-organizational-behavior courses. However, this effort would be useless if I did not address the needs of those most important market players of all: the adopting instructors. How to serve both of these markets and be faithful to what research says? First, I decided to organize the experienced managers' problems into chapters that would be familiar to organizational-behavior instructors, and I placed the chapters in the order usually found in most textbooks and courses. However, instead of calling the chapters Individual Differences and Personality, Motivation, Teams, and the like, I gave them the names of the problems managers would use that knowledge to address: Individual Differences became How to Hire, Motivation became Managing Performance and Managing Incentives, Leadership became Mastering Power. In addition, I also made sure the index included the academic topic names and terms that instructors would expect to cover. In this way instructors could continue to cover the topics they usually did, but could now frame them in ways (I hoped) that would make their relevance and importance to their experienced students clearer. I had faith that others who teach experienced students were as motivated as I was to make the value of organizational behavior clear to these demanding experienced managers, and that they would find my own best case for its value as useful as I would.

Finally, and most importantly, how could I be honest about what the research actually says and still say something useful to practicing managers? We all know that research is often conducted in sterile environments with only limited applicability to the complex multiplex environments in which practitioners work. Those taking practical action cannot "hold everything else constant." Even field-research conclusions may only apply to the particular circumstances of those settings, so I believed that systematic research could be useful, but didn't want it to be used for the kind of dictatorial "do-this" advice that so many overwhelmed managers craved. I tried to address this challenge in three ways.

First, I explicitly stated this conundrum in the first chapter. In the introduction, readers are first warned of the limitations of common sense and our own narrow personal experiences, and then the limitations of scholarly research were described. I advised the readers to treat the scholarly research as additional information—no better and no worse—than the information they have gained from their own experiences. Readers are advised to approach any organizational problem with a good diagnosis by testing their assumptions, finding out how others

Table 21.2 Illustrative Applications Drawn from Research

Application — Get an Honest Assessment of an Applicant's Performance from Others

- Inoculate yourself for confirmation bias before the call by reminding yourself that your first impressions could be wrong and by dwelling on the pain and difficulty of hiring the wrong person.
- Call references before deciding who to bring in for interviews. If applicants do not want a current employer to know they are job hunting, ask to call someone they had worked with in a previous job or someone they trust to keep the search confidential.
- Ask the reference to describe behavior, not the applicant's personal characteristics. Suggest specifics scenarios: "Last time 'X' occurred, could you please describe what happened." You want accurate descriptions, not ill-considered theories.
- Ask questions focused on what successful employees actually do. For example, to assess conscientiousness you might ask, "Has [name] ever missed a deadline? Stayed late to complete an important assignment? Not delivered on what was promised?" Be sure to ask for specific examples.
- Snowball references. Ask each reference to suggest someone else who has worked with the person and so can describe the applicant's performance. If applicants try to restrict you to a narrow list of references, ask why. Persistent managers who ask specific questions about applicants' prior performance can get a lot of information.
- If applicants do not give permission to contact any references until you are about to make them an offer, or if they want to restrict your contacts to a narrow list of people, let them know that this will eliminate them from consideration. Explain that it is your policy to use reference descriptions of past performance in deciding whom to interview for all hiring decisions, and stick to this policy. Good employees will be confident in what you will learn, and poor employees will be eliminated before you have wasted too much time on them.

view the situation, developing alternative explanations, and being clear about the difference between theory and data. They are asked to try to be objective about what they know about the challenge, and what they do not know. This diagnosis, or systematic analysis can then guide them if they need to collect additional information. Once they have as much information as they can practically obtain, they are in a position to see if their own experience or the systematic research can provide the best guidance. Experienced students will never want to throw out their own experience, but they can recognize its limitations and welcome the opportunity to discuss and evaluate it in light of others' experiences and research.

Second, I clearly distinguished what the research says from any practical generalizations from that research. Practical implications are set off in separate boxes, labeled as "applications." An example of applications drawn from research on employee selection appears in Table 21.2. In this way, the experienced students get the clear guidelines for action that they crave, without any dishonest suggestions that the "research says you should do this."

Third, I avoided misleading and potentially embarrassing trendy examples. I felt I really did not have enough information to know exactly why and how today's media darling is successful. Business magazines may praise the executive's employee-centered management practices, but the reality could be a draconian slave-driving climate or the good luck to have

the right product at the right time. We all know that today's excellent company is likely to be tomorrow's failure. I didn't want next month's headline executive indictment for fraud to make the book a laughingstock. If I was to be true to scholarly caution, I needed to acknowledge that, unless I had direct experience with an organization, I really did not know the actual basis for their successes or failures.

Which Publisher?

I began by deciding to solve my own classroom challenge, and I figured that if I just put photocopied manuscript pages in a course reader, that would at least help me as an instructor. But, of course, if I am going to go to all the trouble of writing something this ambitious, it would be nice if others could use it, too. That meant I needed a marketing channel, that is, a publisher. However, careful analysis suggested that what I wanted to do was too different from existing textbooks to be attractive to publishers. After all, I was addressing a problem they didn't believe they had (a textbook that actually was based on research evidence) directed to a market that was too small to be attractive to them. In addition, due to industry consolidation, most textbook publishers already had multiple organizational-behavior textbooks; why would they want another? Producing something this different would be risky for them. They are in the business of assessing markets and then suggesting to textbook authors what to add in the next revision. In addition, even if a publisher did want to publish this kind of textbook, I had a pretty good idea that I would be facing pressures from them to conform to standard textbook format and coverage, pressures in direct conflict with the goals of this textbook. This would not be a contest I could win: if I sign a contract, the publisher owns the book, and if I became troublesome, the publisher could dump me and recruit another author more willing to accept the revisions the editor believed the market wanted.

So this would have been where things stood—me with my photocopied chapters for my own students alone—if I hadn't bumped into Karl Vesper at the University of Washington. He had published his own introductory entrepreneurship textbook himself and had now gone through multiple successful editions. Wow! Karl very kindly spent many hours answering my questions about marketing (I learned this is straightforward for textbooks: just put a free copy into the hands of any potential adopting instructor), the mechanics of producing a book (most of it is easily available through contracted services), and so forth. So instead of writing a prospectus and taking it around to the textbook publishers, I decided to become a micro enterprise and publish it myself (see Pearce, 2009, for the results).

Has It Worked?

In some ways my approach has worked well, and in others I am disappointed. What has worked well was my ability to produce the book and get it into the hands of the instructors who have used it in their courses (and the many managers who have somehow found out about the book). The third edition is in production, and more and more instructors are adopting the book or a few chapters of it for their course readers. I was very worried about the amount of time this effort might require. I found that some aspects take surprisingly little time (sales and fulfillment), some more time than it seems they should have (proofing and correcting the typesetter's pages), and some are more frustrating than I would like (getting the few deadbeat reader services to pay for the books and chapters they have already sold at a profit to students). However, on the whole, it has been worth the time and effort. I now do not need to use consultant-written articles in my executive MBA course; I have been able to cover the costs of putting those photocopied pages into book form and have been able to convey my own enthusiasm for the practical value of organizational-behavior research to more than just the few students who stumble into my own courses.

My area of greatest disappointment is the paucity of good systematic reviews, as described in Briner and Denyer's chapter 7 of this volume, of what organizational-behavior research says that can be used in this textbook. I rely a great deal on my own time-consuming digging in electronic databases and in conference paper and journals' citations, but too often I am forced to read and evaluate research far outside my own specialty. I search in the allied social sciences, and I try my best to be comprehensive, cite sources, and distinguish between what research says and the practical implications of that research. However, I constantly worry that I am not fully and systematically representing what the research evidence tells us when I step outside my own research specialization. Any further development of evidence-based systematic reviews in organizational behavior would be a great service to me, to all textbook authors, and especially to our students.

Better information about what we do and do not know in our field would not only allow us to better represent what we know with some confidence on particular topics, but it could also have numerous other benefits. For example, it could free others to develop their own better, more creative approaches to organizing evidence in ways that can assist managers in their difficult jobs. A growing body of systematically summarized evidence also would make it easy for alumni to keep up, since they could consult the abstracts of such systematic reviews that could be posted online. However, today introductory-organizational-behavior textbooks too often fail to accurately represent what the evidence actually says, and so serve as a reflection of how far organizational behavior now is from an evidence-based discipline.

References

Butler, J. K., & Cantrell, R. S. (1984). A behavioral decision theory approach to modeling dyadic trust. *Psychological Reports, 55,* 19–28.

Changes in Psychological Science (2010). *Observer,* April, 23 (4), http://www.psychologicalscience.org/observer/getArticle. cfm?id=2662.

Davis, M. L. (1971). That's interesting! Towards a phenomenology of sociology and a sociology of phenomenology. *Philosophy of the Social Sciences, 1,* 309–344.

Dunn, J. R., & Schweitzer, M. E. (2005). Feeling and believing: The influence of emotion on trust. *Journal of Personality and Social Psychology, 88,* 736–748.

George, J. M., & Jones, G. R. (2008). *Understanding and managing organizational behavior* (5th ed.). Upper Saddle River, NJ: Pearson Prentice Hall.

Goodman, R. A. (1968). On the operationality of Maslow's need hierarchy. *British Journal of Industrial Relations, 6,* 51–57.

Greenberg, J., & Baron, R. A. (2008). *Behavior in organizations* (9th ed.). Upper Saddle River, NJ: Pearson Prentice Hall.

Hall, D. T., & Nougaim, K. E. (1968). An examination of Maslow's need hierarchy in an organizational setting. *Organizational Behavior and Human Performance, 3,* 12–35.

Hellriegel, D., & Slocum, J. W., Jr. (2007). *Organizational behavior* (11th ed.). Mason, OH: Thomson South-Western.

Herzberg, F. (1987/1959). One more time: How do you motivate employees? *Harvard Business Review, 65*(5), 109–120.

King, N. (1970). Clarification and evaluation of the two-factor theory of job satisfaction. *Psychological Bulletin, 74,* 18–31.

Komorita, S. S., Hilty, J. A., & Parks, C.D. (1991). Reciprocity and cooperation in social dilemmas. *Journal of Conflict Resolution, 35,* 494–518.

Levering, R. (2004). *Creating great places to work: Why it is important and how it is done.* San Francisco, CA: Great Places to Work* Institute.

Locke, E. A. (Ed.) (2000). *Handbook of principles of organizational behavior.* Malden, MA: Blackwell.

Maslow, A. H. (1970). *Motivation and personality.* New York: Harper Row.

Nelson, D. L., & Quick, J. C. (2009). *ORGB.* Mason, OH: South-Western Cengage.

Nolen-Hoeksema, S., Fredrickson, B. L., Loftus, G. R., & Wagenaar, W. A. (2009). *Atkinson and Hilgard's introduction to psychology* (15th ed.). Mason, OH: Cengage.

Osland, J. S., Kolb, D. A., Rubin, I. W., & Turner, M. E. (2007). *Organizational behavior: An experiential approach* (8th ed.). Upper Saddle River, NJ: Pearson Prentice Hall.

Parks, C. D., & Hulbert, L. G. (1995). High and low trusters' responses to fear in a payoff matrix. *Journal of Conflict Resolution, 39,* 718–730.

Pearce, J. L. (2004). What do we know and how do we know it? *Academy of Management Review, 29,* 175–179.

Pearce, J. L. (2009). *Organizational behavior: Real research for real managers.* Irvine, CA: Melvin & Leigh.

Polzer, J. T. (2004). How subgroup interests and reputations moderate the effect of organizational identification on cooperation. Journal of Management, 30, 71–96.

Robbins, S. P. & Judge, T. A. (2011). *Organizational behavior.* Upper Saddle River, NJ: Prentice Hall.

Rousseau, D. M. (2006). Is there such a thing as "EBMgt"? *Academy of Management Review, 32,* 256–269.

Schermerhorn, J. R., Jr., Hunt, J. G., & Osborn, R. N. (2010). *Organizational behavior* (11th ed.). New York: Wiley.

Sniezek, J. A., & Van Swol, L. M. (2001). Trust, confidence, and expertise in judge-advisor system. *Organizational Behavior and Human Decision Processes, 84,* 288–307.

Tavris, C., & Wade, C. (2010). *Psychology* (10th ed.). Upper Saddle River, NJ: Prentice Hall.

Tenbrunsel, A. E., & Messick, D. M. (1999). Sanctioning systems, decision frames, and cooperation. *Administrative Science Quarterly, 44,* 684–707.

PART 5

Criticism

Beyond "New Scientific Management?" Critical Reflections on the Epistemology of Evidence-Based Management

Severin Hornung

Abstract

This essay draws on social theory and philosophy of science to outline controversies about EBMgt as a critical movement versus a one-sided ideological project marginalizing nonmainstream research. Discussed issues include the authority to define evidence, research topics, methods, and evaluation criteria for managerial decisions. A critical and self-reflexive perspective is suggested to enhance awareness of ideological and epistemological constraints that could turn EBMgt into a reloaded version of scientific management.

Key Words: critical management, positivism, ideology, managerial authority, managerial accountability, scientific management, Taylorism, exploitive conditions

"[S]cientific management must inevitably in all cases produce overwhelmingly greater results, both for the company and its employees [. . .] so that they together do the work in accordance with the scientific laws which have been developed, instead of leaving the solution of each problem in the hands of the individual workman."
—*(Frederick W. Taylor*, 2008/1911, p. 90 f.)

"For is it not possible that science as we know it today, or a 'search for the truth' in the style of traditional philosophy, will create a monster?"
—*(Paul Feyerabend*, 1975, p. 154)

"The ruling ideas of each age have ever been the ideas of its ruling class."
—*(Karl Marx and Friedrich Engels*, 1955/1848, p. 30)

Preface: Personal Involvement in Evidence-Based Management

My personal interest in evidence-based management (EBMgt) is partly rooted in the disillusionment of a young scholar realizing that research and

practice are largely unconnected domains, each functioning according to its own set of rules. More often than not, business plays a brutal "profit game" to maximize productivity, revenue, and growth, whereas academia is engaged in an equally competitive "publication game" for personal career opportunities and fame. A lesson learned from field studies is that applied topics of interest to practitioners are often viewed as too descriptive and pragmatic to be of academic value, whereas highly published material is typically indigestible and of little interest to managers. Having been educated in a European tradition of work and organizational psychology emphasizing applied research and humanistic principles, such as worker autonomy, health, and well-being, I find this disconnect to be particularly unsettling.

The existence of a yawning research-practice gap being an undisputable fact, the concept of EBMgt raises the right questions. Joining the collaboration right from its inception, I witnessed how our discussion of EBMgt evolved from a rather blurry and vague idea to an increasingly sophisticated, elaborated concept. Despite our progress, for which this handbook is perhaps the best proof, a number of fundamental issues, such as the political nature and ideological foundations of our field, ethical and moral implications, and epistemological constraints, have been insufficiently addressed in our discussions. The radical criticism of EBMgt that has started to appear in the literature, on the other hand, seems to leave little room for reconciliation.

Based on the conviction that it is not intended to position EBMgt as a counterforce to existing research streams and traditions but, rather, to provide an integrative umbrella to increase the impact of management and organizational research in general, the aim of this chapter is to draw attention to these less salient issues and sketch out ways to address them. That said, the following essay is written in a critical and hopefully thought-provoking manner. The confidence that such a different philosophical perspective is embraced and valued within the EBMgt collaborative is not least based on the positive feedback I received on this chapter from fellow members.

Introduction

EBMgt is an evolving movement, which draws heavily on evidence-based concepts from other fields, most notably medicine and health care (Briner, Denyer, & Rousseau 2009; Sackett, Straus, Richardson, Rosenberg, & Haynes, 2000). Its goal is to promote the uptake and use of best available research evidence to enhance the overall quality of managerial decision-making and organizational practices (Rousseau, 2006). Could there possibly be anything fundamentally wrong with that? At first glance, the obvious answer seems to be "no." Of course, applied research should provide business practice with useful knowledge and decision heuristics; of course it seems desirable that management education should be based on sound research evidence; and, naturally, high quality management decisions and organizational practices seem preferable to uninformed or bad ones. In an attempt to better align management research, education, and practice, EBMgt thus seems to aim at bringing together what belonged together in the first place.

Why, then, has the notion of EBMgt turned out to be such a controversial one? Objections from different perspectives and of varying scope have been raised by a number of scholars. From a systems-theory perspective, Kieser and Leiner (2009) argue that the gap between management research and practice is fundamentally unreconcilable because these two subsystems function according to completely different rules and criteria for evaluating and accepting or rejecting propositions or courses of action. Reay, Berta, and Kohn (2009) have raised issues about the lack of systematic research evidence on the efficacy of EBMgt, thus implying that the whole concept is largely based on rhetoric and—unless and until such proof is provided—appears not substantially different from other management fads and fashions. Using a narrative-theory approach to analyze the literature on EBMgt, Morrell (2008) points out several of its implicit ideological foundations and particularly criticizes the lack of attention to political, moral, and ethical issues. The most radical critique has been brought forward by Learmonth (2006, 2008), who has argued that—from the perspective of critical management studies—the very idea of EBMgt should be rejected as positivistic and poses a threat to methodological and ideological pluralism in organizational studies.

Judging from this array of articulate criticisms, the concept of EBMgt has obviously hit a sore spot. By calling into question the current state of the relationships between management and organizational research, teaching, and practice, it brings to the fore some frictions, tensions, and contradictions within and between these societal subsystems, which are often conveniently ignored or left under the table (Kieser & Leiner, 2009). In this essay, I will review and elaborate on some of the more fundamental criticisms to illustrate the need for EBMgt to develop more self-reflexive qualities by calling into question some of the implicit assumptions that the greater part of contemporary management research is based on.

To the critical mind, the objective to increase the uptake of best available research evidence to improve managerial decision making *indeed* raises a host of questions (Learmonth, 2006; Learmonth, & Harding, 2006). For example, *who* determines what the best evidence is and on *what* topics evidence is gathered in the first place? Improving decisions with regard to *what* criteria or from *which* perspective? In the following, I argue that EBMgt has "poked into a wasp nest" by being both critical and uncritical at the same time—and consequently being criticized for both. However, I also suggest that the resulting controversy can be a healthy and productive one; it offers an opportunity to open up a discussion to reflect on the nature of contemporary management and organizational research and practice. At best, this can aid the EBMgt movement in overcoming some of its unquestioned and overly optimistic—or even positivistic—assumptions by adding a more critical and self-reflexive dimension to the concept, which enhances awareness regarding its own ideological and epistemological constraints and limitations.

The structure of this essay supports its goal to point out and discuss both critical and uncritical or positivistic elements in the concept of EBMgt, and to subsequently provide some recommendations on how to reconcile them. The emphasis will be on fundamental philosophical, ideological, and political concerns, which have received significantly less attention within the EBMgt movement so far—rather than practical, technical, and methodological issues that already have been addressed elsewhere in some detail (e.g., Briner et al., 2009; Rousseau, Manning, & Denyer, 2008). In fact, I will argue that continuing and refining the focus on methods and implementation will not be useful to address the fundamental criticism of EBMgt as an ideological project to advance a particular form of management research while marginalizing others (Learmonth, 2008). Rather, doing so will require unearthing and discussing underlying issues of power, values, and ethics in organizational research and practice. Before turning to the radical critique of EBMgt and its implications, however, the following section will recapitulate the critical core intentions of EBMgt as an outgrowth of scientific rationality, aimed at disenchanting unsubstantiated management and organizational practices based on personal beliefs, lay theories, tradition, or recurring trends and fashions.

Critical Elements: Science as Rationality

In the self-image of its proponents, EBMgt is not an uncritical or reactionary concept. At its core, after all, stands the critique of the status quo in the relationships among management and organizational research, education, and practice (Rousseau, 2006; Rousseau, & McCarthy, 2007). This criticism was born out of the observation that, on the one hand, the uptake of research results in management and organizational practices is low, whereas, on the other hand, the use of practices continues, to which studies attest no positive or even detrimental effects. Examples for tried and tested practices fitting in the former category are goal setting, work design, and feedback; candidates for the latter category are, for example, certain personnel assessment techniques, like graphology, dubious personality tests, or unstructured interviews, as well as management fads and fashions like benchmarking, reengineering,

or downsizing (Pfeffer, & Sutton, 2006; Rousseau, 2006). Reasons for this research-practice gap have been identified in the nature of academic research, in which the development of new constructs and original empirical studies are typically more valued than replicating, integrating, and synthesizing previous work—let alone framing and publishing it in ways that practitioners can understand and use (Rynes, Giluk, & Brown, 2007). Second, it has been pointed out that the prevailing form of management education does not make sufficient use of research evidence compared to others fields—and suggestions about how to improve this situation have been brought forward (Rousseau, & McCarthy, 2007). Indeed, popular textbooks used in MBA classes often seem to emphasize personal-interest stories of CEOs and other "great leaders," case-based learning, in which the criteria for evaluating decisions often remain quite unclear, and so-called "best-practices" of successful firms (even though in today's dynamic economy this success may be short-lived and teaching material may create the unintentionally comical situation of portraying an organization as a role model that has been recently ridden by scandals or gone bankrupt). The motivational models of Maslow and Herzberg—their historical significance notwithstanding—have become prime examples of outdated content of an academic nature that is persistently taught, in spite of weak or contradicting empirical evidence (Rousseau, et al., 2008). Lastly, the critique of EBMgt is also directed at business practice itself, in which time and political pressure often force managers to provide a "quick fix" instead of being given the opportunity to analyze the situation, gather relevant information, evaluate alternatives, anticipate possible outcomes and side-effects, and then make an informed decision (Briner, 1998). Moreover, because there appear to be no objective standards for evaluating managerial decisions, managers are seldom held accountable, even in light of obvious malpractice.

The concerns that EBMgt has raised and solutions it has suggested with regard to the generation, transfer, and application of knowledge in management and organizational research, education, and practice are outlined in more detail elsewhere (e.g., Briner et al., 2009; Rousseau, et al., 2008) and in other contributions to this volume. The major point here is that the idea of EBMgt has grown out of the frustration of organizational researchers with the persistent use of ineffective or unsubstantiated practices, recurring waves of management fads and fashions, and organized unaccountability in business on the one hand; and, on the other hand, the large amounts of theoretical and underutilized research evidence produced by academics, which is comprehensible and of interest mostly to other academics (Rynes et al., 2007). The goal of EBMgt, thus, is to reduce the extent to which the spheres of academia and business are isolated from each other; or—to use the terminology of systems theory—increase the degree to which these two subsystems "disturb" each other in their self-referential and autopoetic (i.e., self-reproducing) functioning (Kieser & Leiner, 2009). Not only does this goal seem theoretically possible, but there are ample historical precedents both in the economic sphere as well as in other areas of society. The increasing use of systematic methods to discover, calculate, and utilize the most effective and efficient means to achieve specified objectives in more and more societal subsystems is characteristic for a process that sociologists have termed *"rationalization"* (e.g., Habermas, 1984). Rationalization, the use of "ratio" or reason to optimize output-to-input relationships is an inherent feature of modernity and closely tied to the rise and proliferation of the scientific method. Basing decisions on systematic empirical data, logic, and calculation, rather than orthodoxy, tradition, dogma, or unsubstantiated beliefs, is at the core of the philosophy of Enlightenment, marking the advent of modernity in Europe during the eighteenth century (e.g., Jacob, 2001). The Enlightenment was a critical movement, advocating the methods of reason and science to dismiss metaphysical explanations, question the rule of the church and aristocracy, educate larger parts of the population, and bring about social change— inspiring the American Revolution and culminating in the French Revolution (Israel, 2009).

Putting EBMgt in the tradition of Enlightenment may appear to be somewhat of a stretch, but helps to better understand the two sides of the "EBMgt coin" on which its proponents and critics have a hard time finding agreement. On the one side, EBMgt is effectively a critical project, advocating use of the scientific method as a way to "debunk" widespread myths, unsubstantiated beliefs, and business practices; and to improve managerial education, decisions, and accountability (Briner et al., 2009; Pfeffer, & Sutton, 2006; Rousseau, et al., 2008). The humanistic core intent of EBMgt becomes evident in the frequently voiced concern for the managed, that is, those who are often subjected to arbitrary or misguided decisions. Moreover, its demand for stronger ties between management research and education seems to mirror the Humboldtian ideal of

unity and freedom of research and teaching in academia (e.g., Ash, 2006). As such, EBMgt appears to revive classic humanistic ideas that are inherent in the concept of scientific rationality as a vehicle for critique, emancipation, and societal advancement.

The second merit of discussing EBMgt in the context of societal rationalization is the promise of getting a better understanding of the fundamental criticisms that have been voiced against the concept. Although there is a broad consensus on the initially emancipatory nature of the Enlightenment, critical scholars have long maintained that, at some point, the specific form of rationality it has advocated in itself has become a tool for societal repression and dominance (Habermas, 1971; Marcuse, 1964). A root cause for this metamorphosis lies in the separation of the authority to define the *ends* ("what") and the ingenuity to discover the optimal *means* ("how") to achieve whatever ends have been specified. In Max Weber's terms, these two different applications of reason refer to issues of *"value rationality"* and *"instrumental rationality"* (e.g., Oakes, 2003). The scientific method is, by definition, an exemplary form of instrumental rationality. That is, it is primarily concerned with finding the right *means*, but, as a general rule, it does not explicitly question the *ends* too much. As such, it is indifferent to whether its results are used to build power plants or nuclear bombs; produce vaccination material or biological weapons; or motivate specified behaviors among software developers, soldiers, or suicide bombers. Therefore, it has been argued that the idea of a neutral science runs the danger of, knowingly or not, providing a willing tool and a rationalization for advancing the particular societal interests of those who possess the power to define objectives, while simultaneously delegitimizing opposing positions.

Uncritical Elements: Science as Rationalization

After briefly highlighting the essentially critical intent of EBMgt, I will now turn to its uncritical assumptions or blind spots. The core of EBMgt forms an optimistic belief in scientific progress, but what it seems to lack, so far, is a critical epistemological debate on the limits of scientific rationality and objectivity in light of the ideological foundations and disparities that characterize our field. Others have started such a discussion and have raised valid concerns, which should be taken seriously and provide a basis for the following arguments (e.g., Learmonth, 2008; Learmonth & Harding, 2006; Morrell, 2008).

The previous section localized EBMgt within the larger project of societal rationalization. Doing so may also help to better understand the discomfort of critical scholars with the concept, which is rooted in a long-standing methodological dispute over scientific positivism and the radical critique of instrumental rationality as a tool to disguise the interests of those in power and exercise suppression over the individual (Adorno & Horkheimer, 2002/1944). Put more simply, science and technology are assumed to be never neutral or universal, but take on specific forms that fulfill the purpose of particular interests in sustaining and reproducing social order or domination (Habermas, 1971). Scientific positivism colludes with this system of anonymous repression by demanding that the status-quo should be taken for granted and at face value—rather than as an object of theoretical deconstruction. The result is that predominant modes of thinking are systematically restricted to a one-dimensional form of instrumental rationality, which refers to optimizing the means to achieve predetermined ends, but does not permit reflecting on or questioning the value of these objectives themselves (Marcuse, 1964). At this point, scientific rationality, which has started out as a medium of critique and emancipation, turns into a rationalization in the sense of an unconscious justification and defense of the particular interests that profit from those—now implicit and, therefore, unquestionable—goals. *The Eclipse of Reason* (Horkheimer, 2004/1947) and the *Dialectic of Enlightenment* (Adorno & Horkheimer, 2002/1944) are key works of the Frankfurt School of critical theorists describing this process in much more sophisticated ways. For the present purpose, the reductionist and fragmentary summary of this stream of thought should suffice, however, to recognize how EBMgt seems to fit into the described pattern of instrumental rationality. That is, it predominantly focuses on technical and practical aspects, but turns a blind eye on the political embeddedness and interest-guided nature of the generation, evaluation, transfer, and application of research evidence. To broaden its scope and transparency, EBMgt needs not only to provide convincing answers to the "how-to" questions, but also needs to deal with questions of "to what end." In the next four sections, I will discuss some of these w-questions that, in my opinion, have not received sufficient attention within the EBMgt movement so far.

What Evidence—and Why?

A fundamental problem pertains to what constitutes or is defined as evidence or, even more ambitious, *"best evidence"* in management and organizational research. The short answer given by advocates of EBMgt is that scientific evidence is ideally based on systematic reviews, using standardized and replicable methods to aggregate, integrate, interpret, and/or explain the results of all available studies relevant to the specific research question (Rousseau, et al., 2008). The role model here is the rigorous process for reviewing and summarizing trial-control studies in medicine as implemented, for example, by the Cochrane Collaboration (Tranfield, Denyer, & Smart, 2003; Higgins & Green, 2009). To evaluate research results, evidence-based medicine adheres to a hierarchy of evidence, which attests the highest value to systematic reviews and meta-analyses of double-blind randomized controlled trials; subsequently, individual nonaggregated randomized controlled trials should be considered, followed by longitudinal cohort studies, case-control studies, and uncontrolled experiments or correlational studies; finally, expert opinions and personal experience form the lowest levels of recognized medical evidence (Sackett et al., 2000; Tranfield et al., 2003). It needs to be stressed that this hierarchy of evidence is by no means undisputed in the medical field. Among others, it has been noted to hold the danger of devaluating common sense, medical expertise, individual treatment of patients, and alternative research designs (e.g., Little, 2003). Aside from probably offending practitioners, transferring this evidence hierarchy into management and organizational research has been described as an agenda to exclude and further marginalize qualitative research approaches, which are more strongly rooted in the social sciences, rather than subscribing to or emulating the methods of natural science (Learmonth, 2008). Similar objections have been raised in health care, where the protagonists of such a radical critique even went so far as to attest the evidence-based medicine movement to have *fascist* tendencies (Holmes, Murray, Perron, & Rail, 2006).

Responding to such criticisms of EBMgt, Rousseau et al. (2008) have outlined the variety and scope of approaches to conduct systematic reviews, including meta-ethnographies of qualitative research. In a similar vein, Briner et al., (2009) have clarified that it would be neither feasible nor desirable for EBMgt to simply adopt the hierarchy of evidence-based medicine and have claimed that a defining feature of the EBMgt movement would be to not privilege one particular type of academic research over another. Although these commitments to inclusiveness and plurality are important, it remains questionable how practicable and credible they really are. The orientation toward the natural sciences and their methods of experiments, quantification, and statistical analysis is a pervasive trend in the social sciences and is deeply engrained in concepts of evidence-based practice (Holmes et al., 2006; Learmonth & Harding, 2006; Little, 2003). Being able to draw on a critical mass of studies using standardized measures and comparable methods, and the availability of well-established statistical procedures for meta-analysis are likely to set quantitative researchers at an advantage in contributing to EBMgt. So, even the explicit inclusion of qualitative research on a theoretical and methodological level might not be able to prevent discrimination on a practical and factual level.

Second, and probably more important, Rousseau and colleagues have countered the criticisms just outlined with rather technical arguments by discussing the ways in which different types of research can be integrated into the method of systematic reviews. However, they have missed the deeper point that some lines of research may just not be compatible with each other, because not only their methods but their underlying worldviews, assumptions, and even the language or jargon they use are so fundamentally different that they do not even share a common understanding of phenomena, concepts, and terminology. Since Thomas Kuhn's (1962) seminal work on the structure of scientific revolutions, we know that such incompatible or *incommensurate research paradigms* are characteristic for scientific progress in general, but they are certainly aggravated by ideological differences in the social sciences. For instance, mainstream management research is primarily concerned with the attainment of organizationally desired objectives (e.g., performance and innovation) or at least seeks to justify any humanistic concern for the working individuals (e.g., satisfaction and well-being) through allegedly positive effects on organizational efficiency and effectiveness. The field of critical management studies, in contrast, focuses on exposing and denouncing "socially divisive and ecologically destructive broader patterns and structures" (Adler, Forbes, & Willmott, 2007, p. 120). Radically critical management and organizational research thus is aimed at overcoming repressive and exploitative conditions and contributing to the social emancipation and psychological development of individuals, groups, and societies in the context of work and employment. Taking into account that wage labor is, by definition, not voluntary, but based on the silent pressure of the economic necessity to generate income, the common ground between performance enhancement and reduction of repressive structures seems fairly small.

To illustrate this point with a more specific example: contemporary mainstream research interprets the phenomenon of affective organizational commitment as a genuine form of emotional attachment based on a personally gratifying employment relationship, in which workers are more than happy to "go the extra mile," partly because they perceive that the organization values their contributions and cares about their well-being (Meyer, Stanley, Herscovitch, & Topolyntsky, 2002; Rhoades & Eisenberger, 2002). An extensive number of studies in various contexts, the use of comparable measures, and already existing meta-analyses make this an appealing topic for a systematic review.

Scholars from a critical and psychodynamic research tradition, however, may have a fundamentally different view on the same phenomenon. In fact, affective commitment can also be interpreted as a kind of Stockholm Syndrome—a psychological defense mechanism to experienced helplessness and lack of alternatives or as a symptom for the domestication of workers by capital through increasingly sophisticated techniques of societal mind control (Braverman, 1974; Robinson, 2004; Marcuse, 1964). From this perspective, affective commitment presents itself as a psychological disability, a form of higher-order alienation separating workers from their genuine needs and true class interests. The important point here is that, no matter how methodologically well it is executed, it appears quite unlikely that research conducted from the perspective of such a labor-control paradigm would be represented in an EBMgt-style research synthesis on affective commitment or related constructs. Moreover, as a principle of EBMgt is the claim to review the *full body* of research relevant to a certain question, focusing on the quantitative mainstream implicitly excludes deviating perspectives and alternative approaches from the realm of science (e.g., Holmes et al. 2006; Little, 2003; Learmonth, 2008). A stronger focus on EBMgt may, regardless of whether intentional or not, further discredit and marginalize such non-mainstream research. To get back to our example, it seems fairly easy and maybe even convenient to brand the interpretation of commitment as a psychologically sublimated form of higher-order alienation as normative or ideological. In fact, however, theories of conflict or convergence of interest in the employment relationship are equally ideological, the latter are just better compatible with the ideology of the Zeitgeist and typically studied with methods the results of which—not coincidentally—are more geared toward the natural sciences and, thus, can be more conveniently treated according to principles of EBMgt.

It seems important to note that the taxonomy of quantitative versus qualitative research is merely one of methodology, whereas the distinction between critical versus mainstream or positivist research refers to the theoretical background and ideological perspective, which determine the content and interpretation of research results (Adler et al., 2007). Principally, both quantitative and qualitative research can be critically oriented, which, in and of itself, is more a matter of degree rather than a dichotomous taxonomy. Because quantitative research tends to take participants' statements at face value, whereas qualitative research offers more possibilities to look beyond or deconstruct this first layer of subjective reality, demarcation lines regarding method and content tend to overlap to some degree, but they are by no means congruent. The arguments just made thus apply to both qualitative research in general, as well as to research conducted from a critical or nonmainstream perspective, regardless of whether it is predominantly based on quantitative or qualitative methodology. The point here is not to say that it is impossible, but that it is definitely harder and, in fact, more unlikely for some research methods, traditions, and topics to be included into an EBMgt-style research syntheses than for others.

The foregoing is my understanding of the real danger that Learmonth (2008, p. 283) points out, when he calls EBMgt a *"backlash against pluralism in organizational studies"* (italics added). Interestingly enough, the controversy between Rousseau and Learmonth is a good example of incommensurate paradigms or different worldviews. The methodological and ideological pluralism Learmonth perceives under attack by EBMgt at least partly corresponds with what Rousseau regards as the fragmentation and specialization that needs to be overcome for the purpose of *"assembling the field's full weight of scientific knowledge"* (Rousseau et al., 2008, p. 475; italics added). Underlying the feasibility assumption of the latter is the optimistic—or rather positivistic—notion that research evidence accumulates and, over time, converges with reality or truth (Popper, 1972). To the former position, the fragmentation in organizational studies reflects the tensions and demarcations between antagonistic societal interests in defining reality. Consequently,

from this perspective, consolidation almost inevitably implies exclusion or marginalization and, eventually, a totalitarian thought reform (Adorno & Horkheimer, 2002/1944; Holmes et al., 2006). Again, it would be too easy to simply ignore or discard these concerns, if EBMgt wants to establish itself as a serious and self-reflective project within social science.

Evidence for What—and for Whom?

Other important issues, which are closely related to the matters discussed in the preceding section, refer to the questions being asked in EBMgt and who asks them. That is, what are the topics that evidence is gathered and synthesized on and from what perspective or with what purpose in mind is this done? Evidence, especially in social science but also in natural science, is by no means neutral, but at least partly socially construed and guided by particular interests (Kuhn, 1962). A prominent example in support of this claim is medical research, where private corporations have long been known for their successful attempts to actively influence and manipulate research outcomes (e.g., Martinson, Anderson, & de Vries, 2005). Most scholars would at least partly agree that from obtaining funding and university positions to publication opportunities, conducting research is inherently a social and political process. In other words, when talking about the uptake and use of best available evidence, we should ask ourselves, why a particular body of evidence is *available* and who it is *best* for. Rogers (2004) has raised a similar argument with regard to EBMgt's role model, evidence-based medicine. His analysis suggests that, by systematically excluding disadvantaged and vulnerable groups (e.g., ethnic minorities, groups of low socioeconomic status, populations from third-world countries, and patients with mental-health problems and co-morbidities) from research commissioning, design, and participation, evidence-based medicine aggravates rather than ameliorates injustice and discrimination in the provision of health care. He concludes that evidence-based medicine theoretically would hold the potential to contribute to improving the health situation of those who most need it. In reality, however, this seems most unlikely due to the inherently interest-guided nature of medical research, where 90 percent of research funding is spent to investigate the diseases of 10 percent of the world's population (Rogers, 2004).

EBMgt, which is leaning so heavily on its medical counterpart, should take these objections very seriously. In fact, in management and organizational research the situation is even more complicated, because the goals or evaluation criteria are more diverse and less specified. That is, determining the efficacy of a medical treatment may require taking into account boundary conditions and ethical questions, however, it is still likely to be less controversial than judging the quality of management decisions. In other words, what would be the equivalent of the patient's health status in EBMgt? Is it organizational performance, productivity or shareholder value—the more the better for those who are managing, or in the name of whom the management is carried out? Is it the complete physical, mental, and social well-being of those who are being managed? Or is it whatever objective the respective decision maker had in mind—which would make EBMgt a willing means to all possible ends?

It is quite common in our field to either implicitly assume or explicitly state that a particular construct, intervention, or management practice would benefit both workers and the organization and, thus, on a broader scale and in the longer term, eventually may also have a positive impact on the economy and society as a whole (e.g., Hodson & Roscigno, 2004). This convenient notion of goal congruence, however, is largely a myth or ideology; at least it remains untested for the most part and is easily falsified by real-world examples. Indeed, some evidence suggests that, in jobs requiring relatively high qualifications, in industrially developed countries, a positive correlation exists between indicators of employee well-being and organizational performance (e.g., Judge, Thoresen, Bono, & Patton, 2001; Harter, Schmidt, & Hayes, 2002). However, the range and boundary conditions for such a joint optimization are likely to be highly restricted. On a world-wide scale, the most profit is still made with the least humane work, including child labor, forced labor, unjustifiable occupational hazards, and poverty wages (International Labor Organization, 2008, 2009). Only the most cynical economists would tell the poverty-stricken and exploited masses in the third world that what is good for their employer is good for them—and vice versa. Moreover, in the industrially developed world, a rising prevalence of mental-health problems, coinciding with a steady increase in productivity can be taken as just one indicator for negative externalities, which are characteristics for the tension between micro- and macroeconomic objectives (e.g., Compton Conway, Stinson, & Grant 2006; Druss et al., 2006).

Sticking with this example, psychopathological effects of work threaten to violate basic human rights for unimpaired mental and physical health and pose a challenge to society as a whole, including enormous costs to health-care systems. Yet, in management and organizational research, comprehensive well-being and positive psychological development of workers often seem to be legitimate objectives *only* to the extent that it can be shown or at least argued for that they are tied to performance, and, thus, taking them into consideration is a profitable deal for the organization (e.g., Knights, 2008). A similar point can be made for other conditions and consequences, which are officially valued in society, but are not regarded suitable as stand-alone objectives in business, such as individual freedom or self-determination, democratic procedures and orientations, dignity and respect in interpersonal work relationships, corporate social responsibility, ecological sustainability, and so forth. Adler et al. (2007, p. 121) bring this criticism to the point when they argue that "prevailing structures of domination produce a *systemic* corrosion of moral responsibility when any concern for people or for the environment requires justification in terms of its contribution to profitable growth."

The point here is *not* that efficiency, performance, or profitability are not legitimate goals, but that they are, by far, not the *only* or—from a societal, let alone an ethical perspective—necessarily the most important or desirable goals. Multiple and potentially conflicting interests and goals are a defining feature of organizational research; the underlying trade-offs and tensions, however, are often not made explicit. If EBMgt has been accused to naturalize managerial interests while suppressing conflicting interests (Learmonth, 2006), this is attributable to the fact that it does *not* disclose or discuss its implicit assumptions on the goals and implications of improved managerial decision making. In my personal understanding, the label EBMgt does not necessarily imply a one-sided subscription to a managerial perspective, the field of critical management studies being a point in case. However, a heads-on discussion on this issue within the EBMgt movement has yet been opened up.

Evidence—and What Else?

It should have become clear by now that evidence does not come in a pure form, but always carries some ideological baggage relating to the underlying worldviews, interests, and objectives. In this regard, the postulate that the major goal of private business is to not only generate but to continuously increase productivity or profits, for example, is as much of a normative statement as the principle that the life, liberty, and dignity of people at work need to be protected at all costs. What does EBMgt have to say on these questions of value-rationality as well as their possible conflicts and prioritization, which, if the goal is to improve the quality of management decisions, are obviously of high relevance? Briner et al. (2009, p. 22) provide some mundane examples of the everyday use of evidence ("Jane is booking a holiday . . ."), but how about the following, slightly more sophisticated uses of evidence: A company is aware of the fact that it sells a dangerous product; to estimate whether it should initiate a recall, it compares the overall costs for recall and repair with the expected number of resulting deaths, severe and light injuries, multiplied by the average out-of-court settlement money for each category. What cineastes may identify as "the formula" that Edward Norton's character applies as a recall coordinator for an insurance company in the movie *Fight Club,* goes back to the real-world case of the Ford Pinto in the 1980s (Birsch & Fielder, 1994). Moreover, a re-analysis of this case from a legal perspective could find no major deviations from common practice in Ford's publicly highly disputed, but distinctively data-based and rationally calculated decision not to make the recall. However, the paper acknowledges that, foremost, the case provides a good example of "how disturbed the public can be by corporate decisions that balance life and safety against monetary costs." (Schwartz, 1991, p. 1014). Likewise, from an economic point of view, it is perfectly rational for an employer to consume or use up an employee's labor power through unsustainably high workload or hazardous working conditions, *if* the associated gains outweigh the costs of hiring and training a new worker. The optimal timing for getting rid of the worn out "personnel resource" in favor of fresh human capital then becomes an optimization problem; its solution will require taking an evidence-based approach, including the extent and likelihood that incurring costs can be externalized to the individual and society (e.g., to government funded social security or welfare programs). In the same vein, it has been pointed out that organizations often treat the deliberate violation of laws as a business decision (e.g., Bakan, 2004). The heuristics that are applied here—comparing the stochastic gains and potential losses—are data-based and very much aligned with the recommendations of rational choice theory.

The list of examples could be carried on. My point here is that managers in business organizations often *do* make rational and evidence-based decisions, which, however, do not conform to ethical and moral standards of large parts of society. Briner et al. (2009) explicitly acknowledge the need to include practitioner judgments, contextual circumstances, and ethical concerns in evidence-based decision making. With regard to the latter, they describe one step in EBMgt as follows: "The views of stakeholders and those likely to be affected by the decision would be considered, along with ethical implications of the decision." (Briner et al., 2009, p. 23). That sounds nice, but—with all due respect—is overly vague and noncommittal. How and what ethical implications should be considered? What if the views of stakeholders and those affected by decision differ? How exactly should their diverging interests and potential trade-offs be taken into account, evaluated, and prioritized? Moreover, the article seems to imply that ethical considerations and values are a subjective and discretionary matter of the decision makers ("In some circumstances, the opinions of stakeholders or ethical considerations may be judged by the decision makers to be much more important than the external research evidence . . ."; Briner et al., 2009, p. 21). However, if EBMgt declares ethics a part of evidence-based decision making, it will need to be much more specific and transparent about the ethical and moral standards that should apply (Morrell, 2008). Again, the medical field might serve as a role model. In medicine, the evidence-based movement is complemented by a highly developed discipline of medical ethics, which is solely concerned with moral values and judgments in medical decision making (e.g., Lakhan, Hamlat, McNamee, & Laird, 2009). In contrast, the field of business ethics is rather underdeveloped. The latest financial crisis, however, has seen a number of politicians and public persons calling for a stronger adherence to socially acceptable ethical standards in business. Overall, it seems that educating managers from an ethical and value-based perspective is equally important and called for as from an evidence-based perspective. EBMgt will have to make sure that the knowledge it provides is used responsibly. It needs to take a firm stance on the ethical standards and values that it calls for to be taken into account in managerial decision making. Failure or lack of courage to fill these blanks with action-guiding content would bring its arguments dangerously close to the infamous slogan of an influential lobby group, claiming that "guns don't kill people, people kill people."

What Is at Stake: EBMgt as New Scientific Management?

The discomfort of some scholars with the concept of EBMgt may be better understood if we take a look at the last major rationalization movement that has claimed to improve the quality of managerial decisions through the use of scientific methods: scientific management or Taylorism (e.g., Littler, 1978). In his lifetime, Frederick W. Tailor was despised by workers and organized labor, who, in the words of a biographer (Kanigel 1997, p. 1), saw in him "a soulless slave driver, out to destroy the workingman's health and rob him of his manhood." In 1911, the notoriety of his system in sparking labor strikes and unrest even resulted in a congressional investigation into the dehumanizing nature of his proposed management practices (Kanigel 1997). Nonetheless, Taylor would not get tired of stating that his system, which substitutes the rule of thumb or tradition for principles based on scientific study of work, would result in enormous gains and benefits for both employers and employees (Taylor, 2008/1911). Indeed, alongside technological progress, extreme division of labor, separation of planning and execution, optimization and predetermination of each minuscule operation based on time and motion studies, and strict pay-for-performance schemes have increased the productive forces within a short period of time so tremendously that historians speak of a second industrial revolution (Littler, 1978). Although evaluations of the contributions of Taylorism vary, there seems to be a common understanding that its success was partly based on the degrading, de-skilling, and dehumanization of work—and the associated shift in power between labor and capital.

Based on the work of Marx, critical scholars have described dominant modes of control in specific phases of industrial development in terms of different forms of subordination or "*subsumption*" of labor by capital (e.g., Burawoy, 1984; Braverman, 1974). The first industrial revolution, characterized by the establishment of dependent wage-labor relationships at the beginning of the capitalist production system, was mainly based on contractual or monetary control mechanisms or, so-called, "*formal subsumption.*" At the core of the second revolution was the transformation of the production process itself, aimed at reducing needed skills, breaking up solidarity among workers, and transferring the de-facto control from labor to management—a process that Marx has termed "*real subsumption.*" All these aims are explicitly stated and embodied in Taylor's system

of scientific management. However, the downsides of Taylorism soon became evident in working conditions that were externally controlled, unchallenging, monotonous, and meaningless, thus frustrating basic psychological needs and functions of work. In the short term, these negative consequences were often met with worker unrest, strikes, and sabotage. In the longer run, they tended to induce passivity and symptoms of learned helplessness and psychological alienation in workers, thus hampering further increases in productivity (Braverman, 1974; Seeman, 1983).

Human relations, sociotechnical design, and quality-of-work-life interventions can be understood as initiatives to address these deficiencies by re-introducing forms of job enrichment, enlargement, rotation, and group work, and/or advocating a joint optimization of technological processes and the human organization of work. Taylorism itself, however, was never really overcome, but rather formed the *basis* for those later developments (e.g., Head, 2005; Littler, 1978). In the same sense as it may be impossible to see the wood for the trees, the basic principles of Taylorism are so deeply engrained in our understanding of work organization that they have become hard to identify. In manual labor, especially in the sweatshops of the third world, however, its purest and more radical variations are still alive and well. The legacy of the scientific management system is what human-rights activists refer to as the "science of exploitation" (Bakan, 2004, p. 66).

Changes in the nature of work in industrially developed societies—the rise of computers and other high technology, knowledge-intensive work, and increasing demands for flexibility—have limited the effectiveness of conventional methods of labor control. Modern work increasingly requires the *whole* person—hands, head, heart, and all. Sociologists and critical scholars have identified this change in the predominant ways that power and domination are exercised in the working process as a shift toward psychological control (Robinson, 2004). The sociological term "*ideological subsumption*" refers to the fact that, in modern organizations, authority and repression are increasingly psychologically internalized, that is, external control turns into a form of self-control or self-exploitation. The tools for the manipulation of workers' minds and emotions in the interest of capital are developed and honed by social scientists (psychologists, sociologists, and human-resource researchers), who, in the tradition of the human-relations movement, may aim toward improving the quality of working life, but simultaneously take the control exercised over workers to the next level. Following this line of thought, loosening the leash of external control mechanisms in exchange for increased self-control, that is, the transformation from a Tayloristic labor camp into a high commitment work system, is not an act of emancipation but one of repression because it increases rather than decreases dominance and psychological dependence (e.g., Braverman, 1974; compare to the concept of *"repressive desublimation"* in Freudo-Marxian terminology; e.g., Marcuse, 1964).

Scientific management has provided a strong paradigm for perfecting the mode of factual control or real subsumption. The modern era of human-resource management and psychologically internalized control or ideological subsumption, so far, lacks such a strong paradigm. Based on the preceding overview of labor-control theory, it should have become clear that scholars from a critical research tradition are rightfully concerned that this and only this is what EBMgt will provide—a psychologically upgraded and refined version of scientific management. However, it is up to the proponents of EBMgt to dispel or at least address these concerns. What differentiates EBMgt from the approach of scientific management? What precautions are taken that EBMgt really serves all its constituents and not management alone? These and other questions have already been raised earlier in this chapter. The hopefully thought-provoking outline of a labor-control theory just offered should illustrate the historical background that demands directing attention to these issues. Moreover, it also serves a second purpose. Labor-control theory provides an established framework of analysis in the social sciences (e.g., Adler at al., 2007; Spencer, 2000). Not everybody needs to agree, but if the majority of readers would jump to the conclusion that there is no place in EBMgt for such a critical perspective, then the controversy would have been resolved as well—in that case, however, by confirming the concerns of the skeptics.

Implications: Making It Critical

Finally, I want to make an attempt to reconcile the outlined perspectives on EBMgt as a critical versus an uncritical project. Based on what has been said earlier, I am ambivalent myself, if this is possible. However, I am also convinced that a serious effort to do so is a necessary and important next step to further and broaden the concept of EBMgt. I have discussed that at the core of the

radical disagreement on the concept of EBMgt are incompatible paradigms about the nature of scientific rationality and progress, giving rise to different views of the field as either (1) fragmented and in need of synthesis, or (2) characterized by methodological and ideological pluralism and diversity. In light of these seemingly unbridgeable differences, I invite readers themselves to adopt a dialectic perspective. At its best, a dialectic reconciliation or synthesis offers an integrating view of two antagonistic propositions: the thesis and antithesis. In doing so, however, it preserves the integrity of both positions by reinterpreting their combined meaning on a higher level of understanding. Thus, the contradictions may not completely disappear, but will take on a different sense and meaning (e.g., Williams, 1989). In the philosophy of dialectic materialism, this three-step approach is expressed in the German word *Aufhebung*, which simultaneously denotes (1) negation, (2) preservation, and (3) elevation. In less philosophic terms, productively dealing with the concept of EBMgt and its critique requires all parties involved to develop tolerance for ambiguity and differing perspectives as well as the ability to step back and take on a meta-perspective.

From such a meta-perspective, both positions warrant consideration and offer valuable insights for a more comprehensive understanding of the nature of management and organizational research. Personally, I agree to some extent with both. There is indeed a huge body of insufficiently integrated and underutilized research, much to bemoan about the current state of management education, as well as a pressing need for more professionalism and accountability in management practice. However, in trying to address these gaps, EBMgt has to be careful not to throw out the baby with the bath water. Concerns that EBMgt might de-facto exclude certain methodologies and nonmainstream research traditions, neglect ethical and moral considerations, and runs the danger of uncritically adopting a managerialistic perspective, are well made. I recommend that, in order for EBMgt to become more mindful of its own underlying assumptions, the discussion of technical and practical issues that Rousseau and others have led should be complemented by an epistemological and an ethical debate on the foundations of management and organizational research. The former should be rooted in the philosophy of science and center around the individual, social, and political influences on the research process and their implications for the specific form and limitations of research outcomes. On a basic level, this includes acknowledging the social construction of research evidence, which is, at least partly, a function of the particular economic context and the interest-guided allocation of resources to certain topics over others. The latter should more explicitly deal with questions of values, that is, what goals does EBMgt support? Which trade-offs does it accept? According to what criteria does it measure the improvement of managerial decisions and define its own success? If EBMgt is serious about the integration of ethics in managerial decisions and organizational practices, it has to promote the development of guidelines for the ethical conduct of managers, addressing moral responsibilities toward all those who are affected by their decisions, such as shareholders, the public, and—probably most important—the managed individuals. Drawing on medicine as a role model may help to strengthen such a value-based perspective, which is rooted in academic research into business, managerial, and applied ethics.

Naturally, these debates are not something that can be led on the side (e.g., in the form of an ethics committee to appease criticism), but need to guide actions and shape the way EBMgt is perceived and advocated by its proponents. To make this clearer, EBMgt recognizes that organizations have multiple stakeholders with potentially differing interests and goals. However, it needs to be more explicit about the fact that these are not necessarily converging, but can imply conflicts and trade-offs (e.g., economic profits, social responsibility, and environmental protection). If decision makers are supposed to take into account the views of stakeholders and those affected by a specific decision, the consequences for these groups need to be assessed and evaluated in the first place, that is, information on the possible trade-offs, side-effects, and downsides has to be provided. As maintaining scientific integrity and independence means not—explicitly or implicitly—subscribing to one perspective over others, EBMgt research syntheses should try to balance different views and interests relevant to the phenomenon under study (e.g., Knights, 2008). EBMgt has been very concerned with replicable and objective methods for reviewing and synthesizing the evidence. An issue it has not addressed is how the research question and consequently the results would differ, if a systematic review on a certain topic was commissioned, for example, by a government agency, a private corporation, a social movement, or a labor union; according to theory, all those perspectives would have to be represented.

As pointed out earlier, EBMgt could all too easily fall into place as the reloaded and psychologically honed version of scientific management. To prevent this risk, it has to be extra careful not to sacrifice scientific objectivity and pluralism for the acceptance of managers, which constitute just *one* group of its stakeholders. Theoretically, there are ample possibilities to make sure that the plurality of research is adequately represented in systematic review projects and that inclusiveness with regard to different research traditions and methodologies is more than lip service. For example, this may be achieved by systematically investigating implications for different groups of stakeholders; prescribing that reviews should comprise both a quantitative and a qualitative part; and the mandatory inclusion of critical positions, counterpoints, or opposing interpretations. I admit, however, that—in light of the necessary efforts and associated complexity—I am not sure about the extent to which these suggestions are practically feasible and realistic. To my knowledge, at least, to date, there is no precedent or example of a research synthesis that systematically adheres to any of the aforementioned suggestions. An alternative venue would be for EBMgt to exercise some more modesty and explicitly acknowledge its own limitations with regard to the objective of including the *full* body of research on a given topic. After all, the points that advocates of EBMgt have made are compelling and applicable for large parts of management and organizational research. Of course, this would do nothing to dispel concerns that the concept aggravates existing imbalances and divides between quantitative and qualitative as well as mainstream and critical research, but at least it would be somewhat more straightforward and transparent.

These unresolved issues notwithstanding, I believe that EBMgt can make an important contribution to the advancement of the field, both in terms of increasing the uptake of relevant research results in managerial decision making, but also by starting a self-reflective discussion about the implicit assumptions underlying contemporary management and organizational research and practice. In this respect, the way may be as important as the goal. That is, the merits of the EBMgt movement should not only be judged by its potential and projected outcomes, but also by the processes it already has set off and will continue to fuel within the scientific community. Not only has it called attention to the lack of alignment and knowledge transfer between organizational research and practice, but the controversial discussion surrounding it has unearthed some usually untapped issues about the nature of our field. The radical critique of EBMgt is as much an ideological critique as it is a critique of ideology in management and organizational research. It reminds us that, although our field has increasingly oriented itself toward natural science and—explicitly or implicitly—asserts to produce generally applicable insights into human behavior that are above and beyond any particular interests, it essentially remains rooted in the realm of political economy. As an applied social science discipline that is concerned with a very specific form of economic organization—typically referring to wage labor in dependent employment relationships—it can never be neutral or beyond ideology. Acknowledging this fact is an important first step. After all, how is EBMgt supposed to promote scientific rationality if it clings to rationalizations about its own ideological roots and philosophical foundations as a science? In more poetic terms, the light of reason cannot shine in an outward direction only, but also needs to encompass its source (Fromm, 1962). As such, self-awareness and self-reflectivity regarding its own epistemological conditions and constraints seems to be an important prerequisite for EBMgt's goal of debunking myths and overcoming widespread illusions in management practice. To me, this seems essential if EBMgt is to live up to its aspiration of becoming an integrating movement within social science rather than a technocratic and interest-guided approach in the tradition of scientific management.

In this chapter, I have offered a number of questions that EBMgt needs to address to overcome some of its blind spots about the political and social construction of evidence. Getting a better understanding of these issues seems to me a precondition for any serious attempt to promote EBMgt. This does not necessarily imply consent. Researchers from different subdisciplines, research traditions, and political positions may come to the conclusion that they agree to disagree. However, making the implicit tensions, divides, and diverging interests explicit and, therefore, subject to open discussion, already seems a major achievement. If it succeeds to continue this process in a spirit of open-mindedness and willingness of all involved parties to consider and accept differing perspectives and face some inconvenient conclusions about the nature of our field, EBMgt has already made an important contribution. In this respect, I tend to conclude with Hodgkinson and Rousseau (2009) that this already seems to be happening.

For the academic debate on EBMgt to eventually translate into more socially, ecologically, and economically responsible and sustainable management practices, which explicitly acknowledge, take into account, and seek to balance the diverging needs and interests of all affected stakeholders, there still seems to be a long and rocky road ahead. Depending on one's perspective, the apparent unsustainability of the current economic system, evident in enduring or more and more rapidly recurring financial, social, and environmental crises of a global scale, can give rise to both optimism as well as pessimism about the necessary momentum to achieve such changes in the near future. One lesson that can be learned from these current events is that any serious attempt to establish and enforce evidence-based standards for managerial practice will need to include some degree of formalization, institutionalization, and sanctioning power. Again, an orientation toward the definition and treatment of professional negligence or malpractice in the medical field might provide a useful role model.

References

Adler, P. S., Forbes, L. C., & Willmott, H. (2007). Critical management studies. *The Academy of Management Annals, 1,* 119–179.

Adorno, T. W., & Horkheimer, M. (2002). *Dialectic of enlightenment* (E. Jephcott, Trans.). Stanford, CA: Stanford University Press. (Original work published in 1944.)

Ash, M. G. (2006). Bachelor of what, master of whom? The Humboldt myth and historical transformations of higher education in German-speaking Europe and the US. *European Journal of Education, 41,* 245–267.

Bakan, J. (2004). *The corporation: The pathological pursuit of profit and power.* New York: Free Press.

Birsch, D., & Fielder, J. H. (Eds.). (1994). *The Ford Pinto case: A study in applied ethics, business, and technology.* New York: State University of New York Press.

Braverman, H. (1974). *Labor and monopoly capital: The degradation of work in the twentieth century.* New York: Monthly Review Press.

Briner, R. B. (1998). What is an evidence-based approach to practice and why do we need one in occupational psychology? *Proceedings of the 1998 British Psychological Society Occupational Psychology Conference,* 39–44.

Briner, R., Denyer, D., & Rousseau, D. M. (2009). Evidence-based management: Concept cleanup time. *Academy of Management Perspectives, 23,* 19–32.

Burawoy, M. (1984). Karl Marx and the satanic mills: Factory politics under early capitalism in England, the United States, and Russia. *American Journal of Sociology, 90,* 247–282.

Compton W. M., Conway K. P., Stinson F. S., & Grant B. F. (2006). Changes in the prevalence of major depression and comorbid substance use disorders in the United States between 1991–1992 and 2001–2002. *American Journal of Psychiatry, 163,* 2141–2147.

Druss, B, G., Bornemann, T., Fry-Johnson, Y. W., McCombs, H. G., Politzer, R, M., & Rust, G. (2006). Trends in mental health and substance abuse services at the nation's community health centers: 1998–2003. *American Journal of Public Health, 98,* S126–S131.

Feyerabend, P. (1975). *Against method: Outline of an anarchistic theory of knowledge.* Atlantic Highlands, NJ: Humanities Press.

Fromm, E. (1962). *Beyond the chains of illusion: My encounter with Marx and Freud.* New York: Simon & Schuster.

Habermas, J. (1971). *Toward a rational society: Student protest, science and politics* (J. J. Shapiro, Trans.). Boston, MA: Beacon Press.

Habermas, J. (1984). *The theory of communicative action volume one: Reason and the rationalization of society* (T. McCarthy, Trans.). Boston, MA: Beacon Press.

Harter, J., Schmidt, F., & Hayes, T. (2002). Business-unit-level relationship between employee satisfaction, employee engagement, and business outcomes: A meta-analysis. *Journal of Applied Psychology, 87,* 268–279.

Head, S. (2005). *The new ruthless economy. Work and power in the digital age.* Oxford, England: Oxford University Press.

Higgins J. P. T., & Green S. (Eds.). (2009). *Cochrane handbook for systematic reviews of interventions* (Version 5.0.2, updated September 2009). The Cochrane Collaboration. Retrieved from www.cochrane-handbook.org

Hodgkinson, G. P., & Rousseau, D. M. (2009). Bridging the rigor relevance gap in management research: It is already happening! *Journal of Management Studies, 46,* 534–546.

Hodson, R., & Roscigno, V. J. (2004). Organizational success and worker dignity: Complementary or contradictory? *American Journal of Sociology, 110,* 672–708.

Holmes, D., Murray, S. J., Perron, A., & Rail, G. (2006). Deconstructing the evidence-based discourse in health sciences: Truth, power and fascism. *International Journal of Evidence Based Healthcare, 4,* 180–186.

Horkheimer, M. (2004). *Eclipse of reason.* London: Continuum Press. (Original work published in 1947.)

International Labour Organization. (2008). *Global employment trends: January 2008.* Geneva, Switzerland: International Labour Office.

International Labour Organization. (2009). *The cost of coercion. Global report under the follow-up to the ILO Declaration on Fundamental Principles and Rights at Work.* Geneva, Switzerland: International Labour Office.

Israel, J. (2009). *A revolution of the mind - Radical enlightenment and the intellectual origins of modern democracy.* Princeton, NJ: Princeton University Press.

Jacob, M. C. (2001). *Enlightenment: A brief history with documents.* Boston, MA: Bedford/St.Martin's.

Judge, T., Thoresen, C., Bono, J., & Patton, G. (2001). The job satisfaction – job performance relationship: A qualitative and quantitative review. *Psychological Bulletin, 127,* 376–407.

Kanigel, R. (1997). *The one best way: Frederick Winslow Taylor and the enigma of efficiency.* New York: Viking Press.

Kieser, A., & Leiner, L. (2009). Why the rigor-relevance-gap in management research is unbridgeable. *Journal of Management Studies, 46,* 516–533.

Knights, D. (2008). Myopic rhetorics: Reflecting epistemologically and ethically on the demand for relevance in organizational and management research. *Academy of Management Learning & Education, 7,* 537–552.

Kuhn, T. S. (1962). *The structure of scientific revolutions.* Chicago, IL: University of Chicago Press.

Lakhan, S. E., Hamlat, E., McNamee, T., & Laird, C. (2009). Time for a unified approach to medical ethics. *Philosophy, Ethics, and Humanities in Medicine, 4* (13). DOI: 10.1186/1747–5341-4-13.

Learmonth, M. (2006). Is there such a thing as evidence-based management? A commentary on Rousseau's presidential address. *Academy of Management Review, 31,* 1089–1091.

Learmonth, M. (2008). Evidence-based management: A backlash against pluralism in organizational studies? *Organization, 15,* 283–291.

Learmonth, M., & Harding, N. (2006). Evidence-based management: The very idea. *Public Administration, 84,* 245–266.

Little, M. (2003). "Better than numbers…" A gentle critique of evidence-based medicine. *ANZ Journal of Surgery, 73,* 177–182.

Littler, C. R. (1978). Understanding Taylorism. *The British Journal of Sociology, 29,* 185–202.

Marcuse, H. (1964). *One-dimensional man.* Boston, MA: Beacon Press.

Martinson, B. C., Anderson, M. S., & de Vries, R. (2005). Scientists behaving badly. *Nature, 435,* 737–738.

Marx, K., & Engels, F. (1955). *The communist manifesto.* Northbrook, IL: AHM Publishing. (Original work published in 1848.)

Meyer, J. P., Stanley, D. J., Herscovitch, L., & Topolyntsky, L. (2002). Affective, continuance, and normative commitment to the organization: A meta-analysis of antecedents, correlates, and consequences. *Journal of Vocational Behavior, 16,* 20–52.

Morrell, K. (2008). The narrative of "evidence based" management: A polemic. *Journal of Management Studies, 45,* 613–635.

Oakes, G. (2003). Max Weber on value rationality and value spheres. *Journal of Classical Sociology, 3,* 27–45.

Pfeffer, J., & Sutton, R. I. (2006). *Hard facts, dangerous half-truths and total nonsense: Profiting from evidence-based management.* Boston, MA: Harvard Business School Press.

Popper, K. R. (1972). *Objective knowledge: An evolutionary approach.* Oxford, England: Oxford University Press.

Reay, T., Berta, W., & Kohn, M. K. (2009). What's the evidence on evidence-based management? *Academy of Management Perspectives, 23,* 5–18.

Rhoades, L., & Eisenberger, R. (2002). Perceived organizational support: A review of the literature. *Journal of Applied Psychology, 87,* 698–714.

Robinson, A. (2004). Between Marxism and populism: Working class identity and bourgeois ideology. *What Next?, 28,* 7–18.

Rogers, W. A. (2004). Evidence based medicine and justice: A framework for looking at the impact of EBM upon vulnerable or disadvantaged groups. *Journal of Medical Ethics, 30,* 141–145.

Rousseau, D. M. (2006). Is there such a thing as evidence-based management? *Academy of Management Review, 31,* 256–269.

Rousseau, D. M., Manning, J., & Denyer, D. (2008). Evidence in management and organizational science: Assembling the field's full weight of scientific knowledge through syntheses. *The Academy of Management Annals, 2,* 475–515.

Rousseau, D. M., & McCarthy, S. (2007). Evidence-based management: Educating managers from an evidence based perspective. *Academy of Management Learning and Education, 6,* 94–101.

Rynes, S. L., Giluk, T. L., & Brown, K. C. (2007). The very separate worlds of academic and practitioner publications in human resource management: Implications for evidence-based management. *Academy of Management Journal, 50,* 987–1008.

Sackett, D. L., Straus, S. E., Richardson, W. S., Rosenberg, W., & Haynes, R. B. (2000). *Evidence-based medicine: How to practice and teach EBM.* New York: Churchill Livingstone.

Schwartz, G. T. (1991). The myth of the Ford Pinto case. *Rutgers Law Review, 43,* 1013–1068.

Seeman, M. (1983). Alienation motifs in contemporary theorizing: The hidden continuity of the classic themes. *Social Psychological Quarterly, 46,* 171–184.

Spencer, D. A. (2000). Braverman and the contribution of labour process analysis to the critique of capitalist production – twenty-five years on. *Work, Employment and Society, 14,* 223–243.

Taylor, F. W. (2008). *The Principles of scientific management.* Charleston, SC: Forgotten Books. (Original work published in 1911.)

Tranfield, D., Denyer, D., & Smart, P. (2003). Toward a methodology for developing evidence-informed management knowledge by means of systematic review. *British Journal of Management, 14,* 207–222.

Williams, H. (1989). *Hegel, Heraclitus, and Marx's dialectic.* New York: St. Martin's Press.

The Politics of Evidence-Based Decision Making

Gerard P. Hodgkinson

Abstract

This chapter argues that evidence-based management is an inherently political project that risks creating an illusion of rationality, a multilayered façade masking underlying fundamental differences of interpretation, purpose, and power among the various stakeholders situated on both sides of the academic-practitioner/policy divide. To avoid this unfortunate scenario, it needs to accommodate on a more systematic basis the important influence of power and politics in organizational life, rather than downplaying them as it currently does, treating political problems as a minor by-product of an otherwise radical improvement to organizational decision processes. Only then will its advancement accelerate the development of work organizations that are more humane and more productive, to the benefit of all stakeholders of the modern enterprise.

Key Words: politics, power, political use of evidence, stakeholders, competition for resources

Introduction

On Thursday October 29, 2009, Professor David Nutt, of Imperial College London, then the UK government's chief advisor on illicit drugs policy, published a briefing paper entitled "Estimating drug harms: A risky business?" In the paper, a transcript of the "Eve Saville Lecture," a talk he had delivered some three-and-a-half months earlier at Kings College London, he reported evidence indicating that tobacco and alcohol were more harmful than a number of illegal drugs, not least LSD, ecstasy, and cannabis. Drawing on his extensive experience as chair of the Advisory Council on the Misuse of Drugs (ACMD), he argued that the classification of recreational psychoactive substances had become a highly politicized process:

> One thing's for sure: at present, experts and politicians don't agree, which is why I think the public debate needs to begin. Who do the public trust more—the experts or the politicians? When we look at the discussion that we had about ecstasy (where the ACMD recommended class B...and the government

maintained it as A), I think there's very little doubt that we, the scientists, won the intellectual argument, but we obviously didn't win the decision in terms of classification. Any agreement will be difficult if we're not talking in the same language about the same relative measures of harm; this is what I am trying to address in this talk. (Nutt, 2009, p. 11)

A press release announcing the publication of the briefing paper stated:

> Professor Nutt argues strongly in favour of an evidence-based approach to drugs classification policy and criticises the precautionary principle', used by the former Home Secretary Jackie Smith to justify her decision to reclassify cannabis from a class C to a class B drug. By erring on the side of caution, Professor Nutt argues, politicians "distort" and "devalue" research evidence. "This leads us to a position where people really don't know what the evidence is", he writes. [http://www.crimeandjustice.org.uk/estimatingdrugharmspr.html] (Accessed at 8:10 P.M., October 1, 2010)

The next day, newspapers and web sites across the world were reporting the fact that Professor Nutt had been sacked by the home secretary. In an interview reported on the Sky News web site, Nutt stated: "I think 'asked to resign' is a euphemism for being sacked . . ." Declaring it a "bad day for science," he explained that: "Politics is politics and science is science and there's a bit of tension between them sometimes." [http://news.sky.com/skynews/Home/UK-News/David-Nutt-Governments-Chief-Drug-Adviser-Is-Sacked-Over-Claims-About-Ecstasy-And-LSD/Article/200910415426304] (Accessed at 8:30 p.m. on October 1, 2010)

At the time of writing this chapter, no less than six further members of the ACMD have resigned in the wake of Nutt's sacking, amid further revelations of political pressure being brought to bear on its work. The seventh advisor to quit, Eric Carlin, resigned in protest over the banning of the party drug mephedrone, classified by the government as a class B substance, in the run up to the 2010 general election. See, for example: http://www.telegraph.co.uk/health/7547605/Eric-Carlin-becomes-seventh-government-drugs-advisor-to-quit.html (Published: 3:18 p.m.. BST 02 Apr 2010); http://www.guardian.co.uk/society/2010/apr/04/eric-carlin-mephedrone-classification (This article appeared on page 31 of the main section of *the Observer* on Sunday, April 4, 2010. It was published on guardian.co.uk at 12.07 a.m. BST on Sunday April 4, 2010.)

The preceding case renders abundantly clear why a chapter on the politics of evidence-based decision making is required in a handbook of evidence-based management (EBMgt). It illustrates the fact that evidence-based approaches to decision making are no less political than other forms of collective decision making (cf. Pettigrew, 1973, 1985; Pfeffer, 1981). All decisions of a sufficient magnitude to warrant the apparatus of an evidence-based approach are ultimately the product of a negotiated order (Walsh & Fahay, 1986), in which the conflicting agendas of multiple stakeholders must somehow be reconciled (Johnson, 1987; Mintzberg, 1983; Pettigrew, 1973, 1985; Pfeffer, 1981). By way of illustration, consider the following scenarios:

• A large general hospital serving a densely populated city is seeking to reduce significant levels of staff turnover within its highly successful neurosurgery unit. Government funded, the highly specialized surgeons, anesthetists, and nursing staff of this unit are being frequently lured into more lucrative positions at a neighboring private sector

hospital. In an attempt to stem the exodus of some of its most talented staff, the hospital's director of human resources is contemplating the introduction of a flexible and highly attractive rewards package, effectively signaling a move away from transactional psychological contracts to relational psychological contracts (Rousseau, 1990, 1995), in the hope that the new deals will engender a sense of loyalty and commitment within this particular unit. In a climate of growing financial stringency, several members of the hospital's board of directors, including the chief executive, are skeptical that the additional costs this will entail are warranted and there are concerns that the policy will create a sense of inequity among the wider workforce. Given the hospital's current finances, there is no prospect that the scheme could be extended to other departments.

• A local U.S. manufacturer of automotive vehicle components is contemplating how best to increase the scale of its operations in order to meet the growing demand for its products. One option it is considering is to outsource some of its contracts to an overseas company located in the Far East. Alternatively, it could embark on an aggressive recruitment campaign within the domestic labor market. However, domestic labor costs are considerably higher, and there is an acute skills shortage, such that it will have to invest in additional training and development should it chose to embark on the latter course of action. Understandably, community leaders and employees are anxious that the company in question should opt to expand its domestic workforce, notwithstanding the additional economic burden that this option would entail.

• In an attempt to raise the productivity of its staff, a major research-intensive university has recently revamped its performance management process, abandoning the predominantly developmental ethos of the previous scheme in favor of a new system, in which staff must meet demanding but achievable targets. At a recent staff meeting, the vice-chancellor justified the launch of the new scheme on the basis of goal-setting theory (Locke & Latham, 1990), citing the extensive high-quality empirical evidence supporting this particular theory (Latham & Pinder, 2005) as a valid foundation for driving the enterprise forward, amid growing competition, to maintain the university's position in global performance league tables.

In each of the preceding cases, from the initial framing of the problem to be addressed, to the gathering of the evidence to inform the decision, to its evaluation, interpretation, and implementation, all aspects of the decision process are inherently political in nature, as is the closely related fundamental question of who is to be involved in each aspect of the process and with what effect. Evidence-based decision making is thus no less political in the context of small to medium enterprises than in the context of much larger organizations and wider policy-making circles, the only substantive differences being the scale of the problems addressed and the range and number of stakeholders affected by the decisions at hand (cf. Bogenschneider & Corbett, 2010; Mintzberg, 1983 Pettigrew, 1973, 1985; Pfeffer, 1981; Pfeffer & Salancik, 1978). The failure to recognize these fundamental truths risks creating an illusion of rationality, a multilayered façade that masks underlying differences of interpretation, purpose, and power among the various stakeholders involved in and affected by the decisions in question (Abrahamson & Baumard, 2008; Pfeffer & Salancik, 1978). Accordingly, this chapter offers a unified treatment of the political dimensions of EBMgt at the levels of policy and practice. It first sketches the political background to the rise of EBMgt and then identifies a range of issues that need to be addressed in order to ensure that its advancement accelerates the development of work organizations that are both humane and more productive, to the benefit of all stakeholders of the modern enterprise.

The chapter is organized in five main sections. Following this introduction, the second section briefly identifies the political backdrop to the rise of EBMgt as an approach to organizational decision making that seeks to incorporate the insights of scholarly research alongside other forms of evidence. The third section demonstrates that in reality evidence-based decision making is an exercise in social construction and that its processes and outcomes are accordingly the product of a negotiated order. The fourth section considers the implications of this analysis for the practice of EBMgt, while the final section summarizes the principal arguments and conclusions.

The Rise of Evidence-Based Management: Politics in the Making

Historical Background

As argued by Hodgkinson and Herriot (2002) a number of the strategic imperatives confronting the applied social sciences, including the management and organizational sciences (MOS), are driving researchers and the users of research away from what might be loosely termed "the scientific inquiry approach" and toward "the problem-solving approach" to knowledge production (see also Hodgkinson, Herriot, & Anderson, 2001; Starkey & Madan, 2001; Tranfield & Starkey, 1998). As illustrated in Figure 23.1, the scientific inquiry approach implies a simple and linear model of knowledge production and application. Common criticisms of this generic approach to knowledge production include the fact that the problems addressed are derived from only a very limited set of stakeholders; dissemination is delayed, and is addressed, for the most part, to this same set of stakeholders; the process of translation from dissemination to practice is not specified; and practice has little or no effect on issues addressed in subsequent work. In marked contrast, the problem-solving approach to knowledge production, represented schematically in Figure 23.2, constitutes a more socially distributed form of knowledge production, in which knowledge is generated in the context of application by multistakeholder teams, drawn from a range of backgrounds that transcend traditional discipline boundaries, and results in immediate or short time-to-market dissemination or exploitation.

Hodgkinson and Herriot (2002) maintain that four major environmental pressures are driving the changing landscape of knowledge production and concomitant shift in emphasis away from scientific inquiry toward problem solving, namely:

1. The changing nature of demand: stakeholders are seeking solutions to problems which increasingly threaten the very survival of their organizations.

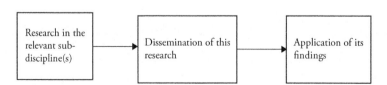

Fig. 23.1 The scientific-inquiry approach to knowledge production.
[Source: adapted from G. P. Hodgkinson and P. Herriot (2002). "The role of psychologists in enhancing organizational effectiveness." In I. T. Robertson, M. Callinan, and D. Bartram (Eds.), *Organizational effectiveness: The role of psychology* (p. 48). Chichester, UK: Wiley. Copyright © John Wiley and Sons, Ltd.]

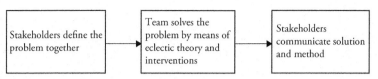

Fig. 23.2 A problem-solving approach to knowledge production.
[Source: G. P. Hodgkinson and P. Herriot (2002). "The role of psychologists in enhancing organizational effectiveness." In I. T. Robertson, M. Callinan, and D. Bartram (Eds.), *Organizational effectiveness: The role of psychology* (p. 49). Chichester, UK: Wiley. Copyright © John Wiley and Sons, Ltd.]

2. Increasingly, the problems confronting organizational stakeholders are new problems, characterized by high levels of ambiguity, such that they defy clear and straightforward definition.

3. Research skills are becoming far more distributed: as firms, charities, and public service organizations increasingly procure the services of highly trained individuals who would previously have only considered traditional university careers, employers are increasingly directing and controlling resources and research activities so as to address their own or their clients' "real" problems.

4. The rise in the Internet and related technologies is such that knowledge that previously might only have been available in highly technical journal articles is becoming increasingly accessible to nonacademics.

Responding to these pressures, over the past decade growing numbers of business-school academics have begun to advance creative solutions born out of a common underlying belief that research can often meet the twin imperatives of scholarly rigor and social usefulness, thereby combining the best of both worlds. This philosophy is gaining momentum among behavioral and social scientists allied to MOS (e.g., Anderson, Herriot, & Hodgkinson, 2001; Dunbar & Starbuck, 2006; Hodgkinson & Healey, 2008a; Hodgkinson & Rousseau, 2009; Hodgkinson & Starbuck, 2008; Huff, 2000; Pettigrew, 1997, 2001; Romme & Endenburg, 2006; Starbuck, 2006; Van de Ven, 2007; Van de Ven & Johnson, 2006), although debate continues (see, e.g., Grey, 2001; McKelvey, 2006; Kieser & Leiner, 2009, 2011).

Viewed in this historical context, the rise of EBMgt is one of a series of important developments over the past decade in MOS that have sought to enhance the robustness of interventions through collaborative working among practitioners, policy makers, and professionally trained academic researchers. Although these developments in general have generated a number of well-documented "success stories"

(for recent overviews see Hodgkinson & Rousseau, 2009; Van de Ven, 2007), the preceding strategic imperatives confronting MOS demand a significant step change, in order to ensure that the key elements of the scientific-inquiry approach continue to meet the needs of reflective practitioners and policy makers (see also Ryan & Ford, 2010). As the marketplace for ideas continues to expand, it is vital that the highest-quality social-scientific evidence available is disseminated as rapidly as possible, in a form that policy makers and practitioners can comprehend. EBMgt has emerged precisely because its emphasis on systematic reviews of the best available evidence as its cornerstone (Briner & Rousseau, 2011a; Briner, Denyer & Rousseau, 2009; Rousseau, Manning, & Denyer, 2008) meets this rapid and accessible dissemination imperative. On closer inspection, however, it becomes clear that, to a much greater extent than in the case of the earlier attempts to bridge the academic-practitioner/policy divide, EBMgt is an inherently political project, with potentially far reaching consequences for research, pedagogy, policy making, and practice, at a time when the funding for university-based research across the globe is coming under increasingly critical scrutiny by governments and other key stakeholders. It is essential, therefore, that the political background to its development is rendered explicit, lest the advocates and practitioners of EBMgt should unwittingly create a façade of rationality of the sort alluded to earlier.

Legitimating Evidence-Based Management

As in the cases of evidence-based medicine (Sackett, Rosenberg, Gray, Haynes, & Richardson, 1996) and evidence-based policy making (Bogenschneider & Corbett, 2010), the advocates of evidence-based management (e.g., Briner, Denyer, & Rousseau, 2009; Briner & Rousseau, 2011a; Pfeffer & Sutton, 2006; Rousseau, 2006) are seeking to establish its legitimacy in the eyes of a diverse and divergent range of stakeholders drawn from the policy making, practitioner, and academic communities. As observed by Morrell (2008, p. 616):

> It would be misleading and overly simplistic to claim that all those pursuing "evidence based" approaches were of one mind. Indeed, they are not even of one label: some eschew the label evidence based and prefer sanitized variants such as "evidence informed" or "evidence aware" for presentational or rhetorical purposes. However...the claims underpinning evidence based approaches can be understood as a shared narrative about the relationship of management research to management practice...As well as consensus over the content of this narrative, it is important to consider the ways in which it is relayed or "told". The power and influence of key actors and networks is such as to support and legitimize the narrative, and to contribute to its being retold in different settings. This is noteworthy because, over and above the inherent appeal of any theory, such contextual factors underpin the likelihood of a school becoming dominant...

It is, in this particular sense, that EBMgt constitutes a political project, which is being driven forward by:

> ...a constellation of specialists, research institutes, funding bodies and political organizations with a common world view, who are powerful because of their shared belief that a particular form of knowledge production is applicable to social problems... (Morrell, 2008, p. 616).

In the UK context, for example, EBMgt can be seen as part of a package of measures that might ultimately contribute to the "impact agenda" of the current UK government in its attempt to ensure a wider contribution from university-based research beyond traditional academic impacts per se. Through the work of its seven Research Councils, which administer the bulk of government-funded peer-reviewed awards across all the major disciplines (along similar lines to the National Science Foundation in the United States), and its forthcoming national evaluation of publically funded academic research, again spanning all disciplines, known as the Research Excellence Framework (REF), which has replaced the previous Research Assessment Exercise (RAE) as one of the primary funding mechanisms for university research, the UK government is evolving a major requirement for all UK academic institutions to demonstrate such wider impact.

The move to EBMgt is one of several approaches that a number of academic management researchers are championing as a way to meet the demands of this requirement (see, e.g., Briner & Rousseau, 2011a; Briner, Denyer, & Rousseau, 2009; Rousseau, Manning, & Denyer, 2008). Other closely related approaches, not least, design science, are also gaining momentum in certain quarters (see, e.g., Denyer, Tranfield, & Van Aken, 2008; Hodgkinson & Healey, 2008a; Hodgkinson & Starkey, 2011; Starkey, Hatchuel, & Tempest, 2009). However, there have also been a number of challenges to the legitimacy of EBMgt, design science, and, indeed, the wider impact agenda in MOS, on both intellectual and ideological grounds (see, e.g., Cassell, 2011; Morrell, 2008; Sandberg & Tsoukas, 2011; Weick, 2001). Some of these objections are based on clear misconceptions (see, for example, the recent interchanges between Hodgkinson & Rousseau, 2009, and Kieser & Leiner, 2009, 2011), whereas others are based on legitimate ideological differences regarding the nature and purposes of social-scientific inquiry (cf. Bartlett, 2011; Baughman, Dorsey, & Zarefsky, 2011; Grey 2001; Learmonth, 2011; Learmonth & Harding, 2006; McKelvey 2006; Sandberg & Tsoukas, 2011; Weick, 2001).

One of the potentially damaging consequences of not reflecting more deeply and critically on the rapidly changing wider political context in which the rise of EBMgt is occurring is that its ascendancy could potentially impact adversely on the required methodological and theoretical diversity of the MOS field. Were alternative approaches incompatible with the prevailing logics of EBMgt and related conceptions to fall out of favor with government policy makers and others with the power to divert resources to the extent envisaged by some critical commentators (e.g., Cassell, 2011; Morrell, 2008), the longer-term consequences would ultimately prove immensely detrimental to the academic, policy making, and practitioner communities alike. Such is the complexity and richness of the challenges confronting contemporary organizations that many problems falling within the purview of MOS cannot be addressed adequately by means of the logic of scientific inquiry alone (cf. Kilduff, Mehra, & Dunn, 2011; Sandberg & Tsoukas, 2011; Wensley, 2009).

As demonstrated by the current financial crises confronting the global economy, approaches antithetical to the EBMgt agenda, on moral, philosophical, scientific, and even aesthetic grounds, each may have a role to play in contributing to the vibrancy and health of management research, policy, and practice. It is essential, therefore, that key sections of the scholarly research community continue to question the central tenets of EBMgt and champion alternatives based on a diverse range of ontological and epistemological positions. The failure to recognize and accommodate theoretical perspectives and research methods antithetical to EBMgt as legitimate forms of management inquiry and render these issues explicitly discussable would constitute an unacceptable form of hegemony, a scenario that needs to be avoided at all costs (cf. Morrell, 2008).

The Political Challenge of Changing the B(i)ases of Organizational Decision Making

A second sense in which EBMgt is arguably a political project, which thus requires political analysis and political situational awareness, is in the sense that its practice demands a fundamental change to the ways in which work organizations (and work-related policy makers) make decisions. As recently observed by Briner and Rousseau (2011a, 2011b), although EBMgt has been defined in a variety of ways, the majority of definitions build on evidence-based notions advanced in medicine and elsewhere. Reflecting this trend, Briner et al. (2009, p. 19) offer a succinct definition of EBMgt, paraphrasing Sackett et al.s (1996) definition of evidence-based medicine, which is convenient for present analytical purposes:

> Evidence-based management is about making decisions through the conscientious, explicit, and judicious use of four sources of information: practitioner expertise and judgment, evidence from the local context, a critical evaluation of the best available research evidence, and the perspectives of those people who might be affected by the decision.

It is clear from this definition that EBMgt seeks to combine key elements of the aforementioned scientific-inquiry and problem-solving approaches to knowledge production, in an attempt to derive workable solutions to the problem or problems at hand. In so doing, its explicit intent is to empower decision makers to weigh and combine the various information sources in accordance with their own critical judgment:

> In some circumstances, the opinions of stakeholders or ethical considerations may be judged by the decision makers to be much more important than the external research evidence and thus be given much greater emphasis in the decision. In other circumstances, there may be little internal evidence available and thus its influence on the decision would

be relatively minor. In all cases, though, the choice to place more or less emphasis on various elements should be made in a mindful, conscious fashion. (Briner et al., 2009, p. 21)

The requirement to blend on an explicit basis the insights of state-of-the-art evidence distilled through a formal evaluation of the pertinent social-science literature with other forms of knowledge and knowing changes fundamentally the rationale on which powerful, politically motivated stakeholders, with potentially conflicting agendas and ideologies, must negotiate and bargain with one another:

> The conscientious use of the four sources of information means that an [evidence-based] approach involves paying careful and sustained attention to sources of what can be potentially different, conflicting, and sometimes difficult-to-interpret information. Being explicit means using information from each source in a clear, conscious, and methodical way such that the roles played by all the information in the final decision are understood. And being judicious involves using reflective judgment to evaluate the validity and relevance of the information from each source. Evidence and information is critically evaluated in relation to the practice context and problem. (Briner and Rousseau, 2011a, p. 7)

As I have observed elsewhere (Hodgkinson, 2011), in seeking to manage uncertainty, senior managers and other influential organizational stakeholders do not typically rely on scientific research; rather, they adopt industry recipes, shared mental models of "what works and what doesn't," acquired through participation in interorganizational social networks (Spender, 1989). Over time, the insights and practices acquired in this fashion, suitably adapted to meet the particular contingencies confronting the individual enterprise, much as a chef adapts a given recipe to the ingredients at hand, become institutionalized and legitimated through the cultural norms and formal requirements of professional bodies and regulatory agencies, in turn stifling further innovation (Abrahamson & Fombrun, 1994). Furthermore, there is also evidence showing that hard-pressed decision makers, particularly senior executives and professionals, base important decisions on expertise manifest as intuitions (see, e.g., Burke & Miller, 1999). Recent advances across a number of basic and applied branches of psychology and MOS lend credence under certain conditions to the validity of intuition and other nonconscious cognitive-affective processes (for overviews see Dane & Pratt, 2007, 2009; Hodgkinson & Healey, 2008b, 2011; Hodgkinson, Langan-Fox, & Sadler-Smith, 2008; Hodgkinson, Sadler-Smith, Burke, Claxton, & Sparrow, 2009; Kahneman & Klein, 2009, 2010; Salas, Rosen, & DiazGrandos, 2010).

In short, politically motivated and powerful actors do not typically rely on formal sources of evidence and ways of knowing as the prime basis of organizational decision making (see also Sandberg & Tsoukas, 2011). Rather, they are inclined to fall back on "practitioner expertise and judgment," just one of the four sources identified by Briner and Rousseau (2011a, 2011b). Despite warnings supported by clear evidence that intuition can only be of positive benefit in situations in which it is possible to identify appropriate cues for its successful deployment on a reliable basis and when there is an underlying body of requisite expertise (Kahneman & Klein, 2009, 2010), as borne out in the fields of evidence-based medicine and evidence-based policy making (e.g., Hunter, 2003) it is unlikely that managers and other key organizational stakeholders will embrace readily new practices that externalize these tacit and informal sources of knowledge and knowing, so as to render them explicit and, thus, open to the scrutiny of potential rivals. To do so would require them to relinquish major sources of power on which they typically rely to drive forward their own agendas (cf. Johnson, 1987; Pettigrew, 1973; Pfeffer, 1981). Furthermore, as observed by Bartlett (2011), in situations in which evidence derived on the basis of systematic reviews challenges the legitimacy of the extant practices of those who wield power within organizations, it is highly likely that the evidence in question will be ignored, rejected, or misinterpreted, an observation borne out by recent findings in social psychology showing that individuals tend to ignore and misinterpret scientific information that is inconsistent with their own viewpoints (Munro, 2010). The validity of these observations can be illustrated conveniently by means of the well-documented case of personnel selection and assessment.

A copious amount of high quality scientific evidence has been accumulated across the globe demonstrating the psychometric superiority of cognitive ability tests, structured interviews, and work-sample tests vis-à-vis a range of less satisfactory alternatives in terms of reliability, validity, and utility. Despite numerous meta-analyses confirming the generalizability of this conclusion (e.g., Hunter & Hunter, 1984; Schmidt & Hunter, 1998), survey after survey has found that organizations typically reject these more effective practices in favor of psychometrically weaker ones, especially traditional interviews and letters of reference, a finding that generalizes across a wide range of different types of organizations, applicant groups, and countries (see, e.g., Bartram, Lindley, Marshall, & Foster, 1995; Hodgkinson & Payne, 1998; Robertson & Makin, 1986; Shackleton & Newell, 1994; Zibarras & Woods, 2010). An obvious explanation for this paradoxical state of affairs, whereby psychometrically robust assessment techniques are rejected in favor of a "stubborn reliance [on] intuition and subjectivity" (Highhouse, 2008), is that they ultimately reduce the latitude of otherwise powerful decision makers to appoint individuals who will fit in with their own agendas, because, in the final analysis, personnel selection and assessment is fundamentally a sociopolitical process, not a psychometric one (Cleveland & Murphy, 1992; Herriot, 1989).

In sum, the extent to which and in what ways organizational decision makers are able and willing to blend the four sources of evidence identified by Briner et al. (2009) is itself the outcome of a fundamental political decision, which both reflects the prevailing ideologies of key stakeholders and bestows a form of rationality on the proceedings. Just as the various contributors to this handbook and its readers will differ in their views regarding the extent to which and in what ways formal social-scientific knowledge can and should predominate over expert judgment and contextual awareness in any given situation, so, too, will the various stakeholders seeking to implement evidence-based approaches to management and organizational decision making in particular contexts of application, reflecting important differences in their goals and underlying sources of power.

Acknowledging the fact that power and politics are indeed fundamental to decision making in organizations, Briner and Rousseau (2011a, 2011b), view the politics of evidence as a potentially significant barrier to the adoption of evidence-based practice:

> Power and politics are fundamental to decision making and also surround the identification and use of evidence in organizations. Senior leaders may feel they have the right or even responsibility to make decisions based on their experience and judgment that seem to fly in the face of the available evidence. The need to be explicit in evidence-based decision making means that those with vested interests in a particular course of action may find it more difficult

to hide such interests. In general, an evidence-based approach may prove challenging particularly in organizations with highly political cultures. Although it is impossible to remove politics from evidence and decision making, evidence-based approaches do at least offer the possibility of making clearer distinctions among politics, values, interests, and other forms of information such as research evidence. The more decision makers are held accountable for their decisions, the more likely they are to welcome such distinctions. (Briner & Rousseau, 2011a, p. 19).

However, it is highly unlikely that organizational decision makers are going to willingly embrace practices that render their differing vested interests explicit. Accountability is a sure-fire recipe for escalating the commitment of politically motivated actors to extant, failing courses of action (cf. Schwenk, 1989; Staw, 1981, 1997). Hence, forcing decision makers to differentiate "politics, values, interests, and other forms of information such as research evidence" is not going to automatically yield less political outcomes; nor is it indeed clear that decision makers will uniformly "welcome such distinctions." Further, as argued by Bartlett (2011), the admission that: "an evidence-based approach may prove challenging particularly in organizations with highly political cultures," is tantamount to an admission that it is only likely to succeed in a small number of highly circumscribed settings and contexts of application, because the cultures of virtually all work organizations are political, a fact recognized long ago by researchers of organizational power and politics (e.g., Johnson, 1987; Mintzberg, 1983; Pettigrew, 1973, 1985; Pfeffer, 1981; Pfeffer & Salancik, 1978).

The Politics of Evidence Construction

More fundamentally, what Briner and Rousseau's (2011a, 2011b) analysis downplays, is that "…the nature of evidence, and importantly, the way it is constructed, is politics, values, and interest laden…Definitions of quality inevitably privilege certain sources and interests, as do definitions of evidence" (Cassell, 2011, p. 23). As demonstrated some 50 years ago by Baritz (1960), the idea that social science can be applied in the workplace in an apolitical and interest-free fashion is a fundamentally untenable proposition. The failure to recognize and accommodate alternative ontological and epistemological positions and perspectives on what constitutes evidence as a basis for informing organizational decisions and explicitly render this issue

discussable when enacting EBMgt would thus constitute a second form of unacceptable political hegemony that, again, must be avoided.

However, even when an agreed philosophy is in place, there is still nonetheless considerable political latitude in terms of how it is to be enacted. Taking the dominant systematic review approach as a working case in point to illustrate what is clearly a much wider issue, the question of how the problem to be addressed is framed, what criteria are to be adopted for inclusion versus exclusion, and the threshold in respect of each inclusion-exclusion criterion are all political issues, in the sense that different stakeholders may well want to contest these microdecisions, each of which will undoubtedly have a fundamental bearing on the answers eventually "revealed" in connection with the focal policy or practice. There is also the question of how the evidence will be interpreted and ultimately implemented once the findings of the systematic review become apparent.

Implicit within the dominant approach to EBMgt outlined earlier is a model of human information processing predicated on the late Herbert Simon's notion of bounded rationality (e.g., Simon, 1955, 1956), which treats social-scientific evidence pertaining to organizational decision problems like any other feature of the decision environment. This model implies that the decision environment is, in essence, an objective entity, and that the reason subjective differences in perception occur is because the objective environment can only be partially comprehended, due to limited processing capacity (i.e., "bounded rationality"). Karl Weick's work, through the interrelated notions of "enactment," "sensemaking" and the "enacted environment" (Weick, 1969, 1979, 1995), challenges this limited view of the environment (which he terms "the perceived environment"), arguing that theories stressing the notion that reality is selectively perceived overemphasize the object → subject relationship, at the expense of the idea that often the subject exerts considerable influence on the object:

> …Managers construct, rearrange, single out, and demolish many "objective" features of their surroundings. When people act they un-randomise variables, insert vestiges of orderliness, and literally create their own constraints…There is a reciprocal influence between subjects and objects, not a one-sided influence such as implied by the idea that a stimulus triggers a response. (Weick, 1979, pp. 164–166)

The concept of enactment refers to the basic process by which organization members actively go about creating their environments, which, in turn, act back on them, as if they were true, objective entities, thereby imposing constraints on what is considered possible; that is, through enactment processes organizational decision makers socially construct key aspects of their material worlds (Weick, 1969, 1979, 1995). Viewed from this social constructionist standpoint, all aspects of evidence-based decision making, from the earliest stages of problem definition, to the gathering and sifting of the evidence (i.e., all forms and sources), to its weighting in determining the final outcome, are each interpretive acts, which ultimately render the entire process just as political as any other collective decision process in which the key actors are seeking to enact alternative visions of the future.

In the words of Learmonth and Harding (2006, p. 247): "…evidence is never simply out there waiting for the researcher to find. Rather, our methods for engaging with the world act to construct 'evidence' in particular ways." It thus follows that this process of "evidence construction" is always going to be an inherently ideological and contestable task—not merely a technical, "scientific" one (see also Cassell, 2011; Learmonth, 2011). In seeking to formalize otherwise informal processes, it really does matter, therefore, that all parties to evidence-based decision making in the workplace, as in any other setting, enjoy situational awareness, politically speaking, lest a facade of rationality should be created through a process in which divergent stakeholders are lulled into a false sense of consensus, founded on a false premise of rationality (i.e., pseudorationality). Again, as Learmonth and Harding put it: "A central concern is to reveal the unobtrusive but constraining operation of power associated with the dominant ways evidence tends to be constructed—and through which alternatives are typically disregarded or rendered invisible…the aim is to highlight how *particular* constructions of evidence have come to be treated as if they were *universal*—thereby promoting and naturalizing conceptions of evidence that tend to perpetuate power, inequalities, and forms of practices that allow for the domination and control of some over others." (Learmonth & Harding, 2006, p. 247).

Just how the power dynamics pertaining to the social construction of evidence in work-related evidence-based decision making can play out at the levels of policy and practice in ways that exclude important forms and sources of evidence that potentially have a major bearing on the problem at hand

can be conveniently illustrated by reference to how the UK Health and Safety Executive (HSE) went about developing its best practice guidelines for the management of occupational stress (Cousins et al., 2004; Mackay, Cousins, Kelly, Lee, & McCaig, 2004; Rick, Thomson, Briner, O'Regan, & Daniels, 2002). In an area that is clearly fraught with political difficulties, the HSE, through a series of consultation exercises with relevant scientific experts and a range of key stakeholder bodies, chose to adopt a particular conception of stress akin to metal fatigue in the field of mechanical engineering. The result is a set of practices and standards that treat all employees on exactly the same basis, regardless of variations in hardiness, Type A Behavior Pattern, and a host of other individual difference variables that have long been well documented in the primary scientific literature as significant moderators of the stressor-strain-stress chain of relationships (see, e.g., Cooper, Dewe, & O'Driscoll, 2001; Ferguson, Daniels, & Jones, 2006). Equally conspicuous by its absence is any notion that the experience of stress is mediated by cognitive-affective processes known to affect the subjective experience of stress in the workplace and in life more generally (cf. Daniels, Harris & Briner, 2004; Lazarus & Folkman 1984; Maslach, Schaufeli & Leiter, 2001).

As observed by Hodgkinson and Healey (2008b) the question of whether a socio-cognitive or objectivist perspective constitutes the most appropriate underlying ontological and epistemological bases for exploring the stressor-strain-stress chain of relationships remains a hotly contested issue. Perrewe and Zellars (1999), for example, have argued for the incorporation of attribution processes in the modeling of work-stress appraisal, whereas others (e.g., Frese & Zapf, 1999; Schaubroeck 1999) maintain that studying the effects of objective environmental features is a more fruitful approach. The HSE's decision to settle on an objectivist conception of stress effectively rendered "off limits" a systematic consideration of individual differences and cognitive-affective processes in the scientific derivation of its policy framework. Had the systematic review that ultimately informed the resulting standards and guidelines for management practitioners (Rick et al., 2002) been predicated on a notion of stress that required a consideration of cognitive-affective appraisal processes and individual differences that are known to potentially mediate and moderate the stressor-strain-stress chain of relationships, arguably, the end result would have been a more sophisticated and contingent set of guidelines and practices. Context-sensitive and, thus, arguably more effective as a basis for combating occupational stress across the board, unfortunately, it is clear that the resulting guidelines and practices would also have been potentially far more costly for employers to implement. The fact that the HSE's systematic review did not address a wider range of factors is a powerful display of how external stakeholders holding scarce financial resources can ultimately determine the overall framing and scientific direction of a given evidence-based project, controlling, for example, which bodies of evidence are deemed admissible and which are not (cf. Pfeffer & Salancik, 1978). In the final analysis, the HSE, the organization that commissioned this particular EBMgt project, is embedded within a wider network of powerful institutional players, which ultimately control the resources on which it is dependent for its own longer-term financial and political well-being. These resources could easily be scaled back or withdrawn altogether in the event that the HSE's scientific outputs were to ultimately cause political embarrassment to the government of the day. Fortunately, however, the fact that the basis on which the evidence underpinning these guidelines and standards has been rendered explicit by means of systematic review means that those stakeholders who might want to contest the scientific adequacy of the project are able to do so.

Given the Political Realities, Where Do We Go From Here?

EBMgt is clearly an inherently political project, but one that is contestable on both sides of the academic-practitioner/policy divide. From an academic standpoint, its more extreme detractors (e.g., Cassell, 2011; Morrell, 2008) are concerned that its champions are seeking to privilege a particular form of inquiry (positivism) and attendant research methods (quantitative techniques) over others, in what is essentially a "soft" (low consensus), applied, divergent, and rural (as opposed to hard, pure, convergent, and urban) field of endeavor (Tranfield & Starkey, 1998). At a time when governments and other key resource providers are seeking to shift the funding base of university academic research in favor of work that will lead to an array of significant impacts on the economy and wider society (going well beyond traditional citation counts and mentions in the mass media), the fear that the EBMgt community could come to dominate the field is not an unreasonable concern. However, it is important to recognize that, although the EBMgt community

is being championed by some highly influential, high-profile scholars—not least several past presidents of the Academy of Management (including the editor of this volume)—it does not enjoy a monopoly of ideas; nor, indeed, unfettered access to the corridors of power.

It is incumbent on EBMgt's critics to advance constructive alternatives and there are signs that this is happening (e.g., Hodgkinson & Starkey, 2011; Sandberg & Tsoukas, 2011; Wensley, 2009). Further, as observed frequently by those promoting EBMgt (e.g., Briner & Rousseau, 2011a, 2011b; Rousseau, Manning, & Denyer, 2008), all forms of evidence, including evidence extracted from studies employing the full range of qualitative methods, are amenable to research synthesis by means of systematic review. The fact that systematic review renders explicit and, therefore, transparent the criteria adopted in a given research synthesis, means that the evidence-base is more easily contested in comparison with the conventional narrative reviews typically favored by evidence-based detractors. These essential points are commonly downplayed or misunderstood by opponents of the very idea of EBMgt and research synthesis (see, e.g., Cassell, 2011; Learmonth & Harding, 2006). Finally, opponents all too frequently misconstrue the EBMgt community as a movement that is committed to positivism (e.g., Cassell, 2011; Morrell, 2008), whereas, like contemporary design science (Hodgkinson & Healey, 2008a; Hodgkinson & Starkey, 2011) and engaged scholarship (Van de Ven, 2007), its epistemological roots lie ultimately in Bhaskar's (1978, 1979) philosophy of critical realism (Rousseau et al., 2008):

> This perspective maintains that all research methods have limits. Rather than advocate one research approach over another (e.g., quantitative or qualitative, laboratory experiment or field study), critical realism makes such a choice unnecessary... The multi-level and socially constructed character of organizations necessitates a critical realist epistemology, which accommodates immediate (i.e., proximal) causal mechanisms coexisting alongside mechanisms at other levels of analysis that operate more distally... scientific knowledge, although general, is also conditional... (Hodgkinson & Rousseau, 2009, p. 540)

The notion that a particular form of EBMgt, one that favors a narrow range of quantitatively based sources of evidence, will ultimately dominate MOS as a scholarly field of endeavor is thus a most unlikely scenario. However, the problems I have identified pertaining to the implementation of EBMgt in practitioner and policy-making circles, run far deeper, and, thus, pose a more difficult series of challenges and dilemmas for its advocates.

At this juncture, it is apparent that all the key stages of evidence-based decision making are fundamentally political in nature, from the definition of the problem at hand, to the judgment calls regarding what will constitute the criteria for inclusion as admissible evidence in the systematic review, to the interpretation of that evidence and its weighting alongside the other forms of evidence gathered as part of the decision process. Arguably, however, the most significant way in which the implementation of EBMgt constitutes a political project is in relation to the question of which stakeholder groups and which particular stakeholders are to be involved in the decision-making process and with what effect.

The question of who is in and who is out at each stage of the process and the extent to which their involvement is meaningful or merely symbolic are always going to be fundamental and potentially vexed political issues. Scientific experts, for example, can be deployed in a host of different ways, from being the mere providers of data, to playing an active role in the definition and scoping of the project, to being full-blown partners in the final outcome(s). As highlighted by the recent sacking of Professor Nutt and the subsequent departures of six further key members of the ACMD, the basis on which each of the different parties to the decision are to be involved in the process needs to be rendered explicit at the outset. The failure to do so can result in a fundamental misalignment of expectations; in the case the ACMD, whereas the committee's members saw themselves as joint decision makers, the government of the day viewed them as holding a mere advisory role. In the final analysis, when faced with a body of evidence and accompanying recommendations that would not sit easy with its fellow parliamentarians, nor, indeed, key sections of the electorate, the government rejected the committee's recommendations. When the committee's leader then rendered his opposition explicit, calling for a wider debate among the public, it exercised its ultimate political sanction by removing him from office! More generally, this case highlights that the fact that "the choice to place more or less emphasis on various elements," even when "made in a mindful, conscious fashion" (Briner et al., 2009, p 21) is also fundamentally a political decision, which, if poorly managed, can result in deleterious political

consequences, to the mutual detriment of the conflicting stakeholders of the decision.

How, then, might practitioners of evidenced-based decision making confront the political realities highlighted by the various cases discussed throughout this chapter, and in so doing, avoid rationality façades? Arguably, this is the most difficult problem to be resolved in ensuring that evidence-based decision making authentically meets the requirements of those stakeholders affected by the decisions enacted, but who so often lack the power to ensure their voices are heard. Recognizing that EBMgt, like most forms of organizational decision making, is inherently political in nature is a necessary but insufficient basis on which to proceed. Rather, its authentic development and application demands that a wider range of stakeholders beyond the dominant coalition is involved meaningfully in the processes of knowledge creation and decision making, from senior, middle, and junior managers to frontline employees, trades unions, government officials (local, regional, and national), to consumer groups, management consultants, pressure groups, and applied social scientists (among others).

The range of stakeholders required for authentic EBMgt varies from one context of application to another. In all cases, however, it is essential that a sufficiently representative cross-section of stakeholders is involved in meaningful ways from the outset. By adopting this approach, the definition and scoping of the problem to be addressed will necessarily result from a social (and political) negotiation among the parties involved.

Inevitably, there are some political trade-offs that need to be considered in the light of the foregoing analysis. On one hand, incorporating in a meaningful fashion a wider range of stakeholders in EBMgt projects will add to the complexity of the attendant decision processes. Wider stakeholder involvement in the way I am suggesting will often add significantly to the costs of the project, both in terms of the manpower requirements and financial resources. On the other hand, there are likely to be significant gains that outweigh these costs, chief of which is the fact that the origins of the problems addressed and the attendant solutions enacted will be grounded better in the working lives and experience of those who must ultimately implement the resulting solutions and live with the consequences.

Enacting this vision of an authentically more inclusive approach to evidence-based decision making is, however, far from straightforward. At the heart of disputes like the ACMD debacle lay fundamental differences in attitudes, values, and beliefs, borne of identity conflicts (Haslam, Reicher & Platow, 2011), sustained by a range of conscious and nonconscious cognitive-affective processes (see, e.g., Amodio, 2008; Dovidio, Pearson, & Orr, 2008; Fazio & Olson 2003, Haines & Sumner 2006; Lieberman 2007). As demonstrated throughout this chapter, evidence-based decision making in the workplace is little different in character from evidence-based decision making in policy-making circles. Union leaders, front-line workers and other stakeholders beyond the realms of management are no less likely to fall back on intuition, expertise and other less formal sources of knowledge and forms of knowing than their management counterparts.

Researchers have barely begun to consider the implications of the many exciting developments at the forefront of the social neurosciences for the design and validation of tools and processes for organizational decision making, innovation, and adaptation (Hodgkinson & Healey, 2008b). Nevertheless, sufficient evidence has accumulated to conclude that "cold cognition enhancing technologies," that is, decision-aiding techniques that seek to foster methodical reflection through explicit conscious reasoning processes, predicated on affect-free conceptions of human information processing, are unlikely to yield the expected benefits (Hodgkinson & Healey, 2011). One thing is clear, however: in exposing the inclusion-exclusion criteria and tabulating on a study-by-study basis the external evidence from the available scientific literature, systematic reviews are a powerful tool for making explicit one of the four key sources of information that feed into evidence-based organizational-decision processes, thus rendering such information amenable to challenge by all with a stake in the attendant outcomes.

Ultimately, however, as observed by Baughman et al. (2011), high quality evidence is a necessary but insufficient basis for practice. It is the quality of argumentation by those who bring bodies of evidence to bear on organizational decisions that determines how it is eventually used:

> The role of evidence is to provide the justification for claims that solutions will be effective or that courses of action should be taken. Accordingly, a critical property of evidence in applied settings is its power to convince, persuade, or influence. What warrants decisions under these conditions . . . is not only good evidence but good argument. Evidence is a part of an argument but clearly not the whole thing. (Baughman et al., 2011, p. 62).

In calling for an "argument-based" approach to decision making in organizations, Baughman et al., "put evidence in its proper place, a place where it will do the most good: as a means and not an end" (Baughman et al., 2011, p. 64). Viewed from this perspective, systematic reviews nevertheless have a potentially valuable role to play, as boundary objects that can help to mediate differences of interpretation and understanding among stakeholders by enabling deeper dialogue.

Conclusion

This chapter has argued that EBMgt is, in a double sense, a political project. In seeking to develop an evidence-based approach to management practice, failing to acknowledge this basic social fact can only serve to amplify the rationality façade that pervades so much of organizational life. In the words of Abrahamson and Baumard (2008, p. 438), organizational façades:

> [hide] the backstage, which if revealed might make organizational stakeholders decide that problems beset the organization. This would cause stakeholders to withdraw their support—they would disinvest, quit, sue, and generally disparage the unveiled organization.

The events surrounding the occasion of Professor Nutt's lecture and associated publication, with which I commenced this chapter, demonstrate the relevance of this observation to evidence-based decision making in general. In exposing the fundamental differences of opinion between the majority of members of the ACMD and the UK government of the day, Professor Nutt revealed the conflicting rationalities of two immensely powerful stakeholder groups. The ACMD believed that, having systematically brought its scientific expertise to bear on the problem at hand, the government could and should have implemented its policy recommendations, whereas the government believed the recommendations of its scientific advisors constituted but one piece of a more complex jigsaw. Once Nutt had exposed the government's approach to evidence-based decision making as a façade, the government sought, through its taking rapid action to remove him, to counterframe the problem as one of its chief advisors having crossed the line from independent advice giver to politically involved citizen, a move that, in its eyes, rendered his position untenable.

Evidence-based decision making, like all forms of organizational decision making, is inherently political. In the final analysis, therefore, as argued by Barlett (2011), in order to realize its full potential, the evidence-based practice movement must ultimately accommodate on a more systematic basis the important influence of power and politics in organizational life, rather than downplaying them as it currently does, treating political problems as a minor by-product of an otherwise radical improvement to organizational-decision processes.

Members of the EBMgt research community must each confront some fundamental political dilemmas and choices. What are we really interested in? Helping management practitioners and policy makers increase the legitimacy of their political decisions by giving them the opportunity to dress them up in the language of EBMgt? Or increasing transparency in decision processes as a way to expose the misuse of power in organizations and to include in meaningful ways those who are normally marginalized or even excluded altogether from these processes? Recognizing that EBMgt is fundamentally political in a double sense forces all that identify with its cause to make clear choices in respect of these matters. This recognition *increases* our responsibility as social scientists to be aware of the (unintended) consequences of its introduction to management practice. To the extent that the embodiment of this philosophy of transparency and participative decision making is embraced by the EBMgt research community at large, much will be accomplished in enhancing the effectiveness and well-being of the full range of stakeholders of the organization. As such, it is a movement and cause with which I will be proud to be associated.

Acknowledgements

The final version of this chapter was completed while I was on sabbatical at the Australian School of Business (ASB), University of New South Wales, and I am grateful to colleagues in the School of Strategy and Entrepreneurship of the ASB for hosting my visit. I am also grateful to Jaco Lok, Denise Rousseau, and two anonymous reviewers for their constructive comments and suggestions on earlier versions of the manuscript. An additional colleague who also offered helpful feedback has chosen to remain anonymous.

References

Abrahamson, E., & Baumard, P. (2008). What lies behind organizational façades and how organizational façades lie: An untold story of organizational decision making. In G. P. Hodgkinson & W. H. Starbuck (Eds.), *The Oxford handbook of organizational decision making* (pp. 437–452). Oxford, UK: Oxford University Press.

Abrahamson, E., & Fombrun, C. J. (1994). Macrocultures: Determinants and consequences. *Academy of Management Review, 19*(4), 728–755.

Amodio, D. M. (2008). The social neuroscience of intergroup relations. *European Review of Social Psychology, 19*, 1–54.

Anderson, N., Herriot, P., & Hodgkinson, G. P. (2001). The practitioner-researcher divide in industrial, work and organizational (IWO) psychology: Where are we now, and where do we go from here? *Journal of Occupational and Organizational Psychology, 74*, 391–411.

Baritz, L. (1960). *The servants of power: A history of the use of social science in American industry.* Middletown, CT: Wesleyan University Press.

Bartlett, D. (2011). The neglect of the political: An alternative evidence-based practice for I–O psychology. *Industrial and Organizational Psychology: Perspectives on Science and Practice, 4*, 27–31.

Bartram, D., Lindley, P. A., Marshall, L., & Foster, J. (1995). The recruitment and selection of young people by small businesses. *Journal of Occupational and Organizational Psychology, 68*, 339–358.

Baughman, W. A., Dorsey, D. W., & Zarefsky, D. (2011). Putting evidence in its place: A means not an end. *Industrial and Organizational Psychology: Perspectives on Science and Practice, 4*, 62–64.

Bhaskar, R. (1978). *A realist theory of science.* Brighton, UK: Harvester.

Bhaskar, R. (1979). *The possibility of naturalism.* Brighton, UK: Harvester.

Bogenschneider, K., & Corbett, T. J. (2010). *Evidence-based policy making: Insights from policy-minded researchers and research-minded policymakers.* New York: Routledge.

Briner, R. B., Denyer, D., & Rousseau, D. M. (2009). Evidence-based management: Concept cleanup time? *Academy of Management Perspectives, November*, 19–32.

Briner, R. B., & Rousseau, D. M. (2011a). Evidence-based I-O psychology: Not there yet. *Industrial and Organizational Psychology: Perspectives on Science and Practice, 4*, 3–22.

Briner, R. B., & Rousseau, D. M. (2011b). Evidence-based I-O psychology: Not there yet but now a little nearer? *Industrial and Organizational Psychology: Perspectives on Science and Practice, 4*, 76–82.

Burke, L. A., & Miller, M. K. (1999) Taking the mystery out of intuitive decision making, *Academy of Management Executive, 12*, 22–42.

Cassell, C. (2011). Evidence-based I-O psychology: What do we lose on the way? *Industrial and Organizational Psychology: Perspectives on Science and Practice, 4*, 23–26.

Cleveland, J. N., & Murphy, K. R. (1992). Analyzing performance appraisal as a goal directed behavior. *Research in Personnel and Human Resource Management, 10*, 121–185.

Cooper, C. L., Dewe, P. J., & O'Driscoll, M. P. (2001). *Organizational Stress: A review and critique of theory, research, and applications.* Thousand Oaks, CA: Sage.

Cousins, R., Mackay, C. J., Clarke, S. D., Kelly, C., Kelly, P. J., & McCaig, R. H. (2004). Management standards and work-related stress in the UK: Practical development. *Work & Stress, 18*, 113–136.

Dane, E., & Pratt, M. G. (2007). Exploring intuition and its role in managerial decision making. *Academy of Management Review, 32*(1), 33–54.

Dane, E., & Pratt, M. G. (2009). Conceptualizing and measuring intuition: A review of recent trends. In G. P. Hodgkinson & J. K. Ford (Eds.), *International review of industrial and organizational psychology* (Vol. 24, pp. 1–40). Chichester, UK: Wiley.

Daniels, K., Harris, C., & Briner, R. B. (2004). Linking work conditions to unpleasant affect: Cognition, categorization and goals. *Journal of Occupational and Organizational Psychology, 77*, 343–363.

Denyer, D., Tranfield, D., & van Aken, J. E. (2008). Developing design propositions through research synthesis. *Organization Studies, 29*, 393–413.

Dovidio, J. F., Pearson, A. R., & Orr, P. (2008). Social psychology and neuroscience: Strange bedfellows or a healthy marriage? *Group Processes and Intergroup Relations, 11*(2), 247–263.

Dunbar, R. L. M., & Starbuck, W. H. (2006). Learning to design organizations and learning from designing them. *Organization Science, 17*, 171–178.

Fazio, R. H., & Olson, M. A. (2003). Implicit measures in social cognition research: Their meaning and use. *Annual Review of Psychology, 54*, 297–327.

Ferguson, E., Daniels, K., & Jones, D. (2006). Negatively oriented personality and perceived negative job characteristics as predictors of future psychological and physical symptoms: A meta-analytic structural modeling approach. *Journal of Psychosomatic Research, 60*, 45–52.

Frese, M., & Zapf, D. (1999). On the importance of the objective environment in stress and attribution theory: Counterpoint to Perrewe and Zellars. *Journal of Organizational Behavior, 20*, 761–765.

Grey, C. (2001). Re-imagining relevance: A response to Starkey and Madan. *British Journal of Management, 12 ,* S27–S32.

Haines, E. L., & Sumner, K. E. (2006). Implicit measurement of attitudes, stereotypes, and self-concepts in organizations: Teaching old dogmas new tricks. *Organizational Research Methods, 9*, 536–553.

Haslam, S. A., Reicher, S. D., & Platow, M. J. (2011). *The new psychology of leadership: Identity, influence and power.* Hove, UK: Psychology Press.

Herriot, P. (1989). Selection as a social process. In M. Smith & I. T. Robertson (Eds.), *Advances in selection and assessment* (pp. 171–187). New York: Wiley.

Highhouse, S. (2008). Stubborn reliance on intuition and subjectivity in employee selection. *Industrial and Organizational Psychology: Perspectives on Science and Practice, 1*, 333–342.

Hodgkinson, G. P. (2011). Why evidence-based practice in I–O psychology is not there yet: Going beyond systematic reviews. *Industrial and Organizational Psychology: Perspectives on Science and Practice, 4*, 49–53.

Hodgkinson, G. P., & Healey, M. (2008a). Toward a (pragmatic) science of strategic intervention: Design propositions for scenario planning. *Organization Studies, 29*, 435–457.

Hodgkinson, G. P., & Healey, M. P. (2008b). Cognition in organizations. *Annual Review of Psychology, 59*, 387–417.

Hodgkinson, G. P., & Healey, M. P. (2011). Psychological foundations of dynamic capabilities: Reflexion and reflection in strategic management. *Strategic Management Journal, 32*, 1500–1516.

Hodgkinson, G. P., & Herriot, P. (2002). The role of psychologists in enhancing organizational effectiveness. In I. T. Robertson, M. Callinan, & D. Bartram (Eds.), *Organizational effectiveness: The role of psychology* (pp. 45–60). New York: Wiley.

Hodgkinson, G. P., Herriot, P., & Anderson, N. (2001). Re-aligning the stakeholders in management research: Lessons from industrial, work and organizational psychology. *British Journal of Management, 12*, S41–S48.

Hodgkinson, G. P., Langan-Fox, J., & Sadler-Smith, E. (2008). Intuition: A fundamental bridging construct in the behavioural sciences. *British Journal of Psychology, 99*, 1–27.

Hodgkinson, G. P., & Payne, R. L. (1998). Graduate selection in three European countries. *Journal of Occupational and Organizational Psychology, 71*, 359–365.

Hodgkinson, G. P., & Rousseau, D. M. (2009). Bridging the rigor-relevance gap in management research: It is already happening! *Journal of Management Studies, 46*, 534–546.

Hodgkinson, G. P., Sadler-Smith, E., Burke, L. A., Claxton, G., & Sparrow, P. R. (2009). Intuition in organizations: Implications for strategic management. *Long Range Planning, 42*, 277–297.

Hodgkinson, G. P., & Starbuck, W. H. (2008). Organizational decision making: Mapping terrains on different planets. In G. P. Hodgkinson & W. H. Starbuck (Eds.), *The Oxford handbook of organizational decision making* (pp. 1–29). Oxford, UK: Oxford University Press.

Hodgkinson, G. P., & Starkey, K. (2011). Not simply returning to the same answer over and over again: Reframing relevance. *British Journal of Management, 22*, 355–369.

Huff, A. S. (2000). Changes in organizational knowledge production. *Academy of Management Review, 25*, 288–293.

Hunter, D. J. (2003). *Public health policy.* Cambridge, UK: Polity.

Hunter, I. E., & Hunter, R. F. (1984). Validity and utility of alternative predictors of job performance. *Psychological Bulletin, 96*, 72–98.

Johnson, G. (1987). *Strategic change and the management process.* Oxford, UK: Basil Blackwell.

Kahneman, D., & Klein, G. (2009). Conditions for intuitive expertise: A failure to disagree. *American Psychologist, 64*(6), 515–526.

Kahneman, D., & Klein, G. (2010). When can you trust your gut? *McKinsey Quarterly, 2*, 58–67.

Kieser, A., & Leiner, L. (2009). Why the rigor-relevance-gap in management research is unbridgeable. *Journal of Management Studies, 46*, 516–533.

Kieser, A., & Leiner, L. (2011). On the social construction of relevance: A rejoinder. *Journal of Management Studies, 48*, 891–898.

Kilduff, M., Mehra, A., & Dunn, M. B. (2011). From blue sky research to problem solving: A philosophy of science theory of new knowledge production. *Academy of Management Review, 36*, 297–317.

Latham, G. P., & Pinder, C. C. (2005). Work motivation theory and research at the dawn of the twenty-first century. *Annual Review of Psychology, 56*, 485–516.

Lazarus, R. S., & Folkman, S. (1984). *Stress appraisal and coping.* New York: Springer.

Learmonth, M. (2011). Where social science and philosophy meet: One explication of the relationship between evidence and theory in management research. In C. M. Cassell & B. Lee (Eds.), *Challenges and controversies in management research* (pp. 212–224). London: Routledge.

Learmonth, M., & Harding, N. (2006). Evidence-based management: The very idea. *Public Administration, 84*, 245–266.

Lieberman, M. D. (2007). Social cognitive neuroscience: A review of core processes. *Annual Review of Psychology, 58*, 259–289.

Locke, E. A., & Latham, G. P. (1990). *A theory of goal setting and task performance.* Englewood Cliffs, NJ: Prentice-Hall,

Mackay, C. J., Cousins, R., Kelly, P. J., Lee, S., & McCaig, R. H. (2004). Management standards and work-related stress in the UK: Policy background and science. *Work & Stress, 18,* 91–112.

Maslach, C., Schaufeli, W. B., & Leiter, M. P. (2001). Job burnout. *Annual Review of Psychology, 52,* 397–422.

McKelvey, B. (2006). Van de Ven and Johnson's engaged scholarship: Nice try, but… *Academy of Management Review, 31,* 822–829.

Mintzberg, H. (1983). *Power in and around organizations.* Englewood Cliffs, NJ: Prentice-Hall.

Morrell, K. (2008). The narrative of evidence based management: A polemic. *Journal of Management Studies, 45,* 613–635.

Munro, G. D. (2010). The scientific impotence excuse: Discounting belief-threatening scientific abstracts. *Journal of Applied Social Psychology, 40,* 579–600.

Nutt, P. (2009). Estimating drug harms: A risky business? Eve Saville Lecture 2009, Centre for Crime and Justice Studies, Kings College, University of London, UK. Retrieved from http://www.crimeandjustice.org.uk/opus1714/Estimating_drug_harms.pdf

Perrewe, P. L., & Zellars, K. L. (1999). An examination of attributions and emotions in the transactional approach to the organizational stress process. *Journal of Organizational Behavior, 20,* 739–752.

Pettigrew, A. M. (1973). *The politics of organizational decision making.* London: Tavistock.

Pettigrew, A. M. (1985). *The awakening giant: Continuity and change in imperial chemical industries.* Oxford, UK: Blackwell.

Pettigrew, A. M. (1997). The double hurdles for management research. In T. Clark (Ed.), *Advancement in organizational behaviour: Essays in honour of Derek S. Pugh* (pp. 277–296). London: Dartmouth Press.

Pettigrew, A. (2001). Management research after modernism. *British Journal of Management, 12,* S61–S70.

Pfeffer, J. (1981). *Power in organizations.* Boston, MA: Pitman.

Pfeffer, J., & Salancik, G. R. (1978). *The external control of organizations: A resource dependency perspective.* New York: Harper and Row.

Pfeffer, J., & Sutton, R. I. (2006). *Hard facts, dangerous half-truths and total nonsense: Profiting from evidence-based management.* Boston, MA: Harvard Business School Press.

Rick, J., Thomson, L., Briner, R. B., O'Regan, S., & Daniels, K. (2002). Review of existing supporting scientific knowledge to underpin standards of good practice for work related stressors — Phase 1. *HSE Research Report 024.* Sudbury, UK: HSE Books.

Robertson, I. T., & Makin, P. J. (1986). Management selection in Britain: A survey and critique. *Journal of Occupational Psychology, 59,* 45–57.

Romme, A. G. L., & Endenburg, G. (2006). Construction principles and design rules in the case of circular design. *Organization Science, 17,* 287–297.

Rousseau, D. M. (1990). New hire perceptions of their own and their employer's obligations: A study of psychological contracts. *Journal of Organizational Behavior, 11,* 389–400.

Rousseau, D. M. (1995). *Psychological contracts in organizations: Understanding written and unwritten agreements.* Thousand Oaks, CA: Sage.

Rousseau, D. M. (2006). Is there such a thing as evidence based management? *Academy of Management Review, 31,* 256–269.

Rousseau, D. M., Manning, J., & Denyer, D. (2008). Evidence in management and organizational science: Assembling the field's full weight of scientific knowledge through syntheses. In A. Brief & J. Walsh (Eds.), *Annals of the Academy of Management, 2,* 475–515.

Ryan, A. M., & Ford, J. K. (2010). Organizational psychology and the tipping point of professional identity. *Industrial and Organizational Psychology: Perspectives on Science and Practice, 3,* 241–258.

Sackett, D. L., Rosenberg, W. M., Gray, J. A. M., Haynes, R. B., & Richardson, W. S. (1996). Evidence based medicine: What it is and what it isn't. *British Medical Journal, 312,* 71–72.

Salas, E., Rosen, M. A., & DiazGranados, D. (2010). Expertise-based intuition and decision making in organizations. *Journal of Management, 36,* 941–973.

Sandberg J., & Tsoukas, H. (2011). Grasping the logic of practice: Theorizing through practical rationality. *Academy of Management Review, 36,* 338–360.

Schaubroeck, J. (1999). Should the subjective be the objective? On studying mental processes, coping behavior, and actual exposures in organizational stress research. *Journal of Organizational Behavior, 20,* 753–760.

Schmidt, F. L., & Hunter, J. E. (1998). The validity and utility of selection methods in personnel psychology: Practical and theoretical implications of 85 years of research findings. *Psychological Bulletin, 124,* 262–274.

Schwenk, C. R. (1989). Linking cognitive, organizational and political factors in explaining strategic change. *Journal of Management Studies, 26,* 177–187.

Shackleton, V., & Newell, S. (1994). European management selection methods: A comparison of five countries. *International Journal of Selection and Assessment, 2*(2), 91–102.

Simon, H. A. (1955). A behavioral model of rational choice. *Quarterly Journal of Economics, 69,* 99–118.

Simon, H. A. (1956). Rational choice and the structure of the environment. *Psychological Review, 63,* 129–138.

Spender, J. -C. (1989). *Industry recipes: The nature and sources of managerial judgement.* Oxford, UK: Basil Blackwell.

Starbuck, W. H. (2006). *The production of knowledge: The challenge of social science research.* Oxford, UK: Oxford University Press.

Starkey, K., Hatchuel, A., & Tempest, S. (2009). Management research and the new logics of discovery and engagement. *Journal of Management Studies, 46,* 547–558.

Starkey, K., & Madan, P. (2001). Bridging the relevance gap: Aligning the stakeholders in management research. *British Journal of Management, 12,* S3–S26.

Staw, B. M. (1981). The escalation of commitment to a course of action. *Academy of Management Review, 6,* 577–587.

Staw, B. M. (1997). The escalation of commitment: An update and appraisal. In Z. Shapira (Ed.), *Organizational decision making* (pp. 191–215). Cambridge, UK: Cambridge University Press.

Tranfield, D., & Starkey, K. (1998). The nature, social organization, and promotion of management research: Towards policy. *British Journal of Management, 9,* 341–353.

Van de Ven, A. H. (2007). *Engaged scholarship: A guide for organizational and social research.* New York: Oxford University Press.

Van de Ven, A. H., & Johnson, P. (2006). Knowledge for science and practice. *Academy of Management Review, 31,* 802–821.

Walsh, J. P., & Fahay, L. (1986). The role of negotiated belief structures in strategy making. *Journal of Management, 12,* 325–338.

Weick, K. E. (1969). *The social psychology of organizing.* Reading, MA: Addison-Wesley.

Weick, K. E. (1979). *The social psychology of organizing* (2nd ed.). Reading, MA: Addison-Wesley.

Weick, K. E. (1995). *Sensemaking in organizations.* Thousand Oaks, CA: Sage.

Weick, K. E. (2001). Gapping the relevance bridge: Fashion meets fundamentals in management research. *British Journal of Management, 12,* S71–S76.

Wensley, R. (2009). Research in UK business schools or management research in the UK? *Journal of Management Development, 28,* 718–727.

Zibarras, L. D., & Woods, S. A. (2010). A survey of UK selection practices across different organization sizes and industry sectors. *Journal of Occupational and Organizational Psychology, 83,* 499–511.

INDEX

Note: Page numbers followed by "*f*" and "*t*" refer to figures and tables, respectively.

A

AACSB. *See* Association to Advance
 Collegiate Schools of Business
AAR. *See* After Action Review
Aarons, G. A., 294–95
ABC analysis, 244
ABI/INFORM, 35, 264
Abrahamson, E., 415
Academic OneFile, 264
academics. *See also* educators; scholars
 Asbury Heights and, 196
 literature reviews, 114
 practitioner resistance to, 132–35
 truthful relationships with practitioners,
  146, 148
Academy of Management (AOM), 63,
 358, 366
Academy of Management Journal, 32
Academy of Management Review, 114
accountability, 287, 411
accuracy mechanisms, 277
action guides, 75
action net, 47
adaptive expertise, 314–16
Adelegan, J. A., 367
Adler, P. S., 396
Adorno, Theodor, 14
Advanced Institute of Management
 Research (AIM), 127
advanced learning, 316–17
advisory groups, 117, 119, 125
Afghanistan, 288
After Action Review (AAR), 352–53
Agarwall, S., 123, 152–53
agency, 47, 213
 theory, 365
Agency for Healthcare Policy and Research
 (AHCPR), 138–39
aggregate evidence, 35
aggregate synthesis, 80
aggregating data, 252, 258
Aguinis, H., 149

AHCPR. *See* Agency for HealthCare
 Policy and Research
AHP. *See* analytic hierarchy process
AIM. *See* Advanced Institute of
 Management Research
Albert Lea, Minnesota, 145, 150
alignment, 236, 239
Allen, David, 153
Allgaier, L., 213
ambiguity, 9, 84, 323, 399, 407
American Revolution, 392
analytic hierarchy process (AHP), 218
analytic plan, 10
Anderson, N., 71
Antman, E. M., 103
AOM. *See* Academy of Management
Argyris, C., 320
Aristotle, 146, 151
Armstrong, J. S., 8, 9, 343
Asbury Heights
 academics and, 196
 background, 191–92
 Carnegie Mellon and, 192
 challenges, 196
 conclusion, 196–97
 management, 192–94
 sales logic model, 195*f*
 what works, 194–96
Asher, Richard, 142
Asher's paradox, 142
Association to Advance Collegiate
 Schools of Business (AACSB), 19,
 358
attribution bias, 5
Aufhebung, 399
Ayres, I., 143, 150, 156–57

B

Baba, M. L., 276
Bader, Rupert, 226
Bain, K., 149
Baker, Timothy, 133

balkanization, 27
Bandolier, 35
Barad, Jill, 155
Barbus, Art, 195
Barends, E. G. R., 343
Barley, S. R., 140
Barnes, D. E., 137
Barnett, S., 315
barriers to communicating academic
 evidence, 166–67, 167*f*
 fostering EBMgt, 169–70
 trustworthy sources and, 170
Bartlett, D., 411, 416
Bartol, Kathryn, 267
Bartunek, J. M., 146, 151, 176
base-rate fallacy, 141
Baughman, W. A., 415
Baumard, P., 415
Baumeister, R. F., 153
Bayh-Dole Act, 136
Beane, Billy, 13, 15
Becoming the Evidence-Based Manager
 (Latham), 69
Begley, S., 134
behavioral integrity, 274
Bekelman, J. E., 136
beliefs, 243, 273, 276, 278–80
 truth and rationality, 285–86
benchmarking, 17, 279, 344, 391
 causal, 280–81
Bero, L. A., 137
Berta, W., 390
Berwick, Donald, 130, 156–57, 188
best available evidence, 5–7, 17
 best available practice and, 32
 critical evaluations, 281
 EBMed and, 38, 238
 nature of, 131
 obtaining, 343, 346–48
 practices, 54
 reporting, 126
 role of, 395

Keppner, C. H., 54
Keynes, J. M., 92
Kieser, A., 165, 390
Kim, Chan, 170
Kim, H., 152
King, Josie, 151
King, Patricia, 283
Kitchener, Karen, 283
knowledge gap, 32–33
knowledge-production problem, 83
knowledge-transfer problem, 83
know-why of practice, 82
Kohn, M. K., 390
Kolb, Deborah, 173, 178–79
Koslowski, B., 315
Kotler, Philip, 170
Kotter, J. P., 145, 151, 156, 171, 175
Kovner, Anthony, 185–86, 270, 297, 303
Kreuter, M. W., 141
Krishnan, R., 85
Kuhn, Thomas, 394
Kumanyika, Shiriki, 137

L

La Belle, A., 366, 370
labor-control theory, 399
Lachman, R., 275
Larcker, David, viii
Latham, G. P., 69, 73, 153, 157–58, 197
Lawler, E. E., 61–62
lay theory, 75
leadership, 27
    development, 67, 246
    five-level, 32
    interventions, 188
    mental models, 238
    research, 370
    theories, 366
    training, 70–71
Leading Change (Kotter), 151, 175
Learmonth, M., 131, 390, 395, 412
learning, 80
    advanced, 316–17
    CLT, 311–13, 316
    from experience, vii
    life-long, 21
    organizational, 32
    SoL, 172, 175
    unlearning, 240–43
"Learning from Samples of One or Fewer,"
    80
Leenders, M., 320
Leiner, L., 165, 390
level-five leadership, 32
Levering, Robert, 380
Levi-Strauss, 152
Lewis, M. E., 13
Liang, B. A., 154
librarians, 125
    libraries, 266–67
    in search for scientific evidence, 262–70
licensing, ix
life-long learning, 21

literature reviews, 113
    by academics, 114
    empirical studies and, 114
    grey literature, 116
    meta-analysis as, 114
    in popular books, 114–15
    textbook, 114
Locke, E. A., 8, 69, 72, 196–97, 267
    summaries, 382
Locock, L., 144
logic models, 9–10, 11*f*
    HR and, 229
    sales in Asbury Heights, 195*f*
logos, 146, 148
lost-before-translation problem, 83
Luckow, David, 152
Luhmann, N., 165

M

MacCoun, R. J., 138
MacGyver medicine, 152
Mackey, T. K., 154
management, 18, 114, 166, 171. *See also*
    critical management; health-care
    management; strategic management
    AIM, 127
    AOM, 63, 358, 366
    Asbury Heights, 192–94
    cafes, 176
    cookbook management, 140
    decision management portfolio,
        199–200, 199*t*
    EBMed and, 26–28
    education practices, 317
    examples of SRs, 117, 118*t*
    professionalization, 28
    research, 19
    researchability of management practice
        misconceptions, 30–32
    SRs, 117, 118*t*
    theory, 318, 320, 323
    Total Quality Management, 56
management and organizational sciences
    (MOS), 406–9
managers, 29, 54, 69
    challenges, 48–49
    decision making, 93
    mental models, 225–28
    middle managers, 297–98
    Rousseau on, 226
    self-training, 174
    senior managers, 296–97, 365–68
    training, 30
    validity and, 32
"The Manager's Workshop 3.0," 174
Mann, C., 131
Manning, J., 80
March, James G., 3, 27, 84, 139
market share, 6–7, 9
Markham, W. T., 150
Marx, Karl, 389, 398–99
Masaru Ibuka, 243
Maslow, Abraham, 380, 391

Maslow's hierarchy of needs, 380
material world, 46–47
Mathieu, Normand, 4, 10
Mauborgne, Renee, 170
Mauffette-Lenders, L., 320
Mauriel, J. L., 273
MAUT. *See* multiattribute utility theory
MBA programs, 29, 71
    case studies in, 171
    curricula, 168
    evidence-based approaches, 124
    teaching for, 73
McCall, Morgan, 177
McCarthy, S., 88, 149, 171
McKinsey, 84
McMaster University, 26, 36, 37
MDMP. *See* military decision-making
    process
measurement error, 252–54
mediation, 93, 103–4, 107
medicine
    cookbook, 38–39, 140, 280
    as discipline, 28
    MacGyver medicine, 152
    naïve image of, 28–30
    practice-oriented outcomes, 67
    randomization in, 31–32
    SRs in, 124
MEDLINE, 34–35
Meehl, P. E., 135
meet the dragon project, 104
mental models. *See also* shared mental
    models
    clarifying objectives, 237
    collaborative modeling scheme, 237
    defined, 225
    establishing roles, 237
    HR, 228
    HR measures and, 237–40
    imperatives for improving, 237
    information processing, 237
    leadership, 238
    of managers, 225–28
    overview, 224
    retooling, 234–37
    role of, 232–33
    team knowledge, 237
    team-shared, 234–37
meta-analysis, 81, 84
    codebook, 101
    criticisms, 85
    in EBE, 95*t*–98*t*, 104–5
    in entrepreneurship, 100–102
    as literature reviews, 114
    OB, 64–65
    procedures, 394
    quantitative, 52
    results, 93
    role of, 99–105
    sophisticated understanding,
        85–86
    studies, 86*t*
meta-cognition, 241

research (*cont.*)
    design and policy evaluation, 83
    DRRC, 318
    EBE, 108
    EBMgt and, 187–88
    evidence-based, 93
    evidence research trinity, 349
    explanatory, 44–45
    findings in professional practice, 52
    full body of, 394, 400
    grounded-theory, 360
    incommensurate research paradigms,
        394
    informed basic, 83
    leadership, 370
    management, 19
    OB, 62–63
    quantitative, 364
    RAE, 408
    REF, 408
    relevant, 17
    scholarly HR, 246–47
    scholars' tradition, 394
    Social Science Research Network, 264
    synthesis, 74
    systematic, 379*t*
    trinity, 349
researchability of management practice
        misconceptions, 30–32
Research Assessment Exercise (RAE), 408
research-based evidence, 369–71
research design, 81–83, 82*f*
researchers, 20–21
    advancing EBMgt, 56
    collaboration, 79
    goal setting and, 312
    OB involvement, 74–75
Research Excellence Framework (REF),
        408
research-practice gap, 72, 73, 391
resource allocation, 84
resource planning, viii
return on investment (ROI), 8, 189, 239,
        297
reverse causality, 256, 259
Reymen, I., 52–54
ride alongs, 148
risk
    in HR, 229–34
    probabilistic risk analyses, 207
Robbins, S. P., 177, 379
Rodgers, R., 87
Rodriguez, Dee Alcott, 177
Rogers, E. M., 290
Rogers, W. A., 395
ROI. *See* return on investment
Romme, A. G. L., 45, 52–54
Rouner, D., 141
Rousseau, D. M., 36, 79–80, 88, 136, 149
    decision making and, 199
    defining EBMgt, 278, 344, 409
    diagnosis and, 171
    evidence and, 175, 193, 360

exercises, 348
    on incentive pay, 350
    on managers, 226
    politics and, 410–11
    on profession, 168
    scaffolding, 240
    scholarly role, 177
    on scientific knowledge, 395
    SRs and, 393–94
Rovelli, Carlos, 12
Rowley, C., 236
Rucci, Anthony, 239
Rundall, T. G., 28–29, 189, 297, 303
Rynes, S. L., 70–71, 107, 132, 135, 142
    on critical thinking, 149
    knowledge quiz, 343

S

Sackett, David, 26, 29–30, 409
    on cookbook medicine, 38–39
    scientific evidence and, 35–36
Salas, E., 236
sales logic model, 195*f*
sample sizes, 5, 80, 104. *See also* small
        numbers
Sanders, K., 70
SAS Institute, vii
Sawitzky, A. C., 295
scaffolding, 240, 316, 318, 323
Schmidt, F. L., 253
Schmitt, Eric, 15
Schneider, M., 81, 85–86
scholars
    HR, 246–47
    research tradition, 394
    staff, 177
scholarship of discovery, 83–84
scholarship of integration, 153
Schomaker, M. S., 151
Schön, Donald, 44, 48, 50, 142, 152
Schools that Learn (Senge), 175
Schrage, Michael, 244–45
Schroeder, R. G., 273
Schwartz, B., 68
"Science by the Pint," 176
Science Direct, 35
science-driven culture, 133
"Science in the News," 176
science of exploitation, 398
science-oriented evidence, OB and, 64–66
The Science of the Artificial (Simon), 44
scientifically proven phenomenon, 6
scientific evidence, 6–7
    accessibility, 34–35, 40
    aggregate, 35
    as higher truth, 35–37
    objective, 38
    Sackett and, 35–36
    teaching, 19
scientific-inquiry approach, 406, 406*f*
scientific knowledge, 5, 395
scientific method, 135–36
scientific positivism, 393

scientific research findings, use of, xxiii,
        3–5
    applications and use, 6–7
    in business syllabi, ix
    implications, 7–8
    organizational facts, 8–11
    peer review, 7
    problems to overcome, 5–6
    professional practice and, 52
    SRs, 7
scientists
    collaboration, xxvi, 37, 66, 75
    communication skills, 134
    information scientists, 125
    practitioner resistance to, 132–35
searching for scientific evidence. *See also*
        literature reviews
    best available evidence, 39, 265
    books, 264, 265
    chaos in, 263–64
    databases, 19, 264–66
    Google, 265–67, 371
    grey literature, 116
    inaccessibility and, 266
    invisibility and, 264–66
    journals, 263
    librarians, 262–70
    libraries, 266–67
    new forms of access, 266–68
    recommendations, 268–69
    roadblocks, 263–66
    websites, 265–66
    Wikipedia, 268
self-awareness, 352
self-efficacy, 142
Self-Guided Field Trip, 344
self-training
    field guides, 175
    managerial simulation, 174
    short video cases, 174–75
    videos, 173–74
    websites, 175
Seligman, Martin, 17
Semmelweis, Ignaz, 143
Senge, P. M., 170–71, 172, 175
serious play, 244–46
Serious Play (Schrage), 244
shared mental models (SMMs),
        224, 246
    enhancing, 234–35
    measuring, 236–37
    retooling, 234
    task elements, 235
    team dynamic elements, 235–36
    teammate elements, 235
sharp-image diagnosis, 171
SHERPA-RoMEO, 269
shifting the burden, 170–71
Shirom, A., 171
Shojania, K. G., 136
SHRM. *See* Society for Human Resource
        Management
Shugan, S. M., 320